Canada: A Short History of Here

Selected Issues in Canadian History

NELSON

NELSON

ISBN-13: 978-0-17-678225-2
ISBN-10: 0-17-678225-7

Consists of Selections from:

Visions: The Canadian History Module Project
P.E. Bryden, Colin Coates, Maureen Lux, Laura Macleod, Lynne Marks, Marcel Martel, Daniel Samson, Colin Coates, Daniel Samson, P.E. Bryden, Maureen Lux, Matthew Hayday, Chris Pennington, Cindy Comacchio
ISBN-10: 0-17-666069-0, ©

Cover Credit:

African Woman Sits With Her Basket, Credit: Library and Archives Canada e010771966 Working men, Credit: Library and Archives Canada C0476150 Shooting the rapids, Credit: Library and Archives Canada C-002774

Contents

● INTRODUCTION

The past is a foreign country; they do things differently there.
—*The Go-Between*, L.P. Hartley (1953)

As editors and authors of the first set of modules in *Visions: The Canadian History Modules Project*, we tried to achieve a number of objectives. We wanted to provide introductory Canadian history students with a solid foundation for learning how to think like a historian in the context of their introductory Canadian history course. We also wanted instructors to be able to choose among a variety of teaching topics set within a common pedagogical framework that would support their students in their aim to become more sophisticated historical thinkers.

Each of the modules is designed to introduce a topic or key question that is commonly taught in introductory Canadian history classes. The short introductions set the basic context for the topic and draw attention to major historiographical themes and issues that have emerged as historians have studied it. They also attempt to show the interplay between the primary and secondary sources and illustrate how historians have used a wide variety of evidence to create their picture of the past. It is important for the students to note, however, that these introductions are merely starting points. Their job is to connect the material in the modules to the course lectures and core textbooks. A set of questions at the end of the introduction presents the framework for thinking critically about the material that follows. Each module contains a selection of primary sources from a broad range of materials, including government documents, diary entries and private letters, contemporary newspapers, and oral history interviews, as well as visual evidence in the form of maps, paintings, illustrations, and cartoons. Finally, a selection of secondary sources, the work of professional historians, foregrounds both the ways in which historians construct a narrative about the past and gives students insights into the differing ways in which evidence can be used.

The use of primary sources in conjunction with secondary sources is an essential component in the postsecondary study of history. To use an analogy, if the textbook for the course tells the overarching story of the history of Canada, the readings presented in these modules provide the rich detail that flesh out particular aspects of that story. They add the details that sensitize students to other viewpoints, other experiences, and other worldviews. If the past is indeed a foreign country, as Hartley said, then these modules are meant to give us an introduction to the tools to understand the assumptions, priorities, culture, and experience of people who lived 20 years ago or 200 years ago.

Learning to approach source material in a careful and nuanced way not only enhances students' ability to think critically, but also helps lower the barriers between the past and the present. It is important to apply these same critical approaches not only to the primary sources, but also to the secondary material. Historical actors are not the only ones influenced by the times in which they live. By showcasing different interpretations of evidence, we hope to help students realize that the past is not a set narrative, but rather that history is an argument created by historians based on how they choose and interpret the available evidence. Just as there are arguments today about issues such as climate change and how to interpret the scientific evidence for human impacts on climate, there are arguments among historians regarding a wide array of issues, from what Confederation meant to whether or not Canadians in the late nineteenth century experienced the secularization of their society.

We have carefully selected material that meets rigorous criteria of readability, significance, and variety. We include modules that cover a variety of approaches—social, political, environmental, religious, and so on—and a wide geographical range. One of the most difficult aspects of creating a reader is the need to exclude topics because of space limitations. In the case of *Visions*, however, the project has been conceived from the start as a living, growing database. We have therefore had the luxury of knowing that topics we were unable to cover in the first release will not be neglected but can be added as the project unfolds. To the instructors using this text we say, if you don't see what you need for your students, please join us!

Laura Macleod (Executive Editor, History)
P.E. Bryden (University of Victoria)
Colin Coates (Glendon College, York University)
Maureen Lux (Brock University)
Lynne Marks (University of Victoria)
Marcel Martel (York University)
Daniel Samson (Brock University)

CONTACT ZONES FROM THE SIXTEENTH TO EIGHTEENTH CENTURY

How Did Aboriginal People Perceive European Newcomers?

Colin Coates

Glendon College, York University

CONTACT ZONES FROM THE SIXTEENTH TO EIGHTEENTH CENTURY: HOW DID ABORIGINAL PEOPLE PERCEIVE EUROPEAN NEWCOMERS?

● **Introduction by Colin Coates**

▲ **Primary Sources**

■ **Secondary Sources**

● INTRODUCTION

Colin Coates

The encounter between Aboriginal peoples in North America and European newcomers changed the lives of people on both continents. While some aspects of this meeting were clearly very negative for Aboriginal peoples, they were not merely the passive victims of European expansion. European newcomers did not dominate Aboriginal peoples from the moment of first encounter. Rather, both groups influenced each other a great deal, and for many decades the Europeans relied on Aboriginal peoples for food and medicine. After all, the fate of the short-lived Viking settlement at L'Anse aux Meadows in northern Newfoundland around the year 1000 indicates that Europeans were not necessarily destined to flourish in the New World. By the sixteenth century, when Europeans returned to this part of the continent, they certainly enjoyed a degree of technological advantage in specific areas such as gunpowder and ships. Still, Aboriginal peoples were clearly better adapted to their terrain and climate.

Moreover, Aboriginal peoples had long experience adjusting to political and economic circumstances. The overview article by Neal Salisbury covers a variety of Aboriginal nations, showing the importance of considering the historical processes underway before the arrival of Europeans. This history of change helps us understand the nature of the contact experience. He also makes the point that the current national boundaries between Canada and the United States are irrelevant to our understanding of the early contact between Aboriginal peoples and Europeans.

One of the earliest records of the encounter of French and Aboriginal peoples is Jacques Cartier's (1491–1557) account of his voyage. But his account may not represent the first time the peoples met. When Cartier came upon Iroquoians at the Gaspé coast in 1535, they were eager to trade with him, an incident that suggests that they had established customs of trading with people who arrived on large sailing ships. Ramsay Cook's article on the extended encounter between the Iroquoians and Cartier and his men shows that not only did the French explorer "discover" North American Aboriginal society, but also the Iroquoians likewise discovered many aspects of European society. The Aboriginals, Cook argues, were not likely impressed. Likewise Cornelius Jaenen reminds us that, in this context, the French were "the other," and that it is important to try to understand Aboriginal attitudes toward the European newcomers. Aboriginal perspectives were not necessarily flattering. The material recorded by French missionary Chrestien Le Clercq (circa 1677) describes the negative Aboriginal attitudes toward many features of French society.

While Aboriginal peoples had many reasons to be wary of the newcomers, a few Europeans demonstrated some sympathy for and understanding of Aboriginal society. Indeed, Cartier and Samuel de Champlain (1567–1635) had visited other parts of the New World before coming to what is now Canada. Champlain in particular developed a broad and complex understanding of Aboriginal society. David Hackett Fisher's recent biography of Champlain argues that the French explorer developed a strikingly enlightened attitude toward Aboriginal society in New France.

In some circles, the exchanges between Aboriginal peoples and Europeans allowed for a new cultural critique to develop within European society. Europeans from the fifteenth to the eighteenth centuries undertook many voyages of exploration around the globe and saw many different societies and customs. One of the images that developed out of these encounters was the "noble savage." This personage exhibited great moral

5

strength while living under more rudimentary conditions than most Europeans. One of the classic texts of this genre, Michel de Montaigne's famous essay, "Des Cannibales" (1580), provides a scathing comparison between contemporary French society and Aboriginal society in contemporary Brazil (at least as far as he understood it). Even though he failed to grasp many features of that Aboriginal society, de Montaigne showed how the Aboriginal peoples' moral code often surpassed that of their French contemporaries.

Another important contribution to the image of the "noble savage" is contained in the works of Baron Louis-Armand de Lom d'Ares Lahontan (1666–1715), a French military official who lived in New France in the late seventeenth century. He provided an influential account of the morality of Aboriginal life in his fictional dialogue between himself and the Iroquois leader Adario. Through this text, which contributed to changing the ways that Europeans understood Aboriginal society, Lahontan uses the literary device of portraying himself as gullible and unable to convince Adario of the virtues of French society. Adario, in contrast, provides a much more convincing account of the superiority of his way of life. Lahontan's work proved to be a significant influence on later Enlightenment thinkers in France. The Enlightenment concept of the "noble savage," while not necessarily doing justice to the complexities and subtleties of Aboriginal life in the New World, created a new image and changed European attitudes about the malleability of human nature.

The "first" encounters occurred over a long time period given the geographical expanse of the continent. The French and later the British slowly extended their reach toward the west, meeting different Aboriginal groups. Because the Rocky Mountains form such a formidable geographical barrier, relations with Aboriginal peoples on the West Coast of what is now Canada were not established until the late eighteenth century, almost 250 years after Cartier's arrival. The earliest newcomers were not always the same mix of British and French explorers. On the British Columbian coast, Russians and the Spanish arrived at the same time as the British. The excerpt from the oral history of the Squamish nation who live near present-day Vancouver deals with the arrival of the first British ship on their shore. It reminds us that "first contact" between Europeans and Aboriginal peoples occurred much later on the West Coast. In all parts of North America, as in other parts of the world, the nature of the contact experience between different peoples was complex, and it led to significant changes in the world views of both sides.

QUESTIONS

1. In the first document, what criticisms did the Mi'kmaq present about the nature of French society in the New World? Would such attitudes have influenced the likelihood of their embracing Christianity?

2. Was the encounter of Aboriginal peoples and Europeans described in "Of Laws" a positive or negative experience for the two sides? Considering that this dialogue was written in the late seventeenth century, was the nature of the cultural interaction different from that for the earlier periods discussed in this section?

3. To what extent are Adario's attitudes about the relationship between the individual and the state similar to attitudes commonly held by North Americans today? Are Adario's or Lahontan's views more "modern?"

4. Evaluate the importance of the technological advances that Europeans enjoyed over Aboriginal peoples. How does the image from Samuel de Champlain's map reflect this technological advantage?

5. Compare the attitudes toward Europeans among the Mi'kmaq in the early seventeenth century and the Squamish in the late eighteenth century? How important are the large differences in time and space?

FURTHER READINGS

Olive Dickason and David McNabb, *Canada's First Nations: A History of Founding Peoples from Earliest Times* (Toronto: Oxford University Press, 2008).

Olive Dickason, *The Myth of the Savage* (Edmonton: University of Alberta Press, 1984)

David Hackett Fisher, *Champlain's Dream* (New York: Simon & Schuster, 2009)

John S. Lutz, ed., *Myth and Memory: Stories of Indigenous–European Contact* (Vancouver: UBC Press, 2007).

Bruce Trigger, *The Children of Aataentsic: A History of the Huron People to 1660* (Montreal: McGill-Queen's University Press, 1976).

▲ Document 1: A Micmac Responds to the French

Chrestien LeClercq

Chrestien LeClercq was a Recollect missionary, who spent twelve years among the Mi'kmaq of the Gaspé peninsula (in present-day Quebec). Having learnt their language, he provides in this excerpt their response to some features of French society.

[...] the Indians esteem their camps as much as, and even more than, they do the most superb and commodious of our houses. To this they testified one day to some of our gentlemen of Isle Percée, who, having asked me to serve them as interpreter in a visit which they wished to make to these Indians in order to make the latter understand that it would be very much more advantageous for them to live and to build in our fashion, were extremely surprised when the leading Indian, who had listened with great patience to everything I had said to him on behalf of these gentlemen, answered me in these words: "I am greatly astonished that the French have so little cleverness, as they seem to exhibit in the matter of which thou hast just told me on their behalf, in the effort to persuade us to convert our poles, our barks, and our wigwams into those houses of stone and of wood which are tall and lofty, according to their account, as these trees. Very well! But why now," continued he, "do men of five to six feet in height need houses which are sixty to eighty? For, in fact, as thou knowest very well thyself, Patriarch—do we not find in our own all the conveniences and the advantages that you have with yours, such as reposing, drinking, sleeping, eating, and amusing ourselves with our friends when we wish? This is not all," said he, addressing himself to one of our captains, "my brother, hast thou as much ingenuity and cleverness as the Indians, who carry their houses and their wigwams with them so that they may lodge wheresoever they please, independently of any seignior whatsoever? Thou art not as bold nor as stout as we, because when thou goest on a voyage thou canst not carry upon thy shoulders thy buildings and thy edifices. Therefore it is necessary that thou preparest as many lodgings as thou makest changes of residence, or else thou lodgest in a hired house which does not belong to thee. As for us, we find ourselves secure from all these inconveniences, as we can always say, more truly than thou, that we are at home everywhere, because we set up our wigwams with ease wheresoever we go, and without asking permission of anybody. Thou reproachest us, very inappropriately, that our country is a little hell in contrast with France, which thou comparest to a terrestrial paradise, inasmuch as it yields thee, so thou sayest, every kind of provision in abundance. Thou sayest of us also that we are the most miserable and most unhappy of all men, living without religion, without manners, without honour, without social order, and, in a word, without any rules, like the beasts in our woods and our forests, lacking bread, wine, and a thousand other comforts which thou hast in superfluity in Europe. Well, my brother, if thou dost not yet know the real feelings which our Indians have towards thy country and towards all thy nation, it is proper that I inform thee at once. I beg thee now to believe that, all miserable as we seem in thine eyes, we consider ourselves nevertheless much happier than thou in this, that we are very content with the little that we have; and believe also

---

Source: Chrestien LeClercq, "A Micmac Responds to the French" circa 1677, in *New Relation of Gaspesia with the customs and religion of the Gaspesian Indians*, ed. by W.F. Ganong (Toronto: Champlain Society, 1910), pp. 103–06.

once for all, I pray, that thou deceivest thyself greatly if thou thinkest to persuade us that thy country is better than ours. For if France, as thou sayest, is a little terrestrial paradise, art thou sensible to leave it? And why abandon wives, children, relatives, and friends? Why risk thy life and thy property every year, and why venture thyself with such risk, in any season whatsoever, to the storms and tempests of the sea in order to come to a strange and barbarous country which thou considerest the poorest and least fortunate of the world? Besides, since we are wholly convinced of the contrary, we scarcely take the trouble to go to France, because we fear, with good reason, lest we find little satisfaction there, seeing, in our own experience, that those who are natives thereof leave it every year in order to enrich themselves on our shores. We believe, further, that you are also incomparably poorer than we, and that you are only simple journeymen, valets, servants, and slaves, all masters and grand captains though you may appear, seeing that you glory in our old rags and in our miserable suits of beaver which can no longer be of use to us, that you find among us, in the fishery for cod which you make in these parts, the wherewithal to comfort your misery and the poverty which oppresses you. As to us, we find all our riches and all our conveniences among ourselves, without trouble and without exposing our lives to the dangers in which you find yourselves constantly through your long voyages. And, whilst feeling compassion for you in the sweetness of our repose, we wonder at the anxieties and cares which you give yourselves night and day in order to load your ship [with cod]. We see also that all your people live, as a rule, only upon cod which you catch among us. It is everlastingly nothing but cod—cod in the morning, cod at midday, cod at evening, and always cod, until things come to such a pass that if you wish some good morsels, it is at our expense; and you are obliged to have recourse to the Indians, whom you despise so much, and to beg them to go a-hunting that you may be regaled. Now tell me this one little thing, if thou hast any sense: Which of these two is the wisest and happiest—he who labours without ceasing and only obtains, and that with great trouble, enough to live on, or he who rests in comfort and finds all that he needs in the pleasure of hunting and fishing? It is true," added he, "that we have not always had the use of bread and of wine which your France produces; but, in fact, before the arrival of the French in these parts, did not the Gaspesians live much longer than now? And if we have not any longer among us any of those old men of a hundred and thirty to forty years, it is only because we are gradually adopting your manner of living, for experience is making it very plain that those of us live longest who, despising your bread, your wine, and your brandy, are content with their natural food of beaver, of moose, of waterfowl, and fish, in accord with the custom of our ancestors and of all the Gaspesian nation. Learn now, my brother, once for all, because I must open to thee my heart: there is no Indian who does not consider himself infinitely more happy and more powerful than the French." He finished his speech by the following last words, saying that an Indian could find his living everywhere, and that he could call himself the seigneur and the sovereign of his country, because he could reside there just as freely as it pleased him, with every kind of rights of hunting and fishing, without any anxiety, more content a thousand times in the woods and in his wigwam than if he were in palaces and at the tables of the greatest princes of the earth.

No matter what can be said of this reasoning, I assert, for my part, that I should consider these Indians incomparably more fortunate than ourselves, and that the life of these barbarians would even be capable of inspiring envy, if they had the instructions, the understanding, and the same means for their salvation which God has given us that we may save ourselves by preference over so many poor pagans, and as a result of His pity ...

▲ Document 2: Of Laws

Baron de Lahontan

These selections show part of the fictitious dialogue between the Baron de Lahontan and the Huron chief Adario. Baron de Lahontan (1666–c. 1716) was a military officer stationed in North America in the late seventeenth century. Disaffected because of ill treatment by his superiors, he returned to Europe and wrote an account that helped create the image of the "noble savage" in European thought. While not entirely reflecting the reality of Aboriginal life or beliefs, the "noble savage" image suggested to European thinkers that humans who lived closer to a natural state enjoyed greater freedoms and lived more honourably than their European counterparts. Lahontan uses himself as a literary figure in this dialogue, and his words do not necessarily reflect his views; rather, they are used to reveal the wisdom of Adario's perspectives. The personage of Adario was patterned after the Huron chief Kondarionk (c. 1649–1701).

Note that these excerpts are from an early English-language translation of Lahontan's original French text. The spelling has been modified only slightly, and where necessary, in order to keep the flavour of the text.

Of Laws

Adario […] let us therefore talk a little of what you call Laws; for you know that we have no such Word in our Language; tho' at the same time, I apprehend the force and importance of the Word, by virtue of the explication I had from you t'other day, together with the examples you mention'd, to make me conceive what you meant. Prithee tell me, are not Laws the same as just and reasonable Things? You say they are. Why then, to observe the Law, imports no more than to observe the measures of Reason and Justice: And at this rate you must take just and reasonable things in another sense than we do; or if you take 'em in the same sense. 'tis plain you never observe 'em.

Lahontan. These are fine Distinctions indeed, you please your self with idle Flams. Hast not thee the Sense to perceive, after twenty Years Conversation with the *French*, that what the *Hurons* call Reason is Reason among the *French*. 'Tis certain that all Men do not observe the Laws of Reason, for if they did there would be no occasion for Punishments, and those Judges thou hast seen at *Paris* and *Quebec* would be oblig'd to look out for another way of Living. But in regard that the good of the Society consists in doing Justice and following these Laws, there's a necessity of punishing the Wicked and rewarding the Good; for without that Precaution Murders, Robberies and Defamations would spread every where, and in a Word, we should be the most miserable People upon the Face of the Earth.

Adario. Nay, you are miserable enough already, and indeed I can't see how you can be more such. What sort of Men must the *Europeans* be? What Species of Creatures do they retain to? The *Europeans*, who must be forc'd to do Good, and have no other Prompter for the avoiding of Evil than the fear of Punishment. If I ask'd thee, what a Man is, thou wouldft answer me, *He's a Frenchman*, and yet I'll prove that your *Man* is rather a *Beaver*. For *Man* is not intitled to that Character upon the score of his walking upright upon two

Source: Lahontan, Baron Louis-Armand de Lom d'Ares, *New Voyages to North-America*, Vol. 2., Reuben Gold Thwaites, ed., (Chicago, IL: A.C. McClurg & Co., 1905), pp. 211 ff.

Legs, or of Reading and Writing, and shewing a Thousand other Instances of his Industry. I call that Creature a *Man*, that hath a natural inclination to do Good, and never entertains the thoughts of doing Evil. You see we have no Judges; and what's the reason of that? Why? We neither quarrel nor sue one another. And what's the reason that we have no Law Suits? Why? Because we are resolved neither to receive nor to know Silver. But why do we refuse admission to Silver among us? The reason is this: We are resolv'd to have no Laws, for since the World was a World our Ancestors liv'd happily without 'em. In fine, as I intimated before, the Word *Laws* does not signifie just and reasonable things as you use it, for the Rich make a Jest of 'em, and 'tis only the poor Wretches that pay any regard to 'em. But, pray, let's look into these *Laws*, or reasonable things, as you call 'em. For these Fifty Years, the Governors of *Canada* have still alledg'd that we are subject to the Laws of their great Captain. We content our selves in denying all manner of Dependance, excepting that upon the Great Spirit, as being born free and joint Brethren, who are all equally Masters: Whereas you are all Slaves to one Man. We do not put in any such Answer to you, as if the *French* depended upon us; and the reason of our silence upon that Head [topic] is, that we have no mind to Quarrel. But, pray tell me, what Authority or Right is the pretended Superiority of your great Captain grounded upon? Did we ever sell our selves to that great Captain? Were we ever in *France* to look after you? 'Tis you that came hither to find out us. Who gave you all the Countries that you now inhabit, by what Right do you possess 'em? They always belong'd to the *Algonkins* before. In earnest, my dear Brother, I'm sorry for thee from the bottom of my Soul. Take my advice, and turn *Huron;* for I see plainly a vast difference between thy Condition and mine. I am Master of my own Body, I have the absolute disposal of my self, I do what I please, I am the first and the last of my Nation, I fear no Man, and I depend only upon the Great Spirit: Whereas thy Body, as well as thy Soul, are doom'd to a dependance upon thy great Captain; thy Vice-Roy disposes of thee; thou hast not the liberty of doing what thou hast a mind to; thou'rt affraid of Robbers, false Witnesses, Assassins &c. and thou dependest upon an infinity of Persons whose Places have rais'd 'em above thee. Is it true, or not? Are these things either improbable or invisible? Ah! my dear Brother, thou seest plainly that I am in the right of it; and yet thou choosest rather to be a *French* Slave than a free *Huron*. What a fine Spark does a *Frenchman* make with his fine Laws, who taking himself to be mighty Wise is assuredly a great Fool; for as much as he continues in Slavery and a state of Dependence, while the very Brutes enjoy that adorable Liberty, and like us fear nothing but Foreign Enemies.
[....]

Adario. I'll tell thee one thing my dear Brother; I was a going one day from *Paris* to *Versailles*, and about half way, I met a Boor [peasant] that was going to be Whipt for having taken Partridges and Hares with Traps. Between *Rochel* [La Rochelle, in southwestern France, one of the main ports linking France and New France] and *Paris*, I saw another that was Condemn'd to the Gally's for having a little Bag of Salt about him. These poor Men were punish'd by your unjust Laws, for endeavouring to get Sustenance to their Families; at a time when a Million of Women were got with Child in the absence of their Husbands, when the Physicians Murder'd three fourths of the People, and the Gamesters reduc'd their Families to a Starving Condition, by losing all they had in the World; and all this with Impunity. If things go at this rate, where are your just and reasonable Laws; where are those Judges that have a Soul to be Sav'd as well as you and I? After this, you'll be ready to Brand the *Hurons* for Beasts. In earnest, we should have a fine time of it if we offer'd to punish one of our Brethren for killing a Hare or a Partridge; and a glorious sight 'twould be, to see our Wives inlarge the number of our Children, while we are ingag'd in Warlike Expeditions against our Enemies; to see Physicians Poison our Families, and Gamesters lose the Beaver Skins they've got in Hunting. In *France*, these things are look'd upon as trifles, which do not fall within the Verge of their fine Laws. Doubtless, they must needs be very blind, that are acquainted with us, and yet do not imitate our Example.

Laboutan. Very fine, my dear Friend; thou goest too fast; believe me, thy Knowledge is so confin'd, as I said before, that thy Mind can't reach beyond the appearances of things. Wouldst thou but give Ear to Reason, thou wouldst presently be sensible that we act upon good Principles, for the support of the Society. You must know, the Laws Condemn all without exception, that are guilty of the Actions you've mention'd. In the first place, they prohibit the Peasants to kill Hares or Partridges, especially in the Neighbourhood of *Paris;* by reason that an uncontroul'd liberty of Hunting, would quickly exhaust the whole Stock of those Animals. The Boors Farm the Grounds of their Landlords, who reserve to themselves the Priviledge of Hunting, as being Masters. Now, if they happen to kill Hares or Partridges, they not only rob their Masters of their Right, but fall under the Prohibition enacted by the Law: And the same is the Case of those who run Salt, by reason that the Right of Transporting it is solely lodg'd in the King. As to the Women and the Gamesters that you took notice of; you can't think sure that we'd shut 'em up in Prisons and Convents, and Condemn 'em to a perpetual Confinement. The Physicians 'twould be unjust to abuse, for of a hundred Patients they do not kill two; nay, on the contrary, they use their utmost efforts to Cure 'em. There's a necessity that Superannuated Persons, and those who are worn out, should put a Period to their Lives. And after all, tho' all of us have occasion to imploy Doctors, if 'twere prov'd that they had kill'd any Patient, either thro' Ignorance or Malice, the Law would not spare 'em no more than others.

Adario. Were these Laws observ'd, you would stand in need of a great many Prisons; but I see plainly that you do not speak all the truth, and that you're afraid of carrying the Thing farther, least my Reasons should put you to a stand. However, let's now cast our eyes upon those two Men who fled last year to *Quebec*, to avoid the being Burnt in *France*. If we look narrowly into their Crime, we'll find occasion to say, that *Europe* is pester'd with a great many foolish Laws.
[…]
Adario. The *French* in general take us for Beasts; the Jesuits Brand us for impious, foolish and ignorant Vagabonds. And to be even with you, we have the same thoughts of you; but with this difference, that *we* pity you without offering invectives. Pray hear me, my dear Brother, I speak calmly and without passion. The more I reflect up the lives of the *Europeans*, the less Wisdom and Happiness I find among 'em. These six years I have bent my thoughts upon the State of the *Europeans*: But I can't light on any thing in their Actions that is not beneath a Man; and truly I think 'tis impossible it should be otherwise, so long as you stick to the measures of *Meum* and *Tuum*. [That which belongs to me or you, i.e., private property] I affirm that what you call Silver is the Devil of Devils; the Tyrant of the *French*; the Source of all Evil; the Bane of Souls and the Slaughter-House of living Persons. To pretend to live in the Money Country, and at the same time to save one's Soul, is as great an inconsistency as for a Man to go to the bottom of a Lake to preserve his Life. This Money is the Father of Luxury, Lasciviousness, Intrigues, Tricks, Lying, Treachery, False-ness, and in a word, of all the mischief in the World. The Father sells his Children, Husbands expose their Wives to Sale, Wives betray their Husbands, Brethren kill one another, Friends are false, and all this proceeds from Money. Consider this, and then tell me if we are not in the right of it, in refusing to finger, or so much as to look upon that cursed Metal.

Lahontan. What! is it possible that you should always Reason so sorrily! Prithee, do but listen once in thy life time to what I am going to say. Dost not thou see, my dear Friend, that the Nations of *Europe* could not live without Gold and Silver, or some such precious thing. Without that Symbol, the Gentlemen, the Priests, the Merchants, and an infinity of other Persons who have not Strength enough to labour the Earth, would die for Hunger. Upon that lay, our Kings would be no Kings: Nay, what Soldiers should we then have? Who would then Work for Kings or any body else, who would run the hazard of the Sea, who would make Arms unless 'twere for himself? Believe me, this would run us to remediless Ruine, 'twould turn *Europe* into a Chaos, and create the most dismal Confusion that Imagination it self can reach.

Adario. You fobb me off very prettily, truly, when you bring in your Gentlemen, your Merchants and your Priests. If you were Strangers to *Meum* and *Tuum*, those distinctions of Men would be sunk; a levelling equality would then take place among you as it now do's among the *Hurons*. For the first thirty years indeed, after the banishing of Interest, you would see a strange Desolation; those who are only qualify'd to eat, drink, sleep and divert themselves, would languish and die; but their Posterity would be fit for our way of living. I have set forth again and again, the qualities that make a Man inwardly such as he ought to be; particularly, Wisdom, Reason, Equity, &c. which are courted by the *Hurons*. I have made it appear that the Notion of separate Interests knocks all these Qualities in the Head, and that a Man sway'd by Interest can't be a Man of Reason. As for the outward Qualifications of a Man; he ought to be expert in Marching, Hunting, Fishing, Waging War, Ranging the Forests, Building Hutts and Canoes, Firing of Guns, Shooting of Arrows, Working Canoes: He ought to be Indefatigable, and able to live on short Commons upon occasion. In a word, he ought to know how to go about all the Exercises of the *Hurons*. Now in my way, 'tis the Person thus qualify'd that I call a *Man*. Do but consider, how many Millions there are in *Europe*, who, if they were left thirty Leagues off in the Forrests, and provided with Fusees [guns] and Arrows, would be equally at a loss, either to Hunt and maintain themselves, or to find their way out: And yet you see we traverse a hundred Leagues of Forrests without losing our way, that we kill Fowl and other Beasts with our Arrows, that we catch Fish in all the places where they are to be had; that we Dog both Men and Wild Beasts by their Footsteps, whether in Woods or in open Fields, in Summer or in Winter; that we live upon Roots when we lye before the Gates of the *Iroquese*, that we run like Hares, that we know how to use both the Axe and the Knife, and to make a great many useful things. Now since we are capable of such things, what should hinder you to do the same, when Interest is laid aside? Are not your Bodies as large, strong and brawny as ours? Are not your Artisans imploy'd in harder and more difficult Work than ours? If you liv'd after our manner, all of you would be equally Masters; your Riches would be of the same Stamp with ours, and consist in the purchasing of Glory by military Actions, and the taking of Slaves; for the more you took of them the less occasion you would have to Work: In a word, you would live as happily as we do.

Lahontan. Do you place a happy Life, in being oblig'd to lye under a pittiful Hutt of Bark, to Sleep under four sorry Coverlets of Beaver Skins, to Eat nothing but what you Boil and Roast, to be Cloath'd with Skins, to go a Beaver Hunting in the harshest Season of the Year, to run a hundred Leagues on Foot in pursuit of the *Iroquese*, thro' Marshes and thick Woods, the Trees of which are cut down so as to render 'em inaccessible! Do you think your selves happy when you venture out in little Canoes, and run the risk of being drown'd every foot in your Voyages upon the Great Lakes; when you lye upon the ground with the Heavens for your Canopy, upon approaching to the Villages of your Enemies; when you run with full Speed, both days and nights without eating or drinking, as being pursued by your Enemies; when you are sure of being reduc'd to the last extremity, if the *Coureurs de Bois* [independent French fur traders] did not out of Friendship, Charity and

Commiseration, supply you with Fire-Arms, Powder, Lead, Thread for Nets, Axes, Knives, Needles, Awls, Fishing-Hooks, Ketties, and several other Commodities?

Adario. Very fine, come, don't let's go so fast; the day is long, and we may talk one after the other at our own leisure. It seems you take all these things to be great hardships; and indeed I own they would be such to the *French*, who like Beasts, love only to eat and to drink, and have been brought up to Softness and Effeminacy. Prithee, tell me what difference there is between lying in a good Hutt, and lying in a Palace; between Sleeping under a Cover of Beaver-Skins, and Sleeping under a Quilt between two Sheets; between Eating Boil'd and Roast Meat, and feeding upon dirty Pies, Ragou's, *& c.* dress'd by your greasy Scullions? Are we liable to more Disorders and Sicknesses than the *French*, who are accommodated with these Palaces, Beds and Cooks? But after all, how many are there in *France* that lye upon Straw in Garrets where the Rain comes in on all hands, and that are hard put to't to find Victuals and Drink? I have been in *France*, and speak from what I have seen with my Eyes. You rally without reason, upon our Clothes made of Skins, for they are warmer, and keep out the Rain better than your Cloth; besides, they are not so ridiculously made as your Garments, which have more Stuff in their Pockets and Skirts, than in the Body of the Garment. As for our Beaver-Hunting, you take it to be a terrible thing; while it affords us all manner of pleasure and diversion; and at the same time, procures us all sorts of Commodities in exchange for the Skins. Besides, our Slaves take all the Drudgery off our hands, (if so be that you will have it to be drudgery.) You know very well that Hunting is the most agreeable Diversion we have; but the Beaver-Hunting being so very pleasant, we prefer it to all the other sorts. You say, we have a troublesome and tedious way of waging War; and indeed I must own that a *French* Man would not be able to bear it, upon the account that you are not accustom'd to such long Voyages on Foot; but these Excursions do not fatigue us in the least, and 'twere to be wish'd for the good of *Canada*, that you were possess'd of the same Talent; for if you were, the *Iroquese* would not Cut your Throats in the midst of your own Habitations, as they do now every day. You insist likewise on the risk we run in our little Canoes, as an instance of our Misery; and with reference to that Point, 'tis true that sometimes we cannot dispense with the use of Canoes, because we are Strangers to the Art of Building larger Vessels; but after all, your great Vessels are liable to be cast away as well as Canoes. 'Tis likewise true, that we lye flat upon the open ground when we approach to the Villages of our Enemies; but 'tis equally true that the Soldiers in *France* are not so well accommodated as your Men are here, and that they are oftentimes forc'd to lye in Marshes and Ditches, where they are expos'd to the Rain and Wind. You object farther, that we betake our selves to a speedy Flight; and pray what can be more natural than to flye when the number of our Enemies is triple to ours. The Fatigue indeed of running night and day without Eating and Drinking, is terrible; but we had better undergo it than become Slaves. I am apt to believe that such extremities are matter of Horrour to the *Europeans*, but we look upon 'em as in a manner, nothing. You conclude, in pretending that the *French* prevent our Misery by taking pity of us. But pray consider how our Ancestors liv'd an hundred years ago: They liv'd as well without your Commodities as we do with 'em; for instead of your Fire-Locks, Powder and Shot, they made use of Bows and Arrows, as we do to this day: They made Nets of the Thread of the Barks of Trees, Axes of Stone; Knives, Needles and Awls of Stag or Elk-Bones; and supply'd the room of Kettles with Earthen Pots. Now, since our Ancestors liv'd without these Commodities for so many Ages; I am of the Opinion, we could dispense with 'em easier than the *French* could with our Beaver Skins; for which, by a mighty piece of Friendship, they give us in exchange Fusees, that burst and Lame many of our Warriors, Axes that break in the cutting of a Shrub, Knives that turn Blunt, and lose their Edge in the cutting of a

Citron; Thread which is half Rotten, and so very bad that our Nets are worn out as soon as they are made; and Kettles so thin and slight, that the very weight of Water makes the Bottoms fall out. This, my dear Brother, is the answer I had to give to your Reflexions upon the Misery of the *Hurons*.

Lahontan.'Tis well; I find you would have me to believe that the *Hurons* are insensible of their Fatigue and Labour; and being bred up to Poverty and Hardships, have another notion of 'em than we have. This may do with those who have never stir'd out of their own Country, and consequently have no Idea of a better Life than their own; who having never visited our Cities and Towns, fancy that we live just as they do. But as for thee, who hast seen *France, Quebec* and *New-England*, methinks thy judgment and relish of things are too much of the Savage Strain; whilst thou prefers the Condition of the *Hurons* to that of the *Europeans*. Can there be a more agreeable and delightful Life in the World, than that of an infinity of rich Men, who want for nothing? They have fine Coaches, Stately Houses adorn'd with Rich Hangings and Magnificent Pictures, Sweet Gardens replenish'd with all sorts of Fruit, Parks Stock'd with all sorts of Animals, Horses and Hounds and good store of Money, which enables 'em to keep a Sumptuous Table, to frequent the Play-Houses, to Game freely, and to dispose handsomely of their Children. These happy Men are ador'd by their Dependants; and you have seen with your own eyes our Princes, Dukes, Marshals of *France*, Prelates, and a Mission of persons of all Stations, who want for nothing, and live like Kings, and who never call to mind that they have liv'd, till such time as Death alarms 'em.

Adario. If I had not been particularly inform'd of the State of *France*, and let into the knowledge of all the Circumstances of that People, by my Voyage to *Paris;* I might have been Blinded by the outward appearances of Felicity that you set forth: But I know that your Prince, your Duke, your Marshal, and your Prelate are far from being happy upon the Comparison with the *Hurons*, who know no other happiness than that of Liberty and Tranquility of Mind: For your great Lords hate one another in their Hearts; they forfeit their Sleep, and neglect even Eating and Drinking, in making their Court to the King, and undermining their Enemies; they offer such Violence to Nature in dissembling, disguising and bearing things, that the Torture of their Soul leaves all Expression far behind it. Is all this nothing in your way? Do you think it such a trifling matter to have fifty Serpents in your Bosom? Had not they better throw their Coaches, their Palaces and their Finery, into the River, than to spend their life time in a continued Series of Martyrdom? Were I in their place, I'd rather choose to be a *Huron* with a Naked Body and a Serene Mind. The Body is the Apartment in which the Soul is lodg'd; and what signifies it, for the Case call'd the Body, to be set off with Gold Trappings, or spread out in a Coach, or planted before a Sumptuous Table, while the Soul Galls and Tortures it? The great Lords, that you call Happy, lie expos'd to Disgrace from the King, to the detraction of a thousand sorts of Persons, to the loss of their Places, to the Contempt of their Fellow Courtiers; and in a word, their soft Life is thwarted by Ambition, Pride, Presumption and Envy. They are Slaves to their Passions, and to their King, who is the only *French* Man that can be call'd Happy, with respect to that adorable Liberty which he alone enjoys. There's a thousand of us in one Village, and you see that we love one another like Brethren; that whatever any one has is at his Neighbour's Service; that our Generals and Presidents of the Council have not more Power than any other *Huron;* that Detraction and Quarreling were never heard of among us; and in fine [in conclusion], that every one is his own Master, and do's what he pleases, without being accountable to another, or censur'd by his Neighbour. This, my dear Brother, is the difference between us and your Princes, Dukes, *&c.* And if those great Men are so Unhappy, by consequence, those of inferiour Stations must have a greater share of Trouble and perplexing Cares ....

▲ Document 3: How the Squamish Remember George Vancouver

The following is an account of the Squamish's first encounter with George Vancouver, as told by Squamish historian Louis Miranda (1892–1990), and presented at the Vancouver Conference on Exploration and Discovery by Chief Philip Joe in 1992. This represents an oral history passed down through the generations since 1792.

Vancouver's journal records that my ancestors who greeted him 'conducted themselves with the greatest decorum and civility.' He certainly liked the fish given and did not mind parting with a few iron tools in exchange. Vancouver took a look around the inlet and then headed into Howe Sound where an incident occurred that you may not be so familiar with, but which has been preserved in Squamish oral tradition.

As my elders tell the story, early one morning in the month called *Tim-kwis-KWAS* 'hot time,' an old man living near the mouth of the Squamish River had gone down to wash. As he raised his head, he saw an 'island' where no island had been before. The old man was alarmed and ran back to his house to wake his relatives. 'There is an island in the sound—a floating island,' he told them. The old man knew it was an island for it had skeletons of trees thrusting skyward. But it was like no island he had ever seen. Word was sent up the Squamish River for the people to come and see the mysterious floating island.

It was decided that the men would go out in their canoes to see the island. As they grew near, they saw that it wasn't a floating island at all, but a very large canoe, a strange canoe. Soon, men appeared and walked around the canoe. But what strange men they were! Every part of their body was covered except for their faces, which were white. My people scrutinized them. Finally, some of the elders came up with an explanation—these people are from the land of the dead. And they are wrapped in their burial blankets!

One of the dead people stepped forward. He had smoke coming from his mouth and it appeared that he was eating fire. The man motioned for my ancestors to go on board. They were hesitant, of course, but after much discussion, one brave young man decided that he would go, and others followed. Instantly, the dead man in the canoe extended his hand. 'Oh, he wants to play the "pulling fingers" game,' the Squamish men told one another. One man stepped forward, spit in his palm, rubbed his hands together, and thrust out his crooked finger. The fire-eating dead man shook his head no, no. 'A stronger opponent is wanted,' the Squamish decided. Another man stepped forward, spit on his hand and got ready to play the game. Again the white man shook his head, no. More Squamish men stepped forward, spit, and extended their finger, until only one man remained—a strong man from up the Squamish River. My people could see that the strangers were talking amongst themselves and we can only assume that they must have decided that this unusual behaviour was the Indian way of greeting. So the white man stepped forward to link fingers with the strong man of Squamish. The Squamish man pulled. He pulled hard. Oh, the smoke-blowing dead man hollered in pain as his finger was disconnected! Some of the Squamish had been sceptical of the strangers. Then they knew. 'Dead people don't feel pain, and this one is certainly having some!'

Fear of the strangers vanished. The Squamish looked around the strange, large canoe and when it came time to leave they climbed down into their own canoes. The white people lowered into the canoes some presents, including a barrel and a few boxes.

Source: Louis Miranda and Philip Joe, in Robin Fisher and Hugh J.M. Johnston, eds., *From Maps to Metaphors*, (Vancouver: UBC Press, 1993), pp. 3–5. Reprinted with permission of the Publisher from *From Maps to Metaphors: The Pacific World of George Vancouver* edited by Robin Fisher and Hugh Johnston. © University of British Columbia Press 1993. All rights reserved by the Publisher.

Back at the village the people huddled around as the men opened the treasure. When they pried the top from the barrel they were pleased to see that it contained good thick hair and face oil, much better than the deer tallow and salmon oil they had in storage. All hands dipped into the barrel and smeared it onto their faces and hair. But soon the oil began to thicken. Their hair got stiff! Their faces got thick! And they could hardly move their jaw! They ran for the water and washed it off. The gift of molasses was then emptied onto the ground.

My people had hoped that the second gift might be less trouble. Inside the box were shiny round pieces that attracted the attention of the women—who saw their value as ornaments—and the children—who thought they made fine toys. For the box of silver coins had no other value to the Squamish in 1792.

The story passed down by my ancestors tells how Vancouver provided gifts of pilot biscuits, whisky, and white flour—unfamiliar foods that they used with results that were initially comical, although history has recorded a less jovial aftermath.

Viewing the explorers' ships as 'floating islands' and the men, themselves, as 'dead people' was not a perspective unique to the Squamish. Our relatives—the Nanaimo Indians—were also visited one night by floating islands. In addition to the fire-eating habit of the strangers, they saw that their feet were wooden and made a great deal of noise when they walked! The Nanaimo people's barrel of molasses was used to mend their canoes, but it was soon found that molasses was as poor a canoe pitch as it was a hair oil.

Apparently Vancouver then sailed north, for his travels up the coast can be traced by the elders' stories of mysterious floating islands that appeared offshore, and then, just as quickly as they arrived, sailed beyond the next point.

Many of you have investigated the naming of the landscape by Vancouver and his Spanish counterparts. But perhaps you are not aware that the Squamish commemorated the historic 1792 meeting in Howe Sound by thereafter referring to the site by the Squamish name *Whul-whul-LAY-ton*, meaning "Whiteman place."

Indian stories and place names, like explorers' journals, are reminders of history that provide a glimpse into another era. As I hope my people's story has demonstrated, our mutual histories since 1792 have been inexorably entwined, although recalled from different perspectives.

This country, which so inspired the explorers and challenged the map makers, was the homeland of the Squamish and our neighbours the Musqueam and the Seleelwat. These beaches gave us shellfish, crabs, and eel grass. The forests and flatlands provided deer, large herds of elk, bear, and mountain goats. Food plants were harvested, and the trees supplied the wood for our houses, canoes, weapons, and ceremonial objects. The bark of red cedars was stripped to make our clothes. The inlet waters provided us with a wide variety of fish and sea mammals, and salmon returned regularly to the streams. And just as Captain Vancouver was said to have shared his molasses, biscuits, and flour, so our people shared our natural resources with those who followed in the wake of the floating islands.

▲ Document 4: Engraving based on a drawing by Samuel de Champlain, 1613

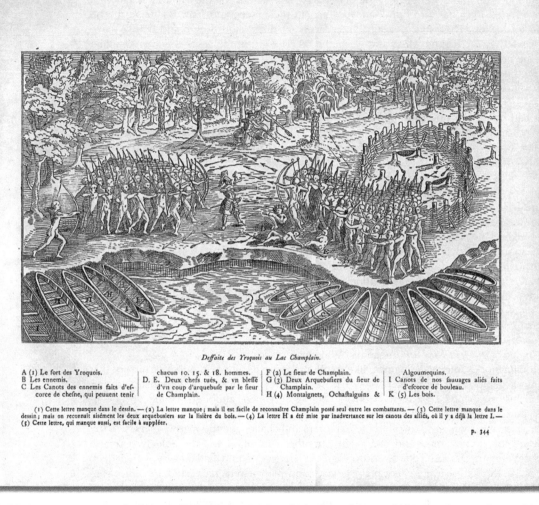

Deffaite des Yroquois au Lac Champlain.

A (1) Le fort des Yroquois.
B Les ennemis.
C Les Canots des ennemis faits d'escorce de chesne, qui peuuent tenir

chacun 10. 15. & 18. hommes.
D. E. Deux chefs tués, & vn blessé d'vn coup d'arquebuse par le sieur de Champlain.

F (2) Le sieur de Champlain.
G (3) Deux Arquebusiers du sieur de Champlain.
H (4) Montaignets, Ochastaiguins &

Algoumequins.
I Canots de nos sauuages aliés faits d'escorce de bouleau.
K (5) Les bois.

(1) Cette lettre manque dans le dessin. — (2) La lettre manque; mais il est facile de reconnaître Champlain posté seul entre les combattants. — (3) Cette lettre manque dans le dessin; mais on reconnaît aisément les deux arquebusiers sur la lisière du bois. — (4) La lettre H a été mise par inadvertance sur les canots des alliés, où il y a déjà la lettre I. — (5) Cette lettre, qui manque aussi, est facile à suppléer.

P. 344

● This is a contemporary depiction of a battle in 1609 in which Champlain used his arquebuse to fire on his Iroquois foes. What conclusions can we draw about Aboriginal–French relations based on this image?

Source: Deffaite des Yroquois au lac Champlain. In Champlain, Samuel de. Œuvres de Champlain / 2nd edition. Quebec : G.-É. Desbarats, 1870. Vol. 3, facing page 196. Archives of Ontario Library, 971.011 CHB http://www.archives.gov.on.ca/english/on-line-exhibits/franco-ontarian/pics/971_001_pg344_battle_520.jpg. LAC C-006780.

▲ Document 5: The Encounter Between Jacques Cartier and the Aboriginal Peoples at Stadaconé

● This image is a much later depiction of the encounter between Jacques Cartier and the Aboriginal peoples at Stadaconé (near present-day Quebec City). Quebec artist Marc-Aurèle Suzor-Côté painted this canvas in 1907. How does this image depict the encounter between the French and the Aboriginal peoples? Which group dominates the image? How well does this painting reflect the attitudes expressed in the readings for this section?

Source: http://www.mnba.qc.ca/Contenu.aspx?page=1529&langue=en. Suzor-Coté, Marc Aurèle de Foy, Jacques Cartier rencontre les Indiens à Stadaconé, 1535, Huile sur toile, 266x401 cm, Museé national des beaux-arts du Québec, Accession No. 34.12. Photograper Jean-Guy Kérouac.

■ Article 1: The Indians' Old World: Native Americans and the Coming of Europeans

Neil Salisbury

Scholars in history, anthropology, archaeology, and other disciplines have turned increasingly over the past two decades to the study of native peoples during the colonial period of North American history. The new work in Indian history has altered the way we think about the beginning of American history and about the era of European colonization. Historians now recognize that Europeans arrived, not in a virgin land, but in one that was teeming with several million people. Beyond filling in some of the vast blanks left by previous generations' overlooking of Indians, much of this scholarship makes clear that Indians are integral to the history of colonial North America.[1] In short, surveys of recent textbooks and of scholarly titles suggest that Native Americans are well on their way home to being "mainstreamed" by colonial historians.

Substantive as this reorientation is, it remains limited.[2] Beyond the problems inherent in representing Indian/non-Indian interactions during the colonial era lies the challenge of contextualizing the era itself. Despite opening chapters and lectures that survey the continent's native peoples and cultures, most historians continue to represent American history as having been set in motion by the arrival of European explorers and colonizers.[3] They have yet to recognize the existence of North American—as opposed to English or European—background for colonial history, much less to consider the implications of such a background for understanding the three centuries following Columbia's landfall. Yet a growing body of scholarship by archaeologists, linguists, and students of Native American expressive traditions recognizes 1492 not as a beginning but as a single moment in a long history utterly detached from that of Europe.[4] These findings call into question historians' synchronic maps and verbal descriptions of precontact Indians—their cultures, their communities, their ethnic and political designations and affiliations, and their relations with one another. Do these really describe enduring entities or do they represent epiphenomena of arbitrary moments in time? If the latter should prove to be the case, how will readings of Indian history in the colonial period be affected?

Far from being definitive, this article is intended as a stimulus to debate on these questions. It begins by drawing on recent work in archaeology, where most of the relevant scholarship has originated, to suggest one way of thinking about pre-Columbian North America in historical terms.[5] The essay then looks at developments in several areas of the continent during the centuries preceding the arrival of Europeans and in early phases of the colonial period. The purpose is to show how certain patterns and processes originating before the beginnings of contact continued to shape the continent's history thereafter and how an understanding of the colonial period requires an understanding of its American background as well as of its European context.[6]

In a formidable critique of European and Euro-American thinking about native North Americans, Robert F. Berkhofer, Jr., demonstrates that the idea of "Indians" as a single, discrete people was an invention of Columbus and his European contemporaries that has been perpetuated into our own time without foundation in historical, cultural, or ethnographic reality. On the contrary, Berkhofer asserts,

> The first residents of the Americas were by modern estimates divided into at least two thousand cultures and more societies, practiced a multiplicity of customs and lifestyles, held an enormous variety of values and beliefs, spoke numerous languages mutually unintelligible to the many speakers, and did not conceive of themselves as a single people—if they knew about each other at all.[7]

While there is literal truth in portions of Berkhofer's statement, his implication that Indians inhabited thousands of tiny, isolated communities in ignorance of one another flies in the face of a substantial body of archaeological and linguistic scholarship on North America and of a wealth of relevant anthropological literature on nonstate polities, nonmarket economies,

Source: Neil Salisbury, "The Indians' Old World: Native Americans and the Coming of Europeans" *The William and Mary Quarterly*, Third Series, Vol. 53, No. 3 (July 1996): 435–58. Reprinted with permission.

and noninstitutionalized religions. To be sure, indigenous North Americans exhibited a remarkable range of languages, economies, political systems, beliefs, and material cultures. But this range was less the result of their isolation from one another than of the widely varying natural and social environments with which Indians had interacted over millennia. What recent scholars of precolonial North America have found even more striking, given this diversity, is the extent to which native peoples' histories intersected one another.

At the heart of these intersections was exchange. By exchange is meant not only the trading of material goods but also exchanges across community lines of marriage partners, resources, labor, ideas, techniques, and religious practices. Longer-distance exchanges frequently crossed cultural and linguistic boundaries as well and ranged from casual encounters to widespread alliances and networks that were economic, political, and religious. For both individuals and communities, exchanges sealed social and political relationships. Rather than accumulate material wealth endlessly, those who acquired it gave it away, thereby earning prestige and placing obligations on others to reciprocate appropriately. And as we shall see, many goods were not given away to others in this world but were buried with individuals to accompany them to another.[8]

Archaeologists have found evidence of ongoing exchange relations among even the earliest known Paleo-Indian inhabitants of North America. Ten thousand years before Columbus, in the wake of the last Ice Age, bands of two or three dozen persons regularly traveled hundreds of miles to hunt and trade with one another at favored campsites such as Lindenmeier in northern Colorado, dating to ca. 8800 B.C. At the Lindenmeier site, differences in the flaking and shaping of stone points distinguished regular occupants in two parts of the camp, and the obsidian each used came from about 350 miles north and south of Lindenmeier, respectively.[9] Evidence from a wide range of settlement sites makes clear that, as the postglacial warming trend continued, so-called Archaic peoples in much of the continent developed wider ranges of food sources, more sedentary settlement patterns, and larger populations. They also expanded their exchanges with one another and conducted them over greater distances. Highly valued materials such as Great Lakes copper,

Rocky Mountain obsidian, and marine shells from the Gulf and Atlantic coasts have been found in substantial quantities at sites hundreds and even thousands of miles from their points of origin. In many cases, goods fashioned from these materials were buried with human beings, indicating both their religious significance and, by their uneven distribution, their role as markers of social or political rank.[10]

While the Archaic pattern of autonomous bands persisted in most of North America until the arrival of Europeans, the complexity of exchange relationships in some parts of the continent produced the earliest evidence of concentrated political power. This was especially so for peoples who, after the first century A.D., developed food economies that permitted them to inhabit permanent, year-round villages. In California, for example, competition among communities for coveted acorn groves generated sharply defined political territories and elevated the role of chiefs who oversaw trade, diplomacy, and warfare for clusters of villages. Similar competition for prime fishing and trading locations strengthened the authority of certain village chiefs on the Northwest Coast.[11] Exchange rather than competition for resources appears to have driven centralization in the Ohio and Illinois valleys. There the Hopewell peoples imported copper, mica, shell, and other raw materials over vast distances to their village centers, where specialists fashioned them into intricately crafted ornaments, tools, and other objects. They deposited massive quantities of these goods with the dead in large mounds and exported more to communities scattered throughout the Mississippi Valley. Hopewell burials differentiate between commoners and elites by the quantity and quality of grave goods accompanying each.[12] In the Southwest, meanwhile, a culture known as Hohokam emerged in the Gila River and Salt River valleys among some of the first societies based primarily on agriculture. Hohokam peoples lived in permanent villages and maintained elaborate irrigation systems that enabled them to harvest two crops per year.[13]

By the twelfth century, agricultural production had spread over much of the Eastern Woodlands as well as to more of the Southwest. In both regions, even more complex societies were emerging to dominate widespread exchange networks. In the Mississippi Valley and the Southeast, the sudden primacy of maize horticulture is marked archaeologically

21

in a variety of ways—food remains, pollen profiles, studies of human bone (showing that maize accounted for 50 percent of people's diets), and in material culture by a proliferation of chert hoes, shell-tempered pottery for storing and cooking, and pits for storing surplus crops. These developments were accompanied by the rise of what archaeologists term "Mississippian" societies, consisting of fortified political and ceremonial centers and outlying villages. The centers were built around open plazas featuring platform burial mounds, temples, and elaborate residences for elite families. Evidence from burials makes clear the wide social gulf that separated commoners from elites. Whereas the former were buried in simple graves with a few personal possessions, the latter were interred in the temples or plazas along with many more, and more elaborate, goods such as copper ornaments, massive sheets of shell, and ceremonial weapons. Skeletal evidence indicates that elites ate more meat, were taller, performed less strenuous physical activity, and were less prone to illness and accident than commoners.[14] Although most archaeologists' conclusions are informed at least in part by models developed by political anthropologists, they also draw heavily from Spanish and French observations of some of the last Mississippian societies. These observations confirm that political leaders, or chiefs, from elite families mobilized labor, collected tribute, redistributed agricultural surpluses, coordinated trade, diplomacy, and military activity, and were worshipped as deities.[15]

The largest, most complex Mississippian center was Cahokia, located not far from the confluence of the Mississippi and Missouri rivers, near modern East St. Louis, Illinois, in the rich floodplain known as American Bottoms. By the twelfth century, Cahokia probably numbered 20,000 people and contained over 120 mounds within a five-square-mile area. One key to Cahokia's rise was its combination of rich soil and nearby wooded uplands, enabling inhabitants to produce surplus crops while providing an abundance and diversity of wild food sources along with ample supplies of wood for fuel and construction. A second key was its location, affording access to the great river systems of the North American interior.[16]

Cahokia had the most elaborate social structure yet seen in North America. Laborers used stone and wooden spades to dig soil from "borrow pits" (at least nineteen have been identified by archaeologists),

which they carried in wooden buckets to mounds and palisades often more than half a mile away. The volume and concentration of craft activity in shell, copper, clay, and other materials, both local and imported, suggests that specialized artisans provided the material foundation for Cahokia's exchange ties with other peoples. Although most Cahokians were buried in mass graves outside the palisades, their rulers were given special treatment. At a prominent location in Mound 72, the largest of Cahokia's platform mounds, a man had been buried atop a platform of shell beads. Accompanying him were several group burials: fifty young women, aged 18 to 23, four men, and three men and three women, all encased in uncommonly large amounts of exotic materials. As with the Natchez Indians observed by the French in Louisiana, Cahokians appear to have sacrificed individuals to accompany their leaders in the afterlife. Cahokia was surrounded by nine smaller mound centers and several dozen villages from which it obtained much of its food and through which it conducted its waterborne commerce with other Mississippian centers in the Midwest and Southeast.[17]

[...] Given the archaeological record, North American "prehistory" can hardly be characterized as a multiplicity of discrete microhistories. Fundamental to the social and economic patterns of even the earliest Paleo-Indian bands were exchanges that linked peoples across geographic, cultural, and linguistic boundaries. The effects of these links are apparent in the spread of raw materials and finished goods, of beliefs and ceremonies, and of techniques for food production and for manufacturing. By the twelfth century, some exchange networks had become highly formalized and centralized. Exchange constitutes an important key to conceptualizing American history before Columbus.

Although it departs from our familiar image of North American Indians, the historical pattern sketched so far is recognizable in the way it portrays societies "progressing" from small, egalitarian, autonomous communities to larger, more hierarchical, and centralized political aggregations with more complex economies. The image is likewise subverted when we examine the three centuries immediately preceding the arrival of Europeans. In both American Bottoms and the San Juan River basin [in present-day New Mexico], where twelfth-century populations were most concentrated, agriculture most productive, exchange most varied and voluminous, and political systems most complex and extensive, there were scarcely any inhabitants by the end of the fifteenth century. What happened and why?

Cahokia and other Mississippian societies in the Upper Midwest peaked during the late twelfth and early thirteenth centuries. Data from soil traces indicate that even then laborers were fortifying Cahokia's major earthworks against attack. At the same time, archaeologists surmise, Cahokia was headed toward an ecological crisis: expanded settlement, accompanied by especially hot dry summers, exhausted the soil, depleted the supply of timber for building and fuel, and reduced the habitat of the game that supplemented their diet. By the end of the fourteenth century, Cahokia's inhabitants had dispersed over the surrounding countryside into small farming villages.[18]

Cahokia's abandonment reverberated among other Mississippian societies in the Midwest. Fortified centers on the Mississippi River from the Arkansas River northward and on the Ohio River appear to have been strengthened by influxes of people from nearby villages but then abandoned, and signs from burials indicate a period of chronic, deadly warfare in the Upper Midwest. One archaeologist refers to the middle Mississippi Valley and environs during the fifteenth century as "the vacant quarter." A combination of ecological pressures and upheavals within the alliance that linked them appears to have doomed Cahokia and other midwestern Mississippian centers, leading the inhabitants to transform themselves into the village dwellers of the surrounding prairies and plains observed by French explorers three centuries later.[19]

The upheavals may even have extended beyond the range of direct Mississippian influence to affect Iroquois and Hurons and other Iroquoian speakers of the lower Great Lakes region. These people had been moving from dispersed, riverside settlements to fortified, bluff-top villages over the course of several centuries; the process appears to have intensified in the fourteenth century, when it also led to the formation of the Iroquois and Huron confederacies. The Hurons developed fruitful relations with hunter-gatherers to the north, with whom they exchanged agricultural produce for meat and skins, and Iroquois ties with outsiders appear to have diminished except for small-scale interactions with coastal peoples to the south and east. Across the Northeast, political life was characterized by violence and other manifestations of intense competition. Whether the upheavals in exchange ties occasioned by the collapse of Cahokia were directly linked to the formation of the Iroquois and Huron confederacies, as Dena Dincauze and Robert Hasenstab have suggested for the Iroquois, or were simply part of a larger process generated by the advent of farming and consequent demographic and political changes, the repercussions were still evident when Europeans began to frequent the region during the sixteenth century.[20]

[...] Combinations of continuity and change, persistence and adaptability, arose from concrete historical experiences rather than a timeless tradition. The remainder of this article indicates some of the ways that both the deeply rooted imperatives of reciprocity and exchange and the recent legacies of competition and upheaval informed North American history as Europeans began to make their presence felt.

Discussion of the transition from pre- to post-contact times must begin with the sixteenth century, when Indians and Europeans met and interacted in a variety of settings. When not slighting the era altogether, historians have viewed it as one of discovery or exploration, citing the achievements of notable Europeans in either anticipating or failing to anticipate the successful colonial enterprises of the seventeenth century. Recently, however, a number of scholars have been integrating information from European accounts with the findings of archaeologists to produce a much fuller picture of this critical period in North American history.

[...] In the Northeast, [...] Iroquoian-speaking villagers on the Mississippian periphery and Archaic hunter-gatherers still further removed from developments in the interior met Europeans of several nationalities. At the outset of the century, Spanish and Portuguese explorers enslaved several dozen Micmacs and other Indians from the Nova Scotia-Gulf of St. Lawrence area. Three French expeditions to the St. Lawrence itself in the 1530s and the 1540s followed the Spanish pattern by alienating most Indians encountered and ending in futility. Even as these hostile contacts were taking place, fishermen, whalers, and other Europeans who visited the area regularly had begun trading with natives. As early as the 1520s, Abenakis on the coast of Maine and Micmacs were trading the furs of beavers and other animals for European goods of metal and glass. By the 1540s, specialized fur traders, mostly French, frequented the coast as far south as the Chesapeake; by the 1550s or soon thereafter, French traders rendezvoused regularly with Indians along the shores of upper New England, the Maritimes, and Quebec and at Tadoussac on the St. Lawrence.[21]

What induced Indians to go out of their way to trap beaver and trade the skins for glass beads, mirrors, copper kettles, and other goods? Throughout North America since Paleo-Indian times, exchange in the Northeast was the means by which people maintained and extended their social, cultural, and spiritual horizons as well as acquired items considered supernaturally powerful. Members of some coastal Indian groups later recalled how the first Europeans they saw, with their facial hair and strange clothes and traveling in their strange boats, seemed like supernatural figures. Although soon disabused of such notions, these Indians and many more inland placed special value on the glass beads and other trinkets offered by the newcomers. Recent scholarship on Indians' motives in this earliest stage of the trade indicates that they regarded such objects as the equivalents of the quartz, mica, shell, and other sacred substances that had formed the heart of long-distance exchange in North America for millennia and that they regarded as sources of physical and spiritual well-being, on earth and in the afterlife. Indians initially altered and wore many of the utilitarian goods they received, such as iron axe heads and copper pots, rather than use them for their intended purposes. Moreover, even though the new objects might pass through many hands, they more often than not ended up in graves, presumably for their possessors to use in the afterlife. Finally, the archaeological findings make clear that shell and native copper predominated over the new objects in sixteenth-century exchanges, indicating that European trade did not suddenly trigger a massive craving for the objects themselves. While northeastern Indians recognized Europeans as different from themselves, they interacted with them and their materials in ways that were consistent with their own customs and beliefs.[22]

By the late sixteenth century, the effects of European trade began to overlap with the effects of earlier upheavals in the northeastern interior. Sometime between Jacques Cartier's final departure in 1543 and Samuel de Champlain's arrival in 1603, the Iroquoian-speaking inhabitants of Hochelega and Stadacona (modern Montreal and Quebec City) abandoned their communities. The communities were crushed militarily, and the survivors dispersed among both Iroquois and Hurons. Whether the perpetrators of these dispersals were Iroquois or Huron is a point of controversy, but either way the St. Lawrence communities appear to have been casualties of the rivalry, at least a century old, between the two confederations as each sought to position itself vis-à-vis the French. The effect, if not the cause, of the dispersals was the Iroquois practice of attacking antagonists who denied them direct access to trade goods; this is consistent with Iroquois actions during the preceding two centuries and the century that followed.[23]

The sudden availability of many more European goods, the absorption of many refugees from the St. Lawrence, and the heightening of tensions with the Iroquois help to explain the movement of most outlying Huron communities to what is now the Simcoe County area of Ontario during the 1580s. This geographic concentration strengthened their confederacy and gave it the form it had when allied with New France during the first half of the seventeenth century.[24] Having formerly existed at the outer margins of the arena of exchange centered in Cahokia, the Hurons and Iroquois now faced a new sources of goods and power to the east.[25]

The diverse native societies encountered by Europeans as they began to settle North America permanently during the seventeenth century were not static isolates lying outside the ebb and flow of human history. Rather, they were products of a complex set of historical forces, both local and wide-ranging, both deeply rooted and of recent origin. Although their lives and worldviews were shaped by long-standing traditions of reciprocity and spiritual power, the people in these communities were also accustomed—contrary to popular myths about inflexible Indians—to economic and political flux and to absorbing new peoples (both allies and antagonists), objects, and ideas, including those originating in Europe. Such combinations of tradition and innovation continued to shape Indians' relations with Europeans, even as the latter's visits became permanent.

The establishment of lasting European colonies, beginning with New Mexico in 1598, began a phase in the continent's history that eventually resulted in the displacement of Indians to the economic, political, and cultural margins of a new order. But during the interim natives and colonizers entered into numerous relationships in which they exchanged material goods and often supported one another diplomatically or militarily against common enemies. These relations combined native and European modes of exchange. While much of the scholarly literature emphasizes the subordination and dependence of Indians in these circumstances, Indians as much as Europeans dictated the form and content of their early exchanges and alliances. Much of the protocol and ritual surrounding such intercultural contacts was rooted in indigenous kinship obligations and gift exchanges, and Indian consumers exhibited decided preferences for European commodities that satisfied social, spiritual, and aesthetic values. Similarly, Indians' long-range motives and strategies in their alliances with Europeans were frequently rooted in older patterns of alliance and rivalry with regional neighbors.[26] Such continuities can be glimpsed through a brief consideration of the early colonial-era histories of the Five Nations Iroquois in the Northeast [...]

Post-Mississippian and sixteenth-century patterns of antagonism between the Iroquois and their neighbors to the north and west persisted, albeit under altered circumstances, during the seventeenth century when France established its colony on the St. Lawrence and allied itself with Hurons and other Indians. France aimed to extract maximum profits from the fur trade, and it immediately recognized the Iroquois as the major threat to that goal. In response, the Iroquois turned to the Dutch in New Netherland for guns and other trade goods while raiding New France's Indian allies for the thicker northern pelts that brought higher prices than those in their own country (which they exhausted by midcentury) and for captives to replace those from their own ranks who had died from epidemics or in wars. During the 1640s, the Iroquois replaced raids with full-scale military assaults (the so-called Beaver Wars) on Iroquoian-speaking communities in the lower Great Lakes, absorbing most of the survivors as refugees or captives. All the while, the Iroquois elaborated a vision of their confederation, which had brought harmony within their own ranks, as bringing peace to all people of the region. For the remainder of the century, the Five Nations fought a gruelling and costly series of wars against the French and their Indian allies in order to gain access to the pelts and French goods circulating in lands to the north and west.[27]

Meanwhile, the Iroquois were also adapting to the growing presence of English colonists along the Atlantic seaboard. After the English supplanted the Dutch in New York in 1664, Iroquois diplomats established relations with the proprietary governor, Sir Edmund Andros, in a treaty known as the Covenant Chain. The Covenant Chain was an elaboration of the Iroquois' earlier treaty arrangement with the Dutch, but whereas the Iroquois had termed the Dutch relationship a chain of iron, they referred to the one with the English as a chain of silver. The shift in metaphors was appropriate, for what had been strictly an economic connection was now a political one in which the Iroquois acquired power over other New York Indians. After 1677, the Covenant Chain was expanded to include several English colonies, most notably Massachusetts and Maryland, along with those colonies' subject Indians. The upshot of these arrangements was that the Iroquois cooperated with their colonial partners in subduing and removing subject Indians who impeded settler expansion. The Mohawks in particular played a vital role in the New England colonies' suppression of the Indian uprising known as King Philip's War and in moving the Susquehannocks away from the expanding frontier of settlement in the Chesapeake after Bacon's Rebellion.

For the Iroquois, such a policy helped expand their "Tree of Peace" among Indians while providing them with buffers against settler encroachment around their homelands. The major drawback in the arrangement proved to be the weakness of English military assistance against the French. This inadequacy, and the consequent suffering experience by the Iroquois during two decades of war after 1680, finally drove the Five Nations to make peace with the French and their Indian allies in the Grand Settlement of 1701. Together, the Grand Settlement and Covenant Chain provided the Iroquois with the peace and security, the access to trade goods, and the dominant role among northeastern Indians they had long sought.[28] That these arrangements in the long run served to reinforce rather than deter English encroachment on Iroquois lands and autonomy should not obscure their pre-European roots and their importance in shaping colonial history in the Northeast.

[...] As significant as is the divide separating pre- and post-Columbian North American history, it is not the stark gap suggested by the distinction between prehistory and history. For varying periods of time after their arrival in North America, Europeans adapted to the social and political environments they found, including the fluctuating ties of reciprocity and interdependence as well as rivalry, that characterized those environments. They had little choice but to enter in and participate if they wished to sustain their presence. Eventually, one route to success proved to be their ability to insert themselves as regional powers in new networks of exchange and alliance that arose to supplant those of the Mississippians, Anasazis, and others.

To assert such continuities does not minimize the radical transformations entailed in Europeans' colonization of the continent and its indigenous peoples. Arising in Cahokia's wake, new centers at Montreal, Fort Orange/Albany, Charleston, and elsewhere permanently altered the primary patterns of exchange in eastern North America. The riverine system that channelled exchange in the interior of the continent gave way to one in which growing quantities of goods arrived from, and were directed to, coastal peripheries and ultimately Europe.[29] [...] More generally, European colonizers brought a complex of demographic and ecological advantages, most notably epidemic disease and their own immunity to them, that utterly devastated Indian communities;[30] ideologies and beliefs in their cultural and spiritual superiority to native people and their entitlement to natives' lands;[31] and economic, political, and military systems organized for the engrossment of Indian lands and the subordination or suppression of Indian peoples.[32]

Europeans were anything but uniformly successful in realizing their goals, but the combination of demographic ecological advantages and imperial intentions, along with the Anglo-Iroquois Covenant Chain, enabled land-hungry colonists from New England to the Chesapeake to break entirely free of ties of dependence on Indians before the end of the seventeenth century. Their successes proved to be only the beginning of a new phase of Indian-European relations. By the mid-eighteenth century, the rapid expansion of land-based settlement in the English colonies had sundered older ties of exchange and alliance linking natives and colonizers nearly everywhere east of the Appalachians, driving many Indians west and reducing those who remained to a scattering of politically powerless enclaves in which Indian identities were nurtured in isolation.[33] Meanwhile, the colonizers threatened to extend this new mode of Indian relations across the Appalachians. An old world, rooted in indigenous exchange, was giving way to one in which Native Americans had no certain place.

Notes

1. See James Axtell, "A North American Perspective for Colonial History," *History Teacher*, 12 (1978–1979), 549–62. The beginning of this shift was signaled by Gary B. Nash, *Red, White, and Black* (Englewood Cliffs, N. J., 1973), and Francis Jennings, *The Invasion of America: Indians, Colonialism, and the Cant of Conquest* (Chapel Hill, 1975).

2. See James H. Merrell, "Some Thoughts on Colonial Historians and American Indians," *William and Mary Quarterly [WMQ]*, 3d Ser., 46 (1989), 108–10, and Daniel K. Richter, "Whose Indian History?" ibid., 50 (1993), 381–82.

3. See Frederick E. Hoxie, *The Indians Versus the Textbooks: Is There Any Way Out?* (Chicago, 1984); Hoxie, "The Problems of Indian History," *Social Science Journal*, 25 (1988), 389–99.

4. A volume that draws on all these approaches is Alvin M. Josephy, Jr., ed., *America in 1492: The World of the Indian Peoples Before the Arrival of Columbus* (New York, 1992). The best surveys of North American archaeology are Brian M. Fagan, *Ancient North America: The Archaeology of a Continent* (New York, 1991),and Stuart J. Fiedel, *Prehistory of the Americas*, 2d ed. (Cambridge, 1992). On languages see Harold E. Driver, *Indians of North America*, 2d ed. (Chicago, 1969), and Joseph H. Greenberg, *Language in the Americas* (Stanford, Calif., 1987), esp. chap. 2. Two especially interesting examples of work that utilizes oral traditions as historical sources to supplement "prehistoric" archaeology are Roger C. Echo-Hawk, "Kara Katit Pakutu: Exploring the Origins of Native America in Oral Traditions" (M.A. thesis, University of Colorado, 1994), and Donald Bahr et al., *the Short, Swift Time of Gods on Earth: The Hohokam Chronicles* (Berkeley, Calif., 1994).

5. On archaeology as a foundation for Indian history see Bruce G. Trigger, "Archaeology and the Image of the American Indian," *American Antiquity*, 45 (1980), 662–76, and "American Archaeology as

Native History: A Review Essay," *WMQ*, 3d Ser., 40 (1983), 413–52. Among works that incorporate archaeology into historical narratives, the most exemplary by anthropologists are Trigger, *The Children of Aataensic: A History of the Huron People to 1660* (Montreal, 1976), and Kathleen J. Bragdon, *Native People of Southern New England, 1500–1650* (Norman, Okla., 1996), and by historians, Daniel K. Richter, *The Ordeal of the Longhouse: The People of the Iroquois League in the Era of European Colonization* (Chapel Hill, 1992). The most thorough argument for the role of indigenous contexts in shaping post-Columbian American history is Francis Jennings, *The Founders of America: How the Indians Discovered the Land, Pioneered in It, and Created Great Classical Civilization; How They Were Plunged into a Dark Age by Invasion and Conquest; and How They Are Reviving* (New York, 1993). But Jennings argues for a pervasive "Mexican influence" in North America by the 15th century A.D. and makes several other inferences that are highly speculative at best. Lynda Norene Shaffer, *Native Americans before 1492: The Moundbuilding Centers of the Eastern Woodlands* (Armonk, N. Y., 1992), is a useful overview by a historian whose interest is world, rather than American, history.

6. The need for an understanding of its West African contexts is equally critical but outside the scope of this article and its author's expertise. For a beginning in this direction see John Thornton, *Africa and Africans in the Making of the Atlantic World, 1400–1680* (Cambridge, 1992), and the review of that volume by Ira Berlin in *WMQ*, 3d Ser., 51 (1994), 544–47.

7. Robert F. Berkhofer, Jr., *The White Man's Indian: Images of the American Indian from Columbus to the Present* (New York, 1978), 3.

8. The basic contribution to the vast literature on gift exchange economies are Marcel Mauss, *The Gift: Forms and Functions of Exchange in Archaic Societies*, trans. Ian Cunnison (London, 1954); Karl Polanyi, *The Great Transformation* (New York, 1944), chap. 4; Marshall Sahlins, *Stone Age Economics* (Chicago, 1972); and George Dalton, "The Impact of Colonization on Aboriginal Economics in Stateless Societies," in Dalton, ed., *Research in Economic Anthropology: An Annual Compilation of Research* (Greenwich, Conn., 1978), 1:131–84. On North America see William A. Turnbaugh, "Wide-Area Connections in Native North

America," *American Indian Culture and Research Journal*, 1:4 (1976), 22–28.

9. Edwin S. Wilmsen, *Lindenmeier: A Pleistocene Hunting Society* (New York, 1974); Turnbaugh, "Wide-Area Connections in Native North America," 23–24.

10. Fiedel, *Prehistory of the Americas*, chap. 4; Turnbaugh, "Wide-Area Connections in Native North America," 24–25; Jesse D. Jennings, "Epilogue," in Jennings, ed., *Ancient Native Americans* (San Francisco, 1978), 651; Barbara Bender, "Emergent Tribal Formations in the American Midcontinent," *American Antiquity*, 50 (1985), 52–62; Lynn Ceci, "Tracing Wampum's Origins: Shell Bead Evidence from Archaeological Sites in Western and Coastal New York," in Charles F. Hayes et al., eds., *Proceedings of the 1986 Shell Bead Conference: Selected Papers*, Rochester Museum and Science Center, Research Records No. 20 (Rochester, N. Y., 1989), 65–67.

11. Fiedel, *Prehistory of the Americas*, 133–43.

12. Joseph R. Caldwell, "Interaction Spheres in Prehistory," in Caldwell and Robert L. Hall, eds., *Hopewellian Studies*, Illinois State Museum, Scientific Papers, 12 (Springfield, 1964), 133–43; David S. Brose and N'omi Greber, eds., *Hopewell Archaeology: The Chillicothe Conference* (Kent, Ohio, 1979); Fiedel, *Prehistory of the Americas*, 240–51.

13. Linda S. Cordell, *Prehistory of the Southwest* (Orlando, Fla., 1984), 207–11; Fiedel, *Prehistory of the Americas*, 209–12.

14. Fiedel, *Prehistory of the Americas*, 251–60; Dan F. Morse and Phyllis S. Morse, *Archaeology of the Central Mississippi Valley* (New York, 1983), chaps. 10–11; Bruce D. Smith, "The Archaeology of the Southeastern United States: From Dalton to de Soto, 10,500–500 P.P.," *Advances in World Archaeology*, 5 (1986), 53–63; Vincas P. Steponaitis, "Prehistoric Archaeology in the Southeastern United States, 1970–1985," *Annual Review of Anthropology*, 15 (1986), 387–93.

15. The successful integration of archaeology, history, and theory as well as the range of approaches possible with these as foundations can be seen by surveying the relevant essays in Charles Hudson and Carmen Chaves Tesser, eds., *The Forgotten Centuries: Indians and Europeans in the American South, 1521–1704* (Athens, Ga., 1994). See also Chester B. De Pratter, "Late Prehistoric and Early Historic Chiefdoms in the Southeastern United States" (Ph. D. diss., University of Georgia, 1983);

Charles Hudson et al., "Coosa: A Chiefdom in the Sixteenth-Century Southeastern United States," *American Antiquity*, 50 (1985), 723–37; David G. Anderson, *The Savannah River Chiefdoms: Political Change in the Late Prehistoric Southeast* (Tuscaloosa, Ala., 1994). The most recent theoretical discussion is Randolph J. Widmer, "The Structure of Southeastern Chiefdoms," in Hudson and Tesser, eds., *Forgotten Centuries*, 125–55.

16. Melvin L. Fowler, "A Pre-Columbian Urban Center on the Mississippi," *Scientific American*, 233 (August 1975), 92–101; William R. Iseminger, "Cahokia: A Mississippian Metropolis," *Historic Illinois*, 2:6 (April 1980), 1–4.

17. Archaeologists disagree as to the complexity and power of Cahokia, but see Patricia J. O'Brien, "Urbanism, Cahokia, and Middle Mississippian," *Archaeology*, 25 (1972), 188–97; Fowler, "Pre-Columbian Urban Center on the Mississippi"; Iseminger, "Cahokia"; Fowler, *The Cahokie Atlas: A Historical Atlas of Cahokia Archaeology*, Studies in Illinois Archaeology, 6 (Springfield, 1989); George R. Milner, "The Late Prehistoric Cahokia Cultural System of the Mississippi River Valley: Foundations, Florescence, Fragmentation," *Journal of World Prehistory*, 4 (1990), 1–43; Thomas E. Emerson and R. Barry Lewis, eds., *Cahokia and the Hinterlands: Middle Mississippian Cultures of the Midwest* (Urbana, 1991). For European accounts of the Natchez and other Mississippians who sacrificed individuals when a paramount chief died see DePratter, "Late Prehistoric and Early Historic Chiefdoms," 64–77.

18. Fowler, "Pre-Columbian Urban Center," 8–11; Iseminger, "Cahokia"; Milner, "Late Prehistoric Cahokia Cultural System," 30–33.

19. Dena F. Dincauze and Robert J. Hasenstab, "Explaining the Iroquois: Tribalization on a prehistoric Periphery," in *Comparative Studies in the Development of Complex Societies*, 3 (Southampton, Eng., 1986), 5, 7–8; George R. Milner et al., "Warfare in Late Prehistoric West-Central Illinois," *American Antiquity*, 65 (1991), 581–603; Morse and Morse, *Archaeology*, chap. 12; Stephen Williams, "The Vacant Quarter and Other Late Events in the Lower Valley," in David H. Dye and Cheryl Anne Cox, eds., *Towns and Temples along the Mississippi* (Tuscaloosa, 1990), 170–80.

20. James A. Tuck, *Onondaga Iroquois Prehistory: A Study in Settlement Archaeology* (Syracuse, N. Y.,

1971), chaps. 2–4; James W. Bradley, *Evolution of the Onondaga Iroquois: Accommodating Change, 1500–1655* (Syracuse, N. Y., 1987), 14–34 passim; Trigger, *Children of Aataentsic*, 1:119–76 passim; Trigger, *Natives and Newcomers: Canada's "Heroic Age" Reconsidered* (Kingston, Ont., 1985), 38–110 passim; Dean R. Snow, *The Archaeology of New England* (New York, 1980), 307–19 passim; Dincauze and Hasenstab, "Explaining the Iroquois." One influential version of the oral account of the Iroquois Confederacy's founding confirms that it occurred against a backdrop of violence among the Five Nations Iroquois and their common enmity with the Hurons; see William N. Fenton. ed., *Parker on the Iroquois*, (Syracuse, N. Y., 1968), bk. 3, pp. 14–29.

21. Neal Salisbury, *Manitou and Providence: Indians, Europeans, and the Making of New England, 1500–1643* (New York, 1982), 51–56; Trigger, *Natives and Newcomers*, 118–44.

22. Christopher L. Miller and George R. Hammell, "A New Perspective on Indian-White Contact: Cultural Symbols and Colonial Trade," *Journal of American History [JAH]*, 73 (1986), 311–28; Trigger, *Natives and Newcomers*, 125–27; Bradley, *Evolution*, chap. 21 Calvin Martin, "The Four Lives of a Micmac Copper Pot," *Ethnohistory*, 22 (1975), 111–33; James Axtell, "At the Water's Edge: Trading in the Sixteenth Century," in Axtell, *After Columbus: Essays in the Ethnohistory of Colonial North America* (New York, 1988), 144–81; Trigger, "Early Native North American Responses to European Contact: Romantic versus Rationalistic Interpretations," *JAH*, 77 (1991), 1195–1215. Compare the barbed Delaware-Mahican tradition of early relations with the Dutch recorded by John Heckewelder in his *An Account of the History, Manners, and Customs of the Indian Nations, Who Once Inhabited Pennsylvania and the Neighbouring States* (Philadelphia, 1819), 71–75.

23. Trigger, *Natives and Newcomers*, 144–48.

24. Ibid., 157–61.

25. See Dincauze and Haasenstab, "Explaining the Iroquois."

26. See, for example, Kenneth E. Kidd, "The Cloth Trade and the Indians of the Northeast during the Seventeenth and Eighteenth Centuries," in Royal Ontario Museum, *Art and Archaeology Annual* (1961), 48–56; Wilcomb E. Washburn, "Symbol,

Utility, and Aesthetics in the Indian Fur Trade," *Minnesota History*, 40 (1966), 198–202; Donald J. Bladeslee, "The Calumet Ceremony and the Origin of Fur Trade Rituals," *Western Canadian Journal of Anthropology*, 7, No. 2 (1977), 78–88; Bruce M. White, "Give Us a Little Milk: The Social and Cultural Meanings of Gift Giving in the Lake Superior Fur Trade," *Minnesota History*, 48 (1982), 60–71, and "A Skilled Game of Exchange: Ojibway Fur Trade Protocol," ibid., 50 (1987), 229–40; Francis Jennings et al., eds., *The History and Culture of Iroquois Diplomacy: An Interdisciplinary Guide to the Treaties of the Six Nations and Their League* (Syracuse, N.Y. 1985), chaps. 1, 4–7; Richard White, *The Middle Ground: Indians, Empires, and Republics, 1650–1815* (Cambridge, 1991), chaps. 2–4 passim.

27. Richter, *Ordeal of the Longhouse*, 30–104.
28. Pennsylvania joined the Covenant Chain early in the 18th century; Francis Jennings, *The Ambiguous Iroquois Empire: The Covenant Chain Confederation of Indian Tribes with English Colonies from Its Beginnings to the Lancaster Treaty of 1744* (New York, 1984), chap. 8; Richter, *Ordeal of the Longhouse*, 105–213 passim.

29. Shaffer, *Native Americans before 1492*, esp. 10–11, 94–96.
30. Alfred W. Crosby, *Ecological Imperialism: The Biological Expansion of Europe, 900–1900* (Cambridge, 1986).
31. Roy Harvey Pearce, *The Savages of America: A Study of the Indian and the Idea of Civilization* (Baltimore, 1953); Richard Slotkin, *Regeneration through Violence: The Mythology of the American Frontier, 1600–1800* (Middletown, Conn., 1973); Berkhofer, *White Man's Indian*.
32. Jennings, *Invasion of America*, pt. 1.
33. For summaries of these developments see Salisbury, "The History of Native Americans from before the Arrival of the Europeans and Africans until the American Civil War," in Stanley L. Engerman and Robert E. Gallman, eds., *The Cambridge Economic History of the United States*, vol. 1: *The Colonial Era* (Cambridge, 1996), chap. 1, and "Native People and European Settlers in Eastern North America, 1600–1783," in *The Cambridge History of the Native Peoples of the Americas*, vol. 1: North America, ed. Trigger and Washburn (Cambridge, 1996).

■ Article 2: Donnacona Discovers Europe: Rereading Jacques Cartier's *Voyages*

Ramsay Cook

Jacques Cartier's *Voyages* is the most informative and reliable French description of the northern coast and the St Lawrence region of North America written in the sixteenth century. The report that the Florentine navigator Giovanni Verrazzano composed for the French king, Francis I, describing the 1524. voyage along the coast from the Carolinas to Cape Breton, captures both the changing topography and the different groups of people who lived on the Atlantic seaboard. But it lacks detail and depth. André Thevet,

Source: From Cook, R. *The Voyages of Jacques Cartier*, 1993, ix–x, xviii–xli. © 1993, University of Toronto Press. Reprinted with permission of the publisher.

cosmographer to Francis I, wrote two works about 'France antartique' during the second half of the century—though he may never have travelled to the St Lawrence area. His works, *Les Singularitez de la France antartique* (1556) and *La Cosmographie universelle* (1575), relied heavily on Cartier, with whom he was acquainted. He provides some fascinating details not found elsewhere—his description of the snowshoe for example—but his reliability is problematic. If Verrazzano approximated Montaigne's 'plain simple fellow' who did not 'construct false theories,' then Thevet exemplified the 'men of intelligence' who could not 'refrain from altering the facts a little' in order to substantiate their interpretation.[1]

Cartier's observations are frequently detailed and include an impressive range of information about the geography, natural history, and ethnography from Funk Island to the Amerindian settlement at Hochelaga at the foot of the mountain he named Mount Royal. The *Voyages*, for over 450 years, have provided almost the only documentation for the beginning of European contact with this region. They reveal a man with both the virtues of an honest observer and the assumptions and preoccupations of a shrewd Breton navigator. Since he interpreted what he saw, he 'never presents things just as they are' and, especially in his discussion of his relations with the people who lived along the St Lawrence, he 'could twist and disguise [facts] to conform to [his] point of view.' Like all historical documents, Cartier's *Voyages* can be both informative and misleading.[2] [...]

The critical test of Cartier's representation of what he saw in eastern North America is [...] his ethnology. For Cartier was, unwittingly Canada's first ethnologist, an activity practiced long before its invention as a science.[3] Cartier's *Voyages* can usefully be put to the test of a successful ethnographer set by Clifford Geertz: 'Ethnographers need to convince us ... not merely that they themselves have truly been there, but ... had we been there we should have seen what they saw, felt what they felt, concluded what they concluded.[4] Historians, from Marc Lescarbot in the seventeenth century to Samuel Eliot Morison and Marcel Trudel in the twentieth, have given Cartier almost uniformly high marks by that standard.[5] Cartier's descriptions of the native people he met carry conviction. But the question may fairly be posed: is it necessary to *conclude* what Cartier concluded, even if his description bears the mark of authenticity? That question can best be approached by focusing on the well-known story of Cartier's troubled relationship with Donnacona, 'the lord of Canada,' and his two sons Dom Agaya and Taignoagny, always remembering that all the evidence about that relationship is provided by Cartier, a judge on his own case.[6]

Can that same evidence be used to discover the voices and motives of Cartier's protagonists, to tease out a dialogue where too often only a single voice has been heard in the past? It is worth attempting, even if the results must be tentative, even conjectural, since it must be constructed from limited, often obscure, clues.[7] Moreover, it is important to realize that, in attempting to reconstruct the Cartier-Donnacona dialogue, the problem of language and communication is enormous. Naturally, on Cartier's first trip, the language barrier was total and native speech was almost always described as a 'harangue' or a 'sermon.'[8] Yet in his account of his contacts with the local inhabitants he confidently describes actions, motives, and relationships as though communication had been fairly straightforward. But was it? For example, he describes the relationship among Donnacona, Dom

Agaya, and Taignoagny as that of a 'father' and his 'sons.' How did Cartier know? The vocabulary compiled on the first voyage does not contain these words. On his second voyage he had, part of the time, the assistance of the two men he had carried off to France. How much French had they learned? How faithfully did they translate their own language that had developed in the North American context into an imperfectly understood European tongue? Many European concepts, as the missionaries would later discover, had no local equivalents.[9] The opposite was almost certainly true: the lack of European words for important Amerindian concepts. The more extensive vocabulary gathered during the second voyage still amounts to little more than a tourist's elementary phrase book: numbers, body parts, food, basic questions and commands. Writing of European accounts of contact with native people, Stephen Greenblatt remarks: 'The Europeans and the interpreters themselves translated such fragments as they understood or thought they understood into a coherent story, and they came to believe quite easily that the story was what they actually heard. There could be, and apparently were, murderous results.'[10] The *Voyages* certainly present a fairly coherent story of the Cartier-Donnaconna relationship. The more that relationship is examined, however, the more obvious it becomes that it was based on a dialogue of incomprehension, a dialogue in which Donnacona's actions were made to speak in European words. It ended, if not in murder, then certainly in tragedy.

IV

Cartier arrived in eastern North America already somewhat familiar with the character of its inhabitants.[11] That doubtless explains the matter-of-fact tone to his description of the scattered groups his expedition came across along the coast of Labrador. In 'the land God gave to Cain' he found a 'wild and savage folk' who painted themselves 'with certain tan colours'—Boethuk hunting seal. Before long he realized that these North American people were not all alike: they spoke different languages, practised contrasting lifestyles, and, he eventually realized, warred against one another. From first contact he feared them or at least doubted their trustworthiness, especially if he was outnumbered. He would retain that suspicion and fear even after numerous experiences of welcoming hospitality, though he would tell

King Francis 1 of 'their kindness and peacefulness'. When forty or fifty canoe-loads of Micmac in the Bay de Chaleur signalled a desire to trade with a French party in one longboat, Cartier 'did not care to trust to their signs.' When they persisted, he drove them off with gunfire. French security and potential dominance was established.

This meeting also suggests that Cartier and his party may not have been the first Europeans whom the local native people had met. They wanted to trade and showed no fear. In fact, by 1534, trade between Europeans—Bretons, Basques, English, and other people who lived and fished on the Atlantic seaboard—had a history of several decades, possibly beginning before Columbus.[12] Cartier provides the first detailed description of the ceremonials surrounding trade when the people he had previously driven off returned on 7 July, 'making signs to us that they had come to barter.' Cartier had brought well-chosen trade goods: 'knives, and other iron goods, and a red cap to give their chief.' The first exchange was brisk, the natives leaving stripped even of the furs that covered their bodies. Three days later, amid ceremonial gift exchanges, dancing and singing, business resumed. The young women hung back, suggesting earlier experiences with European sailors. Cartier watched these events with a careful eye, concluding that 'we perceived that they are a people who would be easy to convert'. This was not an immediate goal, but rather a thought for the future. It was an indication that from the outset the French were fishers of men as well as 'explorers,' and that Cartier saw no reason to accept these 'savages' on their own terms.

At Gaspé Harbour, later in July, Cartier made his first contact with members of the native community to which his future in Canada would be inextricably tied. These were people from Stadacona—Laurentian Iroquoians—making their annual fishing expedition to the east coast. Cartier's reports are the only record of these people who 'disappeared,' probably as a result of warfare and perhaps disease, by the end of the century.[13] His first impression of the Stadaconans is important because it illustrates Cartier's powers of observation again, and also provides a clear insight into his use of the term 'sauvaiges.' He wrote: 'This people may well be called savage; for they are the sorriest folk there can be in the world, and the whole lot of them had not anything above the value of five sous, their canoes and fishingnets excepted. They go quite naked, except for a small skin, with which they cover their privy parts, and for a few old skins which they throw over their shoulders. They are not at all of the same race or language as the first we met. They have their heads shaved all around in circles, except for a tuft on the top of the head, which they leave long like a horse's tail. This they do up upon their heads and tie in a knot with leather thongs. They have no other dwelling but their canoes, which they turn upside down and sleep on the ground underneath. They eat their meat almost raw; only warming it a little on the coals; and the same with their fish [...] They never eat anything that has a taste of salt in it. They are wonderful thieves and steal everything they can carry off'.

For Cartier the word 'sauvaiges' was interchangeable with 'gens,' 'personnes,' 'peuple,' 'hommes du pays,' 'hommes,' 'femmes'—he never used 'Indiens.' This usage suggests that Cartier accepted the Amerindians as human, like himself—a matter much disputed in the aftermath of Columbus's initial encounter with the people in America.[14] That impression is supported by Cartier's belief that the inhabitants of the St Lawrence region could be converted to Christianity; had they not been 'men,' that potential would have been denied. But still they were 'savages,' which apparently meant poverty stricken, lacking in worldly possessions and civic institutions, bereft of religion and culture. (They certainly fulfilled Montaigne's definition: 'we all call barbarous anything that is contrary to our own habits'!)[15] Because of their 'savage,' 'wild' state, their lack of culture, Cartier believed that native people could easily be 'dompter': subdued, subjugated, tamed,[16] or as Biggar says, 'moulded.' Consequently, while native people were accepted as 'human,' they were only potential, not actual, equals of the Europeans. Only if the 'savage' characteristics that made them different were 'tamed' or 'moulded' could they become actual equals. Different *and* equal was inconceivable.[17] Finally, since these Laurentian people were 'savages' without culture, religion, or government, Cartier, like those European explorers who had preceded him, saw no reason to ask permission to explore and eventually settle their lands.

Nothing better emphasizes Cartier's assumptions about his rights—and Donnacona's reaction—than the drama that was acted out on 24 July 1534 at the entrance to Gaspé Harbour. There Cartier presided over the raising of a thirty-foot wooden cross to which was fixed a coat-of-arms bearing the fleurs-de-lys and a board on which was emblazoned the words: 'VIVE LE ROI DE FRANCE.' In the presence of Donnacona's people, the French 'knelt down with our hands joined, worshipping it before them; and made signs to them, looking up and pointing towards heaven, that by means of this we had our redemption, at which they showed many marks of admiration, at the same time turning and looking at the cross'.

Any 'marks of admiration' Cartier thought he detected were soon erased by a vigorous act of protest by native leaders. Cartier's account of this reaction demonstrates that what was viewed as an arbitrary European intrusion into eastern North America was not passively accepted. The protest was led by the person Cartier identified as 'the leader' and 'three of his sons and his brother.' Even the language barrier did not prevent Cartier from understanding—or thinking he understood—the meaning of the demonstration: 'pointing to the cross he [the leader] made us a long harangue, making the sign of the cross with two of his fingers; and then he pointed to the land all around about, as if he wished to say that all this region belonged to him, and that we ought not to have set up this cross without his permission'.

Neither the action of the French, in raising the cross, nor the reaction of the native people is totally unambiguous. Cross-raising, beginning with Columbus, had already become something of a tradition in the Americas. It contained both religious and political symbolism. Cartier had previously raised at least one cross—an undecorated one at St Servan's Harbour in June—and he would raise others later. Some of these crosses were raised unceremoniously and doubtless were intended to function as 'a landmark and guidepost into the harbour'. Though Cartier explained the Gaspé cross that way, its bold symbols of church and state, and the accompanying ceremony, surely represented something more. If it was not an explicit legal claim, recognizable in international law, to French possession of this territory, it was surely at least what Trudel calls 'une affirmation solennelle des droits de la France sur cette terre.'[18] This was not an anonymous directional sign; it distinctly affirmed the French presence. It is also worth emphasizing that in introducing the account of his second voyage, Cartier related his exploration both to the protection and promotion of Catholicism

against the threat of 'wicked Lutherans, apostates, and imitators of Mahomet' and to 'these lands of yours,' 'your possessions,' and 'those lands and territories of yours'. If, then, the crosses were merely traffic signals, they should at least be described as *French* traffic signals.

And what of the native people's protest? Cartier's interpretation of it as a rejection of the French right to act without permission can be seen, at the least, as a sign of a guilty conscience. Certainly he knew that no European sovereign would accept such an act on his or her territory. But did a North American 'leader,' especially one whose home territory was somewhere up the St Lawrence, have the same sense of sovereign or proprietary rights? Was the chief claiming the Gaspé harbour area as his people's fishing and hunting territory? It seems altogether likely. What is beyond doubt is that a protest did take place, a protest Cartier suspected was an expression of territorial jurisdiction. Moreover, Cartier acted quickly and deceptively to quell the protest.

When the chief—we later learn this was Donnacona[19]—completed his 'harangue,' a sailor offered him an axe in exchange for the black bear skin he was wearing. Responding to the offer of barter, Donnacona's party moved closer to the French ship only to have their canoe boarded and themselves taken prisoner, though Cartier did not use that term. On the second voyage he did, however, refer to them as 'captured' and 'seized'. Once on board they were cajoled—'made to eat and drink and be of good cheer' (was the drink alcoholic?)—into accepting the sign-post explanation. Cartier then announced that he intended to release only three of the prisoners—compensated with hatchets and knives. The other two, now decked out in shirts, ribbons, and red caps, would be taken 'away with us and afterwards would bring them back again to that harbour'. Since no destination was announced, it seems entirely unlikely that the two young men, or their father, understood this to mean an Atlantic crossing and a nine-month stay in France. Cartier made the final departure seem amicable, and perhaps it appeared that way to Donnacona's people who, if they understood what was taking place, probably recognized that resistance was hopeless. Cartier admitted that 'we did not understand the parting harangues,' and there is equally no reason to believe that Donnacona understood what Cartier had tried to tell him. At best the day ended in mutual misunderstanding—hardly the basis for an 'alliance.'[20]

In acting as he did—and the action seemed premeditated—Cartier followed an established European precedent. Europeans assumed a right to 'explore' new-found lands and to set up traffic crosses, indicating at least an intention to return and perhaps even staking a claim to possession. So, too, kidnapping native people began with Columbus, and Cartier may even have committed similar actions on earlier voyages to Brazil. Since at the time of the seizure of the natives Cartier had not determined whether to continue his explorations or to return to France before winter, his initial intention may have been simply to make use of the men as short-term guides. More plausible, however, is the view that Cartier planned to take the captives back to St Malo as concrete evidence of 'discovery' and to provide them with language training. With the aid of interpreters and go-betweens, the further penetration of North America, leading to the much sought after route to Asia—Cartier's primary goal—would be expedited. Or so Cartier doubtless hoped.

Exactly how Dom Agaya and Taignoagny, as the young men are identified in the account of the second voyage, spent their time between their arrival in St Malo on 5 September 1534 and their departure for home on 19 May 1535 is unrecorded. Nor is there any direct evidence revealing their reactions to their unexpected discovery of Europe. The harrowing experiences of an eighteenth-century Chinese visitor named John Hu, a man similarly untutored in French language and customs, offer some clues to the complexity of cultural contact: he was driven to such unpredictable behaviour that he was confined to the asylum at Charenton pondering the question, 'Why am I locked up?'[21] The two North Americans survived somewhat better, even though they must often have asked similar questions. They doubtless witnessed many strange and wonderful sights. Yet it seems unlikely that either the standard of living of ordinary Frenchmen—housing, food, or medical care—or the political and religious life of a country wracked with religious strife won their enthusiastic approval.[22] Perhaps they concluded, as Jean de Léry did after returning to France from Brazil, that 'one need not go beyond one's own country, nor as far as America, to see [...] monstrous and prodigious things.'[23]

By the time of their return home, they spoke some French, though the level of fluency cannot have been very high. They had learned to dress in the French manner. They may have calculated, and filed for future use, the comparative values of French trade goods, a knowledge that would earn them the epithet of 'rogues'. They had not been baptized, though they had observed that ceremony and other Catholic rites. To Cartier they may have seemed at least partly 'moulded' or 'tamed,' though he would continue to call them 'sauvaiges.' He apparently believed they were ready and willing to work for him. It was not yet in their interest to disabuse him of that notion. That could wait until they were safely back in Stadacona. Then their actions and attitudes would reveal that they had no wish to go on their foreign travels again.

V

During the winter of 1534–5, Dom Agaya and Taignoagny provided Cartier with much useful information about eastern North America. The French navigator certainly wanted to know whether a route to Asia could be found by continuing westward from the mouth of the St Lawrence. Perhaps they encouraged his hopes that a route existed. What he obviously did learn from them was that their home was far inland, up an enormous river at Stadacona, beyond a rich region known as the Saguenay. It was there that they wished to be returned, not to the Gaspé as their father had been promised. Consequently it was from knowledge gained from the two native men, and as a result of their directions, that Cartier was able to attain his principal geographical achievement: 'he was,' Marcel Trudel noted, 'the first to make a survey of the coasts of the St Lawrence [...] and, what is most to his credit, in 1535, he discovered the St Lawrence River.'[24] In fact, Cartier himself described what happened somewhat more accurately. On Friday, 13 August 1535, sailing from southwestern Anticosti, 'it was told us by the two savages whom we had captured on our first voyage, that this cape formed part of the land on the south which was an island; and that to the south of it lay the route from Honguedo where we had seized them [...] and that two days journey from this cape and island began the kingdom of the Saguenay, on the north shore as one made one's way towards this Canada'. Four days later, when Cartier was in some doubt about the route, 'the two savages assured us that this was the way to the mouth of the great river of Hochelaga [St Lawrence] and the route towards Canada [...] and that one could make one's way so far up the river that they had never heard of anyone reaching the head of it'. Cartier and his crew were the first known Europeans to be guided along the St Lawrence to Stadacona. They then insisted that the guide service be continued further up to Hochelaga. That demand resulted in a crisis in the hitherto satisfactory relationship with Dom Agaya, Taignoagny, and their father.

Not surprisingly, the return of the captives to their people in the Stadacona region was an occasion for great joy. At first the local inhabitants were cautious, even fearful, but once the returning men had identified themselves, the ceremonies and gift exchanges began. On 8 September, near the Ile d'Orléans, 'the lord of Canada' arrived alongside and began a 'harangue,' 'moving his body and his limbs in a marvellous manner as is their custom when showing joy and contentment.' Had Cartier interpreted the body language correctly? At this happy reunion, Cartier reported that the sons informed their father 'what they had seen in France, and the good treatment meted out to them there.' Donnacona expressed his gratitude with warm embraces for the French leader. Bread and wine were shared before the returning travellers departed with their father.

It was not until a week later, during which Dom Agaya and his brother had ample time to discuss their travels in more detail with their father, that Cartier met with them again. He was now impatient to move on, but he detected a marked, disturbing change in the mood of his former companions. Sailing towards Stadacona, Cartier met a large party of native people. 'All came over towards our ships,' he noted, 'except the two men we had brought with us [...] who were altogether changed in their attitude and goodwill, and refused to come on board our ships, although many times begged to do so. At this we began somewhat to distrust them.' Cartier's attitude was obviously changing, too. Nevertheless he believed they were willing to guide him to Hochelaga, a place of whose existence they had apparently informed him.

During the next five days, until Cartier pushed on up-river without his guides, the issue of the continuing service of Dom Agaya and Taignoagny resulted in an almost total break in relations between the Stadaconans and the St Malouins. The issue in dispute was simple. Cartier believed that his interpreters had promised to continue on with him to Hochelaga. Donnacona and his sons (Taignoagny more consistently, it would seem, than his brother) either did not want the French to continue westward at all or at least not without first making some binding commitment or alliance with the Stadaconans. If it is true, as some have concluded, that Donnacona hoped to prevent Cartier from making contact with other native groups so that Stadacona could control trade between the French and the hinterland, or that Donnacona hoped to enlist French military aid against the Hochelagans, there is nothing in Cartier's account to support these speculations.[25] Nor is it fair to accept Cartier's claim that on their return to Stadacona, Dom Agaya and Taignoagny began to 'intrigue' against him.[26] They had, after all, painfully concrete reasons for distrusting Cartier, and legitimate grounds for looking to their own interests in the face of French incursions into their territory. To judge these confusing events—which make it plain that the language barrier had not been effectively breeched—solely from Cartier's perspective implicitly denies the legitimacy of Donnacona's stance. Yet what Cartier viewed as 'treachery,' from Donnacona's point of view was a perfectly reasonable insistence that foreign visitors conduct themselves with due respect for the wishes and customs of their hosts. This is not to argue that the actions of the Stadaconans were so straightforward that Cartier was simply obtuse in failing to understand them. It does have to be remembered that the account of these events is Cartier's and therefore reflects his confusion and suspicion; it does not necessarily represent faithfully the intentions of the other actors whose behaviour may have had a logic of its own. A tentative analysis of a series of events that left Cartier impatient, suspicious, and frightened helps to reveal this logic.

On 16 September Taignoagny informed Cartier that Donnacona was 'annoyed' by the Frenchman's decision to visit Hochelaga and that he would not accompany him. Taignoagny then rejected Cartier's offer of a present—a bribe—in return for disobeying his father. The following day Donnacona appeared, and a ceremony—though Cartier may not have recognized it as such—took place in which the chief presented Cartier with a girl about twelve years old, said to be Donnacona's niece, and two younger boys, one of whom was said to be Taignoagny's brother, though these relationships seem confused. Cartier first understood these gifts as an attempt to convince him to forgo his Hochelaga trip—an apparent bribe. He refused that condition and was then told that the gifts were offered out of friendship and 'in sign of alliance'. Cartier attributed these conflicting stories to Taignoagny, 'as well by this as by other bad turns we had seen him do [...] was a worthless fellow, who was intent upon nothing but treason and malice'. He ignored or disbelieved, or failed to understand, the meaning of a 'sign of alliance.'

It is possible that in order to cement an alliance with the French, Donnacona was proposing a reciprocal gift, an exchange of persons? Cartier was familiar with gift-giving, for he had engaged in it since his first arrival in North America. But he probably did not understand its ceremonial implications in North American native societies, especially that such ceremonies could include the exchange of people.[27] This interpretation is perhaps borne out by the fact that after the Stadaconans failed in what, from Cartier's account, seemed to be a clumsy attempt to invoke the aid of their divinity to frighten the French away from the western trip, a new proposal was advanced. 'Taignoagny and Dom Agaya told the Captain that Donnacona was unwilling that either of them should accompany him to Hochelaga unless he [Cartier] should leave a hostage behind on shore with Donnacona'. It is, of course, possible that Donnacona suspected another kidnapping and wanted a hostage. Alternatively, this proposal may have been a misunderstood attempt to explain the reciprocal nature of the gift-exchange treaty ceremony.

Cartier summarily rejected this new proposal, for he had now completely lost confidence in his former interpreters. He would go without them, sweeping Donnacona's objections aside. But the questions remain: Did Cartier misinterpret Donnacona's objections and the proposal he made? Had Donnacona merely been asking Cartier to complete the reciprocal action that had begun when Cartier accepted the children who had been offered as a 'sign of alliance'? If an alliance had been offered and rejected, was it not quite natural for Donnacona's people to suspect that the French expedition to Hochelaga might have results that would be detrimental to the interests of Stadacona? 'In these primitive and archaic societies'— one might prefer the term stateless societies—Marcel

Mauss wrote in his *Essai sur le don*, 'there is no middle path. There is either complete trust or mistrust. One lays down one's arms, renounces magic and gives everything away, from casual hospitality to one's daughter or one's property. It was in such conditions that men, despite themselves, learnt to renounce what was theirs and made contracts to give and repay.'[28] Cartier had first refused to lay down arms ('to carry them … was the custom in France'); had then insisted that their magic, not his, should be renounced ('their god Cudouagny was a mere fool [...] Jesus would keep them safe'); and finally had refused the reciprocal gift that would have sealed an alliance, even when the lord of Canada's own niece and son were offered to him. Where complete trust might have been established, mistrust, on both sides, resulted.

Unable to understand the framework in which the Stadaconans acted, Cartier was reduced to denunciation, charging his lost allies with ill-will and treason. But the problem was a much deeper one. Cartier had taken Dom Agaya and Taignoagny to France to train them as interpreters so they could act as go-betweens, easing him along his way. On their return to the St Lawrence region armed with their new language skills, they were to act in his interests and aid him in achieving his objectives. In a sense, he expected them to act as Frenchmen. What he failed to comprehend, or accept, was that after a brief nine months of total immersion, Dom Agaya and Taignoagny remained pretty much as they had always been: St Lawrence Iroquoians. Once reunited with their own people, they reverted completely to their own identities and refused to collaborate unconditionally with their former captors.[29] When Cartier learned that what had appeared to be friendship in France had disappeared—a friendship he thought had been affirmed by the welcome he received on his first arrival at Stadacona—he could only explain it by character defects in the native people. They were unreliable, untrustworthy, treacherous rogues—a typical European conclusion.[30] Yet the behaviour that Cartier condemned as 'treason'—a word implying that loyalty was owed to the French— was, by Donnacona's logic, a rejection of that very idea, a rejection of French mastery. The first act of resistance had taken place at Gaspé Harbour. The struggle over Cartier's trip to Hochelaga was but another action in the same drama. Everything was now in place for the dénouement.

VI

Cartier's Hochelaga trip, as he recorded it, stands in marked contrast to the gathering atmosphere of mistrust and confused signals between the French and the Stadaconans. That contrast is seen in the first contact he made with native people up the river: 'they come towards our boats in as friendly and familiar manner as if we had been natives of the country'. Further along Cartier felt the same easy relationship, and at one point allowed a powerful man to carry him ashore 'as if he had been a six-year-old child'. There were gift exchanges; one local leader presented Cartier with 'two of his children,' though only the girl, who was eight or nine, was accepted. The culmination of this almost royal progress came at Hochelaga. As the French approached the village on 2 October they were greeted by 'more than a thousand persons, men, women and children, who gave us as good a welcome as ever father gave to his son [...] They brought us quantities of fish, and of their bread [...] throwing so much of it into our longboats that it seemed to rain bread'.

Cartier accepted this treatment as perfectly natural, perhaps even to be expected from people whom he may have assumed were familiar with Europeans. But what he interpreted as signs of familiarity were quite likely just the opposite, as he may gradually have realized. In fact, the character of the reception the French received at Hochelaga bore the marks of a first contact, one in which the native people mistook the French, marshalled in their armour and speaking a strange language, for something other than ordinary men. Women repeatedly brought their children to be touched, and the women showed none of the shyness evident in those earlier trading sessions when their men kept them at a distance. The next day, within the pallisaded village, a remarkable ceremony took place, one in which Cartier found himself in the role of shaman or healer—and accepted his unexpected casting. Cartier and his men were ushered to the centre of the town square and seated on elaborately woven mats. Soon they were joined by the village's leader, carried in on the shoulders of nine or ten strong men. When he took his seat on a deerskin near Cartier, it became obvious that he was severely paralysed and that he expected to be 'cured and healed' by his visitor. Cartier, taking his cue, 'set about rubbing his arms and legs with his hands. Thereupon this *Agouhanna*

took the band of cloth he was wearing as a crown and presented it to the Captain.' Then the sick, the lame, the blind, and the aged were brought forward for Cartier to 'lay his hands upon them, so that one would have thought Christ had come down to earth to heal them.' Cartier performed his appointed role in the only style he knew, 'making the sign of the cross over the poor sick people, praying God to give them knowledge of our holy faith'. So convincing was his interpretation that the local women tried to prevent the French from leaving by offering large quantities of food. Cartier rejected it for it was unsalted, though he was probably anxious to depart before being called for an encore.

Whether Cartier exaggerated these events of the early days of October 1535, and what exactly they meant to the St Lawrence Iroquoians, can only be guessed at. Certainly they were unlike any other ceremony recorded in the *Voyages*. It was obviously not an occasion for commerce, though some gifts were distributed by the French, for the Hochelagans showed none of the frenzied desire to exchange furs for European goods that was displayed at earlier meetings. Instead, the ritual performed in the village square bore the signs of some prophecy being fulfilled with the arrival of otherworldly healers.[31] Cartier's quick intelligence apparently allowed him to interpret the signals accurately. Perhaps it was the realization that his healing powers were at best untested that led to his hasty departure on the following day 'for fear of any misadventure'. Even the almost worshipful reception of the Hochelagans had not removed Cartier's distrust of the St Lawrence Iroquoians.

The French undoubtedly contrasted the respectful reception they had received at Hochelaga with what they interpreted as the cagey manoeuvring of Donnacona and his sons. Now they set out to return to Stadacona, convinced there was gold and silver to be found somewhere in the region and apparently under the impression that 'the Canadians and some eight or nine other peoples are subjects' of the Hochelagans. Perhaps this belief stiffened Cartier's determination to deal with Donnacona's people more firmly and, if necessary, harshly. The western trip had done nothing to dispel his suspicion that even the friendliest of gesture on the part of the leaders a Stadacona only masked treacherous intentions.

VII

Cartier's peremptory departure for Hochelaga on 19 September doubtless left the Stadaconans displeased, suspicious, and perhaps even hostile. When the French party returned a week later they found that the men they had left behind had built themselves a fort 'with artillery pointing every way'. Obviously relations had deteriorated further. Still Donnacona issued an almost immediate invitation to visit Stadacona—something Cartier had not done before going to Hochelaga, which may have been another cause for Donnacona's earlier unease. On visiting Stadacona, Cartier received a warm and formal welcome. He attached no particular significance to a display of scalps that Donnacona explained had been harvested during a war with the 'Toudamans,' though this may have been a request for French assistance.

During this period Cartier began closer observation of local customs, and concluded that the St Lawrence Iroquoians had 'no belief in God that amounts to anything.' He attempted to inform them about Christianity, but when Donnacona and his sons rounded up the whole village for baptism 'an excuse was made to them': there were no priests to conduct the ceremony and there was no consecrated oil. Whether this was the whole truth is unclear. Cartier had told Donnacona earlier that he had consulted his 'priests' before going to Hochelaga, at the time when an attempt had been made to prevent Cartier's departure by an appeal to the local god. Moreover, a mass was 'said and sung' some months later. If the priests had not died in the interim—and that is possible—then Cartier prevaricated on one of these occasions. It is significant that Cartier refused baptism for two reasons: 'we did not know their real intention and state of mind and had no one to explain to them our faith'. Yet the incident further convinced him that conversion would be easy.

Still, Cartier continued to distrust the Stadaconans, especially his two former guides after they urged their fellows to bargain for better prices. Both on his trip to Hochelaga and after returning, the French had been encouraged by some native people to beware of Dom Agaya and his brother. After a number of small incidents had heightened Cartier's apprehensions, and 'fearing that they should attempt some treasonable design,' he reinforced the fort and ordered a round-the-clock watch, thus provoking annoyance and puzzlement among Donnacona's

followers. Yet by the time winter had set in—and it was a terrible winter—relations had apparently been restored to 'as friendly a manner as before'.

December brought disaster in the shape of a scurvy epidemic, the best-known incident in Cartier's career. Disease was the scourge of sixteenth-century Europeans even more than for pre-contact North American people. In France disease was widespread, often epidemic, and cures were few. In March 1535, prior to Cartier's second trip, an 'epidemic and plague' broke out in St Malo and was perhaps carried up the St Lawrence. Europeans had, however, developed immunities, complete or partial, to a large number of communicable diseases, which meant they were no longer fatal. But European pathogens were largely unknown in America, making measles, small pox, tuberculosis, influenza, and other common diseases deadly. The cures—herbal and spiritual—that North Americans successfully applied to their own illnesses were impotent against the European biological invasion that silently accompanied Columbus.[32] Of course, Europeans could contact unexpected health problems in North America, too.

According to Cartier's account, the 'pestilence' that struck in December broke out first among the people of Stadacona and, despite efforts at quarantine, the French were soon infected. Since Cartier's graphic description of the disease makes it certain it was scurvy caused by a vitamin C deficiency, the suspicion of contagion was unfounded. Moreover, since the native people had an effective cure for scurvy, Cartier's assumption that both communities were suffering from the same illness may be questioned, especially when he reported 'more than fifty deaths' at Stadacona. Perhaps the native people had contracted a French imported virus. That the French brought diseases with them is documented by Cartier's observation that the scurvy remedy that was eventually used 'cured all of the diseases they had ever had. And some of the sailors who had been suffering for five or six years from the French pox [la grande vérole] were by the medicine cured completely'. What this disease really was—syphilis or small pox or something else—is impossible to say. But micro-organisms certainly entered the St Lawrence region with the French, likely began infecting the inhabitants by the early winter of 1535, and may even have played a part in the eventual disappearance of the St Lawrence Iroquoians.[33] Of course, native people suffered from vitamin C deficiencies, too; it is the reported fifty fatalities that suggests scepticism about Cartier's diagnosis.

What is incontestable is that while the scurvy raged through the French camp, afflicting all but three or four and killing twenty-five of the 110 members of the company, Cartier's fears and suspicions—his 'great dread' of the Stadaconans—grew. Utterly convinced that the native people bore the French ill will, Cartier resorted to a series of ruses to disguise the weakness of his stricken contingent from them—instead of asking for assistance. When, for example, a party led by Donnacona set off for the annual winter hunt and did not return exactly when expected, Cartier concluded that 'a large force to attack us' was being assembled. Nor were those suspicions and fears erased by the most obvious sign of Iroquoian good will imaginable in the circumstances. Dom Agaya, who had apparently himself suffered severely from a scurvy-like disease, not only prescribed the cure he had used but even ordered two women to gather the 'Annedda' (white cedar) branches for him.[34] It was not Cartier 'skillfully questioning'[35] Dom Agaya that is noteworthy in this episode, but rather the young Iroquois' quick, willing response to the plight of his one-time kidnappers. That Cartier was blind to this generosity is perhaps seen in his enthusiastic thanks to God, rather than to Dom Agaya, for the miraculous cure.

What even more obviously reveals Cartier's almost paranoid suspicion of the Stadaconans is the evidence that Dom Agaya's gift of the cure did nothing to undermine the 'dread' that Donnacona was plotting an attack on the French. When the headman returned from his trip, accompanied by a large number of hunters, and showed some signs that Cartier interpreted as secretiveness and caution, those fears were heightened. When Cartier learned that 'a leader of that region named Agona' was somehow a problem for Donnacona, he made no offer of support to the old man and his sons or to draw any connection between this problem and Donnacona's mysterious movements. Instead Cartier, 'on being informed of the large number of people at Stadacona, though un-aware of their purpose, yet determined to outwit them, and to seize their leader [Donnacona], Taignoagny, Dom Agaya, and the headmen. And moreover he had quite made up his mind to take Donnacona to France, that he might relate and tell to the king all he had seen in the west of the wonders of the world'. If Cartier believed

that by removing Donnacona's party he could place Agona in power and thus establish French control of the St Lawrence region through a puppet, there is nothing in his account that even hints at such 'a plan for a revolution.'[36]

Every effort was now focused on drawing Donnacona and his supporters into a trap. When the Stadaconans, perhaps suspecting foul play, proved reluctant prey, Cartier took this as a further sign of 'knavishness'. That the Stadaconans had the uneasy feeling that the French were planning a trip for them was revealed by Taignoagny's expression of relief when Cartier assured him that the king had 'forbidden him to carry off to France any man or woman, but only two or three boys to learn the language'. Taignoagny, the supposed scheming rogue, naïvely swallowed this blatant lie and promised to bring his father to the French fort the next day.

That day, 3 May, was Holy Cross Day, an appropriate occasion for a repetition of the events that had taken place at Gaspé Harbour two years earlier. First a cross raising, at a location where a traffic marker was hardly needed. Its Latin letters read: FRANCISCVSPRIMVS, DEI GRATIA, FRANCORVM REX, REGNAT.' Perhaps recalling the earlier ceremony, Donnacona was nervous and reluctant to enter the fort 'to eat and drink as usual'. Cartier became impatient with the cat-and-mouse game: he ordered his men to seize the chief, his two sons, and two others. A desperate attempt by Taignoagny to pull his father back came too late. Once the five 'had been captured and the rest had all disappeared, Donnacona and his companions were placed in safe custody'. They were prisoners.

Donnacona's followers, fully aware of the deadly fire power of the French canon, probably concluded that any attempt to free their leader would result in disaster. One apparent threat was made, but Cartier ordered Donnacona brought on deck to calm his people with the promise that within 'ten or twelve moons' he would return to his homeland. Ceremonies followed on this and subsequent days when Cartier was presented with large quantities of *esnoquy* or wampum, 'the most valuable articles they possess in this world; for they attach more value to it than to gold or silver'. These gestures were surely not made in homage to the French explorer who had deceived them but rather as a pathetic attempt to purchase a guaranteed return passage for their chief and his companions. Cartier generously repeated his promise, for what it was worth, and on 6 May 1536 his ships and their human cargo sailed away.

Cartier probably intended to return to Stadacona the next year, but King Francis was preoccupied by a war with Spain. The return journey was delayed for more than three years. None of the ten native people—the five captives plus five others who were 'gifts'—ever returned to Canada. All but one woman died before Cartier set out again, and she remained in France. She might have brought some embarrassing news had she returned. Before he died, Donnacona had been to court, apparently performing as Cartier had hoped. According to Thevet, he died 'a good Christian, speaking French.'[37] The fate of his companions is unrecorded except that, in all, three were baptized, whether voluntarily, or *in articulo mortis,* is unknown.[38] Probably the diseases that Dom Agaya and Taignoagny had escaped on their first trip now took their toll. Four years was a long time to be away from home. The 'slips of trees and the seeds of the rarest [plants] of Canada' that Cartier presented to Francis I were planted in the garden at Fontainebleau.[39] The 'lord of Canada' and his companions were presumably interred in humbler ground.

When the navigator of St Malo finally reappeared before Stadacona on 23 August 1541, he offered a self-serving account of the fate of the men, girls, and boys he had so callously transported to France. When he met with Agona who, he noted, 'was appointed king there by Donnacona,' Cartier told him that 'Donnacona was dead in France, and that his body rested in the earth, and that the rest stayed there as great Lords, and were married, and would not return back into their country.' The French leader was satisfied that the lie had been carried off convincingly, especially since Agona was now the unchallenged 'Lord and Governor of the Country'.

The third voyage, of which the record is so fragmentary, proved a complete fiasco. The settlement Cartier had been sent to help establish—leadership now rested with Sieur de Roberval—was short-lived. In the spring of 1542 the St Lawrence Iroquoians turned against him. Even Agona, whose loyalty the French so confidently believed had been bought by Donnacona's demise, apparently joined the opposition. Cartier, hoping a fistful of 'Canadian diamonds' would justify his desertion of Roberval, decided to flee.[40] Did he ever suspect that the St Lawrence Iroquoians had finally realized the true fate of Donnacona and the others?

Cartier's failure, for that is what it was, resulted from his ethnology, his attempt to understand the people who lived along the St Lawrence River. His description of them was careful and often perceptive. He leaves the impression of having truly 'been there.' But his judgment, and therefore his representation, of these people was mortally flawed. They existed only in European terms, never in their own, their *alterité* unrecognized because it was unaccepted. Though Cartier successfully mapped the St Lawrence, he misidentified the St Lawrence Iroquoians, who remained as mysterious as the *adhothuys* [belugas] and 'seahorses' [walruses] who played near the mouth of the Saguenay River. For Cartier, a flawed ethnology brought only failure; for Donnacona's people it proved fatal.

VIII

The *Voyages of Jacques Cartier* document the French discovery of the St Lawrence valley. They contain unique geographical, biological, and ethnological descriptions, but they also recount something else. Their pages record the St Lawrence Iroquoians' discovery of France, a country of overdressed and often underfed people, where men grew hair on their faces and did women's work in the fields. Women in France were said to be sexually voracious, babies consigned to wet nurses, and children subjected to harsh discipline. Most families lived huddled together while a few idle men enjoyed extensive estates, hunting and fishing for sport. Theirs was a religion of churches, priests, and preachers warring over dogma. From French ports sailed creaking ships filled with self-confident adventurers and sharp traders who carried arms, ignorant of local customs. These suspicious, scheming intruders brought unknown illnesses, frightened native women, told lies, and shamelessly kidnapped even those who helped them. The French, Donnacona's people might have concluded, 'are wonderful thieves and steal everything they can carry off.'

Notes

1. Laurence C. Wroth, *The Voyages of Giovanni de Verrazzano*, 1524–28 (New Haven and London: Yale University Press 1970), Roger Schlesinger

and Arthur P. Stabler, eds., *André Thevet's North America: A Sixteenth-Century View* (Kingston and Montreal: McGill-Queen's University Press 1986). See also Frank Lestringant, *Le Huguenot et le Sauvage* (Paris: Aux Amateurs de Livres 1990).

2. The Montaigne quotations are from 'On Cannibals' in Michel Montaigne, *Essays* (London: Penguin Books 1958), 108.

3. Numa Broc, *La géographie de la Renaissance* 1420–1620 (Paris: Bibliothèque nationale 1980), where it is said of Renaissance explorers that 'par essence et par vocation, ils seront plus ethnologues que géographes' (80), Margaret Hogden, *Early Anthropology in the Sixteenth and Seventeenth Centuries* (Philadelphia: University of Pennsylvania Press 1964). Michèle Duchet in her *Anthropologie et histoire au siècle des lumières* (Paris: François Maspero 1971), argues that early travelers were not anthropologists in the modern sense because they failed to give up their civilized status 'to become participant-observers' (15). This is an elevated view of modern anthropologists, whose 'science' is effectively questioned in James Clifford, *The Predicament of Culture* (Cambridge, Mass.: Harvard University Press 1988), and by Clifford Geertz in *Work and Lives: The Anthropologist as Author* (Stanford: Stanford University Press 1988).

4. Geertz, *Work*, 16

5. Bruce Trigger's *The Children of Aataentsic: A History of the Huron People to 1660*, 2 vols. (Montreal and London: McGill-Queen's University Press 1976), I, 177–208, and Olive P. Dickason's *The Myth of the Savage* (Edmonton: University of Alberta Press 1984), 163–71, adopt a more sceptical approach to Cartier's evidence.

6. For a reconstruction of Amerindian views of European contact, based on sixteenth-century accounts and anthropological work, see Nathan Wachtel, *The Vision of the Vanquished: The Spanish Conquest of Peru through Indian Eyes 1530–1570* (New York: Barnes and Noble 1977). These rich sources are lacking for the sixteenth century in Canada. See Georges Sioui, *Pour une autohistoire amérindienne* (Québec: Les Presses de l'Université Laval 1989). For a brilliant discussion of the problems of documentation for nonliterate cultures see Inga Clendinnen, *Aztecs: An Interpretation* (Cambridge: Cambridge University Press 1991), 277–94. For an interpretation from an Amerindian perspective see Bernard Assiniw, *Histoire des Indiens du Haut et du Bas Canada* (Montréal: Leméac 1974).

7. On the 'conjectural model' and the use of clues see Carlo Ginzburg,' Morelli, Freud and Sherlock Holmes: Clues and the Scientific Method.' *History Workshop* 9 (spring 1980): 5–36.

8. Cartier used several terms, including 'harangue' (26), 'sermon' (57), and 'prédication et preschement' (54), all suggesting a hortatory tone, a characteristic of formal Amerindian speech.

9. James Axtell, *The Invasion Within* (New York and Oxford: Oxford University Press 1985), 81–3

10. Stephen.J. Greenblatt, *Learning to Curse: Essays m Early Modern Culture* (New York and London: Routledge 1990), 27; see also Stephen Greenblatt, *Marvellous Possessions: The Wonder of the New World* (Chicago: University of Chicago Press 1991), 86–118. For valuable insights into the problem of communications see Lois M. Feister, 'Linguistic Communication between the Dutch and the Indians in New Netherlands, 1609–94,' *Ethno-history* 20, 1 (winter 1973): 25–38, David Murray, *Forked Tongues Speech: Writing and Representation in North American Indian Texts* (London: Pinter Publishers 1991), 1–48, and Robin Ridington, 'Cultures in Conflict: The Problem of Discourse,' in his *Little Bit Knowing Something* (Vancouver: Douglas and McIntyre 1990), 186–205. Charles Darwin's chapter on the Fuegians, in *The Voyages of the Beagle* (New York: Dutton 1977), is an interesting example of the way sixteenth-century attitudes to aboriginal peoples survived into the nineteenth century, though Darwin did recognize that 'wherever the European has trod, death seems to pursue the aboriginal' (418). Of particular interest is his comment on the problem of communication: 'Although all three could speak and understand, it was singularly difficult to obtain much information from them, concerning the habits of their countrymen: this was partly owing to their apparent difficulty in understanding the simplest alternative. Everyone accustomed to very young children knows how seldom one can get an answer even to so simple a question as whether a thing is black or white, the idea of black or white seems alternately to fill their minds. So it is with these Fuegians, and hence it was generally impossible to find out, by cross-questioning, whether one had rightly understood anything

which they had asserted' (198). Inga Glendinnen, '"Fierce and Unnatural Cruelty": Cortés and the Conquest of Mexico,' *Representations* 33 (winter 1991): 65–100

11. Michel Mollat, *Les explorateurs du XIIIe au XVIe siècles: Premiers regards sur des mondes nouveaux* (Paris: J.C. Lattès 1984), 184–5

12. David Beers Quinn, *England and the Discovery of America 1481–1620* (New York: Oxford University Press 1974), chap. 1, and James Axtell, 'At the Water's Edge: Trading in the Sixteenth Century,' in his *After Columbus* (New York: Oxford University Press 1988), 144–81; John Dickenson, 'Les précurseurs de Jacques Cartier,' in Fernand Braudel, *Le monde de Jacques Cartier* (Montreal: Libre-Expression 1984), 127–48

13. Bruce G. Trigger, ed., *Handbook of North American Indians, vol. 15: Northeast* (Washington: Smithsonian Institution 1978), 357–61

14. Anthony Pagden, *The Fall of Natural Man: The American Indian and the Origins of Comparative Anthropology* (Cambridge: Cambridge University Press 1986)

15. François-Marc Gagnon and Denise Petel, *Hommes effarables et bestes sauvaiges* (Montreal: Boréal, 1986), 91–115; Kupperman, *Settling*, 197–40; Montaigne, *Essays*, 108

16. *Cassell's Concise French-English French Dictionary* (New York: Macmillan 1968), 121

17. Tzvetan Todorov, *The Conquest of America* (New York: Harper and Row 1984), 42

18. Marcel Trudel, *Histoire de la Nouvelle-France: Les vaines tentatives* (Montréal: Fides 1963), 82; Brian Slattery, 'French Claims in North America, 1500–54,' *Canadian Historical Review* 59, 2 (June 1978): 139–69, argues convincingly that this act did not represent: a legally recognizable claim, but in dismissing the symbolism he is, I think, too literal. Moreover, he underplays the importance of Cartier's remarks in the introduction to the Second *Voyage*. See also Olive P. Dickason, 'Concepts of Sovereignty at a Time of First Contacts,' in L.C. Green and Olive P. Dickason, *The Law of Nations and the New World* (Edmonton: University of Alberta Press 1989), 232, Cartier's action followed the precedent already set by Columbus on 12 October 1492, when he met his first group 'naked people.' In his brilliant *Columbus* (Oxford and New York: Oxford University Press 1991), Felipe Fernandez-Armesto writes: 'This was

not just a description, but a classification. A late fifteenth century reader would have understood that Columbus was confronting "natural men," not citizens of a civil society possessed of legitimate political institutions of their own. The registering of this perception thus prepared the way for the next step, the ritual appropriation of sovereignty to the Castilian monarchs, with a royal banner streaming and a scribe to record the act of possession'. (82). For a fuller exposition of this argument see the same author's *Before Columbus: Exploration and Colonization from the Mediterranean to the Atlantic 1229–1492* (London: Macmillan 1987), 223–45.

19. Marcel Trudel, 'Donnacona,' *Dictionary of Canadian Biography* (DCB), I, (Toronto: University of Toronto Press 1966), 275–6. This biography, based on the only existing documentation, Cartier's *Voyages,* accepts unquestioningly Cartier's evaluation of Donnacona's actions.

20. Trudel, 'Cartier,' *DCB*, I, 167. There is no documentation for the claim that an 'alliance' was made. Nor is there any evidence that 'Cartier also stated that he wished to take two of Donnacona's sons to France for the winter.' Trigger, *Children*, 182

21. Jonathan Spence, *The Question of Hu* (New York: Knopf 1988), 126. Another suggestive source is Shusaku Endo's stories in *foreign studies* (Seven Oaks, England: Sceptre 1990).

22. Robert Mandrou, *Introduction to Modern France 1500-1640: An Essay in Historical Psychology* (London: Edward Arnold 1975), passim

23. Jean de Léry, *History of a Voyage to the Land of Brazil, Otherwise Called America* (Berkeley, Los Angeles, Oxford: University of California Press 1990), 133

24. Trudel, 'Cartier,' 171, though earlier Trudel gives some credit to the guides. See also Samuel Eliot Morison, *The European Discovery of America: The Northern Voyages A.D. 500–1600* (New York: Oxford University Press 1971), 395–423.

25. Trudel, 'Cartier,' 167; Trigger, *Children*, 187–8

26. Trudel, *Histoire*, 110; Cornelius Jaenen, *Friend and Foe: Aspects of French-Amerindian Cultural Contact in the Sixteenth and Seventeenth Centuries* (Toronto: McClelland and Stewart 1973), 13

27. See Marshall Sahlins, 'The Spirit of the Gift,' in his *Stone Age Economics* (Chicago: Aldine 1972), 149–84, and also a brilliant application of this idea in Peter Hulme, 'John Smith and Pocahontas,' in his

Colonial Encounters: Europe and the Native Caribbean 1492–1797 (London and New York: Methuen 1986), 147–52.

28. Marcel Mauss, *The .Gift: Forms and Functions of Exchange* in *Archaic Societies* (London: Cohen and West 1954), 80; Trigger, *Children*, 187–90

29. Marie-Christine Gomez-Géraud, 'Taignoagny et Dom Agaya: Portrait de deux truchements,' in Alain Parent, *La renaissance et le nouveau monde* (Québec: Musée de Québec 1984), 52–4. This is perhaps the only article on Cartier that attempts to understand the viewpoint of Donnacona's sons.

30. Hulme, *Colonial, 163*; Karen O. Kupperman, 'English Perceptions of Treachery, 1583–1640: The Case of the American Savages,' *Historical Journal 20, 2* (1977): 263–87

31. George R. Hamell, 'Strawberries, Floating Islands, and Rabbit Captains: Mythical Realities and European Contact in the Northeast during the Sixteenth and Seventeenth Centuries,' *Journal of Canadian Studies* 21, 4 (winter 1986–7): 72–4; Christopher L. Miller and George R. Hamell, 'A New Perspective on Indian-White Contact: Cultural Symbóls of Colonial Trade,' *Journal of American History* 73, 2 (Sept. 1986): 311–28. Bruce Trigger, in 'Early Native North American Responses to European Contact: Romantic versus Rationalistic Interpretations,' *Journal of American History* 77, 4 (March 1991): 1195–1215, criticizes the 'cultural' interpretation of

early contact, though he admits that it may apply to first contacts. His position seems unnecessarily rigid.

32. H.P. Biggar, ed., *A Collection of Documents relating to Jacques Cartier and the Sieur de Roberval* (Ottawa: Public Archives of Canada 1930), 51; Alfred W. Crosby, Jr, *The Columbian Exchange: Biological and Cultural Consequences of 1492* (Westport, Conn: Greenwood Press 1972).

33. Bruce G. Trigger and James E. Pendergast, 'The Saint Laurence Iroquoians,' in Bruce G. Trigger, ed., *Handbook of North American Indians,* vol. 15: *Northwest* (Washington, DC: Smithsonian Institute 1978), 36. On syphilis see Crosby, *Columbian*, 122–64, and Claude Quétel, *History of Syphilis* (Baltimore: Johns Hopkins University Press 1990), chap. 1.

34. Jacques Rousseau, 'L'Annedda et l'arbre de vie,' *Revue d'histoire de l'Amérique français:* 7, 2 (Sept. 1954): 171–201

35. Trudel, 'Cartier,' 168

36. Ibid., Trudel, *Histoire*, 110–12

37. Schlesinger and Stabler, eds., *Thevet*, 9; Ch.-A. Julien, *Les voyages de découvertes et les premiers établissements XVe–XVIe siècles* (Paris: PUF 1948), 138–9

38. Trudel, 'Donnacona,' 276

39. Schlesinger and Stabler, eds., *Thevet*, 83

40. Trudel, *Histoire*, 142–68

■ Article 3: The *Other* in Early Canada

Cornelius J. Jaenen

[This article deals with] [...] the image of the "other" at the time of New France, inspired to a certain extent by the magisterial works of Nathan Wachtel, *The Vision of the Vanquished: the Spanish conquest of Peru through Indian eyes, 1530–1570*, trans. by Ben and Siân Reynolds (New York: Barnes and Noble, 1977), Jean Meyer, *Les Européens et les autres* (Paris: Colin, 1975) and Tzvetan Todorov, *The Conquest of America: the question of the other*, trans. by Richard

Source: Cornelius J. Jaenen, "L'autre' en Nouvelle France/ The 'Other' in Early Canada", Historical Papers (Vol. 24, 1989), pp. 1–12 with portions translated from the French. Reprinted with permission from the Canadian Historical Association.

Howard (New York: Harper & Row, 1984) among others. I believe that the issue of the complex relations between oneself and the "other", between identity and alterity exists in all time periods. Nonetheless, I distance myself from those who admire these great historians because I do not conceive of the "other" as being Amerindian, aboriginal, indigenous, seen either as a "cannibalistic and brutish beast" or as a "good man of nature" at the first stage of human history. These historians based their views on texts like the celebrated passage in the *Histoire naturelle* (1761) of Buffon, the naturalist, one of the most widely read works of 18th-century literature:

The American [Indian], it is true, is little less in stature than other men, yet that is not sufficient to form an exception to the general remark—that all animated nature is comparatively diminutive in the new continent. In the [Indian] the organs of generation are small and feeble; he has no hair, no beard, no ardour for the female [...] possessed of less sensibility [sensitivity], yet he is more timid and dastardly; he has no vivacity, no activity of soul [...] he will remain for days together in a state of stupid inactivity.[1]

From this scientific tract, the transition is easy to the polemic work written by Corneille de Pauw, *Recherches philosophiques*, who declared that plants, animals, men and, I presume, even European institutions transplanted to America lost their vigour and strength. From this point, he concluded:

So far we have only considered the peoples of the Americas from their physical attributes, which being essentially tainted, have occasioned the loss of moral faculties: degeneration affects their senses and their organs: their soul has lost in proportion to their body. Nature, having taken everything away from one hemisphere of the globe to give it to another, placed in the Americas only children, who have not yet become men. When the Europeans arrived in the West Indies, in the fifteenth century, not a single American knew how to read or write; there is still today not a single American who knows how to reason.[2]

The polemic served to justify colonization since the Swiss jurist Emmerich de Vattel, the great authority in international law, could conclude that "the people of Europe, too closely pent up at home, finding land of which the [Indians] stood in no particular need, and of which they made no actual and constant use, were lawfully entitled to take possession of it, and settle it with colonies [...]" Still, [the eighteenth-century French philosopher] Diderot could not stop himself from asking if his compatriots would support the same argument in the circumstance whereby Amerindians "brought by chance to your coasts [...] would write in the sand of your shores or on the bark of your trees: 'This land belongs to us!'"[3]

This 18th-century Eurocentrism is hardly surprising to historians, as we are used to making the intellectual effort to place ourselves in the context of the past in which we are interested. But what worries me a little, is perhaps that we ourselves—am I wrong here?— may be too often Eurocentric as well. Is it not true that we always are content with the idea that the "other" in the Americas is always the Amerindian, in the Congo, the Congolese, or in India, the Tamil? The first inhabitants of this vast continent were clearly the Amerindians. Am I wrong, consequently, in formulating the thesis that the "other" on this continent, was and still is the European, whether Viking, Breton or Basque!

As for New France, it seems to me that the French—the *newcomers* of [historical anthropologist] Bruce Trigger and the *virtuous settlers* of [nationalist historian] Lionel Groulx—are the true "others". These "others" appear in a number of guises, from the fisher from St Malo who ravished aboriginal women, the *coureur de bois* rapidly assimilated to indigenous values, to the *Black Robes*, the great Christian shamans, capable of solving droughts and dangerous floods or of avoiding the negative consequences of smallpox. What I want to sketch is the great variety of images, or stereotypes of the "other"—the invader who came from beyond the Atlantic in search of gold, precious stones, a maritime passage, land to cut timber or to grow crops, that is with motives largely incomprehensible to the first inhabitants of this world that would be baptized "the New World."

The European, in this case the French, was perceived by Amerindians, at least by Algonquian and Iroquoian peoples, according to different aspects of his culture and beliefs, as both strangers and strange. In the first place, his physical appearance provided little reassurance. Of course, they appeared to be creatures that resembled the Amerindians, but this meant little in itself, because the moose and the beaver also shared the spirit of life, possessed an intelligence adapted to their environment, and were worthy of respect as "persons", that is in European terms as "persons other than humans." Brother Sagard, Recollect missionary to the Huron, related, "And in this connection I must relate that a savage one day seeing a Frenchman with a beard turned to his companions and said as if in wonder and amazement, 'O, what an ugly man! Is it possible that any woman would look favourably on such a man [...]'"[4]

Was there a link between the physical appearance of this European "other" and his intelligence? The Nipissings were clear on this point, according to Sagard:

It happened that after the interpreter of the Epicerinys had spent two years among them they, thinking they were paying him a compliment, said to him: Well, now that you are beginning to speak our language well, if you had no beard you would have almost as much intelligence as such and such a people, naming one that they considered much less intelligent than themselves, and the French still less intelligent than that people. Thus these good folk judge us to be very unintelligent by comparison with themselves, and at every moment and on the slightest occasion they say to you *Téondion* or *Tescaondion*, that is to say 'You have no sense'; *Atache*, 'ill balanced.'[5]

The missionary Louis Hennepin informs us that certain Amerindians of the *pays d'en haut* [the Upper Country], "added, that we had all Tails like Beasts, that the European Women have but one Pap in the middle of the Breast, and bear five or six Children at a time [...]"[6] This representation of the "other" is worthy of the image of the man of the woods, the *wildeman*, and the world of monsters left to us by the folklore of the Middle Ages.

In fact, in comparison to Amerindians, the French appeared puny, weak and skinny. They had "legs of wool" when it was necessary to traverse the great Canadian forests and "brains of rabbits" as far as the *petite guerre* ["guerilla" warfare tactics] was concerned. This "other" was generally weak in spirit, vain, boasting, boisterous, quarrelsome and, worst of all, without courage and lacking honesty. This was the stereotype of the colonizing Frenchman. Even Amerindian children believed themselves superiors in intelligence to the missionaries, "so good a conceit have they of themselves and so little esteem for others," according to a Recollect father.[7] [The Algonquin chief] Iroquet's band refused to take a young interpreter that Champlain wished to impose on them,[8] and whom they found too weak and inexperienced, "fearing that harm might come to the youth, who was not accustomed to their manner of life, which is in all respects hard, and that if any accident befell him the French would be their enemies."[9]

Can the intelligence—or rather the Frenchman's lack of intelligence—be seen in his material culture? Our historiography has always depicted the primitive "savage" confronting superior European technologies and science. But we should perhaps ask ourselves if the Amerindian found the firearms, the wagons, European clothing, and so on, superior to his own possessions. It is true that in the early 16th century, Gonneville provided important evidence of the first contacts between French and Amerindians and the reactions of the latter: "They were completely amazed by [the] size of the ship, the artillery, the mirrors, and other things that they saw on the ship, and especially by writing that was sent from the ship to the crewmen who were in the villages. These men did what had been asked of them, although the Indians could not explain to themselves how the paper could talk."[10]

However, some twenty years later, Verrazzano remarked that they were not impressed by all the Europeans' products. He tells us:

> They did not esteem the silk, gold or other cloths, and did not wish to receive them. The same was true of metals like iron and steel. Again and again they declared that they had no admiration for the arms which we showed them. They did not want any from us and were only interested in their mechanisms. They even did not wish to receive mirrors: after they looked at themselves in the mirrors, they returned them to us, laughing.[11]

We know that fifty years later, Breton and Norman fishers exchanged knives, combs, needles and bronze pots for beaver and moose hides, a trade that is often qualified as being of unequal value. But I believe that we would do well to ask ourselves how Amerindians perceived these exchanges. If it really involved an unequal exchange, in what ways did they perceive the inequality? Who was fooled? Here is an example which illustrates well the problem: "you [Frenchmen] are also incomparably poorer than we, and [...] you are only simple journeymen, valets, servants, and slaves, all masters and grand captains though you may appear, seeing that you glory in our old rags and in our miserable suits of beaver which can no longer be of use to us."[12]

In answer to Recollect missionaries who wished to make the Amerindians into French people by making them believe that from all points of view the lifestyle of Europeans was superior to their own, a chief of Ile Percée replied that he was astonished that the French had "so little cleverness." Why, for instance, construct houses "which are tall and lofty [...] as these trees [for] men of five to six feet in height, [why do they] need houses which are sixty to eighty?" He continued, "my brother, hast thou as much ingenuity and cleverness as the Indians, who carry their houses and their wigwams with them so that they may lodge wheresoever they please, independently of any seignior whatsoever? [...] [W]e can always say, more truly than thou, that we are at home everywhere [...]"[13] "The other" in this case did not enjoy the liberty which characterized the life of Amerindians. The Frenchman was always, it seems, enslaved to a master, a superior, whether it was an authoritarian head of family, a priest, a seigneur, an officer, a magistrate, a governor, or a king.

How did Amerindians perceive the society that "the other" transplanted to American territory? First of all, it was hierarchical, therefore fundamentally based upon inequalities in all areas, favouring a small class of privileged people, in contrast to the Amerindian society generally lauded for their equality and their fraternity. It was possible to find "the other" authoritarian, intolerant and close-minded. French society focused on profits, often to the point of lacking charity and compassion for one's neighbour. I return to our Gaspesian chief who expressed so clearly his people's sentiments.

Well, my brother, if thou dost not yet know the real feelings which our Indians have towards thy country and towards all thy nation, it is proper that I inform thee at once. I beg thee now to believe that, all miserable as we seem in thine eyes, we consider ourselves nevertheless much happier than thou in this, that we are very content with the little that we have; and believe also once for all, I pray, that thou deceivest thyself greatly if thou thinkest to persuade us that thy country is better than ours. For if France, as thou sayest, is a little terrestrial paradise, art thou sensible to leave it?[14]

If the French were so attached to their inferior lifestyle, it was their choice, but it was not necessary to impose it in America. "*Aoti Chabaya,* [they say] That is the [Indian] way of doing things. You can have your way and we will have ours; every one values his own wares."[15]

The "other's" diet was also disliked: the salted dishes, the bread that tasted of wood ash and the wine which resembled bitter absinthe.

We see also that all your people live, as a rule, only upon cod which you catch among us. It is everlastingly nothing but cod—cod in the morning, cod at midday, cod at evening, and always cod, until things come to such a pass that if you wish some good morsels, it is at our expense; and you are obliged to have recourse to the Indians, whom you despise so much, and to beg them to go a-hunting that you may be regaled. Now tell me this one little thing, if thou hast any sense: Which of these two is the wisest and happiest?[16]

In sum, almost all aspects of life and culture of the European "other" had little attraction for the Amerindians because, among them, individual autonomy and responsibility were the dominant values. The individual recognized no master and was never the subject of coercion. In a culture which held in high regard liberty, they also valued generosity and collective commitment. The conclusion of all these comparisons, according to Chief Gachradodow, in 1744, was a condemnation of European colonization.

The World at the first was made on the other Side of the Great Water different from what it is on this Side, as may be known from the different Colours of our Skin, and of our Flesh, and that which you call Justice may not be so amongst us; you have your Laws and Customs, and so have we. The Great King might send you over to conquer the *Indians,* but it looks to us that God did not approve of it; if he had, he would not have placed the Sea where it is, as the Limits between us and you.[17]

In few realms is the Amerindian vision of the European intruder and of the worth of his own culture better demonstrated than in the responses to evangelization, to the efforts of French missionaries to francisize and christianize the Natives in a context which confused the kingdom of God with the kingdom of France. In responding to missionary intrusion the Native peoples were also responding to a variety of economic, social, and political values and assumptions. The Jesuits, for example, have been praised by some historians for their principle of accommodation to foreign cultures, their cultural relativism. Nevertheless, in the Canadian missions they still worked towards altering to some extent the structures of what they perceived to be a primitive society, to introduce new domestic values, agricultural techniques, a more serviceable political system, formal schooling, and so forth. Amerindian reactions, therefore, were not simply to a new theology or belief system but also to a radically different social organization in which this theology and belief system were embedded. Missionaries, as I have said elsewhere, were aggressive purveyors of a new and supposedly superior way of life, whose purpose was to remake individuals and whole societies in the image of their ideal. The Amerindians dealt with this challenge in a variety of ways and in so doing reveal to us their vision, their perception of this "other being" so intent on converting and transforming them, as well as their view of the culture and beliefs he represented.

It has often been stated that the Amerindians, in general, were attracted by the liturgy and sacraments and were convinced by the preaching of the missionaries. Those who became what some evangelizers called "people of prayer" saw virtues in Catholicism, to be sure, but it is from their point of view that any assessment must be made. Wampum was used in the public confessions that preceded festivals, funeral rites were ended by the interment of the dead "near whom they took good care to bury a sufficient quantity of provisions," in battle a crusader-like cry was raised to the Master of Life, and Christian prayers on crucial occasions could be accompanied by offerings of tobacco and salutations to the sun. Amerindians were able to assimilate the other's religion to their own spiritual concepts. God and devil might emerge from such a fusion with the same appelation, Jesus as the Sun, and the Holy Spirit as Thunder. Some Innu hunters were delighted Jesus had appeared in a dream to promise a successful hunt. They could not understand why their missionary was upset when they recounted how Jesus expected tobacco in return for His intercession. Was He not the Supreme Shaman? Could they not enlist His aid as did their

French brothers in their daily problems? Father Biard had acknowledged that "they accept baptism as a sort of sacred pledge of friendship and alliance with the French." Was the desire of some to convert any less sincere because it seemed to afford access to greater spiritual power, to useful trade and military relations, to possible protection from disease and famine, and to revitalization of one's own spiritual heritage?[18]

Of such Native converts Luc-François Nau was able to write: "I know a great number who serve God as faithfully as is observed in the best regulated religious communities."[19] On the other hand, Corneille de Pauw seriously doubted that, from an objective and detached point of view, this interpretation of conversion was accurate. He quoted from an inquiry into Native beliefs made after the British conquest, therefore a presumably anti-Catholic report: "Several were questioned on the articles of faith which were absolutely unknown to them, although these dogmas had been preached in their country for two centuries. Others had a very uniform notion of the story of Christ. They answered that he was a shaman, French by origin; that the English had hanged him in London; that his mother was French; and that Pontious Pilatous had been a lieutenant in the service of Great Britain."[20] De Pauw attributed this travesty of sacred history more to Native assimilation of the other's religion than to missionary intrigues.

All Amerindian cultures shared an ability to entertain and give assent to a variety of views, even if they were contrary to their better judgement, in what has been called institutionalized hospitality.[21] Sister Duplessis de Ste. Hélène reported that "the greatest number listen to the mysteries which are preached as to a fairy tale" and these left few impressions. The abbé Gaulin believed that they were "sufficiently enlightened to formulate an infinity of difficulties concerning all our mysteries." Did not the soldiers and *coureurs de bois* tell them that "it is the work of a black robe to preach, but one must not be concerned by what he says." So the Baron de Lahontan observed that they listened "to all the Jesuits preached without ever contradicting them, contenting themselves with scoffing between sermons." He explained their viewpoint as he understood it:

When they preach the incarnation of Jesus Christ to them, they reply that is admirable;

when they ask them do they wish to become Christians, they answer that it is laudable, that is to say they will think about it. And if we Europeans exhort them to come in crowds to church to hear the word of God, they say it is reasonable, that is to say they will come; but in the end it is only to obtain a pipeful of tobacco that they approach the holy place; or else to mock our Fathers, as I have said already, for they have such fortunate memories that I am acquainted with more than ten of them who know Holy Writ by heart.[22]

This value placed on deference and detachment was interpreted by the missionaries as dissimulation, which they traced back to their supposedly faulty permissive child-rearing practices: "Dissimulation, which is natural to those Savages, and a certain spirit of acquiesence, in which the children of that country are brought up, make them assent to all that is told them; and prevent them from ever showing any opposition to the sentiments of others, even though they may know what is said to them is not true."[23] Louis Hennepin, true to his own independence of mind, saw this tolerant indifference as part of their conscious antipathy to aggression. He wrote:

Notwithstanding that seeming Approbation, they believe what they please and no more; and therefore 'tis impossible to know when they are really persuaded of those things you have mentioned to them, which I take to be one of the greatest Obstructions to their Conversion; For their Civility hindering them from making any Observation or contradict what is said unto them, they seem to approve of it, though perhaps they laugh at it in private, or else never bestow a Moment to reflect upon it, such being their indifference for a future Life.[24]

The Sorbonne theologians eventually advised the colonial bishop to warn against baptizing those who made their profession of faith "only because they do not wish to contradict the Missionary."[25]

Another response was the assertion of a dichotomous universe, with a present and a hereafter designed for themselves, and separate ones for the "others." The western tribes told Jean-Pierre Aulneau that they "were not made for that religion." Just as there were two paths on earth so there were separate places for the souls of the departed. The Catholic concept of the hereafter was challenged: "This [...] 'tis like all the rest of your fine lies, all the souls, among our people at least, go to the same place; two of our souls came back once and told us all I have said."[26] On another occasion another missionary was interrupted with the same argument: "It's well for those of your Country: but we do not go to heaven after Death. We go only to the Country of Souls, whither our People go to hunt fat Beasts, where they live in greater Tranquility [....]"[27] An Innu shaman said, "Thy God has not come to our country and that is why we do not believe in him; make me see him and I will believe in him." When Paul Le Jeune countered such a statement with the assertion that Jesus Christ had not gone to Europe either, it only brought the noncommittal, "I have nothing to say against all this, for I have not been taught anything to the contrary."[28]

It was commonly believed that the missionaries possessed peculiar spiritual powers. When employed for ends that served their bands and tribes, they were perceived as powerful intercessors. When their intrusion was accompanied by epidemics, famine, or disastrous defeat at the hands of enemies, however, a cause-effect relationship was postulated. So, smallpox and Iroquois assaults on the Huron confederacy brought charges of witchcraft to bear against the missionaries. As a correspondent noted, "They were on the dock as criminals in a council of natives. The fires were lit closer to each other than usual, and they seemed to be so only because of them, for they were esteemed guilty of witchcraft, and of having poisoned the air which caused the pestilence throughout the country."[29] The same charges were not made against the traders, however. A young fisherman reported a visitation dream in which it was revealed to him by louskeha, "the true Jesus," that it was "the strangers who alone are the cause of it; they now travel two by two through the country, with the design of spreading the disease everywhere."[30]

I underscore the fact that there was great tolerance for the religion of the "other," but witchcraft was one of the few crimes in their society punishable by death. One of the first missionaries to come to Canada had opined that "no one must come here in the hope of suffering martyrdom [...] for we are not in a country where the natives put Christians to death on account of their religion."[31] He added that, quite to the contrary, they "leave every one to his own belief." The martyrs, in most cases, were victims of intertribal war.

I believe that the views of Amerindian women deserve attention. They believed that their persons and their social roles were the objects of a two-fold attack on the part of the missionaries—first as women, and secondly as natives. Among the nomadic bands the proscription of polygamy, if adhered to, would have greatly increased a woman's workload. Among the sedentary agricultural tribes the women, especially the "grandmothers" as the Jesuits called the matrons, refused to give up their children to be educated at Quebec. The men as hunters, traders, and warriors might be more amenable to conversion as a means of consolidating their relationship with the French, but the women saw few immediate advantages. What right had the missionary to undermine a woman's authority in the clan, or to assign a man to women's agricultural work? More than one matron drove the converted son-in-law from the longhouse. The men who were appointed "prayer captains" by the missionaries on one reserve exclaimed: "It is you women who [...] are the cause of all our misfortunes. It is you who keep the demons among us. You do not urge to be baptized; you are lazy about going to prayers; when you pass before the cross you never salute it; you wish to be independent. Now know that you will have to obey your husbands and our prayer captains. [. . .]"[32]

This introduction of so-called Christian discipline was deeply resented by many women. At Sillery a runaway wife was returned chained by one foot to her husband. Another woman was beaten by her "young Christian" husband; they were reprimanded but, the *Relations* specify, "especially the woman, who was more guilty than her husband." When a priest suggested that the disobedient had a fire "kindled in the other world" to torment them, women replied "in a deriding way," that, if so, then "the Mountains of the other World must consist of the Ashes of souls." One boldly asserted on another occasion: "I do not recognize any sins."[33]

We can understand why a missionary in the upper country complained that there were "no persons more attached to silly customs, or more obstinate in their error, than the old women, who will not even lend an ear to our instructions."[34] Were they not protecting their culture and traditional belief system? This sometimes required some unusual action. It was a woman who alerted the Huron council to the Jesuit peril: "Do you not see that when they move their lips, what they call prayers, those are so many spells that come forth from their mouths? It is the same when they read in their books. [...] If they are not promptly put to death, they will complete their ruin of the country, so there will remain neither small nor great."[35]

Finally, it might be objected that the missionaries in New France were not without success. Indeed, as I have said, there were conversions at various levels of understanding and for various motives. There were even a few who renounced their identity and heritage to join the "others," saying "I am French." Chief Garakontié of the Onondaga, for example, was derided by traditionalists because "he was no longer a man, that he had become French, that the Black Gowns had turned his head." Even so, the vision of the "other" may not have been what Europeans expected. The Innu are reported to have said their own mass in the absence of missionaries. The Micmacs, we are told, "have often been seen dabbling with, and affecting to perform the office and functions of missionary, even to hearing confessions. [...]" Even more disturbing was the knowledge that Micmac women had taken on a spiritual role in the "new religion" which was not denied them in their traditional religion. "These in usurping the quality and name of *religieuses* [nuns] say certain prayers in their own fashion, and affect a manner of living more reserved than that of the commonalty of Natives, who allow themselves to be dazzled by the glamour of a false and ridiculous devotion." Not only did women dare to take on a role the clergy disapproved of but they were also generally honoured for doing so: "They look upon these women as extraordinary persons, whom they believe to hold converse, to speak familiarly, and to hold communication with the sun, which they have all adored as their divinity." One woman in particular was honoured among the Abenakis. She was 114 years old, and said her prayers on unstrung beads of a rosary which she gave out as relics saying they had fallen from heaven into her hands.[36]

The vision of the "other" in the religious domain was conditioned by the fact that French and Amerindian cultures confronted each other as entities and that, by that fact, the conversion of individuals demanded much more than a superficial revision of personal convictions. Nonetheless, converts and non-converts seem to have been in agreement on one point: the "other" had a lifestyle and beliefs that were appropriate for him, but these should only be adopted after serious reflection. It is true that I have especially used missionaries' writings to show the vision that Amerindians could have of the "other" come from France, but I remind you of a sentence from Montesquieu: "It is necessary for them to tell the truth when they have no interest in hiding it in order to be believed when they wished to lie."

Notes

1. *Buffon's Natural History containing a Theory of the Earth, [....] from the French*, vol. VII (London, T. Gillet, 1807), p. 39.

2. Corneille de Pauw, *Recherches philosophiques sur les Américains*, London, 1770, t. II, p. 153 (translated by editor).

3. Emmerich de Vattel, *The Law of Nations or the Principles of Natural Law*, quoted in Walter B. Scaife, "The Development of International Law as to Newly Discovered Territory", *Papers of the American Historical Association*, 4, 3 (July 1890), p. 275. Diderot, quoted in Yves Bénot, *Diderot: De L'athéisme à l'anticolonialisme*, (Paris; Maspero, 1970), p. 197 (translated by editor).

4. George M. Wrong, ed., *Sagard's Long Journey to the Country of the Hurons* (Toronto: Champlain Society, 1939), p. 137.

5. Ibid., p. 138.

6. Louis Hennepin, *A New Discovery of a Vast Country in America* (Chicago, 1903), vol. 2, p. 84.

7. Wrong, ed., *Sagard's Long Journey*, p. 138.

8. Marc Lescarbot, *The History of New France*, trans. by W. L. Grant (Toronto: Champlain Society, 1914), vol. III, p. 21–22.

9. Ibid., p. 22.

10. "Le Voyage de Paulmier de Gonneville à Brésil (1503–5)" in Ch. A. Julien, *Jacques Cartier: Voyages au Canada. Avec les relations des voyages en Amérique de Gonneville, Verrazano et Roberval*, (Paris, 1981), p. 53 (translated by editor).

11. "Le voyage de Giovanni Da Verrazono à la Francesca (1534) ", ibid., pp. 89–90 (translated by editor).

12. William F. Ganong, ed., Chrestien Le Clercq, *New Relations of Gaspesia with the Customs and Religion of the Gaspesian Indians* (Toronto: Champlain Society, 1910), p. 105.

13. Ibid., pp. 103–04.

14. Ibid., p. 104.

15. R. G. Thwaites, *The Jesuit Relations and Allied Documents*, (New York, 1959), vol. 3, p. 121.

16. Ganong, ed., Le Clercq, *New Relation of Gaspesia*, p. 105.

17. *The Treaty held with the Indians of the Six Nations*, (Williamsburg, 1744), p. 42.

18. W.I. Kip, ed., *The Early Jesuit Missions in North America* (New York, 1846), 166–67; Library and Archives Canada, MG 17, A 7-1, Vol 4, No. 1, "Relation d'une expédition contre les Renards," p. 2658; Thwaites, *Jesuit Relations*, 4:201; 5:223; 8:27–37; 9:213; 11:259. See also James Axtell, *After Columbus* (New York, 1988), Chap. 7.

19. *Rapport de l'Archiviste de la Province de Québec pour 1926–27* (Québec, 1927), 313.

20. De Pauw, *Recherches philosophiques*, 161–62.

21. Calvin Martin, *Keepers of the Game* (Berkeley, 1975), 153.

22. NA, MG 3, Series T, Carton 77, pp. 27, 104; *ibid.*, Series K. Carton 1232, No. 4, p. 112; Baron de Lahontan, *Mémoires de l'Amérique septentrionale* (Baltimore, 1931), 107.

23. Thwaites, *Jesuit Relations*, 52:203.

24. Louis Hennepin, *A New Discovery of a Vast Country in America* (London, 1698), 2:70.

25. Mgr. H. Têtu and Abbé C.-O. Casgrain, eds., *Mandements, lettres pastorales et circulaires des évêques de Québec* (Québec, 1887), 1:447.

26. François du Creux, *The History of Canada or New France* (Toronto, 1951), 1:119.

27. Hennepin, *A New Discovery*, 577.

28. Thwaites, *Jesuit Relations*, 7:101; 11:157.

29. Dom Guy Oury, *Marie de l'Incarnation, Ursuline (1599–1672). Correspondance* (Solesmes, 1971), Lettre XXX, 67–68.

30. Thwaites, *Jesuit Relations*, 20:27–29.

31. Joseph LeCaron, *Au Roy sur la Nouvelle-France* (Paris, 1626), n.p.

32. Thwaites, *Jesuit Relations*, 28:105–07.

33. *Ibid.*, 18:155 and 23:111.

34. *Ibid.*, 54:143.

35. Oury, *Marie de l'Incarnation*, Lettre L, 117–18.

36. LeClercq, *New Relation*, 229–30.

WORLDS OF WORK
Pre-Industrial Work, 1860–1880

Daniel Samson
Brock University

WORLDS OF WORK: PRE-INDUSTRIAL WORK, 1860–1880

● **Introduction by Daniel Samson**

▲ **Primary Sources**

■ **Secondary Sources**

● INTRODUCTION

Daniel Samson

When most people think about history they think of wars and revolutions—the big stuff, with lots of blood, and a certain amount of glory. They don't often think about work. This is odd because it's what most people spend most of their lives engaged in, and from which we derive most of our ability to live and much of our public sense of identity, and where we find many of our best friendships and relationships. This is true today, but it was even more true for eighteenth- and nineteenth-century immigrants, many of whom arrived in the colonies with nothing but their labouring bodies. We also tend to think of immigrants as settlers—as arriving, getting a land grant, clearing the land, and setting up a farm. For many, this was in fact the case. But for just as many—and in some periods more—arrival was followed by a search for the employment that might provide the money they would need to set up that farm, or even to pay rent as a tenant. Indeed, many established farms were economically marginal operations that required the men to spend months away at waged work, which in turn left the work of the farm to the wife and children. This work was usually unskilled—labouring jobs in lumber camps, canal and other forms of construction, or farm labour. For some, this was a transitional phase—a way to get the cash to start the farm or the small workshop—but for many others it was all they would ever obtain. And even for those who successfully established farms, few would establish themselves so well that they could provide for the many sons and daughters that nineteenth-century families produced. Many in the next generation found themselves working in lumber camps, mines, or the farms and homes of their more prosperous neighbours.

The nineteenth century was also a time of significant change in work. Britain was "the workshop of the world," and led the changes that we now call the Industrial Revolution. Whereas up until the late eighteenth and early nineteenth centuries most people worked on farms, this was changing as cities grew and industrial production began to transform where things were produced, how, and by whom. In the past, articles such as fabrics, shoes, tools, and food were produced either in the home or in small local workshops. The advent of new technologies and the new forms of factory production increasingly meant that artisans stopped working for themselves and began working for others in factories. Agricultural production was also changing dramatically, much of it fuelled by mechanization and the consolidation of many smaller farms into larger ones. More machinery and bigger farms meant fewer people were needed in the country. In short, over the course of the nineteenth century, the basic structures of society changed dramatically: people who once lived on a farm in the country, produced for themselves, and achieved a modest independence now lived in a city, worked in a factory, produced for other people, and had become completely dependent on wages and a prosperous industrial economy. In the colonial period, this transformation was not yet complete (indeed, it's still not totally complete today—ask a farmer!), and most people still lived in that older framework. But signs of change were evident.

In this period before those changes, the world of work was remarkably diverse. Because the factory system was not yet established, most goods that were produced in the colonial economy were either staple products (timber, fish, minerals, farm produce), fairly uncomplicated manufactured products such as rope or shoes, or fine-skilled but technologically straightforward goods such as furniture or wooden sailing ships. For most people, at least part of their work entailed some form of labour on a farm. For others, especially in urban centres, skilled work, based in the ancient traditions of apprentices, journeymen, and masters, still prevailed. Opportunities for women were very much restricted, mostly owing to social conventions that frowned on women engaging in the public (masculine) sphere of work. Much of the waged work that was available required little more than a strong body to cut down trees, to paddle a canoe, or to haul nets. All these jobs required skills—a knack, we might say, that allowed the workers to be very good at their jobs, but only the older urban skilled trades had craft guilds that formally taught (and protected) the traditional skills of the Old World. Similarly, and also largely in the cities, opportunities for female employment grew, too, especially in domestic work and education. The growth of a prosperous middle class throughout colonial society meant that there were opportunities to work in wealthier people's homes. Increasingly, too, small artisanal producers expanded their operations, so that, rather than taking apprentices into their homes and businesses, they hired workers. There were many opportunities for work, in a wide range of areas, and these areas themselves were changing.

Sources are one of the major challenges facing the historian of work. While many skilled workers were literate, most unskilled workers weren't, and the result is that our sources tend to be written not by the workers themselves but by their employers and supervisors. And yet even these sources can tell us a lot about class relations, at least from one side of that class divide. The men who journeyed north with Franklin's expedition up the Coppermine River in 1819 were a mixed crew of British officers, French Canadian voyageurs, and Aboriginal guides. While we seldom hear the latter groups' voices, we certainly get a sense of their masters' views of the workers, and even catch occasional glimpses of the servants' views of their masters. Similarly, the newspaper account of the opening of the railway in Albion Mines, Nova Scotia, in 1839 offers us a window not only on the celebration of a technological marvel of the day, but also on how that celebration incorporated the class dynamics of an industrial community. Here, as part of a celebration, relations between masters and servants were quite good, although we can certainly sense elements of conflict. But quite often these relations could break down into strikes, and occasionally even riots. Events in Upper Canada on the still under construction Welland Canal descended into disorder several times in the 1840s, and the letters reproduced here illustrate not only the economic conflicts of early class societies, but also their religious and ethnic dimensions.

Historians have tried to understand the world of work, how it influenced colonial society, how it changed, how these changes affected people's lives, and how they reflected the broader changes of an industrializing world. While work itself was rarely discussed by historians before the 1960s, assumptions about the daily activities of colonial settlers lay underneath the surface. The conventional wisdom went something like this: Most farmers were neither rich nor poor, and all were more or less equal; the *voyageurs* were a group of hardy and colourful men who lived lives of adventure and daring; the advance of the factory system showed Canadians' ingenuity and sense of progress. These positions are in some ways true. But so too is it true that while many farms were expanding and investing in agricultural machinery, many other farms were unable to provide a future for their children, or even to survive; so too is it true that the dangers of the fur trade were many, and the "adventures" often ended in death in the North, and mourning mothers in the East; and so too is it true that the factory system ended many skilled workers' hopes for a respectable and independent future. The historians we read here offer us some sense of that complexity. Very little had changed for the work of the French Canadian *voyageurs* and Aboriginal guides described by Carolyn Podruchny. Their work was extremely dangerous, but their various *rendezvous* also allowed the traders and labourers to make their own world. Women's work, surveyed here by Elizabeth Jane Errington, was much less expansive, but even in their smaller confines women could find their own place. Rusty Bittermann tackles one of the great myths of colonial society—the independence offered by life on the land—and challenges us to think about what this means for our broader understanding of colonial society, and for life on the land today. Finally, T.W. Acheson shows us the important place of the craft traditions in Saint John business and politics, though an importance that was changing. In the city and on the frontier, in the home and across the countryside, work set the pattern for most people's lives.

QUESTIONS

1. What drew people to the different worlds of work that we see in this chapter? What was Franklin paying the Dene for?
2. How vulnerable were workers in the nineteenth century?
3. How independent were workers' actions? Did they, as historians like to say, make their own worlds?
4. How did ethnicity affect one's place in the world of work? Were women restricted in their worlds?
5. How do these historians understand the place of work in nineteenth-century society? Do you see differences that go beyond their choices of subjects? Do they understand work differently?

FURTHER READINGS

Edith Burley, *Servants of the Honourable Company: Work, Discipline, and Conflicts in the Hudson's Bay Company, 1770–1879* (Toronto, Oxford University Press, 1997).

Marjorie Cohen, *Women's Work, Markets and Economic Development in Nineteenth-Century Ontario* (Toronto: University of Toronto Press 1988).

Paul Craven, ed., *Labouring Lives: Work and Workers in Nineteenth-Century Ontario* (Toronto, University of Toronto Press, 1995).

Bryan Palmer, *Working-Class Experience: Rethinking the History of Canadian Labour, 1800–1991,* 2nd edition (Toronto, McClelland & Stewart, 1992).

Graeme Wynn, *Timber Colony: A Historical Geography of Early Nineteenth Century New Brunswick* (Toronto: University of Toronto Press 1981).

▲ Document 1: Chinese Miners Washing Gold

● William G. R. Hind, *Chinese Miners Washing Gold*, 1862. "Move west young man!" was the cry heard throughout North America as eastern farmlands overflowed and gold was discovered in California in 1849. But many of those young men had moved east, from China. By 1871, almost 5 percent of British Columbians were Chinese immigrants. Miners and adventurers came to California, but many moved north as that rush declined and another emerged in the Yukon and British Columbia in the 1860s. Is there anything unusual about these workers?

Source: McCord Museum, Montreal, M609.

● William G. R. Hind, *Resting on the Portage*, 1863.

Source: Library and Archives Canada, C-013980.

▲ Document 3: Shooting the Rapids

● Frances Anne Hopkins, *Shooting the Rapids*, 1879. The long days, sustained hard work, danger, and equally often the sheer boredom of work in the fur trade meant that adventurous representations such as Anne Frances Hopkins' were much less realistic than Hind's unexciting but probably more realistic depiction of fur-trader guides from 1862. While their work was challenging and often dangerous, it was also simply uneventful. These artists both travelled through the west in the 1860s, but offered us very different views of the life of the voyageur. Hopkins's image is much better known than Hind's. Why? How do such representations affect our understanding of fur-trade society?

Source: Library and Archives Canada, C-002774 K.

▲ Document 4: British Naval Officers, *Canadian Voyageurs*, and Chipewyan (Dene) Travel North

NARRATIVE OF A JOURNEY
to the shores of the
POLAR SEA,
in
THE YEARS 1819-20-21-22.
by
JOHN FRANKLIN, Capt. R.N., F.R.S., M.W.S.,
and commander of the expedition.

1820, July 18. EARLY this morning the stores were distributed to the three canoes. Our stock of provision unfortunately did not amount to more than sufficient for one day's consumption, exclusive of two barrels of flour, three cases of preserved meats, some chocolate, arrowroot, and portable soup, which we had brought from England, and intended to reserve for our journey to the coast the next season. Seventy pounds of moose meat and a little barley were all that Mr. Smith was enabled to give us. It was gratifying, however, to perceive that this scarcity of food did not depress the spirits of our Canadian companions, who cheerfully loaded their canoes, and embarked in high glee after they had received the customary dram. At noon we bade farewell to our kind friend Mr. Smith. The crews commenced a lively paddling song on quitting the shore, which was continued until we had lost sight of the houses.
[....]
The wind and swell having subsided in the afternoon, we re-embarked and steered towards the western point of the Big-Island of Mackenzie [...] We coasted along the eastern side of the bay, its western shore being always visible, but the canoes were exposed to the hazard of being broken by the numerous sunken rocks, which were scattered in our track. We encamped for the night on a rocky island, and by eight A.M. on the following morning, arrived at Fort Providence, which is situated twenty-one miles from the entrance of the bay. The post is exclusively occupied by the North-West Company, the Hudson's Bay Company having no settlement to the northward of Great Slave Lake. We found Mr. Wentzel and our interpreter Jean Baptiste Adam here, with one of the Indian guides: but the chief of the tribe and his hunters were encamped with their families, some miles from the fort, in a good situation for fishing. Our arrival was announced to him by a fire on the top of a hill, and before night a messenger came to communicate his intention of seeing us next morning. The customary present, of tobacco and some other articles, was immediately sent to him.
[....]
I endeavoured to explain the objects of our mission in a manner best calculated to ensure his exertions in our service. With this view, I told him that we were sent out by the greatest chief in the world, who was the sovereign also of the trading companies in the country; that he was the friend of peace, and had the interest of every nation at heart. Having learned that his children in the north, were much in want of articles of merchandize, in consequence of the extreme length and difficulty of the present route; he had sent us to search for a passage by the sea, which if found, would enable large vessels to

Source: Sir John Franklin, *Narrative of a Journey to the Shores of the Polar Sea, in the Years 1819-20-21-22* (London, J. Murray, 1824), 301-2, 312-3, 316-8, 321-2, 323-5, 334-5, 338-40, 341-3, 344-6, and 347-51.

transport great quantities of goods more easily to their lands. That we had not come for the purpose of traffic, but solely to make discoveries for their benefit, as well as that of every other people. That we had been directed to inquire into the nature of all the productions of the countries we might pass through, and particularly respecting their inhabitants. That we desired the assistance of the Indians in guiding us, and providing us with food; finally, that we were most positively enjoined by the great chief to recommend that hostilities should cease throughout this country; and especially between the Indians and the Esquimaux, whom he considered his children, in common with other natives; [...] on his return he and his party should be remunerated with cloth, ammunition, tobacco, and some useful iron materials, besides having their debts to North-West Company discharged.

The chief, whose name is Akaitcho or Big-foot, replied by a renewal of his assurances, that he and his party would attend us to the end of our journey, and that they would do their utmost to provide us with the means of subsistence. He admitted that his tribe had made war upon the Esquimaux, but said they were now desirous of peace, and unanimous in their opinion as to the necessity of all who accompanied us abstaining from every act of enmity against that nation. He added, however, that the Esquimaux were very treacherous, and therefore recommended that we should advance towards them with caution.

As the water was unusually high this season, the Indian guides recommended our going by a shorter route to the Copper-Mine River than that they had first proposed to Mr. Wentzel, and they assigned as a reason for the change, that the rein-deer would be sooner found upon this track. They then drew a chart of the proposed route on the floor with charcoal, exhibiting a chain of twenty-five small lakes extending towards the north, about one half of them connected by a river which flows into Slave Lake, near Fort Providence.
[....]

We presented to the chief, the two guides, and the seven hunters, who had engaged to accompany us, some cloth, blankets, tobacco, knives, daggers, besides other useful iron materials, and a gun to each; also a keg of very weak spirits and water, which they kept until the evening, as they had to try their gun before dark, and make the necessary preparations for commencing the journey on the morrow. They, however, did not leave us so soon, as the chief was desirous of being present, with his party, at the dance, which was given in the evening to our Canadian voyagers. They were highly entertained by the vivacity and agility displayed by our companions in their singing and dancing: and especially by their imitating the gestures of a Canadian, who placed himself in the most ludicrous postures; and, whenever this was done, the gravity of the chief gave way to violent bursts of laughter. In return of the gratification Akaitcho had enjoyed, he desired his young men to exhibit the Dog-Rib Indian dance; and immediately they ranged themselves in a circle, and, keeping their legs widely separated, began to jump simultaneously sideways; their bodies were bent, their hands placed on their hips, and they uttered forcibly the interjection *tsa* at each jump. Devoid as were their attitudes of grace, and their music of harmony, we were much amused by the novelty of the exhibition.

August 1.—This morning the Indians set out, intending to wait for us at the mouth of the Yellow-Knife River. We engaged another Canadian voyager at this place, and the Expedition then consisted of twenty-eight persons, including the officers, and the wives of three of our voyagers, who were brought for the purpose of making shoes and clothes for the men at the winter establishment; there were also three children, belonging to two of these women˙.
[....]

August 8.—During this day we crossed five portages, passing over a very bad road. The men were quite exhausted with fatigue by five P.M., when we were obliged to encamp on the borders of the fifth lake, in which the fishing nets were set. We began this evening to issue some portable soup and arrow-root, which our companions relished very much; but this food is too unsubstantial to support their vigour under their daily exhausting labour, and we could not furnish them with a sufficient quantity even of this to satisfy their desires. We commenced our labours on the next day in a very wet uncomfortable state, as it had rained through the night until four A.M. The fifth grassy lake was crossed, and four others, with their intervening portages, and we returned to the river by a portage of one thousand four hundred and fifteen paces.

The chief having told us that this was a good lake for fishing, we determined on halting for a day or two to recruit our men, of whom three were lame, and several others had swelled legs. The chief himself went forward to look after the hunters, and promised to make a fire as a signal if they had killed any rein-deer. All the Indians had left us in the course of yesterday and to-day to seek these animals, except the guide Keskarrah.

[....]

August 13.—We caught twenty fish this morning, but they were small, and furnished but a scanty breakfast for the party. Whilst this meal was preparing, our Canadian voyagers, who had been for some days past murmuring at their meagre diet, and striving to get the whole of our little provision to consume at once, broke out into open discontent, and several of them threatened they would not proceed forward unless more food was given to them. This conduct was the more unpardonable, as they saw we were rapidly approaching the fires of the hunters, and that provision might soon be expected. I, therefore, felt the duty incumbent on me to address them in the strongest manner on the danger of insubordination, and to assure them of my determination to inflict the heaviest punishment on any that should persist in their refusal to go on, or in any other way attempt to retard the Expedition. I considered this decisive step necessary, having learned from the gentlemen, most intimately acquainted with the character of the Canadian voyagers, that they invariably try how far they can impose upon every new master, and that they will continue to be disobedient and intractable if they once gain any ascendency over him. I must admit, however, that the present hardships of our companions were of a kind which few could support without murmuring, and no one could witness without a sincere pity for their sufferings.

After this discussion we went forward until sunset. In the course of the day we crossed seven lakes and as many portages. Just as we had encamped we were delighted to see four of the hunters arrive with the flesh of two rein-deer. This seasonable supply, though only sufficient for this evening's and the next day's consumption, instantly revived the spirits of our companions, and they immediately forget all their cares. As we did not, after this period, experience any deficiency of food during this journey, they worked extremely well, and never again reflected upon us they had done before, for rashly bringing them into an inhospitable country, where the means of subsistence could not be procured.

After starting we first crossed the Orkney Lake, then a portage which brought us to Sandy Lake, and here we missed one of our barrels of powder, which the steersman of the canoe then recollected had been left the day before. He and two other men were sent back to search for it, in the small canoe. The rest of the party proceeded to the portage on the north side of the Grizzle-Bear Lake, where the hunters had made a deposit of meat, and there encamped to await their return, which happened at nine P.M., with the powder. We perceived from the direction of this lake, that considerable labour would have been spared if we had continued our course yesterday instead of striking off at the guide's suggestion, as the bottom of this lake cannot be far separated from either Hunter's Lake or the one to the westward of it. The chief and all the Indians went off to hunt, accompanied by Pierre St. Germain, the interpreter. They returned at night, bringing some meat, and reported that they had put the carcases of several rein-deer *en cache*. These were sent for early next morning, and as the weather was unusually warm, the thermometer, at noon, being 77°, we remained stationary all day, that the women might prepare the meat for keeping, by stripping the flesh from the bones and drying it in the sun over a slow fire. The hunters were again successful, and by the evening we had collected the carcases of seventeen deer. As this was a sufficient store to service us until we arrived at Winter Lake, the chief proposed that he and his hunters should proceed to that place and collect some provision against our arrival. He also requested that we would allow him to be absent ten days to provide his family with clothing, as the skin of the rein-deer is unfit for that purpose after the month of September. We could not refuse to grant such a reasonable request, but caused St. Germain to accompany him, that his absence might not exceed the appointed time. [...]

August 19.—Embarking at seven next morning, we paddled to the western extremity of the lake, and there found a small river, which flows out of it to the S.W. To avoid as strong rapid at its commencement, we made a portage, and then crossed to the north bank of the river, where the Indians recommended that the winter establishment should be erected, and we soon found that the situation they had chosen possessed all the advantages we could desire. The trees were numerous, and of a far greater size than we had supposed them to be in a distant view, some of the pines being thirty or forty feet high, and two feet in diameter at the root.

The united length of the portages we had crossed, since leaving Fort Providence, is twenty-one statute miles and a half; and as our men had to traverse each portage four times, with a load of one hundred and eighty pounds, and return three times light, they walked in the whole upwards of one hundred and fifty miles. The total length of our voyage from Chipewyan is five hundred and fifty-three miles.

A heavy rain, on the 23d, prevented the men from working, either at the building, or going for meat; but on the next day the weather was fine, and they renewed their labours. The thermometer, that day did not rise higher than 42°, and it fell to 31° before midnight. On the morning of the 25th, we were surprised by some early symptoms of the approach of winter; the small pools were frozen over, and a flock of geese passed to the southward. Akaitcho arrived with his party, and we were greatly disappointed at finding they had stored up only fifteen rein-deer for us. St. Germain informed us, that having heard of the death of the chief's brother-in-law, they had spent several day in bewailing his loss, instead of hunting. We learned also, that the decease of this man had caused another party of the tribe, who had been sent by Mr. Wentzel to prepare provision for us on the banks of the Copper-Mine River, to remove to the shores of the Great Bear Lake, distant from our proposed route. Mortifying as these circumstances were, they produced less painful sensations than we experienced in the evening, by the refusal of Akaitcho to accompany us in the proposed descent of the Copper-Mine River. When Mr. Wentzel, by my direction, communicated to him my intention of proceeding at once on that service, he desired a conference with me upon the subject, which being immediately granted, he began, by stating, that the very attempt would be rash and dangerous as the weather was cold, the leaves were falling, some geese had passed to the southward, and the winter would shortly set in; and that, as he considered the lives of all who went on such a journey would be forfeited, he neither would go himself, nor permit his hunters to accompany us. He said there was no wood within eleven days' march, during which time we could not have any fire, as the moss, which the Indians use in their summer excursions, would be too wet for burning, in consequence of the recent rains; that we should be forty days in descending the Copper-Mine River, six of which would be expended in getting to its banks, and that we might be blocked up by the ice in the next moon; and during the whole journey the party must experience great suffering for a want of food, as the rein-deer had already left the river.

He was now reminded that these statements were very different from the account be had given, both at Fort Providence and on the route hither; and that, up to this moment, we had been encouraged by his conversation to expect that the party might descend the Copper-Mine River, accompanied by the Indians. He replied, that at the former place he had been unacquainted with our slow mode of travelling, and that the alteration in his opinion arose from the advance of winter.

We now informed him that we were provided with instruments by which we could ascertain the state of the air and water, and that we did not imagine the winter to be so near as he supposed; however, we promised to return on discovering the first change in the season. He was also told that all the baggage being left behind, our canoes, would now, of course, travel infinitely more expeditiously than any thing he had hitherto witnessed. Akaitcho appeared to feel hurt, that we should continue to press the matter further, and answered with some warmth: "Well, I have said every thing I can urge, to dissuade you from going on this service, on which, it seems, you wish to sacrifice your own lives, as well as the Indians who might attend you: however, if after all I have said, you are determined to go, some of my young men shall join the party, because it shall not be said that we permitted you to die alone after having brought you hither; but from the moment they embark in the canoes, I and my relatives shall lament them as dead."

*The following is the list of the officers and men who composed the Expedition on its departure from Fort Providence:

John Franklin, Lieutenant of the Royal Navy and Commander.
John Richardson, M.D., Surgeon of the Royal Navy.
Mr. George Back, of the Royal Navy, Admiralty Midshipman.
Mr. Robert Hood, of the Royal Navy, Admiralty Midshipman.
Mr. Frederick Wentzel, Clerk to the North-West Company.
John Hepburn, English seaman.

Canadian Voyagers.

Joseph Peltier,	Gabriel Beauparlant,
Matthew Pelonquin, dit Crèdit,	Vincenza Fontano,
Solomon Belanger,	Registe Vaillant,
Joseph Benoit,	Jean Baptiste Parent,
Joseph Gagné,	Jean Baptiste Belanger,
Pierre Dumas,	Jean Baptiste Belleau,
Joseph Forcier,	Emanuel Cournoyée,
Igance Perrault,	Michel Teroahauté, an Iroquois.
Francois Samandré.	
Pierre St. Germain,	Chipewyan Bois Brulés.

▲ Document 5: Agricultural and Domestic Wages

Emigrants Wages in Upper Canada, Distress, &c.

In the recent discussions which have taken place on the condition of emigrants arriving from the Mother Country, many of whom, it must be confessed, are in a state of great wretchedness, the rate of wages has been estimated for both Provinces. In this Province, it is, perhaps, a more difficult matter to fix a standard that in Upper Canada, because few of the inhabitants of French origin have more land than they can cultivate with the aid of their families, and, therefore, they rarely employ hired servants, except in hay time and harvest. In Upper Canada, it is much more common to hire agricultural labourers, and there the rates of wages may be more easily ascertained. We are enabled, on good authority, to state, that in the Newcastle District, in that Province, where the Hon. Peter Robinson is at present engaged in locating settlers, the following were the general prices paid during the past month:

Carpenters, 7s. 6d. per diem | without board
Masons ... ditto ... |

Labourers, by the day, 2s. 6d. to 3s. and found in board. By the month, 40s. to 60s. and boarded, and the same rate is paid to those who engage by the year.

Women servants, living in the family, earn from 15s. to 20s. per month.

It is stated, that the tailors and shoemakers find ready employment in that District; and that a brickmaker, having a little capital to commence with, would find an advantageous opening. Thus, there is encouragement in that quarter, at least, for a portion of the strangers who have arrived this year in our harbour.

A society has been set on foot in Montreal, for the Relief of Destitute Emigrants: the following is the third of a series of resolutions, adopted at the meeting, and really, after all, with temporary shelter, except in cases of sickness, (and that is otherwise provided for,) it is the only relief which Emigrants require.

"That it be an instruction to this Committee, to confine their labours chiefly to the object of forwarding destitute Emigrants to those parts of Upper and Lower Canada, in which they may be most likely to obtain labour and lands". [...]

"Notice. As the public hospitals of this city have been found insufficient to afford medical assistance to the encreasing [sic] number of Emigrants arriving daily, and threatening the city with contagious diseases—the undersigned Medical Practitioners, in conformity with the request made by the Emigrant Society, established to relieve the distress of the destitute emigrants, have associated themselves to conduct a Dispensary, to be connected with the building about to be erected, on the plains of St. Anne, where indigent emigrants may obtain, *gratis*, advice and

Source: "Agricultural and Domestic Wages," *Quebec Mercury*, 28th June, 1831.

medicine every day from 7 a.m. to 8 a.m. upon the recommendation of one of the Committee of said society, signed by

Dr. Stephenson, Dr. Demers, Dr. Vallee".

This is a point to which we have for some time contemplated calling to the public attention. [...]

There is certainly much distress amongst those who remain in the cities, but there is certainly, not a small portion of the emigrants, who, so long as they can subsist by exciting sympathy and extracting alms from the more wealthy, will not make an exertion to gain a livelihood by a more active, but certain operation. From circumstances which have recently come to our knowledge, we are inclined to think that much of this distress arises from an unwillingness on the part of the emigrants to open their eyes to their actual situation, to be convinced that they must submit consequences of the temporary glut of labor the arrival of such unexampled numbers has occasioned, and to take such wages as are going. Two instances have been mentioned to us, from sources every way entitled to credit, where emigrants have refused employment, not because the wages tendered to them were insufficient for their support, but because they not such as they *expected* to obtain. [...]

But although there is a redundance of labor in the immediate neighbourhood of the cities and along the banks of the St. Lawrence, the rate of wages, we have above given, in Upper Canada, shews that labor is not there a superabundant commodity, and there is a demand for it in the Eastern Townships. [...]

We have no wish to discourage any benevolent plan for the relief of emigrants; on the contrary, we shall always feel happy in promoting any thing which may tend to their permanent welfare, but of this we feel certain, that so long as those who are hale and able to work, so long will there be a burthensome list ready to avail themselves of the charitable feelings of the community; and therefore, in administering assistance great caution and discrimination are necessary, or the public will be duped by a set of people who had rather stoop to beg than earn a livelihood by honest labour.

▲ Document 6: Workers, Managers, and Townspeople Celebrate the Dawning Age of Railroads

The first railway built in Nova Scotia (and the second in British North America) had its first public run in September 1839. The railway connected the growing industrial town of Albion Mines with the shipping facilities at nearby New Glasgow. While we should be careful in thinking about the future it signaled (something the participants could not have imagined), it was clearly an important day marked by a very enthusiastic celebration. What is the significance of the carefully ordered parade? What do the parade and the later feast tell us about the nature of class and gender in an early industrial town? The General Mining Association was a British-financed mining company that dominated the coalfields of Nova Scotia from 1827 into the 1870s.

One of the most novel and imposing spectacles ever witnessed in this portion of the world took place on Thursday last on the premises of the General Mining Association. [...]

The event [...] was the running of the locomotive carriages for the first time on the completion of the new Rail Road. [...]

The prediction of an unusual demonstration of feeling was amply verified on the morning of the 19th [September]. At 6 o'clock our little town presented a scene of bustle and agitation, which at that time is rarely exhibited by its peaceful inhabitants. On the arrival of the steamer *Pocohontas* at about half past 6 o'clock, every street and alley was crowded with the votaries of enjoyment making their way in the direction of the boat, and bound for Mount Rundell [the large and by the standards of the day quite luxurious home of the manager of the company] on a pilgrimage of pleasure.

The scene of embarkation was one of great excitement and interest. [...] Half an hour after the tolling of the bell, the note of preparation for the steamer wending her way, having on board upwards of 300 souls, commencing, we have no hesitation in stating as great a portrait of grace and beauty as were ever simultaneously on her deck before. The Albion Steamer, which the agents of the Association had also politely dispatched for the gratuitous accommodation of the Volunteer Artillery Company, arrived some time after the other; they picked up a few choice spirits who were unprepared to be sent in the first boat. These, however, did not long maintain undisturbed possession of the quarter deck—in a short time she was crowded to over-flowing. [...] The tedium of the passage up the river, occasioned by a head wind and a rapid tide against us, was beguiled by a succession of lively and plaintive airs—among which, the "Caledonian Rant", "We'll gang away to yon home" and "The Campbells are coming" may be stated as the most exhilarating and happiest specimens of the musician's art. Our arrival at the New Glasgow bridge was announced by a volley of artillery. [...]

The procession started at McKay's Hotel at 11 o'clock, a.m., and moved off in the following order:

Source: "Albion Mines Locomotive Steam Engine Celebration," *Mechanic and Farmer* (Pictou, Nova Scotia) 25 September 1839.

FIRST

100 horses, mounted by their respective drivers—Horses and men decorated, carrying flags.

Device 1st flag—a large Crown in the centre; a Rose, Shamrock, Thistle, and Mayflower in the corners.

    Motto—Long life to Queen Victoria.

Device 2nd flag—2 horses with 2 wagons, each loaded with coal, coming out of the pit bottom, meeting 2 Colliers going to their work, with picks under their arms.

Motto—Success to the Coal Trade; as the Old Cock Crows, the young one learn.

Device 3rd flag—Blue, Red, and White Silk flag.

SECOND

Enginemen with Flag.

Device—A Steam Engine—Pit Frame etc, drawing coal [much like a steam-driven conveyor belt which lifted the coal out of the shaft].

    Motto—   Long may the Company flourish
                  And their servants rejoice;
                  May Steam Navigation never fail
                  To burn our Coal and send us sale.

FOURTH

Colliers, carrying two Flags.

Device 1st Flag—2 Colliers in the Board [in the mine] at their work, and a horse appearing from behind the Coal, coming out with a Skip load of coal.

    Motto—   Though shrouded in darkness, yet from us proceed
                  A thing that is useful and all persons need.

Device 2nd Flag—A Locomotive engine at one end, a winding engine at the other; in the centre is 2 Colliers meeting, one going from the other to his work.

    Motto—   United we stand, when divided we fall,
                  Unanimous as brethren.

FIFTH

The Freemasons, with Flags and Bagpipes.

SIXTH

The Foundrymen and Blacksmiths, with a Flag.

Device—Archimedes on one side, and Watt on the other.

    Motto—   Ours and for us.

SEVENTH

Bricklayers and Stonemasons, with Flag.

Device—Tools of their Trade.

    Motto—   Success to the Locomotive Engines, and all the Trades belonging
    to the Albion Mines.

NEL

EIGHTH

Carpenters, with a Flag.
Device—Square and Compass, &c.
Motto—   The Albion Mines and Joseph Smith, Esq.

NINTH

Bagpipes.

TENTH

Artillery, with Flags and Band.

ELEVENTH

Visitors on horseback.

The procession returned to the Rail Road station at 1 o'clock, when a salute was fired by the Artillery. The most important part of the ceremony, the running of the Locomotives, was to take place at 2 o'clock, p.m., the intervening time was spent in examining their construction, and admiring these most astonishing monuments of human ingenuity. They are universally allowed by competent judges to be engines of superior manufacture, and the various parts of their machinery are in the highest state of polish and repair. The Locomotives are three in number, and are called the Hercules, the John Buddle, and the Sampson [sic]. [Hercules and Samson were obvious choices for the names of these powerful machines. John Buddle was an important British mining engineer who had business connections with the GMA.]

On this occasion the first two only were called into active service. For though the false Delieah [variant spelling of Delilah, the biblical seductress who was said to have shorn Samson's hair, thus depriving him of his strength] would labour in vain to sap the physical energy of the modern Samson, especially when he has his steam up, yet the others were quite sufficient to discharge the duty, and the great antagonist of the Philistines is kept as a *corps de reserve* to be called into requisition on any pressing emergency.

At the appointed hour the carriages were cleared of the vulgar throng with which they were crowded, and instantly filled with those to whom the gentlemen of the Association had sent tickets of admission. In a few minutes both trains were in motion—the Hercules taking the lead having a train of 35 carriages, containing upwards of 700 souls. The John Buddle with an equal number of carriages and passengers followed in hot pursuit—by Jove it was a splendid sight to see those noble efforts of human mechanism, at the magic touch of the Engineers "walking it off like a thing of life", at a rapidity varying from 10 to 20 miles per hour and each having a tail infinitely longer than that sported by Dan O'Connel [sic] [a reference to Daniel O'Connell who led the fight for Catholic emancipation in Ireland], the representative of all of Ireland!!!

After running two trips in the Locomotive, all workmen again formed in procession and marched to four tables which were spread out for them opposite the office of the establishment, at which not less than 750 individuals partook of a repast. "There was none of your humbugging of French Sauces" but about 1200 lbs. of Beef and Mutton, 6 hhds. [a now antiquated English unit of measure; typically, it was a wooden barrel, the size of which varied (depending on time, locality, and what was being measured) but approximately 60 gallons (250 *l*)] of Ale, with bread and vegetables in abundance, with the other substantial of life, formed the principal items of the Bill of Fare, provided by the generosity of the Commissary General. The masticating apparatus of those seated at the table was speedily in operation, and were it possible that the appetite of the votaries of Epicurus could renew its virginity at every additional supply, we feel confident that the zest with which the *bon vivants* of the Albion Mines relished the good things of this life, could not, even under these circumstances, have been surpassed.

After drinking the health of the Queen, the prosperity of the General Mining Association, and long life and happiness to its Agents, they departed from the tables in the most perfect regularity and order. The Freemasons and Artillery partook of a lunch in one of the new houses, which they washed down with Brandy and water.

In the evening, a dinner was given by Mr. Smith [Joseph Smith, the manager of the Albion Mines] at which 150 persons were sumptuously entertained. On entering the Engine House, which was converted into a Saloon for the occasion, the effect produced on the mind was pleasing in the extreme. At the north end of the room, above the head of the President, the Ensign, and the Union Jack were seen in juxtaposition with the Star Spangled Banner of Republican America, indicative, we presume, of the friendly relations at present subsisting between these two mighty Empires. Two tables, capable of containing 200 persons, were spread on each side of the building. A small table made to cross the others was erected at the northern extremity of the hall, behind which, on an elevation of about two feet, stood the President's Chair. Richard Brown, esq. [The Association's senior manager in Nova Scotia], ("That Prince of Good Fellows") discharged the duty of President, assisted as Croupier by Joseph Smith, Esq., whose gentlemanly conduct during the course of the evening evinced in his anxiety to anticipate the desires of his guests, formed the theme of universal commendation. On the right and left of the President were seated the Hon. William Lawson, and Mssrs. Dickson, Holmes, Hatton, and Archibald, Members of the House of Assembly, and a number of the Clergy and Magistrates of the County. On the removal of the cloth, two carriages, each containing five decanters of wine, traversed both tables, on a *Rail Road*. This device had a capital effect, and its discovery elected a burst of applause from the guests, that shook the tenement to its foundation. In a moment after, away went the *vinous locomotives*, and the votaries of Silenus [a friend and teacher of Dionysus, the god of wine] propitiated the rosy divinity in copious libations of Champagne.

At about 9 o'clock, the scene of festivity was much enlivened by the unexpected appearance of the Ladies, who, at an earlier hour, had been entertained by Mrs. Smith at Mount Rundell [the home of the manager].

Their *entrée* into banqueting hall was greeted by nine deafening acclamations. The standing toasts were cast aside, and "Ladies, Heaven's last best gift to man", given by the President, which was drank with all the honors. The President called upon the individual who had last presented an offering on Hymen's altar, but none forthcoming, one of the fraternity who delight "to roam in bachelor meditation fancy free" discharged this duty in a highly effective manner. After remaining about a quarter of an hour, the Ladies made a precipitate retreat and the Lords of Creation were "left alone in their glory"; during their stay, however, they were much gratified and amused, and the visions of happiness which danced through their mind appeared equally delightful with those "which maidens dream of when they muse on love".

At about 10 o'clock, the President left the Chair, and the guests much gratified with the amusements of the day, departed in quest of accommodation for the night. During the course of the evening, several appropriate speeches were delivered, which, together with the toasts, our limits prevent us from inserting.

▲ Document 7: Correspondence on Strikes at the Welland Canal, Upper Canada, in 1845

THE "GREAT
SWIVEL LINK":
CANADA'S
WELLAND CANAL
TORONTO
THE CHAMPLAIN SOCIETY
2001

Thomas A. Begly to W.B. Robinson
21 September 1842
[NAC, RG 11, Vol. 116 *Letterbook 1838–1842*, #1227]

Mr. Killaly desires me to say that about fifty soldiers are to be permanently stationed at St. Catharines, the same number at Thorold, and the barracks at Broad Creek should be made for seventy five, comfortable dry &c and should be ready as soon as possible. For the Officers he has settled with the Military authorities to make them the usual weekly allowance for lodging. The Officers at Broad Creek Mr. Killaly does not well know what is to be done with but leaves that altogether to you. Mr. Killaly desires me to say that no inducements whatever are being held out to Connaught or other men going over to your work. [...]

Contractors to Magistrates of Niagara District
19 December 1842
[NAC, RG 11, Vol. 65-7, p.9]

We the undersigned Contractors upon the Welland Canal, do most respectfully recommend to the Magistrates of the Niagara District in Special Session assembled to withhold from all applicants Licences for Taverns and Groceries, at the Quarries and the vicinity of the operations upon this Canal, with the exception of those now authorised.

In offering this suggestion, we have in view the quiet and orderly prosecution to this <u>Great Public Work</u> in which we are intimately concerned, and the best interests of the labourers themselves.[1]

Samuel Power to William H. Merritt [Mayor of St. Catharines]
4 January 1843
[AO, F662, MS 74, *Merritt Papers*, Package 15]

[...] my prediction has been fulfilled, and the work suspended between the Junction and Marshville. The army being useless without a magistrate, I had recourse to Mr. Church, and found a willing ally in Mr. McDonagh the R.C. clergyman, who accompanied me to a party of the idlers. They promised to resume work tomorrow. I shall be in Marshville early and hope to see their pledge fulfilled. I also sent Bonnalie for Capt. Farrell, J.P. My reason for mentioning this is to shew the necessity for a resident Magistrate. Mr. Robinsons efforts would I fear be worse than useless as if his purpose were known of appointing his political partisans constables, the riots would occur more frequently, and assume a more

Source: Roberta M. Styran and Robert R. Taylor, The *"Great Swivel Link": Canada's Welland Canal* (Toronto, The Champlain Society, 2001). Reprinted with permission from The Champlain Society.

serious aspect, from the long cherished feelings of hostility existing between the Irish laborers, and the lower class of Orangemen, who it seems are Mr. R's especial favorites. I cordially detest ultra politics of every description, and hope that the laborers may not be unnecessarily exasperated by placing them beneath the surveillance of those whom they view as their old tyrants. While speaking on this subject, I should call your attention to the colored troops, who were <u>not</u> sent to Broad Creek until the sickly season had passed. The Baron de Rottenburg considers them most unsuitable for the duty which they now discharge. It is only by the most rigid discipline that the laborers can be governed but let us not necessarily provoke them. [...]

Hamilton H. Killaly to Rev. William P. McDonagh
7 January 1843
[NAC, RG 11, Vol. 117, *Letterbook 1842–1844*, #1679]

Upon being apprised of the intention of Government to dispense with the services of the Baron de Rottenburgh,[2] I represented to Council the necessity of securing, as far as possible, peace & order along the line of the works on the Welland Canal, which object I consider would be materially forwarded by their authorizing me to avail myself of the influence, which I know you to possess over the laborers, from your profession, from being from the same country with much the greater number of them, and from your being able to address them in their native language.

I have received directions for making this arrangement, and I have, therefore, to entreat that you will not lose a moment in going through the works generally, & exert all your authority, religious & moral, in repressing insubordination, & all tendency to outrage. I need not point out to you the several forcible points, which can be urged to induce them to conduct themselves peaceably. I think it necessary to mention but two matters, first wholly to discountenance the sale & use of spirits on the works, and secondly to represent to them that, <u>most unquestionably</u>, upon any riot of a serious nature occurring, the Government will stop the work wholly for a season and exonerate the Contractors from their obligations so far as time is concerned [...]

Power to Begly
25 August 1843
[NAC, RG 43, Vol. 2097, *Letterbook 1842–1843*, #2671]

[...] I shall now reply to the principal points adverted to in your letter [of the 21st][3] [...]

When the lake fever was raging at Broad Creek to such an extent, that at one time 800 persons were ill and 4 deaths occurred daily. [...]

My monthly reports even monthly descriptions of the frauds of the contractors, and consequent riots among the men, until I became wearied with reiterating the same tale, it may also be recollected that the impossibility of conducting the work under the old form of contract, when in such hands led me to suggest the clauses in the present contracts for the protection of the laborer ... after mature reflection I am convinced that if I should ever again be so unfortunate, as to be placed under similar circumstances in contracts with men strangers to every principle of honesty, and honor, regard to justice & prudence alone must compel me to pursue precisely the same course, and I am certain that the Board on reconsidering all the circumstances of the case will withdraw their censure, which I cannot help feeling was most undeserved. [...]

In opposition to the assertion the additional force consisted of <u>one man</u>, you have the solemn affirmation of Mr. Bonnalie, that he at once placed <u>35 men</u> on the work, and he must from time to time have placed much greater numbers, for I visited the work every week, and almost on every occasion directed him to increase the force on neglected parts but in addition to this his evidence affords a clear proof that the entire force consisting of several hundreds was placed upon the work by my direct orders acting on the part of the Board. [...]

The 3rd point adverted to by the Board is "my countenancing sub-contracting"!! an arrangement against which I have ever protested and prevent which I introduced a clause into the contract. [...]

David Thorburn to D. Daly[4]
10 January 1844
[NAC, RG11, Vol. 68-5 pp. 34–43]

From the riots and disturbances that have recently taken place on the line of the Welland Canal, I have deemed it to be my duty to give you for the information of the Governor General an outline of the proceedings and apparent exciting causes to riot and uneasiness by the labourers as well as the position of matters in general for the prevention of like recurrence. I have therefore the honor to state that for some time past the labourers have shown a disposition to be troublesome and to keep them in check has engaged the attention of Mr. Power the chief Engineer and the Constabulary or Police force, principally under the direction of Messrs MacFarlane and Hobson, J.P.s of the Township of Thorold; these gentlemen are the two Councillors for that Township and have at my request since I left for the Legislature, had a constant care for the preservation of the Peace especially from Thorold Mountain to the upper parts of the works; Mr. Bonnalie the Head Officer of the Police knew this and received from them every aid, instruction, countenance and direction. His general arrangements for the preservation of the Peace could not have been better with his officers, few in number considering the extent of canal from Thorold to Dunnville, Broad Creek and Port Colborne, and the distant stone quarries from the canal in all not less than fifty miles for intelligence has been transmitted to the paper quarter with the least possible delay upon the appearance of an outbreak. Thus giving confidence to the inhabitants of their vigilance and of that of the Civil and Military authorities who have at all times cordially cooperated for the keeping and promoting of order. [...]

Indeed there is no disquiet can occur on any part of the line without the knowledge of the Police. Such being the preventative position on the slightest outbreak steps are soon taken to put it down and to prevent a further extention of it. Indeed had such not been our well regulated position, the result of recent outbreaks must have ended in the loss of human life for an organized system exists amongst the labourers, they are armed with all and every kind of weapon, consisting of guns, pistols, swords, pikes or poles, pitch forks, scythes, &c, &c. They are determined to do evil when they think that by doing so will answer some end consonant with their views which hath no bounds their affrays or riots are against each other or against their contractors as yet in every instance their plans have been promptly met and put down with the destruction of some shanties, cooking utensils &c &c and often broken heads which generally takes place at the commencement of their rows, when uneasiness takes place on any of the works the firing of guns and blowing of horns throughout the night on such works is the sure presage of trouble. Some of the constables have had beatings and one of them, Mr. Wheeler, late a Lieut. of the 5th Bat., incorporated Militia, received from one of them by a gun shot, a ball in his hip and I am sorry to say it there remains for it is too deep seated to be extracted, his health is recovering.

One of the most alarming Riots that has yet been upon the works began at Stone Bridge within one mile of Lake Erie on Monday the 25th Decr. (Christmas Day) caused by the fighting of two drunken men in one of the shantys. Like wild fire the evil spirit ran throughout every work on the whole line when the Cork and Connaught party immediately were roused in the worst character every part of the works were stopped. [...] The Cork men began it, in several instances bodies of four, five and six hundred of them (every one of the men in arms) were met and dispersed, their women & children flew from their shanties for safety, and took refuge where ever they found a door whether it was a stable, barn, dwelling house or even a church, and many of them fled to the woods. The Stone Bridge riot had just commenced when Mr. Bonnalie arrived there when he quelled it, at that place, for the moment with two of his officers, aided by the Contractors, their foremen and some of the well disposed inhabitants and secured a few of the ring leaders as prisoners. Early the following day Mr. McFarland and Capt. Macdonald with a detachment of twenty five of the Coloured Incorporated Militia arrived from Port Robinson by wagon and just in time to prevent a nasty conflict, as a large body of Connaughts came to avenge the wrongs done by the Corkmen to some of their more immediate kindred the preceding day. Mr. Power got there late in the evening and on the following morning I arrived in company with two additional Magistrates. [...]

The first moving cause that excites the trouble is the want of work, if not employed they are devising schemes to procure it, such as driving away the party who are fewest in number who are not of their County. The Corkmen began the Christmas affray, but there is no visible difference with them for either when an opportunity offers will drive off the other.

Another cause is when the wages do not suit, they combine and stop from working indeed the well disposed are compelled to go with the majority for in such cases a patrolling band with bludgeons drive off the workers. The Priest says that Secret Societys exist amongst them binding them by oaths to be faithful to each other. One is called the Hibernian and another the Shamerick Society and that he is unable to break them up.[5]

Some time in Novr. the Contractors by common consent throughout the line dropt the doctor's wages to 2/6 Cy. per day, about the same time provisions advanced particularly potatoes and butchers meat the former of which commodities to 2/6 Cy per bushel, at same time the inclemency of the weather prevented constant work, the combination of such circumstances made their case a hard one particularly for men of families some of whom not able to procure a sufficiency of food even of potatoes, so situated schemes for relief are readily listened to, but unfortunately they too generally rely for assistance through some unlawful proceeding thus adding misery to misery when caught out punished for so doing. The Chief Engineer informs me that the men upon the line will number five thousand and their women and children as many more in all ten thousand people, and that over three thousand cannot find employment, the work does not require more than that number of men [...] seven thousand who earn nothing and those who are employed can put in but little work for a month at this season of the year. I am glad to report that the Contractors are now paying 3/1½ Cy per day. I have not heard of any outbreak among them since the end of the last month, peace and order now reign and I fondly hope will continue not only from the advance of their wages but more particular that their plots and schemes have been promptly met and at once put down and some of their ring leaders are undergoing the sentence of the law while others have been bound over to keep the peace. All those things are quickly known through their Societys.

Mr. Merritt and Mr. Power have desired that I take the general supervision for the preservation of the Peace along the line to which request I have consented, from my general knowledge of the people and of all authorities residing near or in the neighbourhood of the works, occasional visits and from an active correspondence [...][6]

Power to Begly
20 December 1844
[NAC, RG 43, Vol. 2248, *Letterbook 1844–1846*, #5995]
I have been requested by Dr. Campbell to state that during the last two years he has been engaged in attending the laborers employed on the upper part of the line of the Welland Canal & the subordinate servants of the Board stationed in that unhealthy region. That the latter have been unable to pay him in consequence of the very low rate of salaries received by them & that the former were unwilling to remunerate him because they erroneously supposed that he was paid by the Govt. Dr. Campbell has thus sustained a considerable loss & the public have derived great benefit from his services as the attention of a Physician supposed to be in the employment of the Board has doubtless tended to prevent the more frequent occurrence of riots. Under these circumstances I must take the liberty of advising the Board to grant Dr. Campbell's very moderate request that he should receive the same remuneration as one of the Police Officers, his pay to commence from the 1st May last. I can with propriety recommend this measure feeling assured that Dr. Campbell could materially assist Mr. McDonagh in preserving the peace.[7]

Robert Holmes and Dilly Coleman[8] To Merritt
11 April 1845
[AO, F662, MS 74, *Merritt Papers*, Package 15]
From the frequent depredation committed in the village of Port Robinson and its environs Mr. Coleman and myself take the Liberty of addressing a few lines to you upon the subject, the Troops (I mean the Colored Core) were stationed for the Protection of the Inhabitants, along the line of canal but instead of their being a protection they have certainly become a Public Nuisance and are looked upon in that light by the respectable portion of the Inhabitants generally. As we are informed a good deal of pilfering has been committed upon said Inhabitants of said village and Neighbourhood and we want to further add, the Church has been robbed [...] and this morning a most glaring robbery has been committed upon Jesse D. Lacy, Merchant of this place [...] and on passing one of the sentinels he spoke to him making enquiry no doubt if any thing had been discovered by him whilst on duty. Mr. Lacy informed me that Mr. Roberts one of the officers belonging to the Colored Core threatened to report Mr. Lacy for daring to speak to the sentinel to Capt. McDonnell. This morning Mr. McFarland found pasted up near his office an advertisement threatening to burn the premises of Duncan McFarland Esqr, Dilly Coleman [...] and myself, should we dare to enforce the law against certain individuals for selling spiritous liquors without a Licence. We strongly suspect that from certain language used by Capt. McDonnell towards D. McFarland on the previous enquiry that he is the author of the advertisement. I can assure you that such a state of things are not very desirable in this place and the sooner the Troops are removed from this place for the comfort of the Inhabitants the better. We therefore hope that you will use your influence with the Government to get the same removed as we should like a Company of the Rifles instead of the present Company stationed here, and indeed we should much rather be without any troops than to continue the present ones. Mr. McFarland and myself have a good deal of difficulty to contend with as Magistrates sometimes in keeping quiet the labourers upon the Public Works, but I can assure you, that many obstacles are thrown in our way by those from whom we expected assistance to maintain the Dignity of Laws. Should I meet with such Treatment at the hands of Capt. McDonald as I have upon a former occasion I shall feel it my duty, at once to report him to his Excellency as he has conducted himself to me when on the discharge of my duty as a Magistrate, was quite unbecoming any man much less a gentleman holding the situation which he holds in Her Majesty's Service.

Notes

1. The petition is dated at Thorold and was signed by eight contractors or their representatives.
2. Baron George Frederick de Rottenburg (1807–1894) was probably born in England, a son of Baron Francis (Franz) de Rottenburg, who had served with distinction in the British army in the War of 1812. The son apparently followed his father in a military Career, serving in the Militia in Canada West.
3. Power had written to Begly earlier, urging the need to get on with the proposed work on the Welland. The delay was occasioned by the Board of Works' hesitation concerning the precise instrctions to be given regarding the attempt to achieve the Lake Erie level for the Canal. On 1 August, he had said that "however easy it may be for those, who are at a distance, to speculate on the propriety of delaying the work until precise instructions may arrive, it is very different for me surrounded by men infuriated by hunger, to persist in a course which must drive them to despair ..." On the 6th, he pleaded "If the Board will consent to my original design the work can be immediately commenced &c all danger bloodshed & tumult prevented ..." (*ibid*, #2519).
4. Sir Dominick Daly (1798–1868) was an original member of the Board of Works, 1841–46. He refused to serve on the government-appointed Board of Management for the Welland Canal. He was Provincial Secretary at this time.
5. The "Shamerick" Society is probably a spelling variant of "Shamrock." According to Dr. Donald H. Akeson, of Queen's University History Department, "Shamrock" societies were common among first generation immigrants and were probably mutual benefit societies (personal communication 13 August 1998).
6. On 17 January, Thorburn again reported to Daly, describing further violence (NAC, RG 11, Vol. 68–5, Part 1, pp. 49–51).
7. Despite Power's urging, the Board's response was negative. Begly referred Power to a previous communication, nothing that, since this was question "upon which the Executive Government have already determined not to interfere, "the Board could not grant the request (NAC, RG 11, Vol. 118, *Letterbook 1844–1845*, #5397).
8. This letter was marked "Confidential." Holmes was a J.P. and one of the Magistrates involved in the peace-keeping efforts in 1844. In the 1860s and '70s, Coleman was at various times a farmer, grocer, and proprieter [sic] of the Mansion House.

■ Article 1: Making the Voyageur World

Carolyn Podruchny

Voyageurs had much more leisure time during the winter months spent at interior posts than they did during the canoe journeys of the summers. Yet here they also had more time to feel homesick and anxious in the midst of a foreign world. Much of their play was reminiscent of French Canada, such as celebrating annual holidays, drinking, and holding balls; these festivities helped voyageurs create a sense of home away from home. Voyageurs also had the time to create new connections, form new families, and solidify a distinctive society in the Northwest. Their celebrations helped them create new memories and new traditions rooted in their new locations.

An annual schedule of holiday celebrations accompanied the yearly round of labor, which was especially important to the men living at isolated posts, away from their families and friends. Men often journeyed from outlying posts to congregate at larger central forts to celebrate the holidays and gladly risked the dangers and discomfort of winter travel, even a week of walking with snowshoes, to avoid spending a holiday alone.[1] Holidays helped to mark the passage of time and provided structure during the long, dreary, and often lonely months at the interior posts. Coming together to celebrate at specific times helped to generate camaraderie and fellow feeling with one another, their masters, and Aboriginal peoples.

Christmas and New Year were the most popular holidays for the fur traders and were rarely forgotten or ignored. Other holidays that were sometimes celebrated included All Saint's Day on November 1, St. Andrew's Day on November 30, and Easter in early April.[2] Similar celebrations occurred at HBC posts.[3] The occasional mention of celebrations occurred on Palm Sunday, the king's birthday (June 4, George III), and Epiphany, or "Little Christmas" (January 6).[4] Men seemed willing to commemorate any day, regardless of its origins or significance to them, because

Source: Reprinted from *Making the Voyageur World: Travelers and Traders in the North American Fur Trade* by Carolyn Podruchny by permission of the University of Nebraska Press. © 2006 by the Board of Regents of the University of Nebraksa, pp. 174–7, 181, 192–4, and 196–9.

it served as an excuse for a celebration and drams from the bourgeois. Commemorating St. Andrew, the patron saint of Scotland, and observing the birthday of George III, king of Great Britain, were probably holidays introduced by the Scottish and English bourgeois and clerks, while Christmas, New Year's, All Saint's Day, and Easter would have been common celebrations in French Canada.[5] George Landmann noted that in late eighteenth-century Montreal, New Year's Day was "a day of extraordinary festivity, which was extended to the two or three following days. Amongst the Canadians it was [...] the fashion for everybody to visit everybody during one of the three first days of the year, when a glass of noyeau or other liquor was, with a piece of biscuit or cake, presented to the visitor, which, after a hard day's work in calling at some twenty or thirty houses, frequently terminated in sending a number of very respectable people home in a staggering condition toward the close of the day."[6] Feasting, drinking, and levees, or paying courtesy calls on masters (particularly on New Year's Day), were characteristic of celebrations in fur trade society.

The holiday celebrations seemed to follow a formula. Specific rituals and ceremonies, giving the day a sense of orderly formality and tradition, were followed by chaotic parties, where wild abandon and heavy drinking predominated. Alexander Henry the Younger complained on New Year's Day in 1803 that he was plagued with ceremonies and men and women drinking and fighting "pell mell."[7]

During most holiday celebrations at fur trade posts, men generally did not have to work.[8] During the Christmas and New Year's holidays, voyageurs and bourgeois frequently arranged to visit other posts or invited visitors to their post for the day or for the entire holiday season.[9] Many men tried to organize their work schedules so they would not miss any of the festivities. In December 1818 at Tête au Brochet, George Nelson was frustrated by one of his voyageurs named Welles. Nelson had sent Welles to Falle de Perdix on December 23, but Welles returned to the post on December 30, claiming that the snow and ice prevented him from reaching his destination. Nelson suspected that this was a lie and that Welles really wanted to be back at the post for the New Year's celebrations.[10] Men of different companies sometimes put aside their different allegiances to celebrate together. During the Christmas holidays in 1805, XYC employees celebrated with their NWC neighbors at Lac La Pluie.[11] Frequently Aboriginal people came to the posts to participate in the festivities, which helped the traders solidify trading ties and foster goodwill with them.[12] Donald McKay noted that it was customary for Aboriginal people to arrive at the post on all feast days.[13] Voyageurs sometimes visited Aboriginal lodges as part of the day's celebrations.[14] Those Aboriginal people who were closely involved with provisioning and fur trading, such as the "homeguard," celebrated with the traders.

The day's festivities on Christmas and New Year's usually began early in the morning. Voyageurs ceremoniously called on their bourgeois or clerk to formally wish him well and pay their respects.[15] The early morning firing of muskets or cannons usually woke the masters.[16] In 1793 Alexander Mackenzie wrote. "On the first day of January, my people, in conformity to the usual custom, awoke me at the break of day with the discharge of fire-arms, with which they congratulated the appearance of the new year. In return, they were treated with plenty of spirits, and when there is any flour, cakes are always added to the regales, which was the case, on the present occasion,"[17] Like the firing of muskets when a brigade arrived at a post, this salute was a symbolic welcome and a formal honoring of the holiday.

After the firing of muskets, all the residents of the fort gathered together in a general meeting where the bourgeois or clerk would provide regales or gifts to the voyageurs. Depending on the wealth of the post, regales could be as little as a single dram or as much as great quantities of alcohol, especially if there was a shortage of food.[18] At the beginning of 1802, Daniel Harmon gave his men a dram in the morning and then enough rum to drink throughout the course of the day, to help distract them from the scarcity of meat.[19] In an effort to secure more alcohol for the day's festivities, men would go to great lengths to salute their bourgeois or any passing visitor or dignitary, in hopes of gaining a treat.[20] Regales on New Year's seemed to be slightly more generous than those at Christmas, as men were frequently given tobacco in addition to drams.[21] At wealthier posts the men's regales included food, usually specialty items that were hard to procure, such as flour and sugar, though the regale could include meat and grease.[22]

Holding a formal ball was an importation from French Canada, but the dancing and music were culturally distinctive. The "old fiddle and Indian drum" symbolized the mixing of European and Aboriginal forms.[23] Dancing was not restricted to holidays but continued throughout the seasons at fur trade posts. Having dances or "balls" was a fairly common occurrence both at the Great Lakes posts and in the interior.[24] Either fiddlers or singers provided the music. Fast and spirited dancing predominated. The descriptions of the "lively reels" of country dances reflected a rough and tumble joie de vivre that was characteristic of many voyageurs' activities. Balls at Grand Portage during the rendezvous, however, were genteel affairs for the benefit of the bourgeois, with music from the bagpipe, violin, flute, and fife.[25] Yet even at these balls, "country music" combined musical forms from Canada, Scotland, England, and Aboriginal peoples. Dances were often held to celebrate specific events, such as the coalition of the XYC and the NWC in 1804, but the most common occasions were weddings and to honor visitors to the post.[26] Men from different companies frequently attended each others' dances.[27] Sometimes dances were held for no particular reasons other than to have fun and enliven the monotony of post life, especially during the long winters.[28]

The social life and play of voyageurs at the interior posts reveals an interesting tension between old and new social practices. Voyageurs preserved social traditions from French Canada to create a sense of home in the pays d'en haut, which could be overwhelming in its strangeness. Celebrating annual holidays, drinking, and dancing reminded voyageurs of their lives in rural French Canada and allowed them to continue to be part of that social world. Yet the circumstances of the fur trade led to the emergence of new behaviors. Contests and trickery became important because they bolstered the heightened masculinity of the male-dominated workplace, which valued toughness and strength, and the liminal social spaces of canoe journeys and post life. Men made every effort to demonstrate their strength, endurance, and good humor, especially in the face of hardship and privation. They were influenced by the cultural practices they observed among Aboriginal peoples, and imitating Aboriginal peoples became a way of increasing symbolic capital.

How did the liminal position of voyageurs working in the fur trade affect their relationships with one another? How did the men work out the social conventions of their new cultural locations? How were their friendships with fellow voyageurs different from their friendships with men in French Canada? These questions are difficult to answer. The dearth of work on male friendships among habitants makes comparisons especially challenging. A significant drawback in assessing the shape and nature of voyageur friendships is that their lives are mainly visible in the writings of their bourgeois and clerks, who were probably not aware of many of the relationships among their men, and would have little reason to record them in their letters and journals unless the behavior directly affected fur trade work. The documentary record contains descriptions of extremes in behavior, situations that were remarkable or abnormal, and conduct that hindered the workings of the trade. Despite these daunting drawbacks, it is possible to trace the outlines of voyageur camaraderie. In friendships between the men we can see expressions of a voyageur social order, such as an emphasis on good humor, generosity, rowdiness, and strength. In a culture where money and material possessions had limited significance, the quest for a strong reputation became more important.

Politeness was a social convention brought from French Canada. Traveling through the Canadas in the early nineteenth century, John Lambert noted that French Canadians were generally "good-humoured, peaceable, and friendly" and remarkably civil to one another and to strangers. People bowed to each other as they passed on the streets, and men sometimes even kissed each other on the cheek.[29] Similarly writers remarked on the good humor and affection that voyageurs showed to one another and even to their masters. Ross Cox marveled that the men referred to each other as *mon frère* (my brother) or *mon cousin* without being related and that they made up pet names for their bourgeois.[30] Bestowing kinship names on one another may have been a practice borrowed from Aboriginal peoples, who frequently adopted outsiders or assigned them kinship designations to incorporate them into their social order.

Yet civility among voyageurs was often described as "rough," and verbal exchanges were described as the "coarse & familiar language of brother voyageurs."[31] Swearing or blasphemy was not restricted to expressions of anger but was common in many different contexts. Expressions of profanity usually had to do with religious imagery, such as *sacré* (sacred), *mon Dieu* (my God), and *baptême* (baptism), which probably eased tension and poked fun at serious situations.[32] Masters' characterizations of voyageur familiarity and camaraderie as "rough" may reflect the bourgeois' desire to be "civilized."[33] Peter Moogk asserts that verbal and physical abuse among "the lower orders" in New France was commonplace, but it did not mean that habitants were particularly vulgar or wanton people. Bakhtin notes that billingsgate, or curses, oaths, and popular blazons, figured prominently in folk humor in early modern Europe. Abusive language was a mark of familiarity and friendship.[34] The "rough" civility may have found a particularly exaggerated expression in the pays d'en haut. Because the men worked in harsh and dangerous conditions, they wanted to be especially jovial and rowdy to demonstrate their lack of fear and their great strength in living amidst adversity. Rediker suggests that at sea "rough talk" was a way for sailors to express an opposition to "polite" bourgeois customs and their ideals of gentility, moderation, refinement, and industry. He asserts that "rough speech" was a transgressive means to deal with shipboard isolation and incarceration.[35] Likewise rough talk among voyageurs was probably a verbal cue for a distinct masculine identity.

Despite the "rough talk" social conventions among voyageurs stressed charity and generosity, especially in the face of hardship. Voyageurs could demonstrate that they were tough and strong enough to be kind in a brutal environment. If the difficulty of life in the fur trade sometimes caused men to be harsh and cruel to one another, much of this ill will could be expressed in the frequent and usually organized "sport" of fighting. The tension between a desire for equality and the centrality of social ordering influenced relationships among men in both good and bad ways. Voyageurs worked very closely together and relied on one another for survival. Their often deep friendships, however, were threatened by the transience of the job.

How deep did friendships among men develop? Did the homosocial environment, especially on canoe journeys, lead to the development of homosexuality as a normative expression of affection? Did sex between men become a common voyageur pastime? How would this affect the ideal of masculinity central to voyageur culture? Some scholars have argued that masculinity or gendered identities cannot be separated from sexuality and that heterosexuality is often a key part of working men's masculine identity.[36] This construction of masculinity becomes especially problematic in homosocial working environments when men do not have access to women for erotic pleasure. The situation of the voyageurs is historically unusual: they often worked in all-male environments, yet they had access to women of a "savage race." Was heterosexuality constructed in the same way when the sexual "other" was also the racial "other"?

The bourgeois and the clerks portrayed voyageurs as heterosexual and were conspicuously silent on homosexual practices. Masters may have consciously chosen to overlook the occurrence of homosexuality, considering it an unmentionable deviance. The silence may also indicate an ignorance of homosexual practice among voyageurs and Aboriginal men. Or homosexuality may not have existed as a social option for voyageurs who had easy access to Aboriginal women for sex. In any case, the silence demands close scrutiny.

Many all-male sojourners, most notably sailors, have a documented history of practicing sodomy, although it remains a clouded issue.[37] Without being essentialist about the nature of erotic desire, one is not unreasonable to assume that voyageurs sometimes had sexual feelings for each other or participated in sexual acts together. If sexuality is understood to be situational, then men working together in isolated groups probably developed sexual and emotional relationships with one another.[38] The voyageurs who transported goods and furs on the arduous route between Montreal and Lake Superior worked in isolated settings and had limited contact with Aboriginal peoples. These men, however, worked in the trade only during the summer months and returned to their French Canadian parishes, where not only homosexuality but any kind of nonmarital sexual practice was prohibited.[39] Is it possible that in the isolation and freedom of their summer jobs they experimented with different kinds of sexual pleasure? Or were they simply too tired to be interested in sex? Voyageurs who worked in the interior were often cooped up in trading posts, far away from the regulative forces of the Catholic Church and the scrutiny of social peers, and they had the time and leisure to pursue erotic pleasure. Here one might expect to find significant

emotional and possibly sexual bonding. The difficulty of fur trade work and the great risks in canoeing and portaging often created intense bonds of friendship and trust between men.[40] One clue to homosocial practice in the interior may lie in the patterns and rates of marriages between voyageurs and Aboriginal women.

Documentation on sodomy in early modern settings has been found mainly in legal records. I have found no prosecutions for voyageur buggery, or sodomy, in French Canadian courts. The Montreal traders did not impose rigid military discipline on their workers as did the HBC, and thus voyageurs were less socially regulated and freer than HBC laborers.[41] Edith Burley has found a few prosecutions for sodomy among the Orkney men working at HBC posts, but she asserts that "officers appear to have had little interest in the regulation of their men's sexuality and were probably content to overlook their improprieties as long as they did not interfere with the company's business."[42] Was the same true for the Montreal bourgeois? Many violations of contracts and other crimes were not formally punished because legal systems did not exist in the interior. Perhaps because the bourgeois knew they could neither prosecute buggery nor prevent it, they turned a blind eye to it. The silence regarding sodomy in bourgeois writings may reflect that the practice was considered deviant, amoral, illegal, and possibly unimaginable. If sexual contact between voyageurs and masters occurred, it would have been silenced by masters, who did not wish to be incriminated.

Masters may have chosen to overlook sexual relations between voyageurs and Aboriginal men so that they would not threaten trading alliances or create enemies. A substantial group of scholars have explored homosexuality among Aboriginal societies in the cultural form of berdaches.[43] Berdaches occupied "third sex" roles and were sometimes called "two-spirited people." They were most often people who played opposite or both male and female roles and held significant spiritual power, and they often became culture heroes. Although berdaches represented many different configurations of gender roles and sexual practices in different Aboriginal cultures, their widespread presence may indicate that sexuality was not dichotomous in many Aboriginal societies and that there was space for the expression of homosexual desire. Some scholars suggest that berdaches represented forms of "institutionalized" homosexuality. It is possible that the presence of berdaches indicates that homosexuality was permissible in some Aboriginal societies and thus permissible among voyageurs and some Aboriginal men.

It is difficult to know the extent to which the intense physicality of voyageur culture, the worship of masculine qualities of strength and physical endurance, and the scarcity of women enabled experimentation at a sexual level. If such relations among self-identified heterosexual men occurred in this liminal setting, like other forms of play they probably fortified friendships, and increased a sense of collectivity among voyageurs. At the same time, competition over partners and rejected advances probably created tensions and facilitated cultural divisions.

Because voyageurs lived between worlds, they found opportunities to transcend social restrictions learned at their homes in French Canada. In the process of trying out or "playing at" new ways of living, they could reinvent or refashion themselves. The play of voyageurs was influenced by customs brought from French Canada, by new practices learned from Aboriginal societies, and by the everyday life of the fur trade workplace. The working environment especially encouraged new "experimental" behavior because voyageurs were constantly traveling and thus isolated from established communities. Voyageurs' penchant for trickery and play became a tool for carving out the contours of their workspace. Play also became a social space where voyageurs could assert their particular ideal of manhood and where they could appropriate the behavior of Aboriginal peoples in order to be successful voyageurs. By providing a space for voyageurs to test new forms of social behavior, play strengthened voyageurs' social bonds with one another and encouraged camaraderie and a unified identity. At the same time, play became a vehicle through which voyageurs distinguished categories among themselves and deepened occupational fissures determined mainly by job status. It thus had a simultaneously homogenizing and diversifying effect on the voyageurs' world.

Notes

1. Lefroy, *In Search of the Magnetic North*, Lefroy to Isabella, Lake Athabasca, Christmas Day, 1843, 84.

2. For examples of All Saint's Day, see LAC, MG19 CI, vol. 12, November 1, 1804, 25; MRB, MC, C.28, November 1, 1807, 12; and Keith, *North of Athabasca*, 316. For examples of St. Andrew's Day, see OA, reel MS65, Donald McKay, Journal from January to December 1799, November 30, 1799, 43 (my pagination); and MRB, MC, C.24, Sunday, November 30, 1800, 6. For examples of celebrating Easter, see LAO MG19 CI, vol. 1, April 8, 1798, 53; LAC, MG19 CI, vol. 14, April 12, 1800, 23; and OA, MU 842, April 11, 1819, 43.

3. Morton, "Chief Trader Joseph McGillivray"; and Payne, *Most Respectable Place*, 65, 87–92.

4. For an example of celebrating Palm Sunday, see OA, MU 842, April 4, 1819, 42. For examples of celebrating the King's birthday, see TBR, S13, George Nelson's journal, April 1, 1810–May 1, 1811, June 4, 1810, 11 (my pagination); and Landmann, *Adventures and Recollections*, 2:167–68. For and example of celebrating Epiphany, see Henry (the Younger), *New Light*, January 6, 1810 1:165.

5. For comments on New Year's celebrations as a French Canadian custom, see Harmon, *Sixteen Years*, January 2, 1801, 41; see also Grenon, *Us et coutumes du Québec*, 153–68; Lamontagne, *L'hiver dans la culture québécoise*, 101–3; and Provencher, *Les Quatre Saisons*, 449–57, 463–70.

6. Landmann, *Adventures and Recollections*, 1:239–40.

7. Henry (the Younger), *New Light*, January 1, 1803, 1:207.

8. OA, reel MS65, Donald McKay, Journal from January 1805 to June 1806, December 25, 1805, 47 (my pagination); TBR, S13, George Nelson's journal, November 3, 1807–August 31, 1808, December 25, 1807, 14; November 1, 1807, 7; and Henry (the Younger), *New Light*, November 1, 1810, 2:660.

9. OA, reel MS65, Donald McKay, journal from January to December 1799, December 24, 1799, 46 (my pagination); TBR, S13, George Nelson's journal, November 3, 1807–August 31, 1808, December 25, 1807, 14; George Nelson's journal, April 1, 1810–May 1, 1811, December 23, 1810, 39 (my pagination).

10. OA, MU 842 December 23 and 30, 1818, 22–23.

11. Faries, "Diary," December 25–28, 1804 and January 1, 1805, 223–24.

12. Henry (the Younger), *New Light*, January, 1, 1801, 1:162–63; and Harmon, *Sixteen Years*, January 1, 1811 and 1812, 136, 147–48.

13. OA, reel MS65, Donald McKay, Journal from August 1800 to April 1801, December 25, 1800, 17.

14. LAC, MG19 CI, vol. l2, January 1, 1805, 35.

15. LAC, MG19 CI, vol. 14 January 1, 1800, 9; Faries, "Diary," January 1, 1805, 224; LAC, MG19 CI, vol. 8, January 1, 1805, 37; and Keith, *North of Athabasca*, 197.

16. MRB, MC, C.13, January 1, 1800, 11 (my pagination); Henry (the Younger), *New Light*, January 1, 1801 and 1802, 1:162, 192; TBR, S13, George Nelson's journal, November 30, 1815–January 13, 1816, Monday, December 25, 1815, 91; George Nelson's journal and reminiscences, 84; and Franchère, *Journal of a Voyage*, 107–8.

17. Mackenzie, *Voyages from Montreal*, January 1, 1793, 252. On other comments of the long- standing custom, see MRB, MC, C.28, January 1, 1808, 20; Keith, *North of Athabasca*, 326; and Franklin, *Narrative of a Journey*, January 1, 1802, 53.

18. For drams, see LAC, MG19 CI, vol. 1, November 1 and December 25, 1797, 17, 27; MRB, MC, C.24 December 25, 1800, 13; LAC, MG19 CI vol. 6 December 25, 1800, 72; vol. 8 December 25, 1804, 34; and MRB, MC, C.28, December 25, 1807, 20; see also Keith, *North of Athabasca*, 122, 196, 325. For large quantities of alcohol, see LAC, MG19 CI, vol. 67, December 25, 1798, 23; MRB, MC, C.13, December 25, 1799, 10 (my pagination); Harmon, *Sixteen Years*, December 25, 1801,52; and LAC, MG19 CI, vol. 12 November 1 and December 25, 1804, 25, 34.

19. Harmon, *Sixteen Years*, January 1, 1802, 53.

20. TBR, S13, George Nelson's journal, November 30, 1815–January 13, 1816, December 25, 1815, 91.

21. MRB, MC, C.7, January 1, 1794 and 1795, 6, 23; OA, MG19 CI, vol. 1, January 1, 1798, 29; LAC, MG19, CI, vol. 7, January 1, 1799, 24; and vol. 12, January 1, 1805 35.

22. Mackenzie, *Voyages from Montreal*, January 1, 1793, 252, Henry (the Younger), *New Light*, December 25, 1800, 1:161; LAC, MG19 CI, vol. 9, January 1, 1806, 21; Cox, *Adventures on the Columbia River*, 305–6; and MRB, MC, C.8, January 1, 1806, 10.

23. See also Van Kirk, "Many *Tender Ties*," 126–29.

24. For examples of balls at Great Lakes posts, see Pond, "Narrative," Mackinaw, 47; and OA, MU 1146, Frederick Goedike, Batchiwenon, to George Gordon, Michipicoten, February 11, 1812, 1–3. For examples of balls at interior posts, see TBR, S13, George Nelson's Journal, November 3, 1807– August 31, 1808, Fort Alexandria, June 18, 1808, 42;

and Ross, *Adventures of the First Settlers*, Spokane House, summer 1812, 212.

25. Harmon, *Sixteen Years*, Grand Portage, July 4, 1800, 22.

26. TBR, S13, George Nelson's coded journal, June 28 1821 29; Henry (the Younger), *New Light*, September 6, 1810, 2:626; and Faries, "Diary," December 16, 1804, February 24, March 31, April 28, May 12 and 17, 1805, 222, 230, 234–35, 238, 240–41.

27. For an example of NWC and HBC men dancing together at Fort George, see McGillivray, *Journal*, March 22, 1795, 66. For an example of NWC and XYC men dancing together, see Faries, "Diary," January 11 1805, 224–25. For an example of NWC, XYC, and HBC men dancing together at Rivière Souris, Fort Assiniboine, see Harmon, *Sixteen Years*, May 27, 1805, 89–90.

28. Henry (the Younger), *New Light*, January 27, 1810, 2:584.

29. Lambert, *Travels* through *Canada*, 1:173.

30. Cox, *Adventures on the Columbia River*, 306. Also see Ross, *Fur Hunters*, 1:304.

31. TBR, S13, George Nelson's journal "No. 5," 30 (my sequential pagination)/214 (Nelson's pagination).

32. For a few examples see TBR, S13, George Nelson's diary of events, June 18, 1822; Nelson, *My First Years*, 35–36; and Cox, *Adventures on the Columbia River*, 167.

33. See Podruchny, "Festivities, Fortitude and Fraternalism," for a discussion of bourgeois efforts to reconcile what they perceived as "rough" and "gentle" forms of masculinity.

34. Moogk, "Thieving Buggers"; and Bakhtin, *Rabelais and His World*, 5, 16–17.

35. Rediker, *Between the* Devil, 166.

36. Maynard, "Rough Work"; and Blye, "Hegemonic Heterosexual Masculinity."

37. Gilbert, "Buggery and the British Navy"; Maynard, "Making Waves"; T. D. Moodie, "Migrancy and Male Sexuality"; and Chauncey, "Christian Brotherhood."

38. Maynard, "Rough Work," 169.

39. Gagnon, *Plaisir d'Amour*, 12–23.

40. Ross, *Fur Hunters*, 1:303–4.

41. Brown, *Strangers* in Blood, 87–88.

42. Burley, *Servants of the Honourable Company*, 129–30.

43. Harriet Whitehead, "The Bow and the Burden Strap." For a critique of Whitehead's imposition of a two-gender model on Aboriginal societies, see Roscoe, "How to Become a Berdache." See also Williams, *Spirit and the Flesh*. On lesbianism see Allen, "Lesbians in American Indian Cultures."

■ Article 2: Wives and Mothers, School Mistresses and Scullery Maids

Elizabeth Jane Errington

By 1833, the capital of Upper Canada had become a bustling market town. Although many of York's approximately 9,000 residents continued to depend directly on the government for their livelihood, a growing proportion of the local population relied on the retail, manufacturing, or service trades to earn a living. William Ware, for example, sold spirits, wines, and groceries; William Cormack and Co. was a wholesale and dry goods firm. When Anna Jameson arrived in York in 1836, she could purchase supplies at Donald Ross's retail shop on King St. If she did not want to go to the Market House for fresh produce, she could go to Holmes and Co., which was located on Yonge St. The 1833 *York Directory* included twenty-two such retail and wholesale businesses in the community; it also listed dozens of small specialty shops, numerous inns, taverns, hotels, and many small manufacturing establishments.[1]

Almost hidden among the growing number of retail outlets were Mrs Owen's boarding-house, Mrs Bell's candle and soap factory, and the York Hotel, owned and operated by Mrs Jane Jordan.[2] Though many women were probably aware that Mrs Claris' millinery and dressmaking shop had a new supply of the "latest fashions" in August 1833,[3] probably only a few frequented Mrs Shaw's millinery business, which she ran out of her home. Despite the diminutive size of their businesses, these, and many other women were a vital part of the local economy. Like many of their male neighbours, they provided goods and services that residents of this government town needed.

The eclectic commercial scene that was characteristic of York in the 1830s was also apparent in other colonial towns and villages. Small communities such as Cobourg, Picton, and Peterborough supported a butcher, a baker, and a candlestick maker, as well as a number of general stores. An increasing number of towns and villages, including, of course, Kingston and Niagara, also had at least one millinery and mantuamaking shop [a mantua is an Italian-styled gown, fashionable in the eighteenth and nineteenth centuries] and a school for young ladies. And it was not unusual for one of the local boarding-houses, inns, and hotels to be owned by a woman.

In the pre-industrial economy of Upper Canada, women were frequently involved in the marketplace. Although women were "by definition basically domestic,"[4] this did not preclude them from assuming economic as well as familial responsibilities. Many colonial wives were, by necessity, actively involved in the economic affairs of their husbands.[5] Just as Mary O'Brien, Fanny Hutton, Susanna Moodie, and other farm wives helped their husbands plant and harvest, urban women too assisted their husbands in their shops and at their crafts. As was the custom in Europe in the eighteenth century, some artisans' wives "prepared or finished material on which [their] husbands worked."[6] Others cooked and served guests of family inns. When their husbands were ill or away, wives became their "representatives" and even their "surrogates." As Laurel Ulrich has noted, "female responsibility [...] was [...] very broad [...] the role of housewife and the role of deputy husband were two sides of the same coin."[7]

For many women, working beside and with their husbands, fathers, or brothers was not always enough to sustain the family, however. Particularly in Upper Canada's towns and villages, families were units of consumption as well as of production and the family economy was a wage economy.[8] Households depended increasingly on cash to buy goods and services that they did not or could not produce themselves. Women together with the children were often obliged to find waged work to supplement the family income.

In the premodern world, "any task was suitable" for a woman" as long as it furthered the good of the family" and if she was married, it "was accepted by her husband."[9] A woman's opportunity to earn a wage in Upper Canada was determined by a number of factors, including her age, her marital status, her skill, and her available capital. Women were also restricted in their choice of work by where they lived. (Only in urban areas was there sufficient custom actually to set up a dress shop or open a girls' school.) Wage-earning women were also influenced

Source: Elizabeth Jane Errington, "Beyond the Bounds of Domesticity", *Wives and Mothers, School Mistresses and Scullery Maids: Working Women in Upper Canada, 1790–1840* (Kingston and Montreal, McGill-Queen's University Press, 1955), pp. 185–88. Reprinted with permission.

by colonial assumptions about what type of work was appropriate for persons of their sex. Women were not admitted to most crafts. Married women could not own property; legally, they could not hire employees.

As in rural areas, "domestic service was probably the most common waged employment" open to women living in town.[10] To meet the vagaries of seasonal unemployment or those fluctuations in market demand that inevitably affected the income of the family business, married women often sewed, took in washing, became a char, took in a few lodgers, or marketed other "homemaking" skill on a part-time basis.[11] Usually considered unskilled labourers, such women received minuscule wages for their work and coped with often appalling working conditions. Yet a wife's ability to earn even a little money was indispensable to ensuring an adequate family wage.[12]

Though domestic service was the most prevalent type of women's waged work, it was by no means the only one. Many widows who were left "solely responsible for maintaining the family" tried to continue with the family business. With the help of their children, they managed family farms, village stores, or their late husbands' craft shops. In some and perhaps most instances, the death of a husband meant "the destruction of the family economy," however. A number of widows were forced into service; others opened their homes to boarders. After 1820, a growing number of widowed women entered, or often re-entered, one of the "female trades."[13]

Particularly in the second generation of colonial development, a number of women—widowed, single, and married—opened schools for girls, dressshops, and millinery and mantuamaking establishments. Some of these women were recent immigrants who had come to Upper Canada to take advantage of expanding business opportunities and perhaps to escape some of the social and economic strictures that were emerging at home.[14] They were well aware that the chatelaine of the big house needed appropriate clothing, and that Upper Canadian mothers wanted proper schooling for their daughters. Either alone or with female relatives or colleagues, such women opened businesses that consciously catered to these demands.

Nevertheless, relatively few women had the financial resources, skills, and personal confidence necessary to embark on what was inevitably a risky enterprise.[15] The majority of Upper Canadian women were not independent merchants, shopkeepers, or craftswomen who sold their skills in the open marketplace; they were wives and mothers whose primary responsibility remained "the well being of [...] husband and children."[16] Even so, many urban labouring-class women took part in "the common commerce of life" at some time in their lives.[17]

Evidence of women's varied market activities is, for the most part, available only indirectly. Most women who were homemakers for hire, assistants in their husbands' businesses, or small independent tradeswomen were part of the "hidden economy" of Upper Canada.[18] They relied on their local reputation or on contacts made on the street or at the market to gain work. Many of them were undoubtedly part of an informal economy of barter and exchange. However, a growing number of women did sometimes place notices in local newspapers advertising their business. It is these notices, together with brief references in gentlewomen's diaries and aside comments printed in local newspapers that allow us to begin to piece together the world of wage-earning women in Upper Canada's towns and villages.

Notes

1. George Walton, *York Commercial Directory and Street Guide and Register*, 1833–34 (York: Thomas Dalton 1834).
2. *The Patriot*, 8 December 1833; *British American Journal*, 25 February 1834; *The Patriot*, 24 April 1840.
3. *The Patriot*, 2 August 1833. This establishment was also listed in the Directory.
4. Ulrich, *Good Wives*, 36.
5. Ibid., 49. As Tilly and Scott note in *Women, Work, and Family*, 48, a woman in a pre-industrial society "was her husband's indispensable partner." See also the work of Cohen, *Women's Work, Markets, and Economic Development*; Ryan, *The Cradle of the Middle Class*, particularly her discussion of frontier women; Stansell, *City of Women*; Norton, *Liberty's Daughters*; Rule, *The Labouring Classes*; for the later period, Bradbury, *Working Families*.
6. Tilly and Scott, *Women, Work and Family*, 48. See also Sally Alexander, "Women's Work in Nineteenth-Century London," in Mitchell and Oakely, eds., *The Rights and Wrongs of Women*, 59–111, 64–5.
7. Ulrich, *Good Wives*, 50, 37, 47. This, of course, was most graphically illustrated during the American

Revolution. See Norton, *Liberty's Daughters*, Chapter 7; Potter-MacKinnon, *While the Women Only Wept.*

8. Tilly and Scott, *Women, Work, and Family*, 19. See also Bradbury, *Working Families*, Chapter 5.

9. Ulrich, *Good Wives*, 37–8.

10. Stansell, *City of Women*, 12. See also Alexander, "Women's Work," 97–9.

11. See John's "Introduction" to *Unequal Opportunities*.

12. In the pre-industrial world of Upper Canada, as in Montreal in a later period, no one assumed that the male head of the household would, or perhaps indeed even should be able to support his family on one wage: Bradbury, *Working Families*, 13–16. The assumption that the head of the household should be the sole "breadwinner" is quite modern. And although it is to some degree a product of the nineteenth-century middle-class ideology that has been examined so eloquently by Davidoff and Hall, *Family Fortunes* as in so many aspects of this, the rhetoric enunciated by the few did not, nor was it expected to be lived by the many.

13. Tilly and Scott, *Women, Work and Family*, 51, 53, 47.

14. Hammerton, *Emigrant Women.*

15. Ulrich, *Good Wives*, 48.

16. Alexander, "Women's Work," 77.

17. Ulrich, *Good Wives*, 48.

18. Rule, *The Labouring Classes*, 13. See also McCalla, *Planting the Province*, 113, who notes that though women were involved in considerable "productive" work, it "was not captured by standard statistics." Alexander, "Women's Work," 72, found a similar situation in London, England during this period.

■ Article 3: Farm Households and Wage Labour in the Northeastern Maritimes in the Early 19th Century

Rusty Bittermann

One of the most enduring mythologies of rural life in the temperate regions of North America has centred on the freedom resulting from easy access to land. In the New World unlike the Old, the story goes, land was plentiful, free from the encumbrances of a feudal past, and common folk might gain unimpeded access to its abundance and carve an independent niche for themselves. In the 18th and 19th centuries, the mythology was fostered by the effusions of travel accounts and emigrant manuals as well as by the writings of immigrants themselves. Since then it has been broadly sustained in North American historiography.

That the image of the independent yeoman was to a certain degree a reflection of a reality experienced by some rural residents in the Maritimes is indisputable. The opportunities for acquiring an independent rural livelihood were relatively greater in British North America than they were in the Old World. Many transformed these possibilities into reality and achieved a "propertied independence."[1] Those who enjoyed such circumstances, however, were but one component of a larger farming population. And many who came to enjoy a modicum of yeomanly independence only experienced this condition during a fraction of their lives. Like any pervasive mythology, the image of the independent yeoman is partly rooted in a reality. Problems arise, though, when a fragment of the rural experience becomes a characterization of the whole. It is not my intention here to consider how this mythology developed, or to unravel the various strands of peasant dream, liberal ideology, and social critique that have sustained it. Rather, I want to examine what it has obscured, indeed tends to deny: the importance of wage labour to farmfolk in the northeastern Maritimes in the first half of the 19th century.[2] The survey which follows underlines the significance of wages to the farm population and highlights the profile of farm dwellers within the larger labour force.

For many, the quality of land resources available—particularly when coupled with a poverty that diverted labour and capital away from farm improvements and toward the needs of basic sustenance—precluded ever escaping the necessity of engaging in extensive wage work.[3] As the Crown surveyor in Baddeck, D. B. McNab, noted in 1857, there were "hundreds" of farms in this region of Cape Breton

Source: Rusty Bittermann, "Farm Households and Wage Labour in the Northeastern Maritimes in the Early 19th Century," *Labour/Le Travail* 31 (1993), No. 31, pp. 13–45. Reprinted with permission.

where ten, twenty, or thirty years after initial settlement their occupants remained heavily reliant on off-farm employment in order to "eke out the means of a scanty subsistence."[4] In general, he contended, such settlers occupied the difficult hill lands, the backlands, of the Island and tended to be squatters rather than freeholders. The Land Commissioners taking evidence on Prince Edward Island in 1860 heard similar testimony concerning areas of Prince Edward Island, often predominantly occupied by squatters, where few settlers successfully managed to derive the bulk of their livelihood from the soil.[5]

While some households made ends meet by combining wage work with the sale of selected farm "surpluses," often enough exchanging costly foods like butter and meat for cheaper breadstuffs and fish, there were others which appear to have been exclusively, or almost exclusively, reliant on the sale of labour to meet the costs of household goods and food and to procure seed and animal provisions. The ledger books of the North Sydney trader, John Beamish Moore,[6] for instance, reveal a number of backland households whose occupants had nothing but labour to sell during the years of their dealings with him.[7] During the period 1853 to 1860, the members of Angus Link's household paid for their supplies of oatmeal, barley flour, and oats through a combination of Angus's own labour and that of his wife and daughter.[8] So, too, did the Angus McDonald household pay its debts through Angus's own labour and that of his sons and daughter.[9] The debts of the Murduch Ferguson household as well were repaid entirely by Murdoch's labour and that of a female member of the household.[10] Moore's account book reveals something of the seasonality of the pressures on these backland households as well. Between 1853 and 1861, the accounts of those identified as backlanders in his books reveal recurrent debts for hay, barley flour, and oatmeal needed in April and May to replenish exhausted winter supplies, and seed grain (barley and oats) needed in May and June to permit planting another season's crop. Merchant ledgers reveal only a fragment of these patterns. Wealthier members of rural communities as well often took on the role, and assumed the benefits, of acting as provisioners and sources of credit to poorer households through the months of greatest scarcity. It appears to have been particularly common for those acting as road commissioners to sell provisions on credit

during the winter and to retain the road-work returns due to these households the following summer.[11]

Backlanders such as these, though possessing or occupying considerable acreages, were yet compelled by necessity to participate extensively in labour markets near and far in order to make up for the great inadequacies of their farm returns. They were, as the Crown surveyor in Baddeck, D.B. McNab, noted, the New World equivalent of Great Britain's day labourers: they "represent[ed] this class.[12] Quantitative analysis of census data from Middle River in Cape Breton and from Hardwood Hill in Pictou County suggests that in the third quarter of the 19th century, somewhere between a quarter and a third of the households in these agricultural districts of northeastern Nova Scotia needed to earn $100 or more in off-farm income in order to secure a minimal livelihood.[13] At the common agricultural wage rate of roughly 80 cents per day, this would be the equivalent of 125 or more working days.[14] Viewed in another fashion, given an average family food requirement of roughly $200, these farms at best probably derived only half their food needs from their own resources.[15] Data from Middle River confirms as well D.B. McNab's assertion that reliance on off-farm sources of income most often occurred among those who occupied rough hill lands: 84 per cent of the households with negative net farm incomes estimated to be greater than $100 in 1860–61 were those of backlanders.[16] Physical constraints necessitated much of the pattern of adaptation that McNab and others described.

Besides new settlers requiring an income during their years of farm establishment and backlanders grappling with chronic resource problems, analysis of the Middle River census returns indicates yet another stream of rural peoples being propelled into participation in the work force in the mid-19th century and beyond. Estimates of the relationship between farm resources and household needs reveal three basic household categories. At one end of the spectrum there were households, primarily those of backlanders, where farm returns were chronically and substantially short of household subsistence needs—households that of necessity had to look for income beyond the farm across the full course of the family life cycle. On the other extreme there was a significant minority of households, the commercial core of the valley's agricultural economy, where farm production was well in excess of household subsistence needs and the returns from farm product sales were sufficient to permit substantial reinvestments in agriculture and in other pursuits. Members of such households had the option of working for themselves with their own resources or working for others. Wedged between these two strata were families whose condition more closely approximated the image of household self-sufficiency permeating so much of the literature on the rural Maritimes—farms on which the value of production roughly matched current needs. Although they possessed sufficient resources to derive a livelihood from the land, it is clear though, from the census and probate returns, that the resources of many of these households were not expanding at a rate sufficient to permit all their offspring to begin life in similar circumstances. Demographic growth was forcing, and would force, many individuals from an emerging generation within these middle strata households into participation in the labour force.[17]

Throughout the early 19th century, then, substantial numbers of the members of farm households situated in the northeastern Maritimes—new settlers, backlanders (along with others whose farm resources were chronically insufficient for household needs), and some of the offspring of middle-strata households—necessarily had to maintain a significant and regular involvement in the labour force despite the fact that they had access to extensive tracts of land. Added to the ranks of these workers of necessity were many who were drawn for one reason or another by the opportunities afforded by off-farm work, people who might move in and out of the workforce at will alternately deriving a living from farm resources or choosing to participate in the labour force.

Wage work in the timber trade and the shipbuilding industry—agriculture's great rivals for labour in the first half of the 19th century—was, in general, quite different from that in agriculture. This was male employment, and much of the work in these industries was concentrated at sites at some distance from the farms from which many came. Such employment was often for extended periods of time, for woods work was available from late fall until spring, and shipbuilding, when the market dictated, might be conducted on a year-round basis.[18] There were, of course, considerable variations in the nature of the work experience in woods work and shipbuilding.

Some of the employment available within these industries was local and organized in small, perhaps primarily family-based, crews. Hired hands might be added to cluster of brothers cutting logs for the winter or be employed casually in one of the many lesser shipyards turning out modest numbers of smaller vessels. Employment with small local operations where one might return home on a daily basis aided the integration of wage work with farm work. The Irish who settled on the backlands of Lot 29 in southwestern Queen's County, Prince Edward Island, for instance, and who worked in W.W. Lord's timber and shipbuilding operations, were said to have been able to clear their lands and hoe their crops "in spare time."[19] Looking back on his Cape Breton childhood, Aeneas McCharles recalled that his father combined working on his farm in the Baddeck Valley with carpentry work at the shipyards four miles away in the port of Baddeck.[20] Labour in these pursuits, however, was also being organized by capitalists operating on a much larger scale, who relied upon recruiting labourers from beyond the immediate locality of their operations. Entrepreneurs like the Archibalds in Cape Breton and the Popes, Macdonalds, and Cambridges on Prince Edward Island hired scores of men of work at their shipyards, sawmills, and woods operations. So too did their counterparts elsewhere in the region who, even before steam vessels and rail transportation eased the burdens of travel, were drawing labourers from the farms of northern Nova Scotia and Prince Edward Island to work in their operations. By the 1820s and 1830s, farmers in significant numbers were traveling back and forth between the timber camps and shipyards of the Miramichi and their homes in northern Nova Scotia and Prince Edward Island.[21]

Many of those working in these operations were likely to spend part of their lives as bunkhouse men, living at the worksite and labouring on a regular schedule for extended periods of time.[22] In both logging and boatbuilding, wages might be paid partly in kind—shipyards tended to be organized around a truck store—and differentially paid in accordance with a division of labour along skill lines.[23] Farmers and farmers' sons working in the large shipyards shared their workspace with greater numbers than did those in woods camps, and were engaged in work that required more complex forms of organization.[24] The experience of work in the shipbuilding yards that produced large vessels was, as Richard Rice has argued, that of a large, complexly-orchestrated manufactory.

Clearly as the nature of off-farm work varied, so too the ways in which it was integrated into the household economy differed. Daily work close at hand, such as on a neighbouring farm or for a local merchant, permitted, at least in theory, a good deal of flexibility. That farmers and merchants alike required casual labour and employed adults and children, both males and females, meant that various household members might move back and forth between work on the home farm and wage employment. John Beamish Moore's ledger from North Sydney in the 1850s, for instance, shows that the backlander Archy McDonald's household earned wages alternately from Archy's work, that of "his boys," and that of "the girl."[25] The accounts of other backlanders on Moore's ledger show a similar heterogeneity in the composition of household labour made available to the merchant for wages. The same pattern of varying daily movement of different members of the same household in and out of the local agricultural labour force is apparent in the MacNutt farm ledger as men and children, male and female, appear in varying numbers from day to day. One day a father and a couple of sons might be on the pay-roll, another day perhaps only the sons or only the daughters would be employed. There is no way to know whether the pattern was set by demand or by supply, or to discern how in fact those who momentarily disappear from the day book deployed their labour, but clearly local work afforded the possibility of a varied and shifting household response to the needs of the home farm. Local contract work and putting-out work offered similar flexibility. A man who had been hired to mow a field, dig a cellar, or clear land might, particularly if the work was close at hand, exercise some discretion in choosing his hours of employment and integrating such work into other tasks concerning his own resources. As well, he might flexibly use the labour of other members of his household to complete the task. Such would also be the case with the farmer/tailors contracted to sew trousers or for shirtmaking, or the farm women employed by the piece for spinning, weaving, or knitting.

Other employments permitted less flexibility. Some types of work—such as that in shipbuilding, the timber industry, employment with the American fishing fleet, or the construction trades—provided employment almost exclusively for adult males and often entailed working at a considerable distance from one's residence. In homes where the male head engaged in such work, women often were left to manage household and farm for extended periods. Seeking lodgings at a farm house on the Cape Breton-side of the Strait of Canso in the summer of 1831, David Stewart, a Prince Edward Island landlord, and his traveling companion Richard Smith of the General Mining Association, discovered that the man of the farm "was gone to Miramichi to cut lumber."[26] Only Mrs. MacPherson and her two children were home. At midcentury, the Crown surveyor in Baddeck, D.B. McNab, reported that there were "hundreds" of farms located on poorer lands in his region of the Island where the men of the household traveled to "distant parts of the province or to the United States" each summer and left the maintenance of the farm to "their wives and children."[27] With the boom in railway construction and coal mining in the third quarter of the 19th century, a local observer noted that Cape Breton farmers and their sons "by hundreds, nay, thousands, [were] leaving their farms to the women, and seeking employment at the colleries and railways."[28] Some, such as a Highlander born on Lewis residing in Middle River who planted his crop of oats and potatoes and then traveled on foot to Halifax to work on the railway each year, appear to have regularized their patterns of distant wage work so that they synchronized with the seasonal rounds of farming. Come harvest time, the Lewis man would be back in Middle River.[29] In other households the distant wage work of males was made possible because females and children assumed a full array of farm tasks.[30]

Other farm-based workers in the northeast Maritimes, of course, may have resigned themselves to the necessity of perpetually maintaining the dual commitments of self-employment and working for others, or may indeed have embraced wage work never seeking to attain a degree of choice over their involvement in the labour marker.[31] Given the sporadic and uneven nature of the demand for labour in the region in the early 19th century, life without the fall-back of an agricultural holding could be precarious.[32] Rather than working so that they might farm, some, no doubt, farmed so that they might live to work. For many, however, access to the soil held out the hope of achieving control over their time and their labour, and persistence in straddling two worlds constituted a way of resisting the imperatives and dependence of wage work.[33]

We need to look more closely at the transformation of these dreams, which had been closely associated with the myth of the independent yeoman, and at changes in the strategies adopted by working people. Few still maintain that true independence is to be gained by eschewing wage work for agricultural pursuits and by struggling to gain a toehold on the soil. The goal of a "propertied independence" that was embedded in the mythology and once held such an important position in the aspirations of working people of the North Atlantic world has long since lost its lustre. And though many rural residents in the region continue to engage in seasonal work at near and distant job sites, fewer and fewer rely on farming as a means to survive periods when they are not engaged in wage work.[34] Surely these will be key themes for those who would write the environmental history of the region. The decline of the belief that the labourer's salvation was to be found on the land and the decline of agriculture as a safety net have profoundly affected our perception of the significance of arable soil, and of land more generally. For increasing numbers, even of rural residents, it is no longer a matter of importance.

Notes

1. The phrase is drawn from Daniel Vickers' superb analysis of the ideal and some of its implications. Daniel Vickers, "Competency and Competition: Economic Culture in Early America," *William and Mary Quarterly*, 3rd Series, 47:1 (1990), 3–29.

2. The mythology is often incongruously juxtaposed with another reality. Neil MacNeil, for instance, even as he extols the independence Washabuckers achieved on the land, tells of the regular flow of labour southward and of his grandfather's difficult experiences commuting on foot between Washabuckt and a job many miles north in industrial Cape Breton.

3. In his study of farm-making in Upper Canada in this period, Norman Ball notes the presence of immigrants trapped by similar cycles of poverty there. Norman Rodger Ball, "The Technology of Settlement and Land Clearing in Upper Canada Prior to 1840," PhD dissertation, University of Toronto, 1979, 30–2.

4. D. B. McNab to Uniacke, 3 January 1857, Nova Scotia House of Assembly, *Journals*, 1857, app. 71, 421.

5. Ian Ross Robertson, ed., *The Prince Edward Island Land Commission of 1860* (Fredericton, 1988), 136.

6. A number of John Moores lived in and about North Sydney in the mid-19th century. Stephen Hornsby treats this account book as being that of John *Belcher* Moore. The Public Archives of Nova Scotia, though, stand by their description of it as being that of John *Beamish* Moore. Stephen J. Hornsby, *Nineteenth-Century Cape Breton: A Historical Geography*, 72, 138–9; private correspondence with J.B. Cahill, 26 October 1992.

7. These backlanders may have been selling farm products elsewhere, perhaps closer at hand, but the fact that they routinely purchased bulky items, such as 1/2 barrels of flour and bushels of grain from Moore without ever selling farm goods seems to suggest that they had little or nothing to sell.

8. John Beamish Moore Account Book, 1848–67, 14, Micro Biography, PANS.

9. *Ibid.*, 22.

10. *Ibid.*, 23.

11. *Spirit of the Times* (Sydney), 19 July 1842, 347; Captain W. Moorsom, *Letters From Nova Scotia*, 288.

12. Nova Scotia House of Assembly, *Journals*, 1857, Appendix No. 72, 421.

13. Rusty Bittermann, Robert H. Mackinnon, and Graeme Wynn, "Of Inequality and Interdependence in the Nova Scotian Countryside, 1850–1870," *Canadian Historical Review*, (forthcoming March 1993).

14. The estimate of an average agricultural wage for Nova Scotia is drawn from Julian Gwyn, "Golden Age or Bronze Moment? Wealth and Poverty in Nova Scotia: the 1850s and 1860s," *Canadian Papers in Rural History*, 8 (1992), 195–230.

15. Charles H. Farnham, "Cape Breton Folk," *Harpers New Monthly Magazine* (1886), reprinted in *Acadiensis*, 8:2 (Spring 1979), 100. These estimates are considered in detail in Bittermann, MacKinnon, and Wynn, "Of Inequality and Interdependence in the Nova Scotian Countryside," and Rusty Bittermann, "Middle River: The Social Structure of Agriculture in a Nineteenth-Century Cape Breton Community," MA dissertation, University of New Brunswick, 1987, app. IV.

16. Rusty Bittermann, "Economic Stratification and Agrarian Settlement: Middle River in the Early

Nineteenth Century," in Kenneth Donovan, ed., *The Island: New Perspectives on Cape Breton History 1713–1975*, 86–7.

17. *Ibid.*; Rusty Bittermann, "Middle River: The Social Structure of Agriculture in a Nineteenth-Century Cape Breton Community," 157–9.

18. A.R.M. Lower, *The North American Assault on the Canadian Forest: A History of the Lumber Trade Between Canada and the United States* (Toronto 1938), 32–3; Graeme Wynn, *Timber Colony*, 54; Richard Rice, "Shipbuilding in British America, 1787–1890: An Introductory Study" PhD dissertation, University of Liverpool, 1977, 178–81.

19. Mary Brehaut, ed., *Pioneers on the Island* (Charlottetown 1959), 58. On the local organization of farm-based labour for Prince Edward Island's shipyards see too Basil Greenhill and Ann Giffard. *Westcountrymen in Prince Edward's Isle* (Toronto 1967), 56–76; Malcolm MacQueen, *Skye Pioneers and "The Island"* (Winnipeg 1929), 26.

20. Aeneas McCharles, *Bemocked of Destiny: The Actual Struggles and Experiences of a Canadian Pioneer and the Recollections of a Lifetime* (Toronto 1980), 10–1.

21. *Prince Edward Island Register*, 20 October 1825, 3; John MacGregor, *Historical and Descriptive Sketches of the Maritime Colonies of British America* (London 1828), 168: David Stewart's Journal, 31, PAPEI, 3209/28; *Royal Gazette*, 30 May 1837, 3. See too the *Royal Gazette* 26 June 1838, 3, on the theft of £35—a season's wages—from a lumberman returning from the Miramichi woods to his residence in West River, Pictou County.

22. Abraham Gesner, *The Industrial Resources of Nova Scotia* (Halifax 1849), 215–7; Graeme Wynn, *The Timber Colony*, 62; Arthur R.M. Lower, *Great Britain's Woodyard: British America and the Timber Trade, 1763–1867* (Montreal 1973), 189–96. On shipyard/bunkhouse deaths due to drunkeness and violence see the *Prince Edward Island Register*, 25 September 1824, 3; *Prince Edward Island Register*, 27 February 1827, 3.

23. Richard Rice, "Shipbuilding in British America, 1787–1890: An Introductory Study," PhD dissertation, University of Liverpool, 1977, 171, 186–92. The labour contracts from the 1840s entered in Joseph Dingwell's ledger indicate that he paid most of his labourers half in cash and half in "trade." Joseph Dingwell Ledger, Ms. 3554/1, PAPEI. Capt Moorsom's

account of labour relations on the waterfront in Liverpool in the summer of 1828, suggests the reasons for Dingwell's clear indications of the mode of payment in his contracts. There were, he noted, "two scales of value, the "cash price," and the "goods price," and "the various gradation thereof distinctly marked in all transactions between employers and labourers." Moorsom reported a rate of exchange in favor of cash at a ratio of 3 to 4. Captain W. Moorsom, *Letters From Nova Scotia; Comprising Sketches of a Young Country*, 292. For information on Joseph Pope's shipyard and truck store see John Mollison, "Prince County," in D.A. Mackinnon and A.B. Warburton, eds., *Past and Present of Prince Edward Island* (Charlottetown 1906), 86. Lemuel and Artemas Cambridge offered their ship carpenters the choice of employment by the month or payment "by the seam." *Prince Edward Island Register*, 23 May 1826, 3.

24. According to Dougald Henry (b.1817) the modest shipbuilding operation run by the Bells of Stanley River Prince Edward Island employed 30 or more men in the yards. Working days, he relates, began at six with a break for breakfast at 8. For Dougald Henry's account of shipyard life as compiled by Dr. Hedley Ross, see Mary Brehaut, ed., *Pioneers on the Island*, 47.

25. John Beamish Moore Account Book, 1848–67, 22.

26. David Stewart's Journal, 31, PAPEI, 3209/28.

27. Nova Scotia House of Assembly, *Journals*, 1857, Appendix No. 72. 421.

28. *Journal of Agriculture for Nova Scotia*, July 1871, 652.

29. Francis MacGregor, "Days that I Remember," January 1962, Mg. 12, vol. 71, 31, Beaton Institute, Sydney, Nova Scotia.

30. These different patterns of domestic life in poorer households no doubt underwrote the perception that backland women were particularly able workers. Backland girls, notes Margaret MacPhail's character John Campbell, made the best marriage partners as "They can work outside and in and keeps a fellow warm in bed. What else would you want!" Margaret MacPhail, *Loch Bras d'Or* (Windsor, Nova Scotia 1970), 84, 65.

31. Many emigrants had experience with similar work patterns before they migrated. See Barbara M. Kerr, "Irish Seasonal Migration to Great Britain, 1800–38," *Irish Historical Studies*, 3 (1942–3), 365–80;

A.J. Youngson, *After the Forty-Five: The Economic Impact on the Scottish Highlands* (Edinburgh 1973), 182–4; T.M. Devine, "Temporary Migration and the Scottish Highlands in the Nineteenth Century," *Economic History Review*, 32(1979), 344–59; William Howatson, "The Scottish Hairst and Seasonal Labour 1600–1870," *Scottish Studies*, 26 (1982), 13–36; E.J.T. Collins, "Migrant Labour in British Agriculture in the Nineteenth Century," *Economic History Review*, 29 (1976), 38–59, As Maritimers moved on, some carried these patterns of work to new locales. See Aeneas McCharles. Bemocked of Destiny, 28; Neil Robinson, *Lion of Scotland* (Auckland 1952, 1974), 28, 80, 99.

32. Judith Fingard, "A Winter's Tale: The Seasonal Contours of Pre-Industrial Poverty in British North America, 1815–1860," *Historical Papers*, (1974), 65–94; D.B. MacNab to Uniacke, 3 January 1857, Nova Scotia House of Assembly, *Journals*, 1857, app. 71, 421.

33. On the significance of agrarian strategies to working-class struggles in Great Britain and the United States in this period see Malcolm Chase, *'The People's Farm:" English Radical Agrarianism*, 1775–1850 (Oxford 1988); Sean Wilentz, *Chants Democratic: New York City and the Rise of the American Working Class*, 1788–1850 (New York 1984), 164–216, 335–43; Paul Conkin, *Prophets of Prosperity: America's First Political Economists* (Bloomington 1980), 22–58.

34. The terms of eligibility for unemployment benefits have played a role here in forcing some to choose between a state-based or land-based safety net and/or to define themselves as workers rather than farmers.

■ Article 4: Saint John: The Making of a Colonial Urban Community

T.W. Acheson

If merchants and merchant leaders were able to dominate the community agenda, particularly before 1840, the opposition to this domination came not from the manual labourers dependent on their system but from the producers' interest. That interest bound together a number of status groups, ranging from apprentice artisans to shopkeepers to established small manufacturers, led by a petite bourgeoisie of small masters. It is an interest that Michael Katz described as a class in his early work on mid-nineteenth-century Hamilton; in his later study of Hamilton and Buffalo he argued that the journeymen and masters were members of competing classes.[1] Other historians have been more tentative in judgment. All agree that an artisanal interest existed in the eighteenth century and that it was gradually eroded in the face of nineteenth-century industrialism. In her study of nineteenth-century Newark, Susan Hirsch argues that artisan deference to the merchant élite

Source: T.W. Acheson, *Saint John: The Making of a Colonial Urban Community* (Toronto, University of Toronto Press, 1984), pp. 67, 68–71, and 73–77. © 2006 University of Toronto Press. Reprinted with permission of the publisher.

had waned by the time of the American Revolution and that a significant artisanal system in which most journeymen were able to become masters by the time they were forty flourished until at least 1830. A similar community of interest among Kingston artisans is described by Bryan Palmer.[2] British studies suggest that even in the late nineteenth century the aristocracy of labour and a petite bourgeoisie of small proprietors remained closely linked.[3] The experience of the artisan group in Saint John demonstrates that it was not just an economic interest but a politically self-conscious social group.

Artisans composed nearly half the original Loyalist freemen of 1785.[4] Throughout the first half of the nineteenth century they rather consistently composed about a third of freeman admissions, a proportion confirmed by the 1851 Census. Comprising a wide variety of occupations and wide range of incomes, the artisans were always a powerful interest and on a number of important issues they did act as a class. By mid-century they perceived themselves, and were perceived by observers of the scene, as the 'bone and sinew' of the community. In terms of economic function, artisans were distinguished from those of higher and lower status in one important way: other groups were concerned with the provision of services, but craftsmen produced all the goods made in the city apart from the simple mechanical process of sawing deals.

In no way did the early city so faithfully reflect the late medieval origins of its institutions as in the means through which the townspeople organized themselves for the production of goods. Production was equated to craft and each craft was structured around a trade, which in turn was organized on the traditional triad of apprentice/journeyman/master. The importance accorded the trades was reflected in the city's constitution, which attempted to restrict both the franchise and the benefit of the trade to those who had served a satisfactory apprenticeship under a master who was a freeman of the city. The apprenticeship process was central to the trades system.[5] Not only did it provide a critical form of educational and skills development, but it instilled the pride, confidence, and sense of apartness that distinguished the training of professionals. This formation of the artisan usually began in early adolescence when the youth was bound over by his parents to a master craftsman. The standard indenture of apprenticeship was a legal document formally assented to by a magistrate binding the young man to a life of servitude in his master's household for a period of from four to eight years. *The Courier* editor, Henry Chubb, 'voluntarily and of his own free will,' was bound to a master printer for seven years at the age of fifteen. The contract, borrowed from traditional English models, provided that the master should teach the art, trade, and mystery of a printer and provide board, lodging, washing, and a new suit of clothing for his apprentice. In return Chubb was required to serve faithfully, keep his master's secrets and commands, neither to damage nor waste his master's goods. He was further forbidden to commit fornication, contract matrimony, play at cards or dice, buy or sell goods without his master's permission, or frequent taverns or theatres.[6]

The control that masters were given over their charges was an attractive feature to civic authorities since it played an important role in the maintenance of order and good discipline among a large segment of the city's male population during the sometimes difficult passage from adolescence to manhood. The exercise of this authority by the masters was encouraged by Common Council, which placed responsibility for the public misdemeanours of apprentices clearly on the shoulders of the masters.[7] The rigorous control was frequently not appreciated by the prentices, and the search for fugitives became

a regular feature of the daily press before 1850. By 1817, Henry Chubb, now Master Chubb, was beset by problems with his own apprentice, 'Peter James Wade, 16, smart but a drunkard,' who had fled his master's service.[8] Chubb offered 5s. for the return of the apprentice and £5 for information leading to the conviction of those harbouring him. The complaint was not uncommon, but as the law made the harbouring of a fugitive apprentice a hazardous undertaking, most fled the city.[9] As late as 1841, Sam Wilson was arrested for absconding from his master, the sailmaker and assistant alderman Robert Ray, and sentenced to two months at hard labour for assaulting the city marshal who made the arrest.[10]

Despite these commotions, and restrictions, the apprentice system had a good deal to offer young men.[11] In the short run, there was promise of a skill and a paid series of night courses. In the long run, there was a respectable status, admission to the freedom of the city, and the possibility of becoming a master with ownership of a shop.[12] Among a number of Loyalist families, the artisan's status became a tradition that engendered a native tradeocracy comprising an intricate pattern of fathers, sons, grandsons, nephews, uncles, and cousins. Many young second-generation natives could combine a respectable trade with their father's freehold and shop, a sure guarantee of becoming both master and burgher. The Bustins, the Hardings, and the Olives provide characteristic examples of the great trades families of the city. Fifteen Bustins, sixteen Hardings, and sixteen Olives were admitted as freemen between 1785 and 1858. The Bustin clan included five carpenters, four butchers, three harness makers, two masons; the Olives, six ship carpenters, three carpenters, two ship wrights, and a joiner; the Hardings, four tanners, two shoe-makers, and a blacksmith.[13]

Only toward mid-century did the ranks of this tradeocracy begin to break as young third-generation members began to move toward commerce and the professions. The Hardings were particularly successful in this: three became medical doctors, two were merchants, and one entered the law. This mid-century shift out of the trades on the part of young natives is confirmed by the 1851 Census. A sample of 732 east-side households reveals 23 apprentices almost equally divided between natives and Irish arrivals in the 1840s. By contrast the ranks of the young merchants' clerks expanded rapidly in the 1840s and by

1851 their members rivalled those of the apprentice artisans. More than two-thirds of the clerks were natives. Confirmation of the trend out of the crafts, particularly on the part of young natives, is found in the late 1850s in the complaints of *The Courier* editor who bewailed the abandonment of the crafts by young men of artisan families and scolded their parents—particularly their mothers—for denying the dignity of manual work and for placing a premium on any occupation that permitted its occupant to wear a white collar.[14] The decline of the crafts among native families was probably a reaction against the admission of Irish tradesmen who depressed the wages and reduced the importance of the status of artisans. The native-Irish tension was reflected in the matching of masters and apprentices. Native masters accepted only native apprentices, a fact which meant that almost all journeymen boat and coach builders would be natives while the shoemaking trade was given over to the Irish.[15] The native preferences doubtless reflected a traditional pattern of fathers apprenticing their sons to friends and acquaintances in the fathers' craft or in other similar crafts.

The purpose of the apprentice system was to train an exclusive body of skilled workers dedicated to the craft and determined to restrict its practice to those of like formation. The journeymen craftsmen constituted a broad and influential cross-section of the city's population. Together with the masters, they comprised about 35 per cent of the freemen and 35 per cent of all employed males in the city.[16] Thus they easily formed the largest electoral group in the city, outnumbering all commercial freemen by a ratio of two to one.

In 1851, more than three of every four artisans were family heads living in tenements or freeholds of their own. A very small number—about one in fourteen—were single men living with their parents and the remainder—about one in six—were lodgers, one-third of whom lived with employers. Although all were legally required to be freemen to practise their trade, only about two out of five of those in the sample did so. Virtually every master was a freeman but journeymen, particularly in the lesser trades, frequently failed to acquire their freedom. The proportion of freeman rose to half among the native tradesmen, fell to two in five among the Irish, and to little more than one in five among the other groups. It was remarkably low among those of English,

American, Nova Scotian, and Islander origins—doubtless indicating a view toward a temporary residence in the city on the part of members of these groups.

The traditional and emerging trades structures were both plainly visible in 1851. A significant number of master artisans, particularly in the footwear and clothing trades, maintained households that contained both their journeymen and their apprentices. At the other extreme, some individual firms had grown so large that the enterprises might more accurately be described as small factories. Most notable among these were the iron foundaries. The Portland blacksmith James Harris had expanded his operations to include a block of buildings employing more than seventy men and boys. Within the city Thomas Barlow employed another sixty-five, and the city's other founders employed comparable numbers. The wage spread between the blacksmith and the foundry-engineers in the metals trades was no greater than that between the small master cabinet-makers employing a few journeymen in their shops and a leading furniture maker like J. W. Lawrence, who employed sixteen men and boys in making furniture to the value of £2250.[17]

Expanding local markets brought about a rapid change in the structure of the traditional trades. Master tradesmen responded to these opportunities in a variety of ways. Immigration produced large numbers of shoe-makers and tailors. These trades required only limited capital—in some cases artisans even owned their own tools—and the result was a profusion of small shops and small masters.[18] By contrast, those trades permitting the application of steam-generated energy tended to remain concentrated in the hands of relatively few masters who added to their shops and employed an increasingly sophisticated technology.[19] Thus, while the shoemaking shops increased in number, offering numerous opportunities for ambitious young tradesmen to possess their own shops, the tanneries were concentrated in the hands of a few masters who came to employ more men in a more structured fashion and to play increasingly important roles in the life of the city. Daniel Ansley, who entered the trade as freeman tanner in 1809 at the age of eighteen and became a leading master tanner, finally classified himself as a merchant in the 1851 Census. Already possessing substantial shops in the early 1830s, four of the tanners greatly increased their capacity after 1840 by the installation of steam engines.[20]

The same development occurred in the flour trade. Grist-mill owners had constructed sixteen plants by 1840, each costing between £3000 and £5000 and each capable of grinding between 7000 and 12,000 barrels annually.[21] The most important elements in the city's industrial activities were the sawmills and iron and brass foundries, which became increasingly capital intensive as steam engines largely replaced water-driven mills.

The principal masters of that trade provide a useful insight into the successful trades leadership of the city. James Harris came from Annapolis as a young man and began to practise his blacksmith's craft. He gradually added machine, pattern, and fitting shops to his blacksmith's enterprise. In 1831 he added a blast furnace. Over the next few years a stove shop, a car shop, and a rolling mill completed the New Brunswick Foundry. His partner was a Scottish machinist, Thomas Allen, who completed his apprenticeship in Glasgow and settled in Saint John in 1825. Allen's son Thomas apprenticed as a machinist in his father's foundry, and a second son, Robert, became a moulder through the same process; a third son, Harris, studied as a brass founder. All three came to be owners of Saint John foundries by the early 1860s.[22] The Saint John Foundry was established in 1825 by Robert Foulis (a Scottish scientist and inventor and graduate in medicine of Aberdeen University) and was later taken over by a Fredericton merchant, T.C. Everitt, and two Saint John men, John Camber, a blacksmith, and James Wood, a machinist. George Fleming established the Phoenix Foundry in 1835. Fleming had served as a machinist's apprentice at the Dumferline Foundry in Scotland and then had worked as a journeyman in Glasgow, Cork, Pictou, Saint John, Boston, and Baltimore. His partners included a local carpenter, Thomas Barlow, an iron moulder, John Stewart, and later a long-time clerk with the firm, Thomas Humbert.[23] The city's ten iron and brass foundries in 1860 were thus distinguished by their Scottish and native ownership, by their structure as multiple partnerships that enabled them to bring together the necessary capital resources, and by the size of their producing units.

The foundries were the largest producing units in the city by the end of the colonial period. Three hundred journeymen and apprentices worked in them in 1850;[24] by 1873 the New Brunswick Foundry alone possessed a work-force of 300. The foundries were clearly operating on the factory system. In these, as in the bakery, carriage and cabinet making, tanning, and milling trades, the application of steam power and new technology to create a more efficient system of production was well under way by 1840. The founders, of course, were using steam power before 1830. Barzilia Ansley first brought steam power to a tannery in 1838. Thomas Rankine, a product of a Scottish bakers apprenticeship, introduced hand machinery to his business in 1844 and steam power eight years later. G.F. Thompson did the same in the paint trade in 1850. Four years later, Joseph and George Lawrence introduced steam power to the furniture-making firm their father had established in 1817. That same year Jeremiah Harrison applied steam to the carriage-making trade.[25]

The application of newer techniques to the traditional trades and the consequent growth of the firms between 1830 and 1860 certainly led to the growth of a group of prosperous masters having less and less in common with their journeymen and, conversely, limited the opportunities for those journeymen to acquire their own shops.[26] Yet the effect of this should not be overplayed. The growth of larger producing units was a slow process and in most firms involved a master artisan who had been a long-time resident of the city. Most important, apart from the iron foundries and a few sawmills, none of the producing units before 1850 could be described as factories in the sense that they employed more than twenty-five people in a plant powered by steam engines or water paddles. Most Saint John artisans in 1851 worked either in artisans' shops employing no more than five people or in the shipyards.[27] Moreover, the trades represented as much a social as an economic status. James Harris, Daniel Ansley, and the baker Stephen Humbert might become prominent, prosperous burghers, might even hold the Queen's Commission of the Peace with the right to style themselves 'Esquire.' Yet they remained artisans, married the daughters of artisans, and expressed the attitudes and biases of artisans, were perceived as tradesmen by their social superiors, and supported the interests of artisans. Throughout the colonial period—despite the changing structure and work relationships within some trades—that ethos remained a powerful source of identification binding most elements of the trades into a common interest.

This is not to suggest that loyalty to that interest was not sometimes divided or that elements of the interest did not war among themselves. The masters' use of the law to enforce obedience upon the apprentices has already been mentioned. Richard Rice has demonstrated the presence of Friendly Societies of carpenters, joiners, cabinet-makers, and painters as early as 1837, but no evidence that any of them took action against the masters.[28] Confrontations between masters and journeymen, usually over rates of pay or slow payment, occasionally occurred. As early as 1830 the journeymen tailors of the city threatened to withhold their labour until the masters agreed to make payment of wages within three days of the completion of their work and to charge no more than 12*s.* board each week. No further evidence of confrontation occurred until 1841 when a mechanic wrote to the smiths and moulders of the city in the columns of *The News* calling for a one-hour reduction in the workday.[29] In 1856 journeymen printers at *The Courier* withdrew their services because their employer had taken an extra apprentice into the office.[30] Significantly, although Eugene Forsey has provided evidence of a ship carpenters organization, there is no evidence of any confrontations in the shipyards of Saint John.[31]

But incidents of this nature, although indicating an underlying tension within the interest, were relatively few. More important, they were short-lived and left few permanent scars. For the deeply alienated journeyman, Boston lay near and emigration provided a final solution when insoluble problems arose. By contrast, the activities of masters and journeymen, whether working alone or in concert with other groups within the city, revealed something closely resembling a genuine class consciousness.

Notes

1. See M.B. Katz, *The People of Hamilton, Canada West* (Cambridge, Mass. 1975), 27, 311, and with M.J. Doucet and M.J. Stern, *The Social Organization of Early Industrial Capitalism* (Cambridge, Mass. 1982), ch. 1. In his second work, Katz argues that all nineteenth-century urban societies were divided into a business class and a working class and these corresponded to those who owned the means of production and those who sold their labour in return for money. Membership in the class, then, has nothing to do with class consciousness or class awareness; one is a member of a class because of one's relationship to the means of production. It is difficult to quarrel with any objective statement of classification. However, Katz destroys the objectivity of his model by insisting that the business class contains not only 'those individuals who owned the means of production' but also 'those whose interests and aspirations identified them with the owners' (p. 44). Using this definition Katz assigns entire categories of men to the business class: all professionals and even the meanest clerk or school teacher become a capitalist. It is not improbable that a majority of members of the business class did not own the means of production unless it is defined in terms of skills or hand tools. Leaving aside the question of how the historian measures the aspirations of each member of a society—a concept that, in any event, seems very akin to class consciousness—why does Katz assume that no artisan or labourer possessed any aspiration to become a proprietor or at least to better his material lot in life? And if that possibility is admitted, is it possible to assign artisans en masse to the working class?

2. Susan Hirsch, *Roots of the American Working Class: The Industrialization of Crafts in Newark 1800–1860* (Philadelphia 1978), 8, 11, 12, 41; Bryan Palmer, 'Kingston Mechanics and the Rise of the Penitentiary, 1833–1836,' *Histoire Sociale/Social History* (May 1980):7–32.

3. See, for example, Robert Gray, *The Labour Aristocracy in Victorian Edinburgh*.

4. Freemen's roll of the city of Saint John 1785–1862, NBM.

5. A point made by Hirsch in her study of Newark. Palmer, however, sees it as an exploitative arrangement after 1800. See Hirsch, Roots, 6, and Bryan A. Palmer, *Working–Class Experience: The Rise and Reconstitution of Canadian Labour 1800–1980* (Toronto 1983), 28–9.

6. Indenture of Henry Chubb, Chubb Family Papers, NBM.

7. See, for example, the firecracker ordinance of 1819 that provided a 20s. fine against the master of the offender (*City Gazette*, 11 August 1819).

8. *The Courier*, 15 January 1817.

9. See, for example, *The Courier*, 18 January, 25 September, and 15 November 1817.

10. Ibid., 12 June 1843.

11. Despite Katz's contention that few nineteenth-century journeymen became masters, Bruce Laurie

has demonstrated that over half the Methodist and Presbyterian journeymen in 1830 were masters or small retailers by 1850. Hirsch found that most Newark artisans over the age of forty were masters. See Bruce Laurie, *The Working People of Philadelphia 1850–1880* (Philadelphia 1980), 48.

12. See the Mechanics Institute School in *The Courier*, 28 December 1839 and the petition of Peter Cougle for release from his apprenticeship after 3 years, 9 months of service with H. Littlehale, a house joiner. Common Council supplementary papers, vol. 4, 30 June 1842, PANB.

13. These examples are drawn from the Roll of Freeman.

14. *The Courier*, 28 October 1858.

15. These data are drawn from the 1851 Census manuscript sample.

16. On the relative strength of the artisan group in other British North American cities see Palmer, *Working-Class Experience*, 31, and Katz, *The People of Hamilton*, 70.

17. Saint John 1851 Census manuscript, Kings Ward, 238, PANB.

18. As was the case in Newark. See Hirsch, 'Roots', 8.

19. Ibid., ch 2.

20. RLE/834, pe. 91; RLE/845, pe, 208; PANB.

21. RLE/828, pe. 42, 43; RLE/840, pe. 122; RLE/850, 418; *The Chronicle*, 22 March 1839.

22. *St. John and Its Business: A History of St. John* (Saint John 1875), 124, 128–9.

23. Ibid., 125–6.

24. RLE/851, pe. 412, PANB.

25. *St. John and Its Business*, 101, 103, 105, 137.

26. This is what Katz assumed in his work on Hamilton and Buffalo. Crossick, too, has reservations about the closeness of small masters and men in mid-nineteenth-century Birmingham. Hirsch, however, found that small masters in Newark paid fairer wages and kept their firms operating longer in times of adversity than did larger operations. See Crossick, 'Urban Society and the Petite Bourgeoisie,' 322, and Hirsch, *Roots*, 89–90.

27. A useful comparison and discussion of work place forms is found in Bruce Laurie, *Working People of Philadelphia 1800–1850* (Philadelphia 1980), ch. 1.

28. J.R. Rice, 'A History of Organized Labour in Saint John, N.B., 1815–1890' (MA thesis, University of New Brunswick 1968), ch. 1. Rice suggests that collective action by shipwrights and carpenters may have begun in 1799, but it is probable that the principal shipwrights' who composed the organization were the masters, not the journeymen. The earliest active unions were among shop clerks, the semi-skilled and unskilled sawyers, and ship labourers. The first documented instance of artisans taking action against masters occurred in 1864 when the caulkers struck for several months. (ch. ii).

29. *The Courier*, 29 May 1830. Tailors were usually paid half in board and half in cash; *The News*, 17 May 1841.

30. *The Courier*, 20 December 1856.

31. Eugene Forsey found evidence of organizations among sawyers, ship carpenters, carpenters and joiners, tailors, and cabinet-makers between 1835 and 1849. Yet there is no indication of any activity directed against their employers. See Forsey, *The Trade Unions in Canada* (Toronto 1982), 9–10.

CONFEDERATION

What Kind of Country Are We to Have?

P. E. Bryden
University of Victoria

CONFEDERATION: WHAT KIND OF COUNTRY ARE WE TO HAVE?

- **Introduction by P. E. Bryden**

- **Primary Sources**

- **Secondary Sources**

INTRODUCTION

P. E. Bryden

By the 1860s, the British North American colonies of Canada (later to be split into Ontario and Quebec), New Brunswick, Nova Scotia, Prince Edward Island, and Newfoundland were facing a number of threats—both internal and external—that gave leaders in each of the colonies reasons to consider alternative political arrangements.

In Canada, where the *Act of Union*, 1840, had combined the predominantly English Upper Canada with the predominantly French Lower Canada, political progress was increasingly difficult to achieve. Partly, this was because of the convention that recognized the bilingual and bicultural nature of the colony. Leadership of the Canadas was shared between one representative of each half, and legislation, in order to pass, had to secure a majority of support from Canada East and a majority of support from Canada West. The system was known as the double majority, and while it was an effective way of recognizing the demographic reality of the united province, it was a difficult way to govern. The advent of responsible government in 1848, whereby the prime minister and cabinet were obliged to resign if a bill failed to secure majority support in the legislature, ironically made governing even more complicated. With the practice of double majority in place majorities were hard to come by, and by the 1860s the Canadas seemed trapped in a cycle of almost perpetual elections. Clearly, the system had become untenable.

Economic concerns plagued all of the colonies. The free trade agreement that the colonies had entered into with the United States in 1854, known as the Reciprocity Agreement, was not likely to be renewed. Not only had the producers of New England become increasingly vocal in their opposition to allowing Canadian raw materials into the United States duty-free, but also the Civil War had turned sentiment in the northern part of the United States against Britain and her colonies. British North America bore the brunt of that resentment, which had been fuelled by a sense that Britain, officially a neutral observer to the war that was ripping apart America between 1861 and 1865, actually supported the South. The completion of a British ship-building contract that produced the Southern warship the *Chesapeake* was the most convincing evidence supporting Union fears that Britain sided with the Confederacy, but there were other issues as well. Britain's colonies in North America—particularly those in the Maritimes—seemed to develop a strain of anti-Yankee, or anti-Northern, sentiment over the course of the war, and Canada East had proven to be the launching point for a Confederate raid on the Vermont town of St. Alban's in 1864. While the evidence that Britain, and therefore British North America, was actively supporting the Confederacy was scant, it was nevertheless sufficient to raise suspicions and to virtually ensure that the Reciprocity Treaty would be cancelled when its term ran out in 1864. That left the British North American colonies without a clear trading partner, and since all of them relied heavily on external trade, this potentially spelled disaster.

The financial situation in each of the colonies was also such as to make them particularly vulnerable to any fluctuations in international trade. In the Maritime provinces, for example, efforts to complete intercolonial railway projects had left each of the colonies heavily in debt; similar state undertakings in the united provinces of Canada, while not quite so debilitating financially, nevertheless meant that ensuring economic security for the future was imperative.

Defence issues had also begun to concern the tiny British North American colonies. Not only was there a possibility—or, at least, worried colonists believed there was a possibility—that the victorious Union army, the largest standing army the world had yet seen, would turn its attention toward attacking British North America, but there were also fears—and these turned out to be correct—that Irish Americans, or Fenians, would attack British North America to draw British attention to the issue of Irish independence. Moreover, there were also worries about the security of the west. British Columbia, already a colony in the empire, was unlikely to be threatened by American expansion, but the same could not be said for the vast expanse of prairie. American settlers were rapidly filling their own West, and thought that covetous eyes would be cast northward gave British North Americans cause for concern. While Britain was ostensibly responsible for protecting its colonies in North America, the cost of maintaining such an expansive empire was beginning to weigh heavily on them. If there was a way for the colonies to protect themselves, then that would be preferable to the British.

Such was the situation in the British North American colonies in the 1860s. While a confederation of the existing colonies—or at least some of them—was hardly the only solution to the problems each of them faced individually, it was the one solution that seemed most palatable to the most number of colonies. Meeting first in Charlottetown in September 1864, representatives from each of the colonial legislatures began to discuss the possibility of a broader union; they continued the conversation in a more formal way in Quebec City the following month, where the real shape of the potential confederation was debated. The resulting Quebec Resolutions, which are included here, formed the basis for the *British North America Act* that was passed by the British Parliament in 1867, establishing Canada as a new country on 1 July. Examined carefully, the Quebec Resolutions provide some interesting insights into what the men who negotiated the confederation deal thought was important, and what they wanted to protect about their existing system. So too do the excerpts from the debates that occurred in each of the colonies between 1864 and 1867. The comments included here pay particular attention to the institutional shape that the new country would take, and why a federal structure was desirable—or not, as the case may be.

This is a question taken up by the first article included here. Constitutional scholar Peter Russell begins his article "Confederation" by providing a more detailed exploration of the series of events that led to the creation of Canada and discussing the ways in which the colonial legislatures participated in the constitutional process. But having decided that unity would provide a solution to political deadlock, economic uncertainty, and defence concerns, the crafters of the Confederation deal were faced with stickier questions: What shape would this new nation take? How could the structure be massaged in such a way as to serve the needs of the most number of people? How could the shape of Confederation reflect not only British desire to see Canada follow a more independent course, but also concerns in the province of Canada East (later Quebec) that there be clear protection somewhere in the constitution for their language and way of life, and concerns in the Maritimes that the debt incurred over the railway be addressed by the new union? Russell tries to answer some of these questions by examining the contours of the agreement.

P.B. Waite's influential book on the period, *The Life and Times of Confederation,* remains an important study of the events in the colonies in the 1860s. In "Confederation and the Federal Principle," he examines the newspaper articles that reported on the federal nature of the deal that was being hammered out by delegates from the various colonies. In particular, he looks at the response that resulted from the publication of the Quebec Resolutions. Although Confederation was a deal struck among elites, it nevertheless attracted the interest of people across the British North American colonies, who greedily consumed the newspaper reports as they were made available. Christopher Moore also examines the meaning of the deal that was discussed first in Charlottetown, then in Quebec City, and finally with the Colonial Office in London. In his piece "Nation and Crown," he explores the relative power of Britain, the new federal government, and the provincial governments, as well as what the participants understood this new nationality to mean.

While there was much for the people of British North America, as well as for subsequent generations of historians, to discuss about the deal that was worked out, including questions of where sovereignty lay (which all three authors address in their articles), or about what was meant by national identity (as explained by Moore), or about how responsible government or the Senate would work in practice, there has also always been a great deal of debate about the meaning of federalism. It is certainly the aspect of the Confederation agreement that has attracted the most attention from scholars in the twentieth and twenty-first centuries. As a concept borrowed from the United States, the nineteenth-century commentators sometimes expressed hesitation in adapting the structure for Canadian purposes, despite the urging of those supporters that it was a system that would best protect the various interests of all colonies and regions in British North America. The views of both contemporary participants and scholarly commentators are included here, illustrating the differences of opinion that were voiced in the debates surrounding Confederation, the depth of feeling that this supposedly dry political agreement elicited amongst people in the British North American colonies, and the continued vigour of the debate over federalism and the shape of Canadian Confederation.

QUESTIONS

1. In what ways was the process of reaching agreement on a union of British North American colonies in the 1860s different from the way that we would undertake constitutional change now? In what ways was it the same?

2. What were some of the arguments used by Tupper, Tilley and Brown in favour of Confederation? What about the arguments used by people such as John Bourinot of Nova Scotia and Robert Thompson of New Brunswick?

3. Where did the people of British North America see power residing in this new nation of Canada?

4. What evidence can you find in the Quebec Resolutions that the participants at the Quebec Conference were eager to craft a highly centralized form of government? Is there evidence that suggests they were keen to protect the independence of the individual colonies?

5. What evidence would you use to show that Confederation was a compromise? Whose arguments would you use?

FURTHER READINGS

Creighton, Donald, *The Road to Confederation: The Emergence of Canada, 1863–1867,* (Toronto: Macmillan of Canada, 1964).

Martin, Ged, *Britain and the Origins of Canadian Confederation, 1837–67,* (Vancouver: UBC Press, 1995).

Martin, Ged, ed., *The Causes of Canadian Confederation,* (Fredericton: Acadiensis Press, 1990).

Romney, Paul, *Getting It Wrong: How Canadians Forgot Their Past and Imperilled Confederation,* (Toronto: University of Toronto Press, 1999), esp. chapters 6–9.

Saywell, John T, *The Lawmakers: Judicial Power and the Shaping of Canadian Federalism,* (Toronto: University of Toronto Press, 2002), esp, chapter 1.

▲ Document 1: The Quebec Conference, 1864

When representatives of the British North American colonies met in Quebec City in October 1864, they devised a series of resolutions that would form the basis for the creation of the new government of Canada. Below are the 72 resolutions which identify, among other things, the British roots of the constitutional framework, a federal structure, and ways of dealing with some, if not all, of the concerns of the regions. Very few changes were made to the 72 resolutions from the time they were hammered out in Quebec to their appearance in the BNA Act, 1867.

Report

Of Resolutions adopted at a Conference of Delegates from the Provinces of Canada, Nova Scotia and New Brunswick, and the Colonies of Newfoundland and Prince Edward Island, held at the City of Quebec, 10th October, 1864, as the Basis of a proposed Confederation of those Provinces and Colonies.

1. The best interests and present and future prosperity of British North America will be promoted by a Federal Union under the Crown of Great Britain, provided such Union can be effected on principles just to the several Provinces.
2. In the Federation of the British North American Provinces the System of Government best adapted under existing circumstances to protect the diversified interests of the several Provinces and secure efficiency, harmony and permanency in the working of the Union,—would be a general Government charged with matters of common interest to the whole Country, and Local Governments for each of the Canadas and for the provinces of Nova Scotia, New Brunswick and Prince Edward Island, charged with the control of local matters in their respective sections.—Provision being made for the admission into the Union on equitable terms of Newfoundland, the North-West Territory, British Columbia and Vancouver. [British Columbia was the mainland colony, and Vancouver a separate colony composed of Vancouver Island and the Gulf Islands; the two united in 1866 to form British Columbia.]
3. In framing a Constitution for the General Government, the Conference, with a view to the perpetuation of our connection with the Mother Country, and to the promotion of the best interests of the people of these Provinces, desire to follow the model of the British Constitution, so far as our circumstances will permit.
4. The Executive Authority or Government shall be vested in the Sovereign of the United Kingdom of Great Britain and Ireland, and be administered according to the well understood principles of the British Constitution by the Sovereign personally or by the Representative of the Sovereign duly authorized.
5. The Sovereign or Representative of the Sovereign shall be Commander-in-Chief of the Land and Naval Militia Forces.
6. There shall be a General Legislature or Parliament for the Federated Provinces, composed of a Legislative Council and a House of Commons. [The Legislative Council became known as the Senate.]
7. For the purpose of forming the Legislative Council, the Federated Provinces shall be considered as consisting of three divisions:—

Source: *Documents on the Confederation of British North America: A Compilation Based on Sir Joseph Pope's Confederation Documents Supplemented by Other Official Material,* edited and with an introduction by G.P. Browne. (Toronto: McClelland and Stewart, 1969).

1st, Upper Canada; 2nd, Lower Canada; 3rd, Nova Scotia, New Brunswick and Prince Edward Island, each division with an equal representation in the Legislative Council.

8. Upper Canada shall be represented in the Legislative Council by 24 Members, Lower Canada by 24 Members, and the three Maritime Provinces by 24 Members, of which Nova Scotia shall have Ten, New Brunswick, Ten, and Prince Edward Island, Four Members.

9. The Colony of Newfoundland shall be entitled to enter the proposed Union, with a representation in the Legislative Council of four members.

10. The North-West Territory, British Columbia and Vancouver shall be admitted into the Union on such terms and conditions as the Parliament of the Federated Provinces shall deem equitable, and as shall receive the assent of Her Majesty; and in the case of the Province of British Columbia or Vancouver, as shall be agreed to by the Legislature of such Province.

11. The Members of the Legislative Council shall be appointed by the Crown under the Great Seal of the General Government and shall hold Office during Life; if any Legislative Councillor shall, for two consecutive sessions of Parliament, fail to give his attendance in the said Council, his seat shall thereby become vacant.

12. The Members of the Legislative Council shall be British Subjects by Birth or Naturalization, of the full age of Thirty Years, shall possess a continuous real property qualification of four thousand dollars over and above all incumbrances, and shall be and continue worth that sum over and above their debts and liabilities, but in the case of Newfoundland and Prince Edward Island, the property may be either real or personal.

13. If any question shall arise as to the qualification of a Legislative Councillor, the same shall be determined by the Council.

14. The first selection of the Members of the Legislative Council shall be made, except as regards Prince Edward Island, from the Legislative Councils of the various Provinces, so far as a sufficient number be found qualified and willing to serve; such Members shall be appointed by the Crown at the recommendation of the General Executive Government, upon the nomination of the respective Local Governments, and in such nomination due regard shall be had to the claims of the Members of the Legislative Council of the Opposition in each Province, so that all political parties may as nearly as possible be fairly represented.

15. The Speaker of the Legislative Council (unless otherwise provided by Parliament) shall be appointed by the Crown from among the members of the Legislative Council, and shall hold office during pleasure, and shall only be entitled to a casting vote on an equality of votes.

16. Each of the twenty-four Legislative Councillors representing Lower Canada in the Legislative Council of the General Legislature, shall be appointed to represent one of the twenty-four Electoral Divisions mentioned in Schedule A of Chapter first of the Consolidated Statutes of Canada, and such Councillor shall reside, or possess his qualification in the Division he is appointed to represent.

17. The basis of Representation in the House of Commons shall be Population, as determined by the Official Census every ten years; and the number of Members at first shall be 194, distributed as follows:

Upper Canada	82
Lower Canada	65
Nova Scotia	19
New Brunswick	15
Newfoundland	8
and Prince Edward Island	5

18. Until the Official Census of 1871 has been made up there shall be no change in the number of Representatives from the several sections.

19. Immediately after the completion of the Census of 1871 and immediately after every Decennial Census thereafter, the Representation from each section in the House of Commons shall be re-adjusted on the basis of Population.

20. For the purpose of such re-adjustments, Lower Canada shall always be assigned sixty-five members, and each of the other sections shall at each re-adjustment receive, for the ten years then next succeeding, the number of members to which it will be entitled on the same ratio of representation to population as Lower Canada will enjoy according to the Census last taken by having sixty-five members.

21. No reduction shall be made in the number of Members returned by any section, unless its population shall have decreased relatively to the population of the whole Union, to the extent of five per centum.

22. In computing at each decennial period, the number of Members to which each section is entitled, no fractional parts shall be considered, unless when exceeding one half the number entitling to a Member, in which case a member shall be given for each such fractional part.

23. The Legislature of each Province shall divide such Province into the proper number of constituencies, and define the boundaries of each of them.

24. The Local Legislature of each Province may from time to time alter the Electoral Districts for the purposes of Representation in the House of Commons, and distribute the representatives to which the Province is entitled in any manner such Legislature may think fit.

25. The number of Members may at any time be increased by the General Parliament,— regard being had to the proportionate rights then existing.

26. Until provisions are made by the General Parliament, all the Laws which, at the date of the proclamation constituting the Union, are in force in the Provinces respectively, relating to the qualification and disqualification of any person to be elected or to sit or vote as a member of the Assembly in the said Provinces respectively—and relating to the qualification or disqualification of voters, and to the oaths to be taken by voters, and to Returning Officers and their powers and duties,—and relating to the proceedings at Elections,—and to the period during which such Elections may be continued, and relating to the Trial of Controverted Elections, and the proceedings incident thereto, and relating to the vacating of seats of Members and to the issuing and execution of new Writs in case of any seat being vacated otherwise than by a dissolution,—shall respectively apply to elections of Members to serve in the House of Commons, for places situate in those Provinces respectively.

27. Every House of Commons shall continue for five years from the day of the return of the writs choosing the same, and no longer, subject, nevertheless, to be sooner prorogued or dissolved by the Governor.

28. There shall be a Session of the General Parliament once at least in every year, so that a period of twelve calendar months shall not intervene between the last sitting of the General Parliament in one Session and the first sitting thereof in the next session.

29. [Section 29, with its various subsections, laid out the powers that would be held by the federal government. In later versions of the *British North America Act*, it would be renumbered section 91.] The General Parliament shall have power to make Laws for the peace, welfare and good Government of the Federated Provinces (saving the Sovereignty of England), and especially Laws respecting the following subjects:—

    1. The Public Debt and Property.

    2. The Regulation of Trade and Commerce.

3. The imposition or regulation of Duties of Customs on Imports and Exports, except on Exports of Timber, Logs, Masts, Spars, Deals and Sawn Lumber, and of Coal and other Minerals.
4. The imposition or regulation of Excise Duties.
5. The raising of money by all or any other modes or systems of Taxation.
6. The Borrowing of Money on the Public Credit.
7. Postal Service.
8. Lines of Steam or other Ships, Railways, Canals and other works, connecting any two or more of the Provinces together or extending beyond the limits of any Province.
9. Lines of Steamships between the Federated Provinces and other Countries.
10. Telegraphic Communication and the incorporation of Telegraph Companies.
11. All such works as shall, although lying wholly within any Province, be specially declared by the Acts authorizing them to be for the general advantage.
12. The Census.
13. Militia—Military and Naval Service and Defence.
14. Beacons, Buoys and Lighthouses.
15. Navigation and Shipping.
16. Quarantine.
17. Sea Coast and Inland Fisheries.
18. Ferries between any Province and a Foreign Country, or between any two Provinces.
19. Currency and Coinage.
20. Banking, Incorporation of Banks, and the issue of paper money.
21. Savings Banks.
22. Weights and Measures.
23. Bills of Exchange and Promissory Notes.
24. Interest.
25. Legal Tender.
26. Bankruptcy and Insolvency.
27. Patents of Invention and Discovery.
28. Copy Rights.
29. Indians and Lands reserved for the Indians.
30. Naturalization and Aliens.
31. Marriage and Divorce.
32. The Criminal Law, excepting the Constitution of Courts of Criminal Jurisdiction, but including the procedure in Criminal matters.
33. Rendering uniform all or any of the laws relative to property and civil rights in Upper Canada, Nova Scotia, New Brunswick, Newfoundland and Prince Edward Island, and rendering uniform the procedure of all or any of the Courts in these Provinces; but any Statute for this purpose shall have no force or authority in any Province until sanctioned by the Legislature thereof.
34. The Establishment of a General Court of Appeal for the Federated Provinces.
35. Immigration.
36. Agriculture.
37. And Generally respecting all matters of a general character, not specially and exclusively reserved for the Local Governments and Legislatures.
30. The General Government and Parliament shall have all powers necessary or proper for performing and obligations of the Federated Provinces, as part of the British

Empire, to Foreign Countries, arising under Treaties between Great Britain and such Countries.

31. The General Parliament may also, from time to time, establish additional Courts, and the General Government may appoint Judges and Officers thereof, when the same shall appear necessary or for the public advantage, in order to the due execution of the laws of Parliament.

32. All Courts, Judges and Officers of the several Provinces shall aid, assist and obey the General Government in the exercise of its rights and powers, and for such purposes shall be held to be Courts, Judges and Officers of the General Government.

33. The General Government shall appoint and pay the Judges of the Superior Courts in each Province, and of the County Courts in Upper Canada, and Parliament shall fix their salaries.

34. Until the Consolidation of the Laws of Upper Canada, New Brunswick, Nova Scotia, Newfoundland and Prince Edward Island, the Judges of these Provinces appointed by the General Government, shall be selected from their respective Bars.

35. The Judges of the Courts of Lower Canada shall be selected from the Bar of Lower Canada.

36. The Judges of the Court of Admiralty now receiving salaries shall be paid by the General Government.

37. The Judges of the Superior Courts shall hold their offices during good behaviour, and shall be removable only on the Address of both Houses of Parliament.

Local Government

38. For each of the Provinces there shall be an Executive Officer, styled the Lieutenant-Governor, who shall be appointed by the Governor-General in Council, under the Great Seal of the Federated Provinces, during pleasure: such pleasure not to be exercised before the expiration of the first five years, except for cause: such cause to be communicated in writing to the Lieutenant-Governor immediately after the exercise of the pleasure as aforesaid, and also by message to both Houses of Parliament, within the first week of the first Session afterwards.

39. The Lieutenant-Governor of each Province shall be paid by the General Government.

40. In undertaking to pay the salaries of the Lieutenant-Governors, the Conference does not desire to prejudice the claim of Prince Edward Island upon the Imperial Government for the amount now paid for the salary of the Lieutenant-Governor thereof.

41. The Local Government and Legislature of each Province shall be constructed in such manner as the existing Legislature of such Province shall provide.

42. The Local Legislatures shall have power to alter or amend their constitution from time to time.

43. The Local Legislatures shall have power to make Laws respecting the following subjects:—
    1. Direct Taxation and the imposition of Duties on the Export of Timber, Logs, Masts, Spars, Deals and Sawn Lumber, and of Coals and other Minerals.
    2. Borrowing Money on the credit of the Province.
    3. The establishment and tenure of local Offices, and the appointment and payment of local Officers.
    4. Agriculture.
    5. Immigration.
    6. Education; saving the rights and privileges which the Protestant or Catholic minority in both Canadas may possess as to their Denominational Schools, at the time when the Union goes into operation.

7. The sale and management of Public Lands, excepting Lands belonging to the General Government.
8. Sea coast and Inland Fisheries.
9. The establishment, maintenance and management of Penitentiaries, and of Public and Reformatory Prisons.
10. The establishment, maintenance and management of Hospitals, Asylums, Charities and Eleemosynary Institutions.
11. Municipal Institutions.
12. Shop, Saloon, Tavern, Auctioneer and other licenses.
13. Local Works.
14. The Incorporation of private or local Companies, except such as relate to matters assigned to the General Parliament.
15. Property and civil rights, excepting those portions thereof assigned to the General Parliament.
16. Inflicting punishment by fine, penalties, imprisonment or otherwise for the breach of laws passed in relation to any subject within their jurisdiction.
17. The Administration of Justice, including the Constitution, maintenance and organization of the Courts, both of Civil and Criminal Jurisdiction, and including also the Procedure in Civil Matters.
18. And generally all matters of a private or local nature, not assigned to the General Parliament.

44. The power of respiting, reprieving and pardoning Prisoners convicted of crimes, and of commuting and remitting of sentences in whole or in part, which belongs of right to the Crown, shall be administered by the Lieutenant-Governor of each Province in Council, subject to any instructions he may from time to time receive from the General Government, and subject to any provisions that may be made in this behalf by the General Parliament.

Miscellaneous.

45. In regard to all subjects over which jurisdiction belongs to both the General and Local Legislatures, the laws of the General Parliament shall control and supersede those made by the Local Legislature, and the latter shall be void so far as they are repugnant to or inconsistent with the former.
46. Both the English and French languages may be employed in the General Parliament and in its proceedings, and in the Local Legislature of Lower Canada, and also in the Federal Courts and in the Courts of Lower Canada.
47. No lands or property belonging to the General or Local Governments shall be liable to taxation.
48. All Bills for appropriating any part of the Public Revenue, or for imposing any new Tax or Impost, shall originate in the House of Commons or House of Assembly, as the case may be.
49. The House of Commons or House of Assembly shall not originate or pass any Vote, Resolution, Address or Bill for the appropriation of any part of the Public Revenue, or of any Tax or Impost to any purpose, not first recommended by Message of the Governor-General, or the Lieutenant-Governor, as the case may be, during the Session in which such Vote, Resolution, Address or Bill is passed.
50. Any Bill of the General Parliament may be reserved in the usual manner for Her Majesty's Assent, and any Bill of the Local Legislatures may in like manner be reserved for the consideration of the Governor-General.

51. Any Bill passed by the General Parliament shall be subject to disallowance by Her Majesty within two years, as in the case of Bills passed by the Legislatures of the said Provinces hitherto, and in like manner any Bill passed by a Local Legislature shall be subject to disallowance by the Governor-General within one year after the passing thereof.
52. The Seat of Government of the Federated Provinces shall be Ottawa, subject to the Royal Prerogative.
53. Subject to any future action of the respective Local Governments, the Seat of the Local Government in Upper Canada shall be Toronto; of Lower Canada, Quebec; and the Seats of the Local Governments in the other Provinces shall be as at present.

Property and Liabilities.

54. All Stocks, Cash, Bankers' Balances and Securities for money belonging to each Province, at the time of the Union, except as hereinafter mentioned, shall belong to the General Government.
55. The following Public Works and Property of each Province shall belong to the General Government, to wit:—
    1. Canals;
    2. Public Harbours;
    3. Light Houses and Piers;
    4. Steamboats, Dredges and Public Vessels;
    5. River and Lake Improvements;
    6. Railway and Railway Stocks, Mortgages and other Debts due by Railway Companies;
    7. Military Roads;
    8. Custom Houses, Post Offices and other Public Buildings, except such as may be set aside by the General Government for the use of the Local Legislatures and Governments;
    9. Property transferred by the Imperial Government and known as Ordnance Property;
    10. Armouries, Drill Sheds, Military Clothing and Munitions of War; and
    11. Lands set apart for Public Purposes.
56. All lands, mines, minerals and royalties vested in Her Majesty in the Provinces of Upper Canada, Lower Canada, Nova Scotia, New Brunswick and Prince Edward Island, for the use of such Provinces, shall belong to the Local Government of the territory in which the same are so situate; subject to any trusts that may exist in respect to any of such lands or to any interest of other persons in respect of the same.
57. All sums due from purchasers or lessees of such lands, mines or minerals at the time of the Union, shall also belong to the Local Governments.
58. All assets connected with such portions of the public debt of any Province as are assumed by the Local Governments, shall also belong to those Governments respectively.
59. The several Provinces shall retain all other Public Property therein, subject to the right of the General Government to assume any Lands or Public Property required for Fortifications or the Defence of the Country.
60. The General Government shall assume all the Debts and Liabilities of each Province.
61. The Debt of Canada not specially assumed by Upper and Lower Canada respectively, shall not exceed at the time of the Union $62,500,000
    Nova Scotia shall enter the Union with a debt not exceeding $8,000,000
    And New Brunswick, with a debt not exceeding $7,000,000
62. In case Nova Scotia or New Brunswick do not incur liabilities beyond those for which their Governments are now bound and which shall make their debts at the date

of Union less than $8,000,000 and $7,000,000 respectively, they shall be entitled to interest at 5 per cent on the amount not so incurred, in like manner as is hereinafter provided for Newfoundland and Prince Edward Island: the foregoing resolution being in no respect intended to limit the powers given to the respective Governments of those Provinces by Legislative authority, but only to limit the maximum amount of charge to be assumed by the General Government; provided always that the powers so conferred by the respective Legislatures shall be exercised within five years from this date or the same shall then lapse.

63. Newfoundland and Prince Edward Island, not having incurred Debts equal to those of the other Provinces, shall be entitled to receive by half-yearly payments in advance from the General Government the Interest at five per cent. on the difference between the actual amount of their respective Debts at the time of the Union, and the average amount of indebtedness per head of the Population of Canada, Nova Scotia and New Brunswick.

64. In consideration of the transfer to the General Parliament of the powers of Taxation, an annual grant in aid of each Province shall be made, equal to 80 cents per head of the Population as established by the Census of 1861, the population of Newfoundland being estimated at 130,000. Such aid shall be in full settlement of all future demands upon the General Government for local purposes, and shall be paid half-yearly in advance to each Province.

65. The position of New Brunswick being such as to entail large immediate charges upon her local revenues, it is agreed that for the period of ten years from the time when the Union takes effect, an additional allowance of $63,000 per annum shall be made to that Province. But that so long as the liability of that Province remains under $7,000,000, a deduction equal to the interest on such deficiency shall be made from the $63,000.

66. In consideration of the surrender to the General Government by Newfoundland of all its rights in Mines and Minerals, and of all the ungranted and unoccupied Lands of the Crown, it is agreed that the sum of $150,000 shall each year be paid to that Province by semi-annual payments; provided that that Colony shall retain the right of opening, constructing and controlling Roads and Bridges through any of the said Lands, subject to any Laws which the General Parliament may pass in respect of the same.

67. All engagements that may, before the Union, be entered into with the Imperial Government for the Defence of the Country shall be assumed by the General Government.

68. The General Government shall secure, without delay, the completion of the Intercolonial Railway from Rivière-du-Loup through New Brunswick to Truro, in Nova Scotia.

69. The communications with the North-Western Territory, and the improvements required for the development of the Trade of the Great West with the Seaboard, are regarded by this Conference as subjects of the highest importance to the Federated Provinces, and shall be prosecuted at the earliest possible period that the state of the Finances will permit.

70. The Sanction of the Imperial and Local Parliaments shall be sought for the Union of the Provinces, on the principles adopted by the Conference.

71. That Her Majesty the Queen be solicited to determine the rank and name of the Federated Provinces.

72. The proceedings of the Conference shall be authenticated by the signatures of the Delegates, and submitted by each Delegation to its own Government, and the Chairman is authorized to submit a copy to the Governor-General for transmission to the Secretary of State for the Colonies.

▲ Document 2: Federal Union Debates

Once the form of unions was agreed upon by the political elites who met in Charlottetown and Quebec City, it was discussed in greater detail in the legislative assemblies of the various colonies. These debates were as close as the document got to any widespread public consideration.

Nova Scotia House of Assembly, 1865

[Charles Tupper and John Bourinot were both Conservative politicians from Nova Scotia, although only the former participated in the conferences in Charlottetown and Quebec City.]

Charles Tupper: I need not tell the house that a great deal of discussion has taken place in times past as to whether a legislative or federal union would be the best mode by which these provinces could be united, and I believe that I will be able to show this house that whilst a legislative union was really not practically before us—for there were difficulties lying in its path such as to render its adoption impossible—yet the union which was devised by the Quebec Conference possessed all the advantages of both without the disadvantages that attended each separately. No person who is acquainted with the character of legislative union but knows, when it is proposed for a country with the area and extent of territory that British America possesses, its realization is attended with great difficulties, if not with insuperable obstacles. No person who is acquainted with what has taken place in the imperial parliament but knows that great as that country has become under a legislative union, yet the difficulties connected with the union are such as at this moment to be occupying the attention of the foremost statesmen of Great Britain.

The difficulties in the way of a legislative union are that the legislature has not only to be occupied with the discussion of the great and leading questions which touch the vital interests of every section of the country, but to give its attention largely to matters of merely local concern. At present, the [British] parliament is obliged to take up and consider from five to six hundred local bills. When we consider that this body of six hundred men—the most influential and important assemblage of statesmen in the world, are called upon to give their attention upon some five hundred bills, which are not of general but of purely local concern, you can imagine the difficulty of carrying on the legislation of such a country. It is not strange that under such circumstances the parliament is obliged to sit eight out of twelve months in order to accomplish the legislation required at their hands.

If a legislative union were devised for British North America, the people occupying the different sections would not have the guarantee that they have under the scheme devised that matters of a local character would occupy the attention of the local legislatures, whilst those of a general nature would be entrusted to the general legislature. Therefore the scheme that was devised gave centralization and consolidation and unity that it was absolutely indispensable should be given. On the other hand, instead of having copied the defects of the federal constitution—instead of having the inherent weakness that must always attend a system where the local legislatures only impart certain powers to the government of the country—quite a different course was pursued and it was decided to define

Source: Ajzenstat, K., et al. (2003), *Canada's Founding Debates*, pp. 262–65, 269–70, 271–73, 285–90, 295–96, 300–302. © University of Toronto Press Inc., 2003. Reprinted with permission of the publisher.

the questions that should be reserved for local legislatures, and those great subjects that should be entrusted to the general parliament. Therefore, whilst the unity and consolidation connected with legislative union was obtained on the one hand, due care and attention to local matters interesting to each province were provided for by the preservation of local parliaments, and these powers were so arranged as to prevent any conflict or struggle which might lead to any difficulty between the several sections ...

It was proposed ... that all the questions of leading general importance should be entrusted to the general government ... To the local governments were reserved powers of an important character, though of a local interest, which could be exercised without any interference whatever with the unity and strength of the central government ... The local governments would not interfere with the powers of the general government, or weaken its strength and unity of action, but would be able to deal with such questions as touch the local interests of the country—the construction of roads and bridges, public works, civil jurisdiction, etc. ...

Was our representation in the Commons the only guarantee that our rights would not be trampled upon? It is ample security, but I am ready to show the house the most extravagant demand that could enter into the mind of any man was conceded in the scheme of government for these provinces. I need not tell this house of the potent influence that is exercised in legislation by the Legislative Council. We have seen several striking examples of questions on which three-fourths of this body concurred, and yet this house did not succeed in attaining its object because it did not meet with the concurrence of the upper branch. It requires two to make a bargain and pass a law. I ask you, then, if you wish for a guarantee that the security of the people of the Maritime provinces will never be ignored, could you have a stronger one than that 600,000 people in these Maritime provinces should have obtained, under such a constitution, the same representation in the upper branch as was given to Upper Canada with 1,400,000 and to Lower Canada with 1,100,000? This we have for all time to come, although Upper Canada may increase to millions of people. Then I would ask the intelligent people of this country if the parties who devised the constitution did not give us all the security that our rights and interests could demand.

—House of Assembly, April 10, 1865

John Bourinot: [The scheme] provides for a federal union of these provinces. I have no hesitation in saying that if the conference had devised a legislative union, it would have been preferable. Everyone knows what the local legislatures will be under this scheme— very insignificant bodies. Another portion of the scheme provides that the lieutenant governors shall be selected by the governor general at Ottawa. What class of men shall we, then, have for our local governors? These very men who formed the convention. But how would they be looked upon? The position of lieutenant governor would become a mockery in the estimation of the public....

It has never yet been fully explained why we have been given local legislatures in this scheme. It might be satisfactory to the Lower Canadians, but it would never do for these other provinces. The municipal system that is in full operation in Canada West, or the very system of county sessions that exists here now, might have done the work assigned to the local legislatures. If the Lower Canadians would not agree to legislative union, an arrangement might have been made so as to give them the control of those matters in which they felt especial interest without interfering with the rest of the provinces. I am glad, however, that some gentlemen who formed part of the conference had some respect for that section of Canada which has been so trampled upon by the western Canadians for years past. It is known to many that Upper Canada has long been endeavouring to deprive Lower Canada of many of those institutions and rights which they value—the very principle upon which the union was formed it has been attempted to destroy. Just in that way would the Upper Canadians, in case of a confederation, endeavour to override the interests and rights of these Maritime provinces …

—*House of Assembly, April 17, 1865*

New Brunswick House of Assembly, 1865 and 1866

Robert Thomson: By adopting this scheme we surrender our independence and become dependent upon Canada, for this federal government will have the veto power upon our legislation. The 51st section of the scheme says: "Any Bill passed by the General Parliament shall be subject to disallowance by Her Majesty within two years, as in the case of bills passed by the Legislatures of the said Provinces hitherto; in like manner any Bill passed by a local Legislature shall be subject to disallowance by the Governor General within one year after the passing thereof." Here is a written constitution with certain rights given and accorded to the local legislatures, and certain rights are given to the general government. Suppose there is a conflict between the two governments, where is the appeal? In the United States they have an appeal to the judges of the land; but here the general government has an arbitrary veto and we have to submit. I think this is a very serious defect in the constitution.

—*House of Assembly, June 1, 1865.*

Abner McClellan: Another objection taken was, the bills framed by the local legislatures would be liable to be disallowed by the general government. I do not see the point of this objection, as our local bills may now be disallowed by a power farther off, and whereas in the general government we should have representatives to explain and support them, in England we have none at all.

—*House of Assembly, June 2, 1865*

Albert J. Smith: Delegates … have probably taken the idea [for representation by population] from the plan adopted by the constitution of the United States. There they have representation by population in the House of Representatives. But in the Senate it is provided that every state alike send two senators. And it must be remembered that the Senate of the United States has executive as well as legislative functions; it has power even to veto many of the acts of the president. What he does must have their approval and consent. They have a check on the House of Representatives. But under the provisions of this scheme, the people's house will be the all-important and all-powerful branch, for they will be able even to overturn the executive of the country. It is not so in the United States. While the framers of this scheme have copied this provision from the United States, have they given us the same checks as are provided there? Not at all. There every state, large and small, sends one [sic] representative to the Senate.

Thus Canada is not only to have the great majority in the lower house, but in the Legislative Council she is to be represented by forty-eight members, whilst all the lower provinces will only have twenty-four [. . .] It may be asked why we should have an equal number with them in the second branch? I say because they have full power and control in the lower house … In the United States the senators are elected by the people, and not for life, but one-third of their numbers every two years. But here they acknowledge no sway from the people, and with all this Canada is to have a two-thirds majority in that house …

Now how are differences and controversies on this subject to be settled? Have they a superior court to which the matter can be carried as in the United States, where differences between states and the general government can be carried and settled? No, there is nothing of the kind provided. It is not important that there should be some tribunal where disputes of this nature may be settled; and I ask the attorney general to look into the matter and provide for some means of appeal. But even then there is the other power they possess of vetoing any action of the local legislatures. Should we submit that Canada should have the power to abrogate and nullify all or any of our legislation, with no power to which to appeal? They have also left us the power of managing our own private or local affairs, but the question may be raised what is private and local, and then who is to determine?

S. L. Tilley: The honourable member [Smith] stated that it was probable our local legislature would be left without any powers and dwindle down so low that its action would be a mere farce. Now, whatever may be the opinion of the honourable member with regard to this legislature, or of Mr. Brown in reference to the local government of Upper Canada, I believe that our constitution will remain just as it is. It is a fact that out of the whole number of bills passed by this legislature in 1864, all but seven would have come before us in Confederation, and all but three during the last session. No, the work to be performed will not dwindle down to insignificance.

—House of Assembly, June 27, 1866

[Tilley had a long political career in both New Brunswick and Canadian politics, but as premier of the province he was defeated over Confederation in 1865, and then reelected in 1866 in time to bring New Brunswick into Confederation the following year.]

Tilley: He [Smith] says we have not a sufficient number of representatives in the upper branch of the legislature. There might be some concessions made to us in this. When the arrangement was made, and representation by population was conceded, it was considered that there was a great protection given to the Maritime provinces, for New Brunswick was to have one representative for every 25,000 of her population, Lower Canada one to every 50,000, and Upper Canada one to every 75,000 ... In every case the interests of the Maritime provinces are nearly identical, and there is scarcely an important question that can come up in which Lower Canada would not be with us ... Again there is a protection in the fact that the number of representatives in the upper branch cannot be increased by the crown.

—House of Assembly, June 28, 1866

United Canada's Legislative Assembly, 1865

[Brown was a Reformer, founding editor of the Toronto *Globe*, and one of the original supporters of the federal solution to the problems of governing Canada East and Canada West.]

George Brown: I cannot help feeling that the struggle of half a lifetime for constitutional reform—the agitations in the country and the fierce contests in this chamber—the strife and the discord and the abuse of many years—are all compensated by the great scheme of reform which is now in your hands. (Cheers.) The attorney general for Upper Canada [Macdonald], as well as the attorney general for Lower Canada [Cartier], in addressing the house last night, were anxious to have it understood that this scheme for uniting British America under one government is something different from "representation by population"—is something different from "joint authority"—but is in fact the very scheme of the government of which they were members in 1858 ... For myself, sir, I care not who gets the credit of this scheme—I believe it contains the best features of all the suggestions that have been made in the last ten years for the settlement of our troubles. The whole feeling in my mind now is one of joy and thankfulness that there were found men of position and influence in Canada who, at a moment of serious crisis, had nerve and patriotism enough to cast aside political partisanship, to banish personal considerations, and unite for the accomplishment of a measure so fraught with advantage to their common country. (Cheers.) ... But seven short months have passed away since the coalition government was formed, yet already are we submitting a scheme well weighed and matured, for the erection of a future empire, a scheme which has been received at home and abroad with almost universal approval ...

The constitutional system of Canada cannot remain as it is now. (Loud cries of hear, hear.) Something must be done. We cannot stand still. We cannot go back to chronic, sectional hostility and discord—to a state of perpetual ministerial crises. The events of the last eight months cannot be obliterated; the solemn admissions of men of all parties cannot be erased. The claims of Upper Canada for justice must be met, and met now. I say, then, that everyone who raises his voice in hostility to this measure is bound to keep before him, when he speaks, all the perilous consequences of its rejection ...

The very essence of our compact is that the union shall be federal and not legislative. Our Lower Canada friends have agreed to give us representation by population in the lower house, on the express condition that they shall have equality in the upper house. On no other condition could we have advanced a step; and, for my part, I am quite willing that they should have it. In maintaining the existing sectional boundaries and handing over the control of local matters to local bodies, we recognize, to a certain extent, a diversity of interests; and it was quite natural that the protection for those interests, by equality in the upper chamber, should be demanded by the less numerous provinces. Honourable gentlemen may say that it will erect a barrier in the upper house against the just influence that Upper Canada will exercise, by her numbers, in the lower house over the general legislation of the country. That may be true, to a certain extent, but honourable gentlemen will bear in mind that that barrier, be it more or less, will not affect money bills. (Hear, hear.)

Hitherto we have been paying a vast proportion of the taxes, with little or no control over the expenditure. But, under this plan, by our just influence in the lower chamber, we shall hold the purse strings. If, from this concession of equality in the upper chamber, we are restrained from forcing through measures which our friends of Lower Canada may consider injurious to their interests, we shall, at any rate, have power, which we never had before, to prevent them from forcing through whatever we may deem unjust to us ...

For myself, sir, I unhesitatingly say that the complete justice which this measure secures to the people of Upper Canada in the vital matter of parliamentary representation alone renders all the blemishes averred against it utterly contemptible in the balance. (Continued cheers.) But, Mr. Speaker, the second feature of this scheme as a remedial measure is that it removes, to a large extent, the injustice of which Upper Canada has complained in financial matters. We in Upper Canada have complained that though we paid into the public treasury more than three-fourths of the whole revenue, we had less control over the system of taxation and the expenditure of the public monies than the people of Lower Canada. Well, sir, the scheme in your hand remedies that. The absurd line of separation between the provinces is swept away for general matters; we are to have seventeen additional members in the house that holds the purse; and the taxpayers of the country, wherever they reside, will have their just share of influence over revenue and expenditure. (Hear, hear.)

We have also complained that immense sums of public money have been systematically taken from the public chest for local purposes of Lower Canada, in which the people of Upper Canada had no interest whatever, though compelled to contribute three-fourths of the cash. Well, sir, this scheme remedies that. All local matters are to be banished from the general legislature; local governments are to have control over local affairs, and if our friends in Lower Canada choose to be extravagant, they will have to bear the burden of it themselves. (Hear, hear.) ...

But, Mr. Speaker, there is another great evil in our existing system that this scheme remedies: it secures to the people of each province full control over the administration of their own internal affairs. We in Upper Canada have complained that the minority of our representatives, the party defeated at the polls of Upper Canada, have been, year after year, kept in office by Lower Canada votes, and that all the local patronage of our section has been dispensed by those who did not possess the confidence of the people. Well, sir, this scheme remedies that. The local patronage will be under local control, and the wishes of the majority in each section will be carried out in all local matters. (Hear, hear.)

We have complained that the land system was not according to the views of our western people; that free lands for actual settlers was the right policy for us—that the price of a piece of land squeezed out of an immigrant was no consideration in comparison with the settlement among us of a hardy and industrious family; and that the colonization road system was far from satisfactory. Well, sir, this scheme remedies that. Each province is to have control over its own crown lands, crown timber, and crown minerals—and will be free to take such steps for developing them as each deems best. (Hear, hear.)

We have complained that local works of various kinds—roads, bridges and landing piers, court houses, gaols, and other structures—have been erected in an inequitable and improvident manner. Well, sir, this scheme remedies that; all local works are to be constructed by the localities and defrayed from local funds. And so on through the whole extensive details of internal local administration will this reform extend ...

But, Mr. Speaker, I am further in favour of this scheme because it will bring to an end the sectional discord between Upper and Lower Canada. It sweeps away the boundary line between the provinces so far as regards matters common to the whole people—it places all on an equal level—and the members of the federal legislature will meet at last as citizens of a common country. The questions that used to excite the most hostile feelings among us have been taken away from the general legislature and placed under the control of the local bodies. No man need hereafter be debarred from success in public life because his views, however popular in his own section, are unpopular in the other—for he will not have to deal with sectional questions; and the temptation to the government of the day to make capital out of local prejudices will be greatly lessened, if not altogether at an end ... a most happy day will it be for Canada when this bill goes into effect, and all these subjects of discord are swept from the discussion of our legislature. (Hear.)

We had either to take a federal union or drop the negotiation. Not only were our friends from Lower Canada against it, but so were most of the delegates from the Maritime provinces. There was but one choice open to us—federal union or nothing. But in truth the scheme now before us has all the advantages of a legislative union and a federal one as well. We have thrown over on the localities all the questions which experience has shown lead directly to local jealousy and discord, and we have retained in the hands of the general government all the powers necessary to secure a strong and efficient administration of public affairs. (Hear, hear.) By placing the appointment of the judges in the hands of the general government, and the establishment of a central court of appeal, we have secured uniformity of justice over the whole land. (Hear, hear.) By vesting the appointment of the lieutenant governors in the general government, and giving a veto for all local measures, we have secured that no injustice shall be done without appeal in local legislation. (Hear, hear.) For all dealings with the imperial government and foreign countries, we have clothed the general government with the most ample powers. And, finally, all matters of trade and commerce, banking and currency, and all questions common to the whole people we have vested fully and unrestrictedly in the general government. The measure, in fact, shuns the faults of the federal and legislative systems and adopts the best parts of both, and I am well persuaded it will work efficiently and satisfactorily. (Hear, hear.)

—*Legislative Assembly, February 8, 1865*

[A Liberal from the Quebec half of the colony of Canada, Dorion was the first to propose a limited federal association between the two parts of the colony. That did not mean, however, that he supported the extension of federalism any further.]

A.-A. Dorion: The Confederation I advocated was a real confederation, giving the largest powers to the local governments, and merely a delegated authority to the general government—in that respect differing in toto from the one now proposed which gives all the powers to the central government and reserves for the local governments the smallest possible amount of freedom of action. There is nothing besides in what I have ever written or said that can be interpreted as favouring a confederation of all the provinces. This I always opposed …

Now, sir, when I look into the provisions of this scheme, I find another most objectionable one. It is that which gives the general government control over all the acts of the local legislatures. What difficulties may not arise under this system? Now, knowing that the general government will be party in its character, may it not for party purposes reject laws passed by the local legislatures and demanded by a majority of the people of that locality? This power conferred upon the general government has been compared to the veto power that exists in England in respect to our legislation; but we know that the statesmen of England are not actuated by the local feelings and prejudices, and do not partake of the local jealousies that prevail in the colonies. The local governments have therefore confidence in them and respect for their decisions; and generally, when a law adopted by a colonial legislature is sent to them, if it does not clash with the policy of the empire at large, it is not disallowed, and more especially of late it has been the policy of the imperial government to do whatever the colonies desire in this respect, when their wishes are constitutionally expressed …

But how different will be the result in this case, when the general government exercises the veto power over the acts of local legislatures. Do you not see that it is quite possible for a majority in a local government to be opposed to the general government, and in such a case the minority would call upon the general government to disallow the laws enacted by the majority? The men who shall compose the general government will be dependent for their support upon their political friends in the local legislatures, and it may so happen that, in order to secure this support, or in order to serve their own purposes or that of their supporters, they will veto laws which the majority of a local legislature find necessary and good. (Hear, hear.) We know how high party feeling runs sometimes upon local matters even of trivial importance, and we may find parties so hotly opposed to each other in the local legislatures that the whole power of the minority may be brought to bear upon their friends who have a majority in the general legislature, for the purpose of preventing the passage of some law objectionable to them, but desired by the majority of their own section. What will be the result of such a state of things but bitterness of feeling, strong political acrimony, and dangerous agitation? (Hear, hear.)

—*Legislative Assembly, February 16, 1865.*

[Mackenzie would become the first Liberal prime minister in 1872, but in the years leading up to Confederation he was a reform politician in Canada West and a supporter of George Brown.]

Alexander Mackenzie: Some honourable gentlemen have asserted, and truly asserted, that this measure is not as perfect as it might have been—and that it is not as complete as some of us might have desired it to be ... But, where there are two great parties in a nation—as there have been with us—it is quite clear that, when they agree to effect a settlement of the constitutional difficulties which have separated them, this can only be accomplished by mutual compromise to a greater or less extent. And the true question to be determined in this discussion, and by the vote at the close of this debate, is this— whether this is a fair compromise or not. I am prepared to say it is perhaps as fair as could reasonably be expected, and I have therefore no hesitation in giving it all the support in my power. (Hear, hear.) In its main features it is the very scheme which was proposed by the Toronto convention—only carried to a greater extent than the convention thought advisable or possible at the time. The speeches which were delivered at that convention, as well as the resolutions which were passed, showed clearly that it was the opinion of the delegates there present that a Confederation of the whole provinces would be desirable, if it were possible to attain it as speedily as they expected they could obtain a federation of the two provinces of Canada ...

Personally, I have always been in favour of a legislative union where it can be advantageously worked. If it could be adapted to our circumstances in these colonies, I would at this moment be in favour of a legislative union as the best system of government. I believe that is the general opinion of the people in the west. But it is the duty of every public man to shape his course ... according to the circumstances which may prevail locally. And it is quite clear that, if the legislative union could not be worked well with Upper and Lower Canada, it would work still worse with the other provinces brought in. There remained, therefore, in my opinion, no other alternative than to adopt the federal principle, or to dissolve entirely the connection which exists between Upper and Lower Canada at the present moment; and that I would look upon as one of the greatest calamities which could befall us. Even if this scheme were more objectionable than it is ... I would without hesitation accept Confederation rather than dissolution. (Hear, hear.) ...

It is reasonable and just to insert a provision in the scheme that will put it out of the power of any party to act unjustly. If the power that the central authority is to have—of vetoing the doings of the local legislature—is used, it will be ample, I think, to prevent anything of that kind. But the veto itself is objected to ... Well, sir, under the British Constitution, in all British colonies, and in Great Britain itself, there is a certain elasticity to be presumed. Everything is not provided for, because a great deal is trusted to the common sense of the people. I think it is quite fair and safe to assert that there is not the slightest danger that the federal parliament will perpetrate any injustice upon the local legislatures, because it would cause such a reaction as to compass the destruction of the power thus exercised. The veto power is necessary in order that the general government may have a control over the proceedings of the local legislatures to a certain extent. The want of this power was the great source of weakness in the United States. So long as each state considered itself sovereign, whose acts and laws could not be called in question, it was quite clear that the central authority was destitute of power to compel obedience to general laws. If each province were able to enact such laws as it pleased, everybody would be at the mercy of the local legislatures, and the general legislature would become of little importance. It is contended that the power of the general legislature should be held in check by a veto power ... resident in the local legislatures, respecting the application of general laws to their jurisdiction. All power, they say, comes from the people and ascends through them to their representatives, and through the representatives to the crown. But it would never do to set the local above the general government. The central parliament and government must, of necessity, exercise the supreme power, and the local governments will have the exercise of power corresponding to the duties they have to perform. The system is a new and untried one, and may not work so harmoniously as we now anticipate, but there will always be power in the British parliament and our own to remedy any defects that may be discovered after the system is in operation.

—*Legislative Assembly, February 23, 1865*

▲ Document 3: Maps of Canada, 1849 and 1867

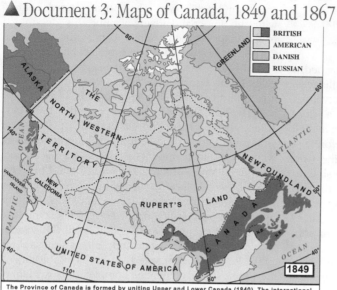

	BRITISH
	AMERICAN
	DANISH
	RUSSIAN

1849

The Province of Canada is formed by uniting Upper and Lower Canada (1840). The international boundary from the Rocky Mountains to the Pacific is described by the Oregon Treaty (1846). The northern portion of the Oregon Territory is called New Caledonia, a name used by Simon Fraser in 1806. The Hudson's Bay Co. is granted Vancouver's Island to develop a colony (1849).

● In mid-19th century North America, British possessions were extended across all of present-day Canada, although only small portions of the territory were actually organized into colonies. These included Vancouver Island on the West Coast, and Canada, New Brunswick, Nova Scotia, Prince Edward Island, and Newfoundland on the East Coast.

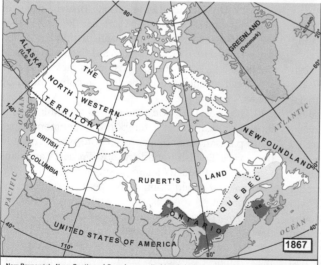

1867

New Brunswick, Nova Scotia and Canada are united in a federal state, the Dominion of Canada, by the British North America Act (July 1, 1867). The province of Canada is divided into Ontario and Quebec. The United States of America proclaims the purchase of Alaska from Russia (June 20).

● Confederation in 1867 redrew some of the boundaries, and established four new provinces—Ontario, Quebec, New Brunswick, and Nova Scotia. Can you see why geography had a great deal to do with the decision to adopt a federal system?

Source: Maps from 1849 and 1867, http://www.collectionscanada.gc.ca/confederation/023001–5000–e.html.

■ Article 1: Confederation

Peter Russell

By the early 1860s Canadian politics had reached a point of deadlock between two sectional alliances: the alliance of John A. Macdonald's Conservatives and George-Etienne Cartier's *Bleus*, with a clear majority in Canada East, was almost evenly matched by the combination of George Brown's Reformers, a growing force in Canada West, and Antoine Dorion's anticlerical *Rouges* in Canada East. English Canadians who had readily accepted equality for the two sections of Canada at the beginning of the union period, when Canada East was considerably larger than Canada West, began to embrace a different principle of political justice once the population ratios were reversed. When Canada West's population came to surpass Canada East's in the 1850s, Brown's cause of 'rep by pop' (representation by population) became increasingly popular with English Canadians and increasingly threatening to French Canadians, who, though still a majority in the eastern section of the province, were now just a third of the Canadian population. Anyone who contemplates a binational, double majority system as the solution to Canada's present discontents should consider the frustrations and animosities generated by such a scheme during the union period.

Much ink has been spilled on whether Confederation was a compact. The compact theory, as we shall see, developed after Confederation.[1] Provincial premiers would base their claim that the Constitution could not be changed without their consent on the argument that Confederation was a contract or treaty between the founding provinces. Defenders of Quebec's right to a constitutional veto would argue that Confederation was based on a compact between the English and the French, Canada's 'two founding peoples.' Historians have had no difficulty in showing that, in a strict legal sense, Confederation could not have been a contract because, in 1867, neither the original provinces nor their people had

Source: Russell, P. (2004), "Confederation" from *Constitutional Odyssey: Can Canadians Become a Sovereign People?* Third Edition, pp. 17–33. © University of Toronto Press Inc., 2004. Reprinted with permission from the publisher.

sovereign legal power. That power rested entirely with the imperial Parliament. But this debunking of the compact theory tends to miss the point that Confederation was based on a political agreement—a deal—first between English and French political elites in the Canadas and then between those Canadians and their Maritime counterparts.

The first stage of this deal occurred in June 1864 when George Brown and his Upper Canadian Clear Grits agreed to participate in a coalition government with their bitter opponents, John A. Macdonald, George-Etienne Cartier, and their Liberal-Conservative followers.[2] Since March 1864 Brown had chaired a parliamentary committee examining various approaches to constitutional reform. This committee ... had at best lukewarm support from the various parties. Macdonald, Cartier, and Galt, as well as some of the Reform leaders, voted against its establishment. Nonetheless, the committee completed its work and, on 14 June 1864, reported that a federal system (for the two Canadas or for all of British North America) was strongly favoured as the solution to Canada's constitutional impasse. A few hours later the Macdonald-Taché coalition was defeated on a vote of confidence. Instead of forcing a dissolution of Parliament and yet another election, Brown, together with some other key Upper Canadian Reformers—to the total amazement of the political pundits of the day—agreed to join Macdonald and Cartier in a Great Coalition solely for the purpose of achieving a constitutional solution along the lines recommended by Brown's committee.

The Great Coalition represented something much more significant than a temporary agreement to set aside partisan differences. At its core was a recognition that if English Canadians and French Canadians were to continue to share a single state, the English majority could control the general or common government so long as the French were a majority in a province with exclusive jurisdiction over those matters essential to their distinct culture. This constitutional agreement was indeed a compromise. For many English Canadians (certainly for John A. Macdonald), federalism was an American abomination, a clear second choice to a unitary state. Not many English Canadians were committed to the long-term survival of French Canadians as a distinct collectivity. On the other side, many French Canadians, including the *rouge* leaders, saw the proposed federation as a sell-out, the latest in a long line of attempts to bring about the 'annihilation of the French race in Canada.'[3] Nonetheless, acceptance of a federal solution was the only possible basis on which leaders from the two sections of Canada could work together on a constitutional accord.

Brown's committee left open the question whether a federation of the two Canadas or of British North America as a whole should be the priority. Brown himself was so anxious to obtain justice for Upper Canada that he preferred the smaller project, since it would be easier to attain. But Macdonald and the Conservatives in the coalition had their eyes set on the larger vision and insisted that it be immediately pursued. An opportunity to do just that was at hand—a forthcoming conference of Maritime leaders to discuss Maritime union. And so the stage was set for the second part of the Confederation deal when Lord Monck, the Canadian governor general, on 30 June 1864 wrote to the lieutenant-governors or administrators of the Maritime provinces asking permission for a delegation from Canada to attend the conference on Maritime union.

Constitutional politics in the Maritimes had been moving in advance of events in Canada. On 28 March 1864 the Legislative Assembly of Nova Scotia adopted Charles Tupper's motion to appoint up to five delegates to meet with representatives of New Brunswick and Prince Edward Island 'for the purpose of arranging a preliminary plan for the union of the three provinces under one government and legislature.'[4] In April, similar motions were passed by the New Brunswick and Prince Edward Island assemblies. The idea of holding a conference on Maritime union did not arise from a ground swell of public opinion. As Creighton summarized the situation, 'It had been strongly resisted in one province, and accepted without any enthusiasm and with a good deal of sceptical indifference in the other two.'[5] Its most enthusiastic supporters were a few business-oriented politicians, who thought it would improve the prospects of an intercolonial rail link, and some imperial officials, who hoped it might be the first step to a larger union of the North American colonies.

Confederation would probably not have occurred without the pushing and prodding of the British Colonial Office and its field officers, the colonial governors. At this stage in the evolution of the British Empire, imperial policy-makers had come to the sensible conclusion that Britain's interests in the North American hemisphere could be more efficiently secured if its scattered colonies were brought together in a more self-reliant political union. Even though the imperial government possessed a full and uncontested legal sovereignty over the colonies, it was no longer willing to use this power in a coercive manner. The Duke of Newcastle, colonial secretary during these critical years, articulated the constitutional convention of the day: 'The initiative in all important internal changes in the colonies must lie with the colonists themselves.'[6] The colonial governors could encourage and throw the formidable weight of their office behind politicians whose ideas were in line with imperial policy; they could manipulate, but they would not dictate. Still, without the coaching, prodding, and fixing of imperial officials, Confederation would probably not have occurred. In the constitutional politics of our own time, for better or for worse, there is really no legitimate counterpart of this imperial steering force.

Through the summer of 1864 the eight members of the Canadian coalition cabinet hammered out a plan for a federal union of British North America. This was the plan they would present at the conference on Maritime union, scheduled for Charlottetown in September. As it turned out, this plan contained the basic elements of the constitution of the new Canada that would come into existence three years hence.

While the politicians were debating and drafting behind the closed doors of the cabinet room, the numerous and lively newspapers of the day carried on a spirited constitutional debate.[7] Among newspapers generally supportive of federation, the fundamental question concerned the division of powers. Today's Canadians will say, Was it not always so? The politicians then, like those of today, were not above using newspaper opinion to bolster their position in constitutional bargaining. Thus, we find George Brown's *Globe* insisting that in the federal system being planned, 'the local governments shall be delegated governments and ... the "sovereign" power shall be vested in the general or federal government.'[8] On the other hand, *La Minerve* was typical of French-Canadian *bleu* papers supporting Cartier and Taché in claiming that under the new federal arrangements, 'Il [le Bas-Canada] aura son gouvernement particulier dont l'autorité s'étendra à tous les objets qui suivent le cours ordinaire des affaires, intéressant de la vie, la liberté et la prosperité des citoyens ... il sera maître chez lui en tout ce qui regarde son économie sociale, civile et religieuse.'[9]

At this crucial stage in constitution making, the coalition cabinet members were not prepared to disclose how they were balancing these conflicting outlooks on the structure of the new federation. They did not want to risk a public row over the details of their constitutional plan. Elite accommodation, the mechanism of consociational democracy, was the order of the day.

At the public level, an attempt was made to forge stronger social links between Canadians and Maritimers. At the very time that the coalition cabinet was hammering out its proposals in the Quebec cabinet room, a delegation of about a hundred Canadians—politicians, journalists, and interested citizens—was travelling through New Brunswick and Nova Scotia. With D'Arcy McGee as their chief troubadour, the Canadians served as Confederation missionaries, mixing with Maritimers at scores of picnics, dinners, and oratorical concerts. They did not debate the constitutional details of the Confederation scheme but endeavoured to kindle Maritimers' interest in becoming part of a larger political community. In this, they clearly had some success. When the *Queen Victoria* sailed into Charlottetown's harbour on 1 September 1864 with eight members of the Canadian Coalition cabinet on board, Maritime interest in the approaching constitutional conference was beginning to match Canada's.

As an instrument for constitution making, the Charlottetown Conference was somewhere between a first ministers' meeting and a constituent assembly of the kind proposed by populist critics in the post-Meech era. This was not a conference of ordinary citizens. All the delegates were politicians—indeed, most were experienced politicians. Included in their ranks were the first ministers or leaders of the largest party and, with the one exception of the Lower Canadian *Rouges*, 'the principal leaders on both sides of politics.'[10] That indeed was a key to success: co-opting political opponents into the negotiating process reduced the political vulnerability of the constitutional proposals that emerged from the conference.

At this stage in their negotiations, the twenty-three delegates (five each from New Brunswick, Nova Scotia, and Prince Edward Island, plus the eight Canadians) did not expose their deliberations to public scrutiny. For five days they met behind the closed doors of Prince Edward Island's Legislative Council chamber. From the outset the Canadians dominated the conference. Brown, Cartier, Macdonald, and the other coalition ministers laid out their plan for a federal union during the first four days. The plan had three basic elements: first, a division of legislative powers that reversed the American system, with the residual power (those powers not explicitly mentioned) assigned to the general (central) legislature; second, a two-chamber federal parliament, with an elected lower house based on rep by pop and an appointed upper house based on sectional (regional) equality, where Canada's two sections and the Maritimes each counted as a section; and, third, a central government that would take over the debts and some of the assets of the provinces.

By the fifth and final day of the Charlottetown Conference it was clear that the second part of the Confederation deal was nearly consummated. While the Maritimers had not accepted all the details of the Canadians' scheme, they did agree to set aside the Maritime union project and to make a federal union of British North America their constitutional priority. On 10 September 1864, three days after the close of the conference, the delegates assembled again in Halifax, where they decided to hold another conference in October at Quebec. At this next meeting they would focus on the confederation of British North America, and invite a delegation from Newfoundland.

The Quebec Conference was structured along the same lines as the meeting at Charlottetown. Again the delegations included both government and opposition leaders. An exception was Newfoundland, whose two delegates, F.B.T. Carter and Ambrose Shea, were not government members—a fact that did not help the prospects of confederation in Newfoundland. The delegations varied in size: Nova Scotia had five members, New Brunswick and Prince Edward island each had seven, and the Canadians were now represented by all twelve members of the coalition cabinet. Each delegation had a vote, except for Canada, which had two. So, in principle, the Atlantic colonies could outvote the Canadians two to one. The thirty-three politicians squeezed into the reading room of Quebec's Legislative Council, where once again the entire discussion took place behind closed doors.

In that stuffy chamber in Québec City over a two-week period in October 1864, details of the new Canadian federation's Constitution were worked out in the form of seventy-two resolutions. The Quebec Resolutions cover nearly all of what was to be contained in the BNA Act. Little was added or changed in the subsequent negotiations and enactment in London.

Most of the constitutional debate at Quebec—and indeed in Canada ever since—concerned the federal aspects of the Constitution. Here is where the British North Americans had to be creative. They were departing from Britain's unitary system and, with the United States in the throes of civil war, the only federal system they knew, the American, seemed thoroughly flawed. Their earlier decision to give the residual power to the central rather than the local legislatures aimed at reversing what many regarded as the most dangerously decentralizing feature of the American Constitution. At Quebec they now spelled out in detailed lists the 'exclusive' legislative powers of both the provinces and the new Canadian Parliament. This may well have muddied the waters, for even though the list of federal legislative powers was simply to be illustrative of the federal Parliament's power 'to make Laws for the Peace, Order, and good Government of Canada, in relation to all Matters not coming within the Classes of Subjects ... assigned exclusively to the Legislatures of the provinces,' the listed powers would come under judicial interpretation to overshadow the general power. Among the explicit federal powers were many of what were then considered the main functions of government: defence, criminal law, trade and commerce, banking, currency, shipping, and interprovincial transportation. But the legislative powers assigned exclusively to the provinces were by no means negligible. They included 'Property and Civil Rights in the Province,' a phrase meant to cover the components of Quebec's civil law (most of the private, commercial, and family law), as well as education, hospitals, and other social welfare activities. The provinces were also given ownership of their lands and natural resources. Two areas, agriculture and immigration, were designated as concurrent fields of legislation, with federal law prevailing in the event of a conflict.

Other features of the structure gave the new federal government a paramount role. Under the fiscal arrangements, the federal government would have access to all modes of taxation while the provinces were confined to 'direct taxation,' licence fees, and royalties. The provinces could not levy customs and excise duties, which at the time constituted 83 per cent of the colonies' revenues.[11] The constitution-makers never conceived of direct taxes on personal and corporate income becoming the milch cow of public finance. The fiscal dependency of the provinces was underlined by building in a complex set of federal subsidies 'in full settlement of all future demands on Canada'—words that should make the Fathers of Confederation blush a little in their graves.

The judicial system was also federally dominated. The key courts for the new federation would be the existing superior, district, and county courts of the provinces, but the judges of these courts would be appointed, paid, and subject to removal by the federal government and Parliament. As for a supreme court, the colonial politicians were happy to carry on with the highest court in the empire, the Judicial Committee of the Privy Council, as Canada's final court of appeal, but if and when a general court of appeal was established for Canada, it would be created by the federal Parliament.

Considerably more contentious was the importation of an element of imperial structure into the federal plan. Just as the British government appointed the Canadian governor general, the federal government would appoint the provincial lieutenant-governors. The lieutenant-governor (in parallel with the governor general's power over federal legislation) could reserve legislation passed by provincial legislatures for consideration by the federal government. Further, just as the British government retained the power to disallow (veto) legislation passed by the federal Parliament, the federal government could disallow provincial legislation. The federal powers of reservation and disallowance were surely the sharpest deviation from the federal principle of government. Their inclusion in the Constitution is a clear indication that many of the constitutional architects, and none more than John A. Macdonald, preferred unitary to federal government.

The point of federal structure that proved most troublesome and took the most time to resolve was the federal Senate. Prince Edward Island and the United Province of Canada had recently shifted from the British tradition of an appointed upper house to an elected second chamber. Some delegates now pressed for a Senate that was directly elected or, as the American Senate then was, elected by the provincial legislatures. The balance of power within all the delegations lay with those who favoured the British parliamentary structure, and the Senate provided for in the Quebec Resolutions was a body appointed for life by the federal government, with full legislative powers except for the introduction of money bills. Even more contentious was the distribution of Senate seats among the provinces. With Newfoundland at the table, the Atlantic delegates now argued that their four provinces should have thirty-two senators—six more than Ontario's and Quebec's twenty-four. In the end, the principle of sectional equality was maintained by a resolution giving twenty-four each to Ontario, Quebec, and the three Maritime provinces (ten each for New Brunswick and Nova Scotia, and four for Prince Edward Island), with a vague promise of 'additional representatives' for Newfoundland.[12] The need for Senate reform was built into the very foundations of Confederation.

While the Constitution drafted at Quebec covered the new federal system in detail, it was relatively silent on other matters that have become of great importance to Canadian constitutionalists. The Fathers of Confederation expressed absolutely no interest in a bill of abstract natural rights. They were prepared, however, to afford constitutional protection to rights or interests that experience had shown were necessary for the peaceable coexistence of two distinct cultural communities. First, the English were assured of the right to use their language in the legislative and judicial institutions of Quebec, where they would be a minority, and the French were given a reciprocal right to use their language in the federal legislature and courts.[13] Second, the denominational schools of the Protestant minority in Quebec and the Catholic minority in Ontario would continue to function on the basis already provided for in law.[14] These two provisions for minority rights were not the only manifestations of cultural dualism in the new Constitution. Another dimension of dualism was the differential treatment of Quebec. Quebec, with its distinctive civil law, was exempt from a clause that envisaged the common law provinces eventually permitting the federal Parliament to take over their jurisdiction over property and civil rights.[15] Special provisions also governed the qualifications of Quebec judges and the appointment of Quebec

senators.[16] Quebec, however, was not the only province to have differential treatment. New Brunswick received a special subsidy over and beyond those provided for the other provinces.[17] The Fathers of Confederation were not strict believers in the principle of provincial equality.

The constitution drafters saw no need to spell out the vital democratic principle that government be directed by ministers who have the confidence of the elected branch of the legislature. Formally, all executive power in both levels of government would 'be vested in the Queen'—a system that has persisted to the present day.[18] The principle of responsible government would continue to depend on unwritten constitutional convention. The only hint of responsible government in the final constitutional text is the reference in the preamble to the BNA Act to a 'Constitution similar in Principle to that of the United Kingdom.'[19]

Aside from some minor changes which each level of government could make on its own, the new Constitution was totally silent on the question of amendment. This void was to be expected. … [T]he Fathers of Confederation assumed throughout that Canada's Constitution would take the form of an imperial statute and, as such, would be formally amended by the British Parliament. Philosophically, this arrangement did not trouble them, nor did they see it as posing any practical problems. Canada's founding fathers suffered even more than the usual hubris that afflicts constitution-makers. As John A. Macdonald was later to explain to Canada's Legislative Assembly, the constitutional drafting was so thorough and detailed that 'we have avoided all conflict of jurisdiction and authority.'[20] Again, posthumous blushes are in order.

With the signing of the Quebec Resolutions on 27 October 1864, substantive constitution making was nearly complete. There were still, however, important political and legal steps to be taken before the Constitution could be put into effect. The seventieth resolution stated that 'the sanction of the imperial and local parliaments shall be sought for the Union of the Provinces on the principles adopted by the Conference.'[21] Enactment of the Constitution by the imperial Parliament was the essential, final legal step. Approval by the colonial legislatures was a political, not a legal imperative. Still, for politicians living under the constraints of responsible government, it was important to secure legislative support for their constitutional plan.

For some commentators of the day, approval by the legislature was not a strong enough measure of popular support. While there were no calls for a referendum or a directly elected constituent assembly, a number of newspapers in Canada West and New Brunswick insisted that sweeping constitutional changes should not be made until they had been tested in a general election.[22] The leading politicians in Canada, including Reform leader George Brown, brushed these demands aside: 'A general election on such an issue, they argued, would be nothing more or less than a plebiscite; and a plebiscite was a dreadful republican heresy, French or American in origin, which would violate all the principles of parliamentary government, without the slightest beneficial result.'[23]

The seventy-two resolutions were debated in both houses of the Canadian legislature. The debate extended over a period of six weeks, from early February to mid March 1865. It was, by any standard, a brilliant debate—by far the best record of the hopes, dreams, and fears of those who supported and those who opposed Confederation. In the end, the supporters of Confederation carried the day, but only after withstanding searing criticism of flaws and inconsistencies in the constitutional plan, especially from the *Rouges* who, as French Canadians, viewed support of the scheme as amounting to treason. The Quebec Resolutions (like the Meech Lake Accord many years later) was a carefully negotiated package deal, so no amendments were allowed. The overall majority in favour of the resolutions was 91 to 33,[24] but support was much stronger among members from Canada West, who favoured Confederation 56 to 6, as compared with members from Canada East, who voted 37 to 25 in favour. Among French-Canadian members the vote was even closer, with 27 for and 21 opposed—a clear majority, but hardly a ringing endorsement from the French component of the political elite.

New Brunswick was the only colony in which Confederation was submitted to the people in an election. Indeed, New Brunswickers went to the polls twice to decide contests between confederates and anti-confederates. In each case it was New Brunswick's mercurial lieutenant-governor, Arthur Gordon, not the politicians, who forced the appeal to the people. Gordon did not like the confederation plan because it did not go far enough in giving absolute paramountcy to the federal government. He threatened to dismiss the pro-Confederation administration headed by Samuel Tilley and appoint other ministers, unless Tilley agreed to hold an election before submitting the Quebec Resolutions to the legislature. Tilley agreed to a dissolution. In the ensuing election, which was conducted at the very time the Canadian legislature was debating Confederation, Tilley and his confederate colleagues were defeated, winning only eleven of forty-one seats. Just over a year later, Gordon, now under strict instructions from the Colonial Office to have Confederation submitted to the legislature, forced the resignation of anti-confederate ministers and dissolved the legislature. This time, the case for a stronger British North American union was bolstered by the massing of Fenians along New Brunswick's border, and the confederates triumphed, taking all but eight of the forty-one seats. Even so, the Quebec Resolutions, although approved by New Brunswick's appointed Legislative Council, were never submitted to its elected assembly.

While Confederation was limping to victory in New Brunswick, it was being pushed off the political agenda in the two island colonies, Prince Edward Island and Newfoundland. On the last day of March 1865 Prince Edward Island's Legislative Assembly, by a vote of 23 to 5, passed a motion rejecting the Quebec Resolutions. The motion had been moved by the premier, J.C. Pope, who had not attended the Quebec Conference.[25] Earlier in that same month, Newfoundland's Legislative Assembly adopted Premier Hugh Hoyles's motion to postpone a decision on Confederation until after the next general election. Although many of the pro-confederation politicians were returned in the election held later in the year, they were considerably outnumbered by those who were opposed or doubtful.[26] Despite considerable pressure from the Colonial Office and the St John's newspapers, Newfoundland's coalition government was not prepared to proceed with Confederation.

In Newfoundland and Prince Edward Island, the politics of Confederation were worked out in a relatively democratic fashion—albeit with a negative outcome. This was not so in Nova Scotia, where opposition to Confederation was, if anything, more intense and articulate than in either of the island colonies. Opposition in Nova Scotia was not to the general idea of a British North American union. Indeed, for that idea, with particular emphasis on the *British* nature of such a union, there was considerable support. Criticism focused on the Quebec Resolutions and especially on the alleged weaknesses of any system of federal government.[27] The anticonfederates found an eminent spokesman in Joseph Howe, a former premier and major force in Nova Scotian politics for over thirty years, who at the time of Confederation was serving as an imperial fisheries officer. Criticism of the Quebec Resolutions dominated a lengthy legislative debate in the Nova Scotia legislature in the early spring of 1865. But the premier, Charles Tupper, was able to avoid a direct test of the Confederation scheme by seeking approval only for Maritime union. A year later, when the Confederation issue was forced by the opposition, with imperial connivance, he managed to corral enough support to win approval not for the Quebec Resolutions but for sending delegates 'to arrange with the imperial government a scheme of union which will effectually ensure just provision for the rights and interests of this Province.'[28]

The Quebec Resolutions were never approved by the Nova Scotia legislature. Indeed, the first time Nova Scotians had an opportunity to give a popular verdict on Confederation they left no doubt about where they stood. In September 1867 in the first Canadian general election, the anti-confederates took eighteen out of nineteen Nova Scotia seats and, in the provincial election, thirty-six out of thirty-eight seats in the Nova Scotia assembly. By then, however, Confederation was a fait accompli.

The implication of Tupper's motion that a new basis for British North American union could be negotiated from scratch had no basis for reality. Macdonald, Cartier, and the other members of the Canadian coalition had no intention of touching their delicate constitutional compromise. If there was any suggestion that the Quebec Resolutions were open to significant amendment, French Canada, in Creighton's words, 'would undoubtedly rise in violent protest.'[29] At the same time, the Canadian politicians did not dare admit publicly that the Quebec scheme was a sealed compact for fear of undermining the cause of Confederation in the Maritimes, which in both Nova Scotia and New Brunswick depended on the credibility of negotiating a different basis for union. The lack of consensus within the Confederation movement was therefore papered over by the political elites.

In December 1866 sixteen of these leaders (six from the Canadas, five each from New Brunswick and Nova Scotia) met for the third Confederation conference in a London hotel room close by the Westminster Parliament. The object of this meeting was not to renegotiate the Quebec Resolutions but to consider some minor modifications and tidying up of loose ends. The only change in the division of powers was to give the federal Parliament, rather than the provinces, jurisdiction over 'Sea Coast and Inland Fisheries.' The Maritime provinces gained a modest increase in their per capita subsidies. Religious minorities in all the provinces were given the right to appeal to the federal government against provincial laws affecting their denominational school rights. A final push by Ontario reformers for an elected Senate was of no avail. The only change made in the structure of the federal upper house was to provide for the appointment of extra senators to break a deadlock between the two houses—a constitutional provision that most Canadians did not realize existed until it was used for the first time in 1990.[30]

With the conclusion of the London conference, the constitution was entirely in imperial hands. Only one further significant change was made—the formal name of the new country. The Fathers of Confederation had favoured the title Kingdom of Canada, but left the final choice to Queen Victoria. It was the Americans who effectively vetoed the monarchical title of kingdom. In their ignorance of the principles of constitutional monarchy they objected to the founding of anything so blatantly non-republican on their border. The Queen then chose the British Americans' second choice: Dominion of Canada. Although this title held out the expansive promise of the Seventy-second Psalm's 'He shall have dominion also from sea to sea,' it struck the British prime minister, Lord Derby, as 'rather absurd.'[31]

In February 1867 the Canadian Constitution, in the form of the British North America Act, was introduced in the House of Lords by the colonial secretary, Lord Carnarvon. The attention of British politicians at the time was fastened on a major development in Britain's constitutional politics, the Second Reform Bill. There was a desultory debate as a handful of Canadian politicians watched the BNA Act go through the two Houses of Parliament. The most vigorous attack came from the few parliamentarians moved by Joseph Howe's petition (supposedly bearing thirty thousand signatures) to postpone further action on the Canadian Constitution until it had been submitted to the people of Nova Scotia in the approaching general election. On 8 March 1867 the BNA Act passed third reading in the House of Commons. It received royal assent on 29 March and was proclaimed in effect on 1 July 1867.

The Dominion of Canada was born, but the constitutional process that brought it into existence provided a thin and uncertain foundation for the birth of a people. True, elected politicians played the leading role in putting the Constitution together, but they were elected on a restricted franchise that excluded unpropertied males and all women.[32] Further, the dominant members, both English and French, showed not the slightest intention of submitting their constitutional handiwork to the people. At the elite level, the process of Confederation produced a wide-based and practical, though not philosophical accord; at the popular level, however, it did not produce a political community with a clear sense of itself. In the language of political science, Canada in 1867 'must be viewed essentially as a political unit that had become amalgamated without necessarily achieving integration.'[33]

For the aboriginal peoples affected by Confederation, the new Constitution was entirely an imperial imposition. There was no thought among the constitution-makers of consulting with the native peoples living on the territory encompassed by the BNA Act, nor did any of the legislative bodies that dealt with the Constitution represent these peoples. The Royal Proclamation of 1763, British North America's first constitution, enacted that the native peoples 'should not be molested or disturbed' on their hunting grounds in the territory reserved to them until the Crown purchased 'their' lands by a treaty of cession. This fundamental aboriginal right was recognized in the subsequent treaties between the British Crown and the aboriginal nations. Although the Royal Proclamation continued as part of Canadian law, the rights it recognized were not explicitly included in the BNA Act.[34] In the 1867 constitution, 'Indians, and Lands reserved for the Indians' were mentioned only as a subject of federal jurisdiction.[35] Aboriginal peoples were treated as subjects, not citizens, of the new dominion.

Not even among the small cadre of politicians who pushed through the Confederation plan was there a clear and common conception of the new nation they were building. As Eugene Forsey was tireless in pointing out, they all recognized they were establishing a new nation-state.[36] Their Constitution provided for the completion of a continental state stretching from Newfoundland to British Columbia,[37] and the lure of performing in this larger political arena was part of their shared vision. But while the Fathers of Confederation thought of themselves as nation-builders, they did not share a common vision of the essential nature of the nation they were building. A few like Cartier espoused the idea, daring in that day, of forming a new 'political nationality' based on deep 'racial' diversity—a society in which "British and French Canadians alike could appreciate and understand their position relative to each other … placed like great families beside each other.'[38] As we have seen, there were marks of this dualistic view of Canada in the new Constitution. But there were just as many Fathers of Confederation, especially in English Canada, who did not share Cartier's ideal of a culturally pluralist nation and who still harboured Lord Durham's dream of building a British North American nation. These Fathers of Confederation could empathize with George Brown, who, writing to his wife at the end of the Quebec Conference, exclaimed: 'Is it not wonderful? French Canadianism entirely extinguished!'[39]

In 1867 there was no need to agree on the fundamental nature of the new Canadian nation because the final custodian of its Constitution was not the Canadian political community but the imperial Parliament. Imperial stewardship of Canada's constitutional politics made it relatively easy to inaugurate Confederation. A new country could be founded without having to risk finding out if its politically active citizens agreed to the principles on which its Constitution was to be based. But if this was a gift, it was a tainted gift. The Confederation compromise was sheltered from the strain of a full public review in all sections of the country, but at the cost of not forming a political community with a clear sense of its constituent and controlling elements. Thus, at Canada's founding, its people were not sovereign, and there was not even a sense that a constituent sovereign people would have to be invented.

Notes

1. For a discussion of the compact theory and its current relevance see Robert C. Vipond, 'Whatever

Became of the Compact Theory? Meech Lake and the New Politics of Constitutional Amendment in Canada,' Queen's Quarterly, 96 (1989): 793.

2. For a detailed account of the events leading to Confederation see Creighton, *Road to Confederation* (Toronto: Macmillan of Canada, 1964).

3. The words are from the newspaper, *Le Pays*, and are quoted in A.I. Silver (Toronto: University of Toronto Press 1982), 38.

4. Creighton, *Road to Confederation*, 32.

5. Ibid., 35.

6. Ibid., 20.

7. For an account of newspaper coverage of Confederation see P.B. Waite, *The Life and Times of Confederation, 1864–1867: Politics, Newspapers, and the Union of British North America*, 2nd ed. (Toronto: University of Toronto Press 1962).

8. Creighton, *Road to Confederation*, 98.

9. Waite, *Life and Times of Confederation*, 139.

10. Creighton, *Road to Confederation*, 188.

11. R. MacGregor Dawson, *The Government of Canada*, 4th ed., revised by Norman Ward (Toronto: University of Toronto Press 1966), 105.

12. Creighton, *Road to Confederation*, 152.

13. Section 133 of the BNA Act.

14. Section 93 of the BNA Act.

15. Section 94 of the BNA Act.

16. Sections 98 and 22 of the BNA Act.

17. Section 119 of the BNA Act. That section is now spent.

18. Section 9 of the Constitution Act, 1867 (the new title of the BNA Act) states that 'the Executive Government and Authority of and over Canada is hereby declared to continue and be vested in the Queen.'

19. Besides responsible government, the other principle incorporated in this phrase is the independence of the judiciary.

20. P.B. Waite, ed., *The Confederation Debates in the Province of Canada, 1865* (Toronto: McClelland and Stewart 1963), 44.

21. Creighton, *Road to Confederation*, 187.

22. Waite, *Life and Times of Confederation*, 122.

23. Creighton, *Road to Confederation*, 189–90.

24. For an analysis see Waite, ed., *Confederation Debates*, xviii.

25. His older brother, W.H. Pope, had attended the Quebec Conference, but in the legislature went no further than proposing that the Island put off its decision until the terms of union had been submitted to the people in a general election.

26. Waite, Life and Times of Confederation, 173.

27. For an analysis see 'The Opposition to Confederation in Nova Scotia, 1864–1868,' in Ged Martin, *The Causes of Confederation* (Fredericton: Acadiensis Press 1990), 114–29.

28. Creighton, *Road to Confederation*, 366.

29. Ibid., 381.

30. The original section 26 provided that the Queen, on the advice of the governor general, could appoint three or six senators (representing equally the three Senate divisions, Ontario, Quebec, and the Maritimes). This was amended in 1915 to provide for four or eight extra senators to accommodate a fourth Senate division consisting of the four western provinces. The Mulroney government used the provision, for the first time ever, in 1990 to ensure passage of its Goods and Services Tax Bill.

31. Creighton, *Road to Confederation*, 424.

32. The first federal election following Confederation was based on the provincial election laws. It is estimated that, on average, about 15 per cent of the population of the four original provinces was eligible to vote. See Reginald Whitaker, 'Democracy and the Canadian Constitution,' in Keith Banting and Richard Simeon, eds., *And No One Cheered: Federalism, Democracy and the Constitution Act* (Toronto: Methuen 1983), 245.

33. Ralph C. Nelson, Walter C. Soderlund, Ronald H. Wagenberg, and E. Donald Briggs, 'Canadian Confederation as a Case Study in Community Formation,' in Ged Martin, ed., *Causes of Confederation*, 85.

34. For an account of the Proclamation and its continuing relevancy in Canada's constitutional system see Bruce Clark, *Native Liberty, Crown Sovereignty: The Existing Aboriginal Right to Self-Government in Canada* (Montreal and Kingston: McGill-Queen's University Press 1990).

35. Section 91(24) of the BNA Act.

36. See, especially, Eugene Forsey, *A Life on the Fringe: The Memoirs of Eugene Forsey* (Toronto: Oxford University Press 1990), chap. 11.

37. Section 146 of the BNA Act.

38. These words are from his contribution to the Confederation Debates. Waite, ed., *Confederation Debates*, 50–1.

39. J.M.S. Careless, *Brown of the Globe* (Toronto: Macmillan 1963), vol. 2, 171.

■ Article 2: Confederation and the Federal Principle

P. B. Waite

Confederation was to be a reality in 1865. Before all else was the determination of the leaders of the movement—Brown, Cartier, Macdonald, Tupper, Tilley, Gray—to strike while the iron was hot. Every delegation to the [Quebec] Conference had represented the two major parties in each colony, and while no one was very sure of Prince Edward Island, Carter and Shea from Newfoundland seemed optimistic and Tupper of Nova Scotia and Tilley of New Brunswick had some cause to be. In Nova Scotia and New Brunswick there seemed no reason why the combined power of the two parties should not be effective. The expiry of the life of the New Brunswick legislature in June, 1865, and that of the Newfoundland legislature in October, 1865, was inconvenient; elections would come too soon to be sure of public opinion. But Tilley and Shea were sanguine of success, and Tupper was, if anything, more so. All was to be in readiness by the spring. Then, Tilley assumed, Confederation would be "a fixed fact."[1] The timetable was breathtaking: Brown was to go at once to England; Galt (and perhaps Brydges) were to go to the Maritimes to discuss the Intercolonial in relation to the existing railway assets of Nova Scotia and New Brunswick.[2] [Alexander Galt was another "father of confederation," a Conservative from Canada East, and C. J. Brydges was the manager of the Grand Trunk railway.] Moreover, the imperial government's enthusiastic approval of the scheme, soon to be forthcoming, was warrant that the full power of the Colonial Office would be placed at the disposal of Confederation. The imperial government would, if requested, legislate the provinces into union in the summer of 1865.[3] "The time is short," wrote Cardwell to MacDonnell, on December 8, 1864. [Edward Cardwell, 1st Viscount Cardwell, was a British politician who, between 1864 and 1866, was Secretary of State for the Colonies in the Colonial

Office in London. He was replaced in 1866 by the 4th Earl of Carnarvon; Sir Richard Graves MacDonell was the lieutenant-governor of Nova Scotia.] His despatch was the reflection of lengthy and recent conversations with George Brown. "The time is short, since those who have undertaken this great measure desire to bring it forward during the ensuing session for the decision of the Imperial Parliament:—and it is impossible to say what evil consequences might not follow the unnecessary interposition of a year's delay. . . ."[4] There was to be no delay. It "only wants the Lower Provinces to say aye, and it is done."[5] "Rarely, if ever," wrote MacDonnell, "has there occurred in history so remarkable and fortunate a concurrence of circumstances to enable distinct Provinces to frame equitable conditions of a Union."[6] There were to be none of the hesitations and fumbling that had characterized so many intercolonial arrangements in the past; the process of joining the colonies together was to be short, swift, and sure.

The Quebec Resolutions were first published on November 8, 1864, little more than a week after the end of the Conference, in *Le Journal de Québec*. Two days later, from another source, they appeared in the Charlottetown *Monitor*.[7] From these two sources they soon spread over all five eastern provinces.[8] Almost every paper published them, in full more often than in part; even a paper as remote from the scene of events as the *Standard,* of Harbour Grace, Newfoundland, took space to print them.[9] They excited much comment. Information had been made public during both Conferences, but except for the brief semi-official report on the Charlottetown Conference, there had been nothing official until Cartier's speech in Montreal on October 29, and Brown's more revealing one in Toronto on November 3. Even these were no more than informative outlines. The battle for Confederation was thus begun long before the legislatures of the several provinces met, and its course was determined, at this critical stage, not by resolutions of legislatures, but by public opinion. In the Maritimes the newspapers, issue after issue, were filled with editorials, letters to the editor, and reports of meetings. Prince Edward Island was the most lively of all. The Saint John *Telegraph* said that the Island papers "come to us completely filled with Confederation. The little Island is determined to assert the truism that small people sometimes make the greatest fuss in the world."[10] But New Brunswick

Source: P.B. Waite, *The Life and Times of Confederation*, Robin Brass Studios, pp. 104–116. Reprinted with permission of the publisher.

papers were little different. Even in the small towns along the north shore of New Brunswick, Confederation became "the subject matter at the corner of the streets, and at 'a thousand and one firesides.'"[11] When the Newcastle Debating Club invited Peter Mitchell and the Attorney General, J.M. Johnson, to publicly discuss Confederation, Newcastle Temperance Hall was filled to overflowing. The crowds at the meetings in Charlottetown, Moncton, Saint John, Truro, and Halifax, testify how powerful—even explosive—an issue Confederation had become. This public discussion continued for many months to come, and crowded every other issue into insignificance.

The Quebec Resolutions, once published, had to be expounded and explained, to be clothed with institutional and political meaning. Tilley and Gray began this process in New Brunswick, a bare week after they had returned from Quebec, and shortly after the Quebec Resolutions had appeared in the Saint John papers. The first meeting, held in Saint John on November 17, was by all accounts not a success since neither Gray nor Tilley seemed to have the broad grasp of the subject necessary to give it coherence. Tilley in particular failed to give any general financial structure for Confederation or to indicate by what means the proposed central government could sustain its admittedly large commitments.[12] One of Tilley's characteristics—his capacity for understatement—showed here to his disadvantage. Tilley lacked the "extraordinary facility of statement which on such subjects distinguishes Mr. Galt. ..."[13]

It was Galt, in fact, who gave the best exposition of any of the delegates. He was the first Canadian minister to give a thoroughly comprehensive analysis of the financial and legal basis for Confederation. His speech at Sherbrooke on November 23 was given before 300 people and took over three hours. It was, despite its length, well received and became at once a textbook for the supporters of Confederation. Widely circulated in all of British North America, it became, as the Saint John *Telegraph* predicted it would, December 19, 1864, "a storehouse from which arms and ammunition may be drawn without limit to defend the holy cause of Confederation. [. . .]" Galt, never one to hide his light under a bushel, mailed off numerous copies of his speech to cohorts in the Maritimes. Tupper wrote, "many thanks for your speech—by far the ablest exposition of the Confederation scheme altho' a little too much from the

Canadian point of view to suit this meridian." Whelan thanked Galt for several copies and for "the immense service you have done to the cause of Confederation. ..."[14] [Edward Whelan was a journalist and one of Prince Edward Island's delegates to the Quebec conference.]

The financial aspect of Galt's analysis is well known and it would be redundant to give it again.[15] But his legal and constitutional analysis was also sound and serves to introduce the British North American reaction to this interesting and complex subject. The proposal is, Galt said, "to go back to the fountainhead, from which all our Legislative powers were derived—the Imperial Parliament—and seek at their hands a measure. ..."[16] The sovereign authority of Westminster simplified wonderfully the task of uniting British North America. All that was necessary was an address to the Queen from each of the colonial legislatures, praying that an act be passed to unite them. There were no ratifying conventions, no elections to decide who should compose them, both of which had made the passing of the American constitution an uncertain, tortuous, even unscrupulous business. The British Parliament had merely to pass an act. Some were, indeed, disturbed by this sovereignty, "one and indivisible," from which all power flowed.[17] A considerable issue was to arise in 1866 in French Canada under this head; it was feared that changes would be silently introduced into an imperial act by delegates in London, against which there could be no recourse.[18]

Some Bleu newspapers recognized that imperial sovereignty could usefully define the powers of the central and local governments and be the guarantor of the constitutional boundaries so established. Such was the clear-headed and sensible view of *Le Courier de St. Hyacinthe*, October 28, 1864:

> Le fait est que les pouvoirs du gouvernement fédéral, comme ceux des corps locaux émaneront également du parlement impérial, qui seul a le droit de les déléguer. Chacun de ces gouvernements sera investi de pouvoirs absolus pour les questions de son ressort et sera également souverain dans sa sphère d'action. ...

Le Courrier du Canada of Quebec expressed similar, though less well-defined, views.

Imperial sovereignty certainly simplified constitutional changes, but even for those with a clear-cut theory of federation, the role of the new central government was rather novel. An intermediate government, between Great Britain and British colonies, so to speak, had never been created before. The London *Times* said that the proposed changes "violate the Constitution of the whole empire."[19] When responsible government had been established in 1848, Britain and the self-governing colonies divided the sphere of government between them. No systematic division was then attempted and Canada had found the omission convenient for pre-empting more for her share as time went on. Nevertheless, the division was not less real for being unsystematic. However, a third government might have seemed rather anomalous. The Montreal *True Witness*, a shrewd judge, said (July 8, 1864) that a central government in British North America would inevitably "encroach upon the legitimate functions either of the Imperial or of the Provincial Government."

Remarks such as this were rare. There were, perhaps, few critics acute enough to recognize the problem. A more convincing explanation is that British North Americans never thought of their central government in quite these terms. The new central government for the Dominion of Canada was simply an expansion of the government of the old Province of Canada. The central government would not be "interposed" between the imperial government and the provincial governments: it would be the provincial governments of old, rolled into one. The really new governments would be the "local" governments, called local and meant to be what they were called, half-municipal bodies, the remnants of the old provincial governments. Galt said as much in Sherbrooke.[20] No great difficulty was therefore anticipated with the new constitutional arrangements. The central government at Ottawa would take over most of the existing functions of the old provincial governments, leaving them with such limited powers and responsibilities that they could be appropriately called "local" rather than "provincial." "The theory will be," said the Montreal *Herald*, June 22, 1864, "that the Federal Government is the fountain of power. ..." The Montreal *True Witness* was afraid this would happen:

We oppose the proposed plan of *Colonial* Federation, since no matter in what terms it may be conceived, it proposes to saddle us with a sovereign central government which in our actual position must derive its authority, not from within, or from the States over which it is to bear rule, but *ab extra*, and from an Imperial Government with which our connection must cease ere many years be past; and to which, and to the plenitude of whose authority, the said central government would then inevitably succeed. Our position would then be that of a subject Province, not that of a State or independent member of a Confederation. (September 23, 1864.)

The French-Canadian Liberals (Rouges) unquestionably sympathized with such a view, but it is safe to say that the prospect intimidated only a few others.

There was thus a general division of opinion in British North America about the kind of government the new colonial union ought to be. Some wanted a federal system in the present-day meaning of the word "federal": that is, a clear recognition of what would now be called "co-ordinate sovereignty,"[21] with the provinces and the central government each having clearly defined powers and protected against encroachment by the other. But this was not a widely held view, nor was it characteristic of those men who created the Quebec Resolutions. The word "federal" was used to describe the Quebec plan, not because it defined the proposed relation between the central and the provincial governments, but because it was the word the public was most familiar with. "It is astonishing," noted the Kingston *British American*, "the looseness with which the term 'federal' is used in these discussions, indicating but an indifferent acquaintance with the actual meaning of the word. . . ."[22] The French Canadians and the Prince Edward Islanders insisted that the constitution be federal, and the constitution was certainly called federal; what it was really intended to be was another matter. The Montreal *Gazette* was not far off the mark when it suggested that the constitution would be a "legislative union with a constitutional recognition of a federal principle."[23] In Britain, Goldwin Smith amplified the point, early in 1865.

They intend to create not a federation, but a kingdom, and practically to extinguish the independent existence of the several provinces. ... They hope, no doubt, that the course of events will practically decide the ambiguity in favor of the incorporating union.[24]

The *Westminster Review* said much the same.[25] This was undoubtedly true of Macdonald, who wanted elbow room for the central power. Tupper of Nova Scotia frankly preferred legislative union. So did Galt. Brown, for the moment at least, was largely satisfied with "rep. by pop." Cartier, like Sir Etienne Taché, was confident, perhaps too confident, that French-Canadian privileges could be defended better by French-Canadian ministers in a central government than by a local legislature.

The members of the Canadian Coalition had originally agreed to address themselves to negotiations "for a confederation of all the British North American provinces."[26] Should this fail to be realized, then the federal principle would be applied to Canada alone. This seemed, on the face of it, simple enough. The question was, what was the federal principle? Macdonald said that under Confederation local matters would be committed to local bodies, and matters common to all to a general legislature. He then went on to say that the general legislature would be constituted on "the well understood principles of federal government." A revealing debate took place on this very point and it was for the government, particularly the French-Canadian members of it, rather embarrassing.[27] What it revealed was that most of the members of the Canadian Coalition government thought of federation largely in terms of the composition of the central legislature. In the lower house there would be "rep. by pop."; in the upper house there would be representation by territory, "equal" representation as the Canadians described it. What could be simpler? Of course local powers would be given to local bodies, but that was taken as a matter presenting little difficulty. The basis of the federal principle lay in the central legislature and in the balance between the House of Commons on the one hand and the Senate on the other. Of the constitution of the House of Commons there could be no doubt, and the constitution of the Senate became of critical importance.

The Charlottetown, Quebec, and London Conferences laboured hard on this very point. It was considered the heart of the system. At the same time, the local governments were apt to be regarded merely as conveniences for dissipating sectional prejudices or absorbing sectional difficulties. Consequently, the division of powers between the central and the local governments which bulks so large in any modern analysis of federation was not a particular difficulty. It never really became so, even when the Maritime delegates appeared on the scene. The general effect was unmistakable. It gave the central legislature and its institutions a preponderant role; it is also the answer to the puzzle of everyone's preoccupation with the Senate. The same problem had existed at Philadelphia seventy-seven years before, and the result was not dissimilar. The Senates of both Canada and the United States caused enormous difficulties, and the division of powers seemed relatively easy. One explanation is that government was neither so pervasive nor so complex in the nineteenth century as in the twentieth. Jurisdictional problems were anticipated by Dunkin and others, but the "difficulties of divided jurisdiction," to use the title of Professor Corry's work,[28] were not very apparent. That the division of powers is the heart of the federal system is a modern proposition, not a nineteenth-century one.

On this point the Quebec Resolutions themselves were enigmatic. No definition of federal was given; perhaps one was not intended. The formal symmetry of the American constitution was probably not even considered desirable. There is much in the argument that Confederation was a practical answer to a political difficulty. "Rarely indeed," said the London *Times*, November 24, 1864, "has constitutional legislation been conducted in so practical and unpretending a style." Macdonald himself has been described as a "natural empiricist in action."[29] Empiricism can be emotional as well as practical and the reference of British Americans to their British political inheritance was both. The Quebec Resolutions remained a working outline; their purpose was practical, their ideas empirical, and their solutions sometimes circumstantial. The Conference had not believed in putting its assumptions into ordered prose; these assumptions remained to be discovered, some implied within the seventy-two resolutions that were the blueprint of the system, others not.

Not without reason did the *Times* of London remark on December 13, 1864, that it was "exceedingly difficult" to construe the clauses on the division of powers. The *Edinburgh Review* said that "the distinction attempted to be drawn between general and local matters is in some respects scarcely traceable. [...]"[30] The Halifax *Morning Chronicle* referred to this question as the "binomial theorem of government."[31] The Montreal *True Witness*, January 13, 1865, cunningly observed that the unintelligibility of the resolutions on the division of powers was inevitable; the Quebec Conference was "attempting to 'define the powers' of a government intentionally armed with indefinite power." That was the matter in a nutshell.

Most British American newspapers fought shy of these thorny problems of political theory, and when analysis of the federal principle was attempted, many newspapers, and not a few politicians, simply bogged down. Ambrose Shea's explanations to the Newfoundland Assembly in February, 1865, were barely comprehensible.[32] The debate in the Canadian Assembly on the "well-understood principles of federal government" largely indicated that they were not well understood at all. Christopher Dunkin's brilliant and devastating analysis in the Canadian Confederation debates was one of the few successful attempts of its kind.[33] Numerous other examples can be given of the difficulty that Canadians and others had in interpreting the division of powers, and, in a more general sense, in understanding the federal principle at all. It was so often referred to in a manner thick with prejudice. The following is from the *Canadian Quarterly Review and Family Magazine* of April, 1865.

The federation and confederation system is the adoption of the principle that *each* member of the *"body politic"* shall, while apparently under the control of a supreme head [,] at the same time possess a separate and independent mind or controlling power, each capable of working, like a *false* rule in arithmetic to the injury of all the other rules or members of the "body politic." [...] A sound system of government requires no *checks* and *guarantees*, for its head is supreme; so all true principles possess internal evidence to prove that they are sound, *immutable* and *ultimate*.

To many sovereignty must reside somewhere and it ought to be at the centre where it belonged. It could be said of the Maritime provinces that their traditions of responsible government made their prejudice against the federal system understandable, but this explanation is less satisfactory for Canada.

Canadians had been familiar with forms of double legislation, with "the Federal principle recognized in the Union Act [of 1840]," as Galt put it.[34] The extension of these devices had grown with the years; by 1864 it had gone so far that the province of Canada was ready to separate into its two halves. Certainly federation had been thought of before as a solution for Canadian difficulties. But after four years of civil war in the United States, fought, it would appear, because of the federal principle, the principle itself was suspect. Indeed the most conspicuous single feature of British North American discussion of Confederation was the prevalent fear of what might now be considered its basic principle. There were exceptions and important ones, particularly the French Canadians, but many Canadians, including a preponderant majority of the English, found the federal principle a wind which, once sown, would reap the whirlwind of civil strife. As the Mount Forest *Examiner* put it,

> ... will the application of the federal principle heal the sectional difficulties under which we labor? On this point we may refer to the experience of our neighbours across the lines, where under the fostering care of this same "Federal principle," the sectional difficulty has grown, in one generation, to proportions so gigantic as to astonish the world by the "irrepressible conflict" waged in its interest.[35]

Or the Ottawa *Union*, September 8, 1864,

> It is not a little singular ... how the federation idea should be taken up in British America at the very time that war, ruin, and demoralization are its effects in the American republic. ... A war of secession in the future ... must flow from copying the errors in statesmanship of our republican neighbours.

The Hamilton *City Enterprise*, October 22, 1864, though more optimistic, was entirely characteristic:

> We do not say nor do we wish to believe the popular cry of today that the federation of the Provinces will bring trouble upon

us if consummated. We would rather trust that our case will prove an exception to the many instances ...

The general proposition was, appropriately, stated by the *Halifax Citizen*, November 19, 1864, "a sectional legislature under a general congress is only a nursery of sectional feeling, a fruitful factory for local jealousies, grievances and deadlocks to progress." Federation was like a drug: efficacious it might be, in small quantities for relieving the pain of the patient, but it was dangerous when used indiscriminately. This quantitative view of federation was a significant feature of Canadian discussion of the subject. "Canadians and Acadians alike will infuse as little of the federal principle into their union ... as will suffice to meet the absolute necessities of the case." Thus the Montreal *Gazette* on August 24. The *Globe*, October 15, was not dissimilar: "Federation is, in a large degrees, but an extension of our political system, and is sustained by precisely the same reasoning as are municipal institutions." This last was too much for the Montreal *True Witness*, and on October 28 it read both papers a lesson in political theory. Federation was not a quantity. It was not analogous to municipal institutions. It differed from a legislative union "not in degree but in kind." There was a "formal and essential difference" between legislative and federal union.

This was a lesson that few British North American newspapers and politicians learned, and their ignorance was indisputably part of their conception of Confederation. With some significant exceptions, they did not believe that federation meant the fundamental recognition of the sovereignty of both central and local governments. They would have regarded with suspicion a principle that would establish such governments in a way that would make each "co-ordinate and independent."[36] If that was the federal principle, they did not want it. Most, however, never fully understood the principle that they were opposing.

It is worth noting a popular and perhaps influential pamphlet published between the Charlottetown and Quebec Conferences, called *A Northern Kingdom*.[37] It was one of many published in 1864, and afterward, on Confederation, part of a considerable body of literature whose uneven merits still remain to be assessed. *A Northern Kingdom* summed up in eighteen pages much of the current wisdom of British North Americans. Its views on federation were repeated again and again.

Federation! Have we not seen enough of federations with their cumbrous machinery of government, well enough in fair weather, but breaking up with the least strain—with treble taxation—with staffs of state functionaries, and of supreme functionaries, and with harassing disputes of various jurisdictions? Shall we not draw wisdom from the errors of others? Must we steer our bark on that rock on which the neighbouring magnificent union has split? . . . The main problems of government have been solved for us. The problem of a federal union has been worked out—a failure. The problem of a Legislative union has been worked out—a success.[38]

The ministerial paper in Quebec, the *Morning Chronicle*, published this extract as the leading editorial, on October 17, while the Quebec Conference was sitting. The Saint John *Evening Globe*, which was to become the foremost advocate of legislative union in New Brunswick, cited it as well on September 26. The pamphlet was quoted and commented upon by many newspapers, and probably achieved a wider currency than any other published at the time.[39] That it did so was as much a tribute to its views as to the succinctness with which they were expressed.

Canadian Confederation was a native creation. There was no intention of imitating the United States. On the contrary, in legislative union, many believed, lay the unequivocal, sovereign design of political excellence. A compromise with the realities of British American political circumstances was necessary, but it was not to be allowed to weaken the structure of the whole. Federation was essential, but it was federation in a unique, and to some at the present time a strange and twisted, form embodied not so much in the relation between the general and the local governments as in that between the House of Commons and the Senate. The great compromise between representation by areas and by population that lay at the heart of the American Congress was understood to be the basis of the federal principle and so accepted; but even here the Senate of Canada was not intended to be similar to its American counterpart. The Canadian Senate was peculiar in its use of regional, as opposed to state, representation. It is conspicuous that no attempts were made in the Quebec Conference, and few outside to develop the American view. Thus, while it is fair to say that the federal principle in its application to the central legislature reflected the American example, it is also probable that American ideas did not, in any sense more specific than this, determine the character of Confederation. The immediate character of Confederation was determined by British North American political experience and political traditions. And it may well be asked if Macdonald did not suspect that the principle of cabinet government might weaken fatally the Senate in its federal capacity, and thus its principal *raison d'être*. Christopher Dunkin was to suggest that the federalization of the Cabinet was inevitable. It is impossible to believe that Macdonald, and perhaps others, were not shrewd enough to see the gist of this point: that a responsible Cabinet would suck in, with silent, inexorable, vertiginous force, the whole regional character of the Senate and with it all the strength that lay in the Senate's regional identities. In circumstances such as these, the question of whether Confederation really was a federation or not was perhaps irrelevant. The French Bleus thought it was, but for a powerful majority of others confederation was an attempt to put aside the insidious federal contrivances that had grown up within the Union of Canada, to relegate the questions that had caused them to the care of subordinate, local legislatures, and to establish at Ottawa a strong, cohesive, sovereign, central government.

Notes

1. Shanly Papers, Tilley to Shanly, Dec. 20, 1864. Cf. Lord Monck, who opened the Canadian parliament in January, 1865 with the hope that it would be the last Canadian provincial parliament ever to assemble. (Monck Papers, Monck to his son, Henry, Jan. 20, 1865.) Cf. also *Sarnia Observer*, June 28, 1867: "in 1864 the universal expectation of the country was that the Federation, either of all the Provinces together, or of the two Canadas together . . . would be carried in about a year from 1864. . . ."

2. P. B. Waite, "A Chapter in the History of the Intercolonial Railway, 1864," *Canadian Historical Review*, XXXII, 4 (Dec. 1951), 356–69.

3. Note the following from the independent *London* [C.W.] *Evening Advertiser*, Jan. 28, 1865: "It is thought desirable, too, that the subject should pass the several Provincial legislatures in time to lay it before the Imperial Parliament during the ensuing

summer, and that all may be prepared for a general election by the end of the year . . . ."

4. Nova Scotia, Lieutenant Governor, Despatches Received, Cardwell to MacDonnell, Dec. 8, 1864. This dispatch had a curious fate. MacDonnell had part of the dispatch (including the quotation above) withdrawn from the regular series and made a Separate. The reason seems to have been that Cardwell's answers to MacDonnell's allegations of personal motives on the part of Tupper and others could hardly fail to be embarrassing if published.

5. Halifax *Morning Chronicle*, Feb. 4, 1865.

6. MacDonnell to Monck, Jan. 9, 1865 (confidential), enclosure in C.O. 42, Monck to Cardwell, Jan. 20, 1865 (confidential).

7. The source of the *Monitor's* information was almost certainly Edward Palmer. W. M. Whitelaw, *The Maritimes and Canada before Confederation* (Toronto, 1934), 265 analyses the differences in the documents printed in Canada and the Maritimes.

8. Halifax Citizen, Nov. 17, 1864; Chatham Gleaner, Nov. 19, 1864; Newfoundland Express, Newfoundlander, St. John's Daily News, Dec. 1, 1864.

9. Harbour Grace *Standard*, Dec. 14, 1864.

10. Saint John *Weekly Telegraph*, Dec. 14, 1864.

11. *Ibid.*, Jan. 11, 1865, letter from "Veni, Vidi," Dec. 31, 1864, from Miramichi.

12. Saint John *Morning Telegraph*, Nov. 19, 1864. See also *infra*, 236.

13. Montreal *Gazette*, Oct. 28, 1864.

14. Tupper to Galt, Dec. 13, 1864; Whelan to Galt, Dec. 17, 1864, in W. G. Ormsby, "Letters to Galt Concerning the Maritime Provinces and Confederation," *Canadian Historical Review*, XXXIV, 2 (June, 1953), 167–8.

15. R. G. Trotter quotes Galt's tables fully in his *Canadian Federation* (Toronto, 1924), 120–2. D. G. Creighton's "British North America at Confederation," an Appendix to the Rowell-Sirois Report uses Galt's work with discernment.

16. Galt's Sherbrooke speech was widely printed. The Toronto *Globe* published it in 12 columns of fine print, Nov. 28, 1864. Extensive extracts appeared in the Saint John *Morning Telegraph*, Dec. 5; Halifax *Morning Chronicle*, Dec. 1; Charlottetown *Examiner*, Dec. 12; St. John's *Courier*, Dec. 21, 1864, to give a few examples. Galt published it himself as *Speech on the Proposed Union of the*

British American Provinces (Montreal, 1864). The above quotation is from page 8 of this edition.

17. *Montreal Herald*, Jan. 18, 1867. E. G. Penny, the editor, published his views in a pamphlet, *The Proposed British North American Confederation: Why It Should Not Be Imposed upon the Colonies by Imperial Legislation* (Montreal, 1867).

18. *Infra*, 276–7.

19. London *Times*, July 21, 1864. Despite these remarks the *Times*, by the end of 1864, was a strong supporter of Confederation.

20. Galt, *Speech on the Proposed Union*, 15.

21. K. C. Wheare, *Federal Government* (London, 1953), 11.

22. Kingston *Daily British American*, Dec. 19, 1864.

23. Montreal *Gazette*, Sept. 9, 1864. Cf. Monck's remark: "So far from the word 'Federal' being an apt designation . . . its general meaning conveys an idea the direct contrary of . . . the intent of the Quebec plan." Monck to Cardwell, Sept. 7, 1866 (confidential), in W. M. Whitelaw, "Lord Monck and the Canadian Constitution," *Canadian Historical Review*, XXI, 3 (Sept., 1940), 301.

24. Goldwin Smith, "The Proposed Constitution for British North America," *MacMillan's Magazine*, March, 1865, 408.

25. "The Canadian Confederacy," *Westminster Review*, April, 1865, 259: "It is impossible to mistake the direction in which these [centralizing] provisions point, and they are calculated to raise the question whether there exists the most perfect conformity and good faith between the semblance and the essence of the yielding to local interests in the name of federation."

26. Toronto *Globe*, June 23, 1864. Also J. Pope, *Memoirs of the Right Honourable Sir John Alexander Macdonald* (Toronto, [1930]), Appendix V.

27. This debate is discussed briefly in P. B. Waite, "The Quebec Resolutions and *Le Courrier du Canada*, 1864–1865," *Canadian Historical Review*, XL, 4 (Dec., 1959), 296.

28. J. Corry, "Difficulties of Divided Jurisdiction," Appendix to Rowell-Sirois Report, 1940.

29. T. W. L. Macdermot, "The Political Ideas of John A. Macdonald," *Canadian Historical Review*, XIV, 3 (Sept., 1933), 264

30. "The British American Federation," *Edinburgh Review*, Jan., 1865, 191.

31. Halifax *Morning Chronicle*, Oct. 16, 1865. Discussed *infra*, 218.

32. St. John's *Newfoundlander*, March 16, 1865. See *infra*, chapter xi.

33. *Infra*, 153–4.

34. Galt, *Speech on the Proposed Union*, 4.

35. Mount Forest *Examiner* (Conservative) quoted in the Toronto *Leader*, July 2, 1864.

36. Wheare, Federal Government, 11.

37. It was written by S. E. Dawson of Dawson & Co., Montreal, publishers. Published anonymously by "A Colonist" (Montreal, Dawson, 1864). S. E. Dawson (1833–1916) was the son of the Rev. Benajmin Dawson, born in Halifax and who came to Montreal with his father in 1847. S. E. Dawson later became owner of the firm.

38. *Ibid.*, 13.

39. E.g., Charlottetown *Examiner,* Oct. 3, 1864; Halifax *Acadian Recorder* Sept. 28, 1864; Saint John *New Brunswick Courier*, Oct. 1, 1864.

Article 3: Nation and Crown

Christopher Moore

Thomas D'Arcy McGee, who turned forty in 1865, was a small, ugly, charming Irish-Catholic journalist with a complicated past. He had been an Irish rebel who recanted, a patriotic American who grew disillusioned, an anti-clerical who had made his peace with the Catholic Church, a reformer who had gone over to John A. Macdonald, and a teetotaller given to alcoholic binges. (Macdonald once instructed him he would have to quit drinking; the cabinet did not have room for two drunks.) In 1857 he had settled in Montreal, launched a newspaper, and got himself into the legislature. His constituents, Montreal's Irish, were a narrow and not always secure power base, but McGee was funny, quick-witted, and a natural orator. He soon became popular in the House, and a prominent, more than a powerful, figure in Canadian affairs.

McGee was barely off the train from Boston in 1857 when he began advocating federal union, westward expansion, and the nurturing of a national literature for Canada. "A new nationality" became his platform and slogan. McGee had good reason to seek a nation. He despaired of Ireland, was an alien in Britain, and resented American intolerance of foreigners and Catholics. He was also a journalist, but unlike George Brown, the millionaire publisher of the *Globe*, or Edward Whelan, who was at least solidly established in his Charlottetown newspaper, McGee always scrambled to make a living. The national vision became a valuable stock in trade.

McGee travelled widely in British North America. With help from railway barons who had their own reasons to encourage such visions, he organized intercolonial good-will trips for politicians and public figures. By 1865, he had been to Atlantic Canada seven or eight times, when many Canadians were still asking him, "What kind of people are they?" Though he had never gone west of Canada West, McGee even outlined a plan for a separate province to be set aside for the native nations on the plains of the far North-West. He had begun to imagine a new country where none existed.

It was a vision upon which he launched many articles and speeches. Amid the tension of the confederation debate in the Parliament of the united Canadas early in 1865, McGee was the first speaker to make the House laugh. It was a feat he achieved consistently in that speech and throughout his public career, but he was just as adept at rolling, patriotic oratory. "I see in the not remote distance," he declared in 1860, when there was no serious prospect of British North American union, "one great nationality bound, like the shield of Achilles, by the blue rim of ocean. ... I see within the ground of that shield the peaks of the western mountains and the crests of the eastern waves." In the confederation debate, he celebrated the beauty of the Canadian land, rejoiced that confederation would elevate "the provincial mind" to nobler contests, and welcomed the advent of "a new and vigorous nationality."[1]

McGee's passionate Canadianism—"not French-Canadian, not British-Canadian, not Irish-Canadian; patriotism rejects the prefix"—disquieted listeners for whom the prefixes defined patriotism. But "a new nationality" had gone into the language. McGee modestly disclaimed sole credit for the phrase (It's always the same, he told the House: "Two people hit upon the same thought, but Shakespeare made use of it first"), but it popped up in many celebratory speeches during the 1860s. Anticipation of a "new nationality" was even written into the Throne Speech that Governor General Lord Monck read to the legislature at Quebec on the eve of the great debate on the Quebec resolutions—inspiring the *rouges*' clever amendment, proclaiming that they were too loyal to want such a thing.

Bleu supporters of the coalition defeated Dorion's amendment, and their unanimity was an early indication that they would not be swayed by attacks on the Quebec resolutions, but they did not much like doing it. McGee defended his phrase, and Macdonald made a point of using "the expression which was sneered at the other evening." But George-Étienne Cartier was careful to say that confederation would create "a political nationality," and he went on to stress that "the idea of unity of races was utopian—it was impossible. Distinctions of this kind would always appear. [. . .] In our own federation we should have Catholic and Protestant, French, English, Irish and Scotch, and

Source: "Nation and Crown" from *1867: How the Fathers Made a Deal* by Christopher Moore. © 1997. Published by McClelland & Stewart Ltd. Used with permission of the publisher.

each by his efforts and his success would increase the prosperity and glory of the new confederacy."[2]

Cartier was glad to escape from awkward questions of nationality to the safer ground of monarchy. He celebrated the benefits of monarchical rule and French Canada's love of monarchy. "If they had their institutions, their language, and their religion intact today, it was precisely because of their adherence to the British Crown," he said. Confederation had been made, he said, "with a view of perpetuating the monarchical element. [. . .] the monarchical principle would form the leading feature." In the Nova Scotia legislature, Charles Tupper said something similar, covering his declaration that the colonies should "advance to a more national position" with assurances that confederation would bind the new nation to the British Crown "by a more indissoluble tie than ever before existed."[3]

McGee, for all his celebration of the Canadian land and the Canadian nationality, took the same stand. "We need in these provinces, we can bear, a large infusion of authority," he said, and he wound up his speech in direct address to Queen Victoria: "Whatsoever charter, in the wisdom of Your Majesty and of your Parliament you give us, we shall loyally obey and fulfill it as long as it is the pleasure of Your Majesty and your successors to maintain the connection between Great Britain and these colonies." Such frankly deferential talk was as common in confederation speeches as talk of the new nationality.[4]

It too had its pitfalls. Confronted with it, Dorion smoothly shifted his line of attack to declare that confederation's advocates were reactionary tories, who "think the hands of the Crown should be strengthened and the influence of the people, if possible, diminished, and this constitution is a specimen of their handiwork." A Halifax newspaper put the same thought more vividly after the Charlottetown conference. When the delegates let their secrets out of the bag, said the *Acadian Recorder*, their constitution would prove to be "a real sleek constitutional, monarchical, unrepublican, aristocratic cat."[5]

This view of confederation—something imposed on cringing colonial Canadians by the reactionary local agents of Imperial dictate—became part of the late-twentieth-century consensus, much more than the confederation-makers' talk of a new nationality. The political scientist Peter Russell opened his survey of Canadian constitutional history, *Constitutional Odyssey*, by quoting a piously deferential Canadian declaration that confederation would "not profess to be derived from the people but would be the constitution provided by the imperial parliament." Taking the statement at face value, Russell identified the 1867 constitution as an Imperial and monarchical imposition. It could not be considered a legitimate beginning for a sovereign community, Russell concluded. Like many theorists and politicians, he declared this failing made the work of the original constitution-makers irrelevant, deserving of the neglect lavished upon it.[6]

Walter Bagehot, who sometimes enjoyed playing the plain journalist taking the mickey out of rarefied theorists, might have enjoyed seizing on lines like these. In parliamentary government, Bagehot had insisted, monarchy was always part of the "dignified," that is, ceremonial side of the constitution. Beneath the trappings of monarchy and aristocracy, which could mislead even the wisest scholars, political power in mid-nineteenth-century Britain, and even more in British North America, was securely in the hands of the representatives of the people. The confederation-makers knew that worshipful addresses to Victoria lent dignity to their business, but they also knew power lay elsewhere. Britain and British North America were disguised republics—in disguise certainly, but certainly republics, if republic meant a government derived from the people.

Bagehot understood as soon as he looked at the Quebec resolutions that the Senate and the governor general were going to be largely powerless in the new Canadian confederation. Dignified for ceremonial purposes they might be, but real power would rest securely in a Canadian House of Commons, elected to represent the Canadian people on a franchise as wide as any then existing in the world. The role of the monarchy was even more illusory. Bagehot did not take seriously the confederation-makers' florid assertions of loyalty and devotion.

In *The English Constitution*, Bagehot had argued that, although the monarchy was integral to British society and tradition, it was not essential to parliamentary government itself. In his confederation editorials, which welcomed the rise of an independent nationality in Canada, he doubted whether Canada needed a monarchy at all. He even suggested that the confederation-makers were not entirely sincere in proposing one. "We are not quite certain this extra and, so to speak, ostentatious display of loyalty was not intended to remove objections which might have been entertained at home," he said of the monarchical clauses of the Quebec resolutions.[7]

Bagehot was wrong to suspect the confederation-makers were insincere about the monarchy. But he would certainly have been right to mock the idea that confederation had been made by Imperial dictate. As late as 1841, Britain had imposed a made-in-London constitution on the mostly unwilling colonists of Upper and Lower Canada. But in 1862, with responsible government firmly established, the colonial minister informed the colonies that, if they worked out a plan of union, Parliament would pass it. When the colonies took up the offer in 1864, the constitution that emerged was indeed what McGee called it: "a scheme not suggested by others, or imposed upon us, but one the work of ourselves, the creation of our intellect and of our own free, unbiased, and untrammelled will." By "us," he meant the legislatures representing the people of British North America.[8]

The confederation deal hammered out by the British North Americans in conference had appalled most of the British colonial officials involved with it. Lacking parliamentary experience, lieutenant-governors like Gordon of New Brunswick and MacDonell of Nova Scotia never fully grasped the compromises that had produced the Quebec resolutions. When the Colonial Office requested clause-by-clause comments on the resolutions, they responded with contemptuous disapproval, demanding an assertion of central power on virtually every point. Officials in London were frequently just as obtuse about the political realities that made federal union a necessity. Expecting deference, not direction, from colonials, they largely ignored the elaborate division of powers worked out in the Quebec resolutions when they began to draft a text for the British North America bill.[9]

Fortunately, British politicians were more realistic. Colonial Office functionaries could still imagine they were administering an empire in North America, but British politicians understood that trying to intervene in Canadian domestic politics meant responsibility without power. Even on a constitutional measure that required action by the British Parliament, they avoided any policy commitment that was not endorsed by the colonial legislatures themselves. The British government formally accepted the Quebec plan for confederation, not merely as advice, but as "the deliberate judgment of those best qualified to decide upon the subject." Bagehot approved. "It is not, that we know of, the duty of Parliament to see that its colonial allies choose constitutions such as Englishmen approve," he said of the Quebec resolutions (though in this case, he did approve and thought Parliament also would).[10]

When Britain's Liberal government collapsed in mid-1866, the outgoing colonial minister, Edward Cardwell, left two questions for his successor, First, could they draft a confederation bill that would get through Parliament quietly, without partisan division? More important, if the staff could draft such a bill, would the provinces accept the text? "This is of cardinal importance," emphasized Cardwell about the second point. His Conservative successor, the thirty-five-year-old aristocrat Lord Carnarvon, agreed. Like his officials, he thought power in the new state ought to be centralized at Ottawa as much as possible. But he understood changes in that direction were possible "only with the acquiescence of the delegates . . . this must depend upon them." Both ministers overruled their advisers to endorse the colonials' choices. When Governor MacDonell of Nova Scotia proved intransigent, he was transferred to Hong Kong, glad to be off to a colony where he could actually wield power. Gordon of New Brunswick held his job only by shelving his doubts about confederation.[11]

George Brown, who went to Britain after the Quebec conference to sound out British reaction, wrote back to John A. Macdonald that the British government might criticize a few details of the seventy-two resolutions, but only for the sake of appearances. "I do not doubt that if we insist on it, they will put through the scheme just as we ask it." Canadian politicians of the 1860s may have been more polite than Pierre Trudeau, who suggested that, since his patriation package had been ratified in Canada, the British Parliament should hold its nose and pass it. But British and Canadian politicians agreed in the 1860s that the political relationship was much the same.[12]

The bill drafted early in 1867 sailed through the Lords and Commons. Britain had been looking forward to British North American union for years, and there was no party division over its terms. This proved fortunate, since the British government was about to collapse in bitter debates about expanding the franchise, and no contentious measure could have passed. Lord Carnarvon, indeed, resigned from cabinet early in March 1867 to protest a bill that would give British men voting rights approaching those long enjoyed by men in British North America, but a new minister shepherded his confederation bill through to the final vote on March 12. Queen Victoria granted the royal assent to the British North America Act on March 29, 1867.

The confederation bill passed so speedily that some of its makers were discomfited. They noticed that even a measure concerning dog licences, introduced in the Commons after second reading of the British North America Act, provoked livelier debate. Macdonald later complained that confederation was treated like "a private bill uniting two or three English parishes," but he would not have tolerated changes to his bill, and British MPs were unlikely to waste time simply dignifying the passage of a bill when their only function was to approve it.[13]

[...] British leaders accepted that they would be obliged to protect British North America if it were threatened, but they were ready to consider granting Canada outright independence if the colonists insisted on it. The confederation-makers, however, were so absolutely sincere in desiring both a monarchy and continued ties to Britain that British observers were struck by the "excessive timidity" with which British North America advanced toward its inevitable independence. Political independence and the "new nationality" somehow lived in harmony with monarchical deference.

They did so because the politicians who negotiated the Quebec resolutions were determined to preserve the pomp and dignity of a constitution modelled on Britain's—and equally determined that having one would not fetter their actions. Bagehot's distinction between the dignified and efficient aspects of parliamentary government had not entered the vocabulary of politics in 1864, but the concept was no mystery to the seasoned parliamentarians who gathered at Quebec. Once they established that the efficient (that is, the power-wielding) parts of confederation were securely in parliamentary hands, they could see nothing but benefits in the dignified aspects Britain could provide in abundance. They were eager to remain loyal subjects of Queen Victoria's Empire, even when there was no pressure on them to remain, even when some in Britain thought they should be striking out on their own.

The confederation-makers of the 1860s had many reasons to avoid challenging the new nation's place in the old Empire, and also one hard, realistic, positive reason to embrace the Empire. In the 1860s, Canada needed Britain, needed it much more than Britain needed Canada. Canadian development depended on British capital, often supported by British government guarantees. Canadian exports depended on access to British markets, assisted by Britain's maternal attitude. Above all, Canada was a small nation sharing a large continent with a huge neighbour, and that meant it needed to shelter under both the military force and the diplomatic influence that only Britain could provide.

D'Arcy McGee caught this sense in his confederation speech. There had always been a desire among the Americans for expansion, he said, "and the inexorable law of democratic existence" in the United States seemed to require appeasing that desire. "They coveted Florida, and seized it; they coveted Louisiana, and purchased it; they coveted Texas, and stole it, and then they picked a quarrel with Mexico, which ended by their getting California. They sometimes pretend to despise these colonies as prizes beneath their ambition; but had we not had the strong arm of England over us, we should not now have had a separate existence." If you seek reasons for confederation under the Crown, he had said earlier, look to the embattled valleys of Virginia, "and you will find reasons as thick as blackberries."[14]

[...] If Canada had somehow been cut loose from Britain's Empire in 1867, it might indeed have survived. With good fortune and American restraint, it might even have achieved its westward expansion. Bagehot breezily concluded in 1867 that, if Canada became wholly independent, merely twenty years of growth would render it able to stand on its own feet, impervious to any American military threat. With or without British support, capital would have come, export markets would have been found. Canada would have developed foreign policies, armed forces, and other attributes of sovereignty merely at a more accelerated pace than it actually did.

But Canadian leaders had to contemplate those twenty years. No Canadian leader was willing to ask Britain to cut ties that would have been cut upon request. In the 1860s, Canada wanted the symbols of monarchy and Empire not least because it urgently needed the benefits of alliance with the most powerful state in the world. In 1864, when he was arguing that the colonies must united to defend themselves better, George-Étienne Cartier said it was a good question whether Britain would fight to help Canada, and a few years later a British statesman doubted whether the colonials would ever fight for Britain in a European war. In fact, the British did accept that, if Canada needed protection, national honour would compel a British response, even at the risk of a nightmare war with the United States. By 1918, sixty thousand Canadian war graves proved the commitment cut both ways, but in the 1860s, Canada needed that alliance far more than Britain did.

There was no debate about monarchy and Empire in the 1860s, because there were almost no voices arguing against them. Financially, economically, politically, culturally, militarily, London was the capital of the world in the mid-nineteenth century, even more than Washington and New York were in the late twentieth. Even Antoine-Aimé Dorion and George-Étienne Cartier could speak unselfconsciously of "home" when they spoke of England. Joseph Howe in his anti-confederate phase did his best to suggest Nova Scotians were choosing between "London under the dominion of John Bull" and "Ottawa under the dominion of Jack Frost," but the confederation-makers assiduously avoided forcing such a choice. Instead, Charles Tupper cited the Maritime provinces' chronic lack of influence in London to prove that "if these comparatively small countries are to have any future whatever in connection with the Crown of England, it must be found in a consolidation of all British North America."[15]

The alliance with Britain, so tangible, so "efficient," in the 1860s, had by the mid-twentieth century dwindled to nothing but dignified traditions. There had been a moment around 1900 when English-Canadian "Imperial federationists" aspired to share in running the British Empire, but Britain's long decline from Imperial might gradually took away most of the benefits the Imperial alliance had offered Canada in 1860 or 1900. Canada and Britain had clearly grown into foreign countries. Incorporating another country's monarchy in its constitution was vastly more anomalous in the 1990s than it had been in the 1860s.

As Walter Bagehot grasped, and the experience of many nations has shown, parliamentary democracy thrives without monarchy. In Canada, an elected governor general, holding the same limited powers as the appointed one, would be more legitimate both in the exercise of those powers in a constitutional emergency and as a Canadian symbol around which the meaning of Canadian nationality could continue to be debated. The inability of modern constitutional negotiators to discuss the head of state surely indicated their inability to respond to Canada's actual situation. A constitutional process that imitated the 1860s by including representatives of all shades of political opinion and by giving them time to debate the issues would surely find that issue arising, among many others. A constitutional process that debated such issues would gain legitimacy whatever it decided.

The monarchy helped the confederation-makers to bypass potentially awkward issues of the "nationality" of the societies being joined by the British North America Act. Nationalism was one of the defining concepts of the nineteenth century, but allegiance to monarchy allowed McGee to boast of a nation even as Cartier and Langevin emphasized that confederation did not require a single tribal nationality. Allegiance, however, was sharply separated from the exercise of sovereign power. Before and after 1867, the confederation-makers consistently identified the legislatures elected by the people as the legitimate source of political authority. Cartier carefully called that "political nationality," and no threat to the French-Canadian nation he represented, but McGee could still frame the question of national allegiance in terms that resonated with men from whom "manliness" was always a vital touchstone. "For what do good men fight?" he asked the legislature. "When I hear our young men say as proudly 'our federation' or 'our country' or 'our kingdom,' as the young men of other countries do, speaking of their own, then I shall have less apprehension for the result of whatever trials the future may have in store for us."[16]

On the eve of July 1st, 1867, George Brown sat in the *Globe* offices in Toronto, back in his favourite role, writing for the newspaper. They were finishing the Dominion Day edition, and Brown wanted the front page for a long article. Maurice Careless captured the scene in his biography. He evoked Brown scribbling relentlessly through the hot night, sweating and gulping down pitchers of water and steadily handing out pages for the typesetters. He continued to write as the harassed night foreman warned that the mail train that would deliver the paper to eastern Ontario would soon be leaving. But the deadline for the eastern mail was missed, and then for the western mail, too. Then "Mr. Brown, all the mails are lost," but Brown kept demanding a little more time. He ignored the pealing church bells at midnight, and he ignored the roar of artillery at dawn. Early in the morning, celebrating crowds gathered on King Street for a copy of the historic edition, and Brown was still writing. Finally, about seven in the morning, Brown declared, "There's the last of it." He handed over the final sheet of a nine-thousand-word history of confederation and went home to bed.[17]

Careless's evocation of the article's creation is wonderful, but Brown's article was really rather dull. Loaded down with a conventional recital of history back to John Cabot, and with reams of unlikely economic statistics, this account by one of the insiders said almost nothing about the way confederation was actually made. Even in its time, it must have been neglected in favour of the *Globe*'s descriptions of how Toronto would celebrate July first: the fireworks, the bonfires, the parades, the boat excursions, the roasting on Church Street of an immense ox purchased by public subscription from a Yorkville farmer, "the new farce 'Dominion Day'" opening at the Royal Lyceum, even the grand balloon ascension hoped for at Queen's Park ("if arrangements can be consummated with parties in New York"). Brown's only really vivid line in the whole historical article was his opening, in which he offered that stirring and ambiguous phrase, "WE hail the birthday of a new nationality."

Brown's true voice, the roar of the passionate politician, ran out more truly in the accompanying editorial. With the first federal election to be held later than summer, he warned with ungrammatical passion that "the only danger that threatens us is les the same men who have so long misgoverned us, should continue to misgovern us still."

These same men were just about to remove Brown from active politics. A year before, he had left the coalition government he had helped create in 1864. Brown had plunged back into partisan politics, intending to make his Ontario reformers the core of a pan-Canadian Liberal Party to sweep John A. Macdonald permanently from office. Macdonald, however, had already drawn many of Brown's natural allies into his own coalition. Brown was no longer exactly "the impossible man," but John A. Macdonald was making it impossible for him to hold on to political power. The Liberals would be badly defeated in the summer elections of 1867, and Brown himself would lose to a Conservative, Thomas Gibbs, who drew many reform votes to the confederation candidate. Brown never sat in the Canadian House of Commons he had done so much to bring into being. He would only go to Ottawa when a later Liberal leader appointed him to the Senate, which Brown helped to ensure would never wield serious political power.

Brown was not too sorry to be out. He preferred journalism to politics and crusades over intrigues. If political success required honing the political adroitness that John A. Macdonald had, it was a price Brown was not willing, and probably unable, to pay.

When Brown and Macdonald were both dead, a wrangle continued among their partisans as to which was the true father of confederation. "Some inspired historians of Canada insist on referring to Macdonald as the father of confederation. He, who tried to prevent it until the lat ring of the bell. To George Brown and to George Brown alone belongs the title," insisted W.T.R. Preston, Oliver Mowat's indispensible "Hug-the-Machine," in his 1927 memoir *My General of Politicians and Politics.*"[18]

The "inspired" historian who provoked Preston to sarcasm may have been Macdonald's first biographer, Sir. Joseph Pope. As a ten-year-old, Pope had watched his father, William Henry Pope, organizing the Charlottetown conference. He grew up to be John A.'s personal secretary and keeper of the Macdonald flame. In *The Memoirs of John A. Macdonald*, which he published upon Macdonald's death, Pope dismissed Brown as a merely sectional leader. Smugly, he quoted Macdonald's patronizing view of his rival: "He deserves the credit of joining me; he and his party gave be that assistance in Parliament that enabled us to carry confederation."[19]

This battle to identify a single hero in the confederation wars was renewed by two Toronto history professors in the 1950s. Donald Creighton relentlessly championed John A. Macdonald ("The day was his, if it was anybody's," was Creighton's take on July 1, 1867) and Maurice Careless insisted there was also a place for George Brown, "the real initiator of confederation." Later, there were ghostly echoes of the search for a father in the debates of the 1980s that set "the Trudeau constitution" against "the Mulroney deal."

Concerning the 1860s, however, the quest for a father has always been misguided. The brilliance of the 1860s process was the way it permitted a George

Brown to make a fundamental contribution to constitution-making, even as it kept him from executive authority. The confederation process let Brown, and much-less-prominent delegates, and even ordinary representatives like those who changed their minds in Nova Scotia and New Brunswick, assert their aims and contribute their ideas without ever achieving unrivalled power. This was the success of a parliamentary process rather than a leader-driven, quasi-presidential one.

A clue to the success of the confederation-makers was inadvertently given in 1865 by one of their most incisive critics. Tearing the Quebec resolutions apart in the legislature at Quebec, Christopher Dunkin seized on some damaging statement made in New Brunswick by George Hatheway, "one of the gentlemen who took part in the negotiations."

"Mr. Hatheway was not here at all," shouted D'Arcy McGee across the floor.

Dunkin was unabashed. "I acknowledge I have not burdened by memory with an exact list of the thirty-three gentlemen who took part in the conference," he said.[20]

Far from being an insult to them or a comment on Canadians amnesiac attitude to history, the anonymity, even in their own time, of most of the makers of confederation suggests a critical ingredient of the constitutional achievement of the 1860s. The constitution-making of the 1860s drew in relatively minor figures from almost every political faction, several of whom dissented from the agreement their meetings reached. Their agreement was then reviewed by rather independent legislatures—four out of five of which at first declined to endorse it. The confederation-makers would have done well to have been more broadly representative, and their confederation might have been received more warmly had they seated even more political factions around the table. Still, their achievement should not be minimized.

In the 1990s, it was impossible for a regional or sectional representative, whether from the West, from Quebec, or from any class or ethnic bloc, to influence constitutional matters without becoming a first minister—or perhaps head of a separate state. Yet a constitution for the twenty-first century would probably require, not eleven first ministers, but several times the thirty-six delegates of the 1860s in order to match the degree of inclusiveness they achieved. The efficient secret of Canada's parliamentary government in the 1860s was its ability to incorporate in constitution-making even those it kept from power. It was an idea the 1860s were lucky to have and the 1990s desperately needed.

Notes

1. Canada, *Parliamentary Debates on Confederation of the British North American Provinces* (Quebec: 1865), p. 125–46.
2. *Confederation Debates*, p. 60.
3. *Confederation Debates*, p. 59; Nova Scotia, *Debates and Proceedings of the House of Assembly 1865* (Halifax: 1865), p. 207–10.
4. *Confederation Debates*, p. 146.
5. Dorion: *Confederation Debates*, p. 255; *Acadian Recorder* (Halifax), September 12, 1864, quoted in Phillip Buckner, "The Maritimes and Confederation: A Reassessment," in *Canadian Historical Review* 61 #1 (March 1990), p. 25.
6. Peter Russell, *Constitutional Odyssey: Can Canadians Be a Sovereign People?* 2nd edition (Toronto: University of Toronto Press, 1993) p. 3.
7. *Economist*, Vol. 2, October 15, 1864, p. 1279.
8. *Confederation Debates,* p. 146.
9. G. P. Browne, ed., *Documents on Confederation of British North America* (Toronto: McClelland & Stewart, 1969), pp. 185–9, Observations and Notes on the Quebec Resolutions, July 24, 1866; pp. 247–62, Initial draft of the BNA Act, January 23, 1867.
10. Browne, ed., *Documents*, p. 169; *Economist*, Vol. 22, November 26, 1864, p. 1455.
11. Browne, ed., *Documents*, p. 180.
12. Joseph Pope, *The Memoirs of Sir John A. Macdonald* (Toronto: Musson, 1927), p. 289.
13. The quotation and much of the detail here are from Ged Martin, *Britain and the Origins of Canadian Confederation, 1837–67* (Vancouver: UBC Press), pp. 284–90.
14. *Confederation Debates,* p. 132; Peter Waite, *The Life and Times of Confederation* (Toronto: University of Toronto Press, 1962), p. 28.
15. Waite, *Life and Times of Confederation*, p. 194; Nova Scotia *Debates* 1865, p. 211.
16. *Confederation Debates*, p. 145.
17. *Globe*, July 1, 1867; Careless, *Brown of the Globe* Vol. II, p. 251–53.
18. W.T.R. Preston, *My Generation of Politicians and Politics* (Toronto: Rose Publishing, 1917), p. 18.
19. Pope, *Memoirs of Sir John A. Macdonald*, p. 274.
20. *Confederation Debates*, p. 541.

AS LONG AS THE SUN SHINES AND THE WATERS FLOW

Treaties and Treaty-Making in the 1870s

Maureen Lux
Brock University

● AS LONG AS THE SUN SHINES AND THE WATERS FLOW: TREATIES AND TREATY-MAKING IN THE 1870s

● Introduction by Maureen Lux

▲ Primary Sources

■ Secondary Sources

● INTRODUCTION

Maureen Lux

Treaties and treaty-making probably marked the very first relations between Aboriginal people and newcomers to northern North America. Fairly equal power relations characterized those early pacts for military or commercial alliance. But the most important document in the history of treaty-making, the Royal Proclamation of 1763, set out the means by which agreements regarding territory could be concluded. Although enacted by the British to create institutions for governing its newly acquired territories after the Seven Years' War, the Proclamation also attempted to keep peace with the Aboriginal nations of the interior by holding back agricultural settlers from the Thirteen Colonies. Thus the Proclamation acknowledged Aboriginal rights to the lands, while also asserting Crown title. The Crown alone could negotiate with Aboriginal people for access to their lands, while the negotiations were required to be conducted in a public forum.

In 1850, in a departure from previous treaties for military alliance or for small parcels of land, the Robinson Treaties with the Aboriginal people of Lakes Huron and Superior regions covered huge districts in preparation for commercial development, and created the precedent for the western Numbered Treaties beginning in the 1870s. Unlike earlier pacts, the Robinson Treaties in what would become Ontario provided for reserve lands, annual cash payments (annuities), and promises of continued fishing and hunting rights. Moreover, it was Aboriginal resistance to incursions into their lands, not royal edict, that forced treaty negotiations.[1]

The Numbered Treaties began with Treaty One in 1871 in southern Manitoba and eventually extended to Treaty Eleven in 1921, which covered a vast segment of the Northwest Territories (see Document 1: Historical Indian Treaties). But this implies an orderly and coherent approach that was far from the case. The Hudson's Bay Company sale of Rupert's Land to the newly created Canadian government in 1869 prompted armed resistance by residents at Red River, who demanded a voice in the new order. The Red River resistance likewise highlighted the need to make some accommodation with Aboriginal peoples of the West who demanded an agreement before they would allow access to their lands.

The first seven treaties to 1877 covered the southern plains from Ontario to the Rockies, serving the government's nation-building project of railway construction and settlement. As the selection from Sarah Carter's *Aboriginal People and Colonizers of Western Canada to 1900* shows, Aboriginal leaders saw the treaties as a way to protect their interests in the land, but especially to ensure the peoples' survival and future livelihood in vastly changed circumstances. The image "Conference with the Chiefs (Treaty One) September 9, 1871" clearly shows that treaty negotiations were conducted in the oral traditions of the Aboriginal nations. The written text of the treaties, however, purported to represent the substance of the agreements. Fundamental misunderstandings emerged about what the parties thought or assumed they were doing when they made the treaties. The concerns varied from one treaty to another, but in general the Aboriginal negotiators, based on their cultural and oral traditions, understood they were sharing the land with the newcomers, not "surrendering" it. As Derek Whitehouse argues in "The Numbered Treaties: Similar Means to Dichotomous Ends" both government and First Nations negotiators understood that treaties were a viable way to meet their respective goals, however much those goals were at odds.

In Treaty Seven, as the selections from *The True Spirit and Original Intent of Treaty 7* makes clear, the surrender of land was not discussed during negotiations; elders understood that the agreement was in fact a treaty of peace. It is clear that the "spirit and intent" of the treaty agreements was not necessarily represented in the written version of the treaties, creating hardship in the immediate post-treaty period and controversy ever since.

Elders have kept their histories alive, but only recently have notions of what constitutes a historical source evolved to include Aboriginal peoples' oral tradition. As we come to understand the treaties as binding agreements made in the presence of the Creator that created a relationship between newcomers (the Crown) and Aboriginal people to share the land and its benefits, and not simply a contract that surrendered the land in return for specific obligations, we can come to realize that indeed all Canadians are treaty people.

NOTES

1. J.R. Miller, *Lethal Legacy: Current Native Controversies in Canada* (Toronto: McClelland and Stewart, 2004), 119, 124; Gerald Friesen, *The Canadian Prairies: A History* (Toronto: University of Toronto Press, 1987), 136.

QUESTIONS

1. Why would Aboriginal elders understand that the treaties were agreements to share, not cede or surrender, the land?
2. Only recently have historians begun to listen to Aboriginal accounts of treaty negotiations. Why?
3. Why were there such fundamental misunderstandings between government and Aboriginal negotiators over what was agreed upon in treaty discussions?
4. The written text of Treaty 7 (Document 8) refers to the Queen and "her Indians." What does this indicate about the Crown's view of the treaty relationship?
5. Why was it important for the government to photograph Mistahimusqua (Big Bear) in chains?
6. On the signature page of the written text of Treaty 7 (Document 8) note the prominence of North-West Mounted Police (NWMP) officers. What does this say about how Canada exerted control over the West?

FURTHER READINGS

Erasmus, Peter. *Buffalo Days and Nights*, ed. Irene Spry, 1976, reprint (Calgary: Glenbow Alberta Institute, 1999).

Miller, J.R., *Compact, Contract, Covenant; Aboriginal Treaty-Making in Canada* (Toronto: University of Toronto Press, 2009).

Morris, Alexander, *The Treaties of Canada with the Indians of Manitoba and the North-West Territories*, 1880, reprint (Toronto: Coles Publishing, 1971).

Ray, Arthur J., Jim Miller, and Frank Tough, *Bounty and Benevolence: A History of Saskatchewan Treaties* (Montreal and Kingston: McGill-Queen's University Press, 2000).

Tobias, John, "Protection, Civilization, Assimilation: An Outline History of Canada's Indian Policy," in *As Long as the Sun Shines and Water Flows*, Ian A.L. Getty and Antoine S. Lussier, eds. (Vancouver: UBC Press, 1983), 13–30.

Treaty Elders of Saskatchewan, with Harold Cardinal and Walter Hildebrant, *Our Dream Is That Our Peoples Will One Day Be Clearly Recognized as Nations* (Calgary: University of Calgary Press, 2000).

▲ Document 1: Historical Indian Treaties

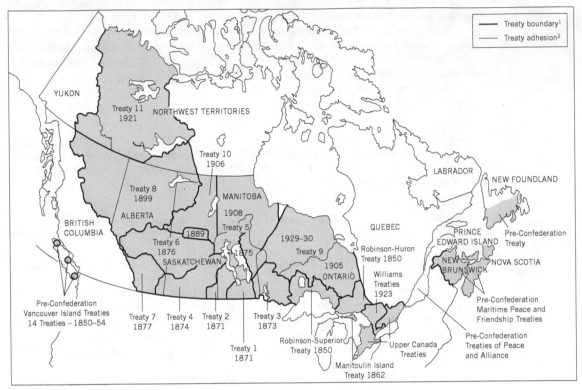

● **Historical Indian Treaties**

Source: Adapted from Canada, Indian Treaties, MCR 4162. "The Atlas of Canada, 1991, Natural Resources Canada, 4 March 2009, http://atlas.nrcan.gc.ca/site/english/maps/archives/5theditions/historical/mcr4162; and from *Ways of Knowing: An Introduction to Native Studies in Canada* 1E. Belanger, Yale D. © 2010 Nelson Education Ltd. Reproduced by permission. www.cengage.com/permissions.

▲ Document 2: Treaty Talks

● "Conference with the Chiefs (Treaty One) September 9, 1871". This illustration, while likely romanticized, clearly shows the oral nature of treaty talks conducted in at least two, sometimes many, different languages. Hand gestures and displays of emotion, crucial to the context of negotiations, become lost in the treaties' written version.

Source: *Canadian Illustrated News*, 09 September 1871, Vol. IV, No. 11, 161. Library and Archives Canada, C056472.

▲ Document 3: Treaty Six

● Page 1 of Treaty Six signed at Fort Carlton and Fort Pitt, 23 August and 28 August, 1876. The images in Documents 2 and 3 refer to different treaties, but all treaties were negotiated using translators, and all treaties were eventually written in English. Imagine how many ways misunderstandings might make their way into the legalistic (and privileged) treaty texts.

Source: Manuscript original of western Treaty 6 (IT296) signed at Fort Pitt on September 9, 1876 by Alexander Morris, Lieutenant-Governor of the Northwest Territories, and representatives of the "Plain and Wood Cree". © Indian and Northern Affairs Canada. Reproduced with the permission of the Minister of Public Works and Government Services Canada (2009). Source: Library and Archives Canada/RG10, Indian Affairs, D-10-a, IT296, Microfilm Reel T-9940/e004156541.

▲ Document 4: Treaty Six Chiefs

● Ahtahkakoop (left front) and Mistawasis (right front) influential Treaty Six Chiefs at Fort Carlton in 1876 (front centre, Chief Flying in a Circle; left rear, Chief Osoup; right rear, Peter Hourie, interpreter). Note the Chiefs wearing their Treaty medal.

Source: Library and Archives Canada, C19258.

▲ Document 5: Mistahimusqua (Big Bear) Cree Leader

● Mistahimusqua (Big Bear) Cree leader who participated in Treaty Six talks at Fort Pitt in September 1876, but refused to sign until 1882. Here he is photographed in chains for his supposed role in the Riel Rebellion 1885.

Source: Library and Archives Canada, C1873.

▲ Document 6: Herd of Buffalo in Foothills of Rocky Mountains

● **What does this image and the next tell you about the pace of change on the prairies?**

▲ Document 7: Pile of Buffalo Skulls, Saskatoon, Saskatchewan, August 9, 1890

▲ Document 8: Text of Treaty 7

Treaty Seven Elders and Tribal Council et al.

The text following contains the articles of the treaty as presented by the treaty commissioners. As is clear from the evidence of the elders, this document does not represent the true spirit and original intent of the treaty that was made at Blackfoot Crossing. The elders say that the treaty as presented to them a year after the negotiations does not contain all of the agreements concluded between the commissioners and chiefs. Many contentious issues concerning the written treaty remain unresolved, especially issues relating to the translation. Many elders have stated that the written treaty they were given was written prior to the arrival of the commissioners, and that agreements made during the negotiations were never incorporated into the final treaty text. The elders feel that much discussion, analysis, and amendment are still required before the written treaty contains the true spirit and original intent of the agreement. In addition to the fundamental issue of whether the treaty represents a land surrender, the elders point to the careless drafting and translation of the treaty.

Elder Louise Crop Eared Wolf* cites examples of gross misrepresentations of names on the treaties as evidence of the incompetence of the translators and those who wrote the treaty. Improper translations and spellings of the Blackfoot names appended to the treaty abound. She identified over eighty errors made by the translators. Some of the worst examples include the recoding of Crowfoot's name as Chapo-Mexico instead of Issapo-maksika; Chapo-Mexico has no meaning and sounds more like an English word. The name of another leading Siksika elder, Old Sun, was recorded as Matose-Apiw, which is simply incomprehensible in Blackfoot. Stamis-cotocar, for Stami-kso-tokan (Bull Head) of the Tsuu T'ina, again has no meaning in Blackfoot, as there are no "r's" in the Blackfoot language. Natose-onistors is a misrepresentation of Natoso-nista, which was wrongly translated as Medicine Calf instead of Powerful Calf. Takoye-stamix is an incorrect representation for Sakoi-yi-stamik (Last Bull, which was also mistranslated as Fiend Bull.) Issokoi-ya-wotanni or Cougar Shield was translated as Sakoye-aowotan, which means Heavy Shield. Crop Eared Wolf points out that this latter translation is an example of a very poor understanding of the language, since even though the words are close in sound—*issokoioyi* for "cougar" and *issokoi* for "heavy"—a real Blackfoot speaker would know the difference. Also Pitah-siksinum, meaning White Eagle, is the wrong spelling and translation of Pitai-siki-namm, which means Black Eagle. Pitah-otsikin, which means "disgusting," was used to represent Pitai-tsi-kinn, which means Eagle Moccasin.

---

*Louise Crop Eared Wolf: "My comments regarding all the mispronounced Blackfoot names of chiefs of the Bloods, Blackfoot, and Piegan give enough evidence to show that the interpreter (James Bird) at the Treaty 7 peace-making agreement was not a fluent speaker of the Blackfoot language at the time. How could he have accurately explained the articles of the treaty if he was unable to master the Blackfoot terms of the names in Blackfoot. My belief is that our ancestors were not made aware of all the English terms of the treaty."

Source: From *The True Spirit and Original Intent of Treaty 7*, Treaty 7 Elders and Tribal Council with Walter Hildebrandt, Sarah Carter and Dorothy First Rider. Chapter 6, pp. 230–31. Montreal and Kingston: McGill-Queen's University Press, 1996. Reprinted with permission from McGill-Queen's University Press.

When recording the names of the Stoney chiefs on the treaty documents, the officials used the Cree language and the not Stoney-Siouan language. Chief Jacob Bearspaw is written as Mas-'gwa-ah-sid, Cree for Bear's Paw, and Chief Jacob Goodstoney is written as Ki-chi-pwat, the Cree word for Big Stoney. The use of Cree to record Stoney names underlines the claim of the Stoney elders that their chief adviser, Reverend John McDougall, officially representing their position during the negotiations, was not a competent translator. McDougall knew Cree but not the Nakota-Siouan language.

The written treaty text below must therefore be read with the understanding that the Treaty 7 elders see it as something that does not fully represent what was agreed to at Blackfoot Crossing.

"THE TREATY WITH THE BLACKFEET; NUMBER SEVEN"

Articles of a Treaty made and concluded this twenty-second day of September, in the year of our Lord one thousand eight hundred and seventy-seven, between Her Most Gracious Majesty the Queen of Great Britain and Ireland, by her Commissioners, the Honorable David Laird, Lieutenant-Governor and Indian Superintendent of the North-West Territories, and James Farquharson McLeod, C.M.G., Commissioner of the North-West Mounted Police, of the one part, and the Blackfeet, Blood, Peigan, Sarcee, Stony, and other Indians, inhabitants of the territory north of the United States boundary line, east of the central range of the Rocky Mountains, and south and west of Treaties Numbers Six and Four, by their head Chiefs and minor Chiefs or Councillors, chosen as hereinafter mentioned, of the other part:

Whereas the Indians inhabiting the said territory, have pursuant to an appointment made by the said Commissioners, been convened at meeting at the "Blackfoot crossing" of the Bow River, to deliberate upon certain matters of interests to her Most Gracious Majesty, of the one part, and the said Indians of the other;

And whereas the said Indians have been informed by Her Majesty's Commissioners that it is the desire of Her Majesty to open up for settlement, and such other purposes as to Her Majesty may seem meet, a tract of country, bounded and described as hereinafter mentioned, and to obtain the consent thereto of her Indian subjects inhabiting the said tract, and to make a treaty, and arrange with them, so that there may be peace and good will between them and Her Majesty, and between them and Her Majesty's other subjects; and that her Indian people may know and feel assured of what allowance they are to count upon and receive from Her Majesty's bounty and benevolence;

And whereas the Indians of the said tract, duly convened in council, and being requested by her Majesty's Commissioners to present their head Chiefs and minor Chiefs, or Councillors, who shall be authorized, on their behalf, to conduct such negotiations and sign any treaty to be founded thereon, and to become responsible to Her Majesty for the faithful performance by their respective bands of such obligations as should be assumed by them, the said Blackfeet, Blood, Piegan and Sarcee Indians have therefore acknowledged for that purpose, the several head and minor Chiefs, and the said Stony Indians, the Chiefs and Councillors who have subscribed hereto, that thereupon in open council the said Commissioners received and acknowledged the head and minor Chiefs and the Chiefs and Councillors presented for the purpose aforesaid:

And whereas the said Commissioners have proceeded to negotiate a treaty with the said Indians; and the same has been finally agreed upon and concluded as follows, that is to say: the Blackfeet, Blood, Piegan, Sarcee, Stony and other Indians inhabiting the district hereinafter more fully described and defined, do hereby cede, release, surrender, and yield up to the Government of Canada for Her Majesty the Queen and her successors forever, all their rights, titles and privileges whatsoever to the lands included within the following limits, that is to say:

Commencing at a point on the international boundary due south of the western extremity of the Cypress Hills; thence west along the said boundary to the central range of the Rocky Mountains, or to the boundary of the Province of British Columbia; thence north-westerly along the said boundary to a point due west of the source of the main branch of the Red Deer River; thence south-westerly and southerly following on the boundaries of the tracts ceded by the Treaties Numbered Six and Four to the place of commencement; and also all their rights, titles and privileges whatsoever, to all other lands wherever situated in the North-West Territories, or in any other portion of the Dominion of Canada:

To have and to hold the same to Her Majesty the Queen and her successors forever:

And Her Majesty the Queen hereby agrees with her said Indians, that they shall have right to pursue their vocations of hunting throughout the tract surrendered as heretofore described, subject to such regulations as may, from time to time, be made by the Government of the country, acting under the authority of Her Majesty; and saving and excepting such tracts as may be required or taken up from time to time for settlement, mining, trading or other purposes by her Government of Canada, or by any of her Majesty's subjects duly authorized therefor by the said Government.

It is also agreed between Her Majesty and her said Indians that reserves shall be assigned them of sufficient area to allow one square mile for each family of five persons, or in that proportion for larger and smaller families, and that said reserves shall be located as follows, that is to say:

First—The reserves of the Blackfeet, Blood and Sarcee bands of Indians, shall consist of a belt of land on the north side of the Bow and South Saskatchewan Rivers, of an average width of four miles along said rivers, down stream, commencing at a point on the Bow River twenty miles north-westerly of the "Blackfoot crossing" thereof, and extending to the Red Deer River at its junction with the South Saskatchewan; also for the term of ten years, and no longer, from the date of the concluding of this treaty, when it shall cease to be a portion of said Indian reserves, as fully to all intents and purposes as if it had not at any time been included therein, and without any compensation to individual Indians for improvements, of a similar belt of land on the south side of the Bow and Saskatchewan Rivers of an average width of one mile along said rivers, down stream; commencing at the aforesaid point on the Bow River, and extending to a point one mile west of the coal seam on said river, about five miles below the said "Blackfoot crossing"; beginning again one mile east of the said coal seam and extending to the mouth of Maple Creek at its junction with the South Saskatchewan; and beginning again at the junction of the Bow River with the latter river, and extending on both sides of the South Saskatchewan in an average width on each side thereof of one mile, along said river against the stream, to the junction of the Little Bow River with the latter river, reserving to Her Majesty, as may now or hereafter be required by her for the use of her Indian and other subjects, from all the reserves hereinbefore described, the right to navigate the above mentioned rivers, to land and receive fuel and cargoes on the shores and banks thereof, to build bridges and establish ferries thereon, to use the fords thereof and all the trails leading thereto, and to open such other roads through the said reserves as may appear to Her Majesty's Government of Canada, necessary for the ordinary travel of her Indian and other subjects, due compensation being paid to individual Indians for improvements, when the same may be in any manner encroached upon by such roads.

Secondly—That the reserve of the Piegan band of Indians shall be on the Old Man's River, near the foot of the Porcupine Hills, at a place called "Crow's Creek."

And Thirdly—The reserve of the Stony band of Indians shall be in the vicinity of Morleyville.

In view of the satisfaction of Her Majesty with the recent general good conduct of her said Indians, and in extinguishment of all their past claims, she hereby, through her Commissioners, agrees to make them a present payment of twelve dollars each in cash to each man, woman, and child of the families here represented.

Her Majesty also agrees that next year, and annually afterwards forever, she will cause to be paid to the said Indians, in cash, at suitable places and dates, of which the said Indians shall be duly notified, to each Chief, twenty-five dollars, each minor Chief or Councillor (not exceeding fifteen minor Chiefs to the Blackfeet and Blood Indians, and four to the Piegan and Sarcee bands, and five Councillors to the Stony Indian Bands) fifteen dollars, and to every other Indian of whatever age, five dollars; the same, unless there be some exceptional reason, to be paid to the heads of families for those belonging thereto.

Further, Her Majesty agrees that the sum of two thousand dollars shall hereafter every year be expended in the purchase of ammunition for distribution among the said Indians; provided that if at any future time ammunition became comparatively unnecessary for said Indians, her Government, with the consent of said Indians, or any of the bands thereof, may expend the proportion due to such band otherwise for their benefit.

Further, Her Majesty agrees that each head Chief and minor Chief, and each Chief and Councillor duly recognized as such, shall, once in every three years, during the term of their office, receive a suitable suit of clothing, and each head Chief and Stony Chief, in recognition of the closing of the treaty, a suitable medal and flag, and next year, or as soon as convenient, each head Chief, and minor Chief, and Stony Chief shall receive a Winchester rifle.

Further, Her Majesty agrees to pay the salary of such teachers to instruct the children of said Indians as to her Government of Canada may seem advisable, when said Indians are settled on their reserves and shall desire teachers.

Further, Her Majesty agrees to supply each head and minor Chief, and each Stony Chief, for the use of their bands, ten axes, five handsaws, five augers, one grindstone, and the necessary files and whetstones.

And further, Her Majesty agrees that the said Indians shall be supplied as soon as convenient, after any band shall make due application therefor with the following cattle for raising stock, that is to say: for every family of five persons, and under, two cows; for every family of more than five persons, and less than ten persons, three cows; for every family of over ten persons, four cows; and every head and minor Chief, and every Stony Chief, for the use of their bands, one bull; but if any band desire to cultivate the soil as well as raise stock, each family of such band shall receive one cow less than the above mentioned number, and in lieu thereof, when settled on their reserves and prepared to break up the soil, two hoes, one spade, one scythe, and two hay forks, and for every three families, one plough and one harrow, and for each band, enough potatoes, barley, oats, and wheat (if such seeds be suited for the locality of their reserves) to plant the land actually broken up. All the aforesaid articles to be given, once for all, for the encouragement of the practice of agriculture among the Indians.

And the undersigned Blackfeet, Blood, Piegan and Sarcee head Chiefs and minor Chiefs, and Stony Chiefs and Councillors, on their own behalf and on behalf of all other Indians inhabiting the tract within ceded do hereby solemnly promise and engage to strictly observe this treaty, and also to conduct and behave themselves as good and loyal subjects of Her Majesty the Queen. They promise and engage that they will , in all respects, obey and abide by the law, that they will maintain peace and good order between each other and between themselves and other tribes of Indians, and between themselves and others of Her Majesty's subjects, whether Indians, Half breeds or whites, now inhabiting, or hereafter to inhabit, any part of the said ceded tract; and that they will not molest the person or property of any inhabitant of such ceded tract, or the property of Her Majesty the Queen, or interfere with or trouble any person, passing or travelling through the said tract or any part thereof, and that they will assist the officers of Her Majesty in bringing to justice and punishment any Indian offending against the stipulations of this treaty, or infringing the laws in force in the country ceded.

In witness whereof Her Majesty's said Commissioner, and the said Indian head and minor Chiefs, and Stony Chiefs and Councillors, have hereunto subscribed and set their hands, at the "Blackfoot crossing" of the Bow River, the day and year herein first above written.

(Signed) DAVID LAIRD,
Gov. of N.W.T. and Special Indian Commissioner.
JAMES F. MCLEOD,
Lieut.-Colonel, Com. N.-W.M.P.
and Special Indian Commissioner

CHAPO-MEXICO(or Crowfoot),	His x mark
Head Chief of the South Blackfeet.	
MATOSE-APIW (or Old Sun),	" x "
Head Chief of the North Blackfeet.	
STAMISCOTOCAR (or Bull Head),	" x "
Head Chief of the Sarcees.	
MEKASTO (or Red Crow),	" x "
Head Chief of the South Bloods.	
NATOSE-ONISTORS (or Medicine Calf.).	" x "
POKAPIW-OTOIAN (or Bad Head).	" x "
SOTENAH (or Rainy Chief),	" x "
Head Chief of the North Bloods.	
TAKOYE-STAMIX (or Fiend Bull).	" x "
AKKA-KITCIPIMIW-OTAS (or Many Spotted Horses).	" x "
ATTISTAH-MACAN (or Running Rabbit).	" x "
PITAH-PEKIS (or Eagle Rib).	" x "
SAKOYE-AOTAN (or Heavy Shield),	" x "
Head Chief of the Middle Blackfeet.	
ZOATZE-TAPITAPIW (or Setting on an Eagle Tail).	His x mark
Head Chief of the North Piegans.	
AKKA-MAKKOYE (or Many Swans).	" x "
APENAKO-SAPOP (or Morning Plume).	" x "
*MAS-GWA-AH-SID (or Bear's Paw).	" x "
*CHE-NE-KA (or John).	" x "
*KI-CHI-PWOT (or Jacob).	" x "
STAMIX-OSOK (or Bull Backfat).	" x "
EMITAH-APISKINNE (or White Striped Dog).	" x "
MATAPI-KOMOTZIW (or the Captive or Stolen Person).	" x "
APAWAWAKOSOW (or White Antelope).	" x "
MAKOYE-KIN (or Wolf Collar).	" x "
AYE-STIPIS-SIMAT (or Heavily Whipped).	" x "
KISSOUM (or Day Light).	" x "
PITAH-OTOCAN (or Eagle Head).	" x "
APAW-STAMIX (or Weasel Bull).	" x "

ONISTAH-POKAH (or White Calf).	His x mark
NETAH-KITEI-PI-MEW (or Only Spot).	" x "
AKAK-OTOS (or Many Horses).	" x "
STOKIMATIS (or The Drum).	" x "
PITAH-ANNES (or Eagle Robe).	" x "
PITAH-OTSIKIN (or Eagle Shoe).	" x "
STAMIX-OTA-KA-PIW (or Bull Turn Round).	" x "
MASTE-PITAH (or Crow Eagle).	" x "
†JAMES DIXON.	" x "
†ABRAHAM KECHEPWOT.	" x "
†PATRICK KECHEPWOT.	" x "
†GEORGE MOY-ANY-MEN.	" x "
†GEORGE CRAWLOR.	" x "
EKAS-KLINE (or Low Horn).	" x "
KAYO-OKOSIS (or Bear Shield).	" x "
PONOKAH-STAMIX (or Bull Elk).	" x "
OMAKSI SAPOP (or Big Plume).	" x "
ONISTAH (or Calf Robe).	" x "
PITAH-SIKSINUM (or White Eagle).	" x "
APAW-ONISTAW (or Weasel Calf).	" x "
ATTISTA-HAES (or Rabbit Carrier).	" x "
PITAH (or Eagle).	" x "
PITAH-ONISTAH (or Eagle White Calf.).	" x "
KAYE-TAPO (or Going to Bear).	" x "

Signed by the Chiefs and Councillors within named in presence of the following witnesses, the same having been first explained by James Bird, Interpreter.

(Signed) A.G. IRVINE, *Ass't Com.,* N.-W.M.P.

J. MCDOUGALL *Missionary.*

JEAN L'HEUREUX.

W. WINDER.

T.N.F. CROZIER, *Inspectors.*

E. DALRYMPLE CLARK, *Lieut. and Adjutant.* N.-W.M.P.

A. SHURTLIFF,

C.E. DENING,

W.D. ANTROBUS, *Sub-Inspectors.*

FRANK NORMAN, *Staff Constable.*

MARY J. MACLEOD.

JULIA WINDER.

JULIA SHURTLIFF.

E. HARDISTY.

A. MCDOUGALL.

E.A. BARRETT.

CONSTANTINE SCOLLEN, *Priest,* witness to signatures of Stonixosak and those following.

CHARLES E. CONRAD.

THOS. J. BOGG.

---

* Stony Chiefs.
† Stony Councillors

Article 1: The Numbered Treaties: Similar Means to Dichotomous Ends

Derek Whitehouse

On 2 August 1871, the Canadian government and the Indians of the North-West Territories signed the first of the Numbered Treaties. By the end of 1877 an additional six Treaties had been negotiated, effectively opening the North-West for settlement. Events leading up to the negotiations, and the negotiations themselves, provide clear evidence that dichotomy existed between the goals that the Indians hoped to achieve through the Treaty process and those the government hoped to attain. The Indians,[1] realizing that their environment was changing, sought to protect their culture from threatening forces such as non-native agricultural settlement and diminishing buffalo herds. The government, meanwhile, strove to encourage the absorption of the Indian cultures into broader Euro-Canadian society, not only because it wanted to open the North-West for settlement, but also because it believed that assimilation was in the best interest of the Indian peoples. Despite the disparity in the objectives that each party sought, both considered the Treaties to be tools that were essential to achieving their goals. Thus, in the first seven Numbered Treaties, the government and the Indians employed similar means toward very dissimilar ends.

Until recent decades, the historical analysis of Canada's past down-played or overlooked the contributions of aboriginal peoples. As James W. St.G. Walker noted of historical works such as Donald Creighton's *Canada: The Heroic Beginnings,* Indians were often presented as "not even minor actors in the Canadian drama, simply stage-props against which others work[ed] out their roles."[2]

A case in point is the work of Allan Harper. In 1947, Harper wrote that, during the Numbered Treaty process, discussion was controlled by the government and "confined to a careful explanation of the terms, answering questions, firmly rejecting exorbitant demands, and dispelling false notions about the government's assumption ofobligations."[3] Similarly, in 1932, G.F.G. Stanley argued that the negotiation of the Treaties "was confined to an explanation of the

terms" by the government and that "the Indians never understood what was happening."[4] Until the 1970s, historians portrayed Canada's aboriginal peoples as passive victims of dominant outside forces.

By the 1970s, however, historians were beginning to revise the image of the Indian peoples as victims. Fur trade historians like A.J. Ray spearheaded the revisionists' efforts. Writing in 1978, Ray argued that historical analyses which assumed "that the Indians were ruthlessly exploited and cheated in all areas and periods by white[s] [...] gives us only half the story."[5] A reinterpretation of Canada's past which recognized the contributions made by the Indian peoples would result in new perceptions of Indians as active and creative agents in the historical process. Ray realized that treating the largely ignored aboriginal peoples as active participants in Canada's past was essential to the appropriate placement of the Indian in the historical record.[6]

While the process of reinterpreting Canada's past began with fur trade historians such as A.J. Ray and Donald B. Freeman,[7] historians working in other fields also reassessed the Indian perspective. Sylvia Van Kirk, for example, argued that the fur trade "was not simply an economic activity, but a social and cultural complex."[8] Consequently, when examining the role that Indian, Métis, and white women had in the fur trade, Van Kirk asserted that the "examination of the role played by women as actors upon the fur trade stage is essential to a full understanding of the complexities" of early Western Canadian society.[9] Thus, in viewing Canada's aboriginal peoples as active agents of history, historians developed new interpretations of economic, social, religious, and political interactions between white and Indian.[10]

J.R. Miller noted, however, that most efforts of historians to restore the Canadian aboriginal to the position of an active historical agent have focused upon the period preceding the 1860s. Indeed, as late as 1990, Miller argued that "studies of Indian-white relations after Confederation [...] have thus far largely proved resistant to reinterpretation."[11]

Articles by Jean Friesen, D.J. Hall, and John Leonard Taylor, however, are notable exceptions in that they demonstrate that the revisionists are no longer emphasizing the pre-Confederation period. Taylor, for example, maintained that the Numbered Treaties were the product of Indian and government interactions, and not, as Harper had argued, the result

Source: *Past Imperfect,* Vol. 3 (1994): 25–45. Reprinted with permission from Derek Whitehouse-Strong.

of the government dictating terms that the Indians had either to "accept or reject."[12] Taylor understood the Treaty process as having been an open negotiation in which the Indians introduced innovations that the government was subsequently forced to accept. If the government had not accepted the innovations, it "would have had even more difficulty getting the treaties, if [it] had been able to get them at all."[13]

Duncan Campbell Scott, Canada's Deputy Superintendent General of Indian Affairs from 1913 to 1932, attested to the underlying continuity of the government's Indian policy some thirty years after the completion of the first seven Numbered Treaties. In 1909, Scott stated that "the true and uniform policy [of the government] [...] has made the Canadian Indian believe the British sovereign is his great parent and [he] himself is a child under beneficent protection."[14] He went on to say that "the happiest future for the Indian race is [...] absorption into the general population, and this is the object of the policy of our government."[15] Toward this goal, the government believed that

> agriculture, education, and religion would, in time, provide the Indian with far more than he had lost. Eventually the settlement of the West would uplift the native from his state [of savagery or barbarism].[16]

The Canadian government genuinely believed that its goal of assimilation was in the best interest of the Indian peoples. The Numbered Treaties were intended to provide the tools which government officials thought were necessary to facilitate this assimilation: reserve agriculture, schools, and missionaries.[17]

Much of the Canadian population shared the government's desire to absorb the Indian peoples into broader Euro-Canadian society. For decades, official documents and reports, and "the works of scientists, social scientists, travellers, humanitarians, and missionaries"[18] had served to shape the perception that assimilation was not only in the best interest of the Canadian population, but also of the aboriginal peoples themselves. As a result of these varied influences, a paternalistic approach to the assimilation of the Indians was seen as both "desirable [...] and necessary. With the Indian as the ward of the state, steps could be taken to protect him from the harmful effects of white culture while teaching him its benefits."[19]

Imperialistic influences also strengthened and confirmed the idea that the assimilation of the Indian was the true and correct policy to follow. Colonies within the British Empire, historian Walter Houghton argued, had been founded

> it was said—and believed—by the generous and altruistic desire of spreading throughout the habitable globe all the characteristics of Englishmen—their energy, their civilization, their religion and their freedom.[20]

Consequently, those directing the government's Indian policy saw themselves as fulfilling this aspect of Britain's destiny. What could be better for an improvident, intemperate, and latently indolent people who were prone to privation[21] than to become active members of a nation destined to assume the role of dominance in the British Empire? The government expected that agriculture would help the Indians overcome the inherent weaknesses that it believed they shared as peoples, and thus it would aid their eventual assimilation into Canadian society. The aboriginal peoples would then become part of that which "represent[ed] man's highest achievement in the development of governmental and social institutions."[22] In order for the Indians to be assimilated, however, the government knew that the cultural identity of the Canadian aboriginals would have to be eliminated. On a cultural level, the Indian would have to adopt the traditions and practices of the white man.[23]

In 1877, the prominent American anthropologist Lewis Henry Morgan put to print a theory, the essence of which many of his era were already familiar with. Morgan asserted that all societies passed through the stages of savagery and barbarism on their way to becoming civilized.[24] Consequently, because passage from one level of development to the next was thought to be unilinear, "each step [...] was regarded as essential to the next and [thus] could not be transcended."[25] According to the unilinear evolutionists argument, it followed that because many of the Indian bands in the North-West engaged in hunting and gathering subsistence, they were in the initial, savage phase of the evolutionary path. Subscribing to Morgan's theory, the government believed that the Indians would have to pass through barbarism, a stage which was characterized by domestication and cultivation, before they could become civilized. Reserve agriculture was, therefore, to be the Indian peoples' "place of probation, a training ground in the lessons of civilization and citizenship."[26]

Besides viewing the Treaties as a means to encourage the assimilation of the Indian, government officials also intended to use the Treaties to open the North-West for settlement in accordance with its national policy.[27] The Royal Proclamation of 1763 made it illegal for anyone, save the Crown, to purchase land in "Indian Country."[28] Although this provision "did not apply to the Hudson's Bay Company lands, [it did] set out the basis" by which these lands would be settled after their transfer to Canada in 1870.[29] It was necessary, therefore, for the government to extinguish Indian title to land in the North-West before settlement could begin. Alexander Morris, the lieutenant governor of the North-West Territories from 1872 to 1876, summarized this objective during the discussions concerning Treaty One and Treaty Two. According to Morris,

> it was desirable to secure the extinction of the Indian title not only to the lands within Manitoba, but also to so much of the timber grounds east and north of the Province as were required for immediate entry and use, also of a large tract of cultivate ground west of the Portage, where there were very few Indian inhabitants.[30]

Regarding the completion of Treaty Three, he continued:

> and so was closed, a treaty, whereby a territory was enabled to be opened up, of great importance to Canada, embracing as it does the Pacific Railway route to the North West Territories—a wide extent of fertile lands, and, as is believed, great mineral resources.[31]

Extinguishing Indian title to land in the North-West so that settlement could commence thus constituted the second goal of the government's Treaty policy.

Morris' words demonstrate that pressures on land, resulting from the government's settlement policy, were the primary motivators behind the government's decision to treat. That settlement pressures were of such great import to the Canadian government can be largely attributed to the fact that, with an annual federal budget of only $19 million and with the construction of a transcontinental railway a national preoccupation, the government was seeking to devote only as many resources as were necessary to negotiating treaties with the Indians.[32] Indeed, Joseph Howe, Secretary of State for the Provinces cautioned Treaty Commissioner Wemyss Simpson to

> endeavour to secure the session [sic] of the lands upon terms as favourable as possible to the Government, not going as far as the maximum sum hereafter named unless it be found impossible to obtain the object for a less amount.[33]

In addition, Prime Minister Alexander Mackenzie pointed out that, when compared to "other countries," Canada's Treaty policy was not only "a humane, just, and Christian policy," it was also "the cheapest."[34] Only when it was so required by settlement pressures, therefore, would the government be induced to negotiate.

The requests of the Indian peoples themselves had little impact on the timing of negotiations when settlement pressures were not at issue. Indeed, some of the bands who would eventually be included under Treaty Six had requested negotiations toward an agreement a full five years before actual proceedings began. The government, however, did little to address the "[general] feeling of discontent and uneasiness," arising from the fact that they had not been treated with, "[that] prevailed [...] amongst the Assiniboines and Crees."[35] Only when the Indians threatened to disrupt survey and telegraph crews was the government finally compelled to negotiate.[36]

Settlement pressure of a different type was the key factor in the government's movement to negotiate Treaty Seven. On this occasion, it was white settlers who pressured the government for an agreement in order to allay growing concerns regarding their own safety. Father Constantine Scollen noted that

> The Blackfeet are extremely jealous of what they consider their country and have never allowed any white men, Half-breeds, or Crees to remain in it for any length of time

[...] [As such, the settlers] are anxious that a treaty be made as soon as possible, so that they may know what portions of land they can hold without fear of being molested.[37]

Consequently, it was again in the government's interest to obtain a treaty, despite the fact that, unofficially at least, the Blackfoot were not seeking such an agreement.

Humanistic, expansionistic, imperialistic, and nationalistic beliefs, values, and ideas thus shaped the Canadian government's Indian policy. Furthermore, it is clear that the government engaged in the treaty-making process for two main reasons. First, negotiations were initiated to facilitate the Euro-Canadian agricultural settlement of the North-West. Second, the Treaty concessions provided the means by which the distinctiveness, uniqueness, and heritage of the Indian could be eliminated, and what was left could be absorbed into the Euro-Canadian culture.

For the Indians, however, the Treaties served an entirely different function. Aware that the Treaties would open the North-West up for rapid settlement, the aboriginal peoples also understood that settlement was inevitable, with or without the Treaties. Consequently, the Indians sought to use the concessions that they gained under the Treaty system to ensure that their culture would survive, an end antithetical to that being sought by the government. To achieve their goal, the Indians, much like the government, expressed an interest in schools and in missionaries and "were desirous of according to the wish of their great Mother" that they "discard their former precarious mode of living and adopt the agricultural pursuits of the white man."[38] Aware that social and economic pressures were making it inevitable that their way of life was coming to an end, the aboriginal peoples sought to adopt a new way of life, one which would allow them to retain their independent cultures.

The Ojibwa and the Swampy Cree, who were among the first Indian peoples to be involved in the Numbered Treaty process, had outwardly expressed concern regarding the "influx of population" onto their lands. Indeed, Alexander Morris noted that "the Indians in Manitoba [...] had in some instances obstructed settlers and surveyors"[39] until their calls for a Treaty were met. Thus, while governmental policy dictated that Treaties were to be negotiated only when so required by settlement pressures, the Indian peoples were still able to "[rush] the government's timetable somewhat."[40]

Concerns about the influx of white settlers also affected the tribes involved in later negotiations. The Plains Cree were aware that great numbers of white settlers would soon be entering their lands. During Treaty Six negotiations, Star Blanket, the Chief of the Wood Indians, cautioned those of his people who opposed the Treaty:

[When the buffalo are gone] what then will be left us with which to bargain? With the buffalo gone we will have only the vacant prairie which none of us have learned to use. Can we stop the power of the white man from spreading over the land like the grasshoppers that cloud the sky and then fall to consume every blade of grass and every leaf on the trees in their path? I think not. Before this happens, let us ponder carefully our choice of roads.[41]

Indeed, in 1875, the Reverend George McDougall had been informed by certain Cree that "they were unanimous in their determination to oppose the running of lines, or the making of roads through their country, until an agreement between the Government and them had been effected."[42] This concern was echoed by the Plains Assiniboine who, on hearing that they would be treated with, informed Alexander Morris that "foolish men have told us that the Great Chief would send his young men to our country until they outnumbered us, and that then he would laugh at us."[43]

The Blackfoot, who in 1877 were signatories to Treaty Seven, also saw the early signs of white settlement. Unlike many of the tribes further east, however, they themselves were not seeking a Treaty. It is likely, nevertheless, that factors such as the diminishing buffalo herds and the steady increase of white settlers into their region would have eventually "disposed the Blackfoot towards making a treaty."[44] Indeed, the likes of the Reverends George and John McDougall and Fathers Scollen and Fourmond had penetrated as far south as the Bow River by 1877. This fact "not only indicates the hold the missionaries were gaining on the prairie Indians but also how much the Blackfoot hold on their native land was slipping."[45]

The Blackfoot's concern over the diminishing buffalo herds had also been voiced by the other Plains tribes who had realized, at least as early as the 1850s, that the herds were becoming more scarce.[46] From that time on, the Cree, for example, had attempted to protect the herds by calling on the government to limit the hunting of these creatures to Indians alone.[47] Yet, it was not until 1876 that "the North-West Council [considered] the framing of a law to protect the buffaloes."[48] Nothing ever came of the Council's consideration, however, and less than three years later the buffalo had disappeared from Canada. Despite attempts to protect the buffalo, the Cree had largely accepted the fact that their way of life was coming to an end. Star Blanket addressed this concern when he said:

> We have always lived and received our needs in clothing, shelter, and food from the countless multitudes of buffalo that have been with us since the earliest memory of our people. No one with open eyes and open minds can doubt that the buffalo will soon be a thing of the past. Will pass? No! They will die and become just a memory unless we find another way.... The mother earth has always given us plenty with the grass that fed the buffalo. Surely we can learn the ways that made the whiteman strong.[49]

Thus, Canada's aboriginal peoples realized that an adaptation to a new way of life was required, and, like the government, most saw agriculture as the answer.

Many Canadians were likely surprised to learn that the Indians were willing to take up cultivating the soil. Most Euro-Canadians believed that Indians resisted change and had lived in their current state for untold centuries. The Methodist missionary John MacLean described Canadian efforts to "civilize" and "uplift" the Indian peoples:

> We wish to make them white men, and they desire to become better Indians. They believe the native culture is best suited for themselves, and having developed under it, and enjoyed it so long, they care not to give it up for an untried system.[50]

The missionary John McDougall, who in 1876 was a commissioner for the government's treaty negotiations, concurred. He wrote that the

> aboriginal man with his traditions unchanged through the centuries met face to face representatives of another old but ever-changing race to negotiate in peace and friendship their future negotiations in this new land.[51]

Much of the Euro-Canadian populace thus believed that the cultures of the Indian peoples were static.

The perception that the Indian way of life was unchanging proved to be unfounded, however. In the two centuries prior to the signing of the Numbered Treaties, many aboriginal peoples had adapted to the new economies that had been created by the fur trade. That the Indians understood the concepts of dynamic economies is evident when one examines the adaptability of the Plains Cree. Prior to European contact, the Cree were primarily woodland hunters and gatherers.[52] After 1670, however, they had assumed a middleman role in the fur trade. When the fur traders themselves began to move into the interior, thus effectively bypassing them, the Cree had adapted again by moving on to the Plains and becoming buffalo hunters.[53] Although they were perhaps caught off guard by the rapidity with which they were required to adapt,[54] the Indian peoples accepted the fact that their lifestyle would have to change again. What the aboriginals were concerned with, however, was the impact that this change would have on their culture.

The desire of Beardy, the Chief of the Willow Crees, to negotiate in a place that "had been revealed to him in a vision"[55] provides clear evidence that the Indians believed the Treaties to be an important means of preserving Native culture. In Cree culture, as in almost all Plains cultures, the dream or vision was of great significance. The Plains Indian perceived dreams to be sources of powerful knowledge and insight. As scholar Joseph Epes Brown argued, the "nature of the received vision often obligate[d] the recipient to externalize the experience and thus ... share the power with the larger community."[56] To ensure that the Treaty would be negotiated successfully and that his people would achieve what they desired from these proceedings, Beardy sought to re-enact his vision. The government negotiators, however, misunderstood his intentions and assumed that Beardy was merely being difficult. Consequently, the government negotiators would only treat with the Willow Crees at the location they themselves had designated.[57]

The Indians of Treaty Six[58] realized that, in order to protect their culture from being destroyed by the inevitable incursion of white settlers onto their lands, they had to reach an agreement with the government. As a result, they took an active role in the Treaty negotiations. Entering the talks, the government was prepared to offer essentially the same concessions that had been granted under the first five Treaties. Regarding Treaty One, the government had intended only to establish reserves and grant annuities in exchange for the surrender of Indian title to their lands. The Indians, however, eventually extracted additional concessions such as the provision of agricultural and educational assistance.[59] Similarly, the Indian signatories to Treaty Three were able to obtain further allowances from the government including an increase in the allotment of land from 100 acres for each family of five to 640 acres and an increase in annuities from \$3 to \$5.[60]

The government had acceded to the Indians' demands as they were consistent with their goals of assimilation. For the Indian peoples to be able to cultivate those reserve lands that were to be set aside for them, they had to be provided with the implements and the knowledge necessary to undertake such a task. As Henry Prince, Chief of the St. Peter's band, asked when he was informed that the government wanted the Indians to take up agriculture but would provide them with only land and annuities, "[How could] the Queen expect the Indian to cultivate the land? They cannot scratch it—work it with their fingers. What assistance will they get if they settle down?"[61] Wemyss Simpson apparently concurred when he wrote that the aforementioned concessions were given "with a view to inducing the Indians to adopt the habits and labours of civilization."[62]

Those concessions which were granted under Treaties One through Five, however, did not fully address the apprehensions that the Plains Cree had concerning the protection of their culture. Consequently, much like the Saulteaux of Treaty One, the Cree were able to demand and receive additions

to the Treaty which the government had not originally intended to grant.[63] These new concessions, namely the granting of \$1000 a year for three years, the medicine chest clause, and the pestilence/famine clause, addressed the concerns of the Plains Cree regarding their adaptation to, and survival in, their new environment.[64]

The government agreed to pay a sum of \$1000 to those bands who were "settled on the reserves and [who were] engaged in cultivating the soil."[65] Consequently, only those Indians who were already considered to be in the process of becoming civilized were to receive benefits from the clause. The government therefore regarded the \$1000 as further contributing to the eventual assimilation of the Indian and achieving the ultimate goal of its Indian policy.

The monetary concession itself had been made in response to Cree demands for "food in the spring" when they began to farm[66] In the spring, and especially during the initial years of cultivation, great expenditures of time and energy would have to be made in ploughing, seeding, and cultivating the land. Consequently, the Indians would have to abandon non-agricultural means of acquiring sustenance, such as hunting, gathering, and trapping, to ensure that their agricultural efforts were as successful as possible. The Indians believed that a secure source of food would assist them in their adaption to reserve agriculture and thus help them to preserve a unique and separate identity in Euro-Canadian society.

With regard to the pestilence/famine clause and the medicine chest clause, both were applicable only to those Indians who had signed Treaty Six.[67] Again, the government considered these concessions as aiding the inevitable assimilation of the Plains Cree as they addressed specific concerns that the Cree had expressed. Alexander Morris was aware that "small-pox had destroyed [the Plains Cree] by hundreds a few years before"[68] and that epidemics of scarlet fever and measles had also recently affected the region. In addition, the fact that the buffalo herds were rapidly disappearing had raised concerns about starvation at a time when adaption to a new method of subsistence, namely agriculture, was required.[69] In the words of Morris, the Indians "dreaded pestilence and famine."[70] The government regarded sustenance requirements as being specific to the Plains Cree alone, however. Indeed, with the exception of "spring provisions for several years" as provided in

Treaty Eight, these "pestilence/famine concessions," or any that were similar, were not repeated in subsequent agreements.[71]

The Indians viewed the pestilence/famine clause as a means of insuring themselves against any hardships that they might have encountered during their initial attempts to cultivate their reserve lands including both crop failure and destruction.[72] Big Child, Chief of the Carlton Indians, noted:

> It is well known that if we have plenty in our gardens and crops we would not insist on getting more provisions, but it is only in the case of extremity and from the ignorance of Indians in commencing to work the land that we speak. We are in the dark. This is no trivial matter with us.[73]

Knowing that the buffalo would soon be gone and that agriculture was to become their main means of support, the Indians were acutely aware of the dangers that could arise if they proved slow to learn proper agricultural techniques or if some disaster befell them. If either situation were to occur without the protection and assistance of the government, the Indians knew that they would starve.

The medicine chest clause addressed specific concerns held by the Cree regarding the aforementioned epidemics that had recently swept through the Plains. As a result of smallpox alone, hundreds of Plains Cree had died and many more had become seriously ill by the early 1870s. In one band alone, over fifty individuals had perished.[74] To make matters worse, during times of affliction many hunters and trappers were either killed or incapacitated to the point where they were unable to perform everyday duties. As a result, starvation and economic difficulties (the latter exacerbated by the need to destroy the property of those who had been infected) often accompanied and outlasted the epidemics. The Indians were aware that a vaccine to combat the disease did exist, but it was not readily available to them.[75] Thus, the aboriginal peoples believed that having a medicine chest on each reserve would help to ensure that both unnecessary deaths and economic hardships resulting from illnesses were minimized.

A consideration of the roles of both the Indian peoples and the Canadian government in the Numbered Treaty process, reveals that both parties sought similar terms to achieve dichotomous ends. While both the Indians and the Canadian government supported the concept of reserve agriculture as outlined in the Treaties, each saw cultivation as a way to help achieve different goals. The Indians recognized that their environment was changing and considered reserve agriculture to be the best method of adapting to a new way of life. In making this transition, however, the Indians attempted to protect their people from being assimilated into white society, thus preserving their separate identities. The government, on the other hand, saw both the Treaties and reserve agriculture as the most practical way to achieve the goals of its Indian policy. By utilizing the Treaties to open up the North-West for settlement, the government hoped to bring about that which it considered to be in the best interest of the Indian peoples: their assimilation into white society.

NOTES

1. It should be noted that many different groups of Indians were involved in the Numbered Treaty process, including various bands of Ojibwa, Cree, Assiniboine, and Blackfoot. For a brief introduction to the first seven of the Numbered Treaties, refer to Gerald Friesen, *The Canadian Prairies: A History* (Toronto. 1987). 138–146.

2. James W. St.G. Walker, "The Indian in Canadian Historical Writing, 1972–1982" in Ian A.L. Getty and Antoine S. Lussier, eds., *As Long as the Sun Shines and the Water Flows: A Reader in Canadian Native Studies,* (Vancouver, 1983), 346. Reprinted from Canadian Historical Association *Historical Papers* (1971), 21–47.

3. Allan G. Harper, "Canada's Indian Administration: The Treaty System," *America Indigena* 7, 2 (April, 1947), 145

4. G.F.G. Stanley, "The Indian Background of Canadian History" in Canadian Historical Association Report (1932), 20. Quoted in Jean Friesen, "Magnificent Gifts: The Treaties of Canada with the Indians of the Northwest 1869–76," *Transactions of the Royal Society of Canada,* Fifth Series, 1. (1962), 42.

5. Arthur J. Ray, "Fur Trade History as an Aspect of Native History" in R. Douglas Francis and Donald B. Smith, eds., *Readings in Canadian History* (Pre-Confederation) (Toronto, 1982), 151

6. Ibid., 149–151
7. See A. J. Ray, *Indians in the Fur Trade 1660–1870* (Toronto, 1974) and A. J. Ray and Donald B. Freeman *Give us Good Measure: An Economic Analysis of Relations Between the Indians and the Hudson's Bay Company Before 1763* (Toronto, 1978).
8. Sylvia Van Kirk, Many Tender Ties: *Women in Fur-Trade Society, 1670–1870* (Winnipeg, 1980), 2
9. Ibid., 8
10. D.J. Hall, "'A Serene Atmosphere'? Treaty 1 Revisited," *Canadian Journal of Native Studies* 4, 2 (1984), 322. Also note works such as J.R. Miller, *Skyscrapers Hide the Heavens: A History of Indian-White Relations in Canada*, rev. ed. (Toronto, 1991) and John Webster Grant, Moon of Wintertime: *Missionaries and the Indians of Canada in Encounter since 1534* (Toronto, 1984).
11. J.R. Miller, "Owen Glendower, Hotspur, and Canadian Indian Policy," *Ethnohistory* 37, (Fall, 1990), 388
12. Harper, "Canada's Indian Administration," 145
13. John Leonard Taylor, "Canada's Northwest Indian Policy in the 1870s: Traditional Premises and Necessary Innovations" in Richard Price, ed., *The Spirit of the Alberta Indian Treaties,* (Montreal, 1980), 6. Also see Friesen, "Magnificent Gifts" and Hall, "Serene Atmosphere."
14. Brian E. Titley, *A Narrow Vision: Duncan Campbell Scott and the Administration of Indian Affairs in Canada* (Vancouver, 1986), 27. For an analysis of the government's Indian strategy prior to the Indian Act and how their post-Confederation goals could be considered to be an extension of a somewhat continuous policy, refer to John E. Leslie and Ron Maguire, *The Historical Development of the Indian Act* (Ottawa, 1978).
15. Ibid., 34
16. Doug Owram, *Promise of Eden: The Canadian Expansionist Movement and the Idea of the West 1856–1900* (Toronto, 1981), 132
17. It should be noted that although missions were outside the purview of the government, both the government and the Indians wished to see them established on reserves. As such, although not prescribed by the Treaties themselves, the establishment of missions was integral to the objectives of both the Indians and the government.
18. L.F.S. Upton, "The Origins of Canadian Indian Policy," *Journal of Canadian Studies* 8, 4 (1973), 5. Alsosee Grant, Moon of Wintertime, 85.
19. Owram, *Promise of Eden,* 132
20. Walter E. Houghton, *The Victorian Frame of Mind: 1830–1870* (New Haven, 1957), 47
21. Marcel Giraud, *The Métis in the Canadian West* Vol. I trans. George Woodcock, (Lincoln, 1986), 349–351
22. Owram, *Promise of Eden,* 126
23. John MacLean, *Indians of Canada: Manners and Customs* (Toronto, 1889), 263
24. Abraham Rosman and Paula G. Rubel, *Tapestry of Culture,* 2nd ed. (New York, 1985), 14. See also Ixwis Henry Morgan, "Ancient Society" in Paul Bohannan and Mark Glazer, eds., *High Points in Anthropology* (New York, 1973), 30-60. Morgan's theory concerning the evolutionary development of societies was an embodiment of Social Darwinism, a theory that held that societal evolution represented progress. Historian, Laurence S. Fallis Jr., noted of intellectual thought in mid-to-late nineteenth-century Canada that the "idea of progress by making change appear to be natural, if not inevitable, made change acceptable." Laurence S. Fallis Jr., "The Idea of Progress in the Province of Canada: A Study in the History of Ideas" in W.L. Morton, ed., *The Shield of Achilles: Aspects of Canada in the Victorian Age* (Toronto, 1968), 173. The "cultural advancement" of the Indian peoples was thus held by much of the Euro-Canadian population as being in the best interest of all concerned, particularly with regard to the Indians.
25. [missing from original document]
26. Ibid., 19. See also Carter, *Lost Harvests,* 36–45 where it is noted that some Indian peoples possessed agricultural experience that pre-dated the Treaty era. Indeed, Carter notes that in "nineteenth-century Manitoba before the treaties of the 1870s, Indian participation in gardening and farming was not uncommon." Ibid., 40
27. Friesen, *The Canadian Prairies,* 184–186
28. Leslie, *The Historical Development,* 3–5
29. Richard C. Daniel, *A History of Native Claims in Canada: 1867–1979* (Ottawa, 1979), 2. As Daniel noted, the terms of the purchase agreement effectively extended the terms of the Royal Proclamation to the newly acquired North-West. Article 14 of the Imperial Order in Council that gave effect to the transfer stated that "[a]ny claims of the Indians to

compensation for lands shall be disposed of by the Canadian government in communication with the Imperial Government; and that the Company shall be relieved of all responsibility in respect to them." Ibid., 1–2

30. Alexander Morris, *The Treaties of Canada with the Indians of Manitoba and the North-West Territories, 1880* (Toronto, reprint, 1971), 26. Morris was the chief negotiator for the crown during the negotiations of Treaties Three, Four, Five, and Six. He also revised Treaties One and Two. Jean Friesen, "Alexander Morris" in Francess G. Halpenny, ed., *Dictionary of Canadian Biography* 11, (Toronto, 1982), 612.

31. Ibid., 46

32. Miller, *Skyscrapers Hide the Heavens,* 162. See also Gerald Friesen, *The Canadian Prairies,* 177–8 regarding the funding that the government supplied for the construction of the C.P.R. including "direct grants of $25 million." Also note Carter, *Lost Harvests,* 22.

33. As quoted in Daniel, *A History of Native Claims,* 6.

34. As quoted in Miller, *Skyscrapers Hide the Heavens,* 162.

35. Morris, *The Treaties of Canada,* 171

36. Ibid., 172

37. Ibid., 249

38. Ibid., 40

39. Ibid., 25–26

40. "Hall, "A Serene Atmosphere," 323. Also see John Tobias, "Canada's Subjugation of the Plains Cree," *Canadian Historical Review* 44, 4 (1983), 519–548. Tobias provides an alternate view to that of Hall. While Hall qualifies his remark with the term "somewhat," Tobias down-plays the government's role, at least with regards to Treaty One. I would argue that until settlement became a governmental priority, the Indians were able to do little to make their demands carry much weight. This is evident in the five-year interval between when the Plains Cree expressed a desire to treat and the beginning of negotiations. Again, in the above case, the government acted only when it perceived that its plans regarding settlement might be threatened.

41. Peter Erasmus, *Buffalo Day sand Nights* (Calgary, 1976), 249. Historian Olive Patricia Dickason makes note of the English spelling of Star Blanket's true Indian name, Ahchacoosacootacoopits, in *Canada's First Nations: A History of Founding Peoples*

from Earliest Times (Toronto, 1992), 300. Similarly, Alexander Morris noted the spelling of Star Blanket's name as Ah-tak-ah-coop in *The Treaties of Canada,* 213.

42. Morris, *The Treaties of Canada,* 173

43. Ibid., 174

44. John Leonard Taylor, "Two Views on the Meaning of Treaties Six and Seven," in Richard Price, ed., *The Spirit of the Alberta Indian Treaties* (Montreal, 1980), 26

45. James MacGregor, *Father Lacombe* (Edmonton, 1978), 233

46. Carter, *Lost Harvests,* 35–36

47. Tobias, "Canada's Subjugation of the Plains Cree," 106

48. Morris, *The Treaties of Canada,* 241

49. "Erasmus, *Buffalo Days and Nights,* 250

50. John MacLean, *Canadian Savage Folk: The Native Tribes of Canada* (Toronto, 1896), 543

51. John McDougall, *Opening the Great West: Experiences oaf Missionary in 1875–76* (Calgary, 1970), 58

52. It should be noted that there is a historical debate concerning the western extent of the Cree borders. John S. Milloy argued for the traditionally accepted interpretation that the Cree "adopted a plains way of life in the 1790s" in *The Plains Cree: Trade, Diplomacy and War, 1790 to 1870* (Winnipeg, 1988), xiv. According to Milloy, the Plains Cree became "clearly identifiable" when they "own[ed] horses" and had "a different relationship to the buffalo herds and to the Europeans" than their Woodland Cree ancestors. Ibid., 23–26. Milloy, argued that the Plains Cree's "transition from beaver to buffalo, from forest to plain, was completed" during the 1790s. Ibid., 27. Dale Russell, however, reinterpreted the archival and secondary resources and contended that the Cree of the mid-1700s did not shift "from the forests to the grasslands. Rather, they were then, and continued to be, a parkland group." Dale Russell, *Eighteenth-Century Western Cree and their Neighbours* (Hull, 1991), 218. Russell believed that the western limits of the Cree had been placed 800 kilometres too far east by previous scholars (Ibid., 212) and that the change in the role of middleman Cree to Plains Cree was gradual and somewhat minimal as they already possessed experience at living in a Parkland environment.

53. Tobias, "Canada's Subjugation of the Plains Cree," 105

54. MacGregor, *Father Lacombe*, 231
55. Morris, *The Treaties of Canada,* 176
56. Joseph Epes Brown, *The Spiritual Legacy of the American Indian* (New York, 1992), 15
57. Morris, *The Treaties of Canada,* 176. See also Ibid., 225.
58. Tobias, "Canada's Subjugation of the Plains Cree," 106–107. It is important to note that not all members of the Plains Cree considered the final text of Treaty Six to be adequate for ensuring the protection of their culture. Big Bear and Little Pine did not sign the Treaty as they believed it would result in a "loss of autonomy" for their people and result in their being "enslave[d]."
59. Hall, "A Serene Atmosphere," 327–331. These concessions took the form of outside promises which were not adhered to by the government until 1875. That the government was willing to agree to these concessions is evident in that Treaty 3, signed in 1873, contained distinctly similar provisos.
60. Gerald Friesen, *The Canadian Prairies,* 141. See also Morris, *The Treaties of Canada,* 320–327.
61. Ibid., 327
62. *Morris,* The Treaties of Canada, 40
63. The additional concessions that were granted to the Indian signatories of Treaty Six were agreed to by the government as they were not considered to run contrary to the government's goal of assimilating Indian culture. As will be seen, these concessions were in fact considered to help facilitate that goal.
64. That these terms were introduced by the Indians is evident in the transcripts of the negotiations. For example, Morris implies as much when he states of the Treaty that "it is more than has been done anywhere else; I must do it on my own responsibility, and trust to the other Queen's councillors to ratify it." Morris, *The Treaties of Canada,* 215.
65. Ibid., 354–355
66. Ibid., 252
67. Ibid., 354–355
68. Ibid., 178
69. George Brown and Ron Maguire, Indian Treaties in Historical Perspective, (Ottawa, 1979). 36
70. Morris, *The Treaties of Canada,* 178
71. Brown and Maguire, *Indian Treaties,* 38
72. Sarah Carter has noted that there were many problems attached to farming in the North-West. "Crops were often damaged by frost and scourged by squirrels, gophers, and dogs. Grasshopper plagues occurred almost annually." Carter, *Lost Harvests,* 42.
73. Erasmus, *Buffalo Days and Nights,* 252. Dickason makes note of the English spelling of Big Child's true Indian name, Mistawasis, in *Canada's First Nations,* 300. Similarly, Alexander Morris noted the spelling of Big Child's name as Mis-tah-wah-sis in Morris, *The Treaties of Canada,* 213.
74. Ibid., 212
75. Ibid., 204–212

Article 2: Canada's Colony and the Colonized

Sarah Carter

'A Unique and Unenviable Place': Canadian Federal Indian Policy

When Manitoba and the North-West Territories joined Confederation in 1870, the vast majority of

Source: Sarah Carter, *Aboriginal People and Colonizers of Western Canada to 1900* (Toronto: University of Toronto Press, 1999), selections from Chapter 6 (pp. 111–130). © University of Toronto Press Inc., 1999. Reprinted with permission of the publisher.

the residents were Aboriginal people, and largely unknown to them, their lives from then on were to be greatly influenced by policies and legislation developed for nearly 100 years in Eastern Canada, and inherited from British imperial practices. The British North America Act of 1867 had given the Canadian federal government jurisdiction over Indians and Indian reserves. In Western Canada, by 1870 there had been over two centuries of European contact, but no formal challenges to Aboriginal land ownership, except within the territory covered by the Selkirk Treaty. The 1870s represents an important watershed for many reasons. The era of efforts to impose the values and institutions of the immigrants or colonists began (although not in earnest until after 1885), and this coincided with the destruction and disappearance of the buffalo economy, just after a devastating epidemic of smallpox and famine. Yet while economic security, independence, and opportunities were to a great extent diminished beginning in the 1870s, Aboriginal people, of course, continued to take action, and make decisions and adopt strategies that influenced the course of events. However, their ability and freedom to control their own lives was increasingly constrained in the last decades of the nineteenth century.

Recent approaches to many of the fundamental documents of Aboriginal and Canadian legal history stress that First Nations were 'not passive objects, but active participants, in [their] formulation and ratification.' To appreciate the meaning of many of these documents then, and the often radically different interpretations of them, it is not enough to have an understanding of the European, written perspective alone. The central policy pursued by the British following the military defeat of the French at Quebec was given expression in the Royal Proclamation of 1763, and this was to form the foundation of the principles governing relations between First Nations and the Crown. The proclamation recognized the 'nations or tribes' of Indians to the west of the British colonies as continuing to own their lands, despite the extension of the new British sovereignty and protection, and directed that the Indians be left undisturbed on these lands. These nations could not sell their lands, however, until they were brought within a colony, and then they could sell only to the Crown, and only through collective and voluntary public action. The proclamation is generally described as a unilateral declaration of the British Crown, but Aboriginal nations played an active role in its genesis, bringing their own considerations, their own power, range of choices, and perspectives, to the agreement. First Nations did not see themselves as dependent, conquered victims of a foreign power, and they proposed peaceful government-to-government relationships of equality, retaining their lands and sovereignty. Different objectives and visions are embedded within the text of the proclamation, and this is why the document is open to differing interpretations.

Beginning in the 1790s, with the arrival of the United Empire Loyalists, the British negotiated treaties with First Nations to permit the expansion of non-Native settlement, generally adhering to the principles established in the Royal Proclamation. At first these were for relatively small parcels of land in exchange for a once-for-all payment. Responsibility for Indian affairs was originally in the hands of a branch of the British military. After the War of 1812, and the decline of the strategic importance of Aboriginal people as military allies, pressure mounted to change the basis of British Indian policy. Missionaries in British North America, as well as a humanitarian lobby in Britain, urged that the Indian Department should take the lead in encouraging Aboriginal people to change their way of life. There was also the example of the United States, where, in the last decade of the eighteenth century, the federal government declared a policy designed to make farmers out of Native Americans, responding to the widely held belief that Native Americans had no choice but to give up their vast tracts of land, with the advantage that they could be taught to farm. From 1828, the British Indian Department sought to foster the creation of self-supporting, as well as self-governing Aboriginal agricultural communities in British North America. In that year the Indian Superintendent of Upper Canada proposed a new function for the department: it would take the lead in 'civilizing' the Indians by encouraging them to settle on reserves, and take up agriculture as a livelihood. Reserves, land set aside for the exclusive use of Indian bands, were now included in the treaties, and the concept of annual payments, or annuities, was introduced. To facilitate the new program, in 1830 in the colonies of Upper and Lower Canada, jurisdiction over the management of Indian affairs shifted from military to civil authorities.

These policies have been assigned 'good marks' by many historians who see in this era the genesis of a humanitarian, benevolent approach to Canada's Aboriginal people. In the British territories, in contrast to the United States (this line of argument goes), there was no hostility, no disposition to eliminate or to coerce; rather, the government played an active role in eliminating reasons for conflict, well in advance of sustained settlement. It is certainly the case that at the same time as the Americans were pursuing the policy of 'removal,' a sizeable portion of the Aboriginal population of the older provinces of Canada remained resident on reserves. Yet there are more cynical views of Britain's 'humanitarian' policy. There was concern about the spread of American 'republican' ideas, and there were good reasons to encourage Aboriginal people to look to Britain as their chief benefactor to gain their loyalty. The concept of reserves and agriculture, which should have ideally allowed Aboriginal people to subsist on a radically reduced land base, permitted a humanitarian veneer to be attached to a policy that was simply aimed at removing an obstacle to non-Aboriginal economic development and settlement.

The direction of the new policy was not entirely unwelcome in the Aboriginal communities. Conscious of the rapid changes unfolding around them, Aboriginal people were not averse to new economic accommodation. With an eye towards preparing themselves to cope with dwindling game and other resources, a number of bands of Upper Canada, even before the adoption of the 'civilizing' program, had used some of the proceeds from land surrenders to fund the establishment of farms and schools with the assistance of missionaries. Aboriginal governments were in favour of agriculture, and the maintenance of the integrity of their society and culture within an agricultural context. For a time beginning in the 1830s there was a progressive partnership in development with Aboriginal governments deciding the degree, nature, and direction of change. They rejected initiatives such as an 1846 effort to introduce the concept of reserve subdivision and individualized property-holding. These councils remained self-governing, with control over their population, land, and finances, until 1860, when responsibility for Indian affairs was transferred from the British government to the government of the United Canadas.

This self-governing status, however, and the progressive partnership, did not last. Colonial legislation of the late 1850s, the transfer of authority over Indian affairs from Britain to the colony, and Confederation radically altered the standing of Aboriginal people. The other parties, groups, or regions that became part of Confederation were consulted and negotiated with, often resulting in contentious and protracted debates. In Canada East, or Quebec, for example, there were concerns about the preservation of their language, religion, culture, and institutions. Aboriginal nations were not consulted, and they were to occupy what historian John Milloy has described as 'a unique and unenviable' place in the new nation. Through the British North America Act, and the legislation aimed at Aboriginal people combined in the comprehensive Indian Act of 1876, the federal government took extensive control of the Aboriginal nations, their land, and their finances. Traditional forms of government were replaced by government/Indian agent–controlled models of government. There was no Aboriginal participation in the formulation and ratification of this legislation; there were protests and objections raised, but these were ignored.

The Indian Act of 1876 incorporated and consolidated earlier legislation of the Assembly of the United Canadas, including the Gradual Civilization Act of 1857 and the Enfranchisement Act of 1869. These acts were based upon the assumption that it was only through individualized property that Aboriginal people could become industrious and self-reliant. With the act of 1857 the Indian Department became an aggressive and disruptive agent of assimilation. It stipulated that any Indian, if he was male, free of debt, literate, and of good moral character, could be awarded full ownership of 50 acres (20 hectares) of reserve land, and would thereby be enfranchised. He would then cut his tribal ties and cease to be an Indian. The goal of full civilization through the enfranchisement of individuals was to be accompanied by the disappearance of Aboriginal communities. In the 1860s there was even more overt encroachment on Aboriginal independence and further destruction of self-government. Enfranchisement had attracted very few qualified candidates, and the tribal governments and their leaders were seen as the obstacles. Self-government had to be abolished. This argument was accepted by the new Canadian government, and the 1869 Enfranchisement Act greatly increased the degree of government control of on-reserve systems. There was to be very little meaningful Aboriginal participation in their own governance. Although chiefs and councillors were to be elected by all male band members over the age of twenty-one, the superintendent general of Indian Affairs decided the time, manner, and place of election, and these officials were to serve at Her Majesty's pleasure, and could be removed by this same official. Band councils were also limited in their areas of jurisdiction, and faced an all-encompassing federal power of disallowance. As historian John Milloy concluded, 'For the original people there was to be no partnership, no degree of home rule to protect and encourage the development of a valued and variant culture, as was the case with French Canada.'

A significant feature of the colonial legislation, later incorporated in the 1876 Indian Act, was the effort to impose Euro-Canadian social organization and cultural values, and English common law, in which the wife was virtually the property of her husband. The act assumed that women were subordinate to males, and derived rights from their husbands or fathers. Women were excluded from voting in band elections and from partaking in band business. They had to prove to government officials that they were of good 'moral' character before they were entitled to receive an inheritance. Beginning with the 1869 act, an Indian woman who married a non-Indian man lost her status as a registered Indian, as did her children. So upon marriage to a non-Indian, the woman would no longer be eligible for residency on reserve land. Even if her non-Indian husband died, her status would not be affected—only remarriage to a status Indian man could reinstate her. On the other hand, white women who married Indian men, and their children, obtained legal status as Indians, and all could reside on reserve land. Another section of the act stipulated that, if an Indian woman married an Indian from another band, she was automatically transferred to the band of her husband, regardless of her personal wishes. This legislation entirely ignored Aboriginal marriage and residency customs, and it was to be keenly resented by women as well as men.

The Indian Act of 1876, which has been described as a 'formidable dossier of repression' and which established race-based laws and limitations in Canada, was originally passed with 100 sections, and this nearly doubled in the next thirty years, to 195. It consigned Aboriginal people to the status of minors; they were British subjects but not citizens, sharing the status of children, felons, and the insane, and it established the federal government as their guardians. Those who came under the act were not allowed to vote in federal or provincial elections, and as they were not voters they were legally prohibited from the professions of law and politics, unless they gave up their Indian status. Through the administration of this act, government agents were able to control minute details of everyday life. There were restrictions on Aboriginal peoples' ability to sell their produce and resources, on their religious freedom and amusements. Many of the clauses of the act were based upon nineteenth-century negative stereotypes of Indians as drunkards, as immoral, as incapable of

handling money. The act criminalized for Indians the consumption of alcohol. It also specifically denied Indians rights available even to complete newcomers to the country. It stipulated, for example, that 'no Indian [...] shall be held capable of having acquired or of acquiring a homestead [...]'

The Numbered Treaties

The First Nations of Western Canada were not informed about this formidable dossier of repression when they entered into treaties in the 1870s. The Indian Act was simply unilaterally imposed, and by not communicating anything about this legislation, government and Crown representatives at treaty negotiations seriously misrepresented the nature of the relationship Aboriginal people were entering into. Aboriginal people were, however, active participants in the treaty negotiations, and the agreements reached reflect the concerns and goals of both sides, although it is now increasingly recognized that these were not fully represented in the written texts of the treaties. There were eight 'numbered treaties' covering the territory of Western Canada (excluding most of British Columbia) made between 1871 and 1899. The written texts of the treaties, prepared well in advance of the sessions, but subject to some change as a result of negotiations, have generally been understood until recently to represent the meaning of these treaties, although that meaning has been open to many interpretations. They have been depicted as just and benevolent instruments through which non-Aboriginal Canada systematically extended its jurisdiction, while offering kindly and generous aid to a population greatly in need of such assistance. The treaties have also been described as tragic misunderstandings, disreputable documents, that were imposed upon a people who had no idea of what was happening. Research that has drawn upon oral history has demonstrated that a focus upon the written text alone projects narrow perceptions of the treaties. The meaning cannot be derived and interpreted from the written words alone as the written texts do not include the Aboriginal understandings. There has also been a Eurocentric tendency to look only at government/and Crown policy and diplomacy with regard to treaty-making, yet Aboriginal societies also had their policy, protocol, ceremonies, and laws. Aboriginal groups had a lengthy history of treaty-making with other First Nations for military, trade, and other purposes. There has been a focus upon the power and authority of the Crown commissioners, but what about the power and authority of the Aboriginal negotiators?

There was significant Aboriginal input with regard to the timing of the treaties, and they were responsible for the introduction of some of the clauses and terms of the agreements. Through treaties Aboriginal people sought to secure not only physical, but cultural survival; to gain assistance in the transition to new economies based on agriculture and husbandry; and to establish peaceful, equitable relations. Canada sought through treaties to acquire legal title to the land in order to complete the transcontinental railway (promised and held out as an enticement to British Columbia in 1871), which would in turn encourage immigration, establish a prosperous economy, and strengthen industry in Eastern Canada. Aboriginal title was to be removed with as little expense as possible, avoiding costly military campaigns. Canadian authorities were also concerned to stop American intrusion north of the forty-ninth parallel, as causes of potential serious international disputes escalated in the 1870s. There were also officials, such as Alexander Morris, who seriously believed that Canadians were honour- and duty-bound to 'elevate' the Aboriginal residents of Western Canada. There was a moral imperative here to export what was perceived as a superior way of life to people assumed to be inferior. It is important to keep in mind that members of a colonizing society can hold powerful convictions that they are behaving altruistically towards the colonized.

Until recently, in written histories the numbered treaties were generally presented as one of the deliberate, orderly, and wise policies pursued by the federal government to ensure the peaceful settlement and prosperous development of the Canadian West. Yet it now seems that there was no particular plan or direction; the pattern and timing of treaty-making, as well as some important clauses, were to a great extent the result of pressure brought to bear by Aboriginal people. In the 1870s Aboriginal people were interested in entering into agreements that could assist them to acquire economic security in the face of a very uncertain future. There was also a great deal of unease and anxiety about the intentions of the government, and concerns were voiced that their land might be taken without consultation. It was learned with alarm that the HBC had 'sold' their land; there had never been any recognition that this company with whom they had traded had any jurisdiction over their land. As legal scholar Sharon Venne recently wrote, 'In present circumstances, it would be tantamount to Pepsi Cola or another such company gaining title to the lands of another country merely by engaging in trading.' Great indignation over the HBC claiming to have sold their land, and then surveying and claiming tracts of land around posts in advance of treaties, was expressed at Treaty Four proceedings: 'A year ago these people [the HBC] drew lines, and measured and marked the lands as their own. Why was this? We own the land; the Manitou [or Great Spirit] gave it to us. There was no bargain; they stole from us [...]' Word of troops stationed at Red River in 1870 heightened fears of hostile intentions. The appearance of railway and telegraph surveyors in advance of treaties caused concern. In central Saskatchewan and in Alberta, the NWMP arrived suddenly in advance of treaties and, without permission or consultation, built posts. Pressure for agreements that would provide economic security was brought to bear through messages, deputations to Crown representatives, and interference with survey work.

The numbered treaties appear to be remarkably similar documents. In each of the written treaties, the First Nations agreed to 'cede, release, surrender, and yield up to the Government of Canada for Her Majesty the Queen,' large tracts of land. They were promised, however, that they could continue their vocations of hunting throughout the surrendered tract, except those tracts taken up 'from time to time for settlement.' Reserves of land were to be set aside. (The precise amount of land varied considerably from treaty to treaty. For example, in Treaties Three, Four, and Five, each family of five was allowed one section, or 640 acres [260 hectares], whereas in Treaties One and Two each family was allotted 160 acres [65 hectares].) These reserves were to be administered and dealt with for the residents by the government. Annual payments (varying from five to twelve dollars) were promised to each man, woman, and child, with bigger payments for chiefs and councillors, who were also to receive suitable suits of clothing. They were promised implements, cattle, and seed for the encouragement of agriculture. In Treaties One to Six, the government agreed to maintain schools on reserves, and, in Treaty Seven, to pay the salary of teachers. The signatories solemnly promised to strictly observe the treaty, to conduct and behave themselves as good and loyal subjects of the Queen, to obey and abide by the law, to maintain peace and good order. Closer inspection of the individual treaties, however, reveals significant differences in the circumstances and negotiating tactics of both sides, and in the written and oral accounts of proceedings. There were unique features to each of the agreements, and different understandings of these agreements emerged.

The earliest of the treaties illustrate the concern about future livelihood that was foremost in the minds of Aboriginal spokesmen, and the effective negotiating skills of Aboriginal leaders. They also indicate that verbal promises and statements were regarded by Aboriginal people as every bit as binding as those which appeared on the written text. The signatories to the 1871 Treaties One and Two were Saulteaux and the Cree of Manitoba. Their concern about future livelihood was shared by Crown negotiators, who clearly indicated that they wished to encourage an agricultural economy. Alexander Morris, who was the Queen's representative in the treaties made between 1873 and 1876 (Treaties Three to Six), felt that it was Canada's duty to make the new wards self-supporting through agriculture. Initially, however, the Crown negotiators did not intend to provide direct assistance in the transition to an agricultural economy in the way of implements, draught animals, and other necessities of a settled and agricultural lifestyle. In Eastern Canada, agriculture as well as education had received official support and encouragement from government, but specific clauses were not included in treaty terms as obligations upon the Crown. This situation changed in the numbered treaties as a result of the bargaining of Aboriginal negotiators. In Treaty One, specific requests were made for implements, cattle, wagons, and housing. The Crown commissioners orally agreed to this assistance, but the clauses did not appear in the printed versions of Treaties One and Two. Controversy soon surrounded the so-called outside promises, the clauses that related to agricultural assistance, and there was discontent over the non-fulfilment of these terms. These were 'outside' only to the non-Aboriginal negotiators to the treaties; to Aboriginal negotiators, who remembered precisely what had been promised orally, they were an intrinsic

part of the treaties. Before the Treaty One negotiations, government surveyor S.J. Dawson had warned his superiors that this would be the case, as 'though they have no means of writing, there are always those present who are charged to keep every word in mind.' Dawson cited the example of an Ojibway principal chief who began an oration by repeating almost word for word what Dawson had said two years earlier. Crown officials agreed to make these a formal part of the treaties in 1875 as a result of the pressure brought to bear by Aboriginal people. The numbered treaties that followed included the terms that provided for agricultural transition in the formal, written treaties.

Treaty Six was made at Fort Carlton and Fort Pitt in 1876 with Plains Cree and Assiniboine. This treaty exemplifies the themes mentioned above; in particular, there was concern about future livelihood. Aboriginal negotiators demanded further clauses that provided for agricultural assistance, and help in making a transition to a new life. As a result of their bargaining, novel terms were added to Treaty Six, including assistance in the event of famine or pestilence, and an additional clause providing for a medicine chest. Reflecting a concern for the future health of their people, the Aboriginal negotiators succeeded in exacting the promise that a medicine chest would be kept at the home of the Indian agent for the use and benefit of the Indians. A troubling aspect of this agreement is that, like Treaty Four, concluded in 1874 at Fort Qu'Appelle with the Cree, Saulteaux, and Assiniboine, a vast number of people, including most of the Cree and prominent leaders, were not informed of the proceedings and were not present. Chief Big Bear, a prominent Plains Cree leader, was not invited by the representatives of the Crown to the original negotiations for Treaty Six.

Studies of Treaty Six that focus upon Aboriginal perspectives reveal fundamentally different understandings of what was agreed to at these proceedings. At the heart of the difference is the certainty that the land was not surrendered, or sold; rather, Aboriginal negotiators agreed to share and to coexist as equals with non-Aboriginals. Given the nature of leadership in Plains societies, and the limits on the powers of the chiefs who entered into treaty, they would not have had the authority to sell or surrender the land. Elders maintain that the land was never sold in the treaty process, and that the wording 'cede, surrender [...]' was not included in the original treaty. They accepted the idea that the Queen wanted to make a treaty to share the land with her people, who were in poverty, and the concept of sharing was acceptable. As Harold Cardinal said in an address to Queen Elizabeth II in 1973, 'Our Treaties were agreements between two peoples from different civilizations to share their resources so that each could grow and successfully meet changes brought on by the passage of time.'

Oral histories with the people of Treaty Seven, made in 1877 with the Siksika, Blood, Peigan, Tsuu T'ina, and Nakoda (Stoney) peoples, indicate that a peace treaty was concluded, not a land surrender. They were asked and agreed to put away their weapons, live in peace and harmony, and share the land. But the emphasis on peacemaking was left unrecorded, and instead land surrender was made the most significant part of the written treaty. In the oral record there is no memory of the issue of land surrender being raised and discussed at the proceedings, and no realization that the land was ceded for ever. There is also little trace of the issue being raised in the documentary record of the treaty proceedings. Government officials were anxious to hastily conclude a treaty with the southern Alberta peoples in 1877, and did not want to raise issues such as land surrender as it could well mean that the treaty would be rejected. The Blackfoot were perceived as war-like, volatile, and dangerous as they were well armed. There was concern about potential Blackfoot alliances with the Lakota, who had defeated Colonel George Custer in 1876 and taken up residence in Canadian territory. To the south, in the spring and summer of 1877, there were numerous small battles between the U.S. military and the non-treaty Nez Percé, whose destination was Canada. The making of Treaty Seven coincided with the Nez Percé moving closer and closer to the camp of Sitting Bull, and there was great alarm about the formation of an alliance.

Research into First Nations' perspectives on Treaty Seven has revealed other factors that would have impeded understanding of the concepts embedded in the written document. In Blackfoot there is no equivalent word for 'cede,' and terms such as 'square mile' could not have been translated properly. In Blackfoot there is now a term for mile (*ni'taa'si*), but it entered the language in the early 1900s with the establishment of mission schools, as

did the term now used for square (*iksisttoyisi*). There was no word for 'Canada,' only a word for the territory of their own nation. The translators at the proceedings were not competent in all of the Aboriginal languages present, nor could they have understood the Victorian jargon of the commissioners. In the written text of the treaty, there are more than eighty examples of gross misrepresentations of the names of chiefs and headmen signatories, clearly indicating that the translators were not real Blackfoot speakers. The names of Nakoda chiefs, who spoke a Siouan language, were recorded in Cree, indicating that the translator for them, Reverend John McDougall, was not competent in their language.

Conflicting perceptions and interpretations of the treaties are at the root of many contemporary issues. Until recently the treaties have been narrowly interpreted by government and in the courts to mean the words on the written documents. Those who prepared these written documents likely did not fully understand or appreciate what the Aboriginal participants believed they had agreed to. From the government's perspective, treaties were straightforward agreements to secure title to land and resources for settlement and development. First Nations draw attention to the verbal promises and the negotiations, and ask that treaties be understood, not according to the technical meaning of the words, but in the sense that they were understood by Aboriginal people. There must be recognition of the 'spirit' of the treaties, and there should be a flexible and generous interpretation of the terms. The Supreme Court of Canada has found that courts cannot begin with the assumption that the written text of the treaties manifests a shared communication between the treaty parties. Instead, the courts must take into account the historical context and perception each party might have as to the nature of the undertaking.

An understanding of the spirit of the treaties also requires an appreciation of Aboriginal concepts, philosophies, and ceremonies. It is consistently explained by Elders of the First Nations that the Creator bestowed sacred responsibilities upon them to act as custodians of the land, and that it could therefore not have been possible for them to even consider breaking this inviolable sacred relationship and to cede, surrender, release, and yield up the land. This would be tantamount to giving up their life. According to Harold Cardinal, to the Cree the treaty relationship is rooted in the principles embodied in the term *meyo witchi towin*, meaning 'good, healthy, happy, respectful relationships among equal parties.' The parties agree to act according to the divinely inspired principles of *wak koo too win*, meaning a perpetual relationship patterned after familial concepts. The relationship with the Crown was understood to consist of mutual ongoing sharing arrangements that would guarantee each other's survival and stability. The concept of *wi taski win*, or sharing the blessing of the land in mutual harmony, provided that the sharing arrangements would be fair to each of the parties, enabling both to enjoy the prosperity of the land and *pim atchi hoowin*, or make a living. Through the pipe ceremonies conducted by First Nations when making treaties for the goals of peace and harmony, the most powerful spirits were called upon to assist in maintaining the peace agreement and accompanying commitments of promises. If the agreement was broken, the powerful spirits of the sun, water, thunder, and wind might unleash their wrath upon the attending parties. The serious consequences to breaking vows made to the spirits was a way of ensuring that peace and harmony would be preserved at all costs. The sweet-grass used in the ceremony represented an undertaking between the parties both that their relationship would be non-coercive and that it would be governed according to precepts of honesty, integrity, good faith, gentleness, and generosity. That these ceremonies took place affirms the sacred nature of the agreements and mutual commitments. As Cardinal wrote in his 1969 *The Unjust Society*, 'To the Indians of Canada, the treaties represent an Indian Magna Carta.'

The North-West Mounted Police

The fact that the non-Aboriginal settlement of Western Canada proceeded relatively peacefully, and that 'law and order' was to a great extent observed, has almost entirely to do with the strategies and actions of First Nations. These strategies, outlined above, featured the negotiation of treaties in order to ensure that resources would be shared, that independence and integrity would be retained, and that a useful partner in the creation of an enriched way of life would be obtained. Aboriginal negotiators solemnly promised that they would in all respects obey and abide by the law. Even leaders such as Big Bear, who rejected 'taking treaty'

for almost a decade, advised and adopted non-confrontational strategies. Despite persistent rumours of Indian 'uprisings' in Western Canada, there were no such events with the exception of Frog Lake (1885; discussed in chapter 7). Promises to maintain peace and good order were observed. Yet credit for the peaceful and orderly settlement of the West is generally attributed in written histories to the NWMP, as well as to the treaties, although these are traditionally perceived as entirely a British-Canadian strategy. Both are often presented as essential components of the vision of one man, Prime Minister Sir John A. Macdonald, who had a grand dream and design for a strong and stable Dominion from sea to sea. While the treaties established the foundation, it was this small force of intrepid few that introduced, and then maintained, law and order, according to many histories of the Canadian West. The force was launched in 1873, and 300 of them, dressed in scarlet to distinguish them from the American cavalry, dressed in blue, made the much-celebrated 'march west' the following year.

A great deal has been written about the Mounties. There are first-hand accounts, academic as well as popular works of history, fiction, and a 'Heritage Minute.' As historian Keith Walden has written, this vast body of literature has made mythic heroic figures of the Mounties. Most of the accounts contain a heavy cultural bias, as they describe these few men as members of a superior and more powerful yet humane culture, bringing stability and peace, law and order, to a wild and savage people in a fretful, uninhabitable land. The force is invariably depicted as having forged outstanding relations with Aboriginal people, who welcomed, appreciated, and respected them. They stopped the whisky trade; pacified warlike Indians; and explained the law to them, administering it in equal doses to white and Indian alike. They stood as sterling examples of manly attributes such as integrity, sobriety, and courage.

As Walden observed, none of this is very plausible as few of the residents of Western Canada could possibly have so willingly accepted the intrusion of outsiders into their affairs. There is an element of plausibility, however. The police were welcomed by some leaders and groups. Red Crow, Crowfoot, and other Blackfoot leaders were grateful that the American whisky trade was curtailed. Major James Walsh *did* forge outstanding relations with Sitting Bull and his people when they sought refuge across the border from 1876 to 1881. Yet the Mounties were outsiders intruding into the lives of Aboriginal people, and their actions were not always appreciated. There were indignant reactions to police posts being placed in the path of the buffalo, without the government first conferring with them about these establishments. A post such as Fort Calgary was placed at a popular camping and fording site without permission or consultation. As Walter Hildebrandt has argued, the police were sent in the vanguard of a 'new order for the white settlers' to pacify the people in what Prime Minister Macdonald called 'that fretful realm' and make the West a safe place to settle. They were more a military, occupying force than a police force. Their function was to assist in expanding British-Canadian influence, without the costs incurred in costly wars of conquest. They served in a military rather than a police capacity at occasions such as treaty negotiations. At Treaty Seven, the police brought and fired cannons, which the Blackfoot found menacing. As agents of the government they assisted in enforcing the Indian Act and related policies of the Department of the Interior and of Indian Affairs, and soon after their arrival they became vital enforcers of extremely unpopular coercive measures and laws that monitored, controlled, and restrained people. They had powers that were unprecedented in the history of police forces; not only did they introduce and enforce Canadian law, they were also given powers as magistrates and so administered the same laws. Many of the predominantly young men who made up the force were also a far cry from the exemplary models of behaviour that most of the police literature would have us believe, and this caused consternation among Aboriginal leaders. The police indulged in considerable drinking, and brawling among themselves and with the 'citizens.'

Missionary John McDougall was critical of the conduct of the police, whom he found to be fond of whisky, drinking all they could lay their hands on, while supposedly putting down the whisky trade. He also felt that some of the laws and policies the police enforced were foolish and unnecessary. Yet despite his criticisms, McDougall contributed to the 'myth of the Mountie.' In his *Opening the Great West*, McDougall wrote that 'here in the mid-summer of 1875 the fact remained that the major sense of all men in this big West was to respect the Police and obey the law. Thus without any bloodshed an immense lawless region was being justly and peaceably administered

[...]' Despite cherished non-Aboriginal origin narratives about Western Canada, the new realm was not, in the last three decades of the nineteenth century, as peaceable as McDougall described, nor was it as lawless as he described in the preceding years. As in other colonial settings, there was considerable resistance to aspects of the foreign presence that caused colonial authorities grave concern, although there was also accommodation to other aspects. Yet it remains the case that in Western Canada there simply was not the record of continuous violence and conquest that characterized not only the western United States, but many of Britain's imperial enterprises. This had as much to do with the strategies and actions of the Aboriginal residents as with the policies of government and the actions of a handful of police.

Bibilography

Borrows, John. 'Wampum at Niagara: The Royal Proclamation, Canadian Legal History, and Self-Government.' In *Aboriginal and Treaty Rights in Canada: Essays on Law, Equality, and Respect for Difference,* ed. Michael Asch, 155–72. Vancouver: University of British Columbia Press, 1997.

Cardinal, Harold. 'Treaty Eight: The Right to Livelihood.' Unpublished LLM thesis, Harvard University Law School, 1996.

Chartrand, Paul L.A.H. *Manitoba's Métis Settlement Scheme of 1870.* Saskatoon: Native Law Centre, 1991.

Flanagan, Thomas, and Gerhard J. Ens. 'Métis Land Grants in Manitoba: A Statistical Study.' *Histoire sociale/Social History 27/23* (1994): 65–88.

Francis, R. Douglas. *Images of the West.* Saskatoon: Western Producer Prairie Books, 1989.

Friesen, Jean. 'Magnificent Gifts; The Treaties of Canada with the Indians of the Northwest, 1869–76.' *Transactions of the Royal Society of Canada,* series 5, vol. 1 (1986): 41–51.

Hildebrandt, Walter. *Views from Fort Battleford: Constructed Visions of an Anglo-Canadian West.* Regina: Canadian Plains Research Center, 1994.

Milloy, John S. 'The Early Indian Acts: Developmental Strategy and Constitutional Change.' In *As Long as the Sun Shines and Water Flows,* ed. Ian A.L. Getty and Antoine S. Lussier, 56–64. Vancouver: UBC Press, 1983.

Morris, Alexander. *The Treaties of Canada with the Indians of Manitoba and the North-West Territories.* 1880. Reprint. Toronto: Coles Publishing, 1971.

Owram, Douglas. *Promise of Eden: The Canadian Expansionist Movement and the Idea of the West, 1856–1900*. Toronto: University of Toronto Press, 1980.

Sprague, D.N. *Canada and the Métis, 1869–1885*. Waterloo: Wilfrid Laurier University Press, 1988.

Stanley, G.F.G. *The Birth of Western Canada: A History of the Riel Rebellions* 1936. Reprint. Toronto: University of Toronto Press, 1975.

Tobias, John. 'Protection, Civilization, Assimilation: An Outline History of Canada's Indian Policy.' In *As Long as the Sun Shines and Water Flows,* ed. Ian A.L. Getty and Antoine S. Lussier, 13–30. Vancouver: UBC Press, 1983.

Treaty Seven Tribal Council, Walter Hildebrandt, Dorothy First Rider, and Sarah Carter. *The True Spirit and Original Intent of Treaty 7*. Montreal: McGill-Queen's University Press, 1996.

Venne, Sharon. 'Understanding Treaty 6: An Indigenous Perspective.' In *Aboriginal and Treaty Rights in Canada: Essays on Law, Equality and Respect for Difference*, ed. Michael Asch, 173–207. Vancouver: University of British Columbia Press, 1997.

Walden, Keith. 'The Great March of the Mounted Police in Popular Literature, 1873–1973.' *Canadian Historical Association Historical Papers* (1980): 33–56.

■ Article 3: The True Spirit and Original Intent of Treaty 7

Treaty Seven Elders and Tribal Council et al.

INTRODUCTION

Otsistsi Pakssaisstoyiih Pi
(the year when the winter was open and cold)

WILTON GOODSTRIKER

Among all First Nations people, there is and has always been a recording of significant events in our history. Our ancestors were just as anxious to leave a record of their story as we are today. I wish that somehow we could let them know that we have remembered, but then again, they probably knew all along that we would.

The stories have been recorded in many forms, through our winter-counts, on the land, but most importantly in the minds and spirit of our people. In these ways, the stories have been passed down from one generation to another throughout the ages.

Throughout this document, we will share the various methods that the First Nations people of Treaty 7 used to record our history.

In the winter-counts of the First Nations of the Treaty 7 area, the year 1877 is referred to as *otsistsi pakssaisstoyiih pi** (Blackfoot—the year when the winter was open and cold). Among the other nations, it is known as "the year when there was great hunger," "the year when the long rains did not come," "the year of starvation and hunger," or "the year when the first snow was late." In any event, to our people it was to be a year which was not going to be normal. To the elders, something was going to be wrong.

It was also the year that a treaty (Treaty 7) was entered into between the First Nations people of this area and the representatives of the Queen of Britain. Interesting is the fact that the treaty did not make its way onto any of the winter-counts of the First Nations people. However, the memory of that occasion is vivid among our people, and the story has been told many times among Niitsitapi (the real people) throughout the years since that time. This story is about *istsist aohkotspi* (the first time that we received gifts and money) at Soyooh

Source: Treaty 7 Elders and Tribal Council with Walter Hildebrandt, Dorothy First Rider, and Sarah Carter, *The True Spirit and Original Intent of Treaty 7* (Montreal and Kingston: McGill-Queen's University Press, 1996), pp. 3–5, 11–15, 111–119, 191–201. Reprinted with permission.

*Blackfoot is an oral language, and over the years several Blackfoot dictionaries have been produced. For consistency in this book, we will use Don Frantz's *Blackfoot Dictionary of Stems, Roots and Affixes* (Toronto: University of Toronto Press, 1995), second edition, unless otherwise noted. This choice is not intended to raise Frantz's dictionary as a final authority for usage, since each Blackfoot tribe has its own legitimate dialect and usage.

pawahko (ridge under water) or Blackfoot Crossing. In our languages there is no word for treaty; the event is simply referred to as *istsist aohkotspi* or *iitsinnaihtsiiyo'pi* (the time when we made a sacred alliance). Among our people, there are several ways to make an alliance and we will examine these closely in the hope that the reader will come to understand the complex ways of our people. The alliance process of the First Nations played a major role at Blackfoot Crossing.

The memory of a people is made accurate with the help of ceremony. This memory is a precious gift among our people.

The Story

"Sit here my child, and watch me close as I prepare the sacred smudge. I will then tell you a story. The reason I will use the smudge is so you will never forget that which I will share with you. And in time, when it is your turn to share, you will share with your children exactly as I will share with you. In this way, things will never change."— Sa'ksisakiaaksin (Laurie Big Plume)

Laurie Big Plume went on to tell me many stories. I remember one time when he told me that "The Christian story always begins with 'In the beginning.' Our story, if we were to write it down, would start with 'Before the beginning.'" I asked him at one point, "How old are our ways?" and he replied, "The ways of the White people are a child compared to our ways."

History has been documented in many ways, and in large part what we know of the past is dependent on information gained through archaeology and to some extent anthropology. Among our people, oral history is perhaps the most accurate. Our people's memory goes back to the beginning of time and in some respects beyond. Our story has come through seven ages, the last one being referred to as *i'kookaiksi* (the age when the people used tipi designs). We are still in this age and will be for as long as the people use the tipi design. This era dates back some five hundred years, and it will be the one that we will concentrate on for the purposes of this document. It is an era that saw the coming of the horse, of the immigrant nations to our land, and of new ways to a people.

One must keep in mind the history of a people when attempting to understand their perspective, their spirit and intent, in their dealings with the new-comers. This story will take you into the world of the First Nations. We will share our history, our alliance process, and our ceremony as they pertain to the treaty. Constant through the ages have been the use of ceremony and the need to document our history accurately. The latter has been done by way of marking in some way on the land, in our winter-counts, and, in all cases, in the oral history, which has been the most accurate method.[...]

Alliances have always been common to our people. There were alliances for trade, for cohabitation of territory. *Innaihtsiini* are sacred alliances of peace between individuals, families, and nations. These alliances find their beginning in the sacred ways of the Plains people, and they go back for thousands of years. Each year one would still witness these in our sacred ceremonies.[...]

STORYTELLING

Storytelling is a great gift among our people. A requirement among our people is for young children to spend much time with grandparents. It is the responsibility of grandparents to teach legends and stories and the ways of our people. In this way a closeness develops between the very young and the old. Our people do not believe in old-age homes.

I was a small child when I witnessed my first storytelling session among the old ones. Those present were my grandfather Many Fingers, Old Man Rabbit, Shot Both Sides, Low Horn, and Old Black Plume. For several days they shared stories, legends, and history. There was always great care in correcting each other when there was error found in one of the accounts. In this way, when everybody left for home, they all left with the same story to be retold at another time. For many years I have heard these stories, and they remained unchanged. It is in this way that our history and heritage have been accurately handed down through the ages. Because our languages are not written, we rely heavily on the oral traditions and on the winter-counts. Among our elders, it is only when individuals could recount stories without error that they were allowed to teach history. When young people were present at these storytelling sessions, they weren't allowed to make noise or be up walking around. From an early age, the young were taught to be careful listeners. A great deal of tenderness and gentleness was required when talking to young people. The elders would talk to the young ones in a low voice, sometimes so low and gentle that the children would think that they were dreaming. In this way a child would never forget.

The teaching of history among our people was given to everyone. Only a select few, however, were privy to sacred teaching, and throughout our recent documented history, this is the information which has been absent. The elders were very careful in the sharing of this kind of information. For the first time, and under the close authority of the elders, this document will attempt to shed some light on those areas which pertain to the events at Soyooh pawahko (ridge under water or Blackfoot Crossing).

SWEETGRASS

The sweetgrass with its three strands represents a harmony which is necessary between the Giver of Life, all that lives, and Mother Earth. It is a harmony which cannot be deliberately imbalanced or separated by man. This is common knowledge among the buffalo people, the Plains tribes. It was this understanding that our leaders and elders took with them to the talks at Blackfoot Crossing in 1877. This was the harmony which for some reason to this point has not been mentioned in the official accounts of Treaty 7. From an early age each young person is taught about this gift of the Giver of Life, and throughout one's lifetime, many times one will experience the ceremonies where it is used. It is a ceremony that played a major part in the talks at Blackfoot Crossing.

THE SACRED SMUDGE

The sacred smudge is a ceremony given to Niitsitapa (the real people) by the Giver of Life. Along with this precious gift there are spiritual laws which govern the use of the smudge: it is used only when there are very important issues to be discussed, the issues cannot be of a negative nature, and spiritual guidance is asked for so that all that will be discussed will be treated with the highest regard for honesty. The sacred smudge is often used in the teaching of sacred information so that the one being taught will never forget. The person teaching or sharing the information will also ask for spiritual guidance, so that he or she will share in exactly the same way as they were taught themselves. When using the smudge, the people present are conducting themselves with the knowledge that the Giver of Life is witness to the proceedings. The smudge is used for cleansing first of all the participants and then the area or environment where the ceremony is being conducted so that everything will be done in a clean and pure way. The ceremony is as old as time and can never change in process because it is a sacred gift to all First Nations. The ceremony itself is a prerequisite to the use of the sacred pipe.

THE STORY OF BLACKFOOT CROSSING

Many stories have been told surrounding the events which took place at Blackfoot Crossing in the fall of 1877, but seldom from the perspective of the First Nations people themselves. In many cases, vivid accounts have been solicited from our people as to the happenings during those few days in September, but noticeable is their reluctance to mention the ceremony attached to the participation of the First Nations. In some instances, the reluctance comes from their not wanting to share that which is sacred; in others, they were not privy to the information. On the part of historians and academics, the reason is oftentimes an ignorance of the complex ways of a people they simply do not know. Thus, in various published accounts, the occasions that involved ceremony are often recorded inaccurately or it is indicated that no record exists of what took place. A good example of this kind of reference is found in documents of the officials at Blackfoot Crossing. The officials simply reported that on the evening of the twentieth there appeared to be much joy and singing well into the night. In actuality, there were prayers and ceremonies in each of the camps of the various nations. This had been going on for several days, and the purpose was to seek guidance as the nations prepared to discuss important issues pertaining to their survival. By that time, all of the various nations were well informed about the deceit that their neighbours to the east and south had experienced at the hands of government and military officials. Many treaties had been entered into, and in most cases, the promises made had been broken over and over. It was common knowledge that the newcomers were not honest people. Before we go into the actual events and talks at Blackfoot Crossing, there is one more ceremony that needs mention, as it was probably the most important ceremony of this occasion. This ceremony took place in the few days prior to the actual discussions of the treaty.

There is a ceremony known to our people as *kano'tsississin* (where everybody smokes ceremony). At times it has been referred to as the "big smoke." It was one of the few ceremonies that brought together all those affiliated in some way with the sacred smudge—elders, medicine pipe holders, members of sacred societies, leaders, and war leaders. One requirement was that those in attendance would bring with them their pipes and knowledge of sacred songs and prayers. The elders conducted the ceremony. They played a key role even in the everyday lives of the people. Important decisions affecting the people were never made in the absence of or without consultation with the elders. The ceremony was, and is, held during the winter moons of our people or, if we use the new calendar moons, from September to March. It began at sundown and ended at sunrise and lasted throughout the night. One could hear the songs and prayers, which are as old as time, with each of the participants asking for guidance in whatever was going to happen. Many of the people in attendance would have their faces painted with sacred ochres to protect them from anything that would be negative in nature. Throughout our recorded history, this painting of the faces has been erroneously termed "war paint." Among our people, there is no such thing as war paint. As with all ceremonies, the sacred smudge was at the centre of all activity. Prior to any pipe being used, the first requirement was to place the sweetgrass on some coals, and in doing this, you would ask the Giver of Life to guide you in what you will say and that you will only hear good things. The pipe would then be taken and again you would ask the Giver of Life to give you courage and strength as the stone of the pipe is strong and that you will talk straight (honestly) as the stem of the pipe is straight. You would then ask the same of those who would join you in smoke.

At Blackfoot Crossing, the ceremony was initiated on the advice of Father of Many Children, who had been present at the signing of the Lame Bull Treaty of 1855. On his urging, the ceremony would give protection against the authorities' apparent disregard of the provisions in the American treaty and the subsequent starvation and hardships of the people. By this time, Father of Many Children was a respected elder and teacher among his people. Many of the participating leaders at Blackfoot Crossing were medicine pipe holders. Each of the five nations had beaver bundles as well as medicine pipes at the time.

Not surprising is the fact that in 1991 the chiefs of Treaty 7, on the advice of their elders, initiated this whole treaty review project by participating in the same ceremony. Their teaching had remained constant in the ways of their people. The songs which were heard were the same songs as those heard in September 1877. This ceremony has remained unchanged throughout the ages, and it is still very much in use today. The chiefs, in authorizing this review, felt that it was important to document the stories of their elders so that, for generations to come, those who would read the story would somehow get a much better understanding of the spirit and intent of the First Nations people with respect to their participation in Treaty 7.

These, then, were some of the ceremonies held in those few days in September of 1877. The sad note is the fact that no descriptions of them found their way into the official accounts of the time. Perhaps those who were responsible for the recording had viewed ceremony as a small detail, insignificant and not worth mention in official documents. To the First Nations people, this was the spirit of the whole process. Only ceremony could seal an accord that would last "as long as the sun would shine, and as long as the river would flow." I once asked Dan Weasel Moccasin where this expression came from. His response was, "The term 'as long as the sun shines and the rivers flow' comes directly out of the way of the pipe. The way of our people is the way of the pipe. Since then there is much sadness each time there is effort to renege on promises they feel were made to them upon a sacred oath."[...]

CHAPTER THREE

The First Nations' Perspective on Treaty 7

WHAT DID TREATY 7 MEAN TO THE FIRST NATIONS?

The leaders who accepted Treaty 7 believed that it was first and foremost a peace treaty. All the Treaty

7 First Nations were unanimous on this point: that through the agreement with the British Crown and the Canadian representatives, the First Nations would cease to war among themselves and that peace would be preserved between the First Nations and the Canadian authorities. Peace and order were essential for the protection of the settler populations that were to be ushered onto the prairies under various schemes initiated within the framework of John A. Macdonald's National Policy. The resulting stability in the newcomer settlements would help to realize the agricultural potential of the West that so many central Canadian explorers and politicians had desired. To some degree the peace process had already been set in motion with the arrival of the North-West Mounted Police in southern Alberta in 1874-75. Their presence and the stability they were able to establish by stopping the whiskey trade were much appreciated by the First Nations people of southern Alberta. Indeed, some historians say that Colonel Macleod became somewhat of a hero among the Blackfoot Confederacy for the authority he was able to establish in the aftermath of clearing Whoop-Up Country of the outlaw traders who had generated so much of the violence that had plagued the territory for the previous decade.

In fact, from the point of view of the elders, it was above all a peace treaty that the Canadian government had desired for this territory. Peace had not been of central importance in the other prairie treaties. The First Nations genuinely appreciated the peace and stability that was brought to the southern territory of the Canadian plains. In return, the First Nations agreed to end hostilities among themselves, promising not to interfere with the peaceful settlement of the newcomer agriculturalists who had been arriving to share the land. There was nothing said among the elders about this peace being in any way linked to giving up land; rather they viewed the peace as being of benefit to all the groups agreeing to the treaty.

In the view of the government, the most significant part of the written treaty involved the surrender of land—not peace. However, peace must have been prominent in the minds of the commissioners who set out to sign Treaty 7, since the tribes of southern Alberta, having had the least contact of any Aboriginal peoples with settler society up to this point, were thought to be a serious threat to settlement.

This fact was most trenchantly underlined by Father Scollen's letter warning the treaty commissioners that these southern Alberta nations were the most "warlike" on the plains. Scollen and others were also concerned about the potential alliance between Sitting Bull's Lakota at Wood Mountain and the tribes of the Blackfoot Confederacy. Thus, it was the Canadian officials, perhaps more so than the First Nations' attending the talks, who wanted to be assured of peace and who raised the issue specifically during the treaty discussions. Certainly they wanted to avoid other international incidents like the one precipitated by the arrival of Sitting Bull or the crisis produced by the Cypress Hills Massacre of 1873.

The First Nations at Blackfoot Crossing were very familiar with the treaty process. Indeed, a number of Blackfoot chiefs had signed the Lame Bull Treaty of 1855, which allowed road development into the West in return for peace with the tribes across the American plains and promised payments to those who signed. This treaty was not understood to be a land surrender but rather a peace treaty, and the tribes at the time were left to move freely over rather large territories. However, the nature of the peace agreed to under Treaty 7 was understood in different ways by the First Nations. Each nation's interpretation of the treaty—just what the peace was to achieve, and who was to benefit—depended on the historical situation that each found itself in at the treaty signing.

The Stoneys, traditional enemies of the other four nations that accepted the treaty, believed that peace meant that they would no longer be fighting with nations of the Blackfoot Confederacy and the other First Nations to whom they had been hostile at various times in the past. As understood by members of the Blackfoot-speaking nations, peace meant not only the kind of peace they enjoyed in the American territories into which their hunting territory still extended, but also the cessation of hostilities with the Stoneys and Cree, and the prohibition of the whiskey trade. But aside from these slight differences in perception, what is clear is that all the First Nations understood the agreement reached at Blackfoot Crossing to be first and foremost a peace treaty. Secondarily, it represented their agreement to share the land and its resources with the newcomers in return for a variety of compensation benefits understood to be their "treaty rights" or "treaty promises."

Blood Tribe

According to Pete Standing Alone, the Blood word for treaty, *innaihtsiini*, means that two sides must "achieve a common purpose." A treaty had to be approached with care and caution. One tried not to be aggressive when negotiating a treaty, as it was a serious undertaking and the consequence of failure might be too great. It was therefore with much gravity that Treaty 7 was pursued. Various interpretive language was used by the Blood elders to describe what the treaty meant to them and their ancestors. Fred Gladstone said that a treaty meant having peace between peoples or tribes; it was a "negotiation between two peoples." Rosie Red Crow indicated that the treaty meant that "we all agreed to be on friendly terms." Wallace Mountain Horse described the treaty process as it had affected the Bloods when they made treaty with both the Cree and the Crow peoples at various times in his memory. He reiterated that the treaty meant an agreement "not to fight anymore." Mountain Horse also discussed the significance of the role of the North-West Mounted Police in pacifying the territory of southern Alberta; this was seen as an important achievement by the Bloods. However, he lamented the fact that the recording of what was said about peace was one-sided, leaving it to look as though the land surrender was the most important issue discussed when in fact for the Bloods peace was most important. Louise Crop Eared Wolf said that the fundamental beliefs of the Bloods would not have allowed them to give away the land: "We believed and understood [that we would] share this territory amongst each other and we also believed that the land could not be given away because of its sacredness; therefore, it did not belong to us or anybody else. The earth is just put there by our creator for only our benefit and use."

Adam Delaney stressed that surrendering land is a concept foreign to the Bloods. Treaties can be made in three situations. Payments are made between in-laws when couples marry; payments can be made between spiritual persons to break a taboo; and finally, treaties are made between nations or tribes to signify peace and friendship or to end wars.

To illustrate the Blood understanding of what happened at Blackfoot Crossing, Louise Crop Eared Wolf related the story of Red Crow: "At the signing of the treaty at Blackfoot Crossing, Red Crow pulled out the grass and gave it to the White officials and informed them that they will share the grass of the earth with them. Then he took some dirt from the earth and informed them that they could not share this part of the earth and what was underneath it, because it was put there by the Creator for the Indians' benefit and use."

Peigan Nation

According to John Yellowhorn, it was the government that wanted the peace treaty, and it was at the government's initiative that the negotiations commenced. People were told that "they would have a much better life if they made the treaty." The reoccurring theme of peace was stated rather differently by Sally Provost: "It's a sign of peace to say we accept the treaty [...] they were just promising and promising, and we were going to get help for the rest of time." That was how important peace appeared to be for the government. Sally Provost also mentioned that the government wanted peace in order to "civilize the Indians." Nick Smith remembered that the main purpose of the treaty was that "we will make peace here with everyone." The "Queen's representatives will make laws for us." Unfortunately, these laws were used "to control us," and the peace that was sued for under the guise of the government "caring for" the First Nations was instead used to restrict and control them. The peace meant that the First Nations' way of life would be changed, for the officials told them, "These are the laws you will abide by." Hugh Crow Eagle remembered his grandfather saying that the treaty was for peace and friendship, "not only with the White man but also with all other tribes that we may have been fighting."

The North-West Mounted Police were considered significant not only for their past service in driving out the whiskey traders but also for enforcing the new laws that were established. Peace would be more complicated than simply not fighting: "You will no longer live the way you were used to. You will be taken care of by the Queen and her representatives. She sent them here. The Red Coat was sent here to watch and take care of you. We will make peace with everyone and we will live in harmony with one another."

For Cecile Many Guns, to make peace meant "no more fighting between anyone, everybody will be friends, everybody will be in peace." Tom Yellowhorn noted with disappointment that the Peigan's initial enthusiasm for the peace treaty grew into bitterness when the seriousness with which they took the agreement was later not reciprocated by the government. In subsequent years the Peigan were "sorry that they made this treaty." For the Peigan the ceremony of peace making was solemn, undertaken with much gravity, especially when they smoked the peace pipe: "They prayed that they would be friends." Yellowhorn thought that the government officials who signed Treaty 7 were serious as well; Macleod in particular was respected. When Macleod said that the First Nations would be thought of by the Queen as "my children," the Peigan thought a great obligation would be attached to so solemn and important a commitment. But disappointment soon followed: "They thought they were going to get money, that they'll own the land and still be free in the country. But this [disappointment] was after, when they found out that they had to stay on the reserves." Macleod had convinced the Peigan that the Queen "was going to treat them good." As Tom Yellowhorn bitterly concluded, in the wake of the treaty "they put up the Indian Act to punish Indian people and protect the White man." In fact, the Indian Act of 1876 had already been enacted.

Elder Ida Yellowhorn remembered: " Long Pipe Woman said that the Peigan leaders understood the making of the treaty as a peace treaty. She said that the leaders said that we should take the White man as our children and share our land with them."

Siksika Nation

The Siksika interpreted Treaty 7 as a commitment to peace in return for government assistance. Philip Many Bears remarked that "the police were to take care of us." For Arthur Yellow Fly, the terms of the peace treaty included "no more killing, no more whiskey trafficking, no more fighting with White men and other Native tribes." The end of warfare and violence was also foremost in the mind of Josephine Weasel Head, who remembered stories about her people deciding that they "wanted to save children from bloodshed and smallpox, also to stop the fighting between tribes." Stemming the violence that accompanied the economic exploitation in the free-wheeling days of Whoop-Up Country was foremost in the memory of Frankie Turning Robe, who stated that "whiskey trading was killing people. Crowfoot was thinking of his people when

he signed." In return for the Siksika's agreement to stop fighting, the Mounties were "assigned to watch over the Native people." There was to be "no more bloodshed between White and Indian."

For Augustine Yellow Sun, peace was agreed to in return for money, freedom to hunt, and rations: "The way I heard it is that treaty money was used to keep us from fighting." The government gave people $12 each for the peace agreement: "The treaty money was used as a token of peace to us at the treaty. Many material things were promised." The Siksika believed the agreement was honestly sought by the government: "We were a treaty people and really thought that we would be taken care of." But Jim Black noted that the Siksika were soon to be disappointed: "Fifty thousand dollars was given out—that was cheap compared to the land we were cheated out of."

To illustrate the point that the Blackfoot tribes had no intention of selling land, Reverend Arthur Ayoungman told a story about Crowfoot that had been related to him by Joe Crowfoot, the grandson of Crowfoot and a former chief of the Siksika himself. A few years after the making of Treaty 7, Crowfoot met with government officials in an evening meeting at his lodge, where a fire was going. Crowfoot took some earth in one hand and, throwing it into the fire, said that the earth would not burn. He then said that if he took money and threw it in the fire, it would burn and disappear. Finally he said that he would rather keep the earth because it will not burn. Ayoungman related the story to underline the contention of the Blackfoot tribes that the earth could not be sold.

Stoney Nakoda Nation

The understanding that Treaty 7 was a peace treaty is very strong among the Stoney. Lou Crawler Sr. recalled that it was "a peace agreement between First Nations and Europe." The nature of the agreement, according to Carl Simeon, was explained by Chief Bearspaw: "He said he [the Stoneys] will camp and live wherever he likes and he will not kill any White man." Della Soldier believed that peace was agreed to in return for land for the Stoney "and to choose more land in the future."

Morley Twoyoungmen remembered leaders of the Stoneys asking why the NWMP cannons were pointed in a threatening manner. The chiefs said, "You talk of peace while there are guns pointing at me. This is not peace … lay down your guns." Similar sentiments were echoed by John and Gordon Labelle. George Ear described the agreement as "a peace treaty between two races." Ear too recalled the request to turn away the cannons "if he [Commissioner Laird] really wants peace."

The Stoneys remembered discussions between their leader Bearspaw and Crowfoot: "Bearspaw told Crowfoot that there were only two options: one was to make war and fight back. But this would make things worse. Women and children will be killed. On the other hand, if we signed the treaty we would be without any worries and would be happy with each other. Crowfoot answered: 'Yes, that is why I want to make peace.'"

"Peace every day" would be valued by the Stoneys according to Joe Brown. "Before there was killing and stealing—because of the killing the treaty was made." The prospect of no more violence was a relief to all sides.

Lily Wesley contended that the peace that was agreed to was not a land surrender; it was meant to "stop the fighting." The stories Wesley remembered suggest that Whites feared an Indian war greatly, that many things were offered to secure peace and that "the White people were very persuasive using slick words." It was clearly the Whites who wanted the treaty most desperately. But according to Wesley, the Stoneys were deceived by the many promises given to get peace. The government ploy was to pacify the tribes initially with false promises so that they would not resist and talk back.

Lazarus Wesley stated that Queen Victoria was highly regarded by the Stoneys and that they solemnly agreed to stop the antagonistic practices that had existed up to that time. The treaty would stop horse stealing, and the parties agree "not to kill each other anymore—to have peace in the land."

In summary, the Stoney attitude was "let's shake hands; as long as we live, we will not oppose each other in any way." This was the meaning that the Stoneys believed both sides understood.

For Lazarus Wesley, the treaty was a comprehensive negotiation between nations: "Countries sign treaties so as not to have war and prevent devastation." The main point of a treaty was "to make peace, to shake hands, to make promises and agreements." In return "we will no longer fight over the land because the NWMP will protect us." Wesley remembered that

John McDougall, as he talked about the treaty prior to the meetings at Blackfoot Crossing, emphasized the peace that was to be gained by accepting the treaty. McDougall vowed: "We will be going to other tribes and tell the others about the [treaty] money to be given out, and that you will lay down your weapons and make peace and there will be no more animosity between the Indian people and the government's people. The government will look after you." The Methodist mission started at Morleyville in 1873 was originally set back in the forest so that it could be defended against attack. Only in 1875, when the NWMP arrived, was the mission church moved to its present location on the valley bench of the Bow River at the junction of Jacob's Creek.

The treaty meant money for Gwen Rider: "It was signed so they would receive money and to have peace." She, like a number of others, stressed that it was the government that wanted the treaty most and this was because "hostility existed between White and Native people."

Bill Mclean had perhaps the most detailed recollection of Treaty 7 as a peace treaty. Mclean remembered the significant role that John McDougall played in talking about the treaty prior to its signing. The missionaries talked about how a treaty would soon be made and the Stoneys would be part of it; they told the Stoneys about a "peace making." There had always been tribal wars but McDougall presented an ominous picture to the Stoneys; he talked about the government's intentions and "how White people would flood the land." Mclean felt that the missionaries had a strategic place among the tribes and acted as government agents, passing along messages the government wanted to get to the First Nations people: "The missionaries told the people when and where the treaty would be made." After reflecting on the nature of this peace making, he concluded that the treaty had been pre-written, even though it ought to have been a matter of "two parties coming together discussing an issue and coming to an agreement." Mclean, like John Snow, thought that the Stoneys had said much more in the treaty making than was recorded; the Stoneys had been able to say what they wanted "but no one wrote it down."

Elva Lefthand recalled that ancestors had talked of Bearspaw having said, " If I sign this treaty, everything I say now will have to be honoured. And there will be no more fighting. The fighting will have to stop." For the Stoneys, peace was the most important reason for accepting the treaty.

Tsuu T'ina Nation

Like the other five nations, Tsuu T'ina emphasized that the treaty was a peace treaty. Hilda Big Crow, Dick Big Plume, Louise Big Plume, Lucy Big Plume, Helen Meguinis, Clarabelle Pipestem, and Rosie Runner all echoed the words of Maurice Big Plume, who said that the treaty meant that Native people and Whites alike would "live as brothers and sisters in peace." The peace, according to Tom Heavenfire, meant that the Tsuu T'ina would be protected: "We were going to live our lives by the laws that White people brought," laws intended to "keep peace" and to "protect families."

CHAPTER FIVE

Treaty 7 in Its Historical and Political Context

INTRODUCTION

Past and present perspectives vie for prominence in the continual debate about what constitutes the history of any event. While the facts of an event remain unaltered, interpretations change and new stories come to light. Such is the case with Treaty 7. The history of Treaty 7, as Treaty 7 people understand it, has always been there, but it has not been part of the mainstream story of Canada. In most historical accounts, Treaty 7 is simply recounted as an event that paved the way to nationhood, making the West safe for settlement by Ontarians and Europeans. But the treaty has a different significance for the Treaty 7 First Nations because in their histories they emphasize issues that have little to do with nation-building. They even disagree with how the Canadian government continues to define its lawful obligations under Treaty 7.

It is only recently that non-Aboriginal Canadians have been willing to listen to what First Nations have to say about their history, and to acknowledge that official histories may have to be changed to accommodate the Aboriginal point of view.

One of the fundamental problems associated with coming to an understanding of Aboriginal-White relations has to do with the fact that Canadian intellectuals generally eschew a colonial framework and scarcely mention imperialism as a factor in the settlement of the West. Told from the point of view of the "victors," or the newcomer settlers, Canadian history emphasizes the perspective of the dominant society. Token recognition is extended to tragedies related to the history of the Aboriginal peoples—the unfortunate disappearance of the buffalo, disease, alcohol—but it is assumed that everything worked out for the best in the long run. Established historians such as Arthur Lower, Donald Creighton, and George Stanley consistently maintain that Canada's Indian policy was honourable, if at times misguided. Intentions were always good. In the long view of Aboriginal-White relations, the "partnership" forged between newcomers and Aboriginal peoples has served both sides well—it was inevitable that Canada's history in the Northwest turned out as it did. The effects of empire-building, according to the establishment historians, has on balance been to the benefit of all concerned in this spread of "civilization." In the words of George Stanley:

The gravest problem presented to the Dominion of Canada by the acquisition and settlement of Rupert's Land and the North-West was the impact of a superior civilization upon the Native Indian Tribes. Again and again, in different places and in different ways, the problem has unfolded itself at the contact of European and savage. Too often the advent of the white man has led to the moral and physical decline of the Native. In Africa, Melanesia and America, the clash of peoples in different stages of development has spelled disaster to the weaker. The European, conscious of his material superiority, is only too contemptuous of the savage, intolerant of his helplessness, ignorant of his mental processes and impatient at his slow assimilation of civilization. The savage, centuries behind in mental and economic development, cannot readily adapt himself to meet the new conditions. He is incapable of bridging the gap of centuries alone and unassisted. Although white penetration into Native territories may be inspired by motives of self-interest, such as trade and settlement, once there, the responsibility of "the white man's burden" is inevitable.[1]

However euphemistically writers like Stanley portray the process, we can no longer ignore colonialism and its imperial context as we write the history of the Canadian West. As cultural critic Edward Said notes:

The global reach of classical nineteenth and early twentieth century European imperialism still casts a considerable shadow over our own times. Hardly any North American, African, European, Latin American, Indian, Caribbean, Australian individual—the list is very long—who is alive today has not been touched by the empires of the past. Britain and France between them controlled immense territories: Canada, Australia, New Zealand, the colonies of North and South America and the Caribbean, large swatches of Africa, the Middle East, the Far East (Britain will hold Hong Kong as a colony until 1997), and the Indian subcontinent in its entirety all these fell under the sway of and in time were liberated from British and French rule.[2]

Imperial powers played a major role not only in physically neutralizing indigenous populations but in creating and sustaining negative images of Aboriginal peoples. The dissemination of these negative images helped those in power justify, to themselves, the removal of Aboriginal peoples from their traditional lands. Said has called this the "struggle over geography": "That struggle is complex and interesting because it is not only about soldiers and cannons but about ideas, about forms, about images and imaginings."[3]

After justifying their right to move into and control new territory, the European powers went wherever they could: "Scarcely a corner of life was left untouched by the facts of empire; the economies were hungry for overseas markets, raw materials, cheap labour, and hugely profitable land, and defense and foreign-policy establishments, were more and more committed to maintaining vast tracts of distant territories and large numbers of subjugated people. When the Western powers were not in close, sometimes ruthless competition with one another for more colonies ... they were hard at work settling, surveying, studying, and of course ruling the territories under their jurisdictions."[4]

The Aboriginal people of southern Alberta were not a pool of cheap labour, nor a new market to be exploited, but they did occupy valuable land and stood in the way of those who wanted to exploit coal, oil, and other minerals in and along the Rocky Mountains. The invasions and intrusions of traders, surveyors, and settlers were experienced by the indigenous people as the National Policy became the driving force behind the Canadian expansion into the Northwest. The same forces at work in other parts of the world were at work in the Canadian West. These forces were defined by Said as follows: "'Imperialism' means the practice, the theory and attitudes of a dominating metropolitan centre ruling a distant territory; 'colonialism,' which is almost always a consequence of imperialism, is the implanting of settlements on distant territories."[5] Imperialism can be exercised in a variety of ways, including force, political collaboration, economic pressure, and social or cultural co-option; it is the process of establishing and maintaining an empire. The accumulation of wealth that invariably takes place is accompanied by productions and portrayals—books, newspapers, visual images—that justify and document the need of the colonizers to dominate the land and make it bountiful in ways that those who originally occupied it have been unable to do. Thus, terms such as "inferior," "subject race," "subordinate people," "dependency," "expansion," and "authority" come into common use by the colonizer.

Those agents of colonialism who exercised power used concepts and languages that gradually became familiar to the colonized and over time became part of the culture of domination. As the agents of empire sought to exploit spices, sugar, slaves, coal, rubber, cotton, opium, tin, gold, oil, and silver, they found it difficult to maintain these huge empires. They needed "immense will and self-confidence even arrogance"[6] in order to rule the indigenous people and convincingly portray them as subordinate, less advanced, and inferior. Thus, a process of "education" began whereby the colonizers tried to persuade the colonized that what the colonizers were doing was right, that they should accept the colonizers' notions of what was best for the lands they were living on. It was, as Stanley put it, the "white man's burden" to persuade the indigenous people that the newcomers' way was the best way. The newcomers promoted the idea of a partnership, but in this partnership the colonizers would try to convince the colonized that what was being done was in their own best interests.

Thus, to understand properly what happened in the Treaty 7 area, one must acknowledge the concepts of imperialism and colonialism, for these concepts shaped the relations between Aboriginal and newcomer, and were behind the forces that permanently changed the landscape and lifestyle of the Aboriginal peoples of the western prairies. The history of Treaty 7 must be broadened to allow the voices of the colonized to be heard.

UNDERSTANDING TREATY 7

The numbered treaties, from 1 to 7, were substantially similar, but each one dealt with particular circumstances and contained distinct clauses. While there can be unanimity on the meaning of certain clauses, in general the texts of the treaties can be interpreted in a variety of ways. It is questionable whether a "mutually understood agreement" was ever arrived at between a people representing a written culture on the one hand and a people representing an essentially oral culture on the other. Indeed, many indigenous cultures throughout the world were at a distinct disadvantage as the nation-states that had been growing since the mid-eighteenth century expanded their interests. In the period from the late eighteenth century to the twentieth century, the world witnessed "the construction of the state in the image and interests of the new middle classes."[7] The expansion of these nation-states saw the subordination of classes, ethnic groups, and races to a dominant class or racial group. The interests of one particular class or group were privileged at the expense of the interests of the others. What emerged in each instance was a so-called national culture that in fact was little more than the culture favoured by those who made up the dominant group or class. By the twentieth century it was clear that the dominant class was the middle class, and its cultural forms and economic interests were favoured. In most nation-states this meant that the culture of the subordinated class, ethnic group, or race was either suppressed or expropriated as nominally part of the "national" culture. National identity and culture were "disseminated throughout the whole of society in several ways, such as the spread of literacy, the 'invention of tradition,' the standardization of 'national' language the establishment of public education, religious evangelism, promotion of economic individualism."[8] What went hand in hand with the valorizing of a national culture was the diminution of other cultures: "Local, 'unprogressive,' and particularist attitudes and practices, such as minority religion, dialect and minority languages, folk customs and traditions rooted in agrarian economy and so on, were either taken over (or tidied up) as folklore of the 'nation' or discouraged and even prescribed as 'superstitious,' 'barbaric' or 'unprogressive.'"[9]

At times the subordinated groups were described in national narratives as "noble savages," especially when any threat from them had dissipated. What they learned from their experiences was that it was best to become assimilated within the dominant culture if they hoped to survive. Their real culture was somewhere far in the distant past: "Nostalgia could be indulged, and the 'primitive people' could be safely used as a moral, because they could not or soon would not pose any political, social or cultural problem in their own right and on their own behalf. Meanwhile the middleclass reformers of the early nineteenth century rapidly developed strategies for 'modernizing' these primitive people, along with the lower classes."[10] While the "noble savage" was idealized, the cultural practices of subordinated groups were belittled. This condemnation included "merely oral culture, communalism (if not communism) and sociability, apparently improvident and opportunistic work patterns and domestic economy, 'immoral' sexual practices, a tendency to nomadism if not outright vagabondage, 'superstitions' or false religion and an ad hoc and adaptive attitude to 'improvement' and new technology, an ad hoc practical approach to leadership, work organization and the 'moral economy' and 'irrational' or merely 'traditional' ideas of social land economic justice."[11]

The dominant middle-class society was either unwilling or unable to see Aboriginal culture as a successful and long-term accommodation to its environment. Thus, the dominant culture that emerged was a literate society directed by Christian principles. In the Canadian West, the dominant culture had a specific agenda: " Just as important were ideas of economic self-sufficiency and individualism and settled, disciplined and investment oriented work habits and domestic economy. These would be supported by a middle-class sexual morality and model of domesticity and reinforced by a more routine, 'orderly' and hierarchical pattern of leadership in work and social life; and a market-oriented, competitive attitude to labour and its rewards. Finally there should be acceptance of regular institutions of surveillance, control and policing."[12] The agents of this European culture, which was making its way across North America in a search for wealth, were not always primarily interested in controlling the indigenous populations—at least not at first. Early in the contact period, they needed the expertise and knowledge of indigenous people in order to establish their own position of strength. The need to denigrate and then to convert and civilize the Aboriginal only came once the economic advantaged had been secured. Those who at first had been important "partners" were soon to become major impediments to "civilization."

By the time the treaties were being negotiated on the prairies, the Euro-Canadian leadership were confident that they were powerful enough to secure agreements that would allow White settlements to be established and to thrive. Unknown to the Aboriginal leadership, the treaties were to privilege the written culture of the dominant society while denigrating the oral culture of the Aboriginal treaty makers. For this newly emerging middle-class power, the land had to be made "bountiful," and in its estimation the Aboriginal peoples had not succeeded in this. There were no cultivated fields or estates by which Euro-Canadians measure success. In fact, when the treaties were being negotiated, the Aboriginal peoples were viewed as an obstacle to the colonization schemes envisaged for the West by Euro-Canadian elites. The treaties were seen by people like Father Scollen, Reverend McDougall, Colonel Macleod, and Commissioner Laird as expedient means of beginning the process of assimilation through which (they believed) the Aboriginal populations would eventually disappear. It is clear that Canadian officials and religious leaders were preparing the Aboriginal population for the White settlers who they knew would be arriving in large numbers to take over the land. These agents of Euro-Canadian society showed scarcely any ability to appreciate the "communal economy and social practices"[13] of the populations with whom they came into contact. They did not approach the treaty process as equals negotiating with equals but rather as superiors with inferiors. This was a major disadvantage for the Aboriginal leadership, who came to negotiate Treaty 7 in good faith. The attitude of the Canadian treaty makers was paternalistic and condescending—they would do what they thought was best for the Aboriginal peoples, even to the extent of ignoring what the Aboriginal leaders clearly wanted to include in the treaty.

Thus, a major problem with the treaties was that ideologically and culturally the treaty makers for the Crown did not respect the Aboriginal leadership and

what it represented: "the white policy-makers' idea of the nature and powers of native chiefs was in part a relic of the earlier political culture of monarchy and court government and the idea that a European monarch was treating a weaker or lesser peer, the chief, in The New World, Africa or Australia."[14] They did not respect the authority or legitimacy of the chiefs with whom they were negotiating, and perhaps they never had any intention of honouring what they were negotiating: "The treaties, circumstances and perceptions of the Canadian Government and its officers profoundly altered the political and social organization of the Native people, according to white assumptions and practices that had been formed in North America but they were also informed by models of social structure and relationships developed in Britain. To some extent, at least, the chiefs were made something like a cross between a Highland laird…[and] an idealized version of the professionalised landed gentleman and the Victorian public school ideal of the gentlemanly public official."[15]

The Aboriginal leaders were allowed to feel that they were negotiating as equals, but the Euro-Canadians did not respect their culture and they saw their nations as inferior. The Aboriginal leaders could hardly be expected to know that these men they were bargaining with in good faith had little resolution to take seriously the discussions that the Aboriginal leadership solemnized by smoking the pipe.

The power relationship between the Aboriginal government and the Canadian government was not equal, and leaders such as Crowfoot and Red Crow were aware that military force was being used to slaughter indigenous people in the United States. By accommodating the newcomers, the Aboriginal people hoped to work out an arrangement to share the land so that both sides could benefit from living side by side. They could not have known that the newcomers expected more than a commitment to share the land, that in fact they wanted to take what they could, even if it meant disregarding the treaties. The Aboriginal leadership did not know about the cultural attitudes that had long been evolving in Europe, which privileged the culture of one class above that of all others. Anything not European was subordinated, and values that were not middle class were dismissed or ignored. What happened in western Canada in the 1870s was only one incident in the global process of subjugation that was played out wherever colonial fragments of the British Empire took hold. There never was a reconciliation between what was actually discussed at Blackfoot Crossing in September 1877 and what was included in the written legal text of the Treaty 7 document. The territorial imperative of the Crown is still imposed today upon the First Nations of Treaty 7.

CONTEXT OF TREATY 7: SOME CONSIDERATIONS

A problem with understanding Treaty 7 arises out of the way in which it has been described and represented to date. Until very recently the treaty has been explained in the context of nation-building, usually in an academic discourse by male writers who are defending a linear approach. Their chosen form is the essay, which usually presumes a monological or single perspective, with a narrator arbitrarily organizing evidence to produce the Truth—a single unassailable verity. Much of the writing done about Treaty 7 assumes this tone of truth, of finality: that we (Euro-Canadians) are right and their (the Aboriginal peoples') opinions are of no consequence. This position has been allowed to go unchallenged—until only very recently—because few of these authors have considered what Aboriginal people themselves thought or think of the treaty; they either never asked, or when they have, they have selectively asked only certain people. The result has been that areas of the treaty that are clearly problematic have been glossed over and the discourse of those who hold power has allowed authors to ignore difficult issues. The consequence has been to discredit the voices of those who disagree with the "official" government line on what the treaty means.

What is clear is that there is no agreed-upon interpretation of Treaty 7; nor is there agreement on what motivated both sides to agree to the treaty. Studies based on a single perspective have failed to stop the nagging questions about the treaty. Over the years academics have come to the recognition that a dialogic (dual or multiple) perspective is needed to understand historical events such as Treaty 7. What becomes evident when a dialogical approach is used is that on some points there is agreement while on others there is divergence of opinion. One of the crucial differences between the perspectives of the Canadian government and the First Nations is that the government side has privileged the written form of representation, while the First Nations side has relied (and still does) on an oral discourse. Thus, while the Crown thought that what was written down was the final word, the Aboriginal people believed that what was said in the discussions at Blackfoot Crossing was as valid as what was written down.

Problems relating to language are at the very core of the Euro-Canadian's difficulty in understanding the Aboriginal world view. The spoken languages of Aboriginal peoples have been ignored by dominant imperial cultures, and the failure to recognize or acknowledge Aboriginal culture constitutes a form of cultural subjugation. As Sakej Youngblood-Henderson has written: "Everywhere we are born into language, everywhere it binds our consciousness. Its mystery and development reflect our particular habits, those of our linguistic heritage. Our language [or languages] contain the essential ways in which we experience and interact with our culture. Thus, our linguistic understanding [the world view in English] is our map that a particular language creates in order to navigate the larger worldview. These understandings become, then, in some sense, most of the worldview."[16]

Youngblood-Henderson argues that the noun-centred objectifying languages of the Eurocentric world view help users of these languages to reify and classify the world environment. By contrast, Aboriginal languages are verb-centred and reflect an apprehension of the world that is in a constant state of flux or change. Thus, there are very few fixed or rigid objects in the Aboriginal world view: "With the fluidity of semantic-phonemes comprising the verb sounds, every speaker can create new vocabulary 'on the fly,' custom tailored to meet the experience of movement to express the very finest nuances of meanings."[17] Youngblood-Henderson maintains that such different ways of seeing the world mean that these languages cannot be easily translated—that simply translating a word by itself does not relay with it the world view that the language as a whole contains.

The fundamental assumptions underlying European and Aboriginal languages are so radically different that simple translation is impossible. For the Aboriginal, "to see things as permanent is to be confused about everything: an alternative to that understanding is the need to create temporary harmonies through alliances and relationships among all forms and forces—this process is a never-ending source of wonder to the indigenous mind and to other forces who contribute to the harmony."[18]

To ignore Aboriginal languages and to insist on assimilation or "cognitive imperialism" is to deny and destroy the Aboriginal sacred understandings. Youngblood-Henderson concludes that "cultural and cognitive racism must be exposed and resolved. Under modern thought, at least in theory, every language describes the world completely, though each in its own way. The Aboriginal languages and worldviews must be strengthened and developed with their own contexts. Any interference is domination, both cognitively and culturally. Thus every Aboriginal language has the right to exist without conforming to Eurocentric languages or worldviews ... The failure to admit differences in worldview is also domination."[19]

Thus, a fundamental problem continues to exist in the discourse between those who have held power and those who have not or those who have represented a new way of life and the indigenous populations.[...]

Notes

Chapter Five

1. Stanley, *The Birth of Western Canada*, 194.
2. Said, *Culture and Imperialism*, 5–6.
3. Ibid., 7.
4. Ibid., 8.
5. Ibid., 9.
6. Ibid., 11.
7. Kelly, "Class, Race and Cultural Revolution," 19.
8. Ibid., 20.
9. Ibid., 21.
10. Ibid.
11. Ibid.
12. Ibid., 22.
13. Ibid., 24.
14. Ibid., 35.
15. Ibid., 36.
16. Youngblood-Henderson, "Governing the Implicate Order," 3.
17. Ibid., 8.
18. Ibid., 9.
19. Ibid., 19.

TRAITORS OR PATRIOTS?

Continentalism and Nationalism
in the Free Trade Elections of 1891 and 1911

Christopher Pennington
University of Toronto

● TRAITORS OR PATRIOTS? CONTINENTALISM AND NATIONALISM IN THE FREE TRADE ELECTIONS OF 1891 AND 1911

● Introduction by Christopher Pennington

▲ Primary Sources

■ Secondary Sources

● INTRODUCTION

Christopher Pennington

Canada and the United States did not enjoy neighbourly relations in the late nineteenth century. The "world's longest undefended border" had yet to come into being, with the two sides maintaining significant military fortifications in case of a repetition of the War of 1812, and diplomatic relations were frosty, hampered by British control over Canadian foreign affairs and recurring disputes over tariffs and fishing rights. Most Americans thought only occasionally about Canadians, and were inclined to regard them as backward colonials who inexplicably preferred to remain subservient to Great Britain. Canadians thought often about Americans, however, and they rarely liked what they saw. The "Yankees" were commonly regarded as an uncultured, greedy, and aggressive people with an alarming tradition of territorial expansion on the North American continent. They had twice attempted to conquer Canada, in 1775 and 1812, and though a third invasion was considered a fading possibility in the late nineteenth century, a few notable American politicians still mused publicly about their "manifest destiny" to someday absorb the Dominion into the United States. This was a doomsday scenario to most Canadians, who were then divided along racial, religious, and linguistic lines, but almost universally agreed that they did not want to become Americans. Across the Dominion, and particularly among imperialist English Canadians, it was thought best to maintain a safe political distance from the United States.

Still, it was difficult not to envy the tremendous population growth, military strength, and economic prosperity of the Americans. This latter attribute was most alluring to Canadians, who had struggled with intermittent economic depressions in the two decades since Confederation. The overtly patriotic "National Policy" of Sir John A. Macdonald, which promised to protect Canadian industries by erecting high tariffs against American and British imports, helped his Liberal-Conservatives to win the election of 1878 and was implemented the next year. The "N.P." propelled the Tories to further electoral victories in 1882 and 1887, but it had limited success as a stimulant to the beleaguered economy. Many Canadians, especially farmers, had become convinced by the late 1880s that gaining unfettered access to the millions of customers south of the border was the key to their economic future. Shortly after the election of 1887, a grassroots farmers' movement in favour of free trade with the United States helped to push the question to the forefront of Canadian politics.

But what kind of free trade, exactly? This was a vital question, because closer economic ties with the Americans might entail closer political ties as well, and that worried many Canadians. The most prominent proposal in the summer of 1887 was "commercial union," which would not only establish complete free trade, but also abolish the customs houses along the Canada—U.S. border and create a common tariff against the rest of the world, including Great Britain. Its foremost champion was Erastus Wiman, a Canadian businessman who had resided in New York City for over 20 years. A bombastic millionaire known as the "Duke of Staten Island," Wiman styled himself as an "envoy extraordinary" whose self-appointed mission was to encourage closer economic relations between his native and adopted lands. He argued not only that Canadian natural products would find a ready market in the United States, a widely accepted theory, but also that Canadian manufacturers—who feared the loss of their privileged position in their home market—could compete on a level playing field with their American counterparts.

NEL

Wiman found it difficult to allay concerns about commercial union's probable economic and political consequences. Could Canadian manufacturers survive? Even if they did, would Ottawa be giving up too much of its sovereignty by having to agree to a common tariff with Washington? What about the damage that would be done to the British connection? Was this just the "thin edge of the wedge" toward eventual annexation? Wiman was widely, if unjustly, suspected of being an annexationist, and this impression was reinforced by his friendship with Goldwin Smith, a world-famous British history professor, controversialist, and longtime Toronto resident. Smith supported commercial union not on its economic merits, but because it might bring about "political union" (he disliked the coercive connotation of "annexation") between Canada and the United States. Smith regarded the American Revolution as a tragedy that had needlessly split the English-speaking peoples of North America. He denounced Confederation as a hopeless failure built upon a national identity that did not exist and, as Smith saw it, the sooner that English-speaking North Americans could be politically reunited, the better. Not surprisingly, his views were regarded as heresy—even treason—by an overwhelming majority of Canadians.

The Liberals, who made Wilfrid Laurier their new leader in June 1887, found commercial union an attractive alternative to the National Policy but worried that its association with Wiman and Smith would raise damaging questions about its political consequences. In February 1888 they settled on a watered-down version, "unrestricted reciprocity," which meant complete free trade with the United States, but without abolishing customs houses or adopting the politically entangling common tariff. Though it was unlikely to be accepted by the Americans (as it would allow British imports to flow freely into the United States through Canada) it proved to be a popular policy among Canadians. The stage was set for a decisive struggle between the National Policy and unrestricted reciprocity, and the Election of 1891 revolved almost solely around this single issue.

Macdonald, who was 76 years old and in failing health, attempted to frame the campaign not as a clash of trade policies, but as an apocalyptic struggle for the future—indeed, the very soul—of Canada. He was assisted by the mid-campaign revelation that the Liberal editor of the Toronto *Globe,* Edward Farrer, had written a top-secret pamphlet advising Americans how to force Canada into annexation. This, Macdonald claimed, was proof that Laurier and the Liberals were conspiring to sell out Canada to the United States, thus committing "veiled treason" against their own country. There was no proof that any leading Liberals had even been aware of the Farrer pamphlet, let alone that they had plotted to have Canada sold to the United States, and the accusations of treason made for an extremely bitter campaign. Still, Macdonald's patriotic plea to Canadians to vote one last time for "The Old Flag, the Old Policy, the Old Leader," as one campaign poster put it, was just enough to ensure the narrow re-election of his government.

Initially, the outcome of the Election of 1891 seemed to serve as a cautionary tale for politicians who might consider reviving the free trade issue. Predictably, none of the four Liberal-Conservatives who followed Macdonald as prime minister after his death in June 1891—Sir John Abbott, Sir John Thompson, Sir Mackenzie Bowell, and Sir Charles Tupper—showed any serious interest in trade negotiations with the Americans. Nor did Laurier and the Liberals, who quietly abandoned their policy of unrestricted reciprocity in 1893 and thereby made themselves "safe" again on the trade question. After the Liberals triumphed in the election of 1896, Laurier maintained the National Policy, though he tweaked it to give a modest preference to British imports. He was fortunate to take office just as the long-struggling Canadian economy finally hit its stride, and the Laurier years proved to be boom years. From 1896 to 1911 the country experienced dramatic economic and demographic growth, fuelled by the arrival of over 2 million immigrants and the rapid settlement of the West.[1] It was because of this remarkable boom that Laurier could make his famous prediction that the twentieth century would belong to Canada.

There would be one more Liberal flirtation with free trade, however. In 1910 Laurier ran into trouble over his government's plans to establish a modest Canadian Navy, comprising five cruisers and six destroyers, instead of contributing money toward the construction of dreadnought battleships that were urgently required by the British Royal Navy. English Canadian imperialists complained that this "tin-pot navy" was not enough, while isolationists in French Canada protested that it was too much. That summer Laurier, looking for an inspiring policy to draw attention away from his naval dilemma, toured Western Canada and was struck by the popularity of free trade in the region. Judging that the issue would be an electoral winner, he entered into negotiations for a trade deal with the obliging Taft administration. The Reciprocity Agreement that the two governments crafted eliminated tariffs on most natural products and reduced them on a long list of manufactured goods. It was a bold reversal of the protectionist National Policy, it was well received in Canada, and it seemed—at first—like a stroke of political genius.

Gradually, however, the Conservatives rallied. Their leader, Robert Borden, spearheaded a coalition against the agreement that incorporated disaffected federal Liberals, Conservative provincial premiers, and Toronto and Montreal businessmen who predicted that economic doom—and possibly annexation—would follow if the National Policy was abandoned. Their slogan was "Canadianism or Continentalism." Its similarity to the emotional appeal made by the Macdonald government in 1891, complete with sinister undertones about Canada being sold out to the United States, was obvious. The difference in 1911 was that, ironically, the Tories could effectively point to the prosperity of the country in the Laurier years as evidence that there was no reason to risk free trade with the United States. For months the Conservatives managed to prevent the Reciprocity Agreement from coming to a vote in the House of Commons, and in July 1911 Laurier called an early election to let the Canadian people settle the issue.

The election of 1911 differed from that of 1891 in that free trade was not the sole issue of the campaign. In Quebec a second prominent concern was the "tin-pot navy," and the Conservatives made a tacit agreement to allow isolationists under the leadership of Henri Bourassa to take the fight to Laurier in that province. The naval issue dogged the Liberals in English Canada, as well. But the Reciprocity Agreement remained the main overall issue, and in the face of hyperbolic Conservative attacks a frustrated Laurier was obliged, as in 1891, to assure voters of his loyalty to Canada in defensive, rather sad campaign speeches. It was not enough. In September 1911 his Liberals were soundly defeated, and Borden and the Conservative Party formed a majority government. It was the end of an era, and the political lesson was clear. Seventy-five years would pass before another Canadian prime minister, this time Brian Mulroney, would take up the banner of free trade with the United States.

This module explores the free trade debates of 1891 and 1911 and what they reveal about Canadian continentalism, nationalism, and anti-Americanism in the late nineteenth and early twentieth centuries. It features an iconic Conservative campaign poster from 1891 and excerpts from the speeches or written statements of leading figures—Erastus Wiman, Goldwin Smith, Sir John A. Macdonald, Robert Borden, and Sir Wilfrid Laurier—that allow them to explain their positions in their own words. The first scholarly

---

[1] Statistics Canada, *Historical Statistics of Canada,* Second Edition (Ottawa, 1983): Section A, Population and Migration, Table A350, Immigrant Arrivals in Canada, 1852–1977.

reading, excerpted from a book by Christopher Pennington, explains why the Liberals adopted unrestricted reciprocity and argues that the election of 1891 was not a struggle between nationalist Conservatives and traitorous Liberals, but a clash of two very different—but equally patriotic—brands of Canadian nationalism. It also notes that the conscious decision of both parties to focus on the trade question, rather than the divisive race and religion question, was essential to the preservation of national unity at that time. The second scholarly reading, by W.M. Baker, reflects on the election of 1911 and on the central place of anti-Americanism in Canadian nationalist thought, while considering other factors that contributed to the Conservative victory in that campaign.

QUESTIONS

1. What were the key features—and the relative advantages and disadvantages—of the National Policy, unrestricted reciprocity, commercial union, and annexation?
2. Why did Goldwin Smith believe that Canada should, and one day would, become a part of the United States? Do you think his arguments are still relevant today?
3. How had Canada's political and economic situation changed from 1891 to 1911, and what impact, if any, did this have on the Election of 1911?
4. Compare Sir John A. Macdonald's address in 1891 to Robert Borden's House of Commons speech in 1911. Was Borden simply reiterating Macdonald's argument against free trade and his appeal to Canadian nationalism, or are there significant differences between the two speeches?
5. Wilfrid Laurier was not known as much of an economic thinker, but in each of these elections he staked his political future on free trade with the United States. Why, in each instance, was he willing to take such a great political risk?

FURTHER READINGS

Robert Hannigan, "Reciprocity 1911: Continentalism and American *weltpolitik*," *Diplomatic History*, vol 4. no. 1 (December 1979): 1–18.

David MacKenzie and Patrice Dutil, *Canada 1911: The Decisive Election that Shaped the Country* (Toronto: Dundurn Press, 2011).

Christopher Pennington, *The Destiny of Canada: Macdonald, Laurier, and the Election of 1891* (Toronto: Allen Lane, 2011).

Paul Stevens, editor, *The 1911 General Election: A Study in Canadian Politics* (Toronto: Copp Clark, 1970).

Patricia K. Wood, "Defining "Canadian": Anti-Americanism and Identity in Sir John A. Macdonald's Nationalism," *Journal of Canadian Studies*, vol 36 no 2 (August 2001): 49–69.

▲ DOCUMENT 1: THE ADVANTAGES OF COMMERCIAL UNION TO CANADA AND THE UNITED STATES

Erastus Wiman

The question of Commercial Union between Canada and the United States is an exceedingly simple one. At the present moment, both countries have a high tariff, and a staff of custom-house officials along the border to enforce it. It is now proposed that there should be no tariff whatever between the United States and Canada, that there should be no custom-houses, and that the barriers that have hitherto prevented the freest intercourse between the two countries should be completely abolished. The proposition, while exceedingly simple in its statement, is freighted with consequences of the greatest import to both countries. It is of rare occurrence in the history of communities, for men to assemble and discuss a question of such magnitude as that of Commercial Union. It is difficult to conceive of a topic of deeper interest, or of wider range, than that which purports to change the economic relations of two countries so vast as the United States and Canada. Recalling great events in history, their importance is measured by the consequences that have resulted from them. The Crusades, the Reformation, the English Revolution, the withdrawal of the American Colonies, the French Revolution, the Napoleonic wars, all stand out in bold relief, because of the momentous consequences to mankind that resulted from them.

The American Revolution is probably, of all others, the event that has had the most direct and most important influence upon the English-speaking race.

In this New World, productive forces have worked out consequences which are almost beyond human computation. It seems as if, in the unfolding of the Providence of God, the discovery and development of America was the one thing needed to fulfill the destiny of His creature, man; for, without this discovery, mankind would never have reached his present material, intellectual and moral progress.

The United States, however, have one advantage over Canada, not of a political character, but which, if it could be secured by Canada, would insures [sic] her success beyond any question. This advantage consists in unrestricted commercial intercourse between the various States. The absence of customhouses between them has done more to make the United States a great and prosperous nation than did the republican form of government. The arteries of commerce, in a greater degree than all else, have served to hold the people together, enriching them with the products and resources of each other.

With a different policy, a policy of isolation of the several States, there would have been no progress in the United States such as the world has witnessed. Many of the States are poor and sterile, some are sandy deserts, while others can produce but one or two great staples. Yet, by a commercial union with each other, they have all developed material prosperity. Mankind in no quarter of the globe has greater cause to rejoice than the inhabitants of the poorest State in the great constellation of commonwealths. They rejoice in the fact that their commercial condition is so shaped as to enable them to participate, without let or hinderance, in the prosperity of the more favored States. Through the free interchange of the rich products of a vast continent, they all reap a benefit, and share in each other's prosperity.

Source: G.M. Fairchild, *Canadian Leaves: History, Art, Science, Literature, Commerce: A Series of New Papers Read Before the Canadian Club of New York* (New York: Thompson & Co Publishers, 1887), 269–281.

With these facts before us, let us now consider what Canada has gained from her isolation from the rest of the continent. Under a different form of government, with a distinctive nationality, a commercial condition has prevailed between Canada and the United States, diametrically opposite to that which has [been] obtained between the various States. Upon the whole, commercially speaking, the results have not been satisfactory to Canada. True she has made some progress; but this is in great part due to the frugality and energy of her people. It is true that her prosperity has been, at times, apparently as great as that of the neighboring States, but it is equally true that her progress has been spasmodic, and that her public debt, her provincial and municipal obligations, and, above all, the private indebtedness of her producers, have assumed alarming proportions. Of recent years an artificial prosperity has been imparted by means of increased taxation, followed by large expenditures for railway improvements that have developed vast regions of country. These outlays have mainly been well directed; they have, beyond doubt, brought within easy access stretches of territory hitherto so isolated as to be valueless. This apparent increase of the wealth of Canada, during the last ten years, from the doubling of railway facilities, is probably greater than that of any one State in the Union, but the price at which the investment is carried by the people of Canada may well be closely watched. If she can, by an enlarged market, [and] higher prices, carry this investment without taxing too seriously the debt-paying power of her people, then these large public and private outlays will bear profitable fruit. But if the heavy load of debt and taxation, now weighing upon Canada, is to be borne in the face of declining prices, of a restricted market, and by an embarrassed agricultural community, it would have been better had such investments never been made.

Large investments in public works and railway improvements are justified only by proportionate increase in trade. No one thing would so much contribute to the increase of traffic as a complete interchange of products between the two countries. The building of the Canadian Pacific Railway is one of the greatest achievements of modern times, following as it does the constant extension of the Grand Trunk system. These two great arteries, with numerous other railways, give Canada means of communication of the greatest magnitude and importance, within her own territory, as well as with the United States.

The wonderful system of waterways with which nature has blessed the Dominion, has been made still more available by the expenditures of vast sums in order to connect them one with another. To-day, the Canadian farmer is paying the interest on these investments. No greater benefit could befall the Canadian tax payer than the stimulation of a trade which would thoroughly utilize these means of communication. A complete interchange of commodities between the United States and Canada, would more than anything else, contribute to that object. Any development within the Dominion itself would also stimulate traffic and increase railway tonnage. These advantages would certainly be largely enhanced by the removal of the barriers which now prevent Canadian commodities from reaching the United States markets. No one longing for the creation of a market could have planned one better suited for Canada than that of the neighboring Republic.

A long residence in New York and a daily contact with the people of the American nation, have imbued me with the belief that no others are so well prepared to become consumers of Canadian products. The country is rich beyond comparison: incomes have reached a point far above those of any other people in the world. There are more individuals in New York who have $10,000 a year, or $200 a week, to spend on their living than in any other city of the world. More are rolling in wealth in the cities of the East and the West than had ever been thought possible. American consumers are in a better financial condition and are more liberal in their expenditures than those of any other country. They want the best products of the soil, and no region is better calculated to furnish these than the Province of Ontario.

The discussion of commercial union has been the occasion for a great display of cheap patriotism. Patriotism, as I understand it, consists in the love of one's country for the furtherance of its best and dearest interests. True patriotism should not obstinately stand in the way of the country's best interests. Love of British institutions, of British connection, cannot be imperilled by a greater development of Canadian resources. No sentimental consideration should stand in the way of a policy which would benefit Canada.

It has been said that in order to arrive at unrestricted reciprocity with the United States, discrimination would have to be enforced against English goods, and that commercial union is but a step to annexation. These two objections are the two strongest arguments brought against the policy of freedom of trade on the North American continent. But when we think of the vast interests at stake, and how great, to the Dominion, the benefits that the measure would bring forth, the interests of the few manufacturers in Great Britain, likely to be affected by the measure, are as a drop in the bucket. It would well repay Canada to guarantee the profit which every exporter of British goods will ever make for the remainder of his life, rather than that there should be any impediment to a union, comercially speaking, between the two great countries of this continent. How many people do you suppose would be affected were Canada to admit American manufactures free, and still impose a duty on English goods? They certainly would not exceed a thousand in number. It is doubtful whether there are five hundred establishments in the whole of Great Britain that have a large interest in the exportation of their wares to Canada. From a close acquaintance with numerous English manufacturers. I believe that they would hail with delight any movement by which the Canadians would be benefitted. Better still, if it should happen that commercial union would so operate as to determine a reduction in the United States tariff—a very likely hypothesis—this alone would offset tenfold the disadvantages that Canada's discrimination against English goods might entail. In other words, the demand for British goods throughout the continent—if a lowering of the tariff of the two countries was to take place—would be far greater than under the existing highly protective policy which prevails against the goods of all nations, both in Canada and the United States.

All great changes are apt to inflict some wrong in a few isolated cases; but progress cannot be retarded by such consideration. A great railway often plays havoc with the symmetry of a farm, cutting it diagonally in two sometimes. The enforcement of a universal law affects many an interest, but that which achieves the greatest good to the greatest number is the standard by which all these matters should be regulated. Commercial union with the United States would confer the greatest amount of good upon the greatest number, therefore, it is difficult to consider with any seriousness the objections urged against it.

Of course, it will be ojected [sic] that if the Yankee manufacturer and merchant are let free into Canada they will crowd out the Canadian manufacturer and merchant. Well, all that need be said in reply is: that if the Canadians cannot hold their own when all the conditions are equal, they don't deserve the name of Canadians. It is the first time in the history of that country that such a disparaging assertion has been made. If the pluck and spirit which conquered Canada has deserted it, it is time we should introduce some new blood in the country.

The talk that any class of Canadians cannot hold their own against any other people on the face of the earth finds no echo in the minds of our fellow-countrymen who have already found a home in the United States. They experience no difficulty in holding their own, side by side, with the Yankees. As mechanics, skilled laborers, railroad men, or as occupants of positions of trust and responsibility, we find everywhere the native born Canadian. Always respected, always self-respecting, sometimes somewhat assertive, always self-reliant and abundantly able to hold his own in a fair field. Have we ever realized the enormous number of Canadians who have already sought the benefits of commercial union with the United States. It is doubtful if, in the history of any country—especially a young country—so large a proportion of the total population has, in so short a time, sought a home outside of it. The census shows the enormous increase of the Canadian element in the American Republic:

Census of 1860—Canadians in United States,   249,970
Census of 1870— "   "   "   "   493,464
Census of 1880— "   "   "   "   717,157
Census of 1885—(estimated)......................   950,000

It appears that to this date, fully one million of Canadians have taken up their abode in the United States A million out of a population of five millions! What a tremendous proportion this is for a country which is making the most desperate efforts to attract immigration within her borders! Surely there is something wrong in all this, especially when we recall the enormous expenditures made, the heavy burdens imposed, to find the most promising portion of the population seeking a home and a future elsewhere. If commercial union did accomplish nothing better than to keep our young men at home, that of itself would be a great advantage.

Not a mother but dreads the day when her boy, her precious boy, will look with longing eyes across the border. What is the future on the farm for the little blue-eyed baby that looks up into its mother's face? If the little one is a boy he will at best inherit his father's fate. The mother knows how hard the father has had to work to earn a livelihood; she also knows what frugality must be practiced to enable them to leave the boy any patrimony. And the dear mother knows that while such a struggle for existence impends, the attractions across the border are forever tempting her beloved son from her side.

But, if the little one in her lap is a girl; if the clear blue eyes look inquiringly into the mother's anxious face, what fate does she read there? If her brothers and half the boys of the neighborhood are leaving the country, how hopeless is her life likely to be? The opportunities for a useful womanhood are lessened. The sweet love that brightens life may never come to her. The delicious odors of the new-mown hay, of the sweet-scented clover, of the forest flowers, may never be associated with that most joyous part of life, when love and betrothal throws a halo over all the world. The budding womanhood will wait in vain for the companionship that should complete her life's joys.

With that far-seeing vision which is innate to a mother's love, she cannot but take a deep interest in any measure calculated to keep her boys at home, in any measure that would secure the happiness and the future of the daughters of this promising land.

No greater calamity can happen to a community than the loss of its young men. The statesmanship that makes Canada less attractive to them than the neighboring country is a failure, no matter how brilliant it may be in other respects. Nothing would so much tend to keep young Canadians at home than unrestricted reciprocity with the United States.

Free American markets for Canadian products would bring such a reward that contentment and prosperity would inevitably follow.

▲ DOCUMENT 2: LOYALTY[1]
Goldwin Smith

You have done me the honour, Gentlemen of the Liberal Club, to desire that I should read you an address on the subject of "Loyalty." I gladly respond to your request. But you will allow me to address you on this occasion as liberal-minded men, not as Liberals in the party sense of the term. I have been asked, as I am with you in this struggle, why I do not join your party? I reply that I am with you and with anyone in a struggle such as that on which you are now entering against Commercial Monopoly and Government by Corruption, and hope with other citizens to do my best in the day of battle; but when I am invited to join a party my answer must be that I have always steadfastly set my face towards national government, and that I and others, if there are any, who think as I do, are more likely to be useful by being true to our own principle, and saying what there is to be said for it, than by compromising it in order to take a more active part in politics.

But to the question. It is not wonderful that you wish just now to get all the information you can about loyalty. The air is full of loud professions of it, and still louder denunciations of disloyalty. The suspicion of disloyalty evidently entails serious consequences, extending in certain contingencies to being sabred by some loyal warrior on the street. What is, perhaps, of more practical importance is that the cry, by its effect on nervous persons, is likely to prevent the fair consideration of questions vital to the welfare of our people....

The loyalty cry is now being raised, in default of any economical argument, to deter the country from accepting the benefits of Reciprocity and to scare it into acquiescence in a policy of which commercial atrophy and the exodus are the visible and inevitable results. Here we see with what curious exactness a Loyalist's virtue follows the lines of his own interest through all their twistings and windings. To exclude British goods by protective duties is perfectly loyal. It is perfectly loyal to wage what in fact is a tariff war against the mother country. But to discriminate against the mother country is disloyal in the highest degree. The very thought of it is enough to almost throw a loyal man into convulsions. Yet discrimination would have no disloyal object. It would be not against England in particular but against all countries alike. It would evince no change of feeling towards the mother country, or towards the political connection. It would not take a penny from the revenue of the Crown or a particle from its power or dignity. It would hardly take away anything from the commercial wealth of the British people. The enhanced value of their Canadian investments which would result from free trade would probably make up to them for the loss which a few exporting houses would sustain. But the same measure would expose the protected manufacturers of Canada to Continental competition. Therefore he who proposes it is a traitor.

Does anyone want to be told what is really disloyal? It is disloyal to assemble the representatives of a particular commercial interest before the elections and virtually sell to them the policy of the country. It is disloyal to seek by corrupt means the support of particular nationalities, churches, political orders, or sectional interests of any kind, against the broad interest of the community. It is disloyal to sap the independence of provinces and reduce them to servile pensioners on the Central Government by systematically bribing them with "better terms" and federal grants. It is disloyal to use the appointments to a branch of the national legislature as inducements to partisans to spend money in elections.

Source: Goldwin Smith, "Loyalty: An Address" delivered before the Young Men's Liberal Club, Toronto, on February 2, 1891 (Toronto: Hunter, Rose & Company, 1891).

It is disloyal to use public works, which ought to be undertaken only for the general good, for the purpose of bribing particular constituencies. It is disloyal to make concessions to public contractors which are to be repaid by contributions to an election fund. It is disloyal to corrupt the public press, and thus to poison the wells of public instruction and public sentiment. It is disloyal to tamper with the article of the Constitution respecting the time of general elections by thimblerigging dissolutions brought on to snap a national verdict. It is disloyal to vitiate the national verdict by gerrymandering. It is disloyal to surrender the national veto on provincial legislation, the very palladium of nationality, out of fear of the Jesuit vote. All corruption is disloyalty. All sectionalism is disloyalty. All but pure, straightforward and honourable conduct in the management of public affairs is disloyalty. If it is not disloyalty to a Crown on a cushion, it is disloyalty to the Commonwealth.

"Loyalty" still has a meaning though the feudal relation between lord and vassal has passed away. It means thorough-going and self-sacrificing devotion to a principle, a cause or the community. All that is contrary to such devotion or tends to its disparagement, is still disloyal.

The question of our political relations is not now before us. We are dealing with the commercial question alone. But suppose the political question were before us, would there be any loyalty in dealing with it frankly and honestly? I say frankly and honestly. There is disloyalty in any sort of intrigue. But who has intrigued? According to the Government organs the country is a nest of conspirators. Everybody who goes to Washington goes for the purpose of conspiracy, as though real conspirators would not have the sense to keep their names out of the hotel book. I have myself been charged in the Government organ with going to Washington to sell the country. I go to Washington every Spring on my way with my wife to a Southern watering-place, and at no other time, mainly for the purpose of seeing personal friends, the chief of whom was the late Mr. Bancroft. I have been charged by the same organ with being a party to bringing American money into the country for the purpose of influencing the elections, the evidence being that my friend, Mr. Hallam, to whom I never said a syllable on the subject of political relations, had proposed to raise a fund for the diffusion of knowledge about the tariff question.[2] Treason is a great crime. If anybody has been guilty of it let him be brought to justice. But it is time that people should know that to charge your fellow-citizens, men in as good standing as yourself, with treason and with trying to sell the country, without any proof of the fact, is a social offence. He who, for the purpose of his own ambition or gain, falsely divides the community on such lines, is himself guilty of the most pernicious treason.

There has just been a meeting of Imperial Federationists, of whose aspiration I desire to speak with all respect. The object of Imperial Federationists is to make a great change in our political relations. They seek to reverse the process of decentralization which, apparently, in obedience to the dictate of nature, has been going on for so many years, to take from Canada a part of her self-government, and to place her again under the authority of a central power. They fancy, indeed, that they can have an Imperial Federation without detracting from colonial self-government. But how could this be when each of the colonies would be subject certainly to military assessments, and probably to fiscal control; for it is hardly possible to imagine a federation with a multiplicity of tariffs, some of them hostile to others, as those of protectionist colonies now are to the mother country? What the plan of the Imperial Federationists is remains a mystery. They tell us not to ask them for a cut-and-dried scheme. We do not ask for a scheme either cut or dried, but only for one that shall be intelligible and a possible subject of discussion. Readjustment of postage-rates is not confederation. However, it lies not in their mouths to say that a proposal of change must be disloyal. If they are at liberty to advocate centralization, "Canada First" was equally at liberty to advocate independence. "Canada First," in its day, was denounced as disloyal. [Canada First was an English-Canadian nationalist group active in the 1870s. Smith was a member before coming to believe, by 1877, that political union with the U.S. was the true and proper destiny of Canada.]

I well recollect when you were told that to speak of Canada as a nation was treason. We have now got beyond that point, I suppose, since adherence to the National Policy is now the height of loyalty. If there is any question of loyalty in the matter it might be thought that they were the most loyal who desired for their country a higher position than that of perpetual dependence. Whether their aspirations were feasible is another question. They hardly took into account the French difficulty, nor did they or perhaps anybody at that time distinctly see what effect the enormous extension of disjointed territory toward the West would have on the geographical unity of the nation. But their aspiration was high; they were responding in fact to the appeal which the authors of Confederation themselves had made to the heart of the country, and never was the name of loyalty more traduced than when they were called disloyal.

There are men living, high in public life and in the Conservative ranks, who signed a manifesto in favour, I do not say of Annexation, which is a false and hateful term, but of political union with the United States. Nothing is more irrational or ungenerous than to taunt people with opinions which they once honestly held and have since not less honestly renounced. It is not for any such purpose that I refer to the Montreal manifesto. [The Montreal Manifesto of 1849 was a document signed by leading citizens of that city that called for annexation to the United States, the point being to lift the Province of Canada out of a serious economic depression by obtaining access to the American domestic market. Several prominent Conservatives, most notably Sir John Abbott (who succeeded Sir John A. Macdonald as prime minister in June 1891), signed the manifesto.]

But such a manifesto could not have been signed by such men if the question were not one which might be entertained without disloyalty, provided always that those who entertain it remain firm, pending its solution, in their dutiful allegiance to their own country. For my own part, being not a politician, but a student, and restrained by no exigencies of statecraft, I never conceal my opinion. I have always deplored the schism which divided our race a century ago. I hold that there was wrong on both sides, and not less on the side of the American Revolutionists than on that of the British Government. I hope and steadfastly believe that some day the schism will be healed, that there will be a moral reunion, which alone is possible, of the American colonies of Great Britain with their mother country, and a complete reunion, with the hearty sanction of the mother country, of the whole race upon this continent. Great Britain will in time see that she has no real interest here but amity and trade. The unity of the race, and the immense advantages of a settlement which would shut out war from this continent and make it an economical whole, will prevail, I feel convinced, in the end over evil memories and the efforts of those who cherish them.

There might be danger and there might be disloyalty in touching this question if there were on the part of Americans any disposition to aggression. But there is none. If the Americans meditated annexation by force, why did they not attack us when they had a vast and victorious army? If they meditate annexation by pressure, why do they allow us bonding privileges and the use of their winter ports? The McKinley Bill was eagerly hailed by Separatists here as an act of American hostility. [The McKinley Bill, passed by Congress in 1890, imposed extremely high tariffs against foreign imports (including those from Canada) into the American market. It was deeply resented in Canada, and used by

Laurier and the Liberals in the Election of 1891 as evidence of the importance of obtaining a free trade agreement with the United States.]

Its object was simply to rivet and extend protection, at the same time catching the farmer's vote, for which politicians fish there with the same bait with which Sir John Macdonald fishes here. Of course as there are paper tigers on our side of the line, there are tail-twisters on the other side. One of the most valiant of them, in the person of Senator Ingalls, has just bitten the dust. The tail-twisters have as much influence there as the paper tigers have here, and no more. These suspicions when unjustified are undignified. They expose us to ridicule, while they prevent us from seeing in its true light and settling wisely the great question of our own future.

Those who say that the country is suffering from a bad fiscal policy and from the corruption of government arc branded as disloyal. They arc charged with decrying Canada by telling this unpleasant truth. Truth, pleasant or unpleasant, can never be disloyal. But let the accusers look back to their own record before 1878, when the opposite party was in power. What pictures of national distress and ruin were then painted! What pessimism was uttered and penned! What jeremiads rung in our ears! Soup kitchens, some thought, were opened not so much for the relief of distress as to present in the most vivid and harrowing manner the state to which Liberal policy had reduced the people. Is it the rising flood of prosperity that is sending so many Canadians over the line? It was disloyal to say that railway monopoly was keeping back the North-west. What do they say about that now?

Is it loyal to turn our Public Schools into schools of international enmity by implanting hatred of the Americans in the breasts of children? The Public Schools are maintained by all for the benefit of all, and it is an abuse of trust to use them for party purposes. Nor does it seem very chivalrous to be inveigling children instead of appealing to men. Celebrations of victories gained in byegone quarrels over people who are now your friends are perhaps not the sort of things to which the bravest are the most prone. Wellington and the men who had fought with him at Waterloo used to dine together on that day. This was very well, especially as those victorious veterans did not crow or bluster. But it forms no precedent for boastful demonstrations by us, who did not fight at Queenston Heights or Lundy's Lane. [The Battle of Queenston Heights, fought on 13 October 1812, was a British victory over an American invasion force in the early months of the War of 1812. The death of Sir Isaac Brock during the battle gave it added significance, and Queenston Heights became a touchstone of Canadian nationalism for generations afterward.]

And when this war spirit is got up, whom are we to fight? The one million of Canadians and their half-million of children now settled on the other side of the line? All the British immigrants who have been pouring into the United States during the last generation? Literally, when we take away from the population of Canada the French and other nationalities, there would be as many men of British blood on the enemy's side as on ours. "Bombard New York!" said a Canadian of my acquaintance; "why, my four sons live there!"

Is it loyal to threaten us with settling questions on horseback, in other words, with military coercion? The English people would not endure such threats from the commanders of the army which won the Alma and Inkerman. I heard one of these tirades read out at a Commercial Union meeting by a tall farmer, who when he had done said, "Now we want no nonsense "—whereat a number of other tall farmers with deep voices cried, "Hear! hear!" There is force enough, let us hope, in the country to vindicate its own freedom of deliberation and its power of self-disposal. The only effect of menaces such as are sometimes heard will be to make our people more deaf than ever to the appeals of British Imperialists who exhort us to maintain a standing army as a safeguard for our independence. Our independence is safe enough from any hostile aggression, and our liberty is safer in our own hands than in those of warriors who propose to decide political questions for us on horseback.

Loyalists appeal to the memories of those who fought and fell at Queenston Heights and Lundy's Lane. [The Battle of Lundy's Lane, fought on 25 July 1814, was one of the largest and bloodiest battles of the War of 1812. Neither side won a clear victory and the battle is best remembered for the heavy losses suffered by both the British and American sides.]

We also appeal to those memories. Honour to the brave who gave their lives for Canada! As they did their duty to their country then by defending her against unjust invasion, they would now, if they were alive, be doing their duty to her by helping to rescue her from monopoly and corruption. Honour, once more, to the truly brave! Let us build their monuments by all means. We are all as ready as any Loyalist to contribute, if only we may be allowed, to make the memorial, like the joint monument to Wolfe and Montcalm at Quebec, a noble and chivalrous tribute to heroism, not an ignoble record of a bygone feud, and to grave on it words expressive not of perpetual enmity, but of the reconciliation of our race.

Let us be true to the country, keep her interest above all other interests, personal, partisan, or sectional, in our hearts; be ready to make all sacrifices to it which a reasonable patriotism demands; be straightforward and aboveboard in all our dealings with public questions, and never, out of fear of unpopularity or abuse, shrink from the honest expression of opinion and the courageous advocacy of whatever we conscientiously believe to be good for the community. So long as we do this, depend upon it, we are loyal.

NOTES

1. Delivered before the Young Men's Liberal Club, Toronto, February, 1891.
2. It has since appeared that the very persons who brought this charge themselves did not scruple to take toll of an American firm for a political purpose.

▲ DOCUMENT 3: ADDRESS TO THE PEOPLE OF CANADA 1891

Sir John A. Macdonald

To the Electors of Canada:—

Gentlemen,—The momentous questions now engaging public attention having, in the opinion of the Ministry, reached that stage when it is desirable that an opportunity should be given to the people of expressing at the polls their views thereon, the Governor-General has been advised to terminate the existence of the present House of Commons and to issue writs summoning a new Parliament. This advice His Excellency has seen fit to approve, and you, therefore, will be called upon within a short time to elect members to represent you in the great council of the nation. I shall be a candidate for the representation of my old constituency, the city of Kingston.

In soliciting at your hands a renewal of the confidence which I have enjoyed as a Minister of the Crown for thirty years, it is, I think, convenient that I should take advantage of the occasion to define the attitude of the Government—in which I am First

Source: *Toronto Empire*, 9 February 1891, reprinted in Sir Joseph Pope, *Memoirs of the Right Honourable Sir John Alexander Macdonald* (Toronto: Oxford University Press, 1894, revised 1930), 772–777.

Minister—towards the leading political issues of the day. As in 1878, in 1882, and again in 1887, so in 1891 do questions relating to the trade and commerce of the country occupy a foremost place in the public mind. Our policy in respect thereto is to-day what it has been for the past thirteen years, and is directed by a firm determination to foster and develop the varied resources of the Dominion by every means in our power consistent with Canada's position as an integral portion of the British Empire. To that end we have laboured in the past, and we propose to continue in the work to which we have applied ourselves, of building up on this continent, under the flag of England, a great and powerful nation.

When in 1878 we were called upon to administer the affairs of the Dominion, Canada occupied a position in the eyes of the world very different from that which she enjoys to-day. At that time a profound depression hung like a pall over the whole country, from the Atlantic ocean to the western limits of the province of Ontario; beyond which to the Rocky Mountains stretched a vast and almost unknown wilderness. Trade was depressed; manufactures languished, and, exposed to ruinous competition, Canadians were fast sinking into the position of being mere hewers of wood and drawers of water for the great nation dwelling to the south of us. We determined to change this unhappy state of things. We felt that Canada, with its agricultural resources, rich in its fisheries, timber and mineral wealth, was worthy of a nobler position than that of being a slaughter market for the United States. We said to the Americans:—"We are perfectly willing to trade with you on equal terms. We are desirous of having a fair reciprocity treaty; but we will not consent to open our markets to you while yours remain closed to us."

So we inaugurated the National Policy. You all know what followed. Almost as if by magic the whole face of the country underwent a change. Stagnation and apathy and gloom—aye, and want and misery, too—gave place to activity and enterprise and prosperity. The miners of Nova Scotia took courage; the manufacturing industries in our great centres revived and multiplied; the farmer found a market for his produce; the artisan and laborer employment at good wages, and all Canada rejoiced under the quickening impulse of a new-found life. The age of deficits was past, and an overflowing treasury gave to the Government the means of carrying forward those great works necessary to the realization of our purpose to make this country a homogeneous whole.

To that end we undertook that stupendous work, the Canadian Pacific railway. Undeterred by the pessimistic views of our opponents, nay, in spite of their strenuous and even malignant opposition, we pushed forward that great enterprise through the wilds north of Lake Superior, across the western prairies, over the Rocky mountains to the shore of the Pacific, with such inflexible resolution that in seven years after the assumption of office by the present administration the dream of our public men was an accomplished fact, and I, myself, experienced the proud satisfaction of looking back from the steps of my car upon the Rocky mountains fringing the eastern sky.

The Canadian Pacific Railway now extends from ocean to ocean, opening up and developing the country at a marvellous rate, and forming an imperial highway to the East, over which the trade of the Indies is destined to reach the markets of Europe. We have subsidized steamship lines on both sides of the ocean—to Europe, China, Japan, Australia and the West Indies. We have spent millions on the extension and improvement of our canal system. We have, by liberal grants of subsidies, promoted the building of railways, now become an absolute necessity, until the whole country is covered as with a network, and we have done all this with such prudence and caution that our credit in the money markets of the world is higher to-day than it has ever been, and the rate of interest on our debt, which is the true measure of the public burdens, is less than it was when we took office in 1878.

During all this time what has been the attitude of the Reform party? Vacillating in their policy and inconstancy itself as regards their leaders, they have at least been consistent in this particular, that they have uniformly opposed every measure which had for its object the development of our common country. The National Policy was a failure before it had been tried. Under it we could not possibly raise a revenue sufficient for the public requirements. Time exposed that fallacy. Then we were to pay more for the home manufactured article than we used to when we imported everything from abroad. We were to be the prey of rings and of monopolies, and the manufacturers were to extort their own prices. When these fears had been proved unfounded we were assured that over-competition would inevitably prove the ruin of the manufacturing industries and thus bring about a state of affairs worse than that which the National Policy had been designed to meet. It was the same with the Canadian Pacific Railway. The whole project, according to our opponents, was a chimera. The engineering difficulties were insuperable; the road, even if constructed, would never pay. Well, gentlemen, the project was feasible, the engineering difficulties were overcome, and the road does pay.

Disappointed by the failure of all their predictions and convinced that nothing is to be gained by further opposition on the old lines, the Reform party has taken a new departure and has announced its policy to be Unrestricted Reciprocity—that is (as defined by its author, Mr. Wiman, *North American Review* of a few days ago) free trade with the United States and a common tariff with the United States against the rest of the world.

The adoption of this policy would involve, among other grave evils, discrimination against the Mother Country. This fact is admitted by no less a personage than Sir Richard Cartwright, who in his speech at Pembroke on October 21st, 1890, is reported to have said:—"Some men whose opinions I respect entertain objections to this (unrestricted reciprocity) proposition. They argue and argue with force, that it will be necessary for us, if we enter into such an arrangement, to admit the goods of the United States on more favorable terms than those of the mother country. Nor do I deny that that is an objection and not a light one." It would, in my opinion, inevitably result in the annexa [sic]—of this Dominion to the United States. The advocates of unrestricted reciprocity on this side of the line deny that it would have such an effect, though its friends in the United States urge as the chief reason for its adoption that unrestricted reciprocity would be the first step in the direction of political union.

There is, however, one obvious consequence of this scheme which nobody has the hardihood to dispute, and that is that unrestricted reciprocity would necessitate the imposition of direct taxation, amounting to not less than fourteen millions of dollars annually, upon the people of this country. This fact is clearly set forth in a remarkable letter addressed a few days ago by Mr. E. W. Thompson—a Radical and free trader—to the Toronto *Globe*, on the staff of which paper he was lately an editorial writer, which, notwithstanding, the *Globe*, with characteristic unfairness, refused to publish, but which, nevertheless, reached the public through another source. Mr. Thompson points out, with great clearness, that the loss of customs revenue levied upon articles now entering this country from the United States, in the event of the adoption of unrestricted reciprocity, would amount to not less than seven millions of dollars annually. Moreover, this by no means represents the total loss to the revenue which the adoption of such a policy would entail. If American manufacturers now compete favourably with British goods, despite an equal duty, what do you suppose would happen if the duty were removed from the American and retained, or, as is very probable, increased, on the British article? Would not the inevitable result be a displacement of the duty-paying goods of the mother country by those of the United States? And this would mean an additional loss to the revenue of many millions more.

NEL

Electors of Canada, I appeal to you to consider well the full meaning of this proposition. You—I speak now more particularly to the people of this Province of Ontario—are already taxed directly for school purposes, for township purposes, for county purposes, while to the Provincial Government there is expressly given by the constitution the right to impose direct taxation. This latter evil you have so far escaped, but as the material resources of the province diminish, as they are now diminishing, the Local Government will be driven to supplement its revenue derived from fixed sources by a direct tax. And is not this enough, think you, without your being called on by a Dominion tax gatherer with a yearly demand for $15 a family to meet the obligation of the Central Government? Gentlemen, this is what unrestricted reciprocity involves. Do you like the prospect? This is what we are opposing, and what we ask you to oppose by your votes.

Under our present system a man may largely determine the amount of his contributions to the Dominion exchequer. The amount of his tax is always in direct proportion to his means. If he is rich and can afford to drink champagne he has to pay a tax of $1.50 for every bottle he buys. If he is a poor man he contents himself with a cup of tea, on which there is no duty. And so on all through the list. If he is able to afford all manner of luxuries he pays a large sum into the coffers of the Government. If he is a man of moderate means, and able to enjoy an occasional luxury, he pays accordingly. If he is a poor man his contributions to the treasury are reduced to a minimum. With direct taxation, no matter what may be the pecuniary position of the tax-payer—times may be hard—crops may have failed—sickness or other calamity may have fallen on the family, still the inexorable tax collector comes and exacts his tribute. Does not ours seem to be the more equitable plan? It is the one under which we have lived and thrived, and to which the Government I lead proposes to adhere.

I have pointed out to you a few of the material objections to this scheme of unrestricted reciprocity, to which Mr. Laurier and Sir Richard Cartwright have committed the Liberal party, but they are not the only objections, nor, in my opinion, are they the most vital.

For a century and a half this country has grown and flourished under the protecting aegis of the British Crown. The gallant race who first bore to our shores the blessings of civilization passed by an easy transition from French to English rule and now form one of the most law-abiding portions of the community. Those pioneers were speedily recruited by the advent of a loyal band of British subjects, who gave up everything that men most prize and were content to begin life anew in the wilderness rather than forego allegiance to their sovereign. To the descendants of those men and to the multitude of Englishmen, Irishmen and Scotchmen who emigrated to Canada, that they might build up new homes without ceasing to be British subjects—to you, Canadians—I appeal, and I ask you what have you to gain by surrendering that which your fathers held most dear? Under the broad folds of the Union Jack we enjoy the most ample liberty to govern ourselves as we please and at the same time we participate in the advantages which flow from association with the mightiest empire the world has ever seen. Not only are we free to manage our domestic concerns, but, practically, we possess the privilege of making our own treaties with foreign countries and in our relations with the outside world we enjoy the prestige inspired by a consciousness of the fact that behind us towers the majesty of England.

The question which you will shortly be called upon to determine resolves itself into this, shall we endanger our possession of the great heritage bequeathed to us by our fathers and submit ourselves to direct taxation for the privilege of having our tariff fixed at Washington, with a prospect of ultimately becoming a portion of the American union?

I commend these issues to your determination and to the judgement of the whole people of Canada with an unclouded confidence that you will proclaim to the world your resolve to show yourselves not unworthy of the proud distinction you enjoy, of being numbered among the most dutiful and loyal subjects of our beloved Queen.

As for myself, my course is clear. A British subject I was born, a British subject I will die. With my utmost effort, with my latest breath, will I oppose the "veiled treason" which attempts, by sordid means and mercenary proffers, to lure our people from their allegiance. During my long public service of nearly half a century I have been true to my country and its best interest, and I appeal with equal confidence to the men who have trusted me in the past and to the young hope of the country, with whom rests its destinies in the future, to give me their united and strenuous aid in this my last effort for the unity of the Empire and the preservation of our commercial and political freedom.

I remain, gentlemen,

Your faithful servant.

JOHN A. MACDONALD.

Ottawa, 7th February, 1881.

▲ DOCUMENT 4: "LAYING OUT THE GRIT CAMPAIGN." (CAMPAIGN POSTER, 1891)

A Conservative cartoonist imagines that the Liberals are secretly conspiring to sell out Canada to the United States. From left to right: the foremost Liberal champion of free trade, Sir Richard Cartwright; Liberal leader Wilfrid Laurier; U.S. President Benjamin Harrison; U.S. Secretary of State James Blaine; Toronto *Globe* editorialist Edward Farrer (holding up a copy of the *Globe*); and Canadian businessman Erastus Wiman. They are all haggling over a "Map of the Canadian States," and the letter in Cartwright's pocket reads, "Senator for the State of Ontario."

Source: Library and Archives Canada, C6539.

▲ DOCUMENT 5: "DIGNIFIED ATTITUDE OF THE LIBERALS." (CAMPAIGN POSTER, 1891)

● Here Wilfrid Laurier and Sir Richard Cartwright kneel in humiliating fashion before James Blaine and Uncle Sam (the personification of the United States), pleading for unrestricted reciprocity. Uncle Sam remarks, "Blaine, if these fellers git into office, Canady is ours!"

Source: National Archives Canada, C6541.

▲ DOCUMENT 6: "THE WAY HE WOULD LIKE IT: CANADA FOR SALE." (CAMPAIGN POSTER, 1891)

● This offensive cartoon depicts Sir Richard Cartwright as a Middle Eastern slave trader (note the turban and darkened skin), selling the bound and helpless Miss Canada to Uncle Sam.

Source: Library and Archives Canada, C6533.

▲ DOCUMENT 7: "THE OLD FLAG, THE OLD POLICY, THE OLD LEADER." (CAMPAIGN POSTER, 1891)

THE OLD FLAG.
THE OLD POLICY,
THE OLD LEADER.

In the most famous image of the Election of 1891, Sir John A. Macdonald sits atop the shoulders of a farmer and industrial worker, holding up a variation of the Red Ensign, the unofficial Canadian flag at the time. The "Old Policy" in question is the National Policy of high tariffs against British and American imports.

Source: Library and Archives Canada, C6536.

▲ DOCUMENT 8: HOUSE OF COMMONS DEBATES, FEBRUARY 9, 1911

Robert Borden

Mr. BORDEN (Halifax). Mr Chairman, the conditions under which I was called upon to speak on a previous occasion in this House, just two weeks ago, afforded little opportunity for grasping the full import of the proposals which have been submitted to parliament and to the country by the government. These proposals are of too grave and serious a character to be considered from a purely partisan standpoint. I desire, therefore, to-day to make a reasonable and moderate presentation of the vies [sic] which I entertain with regard to them without making any attack upon the government or upon any one else. In the first place, I shall direct your attention to the condition to which this country has attained after some forty or fifty years of effort and endeavour, and I shall undertake to demonstrate, in so far

Source: Canada. House of Commons, *Debates*, February 9, 1911, 3294–3316.

as it is within my humble ability, that these are not proposals that should be lightly entered into by the Dominion of Canada at the present time.

I do not agree with my hon. friend the Minister of Finance (Mr. Fielding) when he suggests that there has been ample time for the country to make itself acquainted with the nature of these proposals, and with their probable result, whether that result be considered from the economic standpoint alone, or whether it be considered from the distinct national standpoint which is involved in these proposals ... They are not proposals to be rushed through parliament. They are not proposals which ought to be forced upon the country without the most ample opportunity of consideration and of suggestion, whether to the government or to parliament. What do these proposals embody? They embody practically a new tariff for this country in so far as its tariff relations with the United States of America are concerned. They are of so sweeping an effect that probably no one man, inside or outside of parliament to-day, can accurately or properly estimate what their future result may be. My hon. friend the Minister of Finance has referred to the reciprocity treaty of 1854. He has referred to that treaty as one which conferred great advantages upon this country. I do not propose this afternoon to enter into a consideration of the advantages which may have come to this country during some part of the operation of the reciprocity treaty of 1854, but I would like to point out that this is 1911, and not 1854, and that it is idle for us to attempt to discuss these proposals from the standpoint of 1854, or even from the standpoint of 1866 ...

... What was the condition of this country in 1866? We had not yet formed confederation. There were simply four, or five, or six provinces in eastern Canada, four of which united to form this one, this great confederation. The task which they undertook at that time was, perhaps, as great a task as ever confronted any similar people under anything like the same conditions. What was the task? It was to convery these fringelike communities, scattered along the border land of the United States, into a great and powerful nation, which should maintain its place upon the northern half of this continent under the protecting aegis of the British flag.

The very first of our tasks was to add about 3,000,000 square miles to our territory; to take in the distant province of British Columbia, and all the great uninhabited territory between; to build lines of transportation, to develop and utilize our system of waterways; to bind together into one Dominion the scattered fragments of our country, and last but not least to conserve and to develop the natural resources of untold importance which had come as a priceless heritage to the two great races that had united for the development of this Dominion. Sir, there was something greater than even that: There was the task laid before the people of this country to allay jealousies and prejudices, to create a national spirit, and to bring about that harmony and mutual understanding among the people of these four provinces, and of the other provinces that should be added in the future, which would contribute to the building up of a united and powerful Canada as the greatest of the Dominions which own allegiance to the British Crown. The task before our people was to build up British institutions in this country, to develop them in the spirit in which they had been developed in the mother country, and to do all this under conditions that might well have daunted men of less stout heart, because, it was realized that these fringe-like communities were scattered for 4,000 miles along the territory of a great and powerful nation which must possess a far-reaching influence upon the commercial destiny of this country.

Well, what have we done in that interval of 40 years? Indeed, to mention what we have accomplished it is only necessary to re-echo the statements that have been made over and over again by the Minister of Finance in every budget speech for the last 14 years, and to add to it the record of the advancement in material prosperity of Canada during the past 40 or 50 years, not confining it to 14 years alone. I trust I may be pardoned that remark, because I do not desire to sound any partisan note in the remarks I shall address to the House. Here are the statistics of Canada's trade comparing 1868 with 1910:

TRADE STATISTICS				
	1868	**1910**	**Increase.**	**Percent.**
	$	$	$	
Total Trade	116,000,000	649,000,000	533,000,000	459
Exports	49,000,000	279,000,000	230,000,000	470
Imports	67,000,000	370,000,000	303,000,000	450
Between 1868 and 1910 our exports increased as follows:				
	1868	**1910**		
Produce of mine increased from…	1,225,000 to	$40,000,000		
Produce of fisheries…	3,000,000	15,000,000		
Produce of forest…	19,000,000	47,000,000		
Animals and their products…	7,000,000	54,000,000		
Agricultural products…	13,000,000	90,000,000		
Manufactures…	2,000,000	31,000,000		
Value total field crops last year		533,000,000		
Value total manufactures (estimated) last year…		1,000,000,000		

It is therefore abundantly evident, looking at trade statistics alone, that we have made not only great but marvellous progress in the last 40 years along the path which the people of Canada have been treading, and from which path I trust they will not see fit lightly to depart …

… Look at these evidences of vast progress and prosperity; look at the advancement we have made in founding universities and schools, look at our progress in education. And, last but not least, look at the standard of comfort in life which prevails in Canada to-day compared with that which prevailed in 1868. I know, Sir, that in my own home in the province of Nova Scotia, when I was a boy 40 years ago the comforts of life as they are enjoyed at the present day were unknown to the people then. Observe the growth of our cities. In 1868 Montreal had a population of 100,000; I believe that to-day is has a population of over 500,000. Toronto had a population at that time of 50,000; to-day it is a city of over 400,000. Hamilton had a population of 22,000; now I suppose it has over 80,000. Ottawa then was a town which had hardly escaped the name of Bytown; it had a population of 18,000; now it has a population of 85,000 or 90,000. Take the splendid cities of the west—Winnipeg, Calgary, Regina, Edmonton, Vancouver, Victoria. Some of them were mere wilderness in 1868, and for a long time afterwards. Vancouver, which dates from 1885, is to-day a city of 125,000 or 150,000. Will you tell me that we have not a right to be absolutely satisfied with the material progress, splendid, worldwide in its reputation, which has come to the people of Canada in the last 30 or 40 years? ...

... The Minister of Finance has spoken of the influence of the United States upon the destinies of this country. No one realizes that more fully than I do. A nation of 100,000,000, the greatest manufacturing nation in the world, the greatest agricultural nation in the world, with its boundaries extending along ours for 4,000 miles—why, of course, it must exercise a most profound influence upon the future commercial destiny of this country. I might characterize it even more strongly than I have done. It has been said that they can lower their tariff and change our trade routes. Perhaps they can accomplish something of that kind, but I want to ask you, Mr. Chairman, whether or not it is wise for us to combine with them for that purpose? Wider markets is the cry of the Minister of Finance. If the national issue is to be absolutely disregarded and you are to push the argument of wider markets to its logical, and, I believe, its inevitable conclusion, what will it lead you to? It will lead you to complete free trade and absolute commercial union with the United States. My hon. friend the Minister of Agriculture (Mr. Fisher) smiles at that suggestion. I do not know whether he smiles at the argument or in approval of the suggested ultimate destiny. But I would like to say to him that if it is good to seek wider markets, from which the rest of the empire is excluded, in the United States of America, why not have still wider and wider markets in the United States of America from which the rest of the empire will be excluded? That path has only one termination, and that is absolute commercial union with the United States of America. There cannot be much doubt, I think, about what that would mean. The President of the United States, in his message, on page 6, used very significant words. Speaking of the people of the Dominion, he said: 'They are at the parting of the ways.' They are at the parting of the ways! I think the people of Canada have, indeed, come to the parting of the ways, and that the issue of infinite gravity which is presented to them at the present time is whether they will continue in the work of nation building, in which they have been engaged during the past forty years, whether they will maintain their own markets as they have maintained them during the past forty years, whether they will preserve the autonomy of this country as they have preserved it during the past forty years, or whether they will undo the work which the fathers of confederation began, and which their sons have been carrying out ...

... I trust that the Prime Minister will not proceed hastily with these reciprocity proposals. The country has had very little time to consider them. As far as I am concerned, my opinion with respect to them has, I trust, been made fairly clear to this House this afternoon. I think the Prime Minister would do well to withdraw them from the consideration of the House at the present time, and to await some further developments. We have begun a great work in this country. Two great races whose mother tongues are spoken in this parliament came into the inheritance of this great country under the providence of God. Our fathers endured many hardships and made wonderful sacrifices in planting their homes in this then western wilderness. In time of peril both races have poured out their blood without stint in defence of their common country. In the work of upbuilding a strong nation and a great civilization under the British flag, on the northern half of this continent, they have laboured side by side with mutual sympathy and with high purpose. The heaviest burdens have been lifted, the greatest obstacles have been overcome, the most difficult part of the task has been accomplished. I trust that the Canadian people will not lightly relinquish the task to which their energies and the energies of their fathers have been consecrated for so many years. I trust that the standard will not be thrown aside and the retreat sounded when the battle is more than half won. The self-denials, the sacrifices, the patriotism, demanded of us to-day in order that this nation may maintain and carry out the ideals and the purposes for which it was called into existence are as nothing to those which were required of our fathers who founded this confederation. Loyalty to their memory and to the ideals which they consecrated demands that we should continue with firm heart and unabated hope upon the path on which we entered nearly sixty years ago.

▲ DOCUMENT 9: SPEECH MADE IN COBOURG, ONTARIO, BY SIR WILFRID LAURIER

(Special Despatch to the *Globe*.)

Cobourg, Sept. 5—For two or three startling moments this afternoon it seemed probable that the great Laurier demonstration might end in a tragedy. Sir Wilfrid's address was over, and he had just risen to acknowledge the enthusiasm with which it had been greeted, when there was an ominous crack, followed immediately by a second, a frightened shout from the crowd, and the centre of the temporary platform on which the Premier stood collapsed. It was thronged with humanity at the time, and there was a precipitate scramble, which threatened further disaster. A couple of officers with presence of mind, however, stayed the incipient stampede, and the hundred odd occupants were conducted down from the ten-foot elevation one by one. Finally only the Chairman, the Premier and Hon. Mr. Graham remained standing at the extreme edge supported by the corner wooden upright [George Perry Graham, in 1911 the Member of Parliament for Brockville, Ontario, was Minister of Railways from 1907–1911 in the Laurier cabinet].

The Minister of Railways relieved the tension by commencing his address with the hearty observation: "It is hard to dislodge the Liberal leader from his platform." The great gathering gave vent to its relief in a prolonged cheer.

A Splendid Reception

Cobourg received the Canadian Premier with great enthusiasm. The whole town was a blaze of flags, streamers and bunting. A mammoth procession, headed by bands and a hundred horsemen, escorted him to Donegan Park, a beautiful enclosure situated overlooking the lake. Here were gathered between three and four thousand people, who gave the distinguished visitor the heartiest of welcomes …

… Sir Wilfrid introduced his address with a happy reference to the number of Americans present. Cobourg is the summer home of many residents of the United States, and the Premier wanted to know if the sentiment of reciprocity which had existed in this connection had not been a good thing for Cobourg. It was twenty years since he had first visited the town, and he was impressed with the progress made. It showed that the faulty doctrine of "let well enough alone" had no place in the enterprising makeup of the Cobourg citizen. Had the Government failed to avail themselves of the United States offer of reciprocity the very men who were "parading and perambulating up and down the country denouncing the agreement" would have denounced the government for failing to stand by its professions, "even as I denounce them to you now for renouncing their principles as expressed in years past."

The American Proposals

With all the zeal of new converts, Sir Wilfrid stated, the Americans had urged a larger measure of reciprocity, embracing manufactured as well as agricultural products, but

---

Source: Toronto *Globe*, September 6, 1911, 1, 4.

Canada could not accept the whole of their overtures. "We took the ground, firmly but in a friendly spirit," said the Premier, "that it would not be well at the present time to even consider any exchange of manufactured products, because they have too much the start of us; but we were glad to accept the proposal as regards natural products, because we believed it would not only be without danger, but of great benefit to our people."

Inconsistent Conservatives

The Premier exposed the inconsistency of the present anti-reciprocity Conservatives to the traditions and principles of their former leaders. "The party to-day," he observed, amid laughter and applause, "is like a ship without captain or rudder, tossed on the billows of the sea, or like a fog floating out yonder on the lake. It is always moving, but makes no headway. It is not for me to advise, but, if it were not presumption, I would tell the Conservatives of to-day to gird their loins and fight for principles. This is what made their predecessors great. We have the British system of party government, but to command the confidence of the people there must be more to the platform than 'turn the other fellows out, because we want to get in.' I am a pretty old bird now. (Laughter.) I can read them perhaps better than they think … And I believe I know something of the Canadian people and their ideals and aims. You, my fellow-countrymen, will not be satisfied with efforts to attain office based on setting race against race, east against west. We want no more race and race, no more east and west. Canada at this hour demands men with courage to yield neither to one nor the other. The future of our country claims from us all, Grits and Tories alike, a policy which will unite all diversified aims and aspirations, a policy under which all are cheerfully ready to make sacrifices on the altar of our common country." (Prolonged cheers.) …

… The Annexation Cry

Sir Wilfrid dismissed the annexation cry as unjustifiable and unworthy. "There is another future for Canada and the United States," said he. "It is theirs to share the North American continent, and to co-operate in making its destiny a worthy one. We are the equals of the United States in everything but population. We are their equals in education, in manhood, in civilization. Let us set an example to the world, foreshadowed by the recent treaty of peace between the motherland and the American nation, of two great peoples living separately side by side in peace, amity and friendship. (Cheers.) And I make bold to say that the present arrangement will be a step towards that end. (Renewed cheers.)

Upbuilding of Canada

In concluding, Sir Wilfrid made an eloquent appeal for the upbuilding of Canada as a great nation under the British flag. "I speak now to Canadians as a Canadian. In our party strife let us keep clear of appeals to passion and prejudice. Let us be true to Confederation. Let us strengthen the bonds of unity between the Provinces. In unity, not in discord, lies the great destiny of our country. If the Government should be defeated on appeals to passion and prejudice, I would mourn the defeat far less than the methods which had triumphed. I have ideals for our common country, my fellow-countrymen, ideals I know you share with me. To the people of Quebec and Ontario I appeal to turn a deaf ear to such appeals as these. You cannot build up a country upon them. To the French and the English I give the same word. Our fathers fought, it is true, but we live in better times, thank God. We are brethren now—(cheers)—we are fellow-Canadians, fellow-British subjects. Let us do our duty by ourselves, by our country."

As Sir Wilfrid concluded he was tendered an enthusiastic ovation, which terminated only when the breaking down of the platform startled the cheering throng.

213

ARTICLE 1: THE TWO BRANDS OF CANADIAN NATIONALISM IN THE ELECTION OF 1891

Christopher Pennington

THE QUESTION OF THE HOUR

Laurier was in a tough spot. Commercial union appeared to be making great headway in Ontario, but it was hard for Laurier, who lacked an intuitive feel for Ontario politics, to be sure of its strength. Sir Richard's views had to be taken seriously, if only because many grumbling English Canadian Liberals regarded him as the proper leader of the party. The Liberal press had largely embraced commercial union, and the editor of the *Globe*, John Cameron, was privately nudging him toward a more daring trade policy. Topping it all off, two important Liberal newspapers at opposite ends of the country, the Manitoba *Free Press* and the Halifax *Chronicle*, had recently jumped on the commercial union bandwagon.

On the other hand, the bold course was rarely the correct one in Canadian politics. There were compelling reasons not to do anything rash. First, the Tories were going to raise patriotic bloody hell if the Liberal Party embraced commercial union. They would rally around the National Policy and claim that the apocalypse—meaning the annexation of Canada—was at hand. The next election would revolve around it, and it would be an ugly and divisive election. Second, within the Liberal Party itself there was no consensus on the issue. Would the party as a whole accept commercial union? Edward Blake had never accepted the policy and he was still, presumably, returning at some point to reclaim the leadership. The party would be in a terrible mess if Blake returned to discover, to his horror, that in his absence it had adopted commercial union.

Nobody knew what Laurier was thinking. He had never cared very much about economics, and the Liberals had never bothered to seek out his views on the subject. In fact Laurier was still making up his mind. He had a natural sympathy for free trade, and felt that

some kind of deal with the United States would be good for Canada. It was not the economic merit of commercial union that intrigued him, however, but its potential as an election winner. Laurier was looking for a bold new policy that would divert attention from the divisive race-and-religion issue, put the Tories on the defensive, give the Liberal rank and file something exciting to fight for, and help them to get over the discouraging retirement of Edward Blake.

Still, it would be best to feel out the party before committing to anything. On July 11 Laurier issued an internal circular that, without giving any hint of his own feelings, asked his fellow Liberals for their thoughts on commercial union. It was a smart move, and the results were interesting. Blake did not like it, though he was then vacationing in Europe and seemed reluctant to speak too strongly on the question. James Young, a level-headed party elder who edited the small-town Galt *Reformer*, warned that C.U. was "an anti-national and Americanizing policy." Young published several eloquent letters on "Our National Future" in the Reformer, arguing that the Dominion could not withstand the economic and cultural pressures that would stem from commercial union.[1] Alexander Mackenzie, the former Liberal leader and prime minister, felt that the policy would sever the British connection. "We are to raise a barrier against English trade and so commence a downgrade political life," he protested to Cartwright. "My feelings revolt at the proposal."[2]

These opinions were exceptions to the general rule. Most Liberals who responded to the circular were surprisingly gung-ho for commercial union. The party was obviously yearning for a change from the caution and indecision of the Blake years. Laurier soon reported to Cartwright and Edgar that he was getting almost universally positive feedback from Quebec and the Maritimes. A few letters came in from western Canada, also happy to see the policy under consideration. And in Ontario, where there was the most popular feeling for the scheme, the vast majority of respondents urged Laurier to take the plunge. "In my humble opinion the Liberals have nothing to lose and everything to gain by adopting Commercial Union as <u>the</u> plank in their platform," wrote one Thomas McInnes of Toronto. "If prudently handled I can see no reason why it will not do for them what the national policy cry did for the Conservatives in 1878."[3]

Laurier wanted more time, but he was being pressed to make a decision. On August 2 he was scheduled to speak at a political picnic in Somerset, Quebec, in his first policy speech since becoming the Liberal leader. It was a much-anticipated event, though there were some snickers in the Conservative newspapers that Laurier had chosen for this early test a cautious and obscure venue—small, rural, friendly, and French—rather than a big city in Ontario. Was he afraid, journalists wondered in print, to step in front of an English Canadian audience? And what, if anything, would he have to say about commercial union? Surely the Liberal leader would be compelled by the fast march of Canadian public opinion to make some statement on that controversial subject.

If the Somerset speech was an indication of anything, it was the fact that Laurier did not succumb easily to pressure. His speech was long on pleasant-sounding patriotic sentiments and short on specific policy proposals. He took plenty of potshots at the Macdonald government and devoted considerable time to the subject of national unity. But there was little mention of commercial union, and what he did say was cryptic. "For my part, gentlemen," Laurier carefully remarked, "I am not prepared to say that the advocates and adepts of Commercial Union have as yet very clearly defined their views." Perhaps in time it would be possible to more clearly discern the potential costs and benefits of the proposal. At the moment, however, the Liberal leader would only venture to say, "What lies at the bottom of the idea, what we see clearest in it ... is the conviction that any kind of reciprocity with the people of the United States would be to the advantage of Canada.[4]

That was good enough, for the time being. Laurier had shrewdly kept his options open, and most Liberals were supportive of his cautious approach. But as summer turned to fall, the pressure kept building for the party to come out for commercial union or risk falling out of step with popular opinion. The *Globe* and other leading Liberal newspapers kept beating the drum, as did Ned Farrer at the independent *Mail*. Erastus Wiman, Ben Butterworth, and Goldwin Smith were out stumping in both countries and attracting good crowds wherever they went. At a major interprovincial conference held in Quebec City in late October, five provincial premiers passed a resolution endorsing "unrestricted reciprocity" with

the United States. (Wiman was partly responsible for that, having hustled publicly and privately around Quebec City to get the subject on the conference agenda.)[5] Finally, Sir Richard Cartwright, the financial expert of the Liberal Party and the virtual co-leader in the eyes of many English Canadians, forced his leader's hand by speaking out publicly in favour of the movement.

The Cartwright speech took place on October 12 in the small town of Ingersoll, Ontario, in his home riding of South Oxford. It was a typical Blue Ruin Knight speech, burdened with depressing statistics and a gloomy forecast of the future unless, of course, commercial union was adopted without delay.[6] It was a major event not for the size of the crowd or the quality of the speech, but for the precedent it set. Sir Richard insisted that he was speaking only for himself. He was not committing the Liberal Party to commercial union. But he knew better than that. His voice carried a lot of weight, and he was certainly, perhaps deliberately, making it harder for Laurier to say no to the policy when the time came to make a final decision.

THE NEW DEPARTURE

One leading Liberal who was not impressed with the Cartwright speech was J.D. Edgar, the Ontario organizer who was fast becoming a confidant to his French Canadian leader. Two days after the Cartwright speech he wrote Laurier that it "pleases some but annoys others ... however it is a good 'trial balloon' and we will see better how the wind blows."[7] Edgar also reported that he had just met with Erastus Wiman. That was interesting, because shortly after that meeting, Edgar and Wiman exchanged a series of open letters that would have a profound effect on the debate.[8]

In his letters Edgar criticized the entangling nature of commercial union—especially the necessity of having a common tariff with the United States against all other countries—and suggested that "unrestricted reciprocity" was a more moderate alternative. This was a proposal for complete free trade with the United States, but with the retention of customs houses along the border and the continuing right of each country to set its own tariffs against other countries. It was, in effect, a watered-down version of commercial union. Wiman was not comfortable with it. He knew that unrestricted reciprocity would not go over well in the United States because it would allow British imports to enter Canada at a low tariff rate, then sneak into the United States from Canada tariff-free and compete directly against the products of domestic American manufacturers.

Still, Wiman grudgingly accepted that unrestricted reciprocity might work as an alternative to commercial union. It seemed to be a less radical and less dangerous policy. It allowed Canada to keep control of its own tariff rates, rather than having to set them in lockstep with the United States, and that was certainly appealing. Even Cartwright had admitted to Laurier that most Liberals were "in mortal terror" of having their patriotism questioned by the Tories, and that was sure to happen if they adopted commercial union and were seen to be setting the country's tariff rates in accordance with the wishes of the United States Congress.[9]

Laurier remained undecided. In mid-December he expressed his misgivings in a thoughtful private letter to J.D. Edgar.

> I am afraid this plan of unrestricted reciprocity would be coupled with very many disadvantages. I think it would not do to commit ourselves to any distinct plan in advance. My opinion is that we should first assert the principle that the most unlimited reciprocity, would be for the advantage of both nations, and then let the idea be carried out by treaty negotiations. We must in the discussion keep ourselves in generalities. The moment we attempt to particularize, we will be met by objections upon objections. The only thing we should unreservedly commit ourselves to, should be reciprocity, limited if nothing better can be obtained, unlimited if possible.[10]

That was smart thinking, but a policy of having no policy was not going to be acceptable much longer to the Liberal rank and file. The new year dawned, the next session of Parliament loomed, and the leading figures in the party weighed the risks and possible benefits of the decision that they had to make. Sir Richard Cartwright had been tormented by second thoughts since coming out for commercial union back in October. On January 2 he wrote Laurier to inform him of a change of heart. "I do not think there is any choice left," he declared. "We <u>must</u> make a new departure and there is nothing which will fill the bill half as well as unrestricted reciprocity."[11] Three weeks

later, having mulled the situation a little longer, he had regained his old confidence. "I am ready to tackle the question," he assured Laurier. He wanted to introduce a resolution favouring unrestricted reciprocity, one that would trigger a high-profile debate, in the next session of Parliament.[12]

The final decision was not made until February 22, the day the new session opened in Ottawa. That evening the leading Liberals gathered for a private meeting. There was a clear sentiment in favour of adopting a new trade policy, and the only real question was whether it would be commercial union or unrestricted reciprocity. Laurier was leaning toward the former, but Cartwright and Edgar favoured the latter, and in the end unrestricted reciprocity won out. At a meeting of the full Liberal caucus three days later, the decision to embrace the new policy was made official. It was an important moment in the history of the party and the country, and everyone knew it....

THE LOST LEGACY OF 1891

By the early twentieth century the election of 1891 was already receding from popular memory in Canada. There were several good reasons for that. The election of 1911 superseded it as the cautionary tale of what happened to Canadian parties that pursued free trade with the Yankees. Laurier served so long as prime minister that he became an icon of national unity and prosperity, and few people remembered the self-doubting young leader he had once been. And none of the notorious continentalists of the late nineteenth century remained prominent long after the election of 1891. Edward Farrer, ironically, developed a friendly association with the Laurier government. The prime minister liked Farrer, forgave him his past indiscretions, and entrusted him with various secret missions as a reporter and political troubleshooter for the Liberal Party. Farrer prospered and lived comfortably in Ottawa with his wife, Annie, until his death in 1916.

Goldwin Smith met a more bitter end. Behind the walls of the Grange he railed against society in general and the failure of annexation in particular, never accepting that Canadians did not want to be Americans. As time passed he became isolated from old friends. W.T.R. Preston wrote in his memoirs that Smith was "almost pathetic," trying in vain to convert his dwindling houseguests into annexationists. "The last time I was there he offered me

$60,000 to organize a campaign in favour of annexation," Preston claimed. "I never went again.[13] When Goldwin Smith died in 1910, the obituaries heralded his literary talents, but few Canadians were moved by his passing.

Much sadder was the plight of Erastus Wiman, who suffered defeats and tragedies throughout the later years of his life. His finances evaporated when economic depression struck the United States in the early months of 1893. A year later he was arrested on two charges of forgery, and the trial that ensued resulted in his conviction and imprisonment. He was exonerated two years later, but his career and reputation had been destroyed. Wiman then pleaded with Laurier for a job as an advocate for reciprocity, confessing, "I am not a beggar, but I cannot now work for nothing."[14] His plea fell on deaf ears. He ran for New York city council, hoping to jump from there into Congress, but the voters of Staten Island rejected him. The death of his son Frank in 1896 left him devastated. He suffered a crippling stroke in 1901, and after he died in 1904 Wiman faded quietly into historical obscurity.

The election of 1891, the great moment of truth for each of these continentalists, has never been forgotten by the Canadian people quite so utterly as they have forgotten Wiman. But what traces of the contest linger in our histories are sadly one-dimensional. Even the most fair-minded historians have tended to portray the campaign along the same lines that Macdonald shrewdly drew in the heat of battle. The election of 1891, the story goes, was the great "loyalty election," a climactic battle between the heroic nationalism of the Conservatives and the "veiled treason" of the Liberals. The poster of Macdonald hoisted on the shoulders of supporters, wrapped in the British flag—"The Old Flag, the Old Policy, the Old Leader"—has been the most enduring image of the campaign. And the collapse of the Old Man on the campaign trail, followed by his death only months afterward, has fostered the legend that he literally died saving Canada from being sold out to the United States.

The election of 1891 was a turning point in Canadian history, but *not* because Sir John A. Macdonald saved the Dominion from the veiled treason of Wilfrid Laurier and the Liberal Party. The truth is that the campaign was a struggle between two competing yet equally patriotic visions of the destiny of Canada. Macdonald and the Conservatives sincerely believed that the only way to build a great country was to nurture the British connection, develop a prosperous industrial economy with the help of the National Policy and Canadian Pacific Railway, and resist the assimilating pressure of the United States. There was room in this vision for both English and French Canadians, though the former were naturally more responsive to appeals to the Union Jack. This vision triumphed in 1891, and in consequence the pro-British, anti-American nationalism of the Old Man has been accepted as the definitive expression of Canadian patriotism in the late nineteenth century.

This was not, however, the only brand of nationalism that inspired Canadians in 1891. Wilfrid Laurier and the Liberal Party did not run on a platform of veiled treason. They simply did not accept the national vision of the prime minister, which in their eyes called for dependence on Great Britain, a tariff policy that unfairly favoured an elite class of manufacturers rather than ordinary Canadians, and an irrational fear of the United States. The latter point was the most important. Many Liberals—many Canadians—in the late nineteenth century adopted a continentalist view of the future. They believed that free trade with the United States offered the best chance to achieve the prosperity that had eluded them since Confederation. They still retained an emotional attachment to Great Britain, but they were not swayed by sentiment when they considered what was best for Canada.

These continentalists also saw no reason to fear more intimate relations with the United States. The Conservatives worried constantly that moving Canada closer to the American colossus would ruin the dream of developing not only an independent national economy but also a distinctive national culture and identity. Continentalists such as Erastus Wiman and Sir Richard Cartwright believed that was nonsense. They saw no threat either to Canada's political sovereignty or its national identity in simply trading freely with the United States. Why would Canadians suffer on a level playing field, if they were the equals of the Americans in industry and intelligence? And why would Canadian culture be diminished under free trade, so long as those who valued it were determined to protect and nurture it? The irony of this striking brand of nationalism— this "confident continentalism"—was that it actually made Macdonald out to be the pessimist, the man who seemed to believe that loyalty was, as Erastus Wiman once complained, "an article so precious that it should be put in a glass case to be gazed at, rather than to be in every-day use."[15]

This is what the election of 1891 was really about. It was a struggle between two nationalisms, two visions of the destiny of Canada, and each was patriotic and sincere in its own way. Some schemers really did hope for annexation, and these individuals—Farrer, Smith, and U.S. politicians such as Ben Butterworth—did an untold amount of damage to the continentalist movement in Canada. That does not change the fact that men like Wiman and Cartwright championed free trade, and free trade only. It was not a platform that repelled all Canadians. On the contrary, it is worth remembering that the election of 1891 was a very close contest. Nearly half of the Canadian electorate voted for continentalism, and they did not do so because they were traitors.

There had never been such an intense debate about the destiny of Canada in the course of a federal election, and that alone made the election of 1891 memorable and important. No less important, however, was what the election was *not* about. It was the first time that either a French Canadian or a Roman Catholic had led a federal party into a national campaign, and that historic development came to pass at a time when the race-and-religion question was so toxic that Laurier himself believed his party was doomed under his leadership. He was convinced that no English Canadian Protestant, or too few of them anyway, would support him, simply because that was the way that things were in nineteenth-century Canada. If he had been proved right—if the Liberal Party had been crushed in a campaign that revolved around the ethnicity of its leader—then both parties might well have deduced that in the future only an English Canadian, and preferably one from Ontario where the most voters resided, could lead a national party. The damage to national unity that would have been wrought by such a cynical assumption is all too easy to imagine.

The election of 1891 proved Laurier wrong. It demonstrated beyond a doubt that it was possible for a French Canadian and a Roman Catholic to lead a federal party into a national campaign. The Liberals did not win, but they did not lose because of Laurier. They were defeated on the trade question and by the institutional advantages enjoyed by the Conservatives—their access to patronage, superior campaign funds, an advantage in the party press, and control of the voters lists. English Canadian Liberals did not desert the party because of Laurier. On the contrary, the predominant feeling in the ranks was that he had performed admirably. John Willison, watching Laurier confront the Jesuits' Estates Act controversy directly in 1889, had written, "This man would be a giant in some national crisis."[16] In a letter to Laurier three weeks after the election, Willison expressed his conviction that the Ontario Liberals now shared his views: "But be sure of this, you have now a wonderfully enthusiastic following in Ontario and it is of first-rate importance that you should be in this province as often as possible. You are now in a pre-eminent sense the leader of the party, our people, and I know what I am talking about, are more than proud of the way you managed the campaign, and they want to meet you, cheer you, and encourage you."[17]

The Liberals deserved credit for having the courage to accept Laurier as their leader, but no less important was the fact that the Conservatives resisted the temptation to make him the issue in the election of 1891. In many English Canadian constituencies, it must be remembered, an appeal to prejudice would have played well with the electorate, and the Conservatives felt constant pressure to pander to D'Alton McCarthy, the Orange Order, and the Equal Rights Association.

Sir John A. Macdonald refused to entertain that notion even for a moment. He had spent his life holding the young country together, and it was a measure of his success as a nation-builder—perhaps one of the greatest achievements of his career—that he had lived long enough to see a French Canadian battle him for the office of prime minister. On the trade question, Macdonald fought dirty and made scandalous accusations. Every Canadian knows that he was no paragon of virtue. But he confined the debate to the trade question, and by doing so he prevented race and religion from becoming the main issue during the election of 1891. There was, beneath all the knavery and opportunism, some genuine nobility in Sir John A. Macdonald.

It is important to remember that this nobility, this determination to fight the forces of intolerance that would have happily broken the country, was not confined to Laurier or Macdonald. Canadian politicians had a pretty low reputation among their constituents in the late nineteenth century. The boodling of the era has been well documented, and the sleaziness of certain public figures—McGreevy comes to mind—was certainly nothing to celebrate. Nevertheless, there was a consensus among most federal politicians that preserving the fragile unity of a nation composed of English and French, Protestant and Catholics, was worth risking their political futures. That was a crucial phenomenon, and it transcended party lines even in the heat of the campaign.

No example was more inspiring than that of George Dickinson, the rookie M.P. who voted with Macdonald against disallowance of the Jesuits' Estates Act in the pivotal parliamentary debate of March 1889. Dickinson was aware that he was, as Macdonald lamented, "committing political suicide." He voted with the prime minister anyway, and he did lose his seat in the election of 1891. Dickinson never made it back into the House of Commons. But he was a brave politician, and there were countless brave Canadians who refused to give in to the easy temptation of sticking to their own race or religion in a country that could not survive if they did. That story, no less important than the struggle over the trade question that has always defined the election of 1891, is one that can only be read between the lines.

NOTES

1. James Young to Laurier, 19 November 1887, Laurier fonds, 737, 208153, LAC; Young, *Our National Future: being five letters by James Young in opposition to commercial union (as proposed) and imperial federation, and pointing out what the writer believes to be the true future of Canada as part of North America* (R.G. McLean, 1888).
2. Alexander Mackenzie to Cartwright, 27 September 1887, Private, Sir Richard Cartwright fonds, Correspondence 1884–1899, F24-1, AO.
3. Thomas R. McInnes to Laurier, 16 July 1887, Laurier fonds, 737, 208105, LAC.
4. The English translation of the speech varied significantly in the papers of the day: this particular wording is taken from Joseph Schull, *Laurier*, 205–8.
5. *Proceedings of the Inter-provincial Conference held at the City of Quebec, from the 20th to the 28th October inclusively*, 38; clipping, Halifax *Herald*, 27 October 1887, George Foster fonds, 82, Scrapbook: Unrestricted Reciprocity 1887–89, MG27-IID7, LAC; Toronto *Globe*, 24, 28 October 1887; Halifax *Morning Chronicle*, 25 October 1887.
6. Toronto *Globe*, 14 October 1887.
7. Edgar to Laurier, 14 October 1887, Private, Laurier fonds, 2, 571–72, LAC.
8. Sir James David Edgar, *The Wiman-Edgar Letters: a series of open letters between Mr. J.D. Edgar, M.P., Toronto, and Mr. Erastus Wiman, New York: Unrestricted Reciprocity as Distinguished from Commercial Union*, 1887.
9. Cartwright to Laurier, 29 October 1887, Confidential, Laurier fonds, 2, 579–83, LAC.
10. Laurier to Edgar, 9 December 1887, Private, Edgar fonds, Correspondence, Series A-1-I, AO.
11. Cartwright to Laurier, 2 January 1888, Private, Laurier fonds, 737, 208190, LAC.
12. Cartwright to Laurier, 23 January 1888, Private, Laurier fonds, 737, 208203, LAC.
13. Preston, *My Generation of Politics and Politicians*, 185.
14. Wiman to Laurier, 23 March 1896, Laurier fonds, 70, 21945–46, LAC.
15. Wiman, "The Struggle in Canada," *North American Review*, vol. 152, no. 412 (March 1891): 343.
16. Willison, introduction to *Wilfrid Laurier on the Platform* by Barthe, xix.
17. Willison to Laurier, 26 March 1891, Laurier fonds, 5, 1764-68, LAC.

◼ARTICLE 2: A CASE STUDY OF ANTI-AMERICANISM IN ENGLISH-SPEAKING CANADA: THE ELECTION CAMPAIGN OF 1911

W.M. Baker

Anti-Americanism is a recurring theme in Canadian History. It exists today as it did a century ago. It is one of the solid legs on which that elusive animal, the Canadian identity, stands. Indeed, anti-Americanism is such an important concept in the interpretation of Canadian history that there has long been a need to break it down into its various components.

Source: *Canadian Historical Review*, December 1970, Vol. 51, Issue 4, 426–449. Reprinted with permission from University of Toronto Press Incorporated (www.utpjournals.com).

From the Conquest until well into the twentieth century, anti-Americanism in English-speaking Canada had three ingredients: 1) Canadian attitudes towards the United States; 2) Canadian sentiments regarding Great Britain and the imperial tie; and 3) Canadians' opinions of themselves and their country. The strength of anti-Americanism during this period was dependent upon the particular combination of the three ingredients in existence at any given time. When, for instance, the value of the imperial connection was questioned and Canadians doubted the viability of their own country, as was the case during the middle years of the 1880s, anti-Americanism crept into the recesses of the Canadian landscape. It is necessary, therefore, that the three components of Canadian anti-Americanism be examined in relation to the first decade of the twentieth century before anti-Americanism in the election campaign of 1911 can be considered.

The North Atlantic Triangle during the nineteenth century was characterized by a love-hate relationship. Each one of the three sides expected a great deal of the others, and these high expectations were bound to show their limitations in periods of stress. The Civil War, for instance, placed great tension on British-American relations and, although both sides acted in a diplomatically enlightened manner, severe disappointment, disillusionment, distrust, and even hatred resulted. Fortunately, however, even more fundamental in the long-range relations of the triad were the established bonds of race, religion, law, and philosophy of life. The ancient ties of a common family tree militated in the long run for friendship, not war. Family quarrels, however, are renowned for their virulence. In short, when expectations were not fulfilled, the resulting antagonisms were made worse simply because hopes and basic trusts had been pitched so high. Therefore, a strange paradox existed by which Canada both trusted and distrusted her American neighbour, but, because of Canada's psychological and physical inferiority, Canadians generally chose to emphasize their suspicions of the United States.

The historical development of the North American continent goes a long way in accounting for Canadian attitudes towards the United States. The antagonism which existed between the colonies of France and England during the seventeenth and eighteenth centuries was ended neither by the Conquest nor by the American Revolution. The coming of the United Empire Loyalists, the War of 1812, and the multitude of boundary disputes in the nineteenth century simply confirmed the original conflicts. Throughout the nineteenth century Canadian antipathy towards the United States may have waned at times, but it never disappeared entirely. The tradition of disenchantment with the United States was reinforced in 1903 when the Alaska Boundary Dispute came to a conclusion that was quite unsatisfactory as far as Canadians were concerned. In fact, even the initial discussions on reciprocity between Canada and the United States in 1910 had come about because the United States was using a rather overbearing method to gain tariff concessions.[1] Yet for very practical reasons Canada could not afford to be on bad terms with her great neighbour, and this fact was recognized. Furthermore, the social, cultural, economic, and even family ties between the two countries were close. During the decade from 1901 to 1910, for instance, nearly one-half million Americans became Canadian immigrants and nearly one-quarter million native-born Canadians emigrated, mainly to the United States.[2] The predetermined outlook of a man like Dr O. D. Skelton could not have been completely clouded when he pointed out that such things as trade unions and baseball teams, figures like Roosevelt, and magazines such as *Ladies' Home Journal* were bringing the social relations of the United States and Canada closer together.[3] Even the strongest opponents of reciprocity in 1911 took pains to assure their listeners that they were not antagonistic towards the United States. Conservative leader Robert Borden himself wrote after the election: "The verdict has been given in no spirit of unfriendliness or hostility to the United States and no such spirit exists."[4] Statements such as this show that Canada has seldom been very belligerent in her anti-Americanism. Anti-Americanism in Canada has usually meant simply fear of the United States, that is fear of Americanization and annexation. In this sense the election campaign of 1911 witnessed a great deal of anti-Americanism.

The second ingredient in Canadian anti-Americanism is Canadian feeling towards Britain and the empire. Here again the picture is kaleidoscopic. When Canadians thought about Britain's relationship to Canada they could recall the Family Compact, the repeal of the Corn Laws, the withdrawal of British troops from North America, the Treaty of Washington, and the Alaska Boundary Dispute. This debit side of the ledger was balanced by many happier incidents in the annals of Canadian-British relations. Yet an observer viewing Canadian sentiment in 1903 and shortly thereafter would have found it hard to credit the passionately strong imperial sentiment which was expressed in 1911. This feeling of 1911 did not, however, spring entirely from fear of the United States when the reciprocity agreement was brought forward. The years around the turn of the century had seen the royalist cult of loyalty to "good Queen Victoria" rise to a peak in Canada as the European race for empire had expanded the British empire in area and influence. To a large degree Canadian irritation towards Britain as a result of the Alaska Boundary Dispute was a momentary reaction and these feelings passed quickly. In fact, it was not long after this dispute that the Empire Club of Canada, whose declared purpose was "the advancement of the interests of Canada and a United Empire,"[5] was founded. This reaction against autonomist utterances was reinforced in various ways in the succeeding years. By 1910 imperialism was being discussed favourably in a large number of influential circles. Typical of this is *The University Magazine* which, in 1910 and 1911, had one article on the reciprocity issue, two articles which felt that the development of Canadian autonomy was inevitable and right, and seven articles which favoured closer imperial ties in one way or another. In late 1910 the first issue of the *Round Table* was published and distributed to three hundred subscribers "of real influence in politics, journalism, business, etc."[6] In 1910 not only did the Queen's Own Rifles of Toronto visit England (expenses paid) but also 165 Manitoba teachers toured the same land.[7] Sir James Whitney, the premier of Ontario, spoke in favour of the full Chamberlain policy while he was in England.[8] Sir Edmund Walker was "Imperialistic to the hilt" in urging on 2 December 1910 that Canada should be "a part of the Empire in a wider sense than at present."[9] Even Pauline Johnson, the half Mohawk, half English poetess born at Brantford, Ontario, was not unaffected by imperial sentiment. One of her poems popular as a recitation

at school concerts in this period contains the following stanza:

> The Dutch may have their Holland, the Spaniard have his Spain, the Yankee to the south of us must south of us remain; For not a man dare lift a hand against the men who brag that they were born in Canada beneath the British flag.[10]

A counterattack had begun against the feeling that England was becoming progressively more decadent. The picture of the effectiveness of British diplomacy was being rehabilitated.[11] A number of organizations such as the Empire Club of Canada and the Imperial Order of the Daughters of the Empire had entered upon a period of growth and vitality.[12] The Orange Order was full of advice and wielded considerable influence in favour of imperialism, especially in Ontario and British Columbia.[13] It is also interesting to note that of the 198 speeches given at the 1910 meetings of the various Canadian Clubs throughout the country, none, if one is to judge by titles, dealt with the United States. There is no doubt that on such topics as "Reciprocity and the Empire," Canada's great neighbour was discussed, but in no title do the words "The United States" appear. "Imperial Subjects," in contrast, accounted for no fewer than sixty-five speeches.[14] In short, imperial sentiment was at a very high pitch in 1910 and, as is well-known, even the great issue of 1910, the naval question, was discussed with imperial relations as the central point of attack and defence.

But how did imperial sentiment affect Canadian feelings towards the United States? In 1910 anti-American expressions did not flow from the mouths of politicians or from the pens of editors. Yet, with the strong imperialist background which existed, it can easily be seen that any plan which might challenge imperial ties would find considerable opposition in Canada. While no competitor to the imperial loyalties of Canadians appeared, there was no need for anti-American expressions. Reciprocity was an issue that could and did challenge these loyalties. It is not surprising, therefore, that Borden and other opponents of reciprocity found that Taft's "parting of the ways" speech was effective in consolidating support against reciprocity. Anti-Americanism, or the fear of Americanization or annexation, found a nesting place in the heart of many a Canadian who felt that imperial ties should be strengthened or at least preserved. "To preserve their allegiance to the Empire and to achieve their ambition to become full partner [sic] in its affairs, Canadians must maintain their commercial independence";[15] this was no isolated assessment in 1911.

Anti-Americanism is a three-headed monster, including Canadian opinion of the United States and of Britain, and also the mercurial nature of Canadian attitudes towards Canada itself. There have been times, such as in 1837, 1849, and much of the 1870s and 1880s, when some Canadians have been pessimistic about Canada and its future. This pessimism disappeared during the wheat boom era as the country grew enormously both in production and in capital investments. Canadians were developing a new sense of national identity and pride, and to some extent Canada followed the general trend in this period of rising nationalism which took many forms in many place [sic]. The twentieth century was proclaimed to be "Canada's Century." This optimism was shown in the railway boom and the development of manufacturing. Faith in the future of Canada was also supported by great immigration and quickly-increasing wheat exports. George Foster was quite confident that within a century Canada would have a population of 100,000,000.[16] Other such Utopian forecasts were not lacking. Had Canadians been more unhappy with their lot they might have been less antagonistic to American advances. The argument of "we are doing well, why jeopardize our position?" was frequently used in 1911 and with considerable effect.[17] Even Mackenzie King had the feeling that the *status quo* was best, although in his case political expediency took precedence over economic considerations.[18] Other Liberals also felt complacent or even hostile towards reciprocity, a fact which considerably weakened their campaign. It was also argued that Canada had made herself prosperous despite the hindrances placed in front of her by the United States. George Foster's statement—"Sir, 'I fear the Greeks when they are bearing gifts'"[19]—showed the distrust of the United States which had been engendered by years of American snubs towards Canada and by an abundance of confidence concerning the future of Canada. As well, it was felt that Canada should not allow the United States wastefully to use up Canadian natural resources as she had done with her own.[20] Foster put it this way: "To our present small population they [Canada's natural resources] seem inexhaustible, but we remember that we are trustees for the 100,000,000 people which a century hence will inhabit this territory."[21] Canadians' attitudes towards themselves revealed little desire to gamble with hard-won prosperity. This feeling naturally led to anti-American sentiments.

All three faces of anti-Americanism were visible in the 1911 election, and in a multitude of ways Canadians made themselves aware of their fear of the United States. In Parliament anti-American expressions were guarded, but the speeches of Champ Clark, J. J. Hill, Senator A. J. Beveridge, President Taft, and other apparently annexationist sentiments of American leaders were bandied about. The irrepressible Foster was quite certain that although the American method had changed, the goal was just the same as it had always been. "It is still the conquest of Canada. But it is conquest of Canada by peaceful means and large gifts ... "[22] Yet for all his distrust of the United States, his optimism for Canada's future, and his belief in imperial ties, Foster did not consider himself to be antagonistic to the United States: "[T]here is absolutely the best of friendly feeling between us and our neighbors ... The American people respect and admire us, and they do so for one thing. They respect and admire us because we have clung to our rights, our nationality and our own standards."[23] But his self-proclaimed Canadian national ideals had no room for any "truck or trade" with the Americans. These ideals were: "Canadian natural resources for the purposes of Canadian development, Canadian markets for Canadian producers, Canadian traffic for Canadian carriers, and a Canadian nation with complete freedom of self-government and the closest possible union and co-operation with the British empire."[24] As well, this important Conservative spokesman showed his real antipathy to the United States in the illustrations he used: "A nation has just as much right, and surely an equal duty, to defend its resources from commercial rapine and plunder as to repeal [sic] invaders of its soil."[25] Foster exhibited all three of the ingredients of anti-Americanism. Firstly, he certainly had no great love for the character of Americans or the way the United States had treated Canada in the past. Secondly, he was a staunch imperialist: "[W]e are enamoured of the idea of British imperial trade connections ... Nationhood, race ties, and loyalty to British institutions, are its sources. The desire to consolidate and preserve the Empire of which we form a part is strong with us."[26] Finally, his great faith in the future of Canada was clearly evident.

Borden's position was similar to that of Foster. He was, as Castell Hopkins remarked, "in all his utterances a friend of the United States and an admirer of its national greatness ... "[27] Yet he was quite sure that reciprocity would lead to annexation: "The plain fact is that in entering upon this treaty the people of the United States believe that they are accomplishing the first step towards annexation."[28] Borden was also concerned about the imperial connection and he had an optimistic opinion of Canada's future.[29] In the spring of 1910 he had written to Sir James Whitney, the Conservative premier of Ontario, concerning the establishment of a monthly magazine designed to promote imperial ideas in Canada. Borden had then claimed that such a magazine "would no doubt be of great advantage to the people of this country, whose education in matters of imperial moment is perhaps in some respects neglected."[30] On 19 September 1911 in Halifax he concluded his campaign on the following optimistic note:

I believe that we are, in truth, standing today at the parting of the ways ... We must decide whether the spirit of Canadianism or Continentalism shall prevail on the northern half of this continent ... With Canada's youthful vitality, her rapidly increasing population, her marvellous material resources, her spirit of hopefulness and energy, she can place herself within a comparatively brief period in the highest position within this mighty Empire.[31]

In the provinces similar sounds were heard. Sir James Whitney moved a resolution in the Ontario legislature which showed the three ingredients of anti-Americanism. He asserted that the aim of the United States was to gain control of Canada. The resolution ran as follows:

Canada's tide of prosperity and contentment is still rising and her position and influence as an essential part of a consolidated Empire are becoming more assured. No arrangement with a foreign state should be considered which might even jeopardize the continuance of her present satisfactory condition, much less this Agreement for Reciprocity with the United States of America, negotiated in secret and without any authority from her people, which, if made

effective, would in the opinion of this House to a large extent reverse the policy which has brought Canada to her present enviable position ... would weaken Canada's position and influence as a unit in the British Empire, would frustrate her hopes of nationhood within the Empire, and would lead to Political Union with the United States.[32]

Whitney's attitude towards the United States was not one of violent antagonism. But the Conservative Premier was not averse to appealing to anti-American sentiment among the populace. He reported to Borden during the campaign that he would introduce one of his audiences to the new firm of "Laurier, Taft & Company." Such a phrase had to be handled with finesse, and this Whitney proposed to do: "When I touch upon Taft I shall of course speak of him with respect ... but draw attention to his deliberate meddling with our affairs."[33] It is obvious that Whitney's distrust of the United States was deeply-rooted and, when the election was over and reciprocity had been rejected, he asserted that "our friends over the border will not be apt to attempt any further interference with us."[34]

On the question of imperialism Whitney had long taken an active interest. He claimed, in fact, that "at least eight men out of ten in the Dominion of Canada—except perhaps in Quebec where there are good reasons for a different view—are warmly interested in everything that pertains to the Empire and its future." Whitney himself was in favour of something he rather vaguely termed "sane Imperialism," and criticized everyone from Churchill to Laurier for failing to promote it.[35] He gladly fought the battle for the empire in 1911 and he saw the election results through imperial eyes. In congratulating Borden he wrote: "No such good work was ever done in British America before, and having regard to its effect on the future of the Empire I doubt if any one day's work in England in modern times ever signified as much."[36] Even more striking was Whitney's reply to a cable from H. A. Gwynn of the *Morning Post* in London, England. Gwynn's message had read: "Long live Canada." To this Whitney answered: "Rule Britannia."[37] But the election had national as well as imperial significance for Whitney. Nationalism and imperialism were closely connected, perhaps the same sentiment. After the election he told one correspondent that "Canada is indeed a Nation now."[38]

Robert Rogers, minister of public works in Manitoba, was not to be outdone. He declared that:

Messrs. Fielding and Paterson had bartered away, or tried to do so, the political liberty and fiscal freedom of Canada; that the Republican President of the United States was trying to save his party at Canada's expense and was pledged to lower certain duties anyway ... that the new policy was one of placing the natural resources of Canada open and free to the plundering of the United States; that American fixing and framing of Canadian tariffs and control of Canadian wealth could only have one end.[39]

Rogers felt that there were many other reasons for fighting against reciprocity, including the belief "that the bonds of the Empire should be strengthened, trade relations within the Empire fostered and developed."[40] Thus Rogers, too, evidenced the three ingredients of anti-Americanism in his position on the reciprocity question.

Indeed, the Conservative campaign reiterated these points across the country. H. B. Ames, Conservative member from Montreal, pleaded: "Let us be an independent nation rather than the backyard of the United States. ... Reciprocity is the leak in the dyke."[41] Premiers Rodmond Roblin and Richard McBride, of Manitoba and British Columbia respectively, had very strong imperialist sentiments and were quite happy with the economic development of Canada. This, as well as their intimate connections with, and loyalty to, the federal Conservative party, was instrumental in their campaign against reciprocity. McBride voiced his deep distrust of the United States and his sense of Canadian moral superiority when he asked his listeners: "Are you going to stand firm by British connection, British liberty and British free institutions, or throw these over so as to pander to the many corrupt influences arising and fostered in the United States?"[42] On another occasion he queried whether "anyone had ever heard of Canada, in any business deal with the United States ... getting anything except the short end."[43] Even that grand old pugilist of the Canadian political ring, Sir Charles Tupper, expressed a few words in his usual striking fashion. After claiming that Taft's "parting of the ways" speech was the most convincing argument against reciprocity which Canadians had heard, Tupper continued his post-election speech to the United Empire Club:

I find no fault with him because he was endeavouring to make the United States the dictator of the world by bringing Canada within its folds. They had half the North American continent already, but we had the better half. We have enormous resources, rich soil, and ... gigantic water-power throughout. ... Mr. Taft's speech sank deeply into the heart of every intelligent man in Canada who had to decide on the question ... whether Canada was to be Republican, or to become with the other great dominions and the Mother Country an Empire overwhelmingly strong and in a position to dictate the peace of the world. No person can attach more importance than I do to the position at which Canada has now arrived—a position which will render this Empire the bulwark of the throne and British institutions, a greater Empire than the world has ever seen.[44]

The press expressed a similar variety of anti-American sentiments. Under Sir Hugh Graham, the Montreal *Star*, a leading antireciprocity organ with an average daily circulation of 75,000,[45] disseminated anti-American propaganda both within its pages and by means of pamphlets.[46] Other anti-reciprocity papers made no attempt to hide their anti-Americanism. The Orange *Sentinel* of Toronto of 2 February stated: "In spite of the unfriendliness of our neighbors we have become independent of their trade and are growing more powerful every day."[47] The Saint John *Standard* was more emphatic:

The reception given was partly due to Mr. Fowler's [Conservative candidate in King's-Albert] personal popularity but, in ever larger measure, to the fact that he was the champion of the Union Jack and British connection as opposed to the Stars and Stripes and Yankee domination in Canadian affairs—the domination of a flag which, as one speaker aptly put it, was conceived in treason and born in rebellion.[48]

Across the front page of the Toronto *World* on 21 September appeared the following words: "Which will it be? Borden and King George, or Laurier and Taft?"[49]

Most prominent of individual spokesmen in 1911 was Clifford Sifton.

Other than Laurier, Sifton was still the leading Liberal of all, despite or perhaps even because of his resignation from the cabinet in 1905. Again in 1911 he refused to go along with his chief, and he and certain of his followers worked strenuously to defeat reciprocity. He too held many tenets of anti-Americanism, and even though his expression was temperate it was nonetheless meaningful. Like others he felt that reciprocity would lead to political union.[50] In line with his practice as former minister of the interior he wanted to preserve Canadian natural resources for Canadians and their future.[51] He also saw a threat to imperial unity in reciprocity: "Your publicists who said this trade agreement would bind Canada to the United States and strike a blow at the consolidation of the British Empire were absolutely right and we who fought against it realized that fact and had a full appreciation of its importance."[52] Sifton's historical analysis was that "for the last thirty or forty years we have been either ignored or buffeted by the United States,"[53] but despite this Canada had attained a good economic position, and this should not be thrown away. His conclusion was that "we are putting our heads into a noose" and "if we take the terms we will have to pay the price."[54]

Allied with Sifton was Sir Edmund Walker, a leading Toronto businessman and a staunch imperialist, and also the most prominent of the eighteen Toronto Liberals who broke with the party over the issue of reciprocity. Undoubtedly business interests had a great deal to do with his action, but imperial sentiment was also a strong motivating force. It was Sir Edmund who found the three hundred prominent men to subscribe to the *Round Table*.[55] The question of imperialism had already made Walker unhappy with the Liberals by 1910. He had shown this discontent in a letter to a Conservative MP who had urged Walker to occupy "'the seat beside Mr. Borden as first lieutenant.'" Walker's reasons for refusing were many, but happiness with the Liberal policy on imperial questions was not one of them.[56] Consequently, there was no doubt as to the position he held on reciprocity when it arose. At the Board of Trade protest meeting in Toronto on 16 February 1911 Walker stated what for him was the issue: "The question is between British connection and what has been well called 'Continentalism.'"[57] As well, he had an optimistic vision of the economic future of Canada. He stated in 1906 that "we are on the eve of a great boom. The prospects of the North-West are unlimited."[58] His views on this score had been

reinforced, not changed, by 1911.[59] Fear of Americanization was part of Walker's make-up, and he believed that Canadian nationality would be seriously threatened by the reciprocity agreement.[60] It is not surprising, therefore, to find that he was associated with the mass meeting in Toronto's Massey Hall, held under the auspices of Conservative organizers and the Toronto Eighteen, which was "Imperialistic and anti-American" in tone.[61]

A great number of people, from all walks of life, uttered anti-American statements during the 1911 election campaign. Sir William Van Horne could never be described as "typical," but he was at least a symbol of the strong feeling aroused in 1911. Van Horne, of Canadian Pacific Railway fame, was by no means averse to making an anti-American appeal despite the fact that he himself had been born in Illinois. It was his claim that Canadians, if they accepted reciprocity, were "making a bed to lie in and die in."[62] On another occasion he bluntly asked: "Shall we play gosling to the American fox?"[63] George W. Ross, formerly Liberal premier of Ontario, added that "coercion having failed to bring about the annexation of Canada, commercial privileges were to be adopted as a new and advanced method for the same end."[64] The Baptist minister at Aylmer, Ontario, stated that reciprocity meant absorption by the United States.[65]

Mrs Ewing of Montreal's Women's Branch of the Anti-Reciprocity League sent a petition to the government on behalf of the organization stating "that Reciprocity means Annexation, injury to home life and the marriage tie, a lessening of national religion, morals and patriotism."[66] This was, of course, a severe assessment of Americans, for it was to be by annexation and association that these calamities were to occur. Canadian women were probably led to this belief by articles such as the one which appeared in the *University Magazine* contrasting the prevalence of divorce in the United States and in Canada. This and similar articles are excellent examples of Canadians' belief in their moral superiority over the supposedly rash, spoiled, extravagant Americans who had no loyalty to tradition.[67] Finally on 13 September Henry Joseph, a prominent Jew of Montreal, publicly denounced the reciprocity agreement because it would bring about annexation to a country which was well known for the poor treatment of its Jewish population.[68]

Few of these sentiments were openly belligerent or even very antagonistic. Most of the people who expressed them did so not because of a conscious enmity to the United States but because they felt there was a danger in reciprocity of becoming something they did not want to be—Americans. They appealed to higher loyalties, the nation, and the empire. However, they did so with considerable admiration for American achievements, with much friendliness towards the average American, with the understanding that even annexation was a natural and not an "evil" goal for Americans to seek, and with the trust that the United States and Canada were on sufficiently friendly terms to ensure that no fundamental ill-will would arise from Canadian rejection of reciprocity. Thus one must reassert the conclusion that anti-Americanism in English-speaking Canada in 1911 meant only a desire to remain independent of the United States and to keep, and perhaps strengthen, imperial ties.

This moderate form of anti-Americanism exploited the statements of American politicians and press, factors partly accounting for anti-Americanism in the election of 1911. "Using the unfortunate parting-of-the-ways remark in almost every speech, Borden made Taft his lay-figure, to be stood up and knocked down for the benefit of Canadian audiences."[69] Nor was this the only remark of Taft's that was used, after being wrenched from its economic context, by the antireciprocity forces. In a speech in New York in late April, for instance, the American President had said:

> The forces which are at work in England and Canada to separate her by a Chinese wall from the United States and to make her a part of an imperial commercial band reaching from England around the world to England again by a system of preferential tariffs, will derive an impetus from the rejection of this treaty, and if we would have reciprocity with all the advantages ... *we must take it now or give it up forever.*
>
> ... The government is one controlled entirely by the people, and *the bond uniting the dominion to the mother country is light and almost imperceptible.*[70]

Champ Clark's speech in Congress was even more widely used in Canada. His dream was quite bold: "I am for it [the reciprocity agreement] because I hope to see the day when the American flag will float over every square foot of the British North American possessions, clear to the North Pole."[71] Few Canadians could accept this with the objectivity of the British Ambassador in Washington who characterized Champ Clark as "a rather crude Western man of the 'Chantauqua [*sic*] lecturer' type with a sort of rough humour and picturesqueness of phrase which catches a popular audience, but no knowledge of international relations, much less of international courtesies." To Bryce, the offensive statement had been "blurted out" inadvertently "in the heat of debate." Bryce admitted that many "half-educated Americans" thought that "manifest destiny" would bring about the absorption of Canada, but he asserted that "most sensible men are aware that this is more unlikely now than it ever was before," and he felt that American support for reciprocity was "due to a belief that it will make for cheap food and increased trade."[72]

Many excerpts from the speeches of American politicians and from the pages of American newspapers were widely circulated in Canada. Representative Benjamin K. Focht was quoted as saying: "I don't think Annexation is so far in the future." The Washington *Star* felt that "in time the thoughts of Canadians may turn towards annexation as the most to be desired of all political boons." The *Southern Lumber Journal* demanded immediate negotiations for peaceful annextion "but for Annexation if it should have to come about through conquest." The Philadelphia *Farm Journal* felt that reciprocity "will mean, ultimately, peaceful Annexation. There is no doubt about that."[73] Canadians had not heard statements such as that of Champ Clark very frequently since 1900 and it was upsetting to hear them now. These statements gave credence to the words of Conservatives, such as George Foster, who claimed that reciprocity was simply a means to annex Canada. Americans, by making such distasteful and unfounded statements, were responsible for much of the anti-American sentiment displayed in the Canadian election. Even the Governor General felt that the "foolish speeches in the United States" played a large role in the result of the election.[74]

Anti-American sentiment can partially be accounted for in another way. The immigration of nearly one-half million Americans in the decade from 1901 to 1910 had created problems. Despite the large numbers who emigrated from the United States (497, 249), the number of Canadian residents born in the United States increased by only 175,781 during these years to reach a total of 303,680.[75] But the fact remained that the American-born formed the largest non-native group in Alberta and were an extremely powerful minority in Saskatchewan, and the loudest demands for reciprocity emanated from that region. That there was a clash between the "old Canadian" and the immigrant is seen in the Canadian Manufacturers Association statement of 1910 to the government concerning the farmers' demands for reciprocity:

> Mr. Russell claimed that these Western farmers seemed to ignore everyone but themselves; that Canada had become united, prosperous and strong under a policy of moderate protection; that the present movement was controlled, in the main, by men who were "new Canadians", unacquainted with the history and aims of Canada, the principles of Canadian nationality, the aspirations of British subjects; that these men of the West had come into a rich and easy heritage won and held by a century of Canadian struggle, sufferings, privations, taxation and development in the East...[76]

In 1911 there were many who feared that closer commercial connections would bring these immigrants, of European as well as American origin, into closer social relationships with the United States. It was claimed that because they were not steeped in the tradition of loyalty to "King and country" they would desire political union with the United States. Since many of these immigrants were Americans it also appeared, to some, that reciprocity was being used by the United States and by the American settlers to bring about the annexation of the northwest. Champ Clark and other prominent Americans were quoted in Canada as having intentions of this sort, and the fact that many Americans were settled in the northwest gave the project a certain appeal in the United States.[77] There was, certainly, considerable resentment and distrust in Canada concerning American immigrants and the prairie provinces which so greatly desired reciprocity. One resident of Alberta was quite outspoken in his views:

> We have been in the West 7 years & know it well, our homestead is in a district largely settled by Americans with a minority of British & Canadian settlers. Nearly all will vote Liberal at the coming election because the farmers think they will get better prices for their grain, & cheaper implements under Reciprocity. No other argument or phase of the subject appeals to them. It is worse than useless to talk Imperialism, British preference etc. out here. ... It is quite untrue that the American immigrant becomes a good Canadian.[78]

Ill-will towards the American settler (and other immigrants) spilled over to include the United States itself and was another reason that Canadians distrusted and feared the Americans. Sir Edmund Walker stated that Canadians "must assimilate our immigrants and make out of them good Canadians." He defined a "good Canadian" as one who looked to the British connection, among other things, and he felt that reciprocity was a "deadly danger" because it made assimilation more difficult and doubtful.[79] This distrust of the new Canadians was of enough importance in the election of 1911 to suggest that "Old Ontario" voted against the "new" farmers. Even as far west as Manitoba, which had relatively few Americans, this form of anti-Americanism was used. The Mayor of Winnipeg stated:

> This is our country. We have a right, if our ideals are noble and worthy, that we should have those ideals and purposes realized and maintained. If people come to us it is our duty to persuade them until they see things that are right and best and work with us to realize them. At a time when this difficult task is with us the Government of this country, with no demand from the people, deliberately introduces to the hundreds of thousands of people who are not Canadian and are not British the idea that their material salvation lies with a foreign country.[80]

Winnipeg was, of course, the metropolitan centre of the Prairies. The city would naturally oppose any threat to its dominance and feared that reciprocity would open up new north-south lines of transport, a prospect that Winnipeg could not accept with equanimity. Thus, one further aspect of anti-Americanism in the election was this appeal to the "old Canadian" and the British-born to keep Canada pure from contaminating American influences from both inside and outside Canada. It is significant that

Arthur Hawkes wrote his pamphlet "Appeal to the British Born" mainly for Ontario consumption and left the Prairies virtually untouched.[81]

Though by no means final, the most obvious way in which one can account for anti-Americanism in the election of 1911 is by acknowledging the simple fact that an election is a political act. The Liberal party had apparently won a great victory in negotiating the reciprocity agreement. It was claimed that this was the fulfilment of the dreams of forty years. Although the Liberal party was in a period of serious decline by 1911, the fact remained that the prestige of this victory held considerable political potential. Sir Wilfrid Laurier was confident that the issue of reciprocity would be enough to win the election for the Liberals.[82] The Conservatives therefore had to find an alternative claim. The most obvious tactic was to turn the issue into one of patriotism rather than economics, to appeal to incipient Canadian nationalism and to what was for many an integral part of this nationalism, the imperial tie. The result was anti-Americanism.

Vote-catching, however, was by no means the only factor that influenced the Conservatives. It was sincerely believed that there were dangers inherent in reciprocity. The threats to the British connection and the Canadian nation were more than slogans to the Conservatives and to maverick Liberals such as Sifton. Earl Grey himself acknowledged that the Conservative objections to the Reciprocity Agreement stemmed from sentiments other than "over tenderness for the wellbeing of protected industries. They are prompted by apprehensions as to the effect it may have on Canadian unity and Imperial connection."[83] One cannot doubt the basic sincerity of men such as George Foster who, in the House of Commons, expressed his thoughts in these words:

> I utter the most solemn words I have ever uttered in my life, and I believe them to the very bottom of my heart, that there is danger, and deep danger ahead. The path entered upon leads us away from home to a strange country. I pray, Sir, that the full meaning of this first step may sink into the hearts of members of parliament and into the hearts of the people of this country until there shall burst forth a protest of such strength that the steps contemplated will be recalled to the old paths, leading east

and west, in and out amongst our own people, converging on the great metropolis of the mother land, and which we may follow without uncertainty and without menace to our national existence.[84]

This dislike of Americanization, which is the definition of anti-Americanism in 1911, gave the Conservative party the necessary enthusiasm to carry on a vigorous campaign. A large portion of the campaign was the appeal to the same fears and prejudices which plagued the politicians themselves. The antireciprocity forces had caught sight of a vision, whereas this was conspicuously absent in the Liberal campaign. Even a brief survey of the important speeches in the Commons shows that the dull, factual, unimpressive speeches in favour of reciprocity were no match for the fervent, well-prepared, almost visionary speeches of Borden, Foster, and their compatriots. Thus, the simple fact that there was an election campaign on the issue of reciprocity goes a long way to explain why there was anti-Americanism in 1911. The Conservatives and their allies needed a policy. Moreover this policy was honestly obtained because they did see a threat inherent in the reciprocity scheme. Psychological orientation admirably fitted with the party necessities of the Conservatives.

One final question should be asked. How effective was anti-Americanism in the 1911 election? Did it create a crisis atmosphere which turned the voters away from the Liberal party or are there other factors which explain the Conservative victory? Historians' tools of electoral analysis are admittedly inadequate. Interpreting elections by a recital of the issues and results is the most frequently used method. But an analysis of party organization and past performance are equally important.

It is quite clear that the Liberal party organization was in a deplorable state by 1911. At the beginning of July 1911 A. B. Aylesworth, a prominent Liberal, wrote to Dafoe claiming that an autumn election would give the same or even a larger majority to the government.[85] Lack of accurate electoral analysis plagued the Liberals throughout the campaign, as W. T. R. Preston pointed out shortly after the election: "Only today a letter reached me from the Private Secretary of one of the Ministers saying that the government were coming back stronger than ever. If I had anything to do with the organization that could see no signs of the coming storm I would put my head in ice for the rest of my life."[86] Little help was given the federal Liberals by the provincial Liberals. This fact is especially important, for in this period the connection between federal and provincial parties was extremely close. The commentator on Canadian affairs in the *Round Table* aptly noted that "At the moment the accepted belief that the provinces are reluctant to entrust the control of both federal and provincial affairs to the one party is not strongly supported by the political situation in the Dominion."[87] In fact, the votes in various provincial legislatures on reciprocity resolutions,[88] the results of six provincial elections held late in 1911 and in 1912,[89] and the federal election results[90] run along strikingly parallel courses.

This close connection between federal and provincial political parties severely hurt Laurier in 1911 for the simple reason that the provincial Liberal parties were in a very weakened condition. Indeed, Laurier had no lieutenant in Ontario for much of the 1911 campaign and was forced to handle the local constituency organization himself.[91] In Nova Scotia, despite the fact that the Liberals were in power, "the members of the Provincial Government did not take as active a part in the contest as did most of the other Provincial Governments."[92] In Manitoba, Ontario, New Brunswick, Prince Edward Island, and British Columbia, the provincial Liberal organizations were disorganized, weak, and consequently of little aid to the federal Liberals. Only in Saskatchewan and Alberta could Liberals expect much help from their provincial brothers, and the Liberal premiers, Walter Scott and A. L. Sifton respectively, spoke many times for the federal Liberal party.

The Conservative organizations in these two provinces were moribund if not completely extinguished and the Conservative campaign here was almost non-existent.[93] In contrast, the Conservatives were admirably aided by provincial organizations elsewhere. Premier McBride of British Columbia and several other members of his government carried on an amazing campaign in support of Borden.[94] In Manitoba a vigorous effort was made, especially by Premier Roblin and Robert Rogers, to keep the voters from straying to the Liberal party.[95] Ontario, however, was the most important province in the election of 1911. The co-operation between the provincial and federal organizations was quite amazing.[96] A number of Queen's Park members were induced to become candidates in constituencies where they were likely to win.[97] Accurate estimates and political reports were given to Borden by his organizers in Ontario and the right men were found to stand for election in the proper areas. As a result, as Professor Cuff asserts, "the Conservative Party swept the election of 1911 in Ontario by means of a superior political organization. Powerfully augmented by the many-sided co-operation of the Whitney government, the Conservative machine exercised a vigorous constituency control that took advantage of an increasingly weakening opposition."[98] The analysis made by the Conservative campaign managers gave "no intimation that reciprocity was a controlling factor in their assessment of conditions or predictions of electoral success."[99] In other words "success was apparently coming to the Conservatives by way of superior organization and superior candidates," rather than simply because of the reciprocity issue.[100]

This analysis has serious implications for an evaluation of the effect of anti-Americanism in the election of 1911. If party organization made a Conservative sweep of Ontario likely "no matter what public issue emerged in 1911,"[101] it is probable that reciprocity, with which anti-Americanism was connected, was less significant in the election than historians have asserted. It is perfectly clear that political organization did play a large role in the election and to a considerable extent the battle lines had been drawn before 26 January 1911. British Columbia was upset at the Liberal government's immigration policy respecting orientals and its naval policy.[102] Manitoba, under Premier Roblin, was thoroughly dissatisfied with the handling of the schools question and the problems of boundary extension and control of public lands.[103] In Ontario, the Whitney government held a practically invulnerable position and the bilingual schools question, the *ne temere* decree, and Orange Order proclamations had again made Upper Canadians wary of French-Canadian "encroachments."[104] Moreover, considerable fear for the imperial connection had been aroused over Lauder's stand on the Navy and at the Imperial Conference of 1911. When these considerations are combined with the fact that the provincial Liberal party "had permitted the most brazen machine in Canadian annals to take control of its electoral affairs,"[105] it is not surprising that the Liberals were nearly wiped out in Ontario in 1911. Quebec, of course, was almost exclusively concerned with the naval question, and the Nationalists' attack gave very little scope to anti-Americanism.[106] The local campaigns run by the Conservatives were more efficient and effective than those of the Liberals. The Conservatives were more successful in finding candidates who would appeal to the voters and in getting Conservative supporters to the polls, and, when one considers the fact that Ontario and Quebec were the only provinces in which the Liberals suffered serious losses, it becomes clear that loyalty and the anti-American cry only partially explain the Conservative victory. Given the state of Liberal organization, it would appear that the Conservative party would have been in an excellent position to wage a campaign in 1911 even if the issue of reciprocity had not come to the forefront.

The importance of party organization is also made clear by the fact that the Liberals had a reasonably good case to present to the voters. The policy of not being content when better economic conditions could be obtained was certainly appealing. In dealing with the bogey of annexation Laurier took a firm stand:

> If it be true that President Taft said that Canada is at the parting of the ways I would say to President Taft that he does no [sic] know what he is talking about. I would say to him: We are prepared to meet you in business, but if you want to talk politics, keep to your side of the line and we shall keep to ours.[107]

Premier Scott of Saskatchewan "described the loyalty argument as a 'contemptible reflection' upon the people of Saskatchewan."[108] T. M. Papineau ridiculed those who feared Americanizing influences in Canada by satirically suggesting that international marriages should be prohibited, college fraternities dissolved, American professors in universities discharged, American magazines forbidden, and Easter shopping by Canadians in New York discouraged.[109] This very meagre sample serves to show the possible effectiveness of the Liberal campaign. Unfortunately for the Liberals, these views were not widely disseminated because of the weakness of the Liberal party organization.

However, despite the recognition one must give to the role of party organization in the election of 1911, it is not justifiable to isolate party organization completely from the issues involved. The driving force behind the Conservatives undoubtedly came from the genuine concern of the party workers to "save the country." Qualitative elements such as this cannot be scientifically evaluated, but, from the emotions aroused in 1911 in comparison to other campaigns, it is apparent that the fear of Americanization and annexation was a powerful element in the fight of the Conservatives. It gave them the vigour and the desire to organize for victory. The results of defeat, they felt, would be a disaster for more than the Conservative party alone. Canada itself would be destroyed. Even within the context of party organization and party politics, then, anti-Americanism looms large in the 1911 campaign.

In summary, English-Canadian optimism concerning Canada's future, an upsurge of British imperialism in Canada, and American outspokenness and ingenuousness regarding Canada helped to create a formidable climate of anti-Americanism in 1911. Though this anti-Americanism was expressed in a wide variety of ways in the election of 1911, it was not a vicious feeling generated by fear and hatred. It was rather an almost amicable expression of Canadian independence from the United States in favour of Canadian nationalism and the imperial connection. Many people then and now would say that Canadians were wrong in defeating reciprocity in 1911. Yet even today Canadians hold many of the same fears and prejudices and the same feeling of insecurity and inferiority. Despite the fact, then, that Canada was probably in little danger in 1911, one must agree with Andrew MacPhail that: "[T]here is something noble in this attitude, and something praiseworthy in this spectacle of a whole people swept by a wave of emotion and sentiment. In all sincerity many good and loyal souls were seized by a genuine alarm that their nationality was in danger. They were terrified by the words 'continentalism,' 'annexation,' and 'fusion.' It is all to their credit."[110]

NOTES

1. L. E. Ellis, *Reciprocity: 1911* (New Haven 1939), pp. 35–9.
2. R. Wilson, "Migration Movements in Canada, 1868–1925," *Canadian Historical* Review (CHR), XIII, 1932, 164, 179.

3. O. D. Skelton, "Reciprocity: The Canadian Attitude," *Journal of Political Economy*, XIX, Feb. 1911, 77.

4. Quoted in *Canadian Annual Review* (CAR), 1911, p. 266.

5. Quoted in J. A. Munro, "English-Canadianism and the Demand for Canadian Autonomy: Ontario's Response to the Alaska Boundary Decision, 1903," *Ontario History*, LVII, 1965, 199.

6. Philip Kerr to Sir Edmund Walker, quoted in J. Eayrs, "The Round Table Movement in Canada, 1909–1920," CHR, XXXVIII, 1957, 4.

7. CAR, 1910, pp. 69, 92.

8. *Ibid.*, p. 58.

9. *Ibid.*, p. 85.

10. E. P. Johnson, "Canadian Bora," in *Flint and Feather* (Toronto 1912), p. 82.

11. CAR, 1910, pp. 88–9.

12. *Ibid.*, pp. 123, 125.

13. *Ibid.*, pp. 322–3.

14. *Ibid.*, pp. 306–9.

15. E. R. Gosnell, "British Columbia and British International Relations," *Annals of the American Academy of Political and Social Science*, XLV, Jan. 1913, 9.

16. G. E. Foster, "Canadian Autonomy and American Reciprocity: A Canadian View," *The Nineteenth Century and After*, LXIX, June 1911, 972.

17. Robert Borden's speeches are only one example of this argument. See Canada, House of Commons, *Debates*, 26 Jan. 1911, p. 2497.

18. C. W. Humphries, "Mackenzie King Looks at Two 1911 Elections," *Ontario History*, LVI, Sept. 1964, 206.

19. House of Commons, *Debates*, 14 Feb. 1911, p. 3560

20. CAR 1910, p. 369.

21. Foster, "Canadian Autonomy and American Reciprocity," p. 972.

22. House of Commons, *Debates*, 14 Feb. 1911, p. 3561

23. *Ibid.*, pp. 3556–7.

24. Foster, "Canadian Autonomy and American Reciprocity," p. 971.

25. G. E. Foster, "Reciprocity with the United States," *University Magazine*, IX, Dec. 1910, 560. Foster used another military analogy in his speech in Parliament.

26. *Ibid.*, pp. 560–1.

27. J. C. Hopkins, "Canada's Conservative Policies," *North American Review*, CXCIV, Dec. 1911, 825.

28. Quoted in CAR, 1911, p. 170.

29. *Ibid.*, p. 91.

30. Public Archives of Ontario, Sir James P. Whitney Papers, Borden to Whitney, 6 May 1910, 4 Feb. and 31 July 1911.

31. Quoted in H. Borden, ed., *Robert Laird Borden: His Memoirs* (New York 1938), p. 327.

32. Quoted in CAR, 1911, pp. 97–8; see also p. 226.

33. Whitney Papers, Whitney to Borden, 3 Aug. 1911.

34. *Ibid.*, Whitney to S. A. Baker, 23 Sept. 1911.

35. *Ibid.*, Whitney to Captain Kincaid-Smith, 19 April 1910. See Also *ibid.*, Whitney to Lord Grey, 7 Feb. 1911.

36. *Ibid.*, telegram, Whitney to Borden, 22 Sept. 1911.

37. *Ibid.*, Gwynn to Whitney, 22 Sept. 1911 and Whitney to Gwynn, 22 Sept. 1911.

38. *Ibid.*, Whitney to G. M. Vance, 23 Sept. 1911.

39. CAR, 1911, p. 103.

40. Quoted in *ibid.*, p. 102.

41. Quoted in *ibid.*, p. 156.

42. Quoted in *ibid.*, p. 248.

43. *Ibid.*

44. Quoted in C. Tupper, *Recollections of Sixty Years in Canada* (Toronto 1914), pp.306–7.

45. CAR 1910, Special Supplement, p. 91.

46. Ellis, *Reciprocity: 1911*, pp. 76, 81, 151, 155–8, 177, 178, 181–3.

47. Quoted in CAR, 1911, p. 46.

48. Quoted in *ibid.*, p. 237.

49. Quoted in *ibid.*, p. 202.

50. *Ibid.*, p. 35.

51. CAR 1910, p. 369.

52. C. Sifton, "Reciprocity," *Annals of the American Academy of Political and Social Sciences*, XLV, Jan. 1913, 25.

53. Quoted in CAR, 1911, p. 51.

54. Quoted in *ibid.*, pp. 50–1. James Bryce, the British minister in Washington, felt that although Sifton was an able man he pandered to "the interests" and had no confidence in "moral forces." See Public Archives of Canada (PAC), Grey of Howick Papers, Bryce to Grey, 6 and 10 March 1911. The material concerning Sifton during the 1911 election campaign in the John Dafoe Papers (PAC) and the Sir Clifford Sifton Papers (PAC) was disappointing.

55. Eayrs, "The Round Table Movement in Canada, 1909–1920," CHR, XXXVIII, 1957, 4.

56. G. P. de T. Glazebrook, *Sir Edmund Walker* (London 1933), p. 109.

57. Quoted in Borden, ed., *Robert Laird Borden*, p. 307. For further material on Walker and his imperial sentiments see CAR, 1910, p. 85 and 1911, pp. 48–9. Walker can be taken as typical of the Toronto Eighteen although certain differences were apparent.

58. R. D. Cuff, "The Toronto Eighteen and the Election of 1911," *Ontario History*, LVII, Dec. 1965, 170.

59. For instance, Walker and Sifton were two of the main speakers in a public meeting held in Toronto on 18 May 1910 to discuss the "Conservation of Natural Resources," and the interest of both these men in conservation played a large role in formulating their opinions on reciprocity. See Whitney Papers, circular enclosure, K. Evans to Whitney, 13 May 1910.

60. Cuff, "The Toronto Eighteen and the Election of 1911," p. 174.

61. CAR, 1911, p. 51.

62. Quoted in *ibid.*, p. 54.

63. Quoted in *ibid.*, p. 201.

64. *Ibid.*, p. 35.

65. *Ibid.*, p. 41.

66. *Ibid.*, p. 255.

67. F. P. Walton, "Divorce in Canada and the United States: A Contrast," *University Magazine*, IX, Dec. 1910, 579–96.

68. CAR, 1911, p. 258.

69. L. E. Ellis, "Canada's Rejection of Reciprocity in 1911," Canadian Historical Association, *Annual Report*, 1939, p. 108.

70. Quoted in *ibid.*, p. 104. The italic sections were the words used most frequently by the antireciprocity forces in Canada. After this Taft was more careful, and by August he was actually consulting Laurier as to the course he should pursue on a speaking tour he was about to take. See Grey Papers, Bryce to Grey, 27 Aug. 1911.

71. Quoted in CAR, 1911, p. 62. Apparently Taft was quite annoyed with Clark over this. See Grey Papers, Bryce to Grey, 18 Feb. 1911.

72. Grey Papers, Bryce to Grey, 18 Feb. 1911.

73. CAR, 1911, pp. 65, 67, 68.

74. Grey Papers, Grey to Bryce, 26 Sept. 1911.

75. This is partially explained by the fact that approximately 203,000 natives of the United States emigrated from Canada during these same years. It is also apparent that many of the American immigrants to Canada were not native Americans. Then, too, death took its toll, and children born in Canada were of course classified as native-born citizens. Data drawn from Wilson, "Migration Movements in Canada," pp. 164, 179, and *Report of the Census of 1911* (Ottawa 1913), II, 445.

76. CAR, 1910, p. 336.

77. See CAR, 1911, pp. 63, 65, 67.

78. PAC, Sir Robert Laird Borden Papers, C. J. M. Phelps to Borden, 19 Aug. 1911. John Dafoe, the editor of the Winnipeg *Free Press*, even claimed that a pro-American feeling existed in the West. See Dafoe Papers, Dafoe to Sifton, 7 April 1910. M. E. Nichols, editor of the *Winnipeg Telegram*, felt that there was not "the slightest cause for apprehension insofar as American immigration into this country is concerned." See Whitney Papers, Nichols to Whitney, 30 Nov. 1910.

79. Quoted in Cuff, "The Toronto Eighteen and the Election of 1911," p. 174.

80. Mayor Sanford Evans quoted in CAR 1911, p. 241.

81. Ellis, *Reciprocity: 1911,* p. 169.

82. J. Schull, *Laurier* (Toronto 1965), p. 530.

83. Grey did not agree with their analysis of the probable effect of reciprocity. Grey Papers, Grey to Lord Harcourt, 14 Feb. 1911. Harcourt himself was not alarmed at the prospect of reciprocity resulting in the absorption of Canada, but Joseph Chamberlain, naturally enough, was very concerned and entertained no doubt "of the final result." See *ibid.*, Harcourt to Grey, 1 April 1911 and Chamberlain to Grey, 25 March 1911.

84. House of Commons, *Debates*, 14 Feb. 1911, p. 3563.

85. Dafoe Papers, Aylesworth to Dafoe, 3 July 1911.

86. Sifton Papers, Preston to Sifton, 27 Sept. 1911.

87. *Round Table*, II, 349.

88. In the New Brunswick legislature a proreciprocity resolution was defeated 29 to 15; in Ontario a resolution against reciprocity was passed 74 to 17; in Manitoba the vote was 26 to 12 against reciprocity; in British Columbia there was only one dissentient from an antireciprocity resolution; and the Saskatchewan legislature passed a unanimous resolution in support of reciprocity. See CAR 1911, pp. 96, 101, 102, 105, 108.

89. In Dec. 1911 elections were held in Ontario and Prince Edward Island. In Ontario 83 Conservatives, 22 Liberals, and 1 Labour member were elected. In Prince Edward Island only 2 Liberals in a legislature of 30 members were returned. In 1912 British Columbia elected an all-Conservative legislature

except for 2 Socialists; New Brunswick elected only 2 Liberals of 48 members; Quebec remained in the Liberal fold, with the support of the Nationalists, and elected 64 Liberals compared to only 17 Conservatives; and Saskatchewan elected only 9 or 10 Conservatives in a house of 54. See *Round Table*, II, 348, 712–14.

90. The election results (with those of 1908 in brackets) are as follows:

SEAT DISTRIBUTION		
	Liberal	**Conservative**
Ontario	13 (37)	73 (49)
Quebec	38 (54)	27 (11)
Nova Scotia	9 (12)	9 (6)
New Brunswick	8 (11)	5 (2)
Prince Edward Island	2 (3)	2 (1)

	Liberal	**Conservative**
Manitoba	2 (2)	8 (8)
Saskatchewan	9 (9)	1 (1)
Alberta	6 (4)	1 (3)
British Columbia	0 (1)	7 (6)
Yukon	0 (1)	1 (0)

These statistics have been compiled from CAR, 1908, pp. 229–34 and 1911, pp. 260–5.

91. R. D. Cuff, "The Conservative Party Machine and the Election of 1911 in Ontario," *Ontario History*, LVII, Sept. 1965, 149. See also the recently published paper by P. D. Stevens, "Laurier, Aylesworth, and the Decline of the Liberal Party in Ontario," Canadian Historical Association, *Historical Papers*, 1968, pp. 94–113.

92. CAR 1911, p. 239.

93. *Ibid.*, pp. 243–7.

94. *Ibid.*, pp. 248–9.

95. *Ibid.*, pp. 240–1.

96. The Whitney Papers yield abundant evidence to corroborate this statement. See Whitney to Borden, 27 Jan., 15 April, 2 May, 8 May and 3 Aug. 1911; Borden to Whitney, 4 and 14 Feb., 13 April, 19 July, 31 July and 2 Aug. 1911; and T. Lewis to Whitney, 22 Sept. 1911.

97. Some difficulty arose because Whitney was not consulted about some of these plans, but Borden apologized for this slip-up and amiable relations with the Ontario premier were easily maintained. See Whitney Papers, Borden to Whitney, 13 Apr. 1911 and Whitney to Borden, 15 Apr. 1911.

98. Cuff, "The Conservative Party Machine and the Election of 1911 in Ontario," p. 156. See also CAR, 1911, pp. 224–6.

99. Cuff, "The Conservative Party Machine and the Election of 1911 in Ontario," p. 150.

100. *Ibid.*, p. 155.

101. *Ibid.*, p. 156.

102. M. A. Ormsby, *British Columbia: A History* (Vancouver 1958), pp. 349–50; and Gosnell, "British Columbia and British International Relations," p. 18.

POPULAR VOTE				
	Liberal		**Conservative**	
Ontario	207,078	(224,821)	269,930	(236,919)
Quebec	164,274	(158,393)	159,262	(129,364)
Maritimes	111,652	(103,646)	108,727	(96,846)
Prairies	124,913	(73,982)	89,997	(73,973)
British Columbia	16,350	(7,634)	25,622	(11,302)
Total (including Yukon)	625,096	(568,476)	669,557	(548,494)

103. R. Cook, *The Politics of John W. Dafoe and the Free Press* (Toronto 1963), pp. 39, 41; W. L. Morton, *Manitoba: A History* (Toronto 1957), pp. 312, 323; CAR, 1910, pp. 482–3; 1911, p. 240.

104. CAR, 1910, pp. 322, 323, 358, 411, 419; 1911, pp. 316–26.

105. O. D. Skelton, *Life and Letters of Sir Wilfrid Laurier* (New York 1922), II, 269.

106. The story of the campaign in Quebec and of the Nationalist-Conservative "unholy alliance" can be found in many sources, the best of which are R. Rumilly, *Henri Bourassa: la vie publique d'un grand canadien* (Montreal 1953). pp. 385 ff and CAR, 1911, pp. 179 ff.

107. Quoted in *ibid.*, p. 167.

108. *Ibid.*, p. 243.

109. *Ibid.*, p. 255.

110. A. MacPhail, "Why the Liberals Failed," *University Magazine*, X, Dec. 1911, 571. Lord Grey's sentiments were very similar. See Grey Papers, Grey to Bryce, 26 Sept. 1911.

A NATIONAL CRIME
Residential Schools in Canada, 1880s to 1960s

Maureen Lux
Brock University

A NATIONAL CRIME: RESIDENTIAL SCHOOLS IN CANADA, 1880s TO 1960s

● **Introduction by Maureen Lux**

▲ **Primary Documents**

■ **Secondary Documents**

● INTRODUCTION

Maureen Lux

In June 2008 Prime Minister Stephen Harper stood in the House of Commons to deliver a most unusual speech:

> Mr. Speaker, I stand before you today to offer an apology to former students of Indian residential schools. The treatment of children in Indian residential schools is a sad chapter in our history. [...]
>
> The government of Canada built an educational system in which very young children were often forcibly removed from their homes, often taken far from their communities. Many were inadequately fed, clothed and housed. All were deprived of the care and nurturing of their parents, grandparents and communities. First Nations, Inuit and Métis languages and cultural practices were prohibited in these schools. Tragically, some of these children died while attending residential schools and others never returned home. The government now recognizes that the consequences of the Indian residential schools policy were profoundly negative and that this policy has had a lasting and damaging impact on aboriginal culture, heritage and language. [...]
>
> The government of Canada sincerely apologizes and asks the forgiveness of the aboriginal peoples of this country for failing them so profoundly. We are sorry. [...][1]

The apology and the limited financial compensation for survivors went some way to acknowledge the damage done to many generations of Aboriginal people and their communities. But the formal apology, coming 128 years after the residential school system began, and more than a decade after the worst abuses were widely known, made many wonder whether government efforts were not too little, too late. The Christian churches that managed the schools on the government's behalf had already apologized a few years before, although the Catholic Church issued a Papal apology only in 2009.

The residential schools' tragic legacies—the loss of language and history, damaged lives, and corroded communities—were not unforeseen or unintended consequences, but rather were the *raison d'être* of the schools. Indeed, the foundation of the residential school system rested on what was called in the late nineteenth century "aggressive civilization," or the forced assimilation of Aboriginal people into Christian, capitalist Canadian society by actively repressing their languages, cultures, religion, and medicine. To that end, residential schools, which removed children from their parents' influence, forced them to speak English (or French in Quebec), and indoctrinated them in the Christian faith that denigrated Aboriginal spirituality, became the centrepiece of government policy. For nearly a century, from the 1880s to the closure of most of the schools in the 1960s, the moral authority of the Christian churches joined forces with the legislative and financial power of the state to create and perpetuate the school system. It is important to note that some students had a positive experience at residential schools, and not all Aboriginal children attended the schools. As for the numbers of children enrolled, the *Report of the Royal Commission on Aboriginal Peoples* notes that the records do not allow a precise accounting, but "the impact of the system was felt not only by the children who attended schools but by the families and communities that were deprived of their children and had to deal subsequently with children who returned damaged from the schools. In that sense, communities, parents and, indeed, children later born to former students of the residential schools were all 'enrolled'.[2] At its height in 1931 there were 80 schools in the Northwest Territories and every province except Prince Edward Island, New Brunswick, and Newfoundland. The question must be, why? How did Christian stewardship and state responsibility become so perverted as to create such a tragic end?

In 1879 Canadian Prime Minister John A. Macdonald sent Nicholas Flood Davin, failed Conservative candidate and journalist, to investigate the American Indian Industrial schools and to report on the advisability of establishing such schools in Canada. Davin's confidential 1879 *Report on Industrial Schools for Indians and Half-Breeds* (excerpted here) recommended the establishment of Industrial schools. Davin's consistent and objectionable (to our twenty-first-century ears) references to "race" sheds some light on Victorian perceptions of Aboriginal peoples and the notions of racial superiority that influenced the establishment of the residential school system. As Davin noted, "[…] if anything is to be done with the Indian, we must catch him very young. The children must be kept constantly with the circle of civilized conditions."

As historian John Milloy explains in "The Tuition of Thomas Moore," the state policy of assimilation that attempted to make Aboriginal peoples strangers in their own lands found a most accommodating partner in the Christian churches. But the school system, always underfunded, increasingly forced the churches to economize on food and clothing, while the children spent less time in the classroom and more time working in the fields, barns, kitchens, and laundries to maintain the schools. Despite ample evidence that the "circle of civilized conditions" was creating appalling conditions, those responsible, the churches and government, each blamed the other.

In "The Charge of Manslaughter: Disease and Death, 1879–1946," Milloy examines the dreadful conditions in some of the schools. Rising concerns over costs and the alarming state of the children's health led government and the churches to lower their expectations. The original distinction between Industrial schools (intended to teach trades to older students) and the less expensive boarding schools (for younger students) had become negligible, and after 1923 all were simply known as residential schools.

One of those intimate with the dangerous condition of the schools and the subsequent deterioration in the children's health was the department of Indian Affairs medical officer, Dr Peter Bryce. In the excerpt of his 1922 pamphlet *The Story of a National Crime: Being an Appeal for Justice to the Indians of Canada,* Bryce recounts how the department, especially Departmental Accountant and later Deputy Minister Duncan Campbell Scott, actively suppressed his 1907 report on the conditions of the schools, and ignored his recommendations to ameliorate the children's misery. It is important to note, however, that Bryce's condemnation of the government was motivated not only by the deplorable state of health, but also by his own resentment at being passed over in 1919 for a position in the new federal Department of Health.

School children, their parents, and communities were not passive victims of the assimilationist policies pursued by state and church in the residential schools. Granted, the power relations were hardly equal and the Indian department had considerable resources to force children into school and keep them there. Amendments to the *Indian Act* in 1894 and again in 1920 legislated compulsory attendance at school; police charged parents who refused to comply, and rounded up and returned children who made a run for home. Besides sheer compulsion, there were also the concerted efforts of school principals, Indian Agents, and missionaries to coerce parents and communities to surrender their children. Nevertheless, children and their parents accepted what they could not change, but resisted when and where they could. As historian J.R. Miller explains in "You Ain't My Boss," children and their communities resisted their maltreatment, but their voices were rarely heard beyond the local school. But perhaps ironically, when concerted Aboriginal political action emerged as a national force in the 1960s it was often residential school graduates who were the most effective leaders. The schools themselves created those who mounted the most effective forms of resistance.

Even after the end of the church–state educational relationship in 1969 and the closure of most schools, the story of neglect and abuse was still not widely known beyond the Aboriginal communities that continued to struggle with its legacy. As John Milloy explains, what finally broke the silence was "[...] ironically, the deepest secret of all—the pervasive sexual abuse of the children."[3] In the 1980s, harrowing reports of sexual abuse of non-Aboriginal children at orphanages in Newfoundland and Ontario prompted a public dialogue that eventually listened to Aboriginal revelations of similar abuse. In British Columbia, police uncovered widespread sexual abuse by priests at Williams Lake school; in 1990, Phil Fontaine, chief of the Assembly of Manitoba Chiefs, spoke out about his mistreatment at the hands of priests at Fort Alexander school in Manitoba: "I think what happened to me happened to a lot of people. It wasn't just sexual abuse, it was physical and psychological abuse. It was a violation."[4] Revelations of abuse continued and lawsuits mounted, but it was the aftermath of the failed Meech Lake Accord and the clash between police and Mohawks at Kanestake (Oka) that prompted the establishment of the Royal Commission on Aboriginal Peoples in 1992. With a mandate to explore the relationship among Aboriginal peoples, the government, and Canadian society, and to propose solutions to the problems that plagued the relationship, the Royal Commission reported in 1996. One of its priorities was to investigate the history of the residential schools, and the Commission recommended a public inquiry to allow survivors to tell their stories and begin the healing process. Further, the Commission recommended a compensation package for victims and a government apology. After much prompting and pressure by Aboriginal and non-Aboriginal groups, the apology came 12 years later, while the public inquiry, the Truth and Reconciliation Commission, has yet to begin its work. For very many former students all of this comes far too late, but the opportunity for public debate of this sad history may go some way to honour their memory.

NOTES

1. Prime Minister Stephen Harper's statement of apology, 11 June 2008.
2. Royal Commission on Aboriginal Peoples, *Looking Forward, Looking Back,* Vol. 1, Part 2, Chapter 10, "Residential Schools," n. 15.
3. John Milloy, *A National Crime: The Canadian Government and the Residential School System,* 1879–1986 (Winnipeg: University of Manitoba Press, 1999), 298.
4. *The Globe and Mail,* 31 October 1990, quoted in J.R. Miller, Shingwauk's *Vision: A History of Native Residential Schools* (Toronto: University of Toronto Press, 1996), 328.

QUESTIONS

1. Why was the nineteenth-century policy of "aggressive civilization" actively pursued into the late twentieth century?
2. How was it that the worst abuses of the residential schools did not become the subject of public debate for more than a century? Has there been a public debate?
3. Prime Minister Harper's apology to Aboriginal people is similar to the government's 1988 apology to Japanese Canadians for their internment during World War II. Why

did it take another two decades for an apology to Aboriginal Canadians? Do government apologies create the impression that past wrongs have somehow been corrected or forgiven?

4. What does Davin's 1879 Report tell us about late nineteenth century views of Aboriginal people? What does it say about their views on education? Why were there no plans to train Aboriginal teachers for the schools?

5. Peter Bryce, a physician and powerful public health expert, was eventually drummed out of government service for his public criticisms of the residential school system. What impact would criticisms by the children and their parents have had on the schools?

FURTHER READINGS

Barman, J., Y. Hebert, and D. McCaskill, eds., *Indian Education in Canada, Volume One: The Legacy,* (Vancouver: University of British Columbia Press, 1986).

Dyck, Noel, *Differing Visions: Administering Indian Residential Schooling in Prince Albert, 1867–1967,* (Halifax: Fernwood Publishing, 1997).

Haig-Brown, Celia, *Resistance and Renewal: Surviving the Indian Residential School,* (Vancouver: Tillacum Library, 1988).

Miller, J.R., *Shingwauk's Vision: A History of Native Residential Schools,* (Toronto: University of Toronto Press, 1996).

Milloy, John, *A National Crime: The Canadian Government and the Residential School System, 1879–1986,* (Winnipeg: University of Manitoba Press, 1999).

Royal Commission on Aboriginal Peoples, *Looking Forward, Looking Back,* Volume 1, Part 2, Chapter 10, "Residential Schools," accessed from http://www.collectionscanada.gc.ca.

The following are memoirs by former students or based on interviews with students. See, for example, Celia Haig-Brown, *Resistance and Renewal: Surviving the Indian Residential School* (Vancouver: Tillacum Library, 1988); Isabelle Knockwood with Gillian Thomas, *Out of the Depths, The Experiences of Mi'kmaq Children at the Indian Residential School at Shubenacadie, Nova Scotia* (Lokeport, Nova Scotia: Roseway Publishing, 1992); Basil H. Johnston, *Indian School Days* (Toronto: Key Porter Books Limited, 1988); G. Manuel and M. Posluns, *The Fourth World* (Don Mills: Collier-Macmillan Canada Ltd., 1974); Linda Jaine, ed., *Residential Schools: The Stolen Years* (Saskatoon: University [of Saskatchewan] Extension Press, 1993); Geoffrey York, *The Dispossessed: Life and Death in Native Canada* (Toronto: Lester & Orpen Dennys, 1989); Assembly of First Nations, *Breaking the Silence, An Interpretive Study of Residential School Impact and Healing as Illustrated by the Stories of First Nations Individuals* (Ottawa: First Nations Health Commission, 1994).

▲ Document 1: Report on Industrial Schools for Indians and Half-Breeds

Nicholas Flood Davin

Ottawa, 14th March, 1879
To the Right Honourable
The Minister of the Interior

SIR,—I have the honour to submit the following report on the working of Industrial Schools for the education of Indians and mixed-bloods in the United States, and on the advisability of establishing similar institutions in the North-West Territories of the Dominion.

In accordance with your directions of the twenty-eighth of January, I went to Washington. His Excellency Sir Edward Thornton, the Honourable Carl Schurtz, Secretary of the Interior, and the Honourable E. A. Hayt, the Commissioner of Indian Affairs, secured for me every facility for becoming acquainted with the establishment, cost and practical value of industrial schools among the Indian populations of the United States.

The industrial school is the principal feature of the policy known as that of "aggressive civilization." This policy was inaugurated by President Grant in 1869. But, as will be seen, the utility of industrial schools had long ere that time been amply tested. [...] After eight years' experience of the partial carrying out of these recommendations, the Board pressed for a still more thorough policy; they urged, among other things, that titles to land should be inalienable from the family of the holder for at least three generations. From 1869 vigorous efforts in an educational direction were put forward. But it was found that the day school did not work, because the influence of the wigwam was stronger than the influence of the school. Industrial Boarding Schools were therefore established, and these are now numerous and will soon be universal. [...]

The Indian character, about which some persons find such a mystery, is not difficult to understand. The Indian is sometimes spoken of as a child, but he is very far from being a child. The race is in its childhood. As far as the childhood analogy is applicable, what it suggests is a policy that shall look patiently for fruit, not after five or ten years, but after a generation or two. [...]

[...]

The Indian is a man with conditions of his own, which make civilization a puzzle of despair. He has the suspicion, distrust, fault-finding tendency, the insincerity and flattery, produced in all subject races. He is crafty, but conscious how weak his craft is when opposed to the superior cunning of the white man. [...]

The first and greatest stone in the foundation of the quasi-civilization of the Indians, wherever seen, was laid by missionaries, men who had a supreme object and who did not count their lives dear unto them. Schools are scattered over the whole continent, wherever Indians exist, monuments of religious zeal and heroic self-sacrifice. These schools should be utilized as much as possible, both on grounds of efficiency and economy. The missionaries' experience is only surpassed by their patient heroism, and their testimony, like that of the school teachers, like that of the authorities at Washington is, that if anything is to be done with the Indian, we must catch him very young. The children must be kept constantly within the circle of civilized conditions. [...] The plan now is to take young children, give

Source: Nicholas Flood Davin, *Report on Industrial Schools for Indians and Half-Breeds* (14 March 1879), Library and Archives Canada, MG26A, Sir John A. Macdonald Papers, Vol. 91, 35428-45.

them the care of a mother, and have them constantly in hand. Such care must be *pari passu* with religious training.

[…]

The recommendations I venture to submit are as follows:—

(1.) Wherever the missionaries have schools, those schools should be utilized by the Government, if possible; that is to say, a contract should be made with the religious body controlling the school to board and educate and train industrially a certain number of pupils. […]

(2.) Not more than four industrial boarding schools ought to be established at first. […]

(3.) An industrial boarding school should be established somewhere in the fork of the North and South Saskatchewan, near Prince Albert, in connection with the Episcopalian Church. The land is wonderfully fertile. There are a good many Indians in the neighbourhood. There are Bands of Indians near Carlton and near Dutch Lake. There is plenty of fish and timber.

(4.) In no place could an industrial boarding school in connection with the Methodist body be more properly placed than near Old Bow Fort. The Blackfeet and Stoneys, wild but noble types of Indians, would thus be reached. […]

(5.) At Qu'Appelle it might well be thought we should find an appropriate site for an industrial boarding school to be conducted by Roman Catholics.[…]

(6.) An industrial boarding school, in connection with the Presbyterian Church, should be established on Riding Mountain. […]

The importance of denominational schools at the outset for the Indians must be obvious. One of the earliest things an attempt to civilize them does, is to take away their simple Indian mythology, the central idea of which, to wit, a perfect spirit, can hardly be improved on. The Indians have their own ideas of right and wrong, of "good" Indians and "bad" Indians, and to disturb this faith, without supplying a better, would be a curious process to enlist the sanction of civilized races whose whole civilization, like all the civilizations with which we are acquainted, is based on religion. […]

(7.) Some distinction should be made between the treatment of parents who send their children regularly to the day-school, and of those who are either careless whether their children go to school or not, or who are wholly opposed to their children attending school, as some are. To the first, an additional ration of tea and sugar might be given.

(8.) Where practicable, some inducement of a special nature should be held out to the child.

(9.) As Bands become more amenable to the restraints of civilization education should be made compulsory.

(10.) The character of the teacher, morally and intellectually, is a matter of vital importance. If he is morally weak, whatever his intellectual qualifications may be, he is worse than no teacher at all. If he is poorly instructed or feeble in brain, he only enacts every day an elaborate farce. […]

(11.) In order to secure that the education given would be efficient, there ought to be competent inspection. […]

(12.) Where boys or girls, whether Indians or half-breed, show special aptitudes or exceptional general quickness, special advantages should be offered them, and they should be trained to become teachers and clerks in connection with the Department, as well as fitted to launch out on commercial and professional careers.

(13.) The salary of a teacher must be such as will induce good men to offer themselves. The teacher should be paid according to his qualifications. [...]

I have the honour to be,
Sir,
Your obedient servant,
Nicholas Flood Davin.

▲ Document 2: Anglican Indian School, Siksika (Blackfoot) Reserve

● Anglican Indian School, Siksika (Blackfoot) Reserve, Alberta, ca. 1901–1910. Who might have taken this photograph? Why?

Source: Glenbow Museum, NC-5-1.

▲ Document 3: Students Filling Mattresses with Straw, Kanai (Blood) Anglican School

● Students filling mattresses with straw, Kanai (Blood) Anglican school, ca. 1916. What does this tell you about the kinds of work schoolchildren did? What does it tell you about the living conditions at the school?

Source: Glenbow Museum, NA-1400-31.

▲ Document 4: The Story of a National Crime: Being an Appeal for Justice to the Indians of Canada

Dr. Peter Henderson Bryce, M.A., M.D.

The Story of a National Crime Being a Record of the Health Conditions of the Indians of Canada from 1904 to 1921

I. By Order in Council dated Jan. 22nd, 1904, the writer was appointed Medical Inspector to the Department of the Interior and of Indian Affairs, and was entrusted with the health interests of the Indians of Canada. [...]

For the first months after the writer's appointment he was much engaged in organizing the medical inspection of immigrants at the sea ports; but he early began the systematic collection of health statistics of the several hundred Indian Bands scattered over Canada. For each year up to 1914 he wrote an annual report on the health of the Indians, published in the Departmental report, and on instructions from the minister made in 1907 a special inspection of thirty-five Indian schools in the three prairie provinces. This report was published separately; but the recommendations contained in the report were never published and the public knows nothing of them. It contained a brief history of the origin of the Indian Schools, of the sanitary condition of the schools and statistics of the health of the pupils, during the 15 years of their existence. Regarding the health of the pupils, the report states that 24 per cent of all the pupils which had been in the schools were known to be dead, while of one school on the File Hills reserve, which gave a complete return to date, 75 per cent. were dead at the end of the 16 years since the school opened.

Recommendations of school report 1907

Briefly the recommendations urged, (1) Greater school facilities, since only 30 per cent. of the children of school age were in attendance; (2) That boarding schools with farms attached be established near the home reserves of the pupils; (3) That the government undertake the complete maintenance and control of the schools, since it had promised by treaty to insure such; and further it was recommended that as the Indians grow in wealth and intelligence they should pay at least part of the cost from their own funds; (4) That the school studies be those of the curricula of the several Provinces in which the schools are situated, since it was assumed that as the bands would soon become enfranchised and become citizens of the Province they would enter into the common life and duties of a Canadian community; (5) That in view of the historical and sentimental relations between the Indian schools and the Christian churches the report recommended that the Department provide for the management of the schools, through a Board of Trustees, one appointed from each church and approved by the minister of the Department. Such a board would have its secretary in the Department but would hold regular meetings, establish qualifications for teachers, and oversee the appointments as well as the control of the schools; (6) That Continuation schools be arranged for on the school farms and that instruction methods similar to those on the File Hills farm colony be developed; (7) That the health interests of the pupils be guarded by a proper medical inspection and that the local physicians be encouraged through the provision at each school of fresh air methods in the care and treatment of cases of tuberculosis.

Source: Dr. Peter Henderson Bryce, M.A., M.D., *The Story of a National Crime: Being an Appeal for Justice to the Indians of Canada.* Ottawa: James Hope and Sons, 1922.

II. The annual medical reports from year to year made reference to the unsatisfactory health of the pupils, while different local medical officers urged greater action in view of the results of their experience from year to year. As the result of one such report the Minister instructed the writer in 1909 to investigate the health of the children in the schools of the Calgary district in a letter containing the following:—

> "As it is necessary that these residential schools should be filled with a healthy class of pupils in order that the expenditure on Indian education may not be rendered entirely nugatory, it seems desirable that you should go over the same ground as Dr. Lafferty and check his inspection."

Recommendations based upon examination of 243 school children

These instructions were encouraging and the writer gladly undertook the work of examining with Dr. J.D. Lafferty the 243 children of 8 schools in Alberta, with the following results:—

> (a) Tuberculosis was present equally in children at every age; (b) In no instance was a child awaiting admission to school found free from tuberculosis; hence it was plain that infection was got in the home primarily; (c) The disease showed an excessive mortality in the pupils between five and ten years of age; (d) The 10,000 children of school age demanded the same attention as the thousand children coming up each year and entering the schools annually.

Recommendations, made in this report, on much the same lines as those made in the report of 1907, followed the examination of the 243 children; but owing to the active opposition of Mr. D. C. Scott, and his advice to the then Deputy Minister, no action was taken by the Department to give effect to the recommendations made. [...]

The writer had done no regular inspection work since Mr. D. C. Scott was made Deputy minister in 1913, but had in each year up to 1914 prepared his medical report, printed in the annual report of the Department. [...]

Thus we find a sum of only $10,000 has been annually placed in the estimates to control tuberculosis amongst 105,000 Indians scattered over Canada in over 300 bands, while the City of Ottawa, with about the same population and having three general hospitals spent thereon $342,860.54 in 1919 of which $33,364.70 is devoted to tuberculosis patients alone. The many difficulties of our problem amongst the Indians have been frequently pointed out, but the means to cope with these have also been made plain. [...]

The degree and extent of this criminal disregard for the treaty pledges to guard the welfare of the Indian wards of the nation may be gauged from the facts once more brought out at the meeting of the National Tuberculosis Association at its annual meeting held in Ottawa on March 17th, 1922. The superintendent of the Qu'Appelle Sanatorium, Sask., gave there the results of a special study of 1575 children of school age in which advantage was taken of the most modern scientific methods. Of these 175 were Indian children, and it is very remarkable that the fact given that some 93 per cent. of these showed evidence of tuberculous infection coincides completely with the work done by Dr. Lafferty and the writer in the Alberta Indian schools in 1909.

It is indeed pitiable that during the thirteen years since then this trail of disease and death has gone on almost unchecked by any serious efforts on the part of the Department of Indian Affairs, placed by the B. N. A. Act especially in charge of our Indian population, and that a Provincial Tuberculosis Commission now considers it to be its duty to publish the facts regarding these children living within its own Province.

▲ Document 5: School Boys from Tsuu T'ina (Sarcee) Reserve, 1920

● School Boys from Tsuu T'ina (Sarcee) Reserve, 1920; note the bandages on the boys' heads, likely covering 'scrofula' sores or tuberculosis of lymph nodes of the neck. One-quarter of the boys have their heads bandaged. If these are the 'healthy' boys, what might this say about the other children in the school?

Source: Glenbow Museum, NA-192-13.

▲ Document 6: Schoolchildren at the United Church School on the Stoney Reserve, Morley, Alberta, ca. 1950

● Class in session at the Residential School on the Stoney Reserve, Morley, Alberta. Note the pictures of the Royal Family on the wall. Why would all the children be dressed in their coats?

Source: Glenbow Museum, NA-5719-4.

▲ Document 7: Bed-time Prayers at Girls' Dormitory, Old Sun School, Siksika (Blackfoot) Reserve

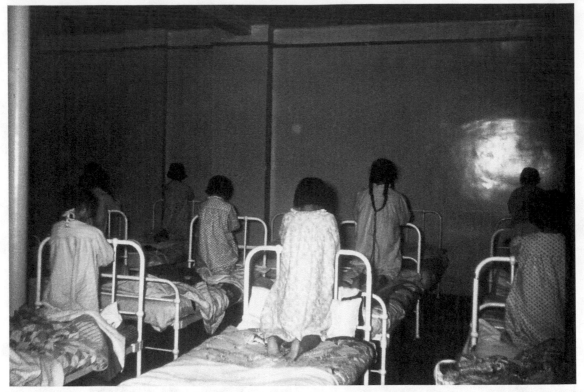

● Bed-time prayers at the girls' dormitory, Old Sun School, Siksika (Blackfoot) Reserve, ca. 1955. Note the ordered beds in the crowded dormitory. Who might have taken this photo? Why?

Source: Glenbow Museum, NA-4817-22.

■ Article 1: The Tuition of Thomas Moore

John Milloy

In its *Annual Report* of 1904, the Department of Indian Affairs published the photographs of the young Thomas Moore of the Regina Industrial School, "before and after tuition." The images are a cogent expression of what federal policy had been since Confederation and what it would remain for many decades. It was a policy of assimilation, a policy designed to move Aboriginal communities from their "savage" state to that of "civilization" and thus to make in Canada but one community—a non-Aboriginal one.[1]

At the core of the policy was education. It was, according to Deputy Superintendent Duncan Campbell Scott, who steered the administration of Indian Affairs from 1913 to 1932, "by far the most important of the many subdivisions of the most complicated Indian problem."[2] In the education of the young lay the most potent power to effect cultural change—a power to be channelled through schools and, in particular, through residential schools. Education would, Frank Oliver, the Minister of Indian Affairs, declared in 1908, "elevate the Indian from his condition of savagery" and make "him a self-supporting member of the State, and eventually a citizen in good standing."[3]

The pictures are, then, both images of what became in this period the primary object of that policy: the Aboriginal child, and an analogy of the relationship between the two cultures—Aboriginal and White—as it had been in the past and as it was to be in the future. There, in the photograph on the left, is the young Thomas posed against a fur robe, in his beaded dress, his hair in long braids, clutching a gun. Displayed for the viewer are the symbols of the past—of Aboriginal costume and culture, of hunting, of the disorder and violence of warfare and of the cross-cultural partnerships of the fur trade and of the military alliances that had dominated life in Canada since the late sixteenth century.

Those partnerships, anchored in Aboriginal knowledge and skills, had enabled the newcomers to find their way, to survive, and to prosper. But they were now merely historic; they were not to be any part of the future as Canadians pictured it at the founding of their new nation in 1867. That future was one of settlement, agriculture, manufacturing, lawfulness, and Christianity. In the view of politicians and civil servants in Ottawa whose gaze was fixed upon the horizon of national development, Aboriginal knowledge and skills were neither necessary nor desirable in a land that was to be dominated by European industry and, therefore, by Europeans and their culture.

That future was inscribed in the photograph on the right. Thomas, with his hair carefully barbered, in his plain, humble suit, stands confidently, hand on hip, in a new context. Here he is framed by the horizontal and vertical lines of wall and pedestal—the geometry of social and economic order; of place and class, and of private property the foundation of industriousness, the cardinal virtue of late-Victorian culture. But most telling of all, perhaps, is the potted plant. Elevated above him, it is the symbol of civilized life, of agriculture. Like Thomas, the plant is cultivated nature no longer wild. Like it, Thomas has been, the Department suggests, reduced to civility in the time he has lived within the confines of the Regina Industrial School.

The assumptions that underlay the pictures also informed the designs of social reformers in Canada and abroad, inside the Indian Department and out. Thomas and his classmates were to be assimilated; they were to become functioning members of Canadian society. Marching out from schools, they would be the vanguard of a magnificent metamorphosis: the savages were to be made civilized. For Victorians, it was an empire-wide task of heroic proportions and divine ordination encompassing the Maori, the Aborigine, the Hottentot, and many other indigenous peoples. For Canadians, it was, at the level of rhetoric at least, a national duty—a "sacred trust with which Providence has invested the country in the charge of and care for the aborigines committed to it."[4] In 1880, Alexander Morris, one of the primary government negotiators of the recently concluded western treaties, looked back upon those agreements and then forward, praying: "Let us have Christianity and civilization among the Indian tribes; let us have a

Source: John S. Milloy, *A National Crime: The Canadian Government and the Residential School System, 1879–1986*. Winnipeg: University of Manitoba Press, 1999, pp. 3–9. Reprinted with permission.

● Thomas Moore, as he appeared when admitted to the Regina Indian Industrial School (Saskatchewan Archives Board, R-82239 [1]). [Source: Saskatchewan Archives Board R-A8223-1]

● Thomas Moore, after tuition at the Regina Indian Industrial School (Saskatchewan Archives Board, R-82239 [2]). [Source: Saskatchewan Archives Board R-A8223-1]

wise and paternal Government…doing its utmost to help and elevate the Indian population,…and Canada will be enabled to feel, that in a truly patriotic spirit our country has done its duty by the red men."[5]

In Canada's first century, that "truly patriotic spirit" would be evident in the many individuals who devoted their "human capabilities to the good of the Indians of this country." In the case of Father Lacombe, Oblate missionary to the Blackfoot, for example, the "poor redman's redemption physically and morally" was "the dream of my days and nights."[6] According to Canada's first Prime Minister, Sir John A. Macdonald, the nation, too, dreamed of discharging its benevolent duty. A national goal, he informed Parliament, was "to do away with the tribal system and assimilate the Indian people in all respects with the inhabitants of the Dominion, as speedily as they are fit to change."[7] With the assistance of church and state, wandering hunters would take up a settled life, agriculture, useful trades and, of course, the Christian religion.

Assimilation became, during Macdonald's first term, official policy. It was Canada's response to its "sacred trust" made even more alluring by the fact that supposedly selfless duty was to have its reward. The Deputy Superintendent General of Indian Affairs, L. Vankoughnet, assured Macdonald in 1887 that Indian expenditures "would be a good investment" for, in due course, Aboriginal people, "instead of being supported from the revenue of the country,…would contribute largely to the same."

Education, as Scott indicated, was the most critical element of this assimilative strategy. Vankoughnet, in his memo of 1887 to the prime minister, was doing no more than reflecting the common wisdom of the day when he wrote:

Give me the children and you may have the parents, or words to that effect, were uttered by a zealous divine in his anxiety to add to the number of whom his Church called her children. And the principle laid down by that astute reasoner is an excellent one on which to act in working out that most difficult problem—the intellectual emancipation of the Indian, and its natural sequel, his elevation to a status equal to that of his white brother. This can only be done through education....Only by a persistent continuance in a thoroughly systematic course of educating (using the word in its fullest and most practical sense) the children, will the final hoped and long striven for result be attained.[8]

"That most difficult problem" was to be solved not only through "persistent" tuition but also, more specifically, by residential school education, which, initially, took two forms: "boarding" schools, which were situated on or near a reserve, which were of moderate size and which taught reading, writing and arithmetic, agriculture, and the simple manual skills required by farmers and their wives; and "industrial" schools, such as Thomas's Regina Industrial School, which were large, centrally located, urban-associated trade schools and which also provided a plain English education. "It would be highly desirable, if it were practicable," the Department wrote in its *Annual Report* of 1890 "to obtain entire possession of all Indian children after they attain to the age of seven or eight years, and keep them at schools...until they have had a thorough course of instruction." The Department was confident that if such a course were adopted "the solution of the problem designated 'the Indian question' would probably be effected sooner than it is under the present system" of day schools.

By 1890, the government had been committed for just over a decade to the development of a system of residential schools of "the industrial type."[9] That commitment had sprung from the recommendations of the now-famous *Davin Report* of 1879. Nicholas Flood Davin, a journalist and a defeated Tory candidate, had been rewarded for his electoral effort by Macdonald with a commission to "report on the working of Industrial Schools...in the United States and on the advisability of establishing similar institutions in the North-West Territories of the Dominion." Senior American officials who Davin visited, Carl Schurtz, the Secretary of the Interior, and E.A. Hayt, the Commissioner of Indian Affairs, evinced the greatest confidence in the efficacy of the industrial school, which was, Davin was informed, "the principal feature of the policy known as that of 'aggressive civilization,'" their policy of assimilation. Day schools had proven a failure "because the influence of the wigwam was stronger than the influence of the school." Indeed, support for this thesis came, he claimed, from Cherokee leaders he met in Washington. They described the "happy results of Industrial Schools" and convinced him "that the chief thing to attend to in dealing with the less civilized or wholly barbarous tribes, was to separate the children from the parents."

Next on Davin's agenda was a trip to the school at the White Earth Agency in Minnesota. He was obviously impressed. The school was 'well attended and the answering of the children creditable....The dormitory was plainly but comfortably furnished, and the children...were evidently well fed." The whole reserve had an air of progressive development, traceable, in the opinion of the agent, to the school. Subsequent meetings in Winnipeg with "the leading men, clerical and lay, who could speak with authority on the subject" must have confirmed his American observations, for Davin's report gave unqualified support to the "application of the principle of industrial boarding schools." He submitted, as well, a detailed plan for beginning such a school system in the west that he probably worked out with those authorities—Bishop Taché, Father Lacombe, the Honourable James McKay and others.[10]

While the *Davin Report* may properly be credited with moving the Macdonald government to inaugurate industrial schools in the 1880s, it is far from being, as it is often characterized,[11] the genesis of the residential school system in Canada. Indeed, when Davin submitted his report, there were already in existence in Ontario four residential schools, then called manual labour schools—the Mohawk Institute, and the Wikwemikong, Mount Elgin, and Shingwauk schools; and a number of boarding schools were being planned by missionaries in the west.

Furthermore, the report does not answer the most important questions about the beginning and intended character of the residential school system.

Why did the federal government adopt a policy of assimilation? What was the relationship between that policy, its ideology and structures, and education, particularly residential schools? Not only are the answers to such central questions not in the *Davin Report*, but neither are they found in any single report in the early years after Confederation. Indeed, to discover the roots of the Canadian residential school system, we must make recourse to the history of the pre-Confederation period of Imperial control of Indian affairs. It was in that earlier era that the assimilative policy took shape with the design of programs for the "civilization" of the Indian population of Upper Canada. The policy was then given a final legislative form, in the first decade after Confederation, with the determination of the constitutional position of Indian First Nations expressed in two early Indian acts: 1869 and 1876.

The Imperial policy heritage of the 1830s, 1840s, and 1850s, supplemented by federal legislation and programming in the first decade of Confederation, was both the context and the rationale for the development of residential schools, which in turn constituted part of the most extensive and persistent colonial system—one that marginalized Aboriginal communities within its constitutional, legislative, and regulatory structure, stripped them of the power of self-government, and denied them any degree of self-determination. As a consequence, Aboriginal people became, in the course of Canada's first century, wards of the Department of Indian Affairs and increasingly the objects of social welfare, police, and justice agencies.

The result of the federal government's colonization of First Nations was sorrowful, indeed. When, in 1946, a joint committee of the House of Commons and Senate met "to examine and consider the Indian Act"[12] and the record of federal administration of Indian affairs, the members found not only a policy that had remained largely unchanged since the Confederation era—"an unwritten heritage of the past"[13]—but also one that had clearly fallen far short of its goal and showed no sign of imminent success. By every indicator—health, employment, income, education, housing—Aboriginal people, far from being assimilated, were still separate and second-class citizens. What unfolded before those parliamentarians was a complex social, economic, and political tapestry with a single unifying thread—growing Aboriginal poverty.

One of the darkest hues in that tapestry came from the fact that the main thrust of the colonial system's assimilative strategy had concentrated on the young, on the thousands of Thomas Moores, boys and girls, Indian, Métis, and Inuit, across the land. They were the vulnerable future of communities and of Aboriginal culture, and they had been removed from their homes and placed in the care of strangers, many of whom were hostile to their culture, beliefs, and language. For the sake of civilization, in the discharge of a national duty, they were placed in the residential schools. For those children and their communities and, indeed, for all Canadians, the consequence of those schools, of Thomas Moore's tuition, has been truly tragic.

Notes

1. For a review of Canadian policy see: J.L. Tobias, "Protection, Civilization, Assimilation: An Outline History of Canada's Indian Policy," in *As Long as the Sun Shines and Water Flows*, edited by I. Getty and A.S. Lussier (Vancouver: University of British Columbia Press, 1983); J.R. Miller, *Skyscrapers Hide the Heavens: A History of Indian/White Relations in Canada* (Toronto: University of Toronto Press, 1989); and O. Dickason, *Canada's First Nations: A History of Founding Peoples from Earliest Times* (Toronto: McClelland and Stewart, 1992).

2. *Annual Report of the Department of Indian Affairs* [hereinafter referred to as the Annual Report] 1911, 273.

3. N.A.C. RG 10, Vol. 6039, File 160-1, MR C 8152, F. Oliver to Joint Church Delegation.

4. *Annual Report* 1891, x.

5. A. Morris, *The Treaties of Canada with the Indians of Manitoba and the North-West Territories* (Toronto: Belfords, Clarke and Col. 1880), 278.

6. N.A.C. MG 27, I C4, E. Dewdney Papers, A. Lacombe to E. Dewdney, 25 November 1889, 2, 189–192.

7. As quoted in M. Montgomery, "The Six Nations and the Macdonald Franchise," *Ontario History* 57 (March 1965): 13.

8. INAC File 1/25-1. Vol. 15, L. Vankoughnet to Sir John A. Macdonald, 26 August 1887.

9. *Annual Report* 1890, xii.

10. *The Davin Report*, 1–17.

11. See for example: J. Barman, Y. Hébert, and D. McCaskill, "The Legacy of the Past: An Overview," in *Indian Education in Canada*, edited by J.

Barman, Y. Hébert, and D. McCaskill, vol. 1: *The Legacy* (Vancouver: University of British Columbia Press, 1986), 6.

12. J. Leslie and R. Macguire, eds., *The Historical Development of the Indian Act* (Ottawa: Depart-

ment of Indian and Northern Affairs Canada, 1979), 133.

13. J. Taylor, *Canadian Indian Policy during the Inter-War Years, 1919–1939* (Ottawa: Indian and Northern Affairs Canada, 1983), 4.

Article 2: The Charge of Manslaughter: Disease and Death, 1879–1946

John Milloy

The provisions of the 1911 contract and the discussions during the negotiating sessions make it clear that there was a crisis in conditions, sanitation, and health in the schools. Neither the Department nor the churches could have pretended otherwise. Dr. P. Bryce's first report was published in 1907 just as the discussions were about to get under way, and another report, by F.H. Paget, a Departmental accountant, which was highly critical of the condition of school buildings, came to hand in 1908. The Honourable S.H. Blake, a lawyer conducting a review of Anglican mission work, who was an influential force in the negotiations, characterized the situation in the schools for the Minister, Frank Oliver, in the most blunt fashion: "The appalling number of deaths among the younger children appeals loudly to the guardians of our Indians. In doing nothing to obviate the preventable causes of death, brings the Department within unpleasant nearness to the charge of manslaughter."[1]

The residential school system began its drift to that "unpleasant nearness" right from its inception. The "appalling number of deaths among the younger children" was the result of removing children, as Blake explained to the minister, from a healthy "out of door life" to the confines of badly constructed schools made worse over time by neglectful and inadequately funded maintenance programs. Perhaps even more pertinent, careless administration of health regulations, a lack of adequate medical services and

Source: John S. Milloy, *A National Crime: The Canadian Government and the Residential School System, 1879–1986*. Winnipeg: University of Manitoba Press, 1999, pp. 77–107. Reprinted with permission.

the effect on children of the harsh and alien routines of education added their deadly weight.

In those hundreds or thousands of deaths (extant records do not allow an accurate count)[2] the churches, Department and government shared complicity.[3] The disease and deaths and the cause of them were known to all. Indian Agent MacArthur commented, in 1910, in view of the situation at Duck Lake, where he estimated that, in the past, nearly fifty percent of the children sent to the school died: "[No one] responsible can get beyond the fact that those children catch the disease while at school" confined for months on end "in a building whose every seam and crevice is, doubtless, burdened with Tuberculosis Baccilli."[4] To those entering the circle of civilization for the first time, the all-too-common conditions could be a shock. For the new Principal of Red Deer school, Dr. J.P. Rice, arriving in 1903 from his comfortable Toronto parish, "the sight of the ragged ill-kempt and sickly looking children was sufficient to make me sick at heart." Enrollment was down due to deaths, the removal of children by their parents, and because the "sanitary conditions of the buildings are exceedingly bad."[5]

It all began with the buildings. Those many schools that were opened by the churches in advance of government grants were routinely "erected on very primitive plans"[6] by amateurs without the guidance of professional architects.[7] They often received grants sight unseen, without any Departmental inspection, and despite the fact that senior officials, like Scott, admitted that they were "intensely apprehensive" about the quality and safety of church-built structures.[8] This was such a common concern that Hayter Reed, when drafting the 1894 regulations, included a proposal that the Department, before any grant was authorized, should have the right to inspect the plans or, if already built, the school premises.[9] Such a regulation, had it been adopted and enforced, may well have been useful for when schools were finally visited; the Department discovered, in some instances, that their decision to proceed had not been wise.[10]

The Department's own record was not a great deal better, however. Benson, in a general assessment of the school system in 1897, pulled no punches: "The buildings have been put up without due consideration for the purpose for which they would be required, hurriedly constructed of poor materials, badly laid out without due provision for lighting, heating or ventilating."[11]

From the outset, schools had been built with an eye to economy. E. Dewdney, who supervised the construction of the first three industrial schools in the west, insisted that they be of the "simplest and cheapest construction." Putting them near railway lines would facilitate the acquisition of construction materials and supplies. In the course of time, he reasoned, with the growth of settlement, construction costs would drop and the schools could be upgraded.[12] That was, it turned out, a foolish assumption. The trains, when they came, brought settlers, but certainly no federal funds for reconstructing schools.

[...]

It is important (and it illustrates the range of problems, rooted in construction deficiencies, siting, and short budgets) to give some indication of the degree of crisis that existed in the fabric of the residential school system as a whole. Moreover, it is important to give an indication of how conscious officials in the Department were, or could have been, of the situation.

A single report, submitted in 1908 by F.H. Paget, an accountant with the Department, gives some sense both of the scope of the problem and of senior Departmental staff's awareness of it. The report was commissioned by the Department during the negotiations for the contracts when information on the condition of the system was vital. It amounted to a review of a cross-section of nearly one-third of the system including both industrial and boarding schools.

[...]

Paget's report revealed that the schools ran the gamut from good to deplorable. The majority—fifteen out of the twenty-one—were in the latter category. He was impressed with the Qu'Appelle School, which was rebuilt after its fire "with all the modern conveniences." Lacombe's High River School "was splendidly conducted,...neat and clean." He was impressed most with the Duck Lake Boarding School, despite what Indian Agent MacArthur said only two years later

about its historic fifty-percent death rate: "Excellent order, neat and clean throughout, [and] very much a self-contained institution, all clothing being made, and meats, roots, grains and vegetable raised."

All of this was overshadowed by Paget's descriptions of schools that did not pass muster. Not surprisingly, Regina and Red Deer topped the industrial school list. Red Deer was "not modern in any respect." Regina was a sorrowful school: "Driving up it looked more like a deserted place than a Government Institution," The "building is old and the floors are worn, the plaster broken and marked in places and the paint worn off." The children "did not have that clean and neat appearance that was in evidence at other schools."

[...]

Finally, the report indicated what was by 1908 a commonplace, the connection between the condition of the schools and the ill health of children, particularly through tubercular infection. Though Paget covered much of the same ground as Bryce's report of the year before had, he had not been directed to check the doctor's findings. He was, however, certainly familiar with Bryce's report and even referred to it obliquely in his description of Old Sun's Boarding School, which he "found to be all that had been said of it by others in regard to being unsanitary and the building unsuitable in every way for such an institution." In addition, he brought forward similar observations of other schools.[13]

The Department, of course, was fully aware, before either the *Bryce Report* or the *Paget Report*, of the plague of tuberculosis affecting the Aboriginal population and the fact that it had insinuated itself into the schools. The tubercular epidemic, which had moved across the country with the tide of settlement, was the result of white presence coupled with the Aboriginal community's lack of immunity to infectious diseases. It was also, however, a consequence of the process of colonization, of the forces that marginalized communities, divorcing them from their traditional life ways. Confinement to reserves and overcrowded European-style lodgings of the lowest quality provided the fertile ground with malnutrition, lack of sanitation, despair, alcoholism, and government parsimony, from which the infection ran its mortal course through communities.

The impact of tuberculosis, statistically expressed, was out of all proportion to the size of the Aboriginal population. A study by Bryce revealed that the rate of tubercular infection for Indians was one in seven "and the death rates in several large bands 81.8, 81.2, and in a third 86.1 per thousand." The "ordinary death rate for 115,000 in the city of Hamilton was 10.6 in 1921."[14]

The tubercular bacilli infested the body in a multitude of manifestations. "Contracted in infancy [it] creates diseases of the brain [tubercular meningitis], joints, bones and to a less degree the lungs [pulmonary tuberculosis or consumption] and ...if not fatal till adolescence it then usually progresses rapidly to a fatal termination in consumption of the lungs."[15] It was signalled by a wide range of symptoms: head and joint aches, pain in breathing, and glandular swelling and eruption (scrofula) being some of the more common ones. In its most contagious phase, that is, consumption, coughing and spitting blood or sputum spread the infection to others; and fever, weakness, and wasting led to death.

One mode of transmission that particularly affected the children in the schools was drinking milk infected with bovine tuberculosis. Industrial and boarding schools kept cows, and the children routinely drank unpasteurized milk. As with the school buildings, the outbuildings for livestock were often a problem. The principal of St. George's School in Lytton, for example, was told by the Department of Agriculture that he would have to pull down his barn because it was a log structure and could not be disinfected. The school had lost eighteen head of cattle in the previous three years.[16]

Not only was it impossible to isolate the schools from the epidemic, but, as well, the schools themselves were expeditors; they aggravated the problem by simulating in an exaggerated fashion many of those problematic conditions that affected reserve communities.[17]

[...]

The root of overcrowded dorms and classrooms, as with the deteriorating condition of school buildings, could be traced back to funding arrangements and particularly to the per-capita system. The critical need that principals had to maintain high enrollments to qualify for the full grant that had been assigned to their school led to practices that contributed directly to the health problem. Pushing enrollments to and past the point of overcrowding was one of these. The Crowfoot School in 1909 provided a striking example

of this. In that year, Duncan Campbell Scott, then the Department's Chief Accountant, had before him a request from the principal for more students and information supplied by Benson that the dormitories were overcrowded and the ventilation was poor. Scott told the deputy superintendent, rather angrily, that of the fifty-two pupils that had been in the school since it had been in receipt of grants eight years earlier, eight had died, seven of those in the school and the other within a month of leaving. Of the thirty-nine children in the school who had been examined in the previous few months by Dr. J.D. Lafferty, twenty-two were infected with tuberculosis in the lungs:

This is what we have to show for an expenditure of $15,611. The outlook for the remaining pupils in attendance is not very bright and there is very little hope that the graduates of the School will attain maturity and be able to exercise any civilizing influence....The accommodation at the School is inadequate for the number of pupils in residence, and the unhealthy pupils should be discharged.[18]

Principals, of course, were contending with problems flowing directly from just the sort of funding that Scott referred to. As the per-capita ceiling remained stubbornly unchanged at $72 until 1911, they could increase their grant only by having their authorized student number raised. Annually, the Department was besieged with such requests. Additionally, principals had to strive to recruit up to the maximum number authorized, which might already have been a figure that permitted the overcrowding of the living spaces of the school, as was evident in the case of Crowfoot and many other schools.

The pressure that principals worked under to secure adequate funds meant that there was a tendency to be less than careful about the condition of the children they brought into the school. In 1907, the Anglican bishop of Caledonia wanted to turn over Metlakatla to government control because of the anxiety, and perhaps the moral disquiet, that he felt over recruitment. He admitted candidly: "The per capita grant system encourages the taking in of those physically and intellectually unfit simply to keep up numbers."[19]

[...]

Of course, neither the principals nor the churches were solely responsible for the schools. If school administrators were driven into excess by funding needs and led there by missionary zeal, they were not restrained in any effective way by the Department. The 1892 and 1894 Orders-in-Council and the 1911 contracts established the government's responsibility for providing medical services to the schools and the Department's right to inspect the schools was made a condition of the grant. Regulations were issued in 1894 and retained, throughout the period, stipulating that children had to have a medical certificate signed by a doctor before admission.[20]

Unfortunately, the implementation of those regulations left much to be desired. There was no regular inspection of the schools nor any guarantee that forms were being filled in or doctors consulted. In 1909, the Departmental secretary sent out new admission and certificate-of-health forms, which he thought were "sufficiently stringent to guard against tubercular children being taken into the school." They were not enough, however, to keep Louise Plaited Hair out of St. Mary's Boarding School on the Blood Reserve. Her form was signed by Dr. O. Edwards and accepted without question by the Department, in 1911, despite the fact that there was evidence that she had contracted tuberculosis. To a question that asked if there were signs of scrofula or other forms of tubercular disease, Edwards had written, "Glands on right neck slightly enlarged."[21]

According to Scott, when he reviewed the situation with other senior officials in 1925, Louise represented hundreds who had been admitted despite the regulations. The "indiscriminate admission of children without first passing a medical examination" continued. It was not only the principals, he realized, but "our own officers who are picking up orphans, delinquents and others, that are causing the difficulty, as occasionally no application forms are forwarded." There had to be, as well, "more careful checking of the medical officers' remarks in the case of all applicants."[22]

The administrative difficulties identified in Scott's review encompassed more, however, than lax implementation of regulations by officials or attempts to evade those regulations by principals desperate to keep up enrollments. The system simply did not have the medical support that the Department was pledged to provide and that was required to properly protect the children and attend to their health needs.[23] That tragic omission had to be laid on the Department's doorstep.

The scope of this tragedy was measured in 1907 by Dr. P.H. Bryce, then the "Medical Inspector to the Department of the Interior and Indian Affairs." He had been appointed to that position in 1904 after a career in public health with the Ontario government. In February 1907, the Deputy Superintendent, F. Pedley, directed him to inspect the schools in the west, reporting particularly on "the sanitary conditions at each of these schools."[24] After visiting thirty-five schools, he submitted his report in November. It was printed and distributed to members of Parliament and to the churches.

[...]

The impact of the report lay not in his narrative of the disease nor in its scientific tone. It was the statistical profile of the extent of the white plague among the children that projected the stunning gravity of his findings.[25] It was the stuff of headlines. The *Ottawa Citizen* on 16 November ran its story of the report under the banner: "Schools Aid White Plague—Startling Death Rolls Revealed among Indians—Absolute Inattention to Bare Necessities of Health."

The article published by *Saturday Night* on the twenty-third of that same month screamed just as loudly. The report should "startle the country" and "compel the attention of Parliament....Indian boys and girls are dying like flies in these situations or shortly after leaving them....Even war seldom shows as large a percentage of fatalities as does the education system we have imposed on our Indian wards." It revealed "a situation disgraceful to the country."[26]

Bryce's statistics were based upon questionnaires that he distributed to all thirty-five schools eliciting the health history of the children who were then, or had been, in the schools. He received only fifteen replies, all from boarding schools founded between 1888 and 1905. Nevertheless, he was convinced that he had "valuable information and food for thought." The information related to the history of 1,537 children. Of these, twenty-four percent had died. Invariably, the cause of death is given as "consumption or tuberculosis," and just as regularly, whenever an answer was given to the question "Condition of the child on entry?," it is "given as good."

The situation was even worse, however, than his initial calculations suggested. The death rate inevitably moved beyond the twenty-four percent mark. Close analysis by Bryce of some of the returns revealed "an intimate relationship between the health of the pupils while in the school and their early death subsequent to discharge." For example, of the thirty-one pupils who had been discharged from the File Hills Boarding School, fifteen left in coffins. An additional seven died from within a few months to three years after returning home. In total, seventy-five percent of those on the discharge roll were actually dead. When the File Hills ratios are applied to Bryce's sample of 1,537 children, it results in an increase from twenty-four percent to forty-two percent as the percentage of those children who died from their school experience. Assuming that these ratios were constant, and projecting them throughout the system in 1907, when there were 3,755 students in the schools, would mean that some 1,614 of those children would die prematurely. And every year more children came into the schools and more became infected.[27]

[...]

With the *Bryce Report* in hand and corroborative comments from local agents, it is not surprising that the Church and Department negotiations turned to the question of the tuberculosis epidemic in the negotiations that took place between 1908 and 1910. In fact, the *Report* had carried recommendations for the reform of the school system. These urged the government to press on with residential education with the stress on reserve-based boarding schools, to place the management of the schools wholly in Departmental hands, relegating the churches to an advisory capacity, and to insure that "the health interests of the pupils be guarded by a proper medical inspection and that the local physicians be encouraged through the provision at each school of fresh air methods in the care and treatment of cases of tuberculosis."[28] Bryce's recommendation of "fresh air methods" was shorthand for sanatoria. This would have been a very expensive approach to the problem necessitating considerable remodelling of buildings and high levels of medical staffing.[29]

Not surprisingly, perhaps, the contract took a different approach,[30] with regulations aimed at improving the medical screening of children entering the schools, ending overcrowding and suggested revisions to the funding system to facilitate better maintenance and improvements in the vital areas of ventilation, health and sanitation. That focus was laid out in a memorandum of agreement sent by the Departmental Secretary, J.D. McLean, to the church representatives who had met with Oliver in November 1910. The contract embodied the conditions upon which the increased grant was to be paid.

"Those conditions require that the school buildings shall be sanitary and that the school management shall be such as to conduce to the physical, moral and mental well-being of the children." The revised per-capita rates were designed to assist in that.

[...]

Unfortunately, the concern for the children reflected in the contract did not give any priority to the improvement of the condition of the schools. By the end of the First World War, it was "business as usual," business as it had been since the 1880s. In 1918, Duncan Campbell Scott briefed the Superintendent General, Arthur Meighen, on the state of Indian education. He reviewed the contract system, pointing out that one of its central purposes had been to deal with the "inadequate" buildings, which "were unsanitary and ... were undoubtedly chargeable with a very high death rate among the pupils." For a few years after 1911, "until the outbreak of the war," the Department, he continued, "had been able to do its share" toward improving conditions. Then, "as the war continued[,] all new projects were abandoned."[31]

While the Department was able to hold the line on per-capita rates, and even managed a $10 advance in 1917, it lost ground in its attempt to fund improvements in the physical condition of the schools. Increasingly, the "circle of civilized conditions" was a crumbling edifice. If it had been Blake who briefed Meighen in 1918, he may well have added to Scott's commentary a sobering reflection; because the Department was still, a decade later, "doing nothing to obviate the preventable causes of death," it continued to be "within the unpleasant nearness to the charge of manslaughter."[32]

[...]

The Department, too, had it within its power to make a greater effort, if not through improved funding, at least through its authority. It could have insisted that its officials carry out inspections and that the churches follow regulations directed to the care of the children. It did not do so. The Departmental watch dog was far from vigilant; it rarely barked and, despite the conditions over which Bryce, Paget, Corbett, local doctors, and even senior Departmental officials had shaken their heads,[33] it certainly did not bite. Grants were not withdrawn, schools were not forced to close or principals to resign. The Orders-in-Council of 1892 and 1894 and the contracts of

1911 were in fact administrative fictions. They constituted powers, authorities, and agreements that did not facilitate effective, efficient, or even what seemed the most constant, goal—economical management.

The reality was that, from the moment the school system was launched in the 1880s and 1890s, it drifted without a firm hand, without concerted intervention. And this was despite the knowledge that many children were held in dangerous circumstances and that the death rate was not only of tragic proportions but was, in addition, undercutting the whole purpose and strategy of the system. Many, many children—perhaps as high as fifty percent according to Scott's estimate—would not "attain maturity and be able to exercise any civilizing influence" in their communities.[34]

A significant cause of this lay with personnel in the Department and in the churches involved directly in the management of the system. These many men and women failed to act decisively in the face of the suffering and death of so many children. They were not alone, however. They were joined in complicity and insensitivity by non-Aboriginal society as a whole. The devastation that the white plague brought to the children in the schools and through their deaths to their parents and communities drew out the fundamental contradiction between the persistent cruelty of the system and the discourse of duty, of the "sacred trust with which Providence has invested the country in the charge of and care for the aborigines committed to it."[35]

It was a contradiction that the country was not prepared to face, and did not in fact face, throughout the rest of this period to 1946. The editor of *Saturday Night* seemed to sense this contradiction from the very moment of the publication of the 1907 *Bryce Report*:

> His report is printed, many people will scan the title on the cover, some will open it, a few will read it and so the thing will drift along another year. And so with the next year and the year after. So will be the course of events...unless public opinion takes the question up and forces it to the front. Then Parliament will show a quick interest, pigeon holes will give up their dusty contents, medical officers will have a wealth of suggestions and the scandalous procession of Indian children to school and on to the cemetery may possibly be stopped.[36]

Of course, none of those conditions was fulfilled. There was no "public opinion," Parliament showed no interest, quick or otherwise, and the children continued to go to the schools and to the schools' cemeteries, as Bryce's pamphlet in 1922 revealed.

In 1922, the issue of Aboriginal people had long since been swept into the darker reaches of national consciousness. The deaths, and the condition of the schools pricked no collective conscience, wrought no revolution in policy, or even any significant reformulation. Sir George Murray's comment in 1830 about the old Imperial policy was just as true nearly one century later. This federal policy "was persisted in...as a matter of routine, [rather] than upon any considered grounds of preference."[37] There was no reconsideration, no second thoughts, no questioning of the assumptions of assimilation or of residential schools as an appropriate method of achieving that end. There appeared to be no thought or reaction at all.

The "routine" of residential education after the industrial school era, in the years after 1923 through to 1946, simply persisted. Unlike so many children, the school system survived the tubercular infection. It even grew, if more slowly than in the initial decades in the life of the system. In 1923, there were seventy-two residential schools. That number grew to a high of eighty in 1931.[38] The number then gradually fell through closures, many because of fires, to seventy-five in 1943.

The much slower rate of growth after the First World War did not indicate any waning in the enthusiasm for expansion. Churches continued to push to open schools in the few remaining untapped educational areas.[39] There were simply not that many areas left. Departmental cooperation continued. Scott, himself, led the way in moving the system into one of those areas—the east, Quebec, and Nova Scotia. The first school commissioned in Quebec was the Anglican Fort George School followed by Fort George Roman Catholic School, and in Nova Scotia the first and only school was the Roman Catholic Shubenacadie School. Scott was particularly dedicated to this latter project: "When we have this school established," he wrote to the Catholic church in 1926, sounding more like Vankoughnet than himself, "one of the desires of my official life will have been accomplished."[40]

As well as there being but limited horizons by the 1920s, finance continued to be a restraint and a detrimental factor in the condition of existing schools. Wartime reductions, which had blighted the program of improvements of 1911, ushered in yet another era of underfunding. Initially after the war, there were advances in the level of per capitas. A $10 increase was authorized in 1919.[41] Other increases followed in 1921, 1924, 1926, and 1931, moving the average per capita to $172.[42] These increases were never enough, however, to satisfy the churches' appetites for government funds nor to prevent them from again "encountering huge deficits."[43]

With the Depression, the situation got worse because, as the minister responsible for Indian Affairs, T.G. Murphy, phrased it, the "financial condition of the country [was] such that economies" were then "imposed on" the government.[44] In 1932, it was "found necessary … to make a flat decrease in per capita grants." Other cuts followed.[45] In 1938, the Committee of Churches Cooperating with the Department of Indian Affairs calculated that between 1932 and 1938 the reductions amounted to a $840,000 loss to the churches.[46]

The Department put the best public face on the situation.[47] Privately, senior staff knew that the per-capita average, claimed to be still about $180 in 1938, was "exceptionally low" and inadequate particularly in relation to the funding available to other residential child-care facilities. R. Hoey, the Department's Superintendent of Welfare and Training, supplied H. McGill, the Director of Indian Affairs, with revealing comparative figures. The government of Manitoba provided per-capita grants of $642 and $550 respectively to the Manitoba School for the Deaf and the School for Boys. Private institutions in that Province were also more generously funded. The Knowles School for Boys in North Kildonan was sponsored by the Community Chest at $362 per boy. The Catholic Church provided St. Norbert's Orphanage with $294 and St. Joseph's Orphanage with a $320 per-capita grant. Finally, an international comparison was not in the Department's favour either. The child Welfare League of America estimated that the average per-capita grant in the United States of large child-care institutions was $541, with the smaller ones running only as low as $313.[48]

The Second World War pulled the country out of the deep economic trough of the Depression, but it brought no benefits to the school system. Wartime military expenditures meant reductions "to almost every appropriation"[49] for the Department and a building freeze. In the face of this, Hoey realized that it would be "exceedingly difficult to secure the funds necessary …at any time during the years that [lay] immediately ahead."[50]

The persistence of underfunding undercut the maintenance and repair of buildings. Under the terms of the 1911 contracts, the Department had been charged with that expense, and, even after the contracts lapsed, it agreed to continue.[51] Indeed, in the relatively optimistic days following the First World War, the policy of the Department was to buy up the church schools and then to be responsible for all capital costs including repairs and new construction.[52] Scott went so far as to propose that the cost of purchasing all the church-owned schools be placed in the supplementary estimates in order that the whole matter "may receive the careful consideration of the government."[53] This would have meant acquiring forty-three of the seventy-five schools then operating in 1922.

The Department's promise and Scott's proposal remained good intentions only. In the early years of the Depression, expenditures (combining the per-capita grants and capital funds) fell from an average of $28,000 per school to $16,000.

By the Second World War, the Department was so far behind that Hoey and P. Phelan, Chief of the Training Division, estimated that they had less than half the funds necessary to meet repair commitments.[54] McGill admitted, in fact, that they had "been experiencing for the [previous] 10 or 12 years the utmost difficulty in securing the funds necessary to keep [the] schools in a state of repair."[55] They were not, he concluded, being maintained "in a reasonable state."[56]

As in the industrial school era, the net result of underfunding could be seen both in the condition of the schools and in the care given to the children. The building stock was in poor shape at the outset. A Departmental survey in 1922 concluded that of the seventy-five schools the great majority were not "modern up to date buildings in good condition," nor were they "adequate for the purpose of Indian education." A smaller number were condemned as "dilapidated and inadequate."[57]

Needless to say, the condition of the system was not improved by the reductions in funding in the 1930s and the wartime freeze. In 1931, one of the system's flagship schools, Shingwauk, was condemned.[58] Long lists of repairs from every corner of the system were submitted and ignored, as were pleas for urgent assistance.[59]

Bad and badly maintained buildings continued to translate into bad health.[60] However, the extent of the tuberculosis problem in the schools in the 1930s and 1940s is hard to assess. There were no reports of the scope or calibre of the Bryce or Corbett reports. Routine agents' reports, which are the most common documentation, are of limited value because agents were not trained medical observers. In many cases, however, the condition of the children was sorrowfully obvious even to such amateurs.[61]

It was obvious, too, from those reports that the Department's administrative system regarding health certificates was still far from watertight. Dr. C. Pitts, who attended the children at Lejac School in British Columbia, certainly held that position. He had special knowledge of the school system because his father was a long-serving principal, and he had friends who were school doctors. He went so far, in 1935, as to suggest that the regulations were a farce and their enforcement a practical impossibility: "As for the general medical examination...this is not done in any other school that I have any knowledge of....Where is the point of this [examination], when I know that were I to apply the standards of health to them that is applied to children of the white schools that I should have to discharge 90% of them and there would be no school left."[62]

An equally serious impediment to any attempt to care for the health of the children was the inability of the Department to acquire funds to underwrite attacks on tuberculosis in the schools. Only at the end of the 1930s did funding for sanatoria treatment appear, and that was largely owing to pressure from the Canadian Tuberculosis Association. No special funds were set aside especially for the schools, however.[63]

The 1920s, 1930s, and 1940s had more in common with the previous Industrial era than underfunding, the woeful condition of the buildings, and the infection and death of children from tuberculosis. Connected to each of these issues, nested in reports on them, is another persistence: abundant evidence of the failure of the churches and the Department to adequately parent these children, to operate institutions that were above reproach as homes and as schools. In part, this was again due to the issue of finance. Whenever correspondence turned to the per capitas or maintenance funds, someone was bound to point out that this affected the children, that it would "render almost superhuman the task of feeding, clothing and treating the children in the manner required by the Department."[64] And there were numerous reports from schools confirming this. Principals were forced to meet budget shortfalls, as the Principal of Christie School in British Columbia, Victor Rassier, O.S.B., had had to do, "by economizing to the bone in every department."[65] And Agent J. Smith at Kamloops School stated: "If the children are to be kept they ought to be reasonably clothed and fed, and this is utterly impossible to do from the present per capita grant."[66]

But the failure to care properly for the children was rooted in more than the issue of funding, and in more than just the difficulties of building and managing the system. The "manner required by the Department [for] feeding clothing and treating the children,"[67] a standard of care, was both an ill-defined and a rarely achieved goal. Bryce, Paget, and Corbett stand as witnesses to the inherent structural flaws in the system. The Reverend Thompson Ferrier comes forward to add to their witness the human failings and the resultant suffering of the children who were neglected by Departmental-church "parents," cruel or incompetent, who presumed that they should and could supplant the childrens' natural Aboriginal parents but who did not consistently carry out their parenting responsibilities.

In July 1925, just three years after Bryce's *Story of a National Crime* was published, Ferrier, who had then been in charge of Methodist industrial and boarding schools and hospitals for twenty-five years, set down on paper his memory of a cross-country tour of those schools when he first took up his position. Only Coqualeetza School in British Columbia was, in his opinion, in good order. The others were not circles of civilized conditions:

> Mount Elgin Institute at Muncey looms up in memory with its untidy yard and a lot of old sheds, outbuildings and dilapidated barns that had passed their day all unconscious of their need of repairs and paint. The main building had accommodation for about one hundred pupils who were receiving such

harsh treatment as to call forth numerous complaints from the Indian people and the Indian department. Several attempts were made on the part of the pupils to burn up the whole business all because it was under the management of a man who had the idea that physical strength was to take the place of what ought to be done by the heart and head in educating and training young life, who believed that it was safer to deal with the hide than the honour of the pupil and a man who took more interest in hydraulics than hygiene.

When Ferrier got to Brandon, he found ninety children who seemed to have the upper hand. They were "destructive, untrained young men and women from thirteen to twenty-three years of age. They were having their own way, smashing everything they could not eat or wear and running roughshod over a discouraged staff. It looked as though the institution had fallen into a pit and was waiting for someone to come and give it a decent burial."

At Norway House, they had a poor barn shaped building with broken doors, worn out floors, no modern conveniences of plumbing, heating or lighting, a cold shell of a place with partial accommodation for about thirty-five pupils who were obliged to live without a balanced ration as there was no garden, poultry or stock. An incompetent staff were trying to penetrate the stronghold of heathenism with the belief that the problem would never be solved. Red Deer was no better. The school comprised a miserable lot of buildings, the boys home being very dark and unsanitary. There was a stable for horses but none for stock. The management was unconscious of the great possibilities of the rich fertile land of the farm and the opportunity presented as a training school for farmers and stockmen. For many reasons the whole institution was very unpopular with the Indian people of Alberta. The office appeared to be used more for a real estate business than to make a contribution toward civilizing and educating the people.

Finally, Ferrier went to the west coast and to Port Simpson, where they "had twenty boys housed in a building and under a management that was a disgrace to the Methodist church."[68]

As had been the case with all the previous reports (Bryce's, Paget's, and Corbett's), none of the conditions described by Ferrier was news to the Department or the churches. They already had a flood of evidence, a spate that continued through to and beyond 1946, that indicated that in too many cases the children were not being adequately fed, clothed, or taught and that discipline often crossed the line into abuse. The vision of life and learning in the "circle of civilized conditions" had not become a reality. The promise that children would receive the "care of a mother"[69] and an education that would elevate the child "to a status equal to that of his white brother" remained unfulfilled.[70]

Notes

1. Anglican Archives, MSCC, Series 2-14, Special Indian Committee, 1905–1910, S.H. Blake to the Hon. Frank Oliver, Minister of the Interior, Sunday Morning, 27 January 1907, printed in *To the Members of the Board of Management of the Missionary Society of the Church of England in Canada*, by The Hon. S.H. Blake, K.C., 21.

2. Given the incomplete state of student records in the school files, it is impossible to arrive at the number of deaths from disease in the schools in any year or decade. Later in the chapter, a sense of how "appalling" the number was is given through percentages supplied in large part by Dr. Bryce. In light of the anecdotal evidence, Bryce's figures seem to have been supported generally by Departmental staff and to have applied nation-wide.

3. There is no statistical base for determining the number of children who died from disease in the schools. The Bryce Report of 1907 gives some indication of death rates when tuberculosis was most rampant (N.A.C. RG10, Vol. 4037, File 317021, MR C 10177, P. Bryce. Report on the Indian Schools of Manitoba and the Northwest Territories, Ottawa, Government Printing Bureau, 1907).

4. N.A.C. RG 10, Vol. 6305, File 652-1, MR C 8682, Agent MacArthur to Secretary, 27 December 1910. To be fair, some children came to school already infected, having contracted the disease in

over-crowded and squalid living conditions in their reserve homes.

5. N.A.C. RG 10. Vol. 3920, File 116818, MR C 10161, Dr. J.P. Rice to C. Sifton, 3 August 1903: M. Benson to Deputy Superintendent General of Indian Affairs, 9 September 1903.

6. N.A.C. RG 10, Vol. 7185, File 1/25-1-7-1, D.C. Scott to Hon. Charles Stewart, 31 October 1927.

7. N.A.C. RG 10, Vol. 4037, File 317021, MR C 10177, D. Laird to Secretary of Indian Affairs, 7 December 1907.

8. N.A.C. RG 10, Vol. 7185, File 1/25-1-7-1, D.C. Scott to Hon. Charles Stewart, 31 October 1927.

9. N.A.C. RG 10, Vol. 3836, File 68557, MR C 10146, H. Reed, Suggestions for the Government of Indian Schools, 27 January 1890.

10. N.A.C. RG 10, Vol. 6467, File 889-1 (1-2), MR C 8785, C. Perry to Dr. H. McGill, 25 May 1900. The Squamish school was a case in point. It was built by the Catholic missionary and funded in 1900 after a direct appeal to Clifford Sifton by the local member of Parliament and the Catholic bishop. It was, when inspected by the Assistant Indian Commissioner of British Columbia, C. Perry, shortly after its opening, in such ramshackle condition that Perry thought it should be closed immediately.

11. N.A.C. RG 10, Vol. 6039, File 160-1, MR C 8152, M. Benson to J.D. McLean, 15 July 1897.

12. N.A.C. RG 10, Vol. 3674, File 11422, MR C 10118, E. Dewdney to Father Lacombe, 22 July 1883; and E. Dewdney to Superintendent General of Indian Affairs, 16 April 1883.

13. N.A.C. RG 10, Vol. 4041, File 334503, MR C 10178, E.H. Paget to F. Pedley, 25 November 1908.

14. Bryce, *The Story of a National Crime*, 11. The Canadian Tuberculosis Association circulated figures that detailed the percentage of Aboriginal tuberculosis deaths by province compared to their percentage of the population. In Manitoba, of the total deaths, forty-one percent were Aboriginal, though Aboriginal people made up only 2.2 percent of the population; in Saskatchewan it was twenty-seven percent of the deaths and 1.6 percent of the population; in Alberta it was thirty-four percent of the deaths and 2.1 percent of the population; and in British Columbia it was thirty-five percent of the deaths and 3.7 percent of the population (Wherrit, *The Miracle of Empty Beds*, 110).

15. Bryce, *The Story of a National Crime*, 11.

16. Wherrit, *The Miracle of Empty Beds*, 16–17; and N.A.C. RG 10, Vol. 6462, File 888-1 (2-3, 6-7), MR C8781, Rev. A. Lett to D.C. Scott, 6 March 1922.

17. Wherrit, *The Miracle of Empty Beds*, 16-17 and 100-103.

18. N.A.C. RG 10, Vol. 6348, File 752-1, MR C 8705, D.C. Scott to Deputy Superintendent General of Indian Affairs, 23 April 1909.

19. N.A.C. RG 10, Vol. 3937, File 120048-1, MR C 10164, Bishop of Caledonia, to A. Vowell, 11 November 1907.

20. See, for example, N.A.C. RG 10, Vol. 6210, File 469-1 (1-3), MR C 7941, Deputy Superintendent General of Indian Affairs to J. Lawlor, 8 November 1894.

21. N.A.C. RG 10, Vol. 1543 [no file number], MR C 14839, J.D. McLean to R. Wilson, 2 October 1909; and D. Laird to R. Wilson, 7 March 1911 (Application for Admission attached).

22. N.A.C. RG 10, Vol. 6015, File 1-1-13. MR C 8141, D.C. Scott to W. Graham, 16 February 1925.

23. See, for example, the explanation from a field official citing the lack of doctors in remote areas as the reason for non-compliance with the medical regulations: N.A.C. RG 10, Vol. 6015, File 1-1-13, MR C 8141, Acting Agent to R. Ferrier, 9 March 1925.

24. N.A.C. RG 10, Vol. 4037, File 317021, MR C 10177, Deputy Superintendent General of Indian Affairs to J.D. McLean, 14 February 1907.

25. N.A.C. RG 10, Vol. 4037, File 317021, MR C 10177, P. Bryce, *Report on the Indian Schools*, 1907, 17–19.

26. N.A.C. RG 10, Vol. 4037, File 317021, MR C 10177. Copies of stories in the *Citizen*, 16 November 1907, and *Saturday Night*, 23 November 1907, as well as the *Montreal Star*, 15 November 1907, are in this file.

27. N.A.C. RG 10, Vol. 4037, File 317021, MR C 10177, P. Bryce, *Report on the Indian Schools*, 1907, 17–20.

28. Bryce, *The Story of a National Crime*, 4.

29. N.A.C. RG 10, Vol. 6039, File 160-1, MR C 8152, Bishop of St. Boniface et al. to R. Rogers, 24 November 1911 and 15 November 1912. Bryce's recommendations may also have been sidelined in the negotiations by political considerations. The Catholic church was opposed to many of the reforms—Bryce's and even some of those eventually included in the contracts. The schools, the church charged, were being "submitted to vexatious requirements by physicians, whose interests therein appear to have been in large measure confined to making unnecessary demands."

30. For further details on the government's approach, see N.A.C. RG 10, Vol. 6039, File 160-1, MR C 8152, F. Oliver to Reverend and Dear Sirs, 21 March 1908. See particularly Oliver's discussion of Winnipeg Resolution No. 7.

31. N.A.C. RG 10, Vol. 6001, File 1-1-1 (1), MR C 8134, D.C. Scott to A. Meighen, n.d. January 1918. The effect of the war on expenditures was dramatic. In 1914, the Department spent on average $8,684 on each boarding school and $16,146 on each of the remaining industrial schools. In 1918, those figures had fallen to $5,738 and $12,338 respectively. Total expenditures for the system fell by thirty-three percent from $811,764 to $542,568.

32. Anglican Archives, MSCC, Series 2-14, Special Indian Committee, 1905–1910, S.H. Blake to the Honourable Frank Oliver, Minister of the Interior, Sunday Morning, 27 January 1907, printed in To the Members of the Board of Management of the Missionary Society of the Church of England in Canada, by The Hon. S.H. Blake, K.C., 21.

33. See, for example, correspondence on the Chapleau School: N.A.C. RG 10, Vol. 6191, File 462-1, MR C 7926, J.D. McLean to Rev. J. Anderson, 29 December 1914; Extract of Inspection Report by W. Hamilton, 3 May 1915; and J. Sheahan, M.D., to J.D. McLean, 2 July 1917. See also the correspondence relating to St. Cyprians: N.A.C. RG 10, Vol. 6368, File 763-1, MR C 8720, Assistant Deputy and Secretary to E. Yoemans, n.d. 1911; S. Stewart to Archdeacon J. Tims, n.d. 1911; J.D. McLean to Archdeacon J. Tims, 22 January 1913; J.D. McLean to Archdeacon J. Tims, 15 February 1913; J.D. McLean to A. Gunn, 15 February 1914; and W. Graham to Secretary, 21 July 1925.

34. N.A.C. RG 10, Vol. 6348, File 752-1, MR C 8705, D.C. Scott to Deputy Superintendent General of Indian Affairs, 23 April 1909.

35. Annual Report 1891, x.

36. N.A.C. RG 10, Vol. 4037, File 317021, Saturday Night, 23 November 1907.

37. N.A.C. C.O. 42/27, G. Murray to J. Kempt (No. 95), 25 January 1830.

38. There was then one school in Nova Scotia, thirteen in Ontario, ten in Manitoba, fourteen in Saskatchewan, twenty in Alberta, sixteen in British Columbia, four in the Northwest Territories, two in the Yukon, and plans for two schools in Quebec.

39. See, for example, N.A.C. RG 10, Vol. 6040, File 160-3A, Part 1, MR C 8153, Rev. T. Ferrier to D.C. Scott, 8 July 1920.

40. N.A.C. RG 10, Vol. 6041, File 160-5, Part 1, D.C. Scott to J. Guy, 11 July 1926. See Appendix, p. 307 herein, for school list, 1931.

41. N.A.C. RG 10, Vol. 6039, File 160-1, MR C 8152, J.D. McLean to Sir James Lougheed, 24 August 1920.

42. N.A.C. RG 10, Vol. 6040, File 160-3, Part 1, MR C 8153, Rev. T. Ferrier to D.C. Scott, 6 December 1921; and Vol. 7185, File 1/25-1-7-1, R.T. Ferrier, Superintendent of Eduacation, Memorandum to File, 5 April 1932.

43. N.A.C. RG 10, Vol. 6040, File 160-3A, Part 1, MR C 8153, Joint Church Delegation to Minister of the Interior, 7 January 1921; Canon S. Gould to D.C. Scott, 23 September 1924; D.C. Scott to C. Stewart, 7 March 1927; and Memorandum to File, 8 February 1926.

44. N.A.C. RG 10, Vol. 6730, File 160-2 (1-3), MR C 8092, T.G. Murphy to Canon S. Gould, 26 April 1931.

45. N.A.C. RG 10, Vol. 7185, File 1/25-7-1, R.T. Ferrier, Memorandum to File, 5 April 1932; and N.A.C. RG 10, Vol. 6041, File 160-5 Part 1, MR C 8153, H. McGill to Rev. J. Scannell, O.M.I., 17 February 1936; and Vol. 7185, File 1/25-1-7-1, Deputy Superintendent General of Indian Affairs, Circular, 26 March 1936.

46. United Church Archives, WMS Fonds, Accession 83.058C, File 3, Memorandum of the Committee of Churches Cooperating with the Department of Indian Affairs in Indian Education, 8 February 1938.

47. N.A.C. RG 10, Vol. 7185, File 1/25-1-7-1. R. Hoey to H. McGill, 4 November 1938.

48. N.A.C. RG 10, Vol. 7185, File 1/25-1-7-1, R. Hoey to H. McGill, 4 November 1938. Hoey provided additional figures that were equally depressing. The Children's Aid Society of Alberta estimated that the minimum per-day maintenance cost for a neglected child was $1. The Ontario figure was slightly lower at seventy-five cents, Manitoba was between sixty-three and seventy-two cents, B.C. was at fifty-seven cents and Saskatchewan was at fifty cents. This worked out to an average of seventy cents. The Department's national average, using its $180 figure, was forty-nine cents, and it was supposed to cover more than just food and clothes.

49. N.A.C. RG 10, Vol. 6041, File 160-5, Part 1, MR C 8153, R. Hoey to Rev. J. Plourde, 15 October 1940.

50. N.A.C. RG 10, Vol. 6730, File 160-2 (1-3), MR C 8092, Director of Indian Affairs to Rev. T. Westgate, n.d. 1940.

51. N.A.C. RG 10, Vol. 6041, File 160-5, Part 1, MR C 8153, D.C. Scott to Charles Stewart, 7 March 1922.

52. N.A.C. RG 10, Vol. 6039, File 160-1, MR C 8152, R.F. Ferrier, Memornadum—Impression of the Interview between Church Representatives and the Superintendent General, 13 April 1922.

53. N.A.C. RG 10, Vol. 6041, File 160-5, Part 1, MR C 8153, D.C. Scott to Charles Stewart, 7 March 1922.

54. N.A.C. RG 10, Vol. 6479, File 940-1 (1-2), MR C 8794, R. Hoey to H. McGill, 16 November 1942.

55. N.A.C. RG 10, Vol. 6479, File 940-1 (1-2), H. McGill to Rev. W. Geddes, 21 November 1942.

56. N.A.C. RG 10, Vol. 6482, File 941-2, MR C 8796, H. McGill to Rev. J. Plourde, 15 February 1940.

57. N.A.C. RG 10, Vol. 6039, File 160-1, MR C 8152, R.F. Ferrier to Charles Stewart 12 May 1922.

58. N.A.C. RG 10, Vol. 6730, File 160-2 (1-3), MR C 8092, Rev. T. Westgate to Secretary, 29 October 1931. It did not, however, close.

59. See, for example, the plight of the Catholic Sturgeon Lake School in: N.A.C. RG 10, Vol. 6041, File 160-5, Part 1, MR C 8153, Bishop J. Guy to Secretary of Indian Affairs, 10 October 1936; and R. Hoey to Father Plourde, 16 October 1940.

60. See, for example, the reports in 1927 from Dr. P. Wilson and C. Perry on St. George's, Lytton, in which overcrowding and defective plumbing, ventilation, and sanitation are charged with the death of thirteen children from mumps and influenza (N.A.C. RG 10, Vol. 6462, File 888-1 (2-3, 6-7), MR C 8781, Dr. P. Wilson to H. Graham, 23 February 1927; and C. Perry to Secretary, 6 May 1927).

61. N.A.C. RG 10, Vol. 6452, File 884-1 (1-3), MR C 8773-8774, Extracts of a Report by C. Perry attached to W. Ditchburn, 16 June 1930.

62. N.A.C. RG 10, Vol. 6443, File 881-1 (1-3), MR C 8767, C. Pitts, M.D., to R.H. Moore, 22 October 1935.

63. See: Wherrit, *The Miracle of Empty Beds*, 107 and 111–14, for a discussion of these events; and INAC File 961/23-5, Vol. 1, G.H. Berry to Major D.M. Mackay. This Inspection Report notes the opinion of Dr. R.N. Dick, who claimed that the children's health, at Kuper Island School, was threatened by budget restrictions.

64. N.A.C. RG 10, Vol. 6041, File 160-5, Part 1, MR C 8153, Rev. U. Langlois, O.M.I., to H. McGill, 28 April 1936.

65. INAC File 951/23-5, Vol. 1, V. Rassier, O.S.B., to The Secretary, 15 April 1934.

66. N.A.C. RG 10, Vol. 3918, File 116659-1, MR C 10161, J. Smith to Assistant Deputy and Secretary, 8 February 1918. For additional examples see: N.A.C. RG 10, Vol. 6327, File 660-1 (1-3), MR C 9807, M. Benson to Deputy Superintendent General of Indian Affairs, 23 December 1903; and N.A.C. RG 10, Vol. 6205, File 468-1 (1-3), MR C 7937, M. Benson to Deputy Superintendent General of Indian Affairs, 26 November 1902.

67. N.A.C. RG 10, Vol. 6041, File 160-5 Part 1, MR C 8153, Rev. U. Langlois, O.M.I., to H. McGill, 28 April 1936.

68. N.A.C. RG 10, Vol. 6040, File 160-3A, Part 1, MR C 8153, Rev. T. Ferrier to C.E. Manning, 1 July 1925.

69. *The Davin Report*, 12.

70. INAC File 1/25-1, Vol. 15, L. Vankoughnet to Sir John A. Macdonald, 26 August 1887.

■ Article 3: You Ain't My Boss:[1] Resistance

J.R. Miller

My grandmother was very, very upset. I distinctly recall the third time—my final year at the Baptist Mission school—when these missionaries came again to take me away, I was at that time living with my grandmother and my aunt ... who was a blind person. They in a sense were my immediate family ... When these missionaries came to the door and they said, 'Well, we have permission to take [named deleted] to this Whitehorse Baptist Mission school,' and they came to physically take me out of my home, I hung on to my grandmother's legs. I was crying, of course, and my grandmother was very angry. She was quite old—in her sixties, probably. I remember her taking her tut as we called it, walking cane—and beating this missionary, this white missionary over the backside, and saying, 'You leave my grandson alone. You are not taking him anywhere.' And my aunt Pat came out— and she was blind then, too—and saying the same thing, supporting her mother. And saying that you cannot take this child from this home no matter what permission you have. They didn't produce any written document at the time ...

My grandmother stood by me, and she was able to drive these white missionaries out of our home. And they finally left in defeat. And this is one Indian child who didn't get to go to the Whitehorse Baptist Mission school forever after.[2]

It is hardly surprising that the excesses that occurred in many residential schools provoked protest and resistance, from both parents and students. In due course, the same grievances would lead to collective recriminations and pressure for change that were transmitted through Indian political organizations. During the first six decades of the modern residential school system, however, opportunities to combine voices of protest were usually limited to the family or the band in the case of adults, and to the level of a dormitory among the student body. Though limited in scope for a long time, the forms that Native resistance took were surprisingly numerous. Among parents and family friends the reactions ranged from complaints, to withholding of cooperation, to violent retribution, to defiance of the underlying assimilative thrust of Indian Affairs policy. Within the ranks of the students themselves, there was a similarly large number of ways in which children and young adults could make their objections known. They could and did complain loudly to their families; they could disturb the schools' routine with behaviour that ranged from a lack of cooperation to outright disruption. When pushed too far to be satisfied by these modest responses, they had available more serious sanctions, such as desertion and destruction. Residential school children and parents protested and resisted in many ways.

The effectiveness of both students' and parents' protests depended on a series of particular, often local, circumstances. Headquarters staff of both government and the missionary organizations were usually inclined to discount complaints from Natives themselves. A Presbyterian group that visited a number of schools in Manitoba and Saskatchewan in 1913 reported dismissively that the complaints about the troubled Crowstand school on the Cote reserve near Kamsack were 'of a stereotype character' and tiresomely familiar.[3] Bureaucrats in the secular realm were usually even less inclined to pay attention to Natives' complaints than were those in the ecclesiastical. However, there were a series of circumstances that could force either or both to be more responsive. A principal who was already under a cloud with his superiors sometimes found it desirable to counteract, if not always to accede to, Indians' complaints. The Indian Affairs department was more inclined to seek a solution to protests if its officials were convinced that ignoring the objections would lead to political complications for which their elected masters might hold them responsible. Missionary bureaucrats were often anxious to conciliate parental opinion in situations where their schools were in competition with institutions of another denomination. Denominational rivalry was an especially sharp goad to action where the competition was between a Roman Catholic and a non-Catholic school. There were few threats more effective than removal of one's children from their school.

Source: J.R. Miller, *Shingwauk's Vision: A History of Native Residential Schools.* Toronto: University of Toronto Press, 1996, pp. 343–374. © University of Toronto Press Inc., 1996. Reprinted with permission from the publisher.

These factors sometimes created circumstances in which protests from parents could have limited effect. Such situations at times allowed Native communities and families to influence, if not control, the way in which individual schools treated their children. What emerges from a survey of the interaction of both schoolchildren and their adult communities is a picture not simply of authority and submission, but of a subtle and shifting interplay of forces. Influence and power could in some instances flow in favour of the Aboriginal constituency, in spite of the apparent dominance of government and church. Although too much should not be made of this phenomenon—it would be misleading to suggest, for example, that Native groups were able to force schools to operate as they wished—it is important to understand that protests and resistance could and did have some effect.

The simplest form of parental protest was a complaint lodged with either a missionary or an official of the Indian Affairs department. The Anglican bishop of Caledonia, for example, reported to Ottawa as follows: '"My child might as well be dead" said one mother bitterly when she found she could not get her child back for eight years.' That was one argument the cleric used to support the government's proposal to place more emphasis on day schools at the expense of industrial schools during the first decade of the century.[4] Complaints about the Anglican T.E. Clarke, principal at Battleford, led the Indian commissioner to dispatch the Department of Indian Affairs inspector to investigate, although dismissal of the principal in this instance did not come for another two years.[5] The Ojibwa whose children attended Wikwemikong in the 1890s proved unable to get the government official to force the missionaries to do anything about their complaints concerning excessive instruction in catechism, though the inspector was prepared to act on a father's fear that it was 'dangerous and indecent for his girl to get on the swing.'[6] And when Mr and Mrs Badger took their objections about mistreatment of their children at the Anglican school at Onion Lake to the DIA, they did get the satisfaction of having the agent report to the Indian commissioner, who quickly issued orders that the overwork and 'the ear-twisting for punishment should be dropped, the latter absolutely.'[7]

Sometimes principals responded to parental criticism themselves, although not always with an eye to correcting the conditions that had given rise to the complaints. Missionary supervisors of schools were often more interested in counteracting public criticism than in resolving the difficulty. The beleaguered Principal Clarke of Battleford, anticipating criticism of his regime at the next diocesan synod and cognizant of the likelihood that Ahtahkakoop (Star Blanket) would attend as a delegate, went to considerable trouble to ensure that friends of his school and of the DIA would be in attendance to counter the critics.[8] Missionaries sometimes found that efforts to involve Native leaders in the deliberations of their organizations provided occasions for criticism, such as the time Chief Rattlesnake told the annual convention of Presbyterian workers in Manitoba and Saskatchewan that he 'wanted [the] children to be taught so that they could help the older Indians. Children [were] not learning fast enough.'[9] On the other hand, the principal of Lestock school interpreted 'a large and representative delegation' that objected to an anticipated cancellation of 'the monthly holiday' as proof that the sisters had blabbed to their charges, and complained to his superior in Ottawa.[10] Other forms of complaint that could have some effect were to the church superiors of those in charge of a school to which parents objected. Two Presbyterian worthies from head office in Toronto collected quite a number of objections to overwork, discipline, and inadequate care at several mission locations, including two boarding schools, on the west side of Vancouver Island.[11] Indians at Sandy Bay reserve in Manitoba forwarded their complaints about the Anglican Elkhorn school through the rural dean and the field secretary of the church's principal missionary organization.[12] And, finally, the disgruntled Ojibwa of Couchiching reserve near Fort Frances, Ontario, demanded a meeting with the Oblate provincial to pursue objections to the way the school in their region was being run.[13]

The aggrieved Couchiching band was engaging in another common form of protest against residential school conditions—the formal petition directed either to Indian Affairs or to church officials. Not all such petitions were critical; there were rare petitions *in favour of* missionaries. For example, the chief and head men of a band whose children attended the Crowstand school, where the principal had resigned because he could not secure adequate housing for his ailing wife, sent a message to the Presbyterian committee in Winnipeg asking 'that your resignation be not accepted and that a house be built for your accommodation.'[14] By far the majority of formal protests, however, criticized school leadership.

In this case, too, there was a familiar pattern of denial on the part of those who were accused of contravening the wishes of parents. A request that the principal of the Alberni school be removed in 1905 because he did not provide adequate supervision of the senior girls met a rejoinder that the letter came from 'the father of the only illegitimate child born of a girl in this Mission in recent years.'[15] Ojibwa in the Shoal Lake area of northwestern Ontario became quite expert in petitioning the Presbyterian officials about aspects of boarding-school administration to which they objected. In 1902 the leading men objected to the administration of the matron, who was perceived to be too strict, with the result that the woman tendered her resignation. She particularly objected to the fact that a contract between the Indians and her church limited what the missionaries could do and required that the children be 'well-treated.'[16] A few years later, the local Indian leadership had to protest again, this time against removal of the missionary who had tried to enforce their wishes in the operation of the school. Chief Red Sky threatened that if the Presbyterians removed this man, 'I will ask the Indian Agent to send the children to another school for we won't have them here at all.'[17] This threat proved unavailing, and the Indian parents found themselves petitioning against excessive corporal punishment the next year.[18]

[...]

A particular source of grievance to parents that might cause them to withhold their children was sickness and mortality at the schools. In northern Manitoba, Native people were 'dumb to entreaties' to send their children to the Methodists' Brandon or Norway House schools. 'Some years ago children were sent to Red Deer. Two have returned, two are at Brandon and will return this summer. The rest, the majority died. Seven were sent to Norway House this past summer. Two are already dead. These things completely knock the attempts re Brandon or Norway House in the head. They just sit right down on a fellow. And one must shut up because there is at least a degree of justice on their side.'[19] The most striking example of withholding children because of a school's bad reputation, particularly for health, was the Presbyterians' Regina school. Parents had

always had problems with the institution, and with its aggressive efforts to fill it with students. One mother even wrote another warning: 'You better bring here your children at once or they will be taken to Regina. They are taking children of[f] the Reserve to Regina. 19 children have been taken from the Reserves to the Regina School.'[20] Problems at the Regina school worsened steadily thanks to incompetent leadership and serious health problems that alienated parents from the institution. The trouble, noticeable early in the century, neared a crisis point towards the end of the decade.[21]

Regina's unhappy experience pointed up several aspects of residential school operations that gave parents at least a narrow area in which to protest effectively. First, when a school was located in a region with numerous institutions, parents had a certain amount of choice. A defective school could be taught a lesson by withholding students. In the southern prairies there were at least a dozen schools serving four denominations in the early decades of the twentieth century, and there were even instances where the same denomination had an industrial and a boarding school within a fairly short distance. The Presbyterians, unfortunately for Regina, operated boarding schools at File Hills in Saskatchewan and at Birtle, Manitoba, in addition to the unpopular industrial school at Regina. A veteran missionary contended 'that the feeling against sending children to the far away Industrial Schools is becoming stronger with the Indians themselves. Many of the old people say, that the worst element on the reserve is to be found among returned graduates who in a year or two, drift down sadly.'[22]

Regina was in bad odour with parents for many reasons. It was distant, run by an unpopular principal, had a reputation for overworking children, and experienced a lot of sickness and death among the students. A missionary on a reserve near the Birtle school reported to Presbyterian head office that 'some of the parents intimate that they will send their children to Birtle when they are bigger. The Regina is looked upon with disfavour. It is a long way off and of the seven who were sent there only one is alive to-day, all the rest dying of tuberculosis. The parents are really afraid to let the children go.'[23] A meeting with a group of parents in the chief's house on Muscowpetung reserve resulted in a list of reasons that explained why, although all wanted education for their children, 'some graduates absolutely refuse to send their children from home any more':

(a) The secrecy observed by most schools as to sickness among the pupils.
(b) The use of the pupils for work about the farm and the school when they should be in the classroom.
(c) The breaking up of their home circle.[24]

As long as there were other schools in the region, parents enjoyed some latitude in seeing that their children were educated without sending them to a distant and threatening institution. Even where dissatisfaction did not reign, 'parents prefer to keep their children in the schools nearest their homes.'[25]

[...]

In some cases, avoidance of schooling appeared to be part of a strategy chosen by the leaders of a particular community. Chief White Bear adhered to Treaty 4 in 1875, but he and his followers clearly were not interested in sedentary agriculture as an alternative to the buffalo economy. Instead, the band selected a reserve with rolling land, lakes, and numerous trees, and it proceeded to develop a mixed economy of hunting, fishing, selling products such as tanned hides and charcoal to townspeople, and limited gardening. As the farmer in charge of the reserve observed in 1897, the White Bear band 'try to live as they did before treaty was made with the North-west Indians.' Their strategy, which was in marked contrast to the Pheasant Rump and Ocean Man bands in the same agency, worked. White Bear lost fewer people to disease compared with these other two bands, and his people maintained themselves well on the varied sources of income.

What was instructive was that White Bear, his sons, and their followers among the leadership rigorously eschewed both missionaries and residential schools. The farmer who commented adversely on their economic activity in 1897 continued his plaint by adding, 'and they will hardly allow any one talk on the subject of education to them, and simply say that their "God" did not intend them to be educated like white people; they will not allow that there would be any benefit to be derived from having their children taught.' Tom White Bear, for example, reportedly would 'not farm or keep cattle himself, and uses all his influence to prevent other Indians from doing

so.' White Bear's son would 'not allow his children to be sent to school, says he would sooner see them dead, and on every chance he gets speaks against education and the Industrial schools provided by the Government.' In an effort to induce White Bear to cooperate on farming and schooling, Indian Affairs deposed him as chief, provoking a kind of boycott by the old chief's followers. When Ottawa noticed in 1897 that there was no chief or councillors on the White Bear reserve, the agent proposed the appointment of a 'good hardworking man, [who] has the best farm and buildings in the Agency, has had five of his children sent to school (three have died there) and does all in his power to help on the work on the reserve, and has a large following.' Eventually, Indian Affairs had to capitulate to the stubborn White Bear traditionalists. Ottawa restored the old chief not long before his death, and the reserve received the day school the leaders sought a couple of years later.[26]

[...]

The ability of parents to resist schools was not confined to the prairie region or to the period before the Great War, when problems of disease and student deaths were at their most intense. In the 1920s the Chooutla school in Yukon experienced severe financial problems because of a persistent inability to get and maintain enrolment at the authorized pupilage. In 1925, when enrolment was ten below the authorized forty, the Anglicans' head office chastised the principal, noting that a loss of 'confidence of the parents' was usually part of the explanation of such problems, along with the competition provided by day schools.[27] The venerable bishop, Isaac Stringer, conceded four years later that the continuing problem of under-enrolment owed much to illness and death at the school, not to mention the fact that 'for some time the idea has gone abroad that the children have not been well fed.'[28] Much later Clara Tizya recalled of the same era that when a girl from Rampart Landing died at Chooutla and 'they sent the body back there were many rumours about the children receiving bad treatment and this scared the parents or gave them an excuse for not sending their children to school.'[29]

[...]

The final way in which the adult community could resist the schools was to persist with the traditional practices that residential schooling was designed to eradicate through assimilation. The Ojibwa at Shoal

Lake in northwestern Ontario had inserted in the 'contract' that they signed with Presbyterian missionaries a provision 'that parents shall be allowed to take their children to their religious festivals, but only one child at a time and the child shall not remain over night.'[30] On the File Hills Colony, which was home to selected graduates from the Lebret and File Hills schools, 'fiddle dances, pow-wows and tribal ceremonies were forbidden.' Nonetheless, Eleanor Brass can 'remember as a child accompanying my parents to some secret fiddle dances held in private homes. There were numerous violin players and the dances were quite lively.'[31]

Charles Nowell used to participate in children's potlatch ceremonies when he was a boy at Fort Rupert, before going to Alert Bay school. When he was twelve, his ailing father sent for him in order to instruct him on the necessity of carrying on the potlatch tradition and to have him use his newly acquired learning—writing—to record essential traditional lore. '"I think the only way for you to remember the main positions and all the ancestors is for you to write them down, because it seems to me that everybody is forgetting all their ancestors and names," said his father. "The first thing, you will write down our ancestors till now." So I did—all our ancestors right down to him.' Soon after having his son record their ancestors, names, position in the clan, the dances and their names—all information vital to the preservation of potlatch practice—Nowell's father 'lay down to sleep' and 'he died.'[32] Nowell as an adult not only observed potlatch practices, but he also helped anthropologists to record for prosperity considerable Kwagiulth heritage.

Other adults, such as the men on a reserve in Manitoba, took action immediately to defend their practices. When the agent and DIA inspector came to the reserve and 'cut down or tore down the booth that had been erected for their dance,' the people were so angry that they boycotted the missionary's services for months afterwards.[33] The centrality of traditional Aboriginal ceremonies to both parents and students from Plains cultures was also demonstrated in the early decades of the modern residential school system by the way in which the onset of dancing provoked a rash of runaways, as at the Regina school in 1891.[34] In some cases, as with the Assiniboine Dan Kennedy, the reaction against church-government efforts to suppress traditional practices came after graduation. Kennedy, a graduate of Lebret, turned out to be one of the most energetic and persistent champions of traditional dancing.[35]

Unlike Dan Kennedy, many residential school children did not wait until after graduation to resist the oppressive program to which they were subjected. Like their parents, the pupils themselves had a variety of means to register their protest and try to change the conditions to which they objected. Even more so than the older generation, they were in a vulnerable position as inmates of institutions staffed by the object of their complaints, facilities that were sometimes far removed from countervailing home influences. However, vulnerability did not mean total incapacity or impotence. Residential school children had a range of sanctions from which to select, although their position usually led them to indirect forms of protest and complaint. They might, for example, seek outside help against the school officials, rather than tackling the situation themselves. Or they might register their objections by lack of cooperation and various forms of 'acting up.' In extreme cases they resorted to avoidance techniques that ranged from getting away from the source of the problem to a direct attack on the school. As was often the case in all sorts of institutional settings, the inmates showed an astonishing inventiveness and energy in combating and trying to reshape the forms and forces that held them.

What gave student opinion at least limited influence was the pupilage system and parents' ability in some situations to withhold their children. These background factors ensured that school authorities, if only sporadically, would make an effort to secure good opinions from the children for home consumption. Censorship could stifle negative reports, but it could not generate positive ones. To get endorsement required effort by the staff. An Oblate wrote enthusiastically from Moose Factory to the principal of the order's Fort George school that parents there 'qui ont des enfants chez vous en recoivent que d'excellentes nouvelles,' and predicted that the 'recrus seront probablement trop nombreuses dans un avenir prochain.' On the other hand, he gently chided the principal for failing to ensure that the children from Moosonee wrote home. 'Les parents des enfants à votre école ont restés surpris de ne pas reçevoir de lettres par les derniers courriers.'[36] In 1936 the official publication of the Chooutla school near Carcross, Yukon, indirectly acknowledged the influence of Native opinion when it congratulated itself on being 'full to over-flowing,' with more 'awaiting admittance.' Chooutla, 'under the popular and efficient leadership of Rev. H.C.M. Grant, its Principal, seems to be more than ever highly regarded by the Indians [sic] parents.'[37] And school officials were quick to celebrate when student opinion seemed favourable, as when Chief Starblanket's son was unexpectedly enrolled in the File Hills school, or a student of the Chapleau institution wrote a positive composition on 'Indian Education' that was published in the Toronto *Globe*.[38] These instances were merely the favourable side of the coin of student opinion. Most of the examples of parental protest and pressure noted above were the result of student complaints, sometimes transmitted surreptitiously by the pupils outside censored channels.

Within the walls of the schools themselves, disgruntled students were most likely to indicate their unhappiness with ridicule and a lack of cooperation. One practice that residential school students shared with pupils everywhere was the use of derisory nicknames for teachers and childcare workers. Among themselves, children at Shubenacadie tagged Sister Mary Leonard, the heavyset supervisor they feared, with the name 'Wikew,' which was Micmac for 'fatty.'[39] At St Philip's school a nun who was particularly hated by the students was known as 'Little Weasel' in Saulteaux.[40] At Shubenacadie during Isabelle Knockwood's time as a student, some 'boys developed nicknames for various nuns based on elaborate and obscene wordplays in Mi'kmaw.' One sister who the boys believed 'was sexually "loose"' was named *Bujig'm*—a nonsense word which sounds similar to *Bijag'n*—which translates literally as "throw it in."' One of the girls would alter Latin words in hymns into ribald Micmac. For example, *Resurrecsit sicut dixit* became *Resurrecsit kisiku iktit*, changing the meaning from 'He said he would rise again' to 'When the old man got up, he farted.' What made the episode all the more delicious was that the sister presiding would stop the singing and 'patiently teach Clara the proper pronunciation. Clara would just stand there and grin. Even the holy ones had to laugh.'[41]

Non-cooperation was more overt than name calling. A former student of the Anglicans' Pelican Lake school vividly remembered an 'older boy' in one of her early classes who never participated in the work of the classroom. He simply sat stolidly at his desk ignoring everything around him.[42] At Moose Factory, Billy Diamond defied a supervisor by refusing to finish his vegetables. The future chief 'sat without eating for eight hours, the plate in front of him and the supervisor pacing behind until finally, at two o'clock in the morning, with the vegetables cold and still untouched, the supervisor caved in and sent the boy up to the darkened dormitory, where dozens of boys still lay with their eyes closed, feigning sleep while they awaited the outcome of the vegetable standoff.'[43] The Methodists' Coqualeetza school in British Columbia recorded in its register of admissions and discharges several students who were 'Discharged because of indisposition for work or study,' or 'Sent away as incorrigible,' or discharged because of an 'indisposition or inaptitude for study.'[44] The Oblate principal at Fort George also expelled a young fellow whom he described as 'unusually stubborn and would not cooperate with school authorities.'[45] Offences might range from refusal to do school work to misbehaviour in chapel; an almost unlimited number of possibilities was available. Isabelle Knockwood delighted in defying Wikew's 'Don't dare move a muscle' at bedtime by 'wiggling my toes under the blankets thinking, "You ain't my boss and I'll wiggle all I want." At the same time, I was looking straight at her wearing the Indian mask which I had discovered over the years she couldn't read.'[46] More overt were the boys at Lytton who threatened the principal to his face that they would steal food if he didn't provide them with better rations. They were pleasantly surprised when their challenge succeeded.[47]

Indeed, the favourite form of misbehaviour among students was stealing food. The young women at Kamloops school organized elaborate schemes to pilfer apples and other food that they shared in the dormitory.[48] Similar stunts were carried out at most schools at one time or another. The boys at Elkhorn in the 1940s killed one of the school's pigs by spraying it with water and leaving it to freeze to death. When the school authorities could not figure out what had killed the pig, they ordered it incinerated. The boys who leapt to dispose of the carcass in fact roasted and hid it, treating the contraband pork as snack for many days.[49] Food pranks that involved staff were fondly remembered. One woman took advantage of the assignment of clearing the staff dining room to sample delicacies with a spoon she had brought. When she found the large jar of horse-radish not to her liking, she spat the condiment back in the jar and screwed the lid on.[50] A male former student of Shubenacadie told Isabelle Knockwood that boys working in the barn sometimes urinated in the milk destined for the sisters and priest.[51] A particularly wicked thrill could be obtained by directing misbehaviour at the religious practices of the missionaries. Some students conscripted into assisting with services indulged in mockery, and a former altar boy recalled how they used to mock the Mass that all were compelled to attend every morning.[52]

More daring—and more rewarding—was theft of communion wine, either by suborning a person who looked after the sacristy or through a nighttime raid.[53] Getting drunk on the stolen wine, however, gave the game away with dire consequences.[54] A man who had attended several residential schools in Ontario recalled that at Shingwauk he and another boy had made homebrew in the attic of the carpenter's work-shop. They had a fright one day when the carpenter smelled something strange and noticed a leak in his shop ceiling. The artisan said that they would have to reroof the building because it was obviously leaking. The boys, who knew better, moved their illegal brew to the barn, where they later got roaring drunk on it.[55]

Another guilty pleasure for multitudes of residential school students was getting around the strict rules on segregation of the sexes. Justa Monk 'had my first sexual experience with another student, a girl I really liked, within the walls of Lejac, just a few feet from one of the brothers who was peeling potatoes at the time.'[56] In some schools, like Shingwauk, where the girls' and boys' dormitories were wings at opposite ends of the same building, contact could be made by going over the rooftop at night—a dangerous resort even if one was not appre-hended.[57] Boys at Blue Quills who thought access to the latest technology was the solution to their isolation discovered that science could be their undoing, too. 'I remember one time we used walkies talkies to socialize with the girls,' recalled one, 'but we were found out because of the wiring system or the pipes. Somehow it got connected with the television and we got caught because our voices came on the television.'[58]

Where the living quarters of the sexes were completely separate, as at Spanish where the girls' school was across the road from the boys', more elaborate arrangements were necessary. There a complicated communications system was worked out, one that, ironically, relied on the daily visit of one of the Jesuits to the girls' chapel to say Mass. A boy who wanted to communicate surreptitiously with a girl would arrange for a message to be slipped into the priest's hatband. When the celebrant reached the vestibule at the girls' school, his hat would be placed on a stand, whence it would be quietly picked up and the slip of paper with the illicit message extracted. A return note could be sent back to the boy with the priest on his return after Mass. Another means used at Spanish capitalized on the fact that shoe repairs were carried out in the cobbler shop in the boys' building. A girl would sew a message into the lining of a pair of boots that was being sent across for repair. This system worked reasonably well, too, although the girls sometimes damaged the newly refurbished boots extracting the return message.[59] Some students simply arranged for regular meeting places and times with either siblings or members of the opposite sex in whom they had a romantic interest.[60] Charlie Nowell in British Columbia eventually got expelled from Alert Bay school when one of his notes to a girl whom he met regularly in the evenings was intercepted by her stepfather.[61] Peter Webster got out of Ahousaht at the age of fourteen when 'I took the blame for the pregnancy of one of my classmates.'[62]

In situations where extensive flouting of the rules about segregation of mature males and females occurred, complications generally ensued. In the early days, a small boarding school such as Alberni on Vancouver Island had considerable difficulty dealing with such a problem. Lax supervision by a trusting matron led to her dismissal, only to be replaced by new officers who upset children and parents by locking the girls in their dormitory every night.[63] At the Anglicans' Sarcee school, similar concerns led to protracted discussions over the design of dormitory windows. The local missionary wanted windows with sashes that could be opened, necessitating, in his opinion, the installation of bars on the outside of the window openings. But the Indian agent ruled that no bars were necessary, leaving the cleric with grave concerns about security.[64] As the new regime at Alberni learned a couple of years after the window debate at Sarcee, open windows led to nocturnal visits, which in the Alberni case led to nailing the windows closed.[65] In extenuation, the Alberni principal contended that 'in other schools similar difficulties have arisen and in Regina we had a share and a great deal more serious than ours.'[66] Indeed, both the Cecilia Jeffrey and the Regina schools had had encounters with the problem. Things so degenerated at the Presbyterian schools that one missionary charged 'the conduct has become almost like that of a brothel instead of a Church home,' while the principal of the File Hills boarding school stated flatly that 'I for one will never consent to send my children that I am treasuring with a mother's love where they would be exposed to such dangers.'[67]

At the Methodists' Brandon school, some of the boys obtained duplicate keys and used them to visit the girls' dormitory before they were caught.[68] When principals at Regina and Alberni responded to renewed scandal by locking the dorms from the outside or by barring the windows, they encountered objections from the Indian Affairs department, which 'objects to the bars lest the building should be a fire trap in case of accident.'[69] Concerns over the students' persistent success in violating the rules against fraternization contributed to the problems that caused closure of both Crowstand and Regina.[70] Others, such as Alberni, carried on for many decades in spite of recurrent problems. At Alberni, the staff put 'a wax stamp and a chain' across the window of the most accessible boys' dormitory, but this merely forced the amorous to take a more dangerous route 'through the window on the west side of the building, and along a ledge of the roof. There was a drop of thirty feet to the ground.'[71] Whether it was a Presbyterian school on Vancouver Island or an Anglican institution near Sault Ste Marie, adolescents found similar ways to flout the rules and get in touch with members of the opposite sex.

Sometimes there was a connection between illicit relations and what was probably the most commonly reported manifestation of student resistance—running away from school. A former administrator of the Pelican Lake school recalled an incident in which an Indian boy who lived with a family in the town of Sioux Lookout paddled across the lake to rendezvous with his girlfriend, a classmate. The following morning they were discovered in a tent not too far off from the school.[72] Although there could be many reasons for students' deserting, the reaction that flight evoked among staff was uniformly negative. For one thing, runaways caused considerable difficulties and anxieties. Early in the century, the missionary principal of Norway House in northern Manitoba had to make a January trip 320 kilometres northeast accompanied by a Mountie to retrieve pupils who had not returned after the summer vacation.[73] At a crasser level, unauthorized absences, if detected by Indian Affairs officials, would lead to a decrease in revenue. For example, when six girls ran away from a Manitoba school 'to attend a dance on the Reserve,' it cost the Anglican Missionary Society a thirteen dollar fee to the police.[74]

[...]

Even more dramatic a form of rebellion than truancy was arson. For students who were unable to escape, often an emotionally satisfying substitute was to attack the school with fire. Once again, as with the problem of runaways, there tended to be a suspiciously high correlation between troubles at a school and a mysterious outbreak of fire. For example, at Wikwemikong in the 1880s, during a period of some tension between missionaries and parents, there were two unexplained fires early in 1885, and another fire at the girls' school in the autumn of 1888 that had definitely been set by two students.[75] At the Presbyterian school at Birtle, Manitoba, a young boy calmly went into the pantry, took matches, and proceeded to set fire to the barn on a September day in 1903.[76] Alberni home burned down in suspicious circumstances in 1917.[77] The Anglicans in the 1920s experienced arson at Alert Bay, which was full to overflowing—sometimes a sign of parental confidence in a school—and at Onion Lake, which was always in some difficulty.[78] The Onion Lake fire in 1928 appeared to be 'copycat' incendiarism: two boys at the Anglican school seem to have been influenced by a recent fire at the neighbouring Catholic school that had completely destroyed the institution. The razing of the Cross Lake school in Manitoba, also in 1928, probably was a coincidence.[79] The Oblates had a suspicious fire at Duck Lake in 1926, and two boys attempted arson at the Sioux Lookout school in 1931. The principal of the Elkhorn residential school was not very pleased when the two would-be arsonists were transferred to his school.[80] The Oblates at Pine Creek, Manitoba, in 1930 had the distinction of double arson, one boy 'having set the church on fire and another boy ... tried to do the same to the School.'[81] In less than a decade after 1936, nine residential schools were destroyed by fires of various origins.[82]

[...]

Arsonists and runaways were merely the extreme of a continuum of unhappy and angry students who, like their parents, often resisted and protested as best they could against the iniquities of residential school life. From complaints, to acts of non-cooperation and defiance, to antisocial actions—these students often expressed by their words and actions what many others felt, others who often were too timid or intimidated to follow suit. What is less clear about resistance by both parents and schoolchildren is how effective their deeds and arguments were. Certainly, when a leading Blood man came to Canon Middleton and objected to his children being taught Blackfoot syllabics, the missionary was more than happy to oblige his desire for solely English instruction.[83] Often missionaries evinced concern to maintain good relations with children and parents, and they trumpeted any small victories they experienced. Kate Gillespie of File Hills was delighted when Chief Starblanket let his son attend the Presbyterian school rather than Catholic Lebret.[84]

[...]

Probably the best symbol of Native resistance to the intrusive and oppressive nature of residential schools was found in the persistence of traditional cultural practices, such as dancing among Plains peoples and the potlatch on the Pacific. That former residential school students, as noted earlier, were among the most energetic in defending the practices that assimilative education was supposed to consign to oblivion is among the most pointed ironies of the history of residential schooling. Also ironic was the fact that, by the time Native resistance led to removal of such coercive elements as the potlatch and prairie dancing bans in the 1951 amendment of the Indian Act, a dramatically new chapter in the residential school story was opening. This instalment—the conclusion, as it turned out—was the increasingly assertive and influential campaign of Native political organizations to eliminate residential schooling in Canada. The irony in this process, which stretched from the first major outpouring of Native political process in the later 1940s to the elimination of government-controlled residential schools in the late 1960s and 1970s, was that it was often former residential school students who provided the most vociferous criticism of education and the most effective political leadership. In helping to shape the generations of political leaders who emerged after the Second World War, residential schools contributed to the most effective of the many forms of Native resistance that had been spawned by these institutions.

So, anyway, after I finished sweeping—she kept following me around like this, cutting me [up], cutting my people up. All of a sudden I just swung my broom like this. 'F you!' Oh, I swore. 'Don't swear.' I said, 'F you.' I kept on. I just went wild. I just snapped. 'You f-ing, fucking...' Oh, did I ever use that F word! Did I ever swear! 'Keep quiet! Everybody's listening.' 'I don't give a damn. I don't give a fuck!' I just went completely wild. And I stood up to her like this.

She said, 'You come upstairs. I'm going to fix you.' 'You're f-ing right I will,' I said. In the meantime, even the boys came running towards the girls' side. And they're all prompting me, 'Don't be scared of her. Keep it up. Keep it up.' They took me upstairs. Those other two—that nun that made trouble for me and another nun—came running. Three of them, they grabbed brooms on the third floor. They beat me up with brooms. Brooms all over. And I grabbed ahold of her ... I grabbed her veil like this. And she was hanging on, and she had me by the hair. And another nun was hitting me all over. I just didn't care. One of them nuns, I grabbed ahold of her like this and swung like this. She landed far [away]. Oh, she landed like at the end of that wall. That's how far [away] she landed. I really went wild that time. And the other one, I grabbed her and flung her like this. And I hung on to this one. And then she told them in French to go. They went crying 'cause I made them cry.

There was me and her now. I said, 'Kill me first; I'm not giving up.' I just hung on to her. Every time she'd hit me, I'd hit her right back. Oh, I had her good. 'Let me go,' she said. I'd jerk her like this. And she'd hang on to it [her veil]. Finally, she said, 'In the name of God, please let me go, Pauline.'[85]

Notes

1. Isabelle Knockwood, *Out of the Depths: The Experience of Mi'kmaw Children at the Indian Residential School of Shubenacadie, Nova Scotia* (Lockeport, NS: Roseway Publishing 1992), 125

2. Interview, 21 June 1990, Whitehorse, with a Han male who attended Whitehorse Baptist Mission school 1951–3 (interview by Lu Johns Penikett)

3. United Church of Canada Archives [UCA], Records of the Presbyterian Church [PC], Foreign Mission Committee [FMC], Western Section [WS], Indian Work in Manitoba and the North West [IWMNW], box 7, file 155, Report of Visit to Indian Missions, 15 Aug. 1913. Other examples concern Mount Elgin in Ontario, both before the Great War (ibid., A. Sutherland Papers, box 8, file 154, T.T. George to A. Sutherland, 27 May 1908, and Sutherland to George, 3 June 1908) and during the 1940s (ibid., E.E. Joblin Papers, box 1, file 3, Notes on the Survey of the Education of Indian Children in Western Ontario, 15 Sept. 1943). In commenting on complaints made in the 1890s about the Wikwemikong schools on Manitoulin Island, the Jesuit historian noted, after conceding that Indian Affairs investigated parental complaints, that the outcome 'shows that the Indians were still capable of thinking and speaking nonsense.' Regis College Archives, Father Julien Paquin, 'Modern Jesuit Indian Missions in Ontario' (unpaginated manuscript)

4. General Synod Archives [GSA], GS 75-103, Papers of the Missionary Society of the Church in Canada [GS 75-103], Series 2-14, Special Indian Committee [Series 2-14], box 19, S.H. Blake correspondence, file Mar/08–June/09, F.H. DuVernet to S.H. Blake, 23 Mrch 1909, enclosing copy DuVernet to Secretary, Department of Indian Affairs, 23 March 1909.

5. National Archives of Canada [NA], MG 29, E. 106, Hayter Reed Papers, box 20, 1255, H. Reed to Inspector J.A. Macrae, 30 June 1892.

6. Paquin, 'Modern Jesuit Indian Missions'

7. NA, Records of the Department of Indian Affairs [RG 10], School Files, vol. 6320, file 658-1, part 1, 305595, (copy) David Laird to Indian Agent Sibbald, 28 Nov. 1906,' enclosed with Laird to Secretary, DIA, 4 March 1907. Laird continued to the Agent: 'When the children have sore necks or are tender about the throat, this sort of punishment is cruel. 'I think it would be well to call the meeting of Indians you propose, speak to them in a persuasive manner, assure them the overwork and ear-twisting will be discontinued, and tell them the Indian Commissioner [Laird] and the Department are most anxious that they should send their children to school.'

8. Reed Papers, vol. 12, file 'Rev. T. Clarke 1891-92,' 132, T. Clarke to Hayter Reed, 14 July 1891

9. Archives of the Manitoba and Northwestern Ontario Conference of the United Church of Canada, University of Winnipeg [UCA-Wpg], Minute Book of Presbyterian Workers among the Indians, Synods of Manitoba and Saskatchewan, 1909–1915, 68, Fifth Convention, Crowstand school, 23–24 July 1912

10. Archives Deschâtelets [AD], L 535 .M27L 349, William Moss, OMI, to J. Magnan, OMI, 18 April 1932. Father Moss was replaced as principal shortly after this incident. Ibid., 351, J. Magnan to A.S. Williams, 21 May 1932

11. PC, FMC, WS, Indian Work in BC [IWBC], box 1, file 16, Hamilton Cassels and Andrew Jeffrey to R.P. MacKay, 4 Aug. 1897

12. GS 75-103, Series 2-15, Papers of the MSCC [Series 2-15], Records of the Indian and Eskimo Residential School Commission [IESRC], box 21, 9, Minute of 28 Aug. 1928. In this case, since the principal at Elkhorn had already rejected similar complaints, 'No further action was considered necessary' by the central body.

13. AD, L 912 .M27C 195, Maurice Bruyere and Joe Mainville to Rev. Fr. Magnan, Provincial OMI, nd [1933]. The following year a new principal was appointed and, apparently, conditions improved for a number of years. However, by the end of 1940, the president of the Columbus Indian Mission Club on the reserve was objecting to another deterioration in conditions at the school.

14. UCA-Wpg. A.B. Baird Papers, box G, G 1393-4, A.B. Baird to Rev. C.W. Whyte. The principal's resignation (Whyte to Baird, 12 March 1897) is ibid., G 1214-18.

15. PC, FMC, WS, IWBC, box 3, file 174, A.W. Vowell to Dr John Campbell, 13 May 1905 (enclosing letter from Dan Watts, Big George, Tatoosh Jimmie George, Tyee Bob of 6 May); ibid., James R. Motion to R.P. MacKay, 27 May 1905. Swewish, who claimed to be 'chief of the Shesaht people,' later wrote to denounce the petitioners and to endorse the work of the principal. Ibid., file 75, Shewish to R.P. MacKay, 5 July 1905 (translated and typed by James R. Motion)

16. PC, FMC, WS, IWMNW, box 2, file 41, petition from Shoal Lake Reserve, 22 Sept. 1902 (enclosed with A.G. McKitrick to MacKay, 23 Sept. 1902); ibid., Maggie A. Nicoll to R.P. MacKay, 23 Sept. 1902;

ibid., file 42, same to same, 13 Oct. 1902; ibid., file 40, same to same, 25 Aug. 1902. See also ibid., box 3, file 55, J.O. McGregor and Sarah McGregor to R.P. MacKay, 27 Nov. 1903, in which a new principal and matron complained that the missionary, A.G. McKitrick, interfered with their work by insisting that the original promise 'that the children would not be taught religion' be honoured.

17. Ibid., box 5, file 95, Petition dated Shoal Lake, 4 March 1907, to Foreign Mission Society, Toronto (interpreted by Miss Mary Begg and transcribed by Miss E. Robertson, teacher)

18. Ibid., file 111, Report of the Subcommittee of Synodical Indian Mission Committee, Manitoba and Saskatchewan, July 1908. See also ibid., box 6, file 117, Agnes Sibbald to Rev. Dr J. Farquharson, 30 Jan. 1909.

19. Ibid., W.W. Shoup (Nelson House) to A. Sutherland, 17 March 1907

20. Reed Papers, vol. 19, file 'May 1891,' 619, Knatakasiwisine (Piapot Reserve) to D[ea]r Sister in law (Mrs Mistassini], 21 May 1891

21. PC, FMC, WS, IWMNW, box 1, file 24, J.A. Sinclair to R.P. MacKay, 19 April 1901; ibid., box 5, file 115, (copy) R.P. MacKay to J. Farquharson, 30 Nov. 1908; ibid., file 116, J. Farquharson to R.P. MacKay, 3 Dec. 1908

22. Ibid., box 4, file 70, Neil Gilmour (Norway House) to R.P. MacKay, 11 Feb. 1905. Gilmour was referring specifically to 'the reserves that form the Regina School constituency.'

23. Ibid., file 72, F.O. Gilbart to R.P. MacKay. 28 April 1905

24. Ibid., box 7, file 145, W.W. McLaren, report on tour of reserves and schools in southern Manitoba and southern Saskatchewan, 22 April 1912

25. Report of Deputy Superintendent General James A. Smart, in Annual Report of DIA for 1900, Canada, *Sessional Papers [CSP] (No. 27) 1901,* xxxiii. The deputy minister went on: 'equally natural is it for the teachers of boarding schools to desire to retain their pupils instead of drafting them to the higher institutions.'

26. The materials for the White Bear story, which were assembled by Mary Miller for my benefit, are found in RG 10, Black Series, vol. 3940, file 121,698-13, part 0; and Annual Reports of the Department of Indian Affairs, 1880–1906. The materials quoted are from letters written in 1897, and from the report for 1897. Concerning the resistance to residential schooling, the 1897 department report (*CSP[No. 14] 1898,* 161) was clear and revealing: 'There are twenty-five children of school age in the band, and seven of them are attending the industrial schools at Regina, Qu'Appelle and Elkhorn. It is very difficult to get the parents to allow the children to be sent away to school, more especially those Indians who are in any way connected with the deposed chief White Bear and his sons, who will have nothing to do with anything in the shape of education, and who try to live as they did before treaty was made with the North-west Indians.'

27. Archives of Yukon [AY], Anglican Diocese of Yukon Records, box 7, file 9, T.B.R. Westgate to W. Barlow, 7 July 1925

28. Ibid., I.O. Stringer to T.B.R. Westgate, 21 Oct. 1929. Westgate, the Anglican's head man in missionary work in Canada, in turn lamented to DIA that an enrolment of twenty-six in a school with a pupilage of forty meant serious financial problems for the school and the church. Ibid., T.B.R. Westgate to Secretary, DIA, 16 Dec. 1929

29. L.G.P. Waller, ed., *The Education of Indian Children in Canada* (Toronto: Ryerson Press 1965), 103–4. Mrs Tizya also recalled: 'And so, for the next 25 years, no children were sent out to the Carcross Indian Residential School and it was for this reason that we decided to bring our children out to where they could become educated. We realized that we could not do anything for our children in an atmosphere where no one else cared about his children' (104).

30. PC, FMB, IWMNW, box 1, file 33, 'Agreement' of 14 Jan. 1902 enclosed with J.C. Gandier to R.P. MacKay, same date. The first clause of the agreement provided: 'That while children are young and at school they shall not be baptized without the consent of their parents …'

31. Brass, *I Walk in Two Worlds,* 13

32. Clelland S. Ford, *Smoke from Their Fires: The Life of a Kwakiutl Chief* (New Haven, Conn.: Yale University Press 1941), 85–6 and 107

33. PC, FMC, WS, IWMNW, box 3, file 46, D. Spear to R.P. MacKay, 26 Feb. 1903. The agent's visit had occurred a little before Christmas.

34. Baird Papers, box 3, E1156-9, A.S. McLeod to A.B. Baird, 4 June 1891

35. See PC, FMC, WS, IWMNW, box 4, file 59, E. MacKenzie to R.P. MacKay, 7 March 1904; James R.

Stevens, ed., *Recollections of an Assiniboine Chief* [Dan Kennedy, Ochankuhage] (Toronto: McClelland & Stewart 1972), 103–4. See also RG 10, Black Series, vol. 3825, file 60, 511-1, J.D. McLean to Indian Commissioner, 5 Jan. 1903: 'Chief Wanduta, of the Oak River Sioux Band, has called at the Department with his son, who is a graduate of the Brandon Industrial School.'

36. AD, LCB 3445 .G46M 65, J. Cyr, OMI, to Father Labrèche, 13 Feb. 1944 [families that have children at your school have received only excellent reports, (and) recruits probably will be too numerous in the near future]; ibid., 66, same to same, 28 March 1944 [families of children at your school remain surprised at not receiving letters by the last mail].

37. AY, Anglican Yukon Records, *Northern Lights* 25, 4 (Nov. 1936): 3

38. PC, FMC, WS, IWMNW, box 3, file 55, K. Gillespie to R.P. MacKay, 20 Nov. 1903; *Globe,* 9 Oct. 1926, 'Certified by G.T. Snowden, Acting Principal,' The published letter was noted by the Anglicans' missionary body: GS 75-103, Series 2-15, box 21, 812

39. Knockwood, *Out of the Depths*, 32. The students had other, somewhat less derogatory names in their own language for other sisters.

40. Joe Severight interview, Cote Reserve, 19 Feb. 1992. Mr Severight also recalled that some boys— 'peeping Toms,' he called them—spied on two of the sisters, whose bedroom adjoined the boys' dormitory.

41. Knockwood, *Out of the Depths,* 124

42. Interview with an Ojibwa woman who in the 1940s attended Pelican Lake from age seven until about age eleven, 2 Feb. 1991, Sioux Lookout, Ont. She recalled that this boy ran away several times and was strapped for it once.

43. Roy MacGregor, *Chief: The Fearless Vision of Billy Diamond* (Toronto: Penguin 1989), 25–6. The episode clinched young Billy's role as leader of the students.

44. Vancouver, United Church of Canada Conference of BC Archives, Coqualeetza Register of Admissions and Discharges, numbers 38, 049, 89, and 90

45. AD, LCB 3346 .G46M 112, (copy) W.S. Gran to Regional Supervisor, 14 Feb. 1961

46. Knockwood, *Out of the Depths*, 125

47. 100 Verna J. Kirkness, ed., *Khot-La-Cha: The Autobiography of Chief Simon Baker* (Vancouver/Toronto: Douglas & McIntyre 1994), 36–7

48. Haig-Brown, *Resistance and Renewal,* 89–90

49. Telephone interview with Ernest Hall, 3 Aug. 1993. I am indebted to Regina writer Jim Anderson, who first told me of this incident.

50. This anecdote was told by an unidentified woman, who said that it had been experienced by another woman, during a public session of the 'Journey to Healing' Conference, 26 Sept. 1991, Saskatoon.

51. Knockwood, *Out of the Depths*, 55. The workers knew which milk was headed for the staff dining room because it always came from the cows that gave milk of higher quality than the rest.

52. Interview, 21 Jan. 1992, Saskatoon, with male Saulteaux student who attended St Philip's, 1955–62, and Marieval 1962–5

53. Haig-Brown, *Resistance and Renewal,* 91, recounts an organized system at Kamloops for the theft and sale of eucharistic wine.

54. Joe Severight interview. Mr Severight, who attended St Philip's school in the 1930s, recalled that he and his companions were punished—after they had sobered up.

55. A male (surname Kakeegesic) who attended Chapleau, Moose Factory, and Shingwauk schools, speaking at the public session of Shingwauk reunion, 4 July 1991

56. Bridget Moran, *Justa: A First Nations Leader* (Vancouver: Arsenal Pulp Press 1994). 54. On another occasion, 'Sister Alphonse saw me kissing a girl in the priests' dining room' and 'started slapping me. I grabbed her wrists and squeezed them hard and I said to her, "You're not my teacher now,"' Ibid., 55

57. Recollection in public session at Shingwauk reunion, 4 July 1991

58. Diane Persson, 'The Changing Experience of Indian Residential Schooling: Blue Quills, 1931–1970,' in Jean Barmen, Yvonne Hébert, and Don McCaskill, *Indian Education in Canada*, vol. 1: *The Legacy* (Vancouver: University of British Columbia Press and Nakoda Institute 1986), 164

59. Interview with Miss Ann Berrigan, SFM (La Société des Filles du Coeur de Marie), Montreal, 16 Oct. 1990. Students at St Philip's school in the 1950s used a wood box as a 'drop' for messages between boys and girls. On one occasion, a staff member found a note, assembled the students, and read the message aloud to embarrass those involved. Interview, 21 Jan. 1992, Saskatoon, with male Saulteaux student of St Philip's, 1955–62, and Marieval, 1962–5

60. Interview, 15 Dec. 1987, Regina, with Joy Mann

61. Ford, *Smoke from Their Fires*, 104–5

62. Peter Webster, *As Far as I Know: Reminiscences of an Ahousat Elder* (Campbell River, BC: Campbell River Museum and Archives 1983), 42

63. PC, FMC, WS, IWBC, box 1, file 22, M. Swartout to R.P. MacKay, 22 Feb. 1899; ibid., file 23, K. Cameron to R.P. MacKay, 30 May 1899; ibid., B.I. Johnston to R.P. MacKay, 17 June 1899

64. Calgary Indian Missions Papers, box 3, vol. 1, 124–7, J.W. Tims to Mr Scott, 11 Aug. 1903

65. PC, FMC, WS, IWBC, box 3, file 72, K. Cameron to R.P. MacKay, 1 and 25 March 1905: ibid., Mrs J.R. Motion to R.P. MacKay, 29 March 1905

66. Ibid., file 75, J.R. Motion to R.P. MaKay, 17 June 1905

67. Ibid., IWMNW, box 3, file 55, A.G. McKitrick to R.P. MacKay, 14 Nov. 1903; ibid., box 5, file 74, Kate Gillespie to R.P. MacKay, 22 June 1905

68. Ibid., box 6, file 123, W.W. McLaren to R.P. MacKay, 5 July 1909. McLaren also noted of Brandon, 'The older boys too whenever they got a chance when on leave down town often frequent the redlight district of the city.'

69. Ibid., box 5, file 1095, (copy) D.M. Laird to Rev. Sir, 14 Jan. 1908; ibid., BFM, Correspondence with WFMS, box 1, file 24, (copy) R.P. MacKay to Mrs C. Clark, 5 May 1910

70. For a sample of the material on the Crowstand dormitory problems, see PC, FMC, WS, IWMNW, box 5, file 99, (copy) E. McWhinney to J. Farquharson, 8 July 1907.

71. PC, BFM, Correspondence with WMS, box 5, file 84. Helen W. Horne, assistant secretary for Indian Work, WMS to J.H. Edmison, 6 Jan. 1923; Chief Earl Maquinna George's Life Story (typescript), 25

72. Derek and Hazel Mills interview, 2 Feb. 1991, Sioux Lookout, Ont.

73. UCA-Wpg. J.A. Lousley Autobiography (manuscript), chapter 11, 2–3

74. GS 75-103, Series 2-15, box 20, minutes of 23 Oct. 1924. See also Archives of Yukon, YRG 1, Series 1., vol. 11, file 2335, part 6, (copy) John Hawksley (DIA) to Rev. Principal, Chooutla Indian School, 20 July 1932.

75. Paquin, 'Modern Jesuit Indian Missions': and 'Synopsis of the History of Wikwemikong'

76. PC, FMC, WS, IWNMW, box 3, file 53, E.H. Crawford to R.P. MacKay, 30 Sept. 1903

77. PC, BFM, Correspondence with WMS, box 4, file 61, Jessie Wilson to R.P. MacKay, 31 May 1917

78. GSA, M 75-1, Bishop Lucas Papers, box 2, Minutes of Commission, 23 Oct. 1924 re Alert Bay; GS 75-103. Series 2-15, box 21, Minutes of 6 March 1928

79. AD, LC 6201 .K26R 1, clipping from *Le Patriote*, 21 Oct. 1931

80. AD, HR 6671, .C73R 47, (copy) J. LeChevalier, OMI, to W.M. Graham, 4 May 1926, concerning Duck Lake; GS 75-103, Series 2-15, box 22, Minutes of 7 April and 30 April 1931

81. RG 10, School Files, vol. 6041, file 160-5, part 1, J. Magnan, OMI, to Duncan C. Scott, 2 Dec. 1930

82. Joblin Papers, box 1, file 3, (copy) R.A. Hoey to G. Dorey, 29 May 1944. With all these fires, missionaries might be forgiven the odd bit of paranoia. The Oblates, for example, thought that a fire at Fort Frances school had been set by an American socialist in revenge for the principal's discouraging organizing on the nearby reserve. *Missions*, no. 214, (Sept–Dec. 1921): 307–8

83. Middleton Papers, box 2, file 7, (copy) S.H. Middleton to Roberta Forsberg, 7 Nov. 1960

84. PC, FMC, WS, IWMNW, box 3, file 55, K. Gillespie to R.P. MacKay, 20 Nov. 1903

85. Interview with Pauline Pelly, former St Philip's student, 6 Sept. 1991, Saskatoon. The altercation between Pauline and the sister lasted some time, and eventually the confrontation shifted to the student's home on the reserve, because the principal followed her there. Pauline's father sternly admonished the Oblates for the behaviour of the sister and the principal.

CONSTRUCTING A CANADIAN ICON

The Medicare Debate to the 1960s

Maureen Lux
Brock University

CONSTRUCTING A CANADIAN ICON: THE MEDICARE DEBATE TO THE 1960s

● **Introduction by Maureen Lux**

▲ **Primary Sources**

■ **Secondary Sources**

● INTRODUCTION

Maureen Lux

Canadians take great pride in their national health insurance program, or Medicare. As an icon of Canadian identity, it is one of the few issues on which we can agree, and although we love to complain about it, voters consistently tell politicians to keep their hands off Medicare. In 2002, in response to another "crisis" over healthcare costs and increasing wait times for treatment, Roy Romanow led a Royal Commission on the future of health care. He found that Canadians strongly support Medicare's core values of "equity, fairness and solidarity. These values are tied to their understanding of citizenship."[1] In November 2004 the CBC asked its audience to name the "greatest Canadian of all time." Canadians overwhelmingly chose a politician—T.C. (Tommy) Douglas—for his role as the "Father of Medicare."

The notion that Medicare was born of a single parent is a simplification, of course. Moreover, only about 70 percent of services (doctor visits and hospital treatment) are financed by taxation; private payments cover the other 30 percent, which includes such services as dental care and prescription drugs.[2] But there can be no question that Medicare has come to define what it means to be Canadian, even though the national program, not established until 1968, is fairly recent. It might seem strange that an insurance program should carry such importance, but Medicare distinguishes Canadians from Americans and allows Canadians to feel not a little superior.

It was not always so. The national health insurance program, like much public policy, emerged out of struggle between a vision of a much more comprehensive program and the demands of Medicare's opponents.

In June 1944 Saskatchewan elected the Co-operative Commonwealth Federation (CCF, later NDP), the first social democratic government in North America, led by Tommy Douglas. The CCF ended the decade-long Liberal party rule and captured 47 of 52 seats in the provincial legislature. Douglas' CCF emerged out of the social, political, and economic circumstances of the province, especially the searing experience of the Depression.

The international economic decline began in the late 1920s, and the Canadian economy reacted quickly since Canada exported so much of its resources. In the prairie West the "Dirty Thirties" began in 1931 with the weather: hot, dry winds blew month after month, year after year, drying fields, destroying crops, covering everything with dust. Some years were worse, some better, but by 1938 the drought led to a plague of grasshoppers that ate anything that managed to stay green.[3] Worse yet, the international market for prairie grain collapsed, leaving farmers with accumulated debt and little income. Unemployment rose to dangerous levels in central Canada when prairie farmers could no longer afford the cars, tractors, radios, and refrigerators that the factories produced. Understandably more than a quarter-million people gave up on the place and left the prairies in the 1930s, but what is surprising is how many remained. Municipalities, responsible for assistance, made the experience of collecting "relief" in the form of vouchers for food and clothing sufficiently humiliating in order to deter all but the most destitute. It seemed to many during the Depression that capitalism itself could not, or should not, survive.

The CCF's political and ideological program, a practical blend of socialism and Christian values, was spelled out in the Regina Manifesto at its founding meeting in 1933. The CCF, declared the Manifesto, would not rest until cooperation replaced competition, until socialism replaced capitalism.

> We aim to replace the present capitalist system, with its inherent injustice and inhumanity, by a social order from which the domination and exploitation of one

class by another will be eliminated, in which economic planning will supersede unregulated private enterprise and competition....[4]

This Depression-inspired document called for wide-ranging social and economic change, including socialized health services and "insurance covering illness, accident, old age and unemployment."[5] During the Depression doctors' bills were often the last to be paid, if they were paid at all. A survey of rural physicians in the early 1940s found that most worried that private practice was no longer possible. One physician despaired: "Any system is to be preferred to the present. Collections appear hopeless."[6] By 1943 the Canadian Medical Association (CMA) endorsed a scheme of compulsory medical insurance, acknowledging the Depression's impact on the health of Canadians, as well as its impact on doctors' incomes.[7] As Bothwell and English argue in "Pragmatic Physicians" included here (Article 1), organized medicine's stance on health insurance waxed and waned depending on the economic climate. By the 1930s its solid support for 'socialized medicine', led by government, reflected doctors' plummeting economic and social position. But this was the last time organized medicine would agree on the need for a comprehensive program of health insurance; in the postwar period organized medicine was the most strenuous opponent of Medicare.

The CCF's first electoral victory came not during the Depression but in 1944 during wartime's full employment. Certainly the memory of the Depression was still vivid for voters, but the CCF also appealed to voters by tempering some of the Manifesto's more radical proposals. Just as important to the victory was Douglas himself. A Baptist preacher in Weyburn, Saskatchewan, he was a fiery campaigner and a gifted speaker. One of his more famous speeches, "Mouseland," is reproduced here. He used humour, sarcasm, and allegory to criticize the economic and political status quo, which appealed to hardworking Canadians. Another of his famous speeches, "The Cream Separator," likened economic society to the cream separator where milk (produced by farmers) was churned by workers, to separate the skim milk from the cream, which was consumed by the "corporate elite" that owned the machine. The farmer and worker were made to fight over the thin skim milk, and each blamed the other. And when there was too much cream and the corporate elite couldn't consume it all, the worker was laid off and markets for farmer's milk disappeared. The moral of the story, and the promise of the CCF, was that one day the farmers and workers would take control of the machine "so that it begins to produce homogenized milk in which everybody'll get a little cream."[8]

Douglas as premier and minister of health committed his government to health insurance. A rough chronology of events leads to the impression that Saskatchewan led the way: in 1947 Saskatchewan established hospital insurance; a national hospital insurance program followed in 1958; in 1962 Saskatchewan enacted universal health insurance after a bitter doctor's strike; in 1968 the federal government developed a national health insurance program. But such a chronology dismisses the struggles and compromises that lay behind the policies; it creates the notion that the development of Medicare was a story of inevitable progress. History rarely happens that way.

In July 1962 Saskatchewan doctors withdrew their services, hoping to force changes to the government's medical insurance plan. "Keep Our Doctors" committees formed in reaction to a well-funded propaganda campaign that threatened the province's doctors would leave rather than work under the government plan. The images of protest and conflict reproduced here suggest that many Saskatchewan residents supported the physicians and loudly opposed health insurance. The bitter three-week doctors' strike ended with a compromise agreement that allowed physicians to work on a fee-for-service basis rather than as salaried employees; they could continue to see patients in their private offices rather than as part of a healthcare team in clinics. Medicare emerged out of this sort of protest and compromise.

Gerard Boychuk's article is part of a larger work that examines the history of health insurance in a comparative North American political framework that asks why Canada established a national insurance program while the Americans did not. His perspective is thoroughly political, and he concludes that the debate over health insurance in each country was fundamentally influenced by the larger political temper of the 1960s. American public policy, influenced by the politics of civil rights and "race," fragmented into a system of private health insurance, while Canada, threatened by Quebec nationalism, worked to integrate citizens into a national program. Boychuk's approach suggests that Medicare and its "core values" emerged by political negotiation from above rather than social pressure from below. But Boychuk does suggest an intriguing notion of how Medicare grew to iconic status in Canada.

Alvin Finkel's chapter highlights the material basis of public policy and the struggle between Medicare's proponents and its detractors. Finkel does not ignore politics, but he emphasizes the contingency of history. Nothing about Medicare was inevitable, and the program that emerged was less than its founders desired, but more than its opponents wanted.

NOTES

1. Roy Romanow, *Building on Values: The Future of Health Care in Canada* (Ottawa: Final Report of the Royal Commission on the Future of Health Care in Canada, 2002), xvi; Romanow was Saskatchewan's premier from 1991 to 2001.
2. Gregory P. Marchildon, *Health Systems in Transition: Canada* (Toronto: University of Toronto Press, 2005), 39.
3. Gerald Friesen, *The Canadian Prairies: A History* (Toronto: University of Toronto Press, 1987), 386.
4. Quoted in A. W. Johnson, *Dream No Little Dreams: A Biography of the Douglas Government of Saskatchewan, 1944–1961* (Toronto: University of Toronto Press, 2004), 21.
5. Johnson, 22.
6. Quoted in Gerard W. Boychuk, *National Health Insurance in the United States and Canada* (Washington: Georgetown University Press, 2008), 103.
7. Bernard Blishen, *Doctors and Doctrines: The Ideology of Medical Care in Canada* (Toronto: University of Toronto Press, 1969), 147.
8. Quoted in Dennis Gruending, ed., *Great Canadian Speeches* (Markham, ON: Fitzhenry and Whiteside, 2004), 152–3.

QUESTIONS

1. If Medicare was so important to Canadian identity, how can you explain the opposition to its implementation?
2. How did Medicare move from a contentious issue to an icon of identity so quickly?
3. As the Americans currently debate a public health insurance scheme, can you see parallels with the Canadian debate?
4. How does Finkel's approach differ from Boychuk's? Why?
5. In Douglas' "Mouseland" speech, who are the cats? Who are the mice?

FURTHER READINGS

Badgley, Robin F., and Samuel Wolfe, *Doctor's Strike: Medical Care and Conflict in Saskatchewan,* (Toronto: Macmillan, 1967).

Blishen, Bernard, *Doctors and Doctrines: The Ideology of Medical Care in Canada,* (Toronto: University of Toronto Press, 1969).

Boychuk, Gerard W., *National Health Insurance in the United States and Canada,* (Washington: Georgetown University Press, 2008).

Johnson, A. W., *Dream No Little Dreams: A Biography of the Douglas Government of Saskatchewan, 1944–1961,* (Toronto: University of Toronto Press, 2004).

Marchildon, Gregory P., *Health Systems in Transition: Canada,* (Toronto: University of Toronto Press, 2005).

"Medicare: A People's Issue," accessed February 1, 2010, from http://scaa.sk.ca/gallery/medicare/index.php.

Romanow, Roy, *Building on Values: The Future of Health Care in Canada*, (Ottawa: Final Report Royal Commission on the Future of Health Care in Canada, 2002).

▲ Document 1: Mouseland

Tommy Douglas

Mouseland was a place where all the little mice lived and played, were born and died. And they lived much the same as you and I do.

They even had a Parliament. And every four years they had an election. Used to walk to the polls and cast their ballots.

Some of them even got a ride to the polls. And got a ride for the next four years afterwards too. Just like you and me. And every time on election day all the little mice used to go to the ballot box and they used to elect a government. A government made up of big, fat, black cats.

Now if you think it strange that mice should elect a government made up of cats, you just look at the history of Canada for the last ninety years and maybe you'll see that they weren't any stupider than we are.

Now I'm not saying anything against the cats. They were nice fellows. They conducted their government with dignity. They passed good laws—that is, laws that were good for cats. But the laws that were good for cats weren't very good for mice. One of the laws said that mouse holes had to be big enough so a cat could get his paw in. Another law said that mice could only travel at certain speeds—so that a cat could get his breakfast without too much effort.

All the laws were good laws, for cats. But, oh, they were hard on the mice. And life was getting harder and harder. And when the mice couldn't put up with it any more, they decided that something had to be done about it. So they went en masse to the polls. They voted the black cats out. They put in the white cats.

Now the white cats had put up a terrific campaign. They said: "All that Mouseland needs is more vision." They said: "The trouble with Mouseland is those round mouse holes we got. If you put us in we'll establish square mouse holes." And they did. And the square mouse holes were twice as big as the round mouse holes, and now the cat could get both paws in. And life was tougher than ever.

And when they couldn't take that anymore, they voted the white cats out and put the black ones in again. Then they went back to the white cats. Then to the black cats. They even tried half black and half white cats. And they called that coalition. They even got one government made up of cats with spots on them: they were cats that tried to make a noise like a mouse but ate like a cat.

You see, my friends, the trouble wasn't with the colour of the cat. The trouble was that they were cats. And because they were cats, they naturally looked after cats instead of mice.

Presently there came along one little mouse who had an idea. My friends, watch out for the little fellow with an idea. And he said to the other mice, "Look, fellows, why do we keep electing a government made up of cats? Why don't we elect a government made up of mice?" "Oh," they said, "he's a Bolshevik. Lock him up!" So they put him in jail.

But I want to remind you: That you can lock up a mouse or a man but you can't lock up an idea.

Source: T. C. Douglas, "Mouseland" (c. 1944). Originally broadcast on CBC Radio News Special, January 1, 1961. Reprinted with permission from the Canadian Broadcasting Corporation. To hear Tommy Douglas' speech, go to http://archives.cbc.ca/politics/parties_leaders/topics/851/

Source: Saskatchewan Archives Board S-A998.

▲ Document 3: All Doctors Are Out

Source: Courtesy of the *Regina Leader Post*.

▲ Document 4: The Doctors' Position

June 16, 1962

The Doctors' Position on Medical Insurance

Doctors do not object to the Saskatchewan Government-controlled medicare plan because of money. Even Government leaders admit that doctors would get more money under the Act. **So it is not a matter of fees or of money.**

Genuine medical insurance is something every doctor wants to see. But this plan proposed by the Government, no matter what the Government says, is much more than just medical insurance. It places the control of medicine in the hands of the Government and a political Commission.

In an effort to solve the impasse with Government, your doctors proposed that the Cabinet accept an insurance plan similar to the one which has been so successful in Australia. This would have provided you with all the benefits of the Government Plan **but it would have prevented Government control of medical practice.**

The Government, by its actions, has indicated that it will accept no plan other than its own Act because it wants absolute control over doctors and patients. These controls are long-term rather than immediate. Many of them will not appear in the first draft of Commission regulations. However, these regulations can be changed any time at the whim of the politicians and the politically appointed Commission. **Subsequent versions will contain more and more controls.**

Both Government and the Commission have given doctors their "assurance" they do not want to control doctors. **They have "promised" this and "promised" that** in recent weeks in an attempt to manoeuvre the doctors into accepting their Act.

WHY

can't the doctors accept this act?

POLITICAL MEDICINE

Your doctors are concerned about the future quality of medical care. We believe that you, too, are concerned that the medical care you will receive in the future will be of the same quality that you have received in the past. We don't believe that you want to have your doctor directly responsible to politicians or a Commission which is politically controlled.

CONTROL

This Act provides for control of patients as well as doctors. The Commission takes away your rights whether you would want them to or not. It controls doctors in a very special way—as we understand Section 49(1)(g), the Commission has the right, for example, to tell doctors where to practice, whom they may care for and how they may provide care. **We believe that you would react as the doctors have done because you would not tolerate such control by Government for one minute.**

POLITICAL ASSURANCES

Government spokesmen have admitted that these controls exist in the Act but they say that they will never use them. Your doctors wonder why they were written into the Act, if the politicians don't intend to use them. We consider that the health of our patients and the future of the practice of medicine are too important to depend on the promises of politicians. Promises are too easily broken and in the experience of the doctors of Saskatchewan in dealing with this government, promises have been broken too many times in the past.

BROKEN PROMISES

Doctors were promised by "duly elected representatives" that they would have an opportunity to study this Act before it was presented to the Legislature.

THIS PROMISE WAS NEVER KEPT

Our then "duly elected" Premier T. C. Douglas promised us that any plan must be acceptable to those giving the services as well as those receiving them.

THIS PROMISE WAS NEVER KEPT

"Duly elected representatives" promised that the Thompson Committee would have ample time to study and report on all the health needs of the people before legislation was introduced.

THIS PROMISE WAS NEVER KEPT

These are just three examples of broken promises. There are many more. Would you, under these circumstances, place any trust in the promises of "duly elected" politicians?

We ask all thoughtful citizens to consider this question— Could you bring yourself to accept such an Act and such a Commission?

Your doctors face a dilemma. They have decided that they cannot continue in practice under this Act after July 1st. They hope that you, as free men, will appreciate their position. What is at stake is the future quality of medical care and the right of doctors to practice medicine without political direction.

WE ASK THAT YOU SUPPORT THE IMMEDIATE WITHDRAWAL OF THE GOVERNMENT PLAN AND RESUMPTION OF NEGOTIATIONS ON A BASIS ACCEPTABLE TO THE PROFESSION

(Authorized by the Saskatchewan Division of the Canadian Medical Association)

Source: Courtesy of the Saskatchewan Division of the Canadian Medical Association.

▲ Document 5: Hanging T. C. Douglas in Effigy, July 1962

● **Hanging Douglas in Effigy During Rally in Support of Striking Doctors, July 1962. Why are these women so angry? What role did the media have in the Doctors' strike?**

Source: Saskatchewan Archives Board RB-39801.

▲ Document 6: Rally in Support of Doctors, July 1962

● What do these images of the July 1962 rally indicate about the doctors' supporters? By their professionally produced protest signs, and their clothes, can you make some assumptions about their social and economic position in society? What groups did not attend the rally?

Source: Courtesy of *The Leader Post*.

▲ Document 7: Rally in Support of Doctors, July 1962

Source: Morris Predinchuck, Saskatchewan Archives Board, Morris Studio Fonds.

Article 1: Pragmatic Physicians: Canadian Medicine and Health Care Insurance, 1910–1945

Robert S. Bothwell and John R. English

It has become a ritual in Canada to view the medical profession as unalterably opposed to state-sponsored health insurance. It is usually assumed that this is so, was so, and has always been so.

In fact, the history of the medical profession's attitude to health insurance belies this common stereotype. The first mention of health insurance in the *Canadian Medical Association Journal* was in 1912. Lloyd George had just introduced his famous Insurance Act in Great Britain, and Canadian doctors took note of this new phenomenon. In the words of the editor of the *Journal,* the conservative Sir Andrew Macphail, "a spirit of charity will be replaced by a cold official atmosphere. When physicians become civil servants, those who peculiarly adapted for healing the sick will be automatically forced out of the service and into private practice." Prophetic words perhaps, and similar reservations were expressed in 1914 by Dr. A. R. Munroe of Edmonton, who claimed that Lloyd George was "exploiting the medical profession either in the name of charity of religion." Nevertheless, Munroe believed that commercial methods of insurance should be studied and that the medical profession could agree on four points: universal access to medical care; no "charity" treatment; increases in doctors' incomes; the need to have insurance schemes calculated on the basis of "the medical schedule of fees." Munroe added that it was "worth every man's while studying."[1] Who could disagree?

Macphail and Munroe assumed that health insurance would be a long time coming to Canada. The First World War, however, created an atmosphere of mutual sacrifice and an acceptance of state

involvement in a broader range of social services than hitherto contemplated. In 1917 the president of the CMA, Dr. A. D. Blackader, reflecting the anti-materialist sentiments so prevalent during the war, warned the CMA that it must avoid the imputation of "mercenary reasons" in its opposition to health insurance. Moreover, all doctors should now begin to prepare for the consideration of health insurance in Canada, and in this process the CMA should seize the initiative "to safeguard the true interests of our own profession."[2]

Still, by the war's end in 1918 no prominent Canadian doctor had explicitly stated a preference for state-directed medicine. But in 1919 Professor D. F. Harris told the Association of Medical Health Officers of Nova Scotia that since preventive medicine was already and properly the concern of the state, curative medicine should be a state concern as well. This was a fairly common attitude among public health doctors, who, being already civil servants, could see few terrors and no degradation in the prospect of universal state medicine. In the same year the first Royal Commission was appointed to study health insurance, in British Columbia, and its Report recommended a state-supported system of health insurance.[3]

The British Columbia government, however, took no action on the Royal Commission Report, because, as Premier Oliver informed the legislature, there was much doubt that health insurance was a provincial responsibility. The Royal Commission recommendation was therefore ignored, and medical insurance, like so many wartime social schemes, was all but forgotten during the 1920s. When the general secretary of the CMA, Dr. T. C. Routley, told Saskatchewan doctors in 1923 that health insurance was a serious proposition which deserved study, the secretary of the Saskatchewan Medical Society replied that he was "sure that this is just a flight of imagination in Dr. Routley's mind, and if he keeps quiet about it the country will never hear of it again."[4]

In fact, the country did begin to hear about health insurance again in 1928 and 1929 when a parliamentary committee held hearings in Ottawa to determine Canada's social security needs. Health insurance, the committee decided, was one of the needs, but the committee bowed to an advisory legal opinion which stated that social security was really

Source: Robert S. Bothwell and John R. English, "Pragmatic Physicians: Canadian Medicine and Health Care Insurance, 1910–1945" in SED Shortt, ed., *Medicine in Canadian Society: Historical Perspectives* (Montreal: McGill-Queen's University Press, 1981), pp. 479–493. Reprinted with permission.

the responsibility of the provinces. This did not prevent the House of Commons from debating health insurance, which it did annually, but it did insure that health insurance would be talked out every time.

The CMA itself discussed health insurance once again in 1929. In a debate at the annual meeting that year speakers indicated uncertainty, opposition and, in a few cases, support for health insurance. Dr. T. B. Green of British Columbia claimed that in his association meetings he had "never heard, with one exception, any voice favouring health insurance." On the other hand, Dr. George Wilson of Toronto stated his belief "that state medicine is coming and we need not fight against it. It behoves {sic} this Association to get behind it and direct it." Speakers from eastern Canada tended to be less specific than those from the West. One doctor from Saint John hoped that the idea of health insurance "will die before it reaches us," but was willing to support an investigation, providing that it was done "as quietly as possible, let those {of us} in the East may hear of it."[5]

In the same year the British Columbia government abandoned its position that health insurance was a federal matter and appointed yet another Royal Commission to consider the possibilities of a provincial scheme. Before the commission submitted its report in 1932, a general economic depression had settled over the country, a depression which fundamentally altered both the state's and the medical profession's perspective on health insurance.

Quite suddenly the CMA began to perceive health insurance not as a threat but rather as an antidote for the economic ills of the profession. The CMA's Committee on Medical Economics pointed out how severely doctors were affected by the depression. In a survey of doctors in Hamilton, which the committee carried out in 1933, it was found that doctors' practices had declined in volume by 36.5 percent between 1929 and 1933. Even worse, in 1929 77.5 percent of doctors' work was remunerative; in 1932, the proportion had fallen to 50 percent. Almost half of the doctors surveyed claimed that their professional income was insufficient to pay their expenses and provide the necessities of life. The respondents estimated that only 30 percent of the population was willing to pay for medical care, and that many patients failed to secure medical attention early enough in cases of serious illness solely because they could not afford it.[6]

In rural areas the situation was reportedly even more desperate. Dr. Ward Woolner of Ayr, Ontario, described his own experience in an article in the *CMA Journal*:

> Since 1929, rural areas have many families who cannot pay anything to their doctor. Even farmers, who a few years ago were considered well to do—had electricity installed, had motor cars and telephones— cannot pay for medical care today. We are asked to accept all kinds of produce on our accounts. The writer received over twenty chickens, several ducks, geese, a turkey, potatoes and wood on account during last winter. Many country doctors have trouble collecting sufficient to purchase the bare necessities of life.[7]"

Dr. Woolner concluded that only a province-wide scheme of medical care could alleviate the situation. Many others had come to the same conclusion.

In 1932 the Province of Quebec Medical Association recommended a system of compulsory health insurance to cover complete service, cash benefits, and the right to free choice of physician by the patient.[8] The B.C. Royal Commission set up before the depression reported in favour of a health insurance plan covering employed persons making less than $2,100 per annum. The unemployed, however, were still left to charity. This meant, inevitably, that indigents would continue to receive a considerable amount of free service from doctors, or continue to add to the municipal relief burden. Doctors generally found this to be intolerable, and, in response to the British Columbia proposals, the CMA instructed its economics committee to prepare its own health insurance plan.[9]

Medical care for the unemployed and payment for such care was the CMA's greatest concern. Accordingly in 1933, Dr. Routley, the CMA's general secretary, went to see Prime Minister Bennett about the problem. He pointed out to Bennett that the doctors were in effect providing their own subsidy to the unemployed by giving free service, but Bennett offered little hope of federal aid. With no solution in sight, the editor of the *Bulletin of the Vancouver Medical Association* called for the "socialization" of medicine. He urged doctors to accept a situation that was not only unavoidable, but actually desirable. A generous response from the medical profession would restore doctors' self-esteem and return "the medical profession to the pinnacle on which it once stood, and from which to a great extent ... it has fallen.[10]

The CMA Committee on Economics finally presented its "Plan for Health Insurance in Canada" to the CMA's Council in 1934. The committee pointed out that provincial and municipal governments had shirked their responsibility for the provision of medical care for the indigent. The only solution to the problem was "State Health Insurance." State health insurance would be organized as a division of provincial departments of health and a central health insurance board, "representative of all interested parties," would furnish advice. The supervision of the plan would, of course, be handled by doctors, who would ensure that "the systematic practice of preventive medicine" would be properly carried out. The plan covered indigents, whose premiums would be paid for by the state, as well as single persons with incomes below $1,200 and families with incomes below $2,400. Above those income levels, participation in the plan would remain voluntary. The committee did not specify how doctors should be paid, although they noted that in sparsely populated rural areas doctors would have to rely on a contractual salary.[11]

In the same year, the president of the Toronto Academy of Medicine, Dr. E.A. McDonald, argued in his presidential address for state medicine. Doctors, he claimed, were "being driven into the indigent class" because they were forced to treat penniless patients free of charge. He advocated that Canada follow the British model for health insurance, but he recommended rather more generous salaries than the British paid. The general practitioner, McDonald suggested, "shall be paid a salary sufficient to enable him to live in comfort and continue his post-graduate studies to enable him to keep abreast of the progress of medicine, say, $6,000.00 per year." Specialists would be paid proportionately more, "say $8000 to $10,000 yearly." In 1930–31 the average male wage-earner in Canada was estimated to have earned only $927 per annum, and the salary of a member of Parliament was $4,000. It is therefore unlikely that McDonald's salary proposals met with much favour outside the medical profession.[12]"

When British Columbia introduced a draft health insurance scheme in 1935, the medical profession began to realize that health insurance presented many difficulties which had not been anticipated. By the time the draft pill became law in 1936, the B.C. medical profession was thoroughly alarmed. The Health Insurance Act proposed a restricted coverage—wage-earners making less than $150 a month, leaving out domestic servants, casual labourers, the indigent, part-time workers, and recipients of old age pensions and mothers' allowances. In short, those least likely to pay their accounts remained uninsured. The act was, the *Bulletin of the Vancouver Medical Association* declaimed, "a pale shadow of its former self, anaemic and paralyzed in its lower limbs, or its lower income levels, if you prefer." Equally disturbing was the act's failure to make specific provision for the rates and manner of payment and to give doctors a large role in the act's administration. Subsequent negotiations with the doctors failed to produce agreement, and the government postponed implementation of the scheme—indefinitely, as it turned out.[13]"

The British Columbia experience, however, did not cause Canadian doctors to reject the concept of health insurance. Indeed, the problem was that governments were not prepared to go far enough. In some provinces, therefore, the medical associations took the lead in developing voluntary health care schemes. In 1937, Manitoba began the study of voluntary hospital insurance (Blue Cross) and by 1939 the plan was in operation. Other Canadian provinces soon followed. In Ontario, Associated Medical Services and the Windsor Medical Services were established in 1937; both were sponsored by the OMA. A similar scheme was put into operation in Regina in 1939.[14]

These plans were local in coverage and voluntary in nature, and it seems that the CMA regarded them as a stop-gap. In 1939, the CMA's Committee on Economics reported that it had completed a comprehensive study of the working of health insurance in other countries, but recommended that the task of completing a health insurance plan had to be left to the government: "the Government must be the lead horse and ... the Canadian Medical Association should be an essential and recognized running mate." The lead horse soon came round the corner, in the person of Dr. J.J. Heagerty, the director of public health for the federal Department of Pensions and National Health.

Before 1939, Pensions and National Health had failed to win, show, or place in the health insurance sweepstakes. It was regarded in Ottawa as a mediocre department filled with second-raters. Its functions were confined to house-keeping on the health side, and it had never developed a comprehensive approach to health insurance, which it believed was a provincial responsibility. But in September 1939, Pensions and National Health acquired a new minister, Ian Mackenzie, who had been hastily transferred from the sensitive Department of National Defence on the outbreak of war. Mackenzie was naturally anxious to re-establish his reputation, and within months he had adopted social welfare as his instrument.

In January 1941, the King government summoned a Dominion-Provincial Conference to discuss the recommendations of the Rowell-Sirois Royal Commission. One of the special studies prepared for the commissioners by A. E. Grauer dealt with public health, which Grauer reported was in dismal shape. As Ottawa prepared for the conference, Mackenzie approached the deputy minister of finance, Clifford Clark, to ask that "consideration {be] given to the possible inclusion of public health as one of the subjects for discussion." "Someone," Clark rudely noted, "has called his attention to Professor Grauer's report."[16] While Mackenzie did not succeed in having health insurance placed on the agenda, he did create the impetus within his own department for a re-examination of the possibilities of health insurance.

A small committee, chaired by Dr. Heagerty, reported in January 1941 that "The principle of health insurance is approved." Its recommendations were to form the nucleus of the future federal health insurance scheme. The committee urged that public health (Heagerty was a public health doctor) be "an integral part" of any health insurance plan, that coverage be universal below a certain income level, and that provincial departments of health administer the plan in consultation with medical practitioners.

In October 1941, the CMA's executive visited Ottawa, where they were informed by Mackenzie of the work in progress. Mackenzie emphasized that nothing had been decided as yet, and that he wished to keep in touch with the doctors. A subcommittee of seven, including Routley, was appointed for this purpose. More important, the CMA itself in the same year approved the principle of health insurance, expressing reservations mainly about direct employment of doctors by the state.

The stumbling block was not the medical profession but rather the federal Department of Finance.

Pensions and National Health's early proposals envisaged a federal enabling act which would authorize federal contributions to provincially legislated plans. These plans would have to exclude indigents, but would allow fairly comprehensive medical treatment. In a letter to the minister of finance, Mackenzie estimated the cost of the program at $20 million, but alas, the Finance Department did not believe Mackenzie, and the minister's project was returned to him with a recommendation for more study.[17]"

An exchange of letters in the *CMA Journal* of April 1942, between Heagerty and Routley, was intended to show that a health insurance bill was very near—something that was far from the truth. Dr. Routley sounded the alarm: the doctors must consider their position before it was too late. A great change was coming, and the CMA must be in the vanguard. Routley urged all doctors to join the CMA so that the CMA's answer to the anticipated question "Whom do you represent?" would be too embarrassing. To the current wartime slogans of "Remember Hong Kong! Remember Pearl Harbor!" Routley suggested adding, "Remember Great Britain, and remember New Zealand when you think of Health Insurance!"[18]

At the annual meeting of the CMA in June 1942, the results of a questionnaire on health insurance were tabled. The 2,500 doctors who replied strongly supported the 1934 principles. They wanted: "an independent Health Insurance Commission" in each province, "the majority of whom shall be representatives of organized medicine"; medical care for indigents paid for by the government; freedom of choice for physician and patient; remuneration "according to the method or methods of payment which [doctors] select." With this mandate the committee of seven could take the initiative in defining more precisely the association's attitude towards the prospective health bill.[19]

The next draft of Heagerty's bill reflected the CMA's concerns. There was to be both a dominion Council on Health Insurance and separate provincial councils, with a majority of the membership being practising doctors. There was to be fee for service payment, and all indigents were to be included. In effect, Heagerty's bill gave the doctors everything they wanted. As far as Pensions and National Health were concerned, the bill was complete by December 1942, "except as to matters relating to costs." But costs, as it turned out, were close to the heart of the matter.

On 18–19 January 1943, a special meeting of the CMA Council was convened in Ottawa. (Heagerty and his deputy minister, Dr. Wodehouse, were members of the council.) The meeting adopted two resolutions:

1. The Canadian Medical Association approves the adoption of the principle of health insurance.
2. The Canadian Medical Association favours a plan of health insurance which will secure the development and provision of the highest standard of health services, if such plan be fair both to the insured and to all those rendering the services.

The *CMA Journal* approvingly noted that Heagerty and Wodehouse's attitude throughout was one of satisfying frankness. While the council was pleased with the progress made to date, it nevertheless refrained from approving the specific plan put forward by Pensions and National Health.[20]

Heagerty and Wodehouse had achieved a qualified success on the medical front, but Mackenzie, their minister, had lost the political battle for immediate implementation of the plan. The day after the CMA Council approved the principle of health insurance, Mackenzie learned that the cabinet would not support the enactment of health insurance in 1943. Instead, Heagerty's draft bill would be sent to a House of Commons committee, the Committee on Social Security, for study.

The Special Committee on Social Security convened in March 1943. It held four months of frequently wild and woolly sessions as lawyer-MPs and medical MPs had at one another. Routley and Dr. A. E. Archer, the CMA president, appeared on behalf of the association. Routley repeated the conclusions of the special council meeting of the previous January: the doctors anticipated "great and in some respects unwelcome changes," but they had accepted the principle of health insurance. Reflecting a common fear among doctors that politicians would meddle in their daily work, Routley warned the committee that health insurance must be run by a "nonpolitical independent commission."

Other medical opinions were given at the hearings. The Catholic Hospitals Council's representative told the committee that they feared a loss of autonomy and confessional identity in a national hospital scheme; the majority of Canadians, after all, were Protestants. The osteopaths, the chiropractors, the Christian Scientists, and even the "Anti-Vaccination and Medical Liberty League of Canada" came forward. The gist of their testimony was objection to the predominant role of" doctors in the administration of health insurance, and the restriction of benefits to strictly medical forms of treatment. Heagerty firmly rejected their arguments, insisting on the control of all medical treatment by the medical profession.

Finally, in July, the committee reported to the House of Commons that it thought that the principle of health insurance was a good one, and that the government should scout out the provinces' reactions. In the meantime the committee should be reconstituted next session. Heagerty's project had survived, chloroformed.[21"]

The CMA, which may have been disturbed by the attitude of some who had appeared before the Social Security Committee, seemed to welcome this pause. An August 1943 editorial in the *CMA Journal* saw the delay in Ottawa as providing an opportunity to think things over. Archer echoed this sentiment in his presidential address, and while not repudiating the CMA's support for the principle of health insurance, he suggested that health insurance should be delayed until after the war.[22] The doctors' hesitations gained force in December 1943 when a financial committee on health insurance reported that health insurance would cost the federal government approximately $100,000,000, four times as much as Mackenzie's original estimate. This report undermined much of Heagerty's testimony to the Special Committee. This committee's conclusions did not become public for a few months and in the meantime, the *CMA Journal* described Heagerty's testimony on finance as "not always consistent." Heagerty, who must have known by this point that his financial estimates were unsound, tried to reply that the criticisms were "erroneous" and unjust. As the chairman of the B.C. Division of the CMA's Committee on Economics observed, "Dr. Heagerty's subsequent reaction has seemed to rather prove that we have hit a tender point."[23]

The tone of the discussion had changed, a fact noted by Dr. M. G. Burris in a letter to the *CMA Journal* in March 1944:

The profession of Canada as a whole is only now realizing the true nature of the proposed Bill. In my opinion the section of the profession included within the Canadian Medical Association has been altogether too complacent and too compliant in the matter hitherto. We have proceeded apparently in the belief that State control was inevitable and as if the legislation had already been enacted. We have neglected to examine adequately the theories underlying and the theorists responsible for the present situation. The philosophy of the proposal is as plain an example of National Socialism and State Control as one could imagine or desire.

The *Journal* also took note of the American Medical Association's hostile attitude on health insurance, an attitude quite unlike the CMA's "too complacent and too compliant" attitude. The *Journal* also began to publish unfavourable comments on the proposed measures for British health insurance, in one case repeating a warning issued to Canadian doctors by Lord Dawson of Penn, "Chief Physician to His Majesty the King."[24]

It was, however, the Health Insurance Act passed by the Saskatchewan legislature in the early spring of 1944 which crystallized doctors' fears about politicians and their use of health care schemes. The Saskatchewan medical profession strongly protested "the fact that no opportunity was given to make representations on this bill and the hasty manner in which it was rushed through in the last hours of the legislature." They were understandably alarmed that no provision had been made for the representation of doctors on the Health Insurance Commission. The responsible minister replied that the bill was merely an enabling act and that no health insurance could be set up immediately under its provisions. Nevertheless, the doctors treated this Saskatchewan experience as an evil omen. The profession, Saskatchewan doctors argued, had been subjected to slanders and abuse. Rather plaintively, they summed-up their position: "We all know that individually, the doctor is everyone's friend but as a group we are regarded as anything but that."[25]

The fears of the Saskatchewan doctors were premature: there was no possibility that a poor province like Saskatchewan could finance a health insurance scheme without federal aid. Just as the Patterson government in Saskatchewan was passing its "innocuous enabling act," the federal scheme was collapsing in Ottawa, the victim of miscalculations and political exigencies. When the Mackenzie King government decided to proceed with family allowances, health insurance was abandoned and not revived as a separate measure. Far from being imminent and inevitable as CMA President Archer had claimed in 1943, a comprehensive health insurance scheme was a generation away. By the mid-1960s when the Pearson government introduced medicare, the Heagerty plan was all but forgotten; so too was the CMA's previous support for health insurance for Canadians.

The CMA's support for health insurance in the 1930s and early 1940s contrasted strongly with organized medicine's opposition to health insurance in the United States and Britain. Indeed, in the 1930s and even in the early 1940s, the most vocal supporters of health insurance were prominent members of the Canadian medical profession. It was always a qualified support and enthusiasm varied inversely with the economic condition of the profession. It also seems that the greater the degree of familiarity with the politician and his schemes, the greater were the doctors' doubts. Nevertheless, to the "indigent" medical profession of the 1930s, health insurance promised paid accounts and security. In the 1940s and 1950s there appeared to be better ways, and the medical profession then chose to confront the perils of prosperity alone, without the politician's help.

Notes

1. *Canadian Medical Association Journal* (hereafter *CMAJ*) 3 (1912): 228; ibid. 4 (1914): 1112.

2. Ibid. 7 (1917): 582.

3. H. E. MacDermot, *History of the Canadian Medical Association,* 2 (Toronto, 1958): 60–61.

4. Cited in ibid., p. 61.

5. A transcript of this discussion may be found in ibid., pp. 61–64.

6. *CMAJ* 31 (September 1934), Supplement: 51.

7. Ward Woolner, "Medical Economics in the Rural Districts of Ontario," *CMAJ* 30 (1934): 307.

8. *CMAJ* 31 (September 1934), Supplement: 51.

9. H. E. MacDermot, "A Short History of Health Insurance in Canada," *CMAJ* 50 (1944): 448–49.

10. Cited in ibid.

11. Report of the Committee on Economics, "A Plan for Health Insurance in Canada," *CMAJ* 31 (September 1934), Special Supplement: 25–62.

12. E. A. McDonald, "State Medicine," *CMAJ* 31 (1934): 666–67.

13. Reproduced in *CMAJ* 34 (1936): 685.

14. *Royal Commission on Healthy Services* 1964 1: 387-88.

15. Cited in MacDermot, *History of the CMA,* p. 73.

16. Clark to Alex Skelton, 23 December 1940, RG 19 E2C, v. 108, Public Archives of Canada. See, generally, R. S. Bothwell, "The Health of the People," Paper presented to Canadian Historical Association Annual Meeting, June 1975. Reprinted in John English and J. Stubbs, eds., *Mackenzie King: Widening the Debate* (Toronto: Macmillan, 1978), pp. 191–220.

17. See Bothwell. "Health of the People," pp. 11–13.

18. *CMAJ* 46 (1942): 390–91.

19. Ibid. 47 (1942), Special Supplement: 3-5

20. Ibid. 48 (1943): 93.

21. Canada, House of Commons, Special Committee on Social Security, *Minutes; Journals of the House of Commons,* 23 July 1943.

22. *CMAJ* 49 (1943): 123–27.

23. Ibid. 50 (1944): 72, 174–75, 276.

24. Ibid., pp. 164–65, 276.

25. Ibid., pp. 273–74.

Article 2: Excerpts from National Health Insurance in the United States and Canada

Gerard W. Boychuk

Federal Failure, Provincial Success— Reform in Canada, 1945–49

The Failure of Comprehensive Health Insurance at the Federal Level

The initial push for public health insurance reform in the World War II period took place at the federal level in Canada. Federal proposals in the early 1940s initially contemplated a federally administered system of comprehensive health insurance coverage. Others proposed federal matching grants for provincial provision of public insurance for a similarly comprehensive range of health services. Finally, others recommended leaving health insurance completely to the provinces. The system that emerged roughly fifteen years later was a federal–provincial system limited to hospital insurance that, while setting broad national principles, left administration to the provinces—a system that none of the early proponents of reform had envisioned. In large part, this outcome reflected the degree to which public health insurance reform was intertwined with territorial politics and was the result of a reform process in which successful outcomes were highly tenuous. In contrast with early proposals for reform illustrating the different visions—one federalist and one provincialist—informing proposals for public health insurance reform, more moderate proposals (tilting toward the latter vision) came to dominate but even these initially floundered on the shoals of the territorial politics inscribed in Canadian federal–provincial relations.

...

After securing reelection, the Liberal government included public health insurance reform as part of the broader package of "Green Book Proposals" for postwar reconstruction in 1945. The federal government, at the Dominion–Provincial Conference on Post-War Reconstruction of 1945, offered grants-in-aid for medical, hospital, dental, pharmaceutical, and nursing benefits. The terms of the proposals were very open-ended, and "the original plan for national legislation in the interests of promoting national uniformity and adequacy had been dropped" (Guest 1997, 132).

The government of Québec rejected the social insurance proposals. Other elements of the overall package also met with serious provincial resistance.[1] Despite the softening of federal proposals as outlined above, the Québec premier opposed federal proposals on the basis that they were "incompatible with the autonomy of the province" and "would inevitably lead to interference in all these fields which ought to be free of Dominion authority."[2] Of course, the provincial government had no plans of its own to enter the public health insurance field; rather, it was protecting existing arrangements in which the Catholic Church had largely assumed the responsibility for providing the province's health services. The provincial government was not willing to be subjected to the political pressure that would have undoubtedly been generated by a federal cost-sharing program. Nor was it willing, on principle, to cede the initiative to federal social policy in an area of provincial jurisdictional competence. As a result of the inability to achieve federal–provincial consensus on this and other issues, the "entire package was jettisoned and the first significant plan for a comprehensive medical care system in Canada was stillborn" (Guest 1997, 132).

...

Hospital Insurance in Saskatchewan

The story of the emergence of public hospital insurance in Saskatchewan in this period is more complex and nuanced than is often portrayed. Public health insurance did not emerge simply as the natural result of a government with a socialist public philosophy holding power in a parliamentary system. The outcome was far more contingent than such an interpretation suggests and dependent on the perception—mistaken though it was—that a federal program for cost-sharing health insurance was imminent.

Necessity as the Mother of Reform

Various government programs in the hospital and medical-care sectors had developed incrementally over a long time in Saskatchewan—less as a matter of ideological predisposition than as a response to necessity. First allowed under provincial legislation in 1916, Saskatchewan had, in various localities, municipal doctor arrangements by which physicians in rural municipalities were paid a stipend by the municipality to supplement their fee-for-service income (Houston 2002, 23).[3] This was seen as a pragmatic response to an immediate problem—the difficulty of retaining physicians in sparsely populated agricultural areas especially during economic downturns that, in a one-crop agricultural economy subject to drought and other natural hazards and based on world commodity prices, were not infrequent.[4]

The Depression and its aftermath provided a strong impetus for some government intervention to provide health services in Saskatchewan. In a survey of ninety rural physicians in the early 1940s, the response was "almost unanimous in declaring that private practice was no longer feasible" (Houston 2002, 36). One particular reply captures the urgency of the mood of rural physicians: "Any system is to be preferred to the present. Collections appear hopeless. I do not know how medical men can hope to carry on out here under present and future conditions" (Houston 2002, 36).[5]

In keeping with the existing pattern of local development, universal hospital and medical insurance first came into being on a regional rather than provincial basis. The Swift Current area in southwestern Saskatchewan was drought stricken and facing serious doctor shortages (Houston 2002, 82). As the private health care system faltered, some sort of public plan appeared to be a necessity. By special legislation, the Swift Current Health Region was created, and universal medical and hospital care was implemented in the region in mid-1946—half a year before universal hospital insurance would be offered across the province. Physician support for such an initiative was split between rural doctors, some of whom believed that they could not continue to practice under existing conditions, and urban doctors, who did not share the plight of their rural colleagues. Physicians in the province's two urban areas, Regina and Saskatoon, "looked askance at this experiment in 'socialized medicine'" (Houston, 2002, 84).

These early programs of government intervention in the provision of health services had resulted in public opinion that was favorably predisposed toward public health insurance and led the Saskatchewan College of Physicians and Surgeons as well as the Saskatchewan Association of Rural Municipalities to endorse public hospital insurance (Taylor 1978, 79).

The Role of the Cooperative Commonwealth Federation

It is tempting to assume that since a provincial hospitalization program was implemented after the election of the Cooperative Commonwealth Federation (CCF) in 1994 that it was implemented as a result of that election.[6] The reality is again more complex. As argued above, necessity placed health care on the political agenda. The proposals for health insurance reform at the federal level provided a template for reform as well as the likelihood of future federal cost-sharing. The Liberal government in Saskatchewan in 1944 had already adopted enabling legislation to allow for Saskatchewan's participation in a federal health insurance program before the CCF's election (Naylor 1986, 129).

Hospital insurance proposals that emerged under the Liberals prior to the CCF's election placed public provision on a social insurance basis (e.g., requiring contributory premiums) and limited its provision to hospitals. These design decisions came from an abiding belief on the part of Saskatchewan policymakers that a federal cost-sharing program was imminent. The Select Special Committee on Social Security, which had been appointed by the governing Saskatchewan Liberals, had considered both direct state provision of medical services as well as public health insurance but concluded that "since federal assistance was a prerequisite to the adoption of a scheme of health services in Saskatchewan, and inasmuch as the Dominion government would probably determine which of the two systems it could support, the choice for Saskatchewan was not theirs to make" (Taylor 1978, 76). The Liberal government came to the same conclusion—a plan in Saskatchewan required prior action by the federal government. The Liberals passed enabling legislation for public health insurance that allowed the province to implement a health insurance plan as soon as a federal program was announced (Taylor 1978, 77).

In contrast to these tentative proposals for hospital insurance, the CCF was firmly committed to socialized health services and had been since the Great Depression. In its Regina Manifesto of 1933, the CCF called for "socialized" health services. Health, hospital, and medical services would be "publicly organized"—moving health services from the existing system based on private enterprise to making such services freely available on the same basis as education—the same principle underpinning proposals in the state of New York in 1939 (CCF 1933).[7] The 1944 CCF campaign under T. C. "Tommy" Douglas focused on the issue of health service but argued that health insurance akin to that proposed by the Heagerty committee would be inadequate (Naylor 1986, 137).

Immediately after being elected in 1944 the Douglas government appointed a health commission under Henry Sigerist, a professor of medical history at Johns Hopkins University (Houston 2002, 69). Following the recommendations of the Sigerist report, the province first moved to provide comprehensive health care for social assistance recipients, pensioners, and widows on the fee-for-service basis (Houston 2002, 72). The plan was in operation by January 1, 1945, and provided medical, hospital, and dental care and pharmaceuticals on a means-tested basis for recipients of Old Age Assistance and social assistance (Taylor 1954, 751–52).

At the same time, the government began making plans for universal hospital insurance. As had been the case under the Liberals, the CCF considered it essential that the hospital insurance plan be designed to meet federal requirements (Taylor 1987, 98).[8] It jettisoned its commitment to socialized health services and, instead, adopted the approach that had been initiated under the former Liberal government—universal premium-based insurance limited to hospital services.

Strategic Miscalculation

The Dominion–Provincial Conference on Reconstruction had been launched but not concluded when the Saskatchewan government decided to move ahead with hospital insurance (Taylor 1978, 69). Believing that having a public health insurance program up and running successfully before the next election would be crucial to their reelection, the Saskatchewan officials proceeded with the hospital insurance initiative and took "the gamble to introduce the program before the federal policy had been decide upon" (Taylor 1990, 72–73). The Saskatchewan government, of course, could not know that the federal–provincial negotiations would break down and that federal cost-sharing would, as a result, not be available for another dozen years.[9] As it stood, the provincial government was now publicly committed to instituting a hospital insurance program, and province-wide universal hospitalization insurance became available on January 1, 1947. Given the belief that federal support was essential, the Saskatchewan government would certainly not have proceeded with the hospital insurance plan had it realized that no federal cost-sharing would be forthcoming for more than a decade. The expectation of federal cost-sharing temporarily suspended the constraining dynamics typically faced by provinces attempting to implement major social programs on their own.

The crucial contribution of the CCF government in Saskatchewan in this period was not to be the first provincial government to seriously pursue reform (which the government of British Columbia had done a decade earlier) or to be the only provincial government to undertake reforms (as discussed below, British Columbia adopted a program of social assistance medical care at the same time as Saskatchewan and would implement universal hospital insurance two years after Saskatchewan) or even to be the originator of the idea of public health insurance (in this period forceful impetuses for reform existed in Ottawa including, for example, the Heagerty committee, which had a great influence on debates in Saskatchewan).

Rather, the major contribution of the CCF government was to follow through with the implementation of its hospital insurance program even after its strategic miscalculation in regard to federal cost-sharing became clear. Despite the serious setback represented by the failure of the Conference on Reconstruction to produce cost-sharing, the Saskatchewan government implemented hospital insurance in an administratively effective and politically adroit manner—providing an impressive example that every single other provincial government sent a delegation to Saskatchewan to study. Had the Saskatchewan government wavered or, alternatively, been less successful in its implementation of hospital insurance (as would later be the case in British Columbia), the historical development of public health insurance in Canada would undoubtedly have taken a significantly different path.

National Public Hospital Insurance and Medical Care Insurance in Saskatchewan, 1950–62

The advent of hospital insurance at the provincial level did not automatically translate into the successful implementation of a hospital insurance program at the federal level. Instead, the failure of the federal–provincial negotiations in 1945 pushed subsequent reforms at the federal level into a period where they would have to be undertaken without the support of the medical profession and, as outlined in the following section, under political leadership considerably less predisposed toward direct public intervention in the health insurance field. Neither the federal government nor the Ontario government—whose agreement was key to the adoption of a federal plan—was enthusiastic about the prospect of public intervention in the health insurance field. Despite provincial precedents, the outcome remained far from assured and subject to the vagaries of the politics of Canadian federalism.

Nevertheless, as a result of federal–provincial dynamics, the federal government and Ontario provincial government became caught up in a game of one-upmanship driven by electoral pressures—the result of which was the hospital insurance program, which still constitutes one of two major planks of Canadian medicare today. A number of characteristics of the emergent system now seen as representative of the philosophical underpinnings of health care in Canada (such as universality and first-dollar coverage) came about as pragmatic responses to the immediate administrative problems of implementing a federal–provincial program.

One major consequence of federal cost-sharing for hospital insurance was to set the stage for the inception, four years later, of public insurance for physician care in Saskatchewan. Medical care insurance faced vociferous opposition in Saskatchewan from the medical profession, business, the media, and significant segments of the public—echoing earlier debates over public health insurance in the United States. However, in this case, reform would ultimately be successful.

National Hospital Care Insurance in Canada

In comparison with 1945, none of the key protagonists by the early 1950s—including the prime minister and federal government, the Ontario government, and the CMA—was keen on the idea of public health insurance. St. Laurent as leader of the Liberal Party was clearly not predisposed toward public health insurance although the Liberal cabinet was deeply split philosophically. On the other side of this debate, Paul Martin Sr., as minister of health, was a strong proponent of national health insurance and, over the period that hospital insurance was debated in the federal government, his support and influence in the cabinet grew (Taylor 1987, 128). At the provincial level, the governing Conservatives in Ontario were committed to the principles of free enterprise and limited government, and many individual members of the government were ardent opponents of government health insurance (Taylor 1987, 110, 118–19).

...

Certain characteristics of the hospital insurance plan as adopted later contributed to the rise of public health insurance to iconic status in Canada. They also helped foster public health insurance's role as a powerful tool of territorial integration. However, it is critical to note that, for the most part, these characteristics were incidental elements of the federal plan.

Certainly the federal program recognized and reinforced a central role for the provinces in shaping their own hospital insurance programs. The program was relatively conditional and certainly more highly conditional than future programs, such as federal cost-sharing for medical care insurance, would be. However, at the same time, it was not nearly as specific in its conditions as the initial federal proposal (based on the Heagerty recommendations) had been in 1943. The sequencing of events was crucial in this outcome. The failure of federal reforms in 1945 had opened up political space for the provinces to proceed on their own, and some of them did. In the wake of provincial experimentation, the federal government simply could not enforce a specific model of hospital insurance on the provinces once four provinces already had programs fully operating (Taylor 1987, 202).

At the same time, the federal conditions on cost-sharing for hospital insurance introduced elements that helped make public health insurance a symbol of national unity and identity—including universality and public insurance as an entitlement unrestricted by payment of premiums or coinsurance fees. Policymakers, however, did not deliberately intend either of these outcomes. Despite later revisionist histories that elevated universality to iconic status as a philosophic principle underpinning the health care system in Canada, the requirement that insurance be universally available on uniform terms and conditions simply meant that federal cost-sharing funds could not be used to subsidize insurance provision through private plans—thus banning the transfer of public funds to private control. This provision reflected a desire to keep direct public control over public funds more than a commitment to egalitarian ideals (Naylor 1986, 166).

...

Medical Care Insurance in Saskatchewan

The advent of federal cost-sharing for hospital insurance allowed the provincial government in Saskatchewan the financial latitude to move ahead with medical care insurance. In stark contrast with the earlier development of hospital insurance in Saskatchewan, the decision to embark on public medical care insurance was made with no expectation that federal cost-sharing would be forthcoming and was truly a decision to "go it alone." There were, of course, strong precedents on which to base the expansion of health insurance to the coverage of physician services in Saskatchewan, including the hospital insurance scheme that had in been in operation for roughly fifteen years as well as the more geographically limited experiment in comprehensive coverage in the Swift Current Region. Nevertheless, from the outset the success of this venture was far from assured. Despite contemporary claims that Saskatchewan had a political culture strongly predisposed toward public medical insurance, the endeavor encountered serious resistance from the medical profession, broad segments of the public, and the media. Despite this opposition, universal medical care insurance became a reality—but only after a bitter twenty-three-day physician strike that made news around the world.

...

The doctors had already experienced some success in forestalling earlier attempts at expansion of public insurance coverage for physician services at the regional level. In 1955 proposals for two additional comprehensive regional medical care plans (following the model of the Swift Current plan) were subject to referendums in their respective areas. The college and its voluntary prepayment plans launched a massive publicity campaign contributing to the resounding defeat of medical care in both regions (Taylor 1990, 98; Naylor 1986, 179). These earlier battles had contributed to reinforcing the solidarity of the profession as well as steeling their resolve to resist further expansions of public medical care insurance (Taylor 1990, 98).

The doctors had also aggressively adopted a strategy of expanding physician-controlled voluntary prepayment plans (Taylor 1990, 98). Roughly 40 percent of the population was already covered under enrollment in the two profession-sponsored plans (Naylor 1986, 179; Taylor 1987, 266n71). Furthermore, the province also had a categorical system of comprehensive coverage for recipients of old-age pensions and social assistance for more than sixteen years at the time when universal medical care insurance became a reality. Thus roughly one-quarter of the Saskatchewan population has "more or less" comprehensive coverage for medical services under various public programs including the Swift Current plan for comprehensive health service coverage in that region, the social assistance medical care program, and the municipal doctor contract system (Naylor 1986, 177). Only the remaining one-third of the population was without medical care coverage.

In addition to its own considerable political power, the College of Physicians and Surgeons received the support of extraprovincial interests including the CMA and the insurance industry, which were both committed to defeating public physician service insurance in Saskatchewan. This support significantly increased the pressure the college could bring to bear on the provincial government (Taylor 1990, 105). The Saskatchewan government was confronted not only by its own physicians but also by the national profession.

...

Finally, the coalition of interest opposed to the Saskatchewan plan was as broad as the coalition resisting public insurance in the United States. In the 1960 provincial election the college was joined in its opposition to public medical care insurance by the Saskatchewan Liberal Party, the dental and pharmaceutical associations, and the Chambers of Commerce (Taylor 1990, 104). During the actual doctors' strike in 1962, the press was universally critical (Taylor 1990, 118–19). Popular resistance to medical care insurance was organized through the development of a series of Keep Our Doctors Committees, which were vocally and vociferously opposed to the plan. These committees staged a series of impressive public rallies against the medical insurance plan.

The anti-insurance coalition also used rhetoric as drastic and misleading as the AMA campaigns in the United States. As noted by Lord Taylor, a leading figure in resolving the Saskatchewan doctors' strike, "'The American Medical Association was at this time, hysterically opposed to Medicare; and it endeavored, not without some success, to communicate its hysteria to the doctors and the public in Saskatchewan" (quoted in Taylor 1990, 121). Organized medicine in Saskatchewan portrayed public health insurance as communistic and a threat to freedom. Typical press coverage in Saskatchewan referred to the medical insurance program as "ferocious" and the government as "dedicated to the destruction of our economic system" (Taylor 1990, 118–19).

The 1962 Doctors' Strike and Its Resolution

In response to the announcement of Premier Douglas during a provincial by-election campaign in early 1959 that the provincial government intended "to embark upon a comprehensive medical care program that would cover all our people," the college emphasized its support for voluntary prepayment plans that, in this case, it controlled.[10] To the degree the college was willing to countenance a role for government in health insurance, it argued in favor of the CMA policy of subsidizing coverage for low-income people provided through voluntary agencies (Taylor 1990, 106). As outlined above, the college waged a massive publicity campaign in the 1960 election.

Initially the CCF government was far from certain as to how the public would react to the plan (Taylor 1987, 269). In the 1960 election the government received only 40 percent of the vote. In reaction to these results, "the college contended that the election, which had been virtually converted into a referendum on medical care insurance, had indicated

majority opposition to the government's policy" (Taylor 1990, 104). In the 1962 federal election the CCF was badly beaten in Saskatchewan (including the defeat of former CCF premier Tommy Douglas who had left provincial politics to run federally), and this defeat was widely perceived to be a reaction against public medical care insurance (Taylor 1987, 300). Nevertheless, an internal assessment presented by the head of the college to the CMA in July 1962 noted: "Over the past two and a half years, the public in that province seems to have accepted and approved of the fact that they will be provided with some form of plan for comprehensive, all-inclusive medical care insurance" (Taylor 1990, 114). Rather than responding to public opinion demanding public insurance, the CCF was shaping public opinion.

Despite the strident opposition of the profession, legislation was introduced and passed in the fall of 1961 making provision for a compulsory, premium-based system of public medical insurance. In response, the primary objective of the college was to preserve a role for the prepayment plans in the expectation that the CCF government would be replaced after the next election. If the move to public insurance was to later be reversed, the college believed it was critical that the prepayment plans survive so they might provide a voluntary alternative to the public program (Taylor 1990, 116). In response to the college's refusal to even negotiate in regards to a public plan, the government offered a major concession: The doctors could directly bill their patients who would then be reimbursed by the public plan according to the negotiated fee schedule. The college rejected the concession and called again for a system of subsidization of voluntary plans (Taylor 1990, 109). The gulf between the two sides could not be bridged, and on July 1, 1962, the doctors withdrew their services.

The strike presented huge political risks for both sides—no one knew where the public would lay blame if deaths were attributed to the strike (Taylor 1987, 314). Under mounting pressure, after twenty-three days an agreement was reached as a result of a major concession on both sides. The medical profession agreed to accept that the plan would be universal and compulsory with the government collecting premiums and disbursing payments. For its part, the government agreed that the existing organizational structure of the voluntary plans remain in place to act as billing and payment agents for physicians who did not wish to deal directly with the government health commission (Taylor 1990, 125).[11]

With the strike ended, universal compulsory public health insurance for physician services was fully in operation in the province of Saskatchewan although the physician-controlled prepayment plan organizations remained in place. The medical profession viewed the end of the strike as a cease-fire rather than a cessation of hostilities (Taylor 1987, 325–27). As the profession's leadership had hoped, twenty-one months later, in early 1964, the CCF government fell and the Liberals, who had opposed the public medical insurance plan and supported the doctors, were elected. But "to the surprise of the public and the dismay of the profession, the Liberal government did not change the format of the program, and the profession-controlled plans were never returned to their prior status" (Taylor 1990, 129). Comprehensive universal compulsory health insurance in Saskatchewan had become a reality.

Medical Care Insurance in Canada, 1962–84

I suppose we'll be proposing grocery-care next.
—Ernest Manning, Premier of Alberta

The principles of the Canada Health Act began as simple conditions attached to federal funding for medicare. Over time, they became much more than that. Today, they represent . . . the values underlying the health care system. . . . The principles have stood the test of time and continue to reflect the values of Canadians.
—Roy J. Romanow, *Health Canada Act Overview*

It is difficult to overstate the seriousness of the crisis facing Canadian unity during the period in which medical care insurance was debated and introduced. As *independentiste* sentiment in Québec flared, bombings first took place in Québec's largest city, Montréal, in 1963. The tension reached crisis proportions seven years later when, in the wake of the

kidnapping of the British Trade Commissioner James Cross and kidnapping and murder of Québec cabinet minister Pierre Laporte, the federal government temporarily suspended civil liberties across Canada on the basis of "apprehended insurrection" in Québec. Over this period, the rise of the militant separatist movement, the Front de Liberation du Québec (FLQ), as well as the creation of nonviolent parties dedicated to the establishment of an independent Québec by constitutional means—such as the Rassemblement pour l'Indépendence Nationale in 1960 and Ralliement National in 1966, which were both superseded by the Parti Québécois (PQ) in 1968—signaled the force of this challenge to Canada's territorial integrity.[12] It was from within this context that a national system of medical care insurance emerged in Canada.

. . .

The development of national public medical care insurance in Canada is often viewed as the result of a relatively natural evolution flowing out of earlier federal and provincial policy innovations such as universal hospital care insurance at the federal level and medical care insurance in Saskatchewan. The development and consolidation of national universal medical care insurance, however, in the period from the mid-1960s to the mid-1980s was highly tenuous. In this contingent process of development, the conjuncture at key points between the politics of health care and politics of territorial integration played an important role. Powerful political currents—especially those developing in Québec—provided a central dynamic driving the development of a national system of medical care insurance designed to touch the lives of all Canadians regardless of where they lived.

. . .

Political Resistance to Federal Medical Care Insurance

While it is often argued that the development of public medical care insurance in Saskatchewan set in motion positive feedback dynamics that created pressure for federal reforms, the political context for federal medical care insurance proposals in the wake of the developments in Saskatchewan was not particularly propitious. Although universal public medical care insurance had been implemented in Saskatchewan, this development, in itself, triggered negative feedback dynamics auguring against the adoption of a similar program at the federal level. First, it generated even more serious resistance by the CMA to public physician-care insurance at the national level than had existed prior to the Saskatchewan experiment. Second, it contributed to the adoption of alternative health insurance plans in other provinces. Finally, it created serious concern at the federal level about the degree of resistance that a federal program might encounter.

One of the crucial effects of Saskatchewan adopting medical services insurance was to steel the CMA's resolve against compulsory public insurance for physician services. Organized medicine in Canada viewed the development of public medical care insurance in Saskatchewan as a "serious breach" (Taylor 1990, 129). In response to the developments in Saskatchewan, the president of the CMA made a "ringing call to the profession to reinforce the private governmental structure it had created to prevent any further breach in the system. And it made very clear its fear of, and determination to exclude, any other influence in the arrangements the profession controlled" (Taylor 1990, 130). As the CMA campaigned vigorously against national medical insurance, it issued constant warnings that "the introduction of medical care insurance, which they pejoratively referred to as socialized medicine, would lead to an exodus of doctors from the country" (Taylor 1990, 26).

...

Finally, the Saskatchewan experience generated considerable concern among federal policymakers. The difficulty of implementing medical care insurance in Saskatchewan demonstrated just how politically risky the venture would be for a minority Liberal government at the federal level. Certainly, the Saskatchewan doctors' strike removed any perception at the federal level that medical care insurance would be a natural evolution from hospital care insurance.[13] Federal policymakers were acutely aware that there was "a hell of a lot of opposition" to the plan in Saskatchewan. In light of the developments in Saskatchewan, the federal decision to proceed would have to be made on the assumption that an expansion of public health insurance would be campaigned against vigorously—which it was, especially by the insurance industry, which argued that the federal proposals would "ruin the nation."[14]

The omens for the successful achievement of a national plan "now were increasingly dark" (Taylor

1990, 144). In the view of the CMA, "The odds in favor of the market-economy approach . . . were shifting most favorably" (Taylor 1990, 140). Encouraged by these outcomes, the CMA was stepping up its publicity campaign against universal compulsory public health insurance as well as directly lobbying at the highest political levels.[15] Furthermore, public support of compulsory public physician-care insurance was weak. In a public opinion poll conducted in the fall of 1965 as the government was preparing to introduce legislation, support for a voluntary plan (52 percent) outstripped support for a compulsory plan (41 percent) by a significant margin.[16]

The provinces, on the whole, were recalcitrant. At the annual Provincial Premiers Conference, "so strident were the tones, so angry the voices, and so vehement the opposition that one journalist summed it up, 'The federal government's proposed legislation lies torn, tattered, and politically rejected'" (Taylor 1990, 149). When the federal government announced its medical care insurance proposals in 1965, Premier of Alberta Ernest Manning commented acerbically, "I suppose we'll be proposing grocery-care next."[17]

Nevertheless, the Liberal minority government elected in 1963 and reelected as a minority again in 1965 persevered in pursuing a national plan, and the federal government eventually pushed through a conditional cost-sharing program for public medical care insurance. Of course various compromises were made. For example, the medicare program would have "principles" rather than "conditions," a semantic measure intended to make the plan more palatable to the provinces. These principles, later to become enshrined in the CHA, were portability, public administration, comprehensiveness, universality, and accessibility.[18]

From the outset the Québec government flatly refused to participate in any federal scheme in an arena of primarily provincial jurisdiction. Premier of Québec Jean Lésage argued that Québec would bring in its own plan of medical care insurance but that "when our plan is introduced, it will be operated outside any joint Federal–Provincial program in line with our general policy of opting out of all areas within our competence" (quoted in Taylor 1990, 147).[19] The Québec position had been and remained clear: its overriding objectives were complete provincial autonomy in all areas of provincial jurisdiction and securing the financial capacity to fund programs in these areas independently of conditional federal transfers.

This provincial recalcitrance was overcome, however, by a brilliant federal maneuver of dubious constitutional legitimacy—certainly breaking the spirit, if not the letter, of the Canadian constitution. In the fall of 1968 the federal finance minister announced an increase of 2 percent in federal income tax. Although it was formally called the social development tax (as it would have been unconstitutional for the federal government to levy a health care tax), the tax was clearly intended to finance federal contributions to health insurance. Taxpayers in all provinces would be, in essence, paying for medical care insurance regardless of whether or not their province had a program eligible for federal cost-sharing. This action created significant political pressure on provincial governments to acquiesce to the program (Taylor 1987, 392). As a result, all provinces, even those that were less than enthusiastic about the federal plan, such as Québec, quickly developed programs eligible for federal cost-sharing (see table 8.1).

In a context in which provinces could opt out of established programs, a new cost-sharing program offered unique opportunities for renewing a strong federal role. Constitutional questions aside, the relevant political question was whether public opinion in favor of universal medical care insurance was sufficiently strong in Québec that the federal government could put pressure on the provincial government that it could not resist. Federal policymakers were well aware that universal public medical care insurance has as much popular appeal within Québec as anywhere else.[20]

...

The political prospects for a straight federal program of either a universal or categorical (e.g., limited to children) variety were radically transformed by a number of factors. The first was the report of the Royal Commission on Health Services (Hall Commission) in 1964. The Hall Commission provided, in large part, the philosophical rationale for the expansion of universal public insurance to medical care.[21] The Hall Commission, reflecting its own concern with issues of territorial integration, recommended a "Health Charter," the essence of which was as follows: "The achievement of the highest possible health standards for all our people must become a primary objective of national policy and a cohesive factor contributing to national unity. . . . The objective can best be achieved

through a comprehensive, universal Health Services Program for the Canadian people" (Taylor 1990, 135).[22]

...

As Kent outlines, the role of Québec was "absolutely crucial" to the endorsement of medical care insurance by the federal government: "There would have been no Canadian welfare state if pre-1960 Québec politics had continued."[23] Changes in Québec were "absolutely essential to moving ahead." The new Lésage government was as keen on social policy as was the federal Liberal government. Federal officials perceived the Pearson government and Lésage government of Québec as having the same broad objectives in health care, and federal officials believed that a federal cost-sharing program could be made politically acceptable even in light of Québec nationalism. In so doing, the federal cost-sharing proposal for medical care was significantly different from cost-sharing for hospital care, with the former being based on broad principles rather than federal monitoring of a detailed program. Federal policymakers fashioned a proposal that proved impossible for the Liberal government in Québec to resist.

As soon as the federal government announced its intentions to initiate a federal cost-sharing program for medical care insurance, the Québec government declared that it intended to bring in its own program outside the rubric of any federal shared-cost plan (Taylor 1987, 356). To this point, there had been very little government action in Québec to support this claim. It was after the conference that the Québec premier "set events in motion," announcing that health insurance would be introduced the following year and establishing a committee to study the issue (Taylor 1987, 386, 392). The two governments now were jockeying to be the first to occupy the political space created by the issue of medical care insurance—engaging in competitive state-building, to use Banting's apt phrase.

Although the Liberal government in Québec was replaced by the Union Nationale government in mid-1966, the Québec government continued to insist that it had full jurisdictional competence over health care and demanded that the federal government cede further tax room and return to Québec the tax capacity that it required to exercise this competence (Taylor 1987, 386). Despite the fact that the influential Castonguay committee (which had been appointed by the Québec Liberals) recommended the establishment of a comprehensive, universal provincial health insurance program, the Union Nationale publicly committed itself to a policy of subsidizing health insurance provided to those with low income through existing agencies (Taylor 1987, 389–90).

Two factors combined to make this policy position futile. First, the structure of the federal "health insurance tax" meant that even if the Québec government were to refuse to go along with the federal plan, Québec citizens would still be taxed and the proceeds transferred to other provinces. Of course the Québec government (and some Québec members of parliament) vociferously protested against the federal position; however, the federal government, from the outset, refused to budge. As the national program was implemented and Québec stayed out, federal intransigence was reinforced by the election results of 1968: "The federal government with its recently acquired large majority in the Commons, and especially its success in Québec, was in no mood to compromise" (Taylor 1987, 392). Second, the position of the Québec government ran against strong public support for medicare inside the province of Québec—a factor that the federal government was counting on. Support for the federal medicare program in Québec proved to be higher than in any other region in Canada by a considerable margin (see table 8.2).

Given the immense pressure on the Québec provincial government generated by federal maneuvering, it seemed largely a foregone conclusion that Québec would eventually join the program despite its efforts to resist (Taylor 1990, 150).[24] Regardless of aspirations to exercise full provincial autonomy, the Québec government could not resist the federal offer even in the face of federally stipulated "national principles."

The Iconic Status of Health Care in Canada, 1984–2008

National Unity and National Distinctiveness

Support for public health insurance became increasingly strongly linked to issues of national unity as well as Canadian distinctiveness. In a 1978 poll, 72 percent of respondents agreed that medical care "should be guaranteed by the government" (Mendelsohn 2001, 28). By 1985, 95 percent of Canadian respondents agreed. In 1965, 52 percent of people responding to a poll favored a voluntary plan while only 41 percent favored a universal plan, and in 1968, only 55 percent of respondents (and less than half in Ontario) felt that the federal government should bring in Medicare as it had promised (Taylor 1987, 391). In contrast, by 2000, 88 percent of respondents said that it was "very important" to them to have a "strong national system of publicly funded health care"—only 3 percent felt it was "not important" (Mendelsohn 2001, 25). As Marmor and coauthors noted: "None of the major studies of the origins of Medicare [in Canada] . . . have concluded that the overwhelming support for the egalitarian values of the Medicare program preceded the passage of

● **TABLE 8.2**

Support for Medicare, Canada, by Region, 1968 (Percentage)

	NATIONAL	QUÉBEC	ONTARIO	WEST
Federal government should bring in:				
Medicare as promised	55	64	49	55
Medicare should be postponed	19	20	19	19
Medicare should be dropped	19	12	23	19
Can't say	7	4	9	7

Source: Taylor 1987, 391.

national health insurance legislation." Rather, "the values expressed by the . . . operating principles of Medicare . . . have in large measure arisen from Medicare's performance, not its origins" (Marmor, Okma, and Latham 2002, 16). Public support for the program is not explained solely by its performance, however. These shifts were also related to public perceptions of the role of health insurance in fostering national unity and defining a national identity precisely as intended, though to a degree not anticipated by, federal policymakers.

Public Health Insurance, Citizenship, and National Unity

Public health insurance has come to be seen in Canada as a right of citizenship. In a 1998 poll 69 percent of respondents agreed (48 percent agreed "completely") and only 11 percent of respondents disagreed that "Medicare is a right of citizenship" (Mendelsohn 2001, 28) Perceived in this way, health care fosters national unity by defining the national community as the community through which this right is granted. The central principles of the CHA, especially universal coverage, equal access, and cross-provincial portability of benefits, "have come to define the citizenship dimensions of health provision in Canada" (Maioni 2002). When asked in a 1994 poll to identify what "most ties us together as a nation," the two responses garnering substantial agreement were health care and hockey (Stanbury 1996).

The corollary of perceiving health care as a right is the demand for a high degree of national uniformity in the provision of public health services. The degree of provincial variability that is politically acceptable in delivering a service that is a right of national citizenship is necessarily limited. In a 1996 poll 63 percent of respondents felt that it was "very essential" to have national standards for health care across the country while another 25 percent felt it was somewhat essential (Mendelsohn 2001, 80).[25] The federal role in health care through its link with citizenship is imbued with considerable symbolic significance. As Maioni puts it:

> The federal government can claim to have "nationalized" health care and promoted "equal citizenship" among Canadians and guaranteed health benefits to all. In debates about provincial autonomy, national unity,

or constitutional renewal, this is of enormous significance: the federal government has no constitutional role in health care but can claim to defend the "integrity" of the popular features of the "Canadian" health care model. The federal government achieves clout without the headache of administering and budgeting for health care services. (2001, 100)

All relevant political actors "recognize the extent to which disputes about health care involve struggles over economic and political space in the federation" (2001), 88).

...

Footnotes

Federal Failure, Provincial Success—Reform in Canada, 1945–49

1. Another unresolved issue was tax rental—an arrangement by which the provinces during wartime had ceded certain issues of provincial taxation to the federal government in return for unconditional federal grants. The agreement proposed an extension of these arrangements. Both Ontario and Québec opposed the proposals. The former disagreed with the structure and level of proposed federal compensation for ceded tax room (Naylor 1986, 133–4). However, the Premier of Québec, Maurice Duplessis, objective on the basis of constitutional principle—arguing that the proposals undermined the federal–provincial division of powers enshrined in the British North America Act, Canada's central constitutional document at the time.

2. Premier Maurice Duplessis quoted in Taylor and friends 1987, 62–63).

3. According to C. Rufus Rorem, a researcher for the U.S. Committee on the Costs of Medical Care (CCMC) who studied the Saskatchewan municipal doctor system in the period, "Each of the municipalities which has adopted the municipal doctor system had already had unsatisfactory experiences with the conventional methods of private practice.... In several instances a local physician placed before the municipality the alternative of employing him on an annual salary or having him move to another

community." The CCMC in the United States recommended that a similar program be implemented in particular areas in the United States.

4. An important innovation in 1941 was a municipal system of tax prepaid hospital and physician care that allowed residents to choose from any doctor or hospital anywhere in the province (as opposed to limiting choice to salaried doctors in that particular municipality) (Houston 2002, 78).

5. Full results of the survey are reported in the Saskatchewan Medical Quarterly.

6. The CCF philosophy, although it clearly could be considered a democratic socialist party, was at root an extension of the "social gospel" vision. This vision originated in the United States: it was influential after the Civil War and peaked during the Progressive Era (from the turn of the century to the end of World War II). For an overview of the social gospel doctrine in the United States, see Morone (2004).

7. Under the heading "Socialized Health Services—Publicly Organized Health, Hospital and Medical Services," the Regina Manifesto states: "Health services should be made at least as freely available as are educational services today. But under a system which is still mainly one of private enterprise the costs of proper medical care, such as the wealthier members of society can easily afford, are at present prohibitive for great masses of the people. A properly [i.e., publicly] organized system of public health services including medical and dental care . . . should be extended to all our people in both rural and urban areas" (CCF 1933).

8. Thus, for example, the decision to make the plan a contributory social insurance program based on premiums was in direct response to the Green Book proposals, which emphasized premiums (Taylor 1990, 70).

9. The provincial legislation was passed in February 1946, and the federal–provincial negotiations ended in failure in early May 1946 (Taylor 1990, 58).

National Public Hospital Insurance and Medical Care Insurance in Saskatchewan, 1950–62

10. At the first opportunity following Douglas's speech, the College of Physicians and Surgeons unanimously passed a resolution avowing that "medical care has always been readily available to the public regardless of ability to pay, and that no one has ever been denied medical attention because of his financial position"; "we firmly believe that the standards of medical services to the people will deteriorate under such a system"; and "we oppose the introduction of a compulsory government-controlled, province-wide medical care plan and declare our support of, and the extension of health and sickness benefits through indemnity and service plans" (Taylor 1990, 100–101).

11. As a result of this compromise, doctors had a number of choices of ways to practice (a) receiving direct payments from the commission as payment in full (either salary or fee for service); (b) billing through a voluntary agency (and accepting billing as payment in full); (c) billing payments at doctors' sole discretion (providing an itemized list so that the patient could apply to the commission for reimbursement from the minimum fee schedule); (d) practice entirely for private fees (no itemized statement required) (Taylor 1990, 125–26). Initially it appeared as if the voluntary agencies (option B) would become a key component of the new system. Direct billing of the government, however, came to supercede billing through voluntary agencies: "In 1963, the proportion of physicians billing the commission directly was minimal, amounting to only 21.5 percent. By 1970 this proportion had increased to 51.5 percent, with the proportion billed through the prepayment plans declining from 68.0 percent to 40.5. With the proportion continuing to decline, in 1988 all physicians' claims were sent directly to the commission" (Taylor 1990, 129).

Medical Care Insurance in Canada, 1962–84

12. The territorial challenges facing the federal state were not limited to those emanating from Québec. As contemporary observers noted at the time, even had Québec remained quiescent, "the pressures for decentralization have been so fired up by resurgent provincialism that many have questioned the very survival of the federal government as a decisive body" (Black and Cairns 1966, 34).

13. Tom Kent, principal assistant to Prime Minister Lester B. Pearson, interview with author, April 2005.

14. Ibid.

15. The CMA executive met with the minister of health and prime minister in June 1965 (Taylor 1990, 141).

16. When asked about the apparent support in public opinion polling for a voluntary plan rather than a compulsory plan, Tom Kent emphasized that senior policymakers did not put much stock in public opinion polls—believing that the answers were largely shaped by the way the questions were asked. They believed that, in the last analysis, a straight public plan was "what people would vote for." As Kent points out, the real evidence of public support for the proposal was that it was voted for unanimously in the House of Commons. Kent, interview.

17. Ibid.

18. For an overview of these principles, see chapter 9. The federal contribution would match total spending by all provinces with this total amount being divided among provinces on a per capita basis.

19. Rather than calling for federal financial aid for health care (or any other specific program area), the Québec government called for the federal government to "make it easier for provinces to exercise their constitutional powers, for example, by rectifying the present system of sharing revenue sources in Canada" (Lésage quoted in Taylor 1990, 147). This continues to be the position of the Québec government in 2008.

20. Kent, interview.

21. The Hall Commission was appointed in mid-1961 and issued its report three years later, in mid-1964.

22. The report recommended public insurance coverage of a comprehensive range of services including medical services; dental services for children, expectant mothers, and public assistance recipients; prescription drug services; optical services for children and public assistance recipients; prosthetic services; and home care services.

23. According to Kent, far more than people appreciated, there was a real alliance between the Lésage and Pearson governments (Kent, interview). According to Peter C. Newman, "Pearson's main policy preoccupation was his attempt to sponsor some kind of accommodation between Québec and the rest of the country" (Newman 1968, 45).

24. Québec Premier Bertrand was resigned: "Ottawa has placed us in a position where we might be one of the last provinces to sign. . . . Either Quebec joins the programme, and thus flies squarely in the face of the Canadian constitution, or else we do not join up and thus deprive our people of a lot of money to which they have the right. What does one do in a case like this? Don't we have to be realistic and make the best of the situation, that is, sign the agreement with Ottawa, counting on its being the last time?" (Taylor 1987, 392).

The Iconic Status of Health Care in Canada, 1984–2008

25. In a 2000 poll, just under 60 percent of respondents felt that the federal government "should ensure that all Canadians, no matter where they live, have access to similar levels of health care services" (Mendelsohn 2001, 77).

Alvin Finkel

"The government sponsors the TB testing of cattle, pays for loss and has blood testing every year free of charge. What about humans? Let's take our hats off to Russia as far as health is concerned."[1] This was the conclusion of a group of farmers in Seaforth, Ontario, meeting in late 1943 to discuss the idea of a national universal medical care program. Sponsored by *Farm Radio Forum*, a CBC radio series, groups of farmers across the country responded to the proposals that were being mooted for state medical insurance. But the proposals being discussed were more radical than Canada's current medicare system. Medical care was to be removed from the private marketplace completely, and the costs of hospital care, doctors' visits, pharmaceutical costs, dental care, and eye care were to be covered by a state-funded regime.

The farmers' groups revealed that conditions of health care in Canada, particularly in rural areas, were often grim. For example, a farmer in Elderbank, Nova Scotia, stated "Our doctor has 275 miles of highway to travel. Many do not consult him because of cost of services. Immediate federal action is needed." In Leader, Saskatchewan, another reported: "Our school is never visited by either doctor or nurse. This fall one family had a child with contagious disease…finally the school was closed up, as teacher and all pupils were sick. Mothers here, who never have a doctor at the birth of a child, least of all pre-natal care, most of them are wrecks and old long before their time."[2] Polls suggested that a national medicare scheme was the most popular reform discussed during the Second World War and its aftermath. In both 1944 and 1948, 80 per cent of Canadians expressed support, with the Québécois sharing this sentiment despite the claims of their provincial government and the Catholic Church that national medicare posed a threat to Quebec's traditions of individualism and Church control of social services.[3]

Source: Alvin Finkel, "The Medicare Debate, 1945–80," *Social Policy and Practice in Canada: A History* (Waterloo, ON: Wilfrid Laurier University Press, 2006), chap. 8. Reprinted with permission from Wilfrid Laurier University Press.

The dismal state of health services across the country fuelled the demand for state action. Canadians had reason to believe that they did not enjoy the full benefits of the medical knowledge of their time. While Sweden and New Zealand, both with universal state medical programs, had the world's lowest infant death rates in 1942—29 per 1,000 live births—Canada's rate was 54: In all provinces, the infant mortality rate in rural areas was higher than the urban rate, usually quite significantly, for example 79 to 51 in Nova Scotia, 76 to 43 in Manitoba, and 63 to 30 in British Columbia. Significantly, Saskatchewan, where pressure from women's groups in the interwar period had led to the hiring of municipal doctors and the creation of "union" hospitals (hospitals operated by several municipalities uniting to pay for their construction and operation), had the country's lowest rural death rate for infants. In that province, 52 children per 1,000 died in their first year of life compared with 43 in the province's cities.[4]

Still, the State Hospital and Medical League of Saskatchewan estimated that 34 per cent of all deaths were premature and that half of all provincial residents suffering disabling illnesses could have been free of disease if preventive care had been applied. As Tommy Douglas, soon-to-be-premier of that province and generally regarded as the "father of Canadian medicare,"[5] noted in a broadcast in 1943, "If the average person were checked over by a clinic at stated intervals, and treatment were available before the illness had reached a critical stage, not only would we live longer but the cost of health services in the aggregate would be less than it is now."[6] The National Committee for Mental Hygiene reported in 1939 that only 10 per cent of Canadians could comfortably pay for their medical services in a free-market system while 25 per cent were completely dependent on charity; the remaining 65 per cent could pay for normal services but were forced into debt or rejection of treatment if an operation or long-term care was required.[7]

Yet, despite popular support for medicare, it was not implemented in the early postwar period and, over the next two decades, pro- and anti-medicare forces were locked in constant battle. Advocates of medicare seemingly won, but the program that emerged disappointed them both in the limitations of its coverage and the structure of medical care that it embraced. This chapter explores the structures of political decision making, formal and informal, that resulted in the creation of a particular type of medicare in 1968.

From the Green Book to Hospital Insurance

Though the federal government balked at the potential costs of national health insurance in 1945, it recognized that Canadians expected governments at all levels to invest in health care.[8] In 1948, it announced a program of conditional health grants to provinces to build and operate hospitals, train medical personnel, and carry out health research. The wealthier provinces, in turn, also provided funding to expand their network of hospitals and to increase the number of graduates from medical schools. From 1948 to 1953 alone, forty-six thousand hospital beds were added across Canada.[9]

Saskatchewan had elected a CCF government led by T. C. Douglas in 1944, and it had pledged to take steps towards the creation of a universal medicare scheme. Despite the unavailability of matching federal funds after the collapse of the Green Book process, Saskatchewan forged ahead with plans to create universal hospital insurance in the province and end the distinction in hospitals between paying clients and charity cases. It immediately undertook a hospital construction project to ensure that most residents lived close enough to a hospital to receive care close to home. Then it legislated tax-funded hospitalization insurance in 1947, becoming the first jurisdiction in North America to implement such a program. The province's general revenues as well as a prepaid monthly premium levied on families and singles would pay the costs of insuring that need, and not financial means, determined who used 'Saskatchewan hospitals. Saskatchewan physicians largely supported this measure, while hospital administrators who opposed the legislation kept quiet after the premier threatened that the province could take control of the hospitals if the existing administrators no longer wished to run them.[10]

British Columbia's Coalition government of Liberals and Conservatives faced serious competition from that province's CCF and also decided to implement a universal hospital insurance program, financed by premiums and a 3 per cent sales tax. Claiming that it wanted to blend the concepts of private and public responsibility, it included "co-insurance" (user fees) within its hospital insurance program, despite protests from the CCF and the labour movement. Alberta presented yet a third model for paying hospital and other medical bills. Decrying both compulsory participation and centralization, the government established a series of health districts in 1946. District boards, which included both physician and consumer representatives, negotiated a health insurance scheme with municipalities, including the services to be covered for a maximum payment of $10 per adult. While most costs were borne by the voluntary subscriber to the insurance scheme, hospital fees were set at $1 per day, with the municipality and the province splitting the remaining operating costs. Manitoba and Newfoundland also had voluntary programs, which had been established before Newfoundland joined Canada, enrolling about half the province's population.[11]

Louis St. Laurent, like Mackenzie King, was less than enthusiastic about the federal government creating a national health insurance scheme. But he was under tremendous pressure from the five provinces that were heavily subsidizing patients' costs to implement a national program and lift at least half the burden of costs from the provines.[12] Ontario weighed in on the provinces' side in 1955. About 70 per cent of Ontario residents enjoyed some form of hospital insurance coverage, but Premier Leslie Frost faced public pressure for the government to fund hospital insurance. This included pressure from hospital authorities. The community elites that ran the hospitals had been dealt a body blow by the Depression, as the number of paying customers dwindled while charity cases climbed. In the postwar period, they came to believe that their institutions needed the economic stability that public insurance alone could provide.[13]

Frost responded by insisting that federal involvement was required, a viewpoint he stressed at federal-provincial discussions on hospital insurance. These discussions led to the Hospital Insurance and Diagnostic Services Act of April 1957, which established a formula for federal grants to provinces that implemented a provincial hospital insurance scheme. About half of all hospital costs would be borne by the federal government. The provinces chose the method of financing for their plans, but there were penalties for provinces that levied user fees. Passage of the legislation was eased by the lack of opposition from the Canadian Medical Association (CMA), which, since 1949, had supported user-pay hospitals.[14] Their change of heart was dictated by the need to assuage public anger regarding high costs for hospital stays and to avoid more radical medicare programs that included costs of doctors' visits. The private insurance companies were the big losers in the debate, but were determined to fight to maintain the rest of their health insurance business by denouncing further state intervention in medical care.

Towards Medicare

The CMA's rejection of public hospitals insurance in 1949 was part of a broader rejection of health insurance by Canadian doctors after the war. With average incomes rising quickly, physician groups expanded or launched health insurance plans that proved successful beyond the doctors' expectations. The plans tabulated total annual medical bills for given populations and set insurance rates that would yield the income expected by physicians plus administrative costs needed to run the plan. For physicians, it meant that they collectively set the rates for various types of treatment. Private insurance companies, which covered over 1.5 million Canadians in 1962,[15] were required to accept the physician-dictated rates as the price for having a place in the health insurance industry.

By contrast, if governments were to get involved in medical insurance, it was likely that they would require physicians to accept lower rates for various procedures as a means of reducing overall medical costs. In the United States, the growth of the private health insurance industry, also dominated by physicians, gave the American Medical Association (AMA) an incentive to spend lavishly to lobby politicians and propagandize Americans regarding the evils of a public health insurance program. Their efforts forestalled President Harry Truman's plans in the late 1940s to introduce a national universal medical insurance scheme despite widespread popular support for such a policy. In the context of the Cold War, the AMA painted state medicine as an exemplar of the programs that unfree Communist states imposed upon their hapless citizens, an image that was ironic in light of the introduction of state medicine in Britain and other European democracies. Supported by big business organizations, the AMA developed an impregnable opposition to state

medicine in Congress that united northern Republicans with southern Democrats, the latter often wealthy conservatives elected from pro-medicare constituencies but able to avoid the issue by making the preservation of racial segregation the key to their election strategies.[16]

At the federal-provincial conference in 1955, St. Laurent indicated that the federal government would only consider a national health insurance program when a majority of provinces representing a majority of citizens were prepared to institute provincial programs. The three Atlantic premiers responded that they could only consider a program if the federal government promised in advance to provide most of the funding. The premiers of Alberta and Manitoba wanted more unconditional grant money from the federal government in preference to universal medicare, and wanted any universal scheme to incorporate the private insurance schemes already in operation rather than replace them with a public plan. Ontario was only willing to commit to a national study of the possible scope and costs of a federal health scheme while Premier Duplessis of Quebec a federal program.[17]

As with hospital insurance, it was the provinces that stepped up to the plate first to offer universal programs and then put the federal government on the hot seat for failure to make such provision a national responsibility. Once again, it was Saskatchewan CCF government that led the way. Tommy Douglas, running for re-election in 1960, announced that with the federal government now paying half of Saskatchewan's hospital bills, his government could afford to implement universal medicare. Both the urban and rural poor, including most farmers, were unable to buy medical coverage, and the Saskatchewan government, like other provincial governments, was picking up the tab for medical bills for a growing section of the poor. It argued that this was unfair, first because it stigmatized those required to rely on state aid and discouraged them from seeing doctors, and second because it placed heavy financial burdens on the state that a universal plan would offset with the tax or premium contributions of the better-off, which the private insurers claimed for themselves. But Saskatchewan faced a huge fight in implementing its program.

Saskatchewan had played a pioneering role in the provision of medical services in Canada. Its municipal doctor schemes and union hospitals of the interwar period, the result of the work of the farm women's movement, and particularly Violet McNaughton, challenged the notion of health as a commodity to be purchased by those with the wherewithal to do so. Nonetheless, such programs relied on voluntary participation by doctors rather than state coercion. The CCF's experiments with full-state operation of medical services before the 1960s were limited to a few areas of the province in which the government was able to enlist the support of progressive-minded physicians. However, after the government announced its intentions to have a province-wide medical insurance scheme, a community clinic movement sprang up, a natural outgrowth of the populism that had produced both the major farm movements in Saskatchewan and the CCF itself. Health clinics with a holistic model of health, in which nurses, social workers, nutritionists, and dentists worked alongside doctors, enrolled about fifty thousand people in thirty-five regional associations in a province of less than 1 million people.[18]

Most physicians had no intention of becoming salaried professionals working in state-run clinics whose policies were determined by elected boards of non-physicians. In line with the CMA, which aided them in carrying out an extensive propaganda campaign against the government's plan, Saskatchewan doctors insisted that individuals and families should pay their medical bills via private insurance. If the province insisted that all citizens should be insured, it should direct them to buy insurance from a private plan. Only the poor should have their bills paid by the state, with the state paying physician-dictated rates for services that private plans paid. In July 1962, when the government proved adamant that it would proceed with its plans, the Saskatchewan branch of the CMA organized a withdrawal of physician services.[19]

Upper- and middle-class supporters of the physicians formed "Keep Our Doctors" committees that accused the government of imposing an unworkable policy for socialist ideological reasons. The corporate-owned daily papers, always hostile to the CCF government, terrified people by suggesting that the province might lose most of its doctors. With both the CMA and national business organizations spending extravagantly to reinforce this message through television and radio advertising, as well as by using the appearances of "expert" witnesses on news shows, Saskatchewan residents were subjected to non-stop propaganda against state medicare. This was offset by the support for medicare from the Saskatchewan Federation of Labour and the major farm organizations, though these groups had limited access to the media.

The doctors' strike ended after twenty-two days as a result of government negotiations with the Saskatchewan branch of the CMA, in which the doctors conceded a universal state program and the government conceded many of the demands of the doctors. There would be no salaries for doctors or payments by the number of patients that they served. Instead, fee for service, the principle that governed private insurance plans, would remain sacrosanct. Doctors would continue to operate from their own private offices, and not only would doctors not be forced to participate in a community clinic, but those who chose to practise in a clinic would receive direct funding from the state rather than have to deal with the community clinic board. Finally, doctors would have the choice of participating directly in the state plan either by requiring patients to pay bills and then bill the plan or by staying out of the plan altogether and billing patients with whatever fees they deemed appropriate. This was simply a face-saving measure since both sides understood that most patients would choose to patronize doctors who were in the prepaid medicare scheme.

The Hall Commission

Saskatchewan's decision to launch a compulsory, state-run medicare scheme placed pressure on the national political parties to respond to demands from Canadians in all provinces for universal medical insurance. The NDP made implementation of a national medicare scheme a central plank in its platform. Out of office, the Liberals as well recommitted themselves to the national medicare program that they had promised in the 1945 election but had never delivered. Business stalwarts among former ministers, including C. D. Howe, Charles Dunning, and Brooke Claxton, opposed medicare. But the reformers who had taken over the party machinery in the late 1950s convinced delegates at the 1961 national convention to recommit the party to a national medicare program.[20]

While John Diefenbaker faced fewer demands within his party for state medicare, and considered business pressures against such a measure, he was leery of simply dismissing any solution that might appease public demands for guaranteed access to medical care.

He turned in 1961 to Justice Emmett Hall, a fellow Saskatchewan Conservative, to head a commission to study options for improving the health care available to Canadians. Commentators assumed that the commission, largely composed of hand-picked Tory supporters, would opt for a non-compulsory scheme.

While the commission deliberated, the Social Credit governments of Alberta and British Columbia attempted to counter the "socialist" Saskatchewan scheme with state programs that avoided "coercion" of doctors or "conscription" of citizens into a state plan. First, Alberta in 1963, and then British Columbia in 1964, announced voluntary plans that directed most residents into existing doctor-controlled and insurance-company plans, but provided state subsidies for the poor so that they could also receive coverage. The Alberta plan was endorsed by the provincial College of Physicians and Surgeons, which the government consulted as it set the premium and determined what services were covered. Such plans left many families who were just above the low-income cut-offs in the position of having to decide whether they could afford the high costs of private insurance or should risk going without coverage. Even in wealthy Alberta, the province calculated that only 60 per cent of provincial residents were covered by the voluntary medical-care scheme.[21]

The commission heard ample testimony from organized groups as well as individuals who favoured the Alberta and British Columbia approach over the Saskatchewan plan. While 40 per cent of Canadians had no medical insurance and many more had coverage only for catastrophes, elite groups that opposed a universal state program, led by the CMA and the Canadian Chamber of Commerce, insisted that only 15 per cent of Canadians were unable to afford medical coverage.[22] This figure seemed suspicious in light of a Statistics Canada study in 1961 that placed 27 per cent of Canadians below the poverty line and another 14 per cent on or just over that line.[23] However, to admit that private medical insurance was a hardship for almost half of the population would weaken the argument against state medicine.

Medicare's Opponents

Supporters of continued privatization and voluntary participation in medical insurance included the Canadian Medical Association, the Canadian Dental Association, the Canadian Chamber of Commerce, the entire private insurance industry, the pharmaceutical industry, and representatives of most other industries. The premiers of British Columbia, Alberta, Manitoba, and Ontario opposed medicare while Quebec's Premier Lesage was opposed to federal legislation in a sphere of provincial competence. The Atlantic premiers generally supported medicare but wanted the federal government to pay the lion's share of the costs and to give them time to phase in any universal program because they faced shortages of medical personnel. Only Woodrow Lloyd in Saskatchewan was an unequivocal supporter of a fully state-operated scheme.[24]

The advocates of private insurance used a variety of arguments before the commission. For example, the British Columbia Medical Association, following the lead of the CMA,[25] argued that the monies that medicare would absorb could be better spent on "scholarships for medical students, to add rehabilitative and chronic care kids to our hospitals, to extend our mental health programme, and for many other important services." Directing taxes instead towards paying medical insurance was "foolhardy" because it meant "providing a service to those who are already providing it for themselves, as most British Columbians are doing through our system of voluntary health insurance."[26]

The CMA's brief added that the hospital insurance program, which the physicians regarded favourably, had expanded demand for hospital beds. The federal and provincial governments, it suggested, having created this demand by making hospitalization a free good, now had to cough up the money for more beds. Implicit, however, in this argument was that prior to the existence of a public program, the real health needs of the population, in the area of hospitalization, had been underserved despite the availability of private hospitalization insurance.[27] Nor did the physicians try to claim that private health insurance was meeting everyone's needs. They conceded that to achieve universal medical insurance coverage, about 3 million Canadians would have to have their bills paid by taxes collected from the rest of Canadians, who, in turn, would also have to pay for their own private insurance.

The CMA, while avoiding the Cold War rhetoric of its American counterpart in its opposition to state medicine, emphasized that doctors as a group would be hostile to state medical insurance and even more hostile to any efforts by the government to move them away from individual practice into group settings that might also include other types of medical practitioners. "Physicians by nature and by training are strongly individualistic and it is not given to all doctors to function happily and efficiently as a member of a group." It could lead, in any case, to "assembly-line medicine."[28]

The Canadian Dental Association (CDA) also claimed that state monies could be better directed at other goals than a national insurance program. Admitting that most Canadians had little or no access to dentists, they pointed out that there was a dismal ratio of dentists to population—1 to 3,000, compared with 1 to 1,900 in the United States, with regional gaps that were best demonstrated by Newfoundland and Labrador's ratio of 1 dentist per 11,000 residents. If all Canadians suddenly had access to dental services, there would simply be too few dentists to accommodate them. Steps to increase the number of dentists would have to precede the implementation of any government plan, and, in any case, any such plan had to be placed under the control of dentists. The dentists called for greater state funding for dental programs and lower fees for dental students.

The dentists admitted that "education and income separately and together are strongly associated with going to the dentist." Yet the dentists largely ignored their own insight that money kept many Canadians from properly caring for their teeth, focusing instead on "people's lack of interest in preventative measures" as the way to improve dental health. They recommended that provinces make fluoridation of water supplies mandatory for municipalities, that Canadians consume less sugar, and that more government funds go to dental research. While cool to state involvement in dentistry, outside of dental education and research, the CDA did recognize some need for governments to fund potential consumers of dentists' services. Like the physicians, they supported state funding of necessary services for destitute Canadians. If governments were going to provide state dental service programs, they should restrict their programs to children.[29]

Not one recognized organization of health professionals in Canada placed itself on record as supporting medicare, with the exception of the nurses'

association in Saskatchewan where medicare already was an established program.[30] The rest of the nursing profession in Canada, which later would become a militant supporter of public medicine, restricted itself to calling for greater public support for nursing education and better salaries for nurses.[31]

Both pharmacists and the pharmaceutical industry strongly opposed inclusion of prescription drugs in a state medical insurance plan, since it carried the implicit threat of state regulation of drug prices. The Canadian Pharmaceutical Manufacturers' Association (CPMA) reported soothingly that competition was lively at the manufacturing and retail levels of the industry: "The competitive aspect of research and development, combined with behaviour of prices and promotional activities, indicates that a satisfactory level of competition exists in the industry. Furthermore, this competition is directed in a manner which is socially desirable. Growth, product development and the general level of prices have been favourable rather than unfavourable to the consumer."[32] The pharmaceutical manufacturers assured the commissioners that after-tax profits of the industry were modest and the industry's expenditures on promotion were fairly restrained and served the purpose of informing physicians and others about useful pharmaceuticals.

In fact, the industry's profits, measured as a percentage of invested capital, were double the average for Canadian industries as a whole from 1953 to 1958. A study prepared in 1961 for the federal Department of Justice by the director of Investigation and Research, Combines Investigation Act, noted that apart from making large profits, the industry was absolutely profligate in its promotion expenditures, as it worked tirelessly to press physicians to use various new drugs. Patent laws protected drug companies that developed a new pharmaceutical product, and it was the knowledge that they had a monopoly for many years over a particular drug that caused pharmaceutical companies to spend millions trying to convince physicians to prescribe their product.

But, while monopolistic practices affected only "certain drugs" at the manufacturing level, the retail level was a dead loss to market forces despite being wholly private. Wrote the justice investigator: "The practices of retail druggists ... have resulted in the virtual elimination of price competition at the retail level."[33] Such monopolistic practices did not lead to calls for either a public takeover of the manufacture and distribution of pharmaceuticals in Canada or for new public regulations over the industry from any segment of the health care industry. Health care providers, such as doctors, dentists, and pharmacy owners, had a common interest in establishing a high price for their services, and happily confounded private provision with competition and efficient pricing.

Ultimately, the two arguments that were heard most frequently to discredit a compulsory public medical system were that it would deprive health practitioners of the freedoms that all business people ought legitimately to have in a democratic society, and that it would be so costly as to provoke crushing levels of taxation that would destroy Canada's industrial competitiveness. The CMA stated starkly: "We consider government intervention into the field of prepaid medical care to the point of becoming a monopolistic purchaser of medical services, to be a measure of civil conscription. We would urge this Royal Commission to support our view that, exclusive of states of emergency, civil conscription of any segment of the Canadian population is contrary to our democratic philosophy."[34] Premier Leslie Frost of Ontario was prominent among anti-medicare politicians to invoke the industrial competitiveness argument. The country, he averred, "has already become a high cost economy. And that is affecting our trading and developmental position."[35]

Medicare's Supporters

Medicare's supporters suggested that Canadians had collective rights to the best medical treatments that were available regardless of income, and that the right of individuals to receive affordable medical service outweighed the alleged rights of medical practitioners to price their services as they deemed best. Despite the crushing majority support for medicare evident in opinion polls, few Canadians were willing to come forward as individuals and suggest that they had received second-rate medical treatment because they were poor. A careful scouring of the thousands of briefs before the Hall Commission reveals only one case where an individual Canadian denounced her doctors for providing her family mediocre care because of their inability to pay. Her physician's scathing personal attack upon her in response demonstrated why few

Canadians had the temerity to reveal personal cases of receiving poor treatment or being driven to bankruptcy to obtain necessary medical attention.[36] Instead, the horror stories that the commission heard as well as the main arguments countering the claims of private medicine came from organizations. Trade unions, social worker and welfare organizations, farmers' federations, and the United Church of Canada convinced the commissioners that they should adopt an ambitious national program.

The Canadian Association of Social Workers placed the case before the Hall Commission that programs that limited free state care to the destitute, which were in operation in many Canadian provinces, did not work. Many were deterred from seeking medical assistance at clinics because several hours might be required for them to fill out forms at the accounting department. Meanwhile, many people of middle means who did not qualify for the state care available to the indigent avoided seeking medical care because "it is going to come out of the food budget, or come out of the youngsters' clothing budget or something like this." The social workers observed that the stigma of receiving a charitable service discouraged usage of the service. It also created problems regarding the proper cut-off income for recipients. Better to have medicare available to all Canadians so that no one had to see it as either a special right or a special shame.

The social workers unsurprisingly made a strong pitch for closely co-ordinating health and welfare services so as to improve the physical and mental health of the population. Many of their clients suffered poor health because of poor housing and the stresses that resulted from limited incomes. They also called for the definition of medical services under medicare to include convalescent hospitals, home care and replacement homemakers for convalescing mothers, and the provision of prosthetic appliances.[37]

The Canadian Federation of Agriculture (CFA) and several other major farm groups appeared before the commission and indicated that the majority of farmers could not afford private health insurance.[38] The United Church of Canada, whose General Council had called for a contributory national health plan since 1952, confirmed the CFA's impressions. The United Church brief added that urban immigrants, particularly unskilled workers from southern Italy, were perhaps even more vulnerable. These people were underpaid, ill-housed, insecure about their income, and prone as a result to both physical and mental illness. Yet they were too impoverished to be able to set aside the money for private health insurance.[39]

But the trade union movement probably proved the most effective in demolishing the arguments of industry and physicians that Canadians were gradually meeting their medical needs privately. In the postwar period, the trade union movement, which enrolled about a third of Canadian workers thanks to wartime and early postwar organizing successes, had succeeded in winning a variety of "fringe benefits" for their members in addition to wage increases and improvements in working conditions. A medical benefits package had become a common gain for trade unionists, and such prepaid medical insurance swelled the numbers of families whom the private insurance companies could claim as they pooh-poohed the need for a public program.

Unions' characterizations of the limitations of private coverage undermined such insurance industry boasting. National, provincial, and labour federations complained to the Hall Commission that the profit-driven insurance schemes that enrolled their members tended to severely restrict or deny coverage altogether in such areas as preventive health services, rehabilitation, mental health, dental services, and social services. Prescription drugs, nursing aid, appliances, eyeglasses, and hearing aids were rarely covered. Yet most of these plans had "costly deductible and co-insurance charges." As the Canadian Labour Congress (CLC) concluded, "It is too much to expect that a complete range of services can be made available on a universal basis to the Canadian people within the near future through the mere extension of the private pre-payment schemes. It is not physically financially nor administratively possible."[40]

The CLC led the way in labour's deliberations before the commission, answering point-by-point the claims made to the commission by the CMA. It noted that, even using the CMA's definition of poverty, 4.5 million Canadians would require that their medical bills be paid for by the state. Apart from the layouts for these people, the state would have to spend millions in carrying out the means tests necessary for determining who was eligible, in the process of stigmatizing them.[41]

Trade union federations in poorer provinces emphasized the disparities in medical services among Canada's regions that resulted from a market-driven allocation of resources. In Newfoundland, for example, the number of doctors per capita was less than half the Canadian average, while many rural areas had no physicians at all. The imbalance in the availability of nurses with the rest of Canada was similar. There were few dentists outside the two major cities, and St. John's institution for the aged and infirm was "a blot on the decency of the Canadian nation." Not only was a national medicare plan needed, according to the Newfoundland Federation of Labour, but such a plan had to provide for regional hospitals and clinics to be built and staffed in deprived provinces.[42]

The Hall Report and the Implementation of Medicare

Emmett Hall and the majority of his fellow commissioners were won over, in large part, by the values and arguments of the supporters of a universal medicare program. Their 1964 report made some obeisance in the direction of business and physicians by recognizing that no doctor should be forced to join a national medicare program, and that doctors should remain in private practice even if they joined medicare rather than becoming civil servants working in government offices. Even more of a victory for the physicians was the commission's rejection of the National Health Service model of salaried physicians, which the labour movement had endorsed. Instead, the commissioners supported continuation of the fee-for-service model which was a hallmark of private insurance.[43]

However, the overall direction of the report reflected the persuasiveness of the opponents of the argument made by businesses and physicians. Wrote the commissioners: "The achievement of the highest possible health standards for all our people must become a primary objective of national policy and a cohesive factor contributing to national unity, involving individual and community responsibilities and actions. This objective can best be achieved through a comprehensive, universal Health Services Programme for the Canadian people." "Comprehensive," in Hall's view, included "all health services, preventive, diagnostic, curative and rehabilitative, that modern medical and other services can provide."[44] This meant that governments should not only provide universal coverage for physicians' services and for hospitalization but should also cover prescription drug payments for all Canadians, home care and prosthetic services as required, dental services for children, expectant mothers, and public assistance recipients, and eyecare for children and the poor. Most of these programs would exclude user fees, though each prescription would bear a dollar user fee and adults would be expected to pay one-third the cost of eyeglasses, which would however be free for children.[45] Taxation would pay for all Canadians to be covered by the national health program. In short, Hall had rejected the voluntary medical insurance schemes that Ontario, Alberta, and British Columbia had proposed as alternatives to the potential of full coverage to all Canadians for all necessary medical services.

Hall recommended that the federal government pay half the costs for any provincial medicare scheme that provided universal coverage. The provinces could determine their priorities in terms of the various components of the medicare scheme and the timing of their introduction. Federal government grants would help to establish the training programs required to produce the additional personnel needed once medical services were universally available, as well as he facilities required to build the medical and dental clinics to house these services. The federal government would, for example, share with the provinces the costs of building mental health wings in regular hospitals so that most inmates of mental health institutions could receive care in their community. It would also aid the provinces in providing funds that allowed parents to raise mildly intellectually disabled children at home.[46]

The Hall Report put pressure on Lester Pearson's Liberal government, which had been elected in 1963, albeit without a parliamentary majority, to live up to its medicare promises. The Liberals had promised a national medicare program that would provide comprehensive services free of charge to children till they left school and to Canadians over sixty-five years of age. Everyone else would have services by general practitioners, specialists, and surgeons, along with diagnostic services, covered, except for the first $25. Even the left-wingers in the government were taken aback by the scope of services that Hall wanted a national program to cover. For a year the government waffled, and even in the throne speech

of 1965, the government committed itself to medicare in only the vaguest terms. The NDP, which had endorsed the Hall Report *in toto*, demanded that the government implement its full set of recommendations immediately.[47]

An exhaustive review of the Hall recommendations by the Department of National Health and Welfare demonstrated the substantial bureaucratic support for the tenor of the reforms proposed by the commissioners. Department officials endorsed Hall's views that "deterrent fees," that is user fees, could not be allowed for basic services because they contradicted the principle of universal availability of medical services. Federal funding of medical services along the lines of the existing federal formula for hospitals was "fundamental in making the most effective use of the nation's health resources to achieve the highest possible health standards for residents of Canada." The bureaucrats also endorsed the children's dental program and subsidizing of prescription costs, but with Finance and Privy Council officials serving as observers to the committee's deliberations, they couched such support with indications that both of these sets of services should be phased in over an unspecified period. Potential costs also caused the officials to reluctantly oppose Hall's embrace of government financing of home care.[48]

The eventual compromise reached within the government called for medicare to be introduced in phases. The first phase would add physician and diagnostic services to the existing hospitalization coverage, while other components of the Hall vision would be introduced as fiscal means became available. In practise, though few Canadians could know it at the time, there would be no second phase for medicare at least during the twentieth century.

The government had a built-in excuse for delay because of the need to convince the provinces to implement medicare programs. There were meetings in April and May of 1965 in which federal officials representing the cabinet and the Department of National Health and Public Welfare along with the Department of Finance heard the views of ministers of health and their officials from the provinces. Two federal–provincial conferences that year also provided the provinces with a forum for their disparate views, but provided little detail from Pearson regarding the federal government's plans. Pearson did, however, insist that the federal government, following Hall, would insist that federal funds would only to go provincial programs that met four criteria: comprehensive coverage of physicians' services, universality of coverage, public administration, and portability of services so that citizens were covered when they lived outside of their home province.[49]

In Quebec, an exhaustive provincial review of social programs, headed by Claude Castonguay, had recently begun and tentatively looked favourably upon a program of universal medicare. Federal dollars to help fund such a program were desirable, but federal input into the design of the program was unacceptable. Alberta's Premier Manning continued to fulminate against any program that was universal and that did not involve co-insurance. His government was furious that Ottawa had penalized the province financially for its insistence on user fees in the hospitalization plan. Ontario, Manitoba, and British Columbia also insisted that provinces have more scope for the design of medicare than Pearson's four principles might allow. Other provinces accepted the principles of the Hall Report but wanted sufficient federal funding to make it affordable for them to establish a program. Only Newfoundland was anxious for a federal plan to be legislated immediately, though New Brunswick was committed to establishing a plan and Saskatchewan wanted a federal contribution to its program.[50]

The Liberals called a federal election in late 1965 but narrowly failed again to form a majority government. Their commitment to a modified version of the Hall recommendations during the election left them little alternative afterwards but to legislate a medicare bill. In 1966, the government introduced legislation to provide an average of 50 per cent of the costs of provincial schemes that met the four medicare principles (a formula was used that would provide a larger portion of federal funds per capita in poorer provinces),[51] but the legislation lacked a date for implementation. Initially, Pearson aimed for 1 July 1967, the one hundredth birthday of the country. However, continued provincial reluctance to accept the federal principles argued against such speed, as did the change in the balance of forces in the Liberal cabinet after the election.

Walter Gordon, the progressive finance minister, took responsibility for having advised Pearson to hold an early election, and resigned from cabinet.

His replacement, Mitchell Sharp, held views similar to those of organized business and appeared in no hurry to implement medicare, which he claimed could have an undue impact on the federal treasury. Robert Stanfield, the new leader of the Conservative party, denounced "a vast new spending program."[52] But Sharp and his supporters were only able to delay medicare's implementation by one year.[53] On 1 July 1968, funds would be available to provinces with a medicare scheme that met the four principles of medicare. Still, the division within the Pearson cabinet encouraged provinces that opposed universality and public administration to move slowly. Only Saskatchewan and British Columbia presented plans in the month after the medicare deadline and began to receive federal funding in July.

By then, the dithering Pearson had been replaced as head of the government by the more decisive Pierre Elliott Trudeau. Trudeau scotched any further attempts from within the cabinet or the provinces to allow for either delays or modifications of the medicare legislation. Within a year all provinces but Quebec had announced plans that met the criteria of the Medical Services Act of 1968. Quebec entered the plan in 1972.[54]

Medicare, Health, and Hierarchy

The Hall Report was less about health overall than about how to ensure that access to physicians was generally available and that physicians were adequately paid.

Hall did not challenge the medical profession's monopoly over medical care. The commissioners heard a variety of briefs from non-allopathic healers, but they largely accepted the equation of physicians with healing. Even the officials of the Department of National Health and Welfare who reviewed the report's recommendations observed the narrowness of Hall's focus: "Attention in the Recommendations was actually focused on personal health services provided mainly by physicians and others in private practice to the exclusion of public health services."[55]

In addition, the commissioners paid little attention to environmental pollution, which a few trade briefs suggested was a factor in the health of individuals.[56] They had little to say about the roles of fitness, stress, nutrition, and poverty, outside of its impact on ability to pay medical bills. Industrial accidents were not addressed. The commissioners gave no consideration to the community-care model, which had already been piloted in Saskatchewan, accepting unquestioningly a hierarchical model of medical care in which physicians dictated the roles of other medical practitioners and patients had no input into either the character or payment structures of services.[57]

Native Peoples and Medical Care

Nothing illustrated better the argument that physician care alone could not guarantee a healthy population that the continued oppression and suffering of indigenous Canadians. In 1977, when the average age of death for Canadians was 66, the comparative figure for natives was 42.4 years. They were four times as likely to die violent deaths in their twenties or thirties as other Canadians. Babies on reserves died in large numbers of gastroenteritis and pneumonia, diseases of poverty. Waters upon which Natives depended for their fish were often poisoned with waste mercury from chemical plants. On poor, isolated reserves with shabby housing and few facilities, Native children sniffed gas while their parents abused alcohol. Though the residential schooling system, which snatched children from their parents and placed them in environments where physical and sexual abuse were often rife, was being phased out, its scars on the Native psyche were reflected in substance abuse and poor parenting skills.

These woes were compounded by a lack of health workers, including doctors and nurses, on many reserves. There were only ten physicians and 221 nurses of Native descent in Canada in the mid-1970s and there was no national program to change this situation.[58] The federal government had over time taken a degree of responsibility for Native health care, always claiming, however, that constitutionally it was not compelled to do so. Until 1945, Indian Affairs had authority over Native health. After 1945, the Department of National Health and Welfare (DNHW) was given charge of this responsibility, and in 1962, a branch of DNHW called Medical Services was formed with a variety of programs under its control, including the former Indian Health Services.[59]

Community control initiatives at the grassroots attempted to compensate for government indifference and to pressure the federal government to provide Native communities with the wherewithal to deal with both their social and health needs. Reserves began to organize their own community medical schemes to hire doctors and nurses, to make up for the lethargy of Medical Services and to establish the right of Native communities to govern themselves in all areas, including health services. Native nurses formed an organization to promote nursing as an occupation for Native girls. Shamanistic healing practices, long suppressed by the colonial authorities on reserves, but never completely eradicated, made a comeback. The colonialism experienced by Native peoples and the health of the Aboriginal population seemed inextricably linked, and campaigns for community control over health services formed part of the struggle to shed the legacy of paternalistic, remote control by Ottawa over Native lives.[60]

The creation of a national network of provincial medicare programs, all subscribing to the principles of comprehensiveness, universality, portability, and public administration, represented a major victory for progressive forces in Canada, backed by overwhelming public opinion. The combination of public campaigning by important social movements, including labour, farmers, and social workers, with support from key elements of the Liberal Party and the civil service, resulted in a Tory-appointed royal commission failing to suggest some sort of public–private mix that largely subordinated health service provision to profit-seeking health insurance companies and physicians. In turn, this led the Liberal government, divided for two decades on whether to implement its promises originally made in 1919 for a national public program, to finally deliver.

The success of reformist forces in Canada in the area of medicare was a contrast with the United States where the politics of race, the lack of a social-democratic party, the bias of public expenditures towards military spending, and the immense power of organized medicine continued to prevent the introduction of a universal medicare program. As Canada legislated universal medicare, American President Lyndon Johnson, spending billions of dollars on an unpopular war in Indochina, felt only able to support medicare for the elderly and a Medicaid program for the destitute that held down costs for medical services for the poor by sending them to special medical clinics, which were generally understaffed and involved long waits for service.[61]

By contrast, Canada's "first phase" of medicare provided far less comprehensive coverage for illness prevention and treatment than the National Health Service in Britain and similar programs in Scandinavia and Holland. The Soviet Union and its Cold War satellites in eastern Europe all provided sweeping free comprehensive medical care programs. The Hall Commission had looked to western European models rather than the United States in framing its recommendations, and the government rhetorically accepted the commission's conclusions. In practice, the desire to keep costs down resulted in a watering down of Hall's proposals that saw medicare's "first phase" limited to coverage of visits to hospitals and physicians, and diagnostic services. Further phases were not legislated. The late 1960s represented the high point of social reform rather than a first installment on social reforms that would fundamentally redistribute wealth in Canada. The next three chapters examine areas in which the postwar welfare state largely failed to meet the needs of Canadians—daycare, housing, and poverty.

Notes

1. Health Study Bureau, *Review of Canada's Health Needs and Insurance Proposals* (Toronto, ON: Health Study Bureau, 1946), 41.

2. Ibid., 40–3.

3. Malcolm G. Taylor, *Health Insurance and Canadian Public Policy: The Seven Decisions That Created the Canadian Health Insurance System* (Montreal, QC: McGill-Queen's University Press, 1978), 166.

4. Health Study Bureau, *Review of Canada's Health Needs*, 3–4.

5. Historian Georgina Taylor nuances the notion of medicare having been single-parented by a male, recalling that farm women, led by Violet McNaughton, had created the prototypes of medicare at a municipal level in the province. See Georgina M. Taylor, "'Ground for Common Action': Violet McNaughton's Agrarian Feminism and the Origins of the Farm Women's Movement in Canada" (PhD thesis, Carleton University, 1997). See also Georgina M. Taylor, "'Let Us Co-operate': Violet McNaughton and the Co-operative Ideal," in *Co-operatives in the Year 2000: Memory, Mutual Aid, and the Millennium*, ed. Brett Fairbairn and Ian Macpherson (Saskatoon, SK: Centre for the Study of Co-operatives, University of Saskatchewan, 2000), 57–78.

6. "CCF Broadcast by T. C. Douglas, MP," William Lyon Mackenzie King Papers, MG 26, J1, Vol. 346, p. 297811, *Library and Archives of Canada* (LAC).

7. Ibid., p. 297809.

8. Many organizations expressed disappointment that the promised national health insurance program did not materialize. For example, the National Council of Women of Canada voted at their 1947 convention to "commend the Dominion Government on the Health Insurance Plan already prepared and urge its implementation as soon as possible." "Resolutions, Annual Meeting, held in Regina June 6–11, 1947," National Council of Women of Canada (NCWC) Papers, MG 28 I 25, Vol. 90, File 1, LAC.

9. Malcolm G. Taylor, "The Canadian Health-Care System: After Medicare," in *Health and Canadian Society: Sociological Perspectives*, 2nd ed., ed. David Coburn, Carl D'Arcy, George M. Torrance, and Peter New (Toronto, ON: Fitzhenry and Whiteside, 1987), 74.

10. Duane Mombourquette, "'An Inalienable Right': The CCF and Rapid Health Care Reform, 1944–1948," in *Social Welfare Policy in Canada: Historical Readings*, ed. Raymond B. Blake and Jeff Keshen (Toronto, ON: Copp Clark, 1995), 298–302.

11. Taylor, "The Canadian Health-Care System," 74, 84; Margaret A. Ormsby, *British Columbia: A History* (Vancouver, BC: Macmillan, 1958), 487; Alvin Finkel, *The Social Credit Phenomenon in Alberta* (Toronto, ON: University of Toronto Press, 1989), 123.

12. Eugene Vayda and Raisa B. Deber, "The Canadian Health-Care System: A Developmental Overview," in *Social Welfare Policy*, ed. Blake and Keshen, 315.

13. David Gagan and Rosemary Gagan, *For Patients of Moderate Means: A Social History of the Voluntary Public General Hospital in Canada, 1890–1950* (Montreal, QC: McGill-Queen's University Press, 2002).

14. Brief of Canadian Medical Association, April 1962, Canada, Royal Commission on Health Services, RG 33, Series 78, Vol. 19, File 278, LAC.

15. "Brief from Great West Life and Metropolitan Life Insurance Company," n.d., Royal Commission on Health Services, Vol. 15, Exhibit 200.

16. Monte M. Poen, *Harry S. Truman Versus the Medical Lobby: The Genesis of Medicare* (Columbia, MS: University of Missouri Press, 1979); Lawrence R. Jacobs, *The Health of Nations: Public Opinion and*

the Making of American and British Health Policy (Ithaca, NY: Cornell University Press, 1993).

17. "Reports of 1955 Federal-Provincial Conference," Department of National Health and Welfare Papers, RG 29, Vol. 918, LAC.

18. Joan Feather, "From Concept to Reality: Formation of the Swift Current Health Region," *Prairie Forum* 16, 1 (Spring 1991): 59–80; Joan Feather, "Impact of the Swift Current Health Region: Experiment or Model," *Prairie Forum* 16, 2 (Fall 1991): 225–48; Stan Rands, "Recollections: The CCF in Saskatchewan," in *Western Canadian Politics: The Radical Tradition*, ed. Donald C. Kerr (Edmonton, AB: NeWest, 1981), 58–64.

19. On the doctors' strike, see Robin E. Badgley and Samuel Wolfe, *Doctors' Strike: Medical Care and Conflict in Saskatchewan* (Toronto, ON: Macmillan, 1967).

20. P. E. Bryden, *Planners and Politicians: Liberal Politics and Social Policy, 1957–1968* (Montreal, QC: McGill-Queens University Press, 1997), chap. 2 and 3.

21. Finkel, *The Social Credit Phenomenon*, 144; "Discussions with Provinces on Health Services Matters," Meeting with Alberta Officials, 22 April 1965, Department of National Health and Welfare Papers, RG 33, Vol. 45.

22. Evidence of Canadian Medical Association, April 1962, Canada, Royal Commission on Health Services, Vol. 19, File 278; Evidence of Canadian Chamber of Commerce, March 1962, Vol. 14, File 188.

23. Canada, Economic Council of Canada, *The Challenge of Growth and Change*, Fifth Annual Review (Ottawa, ON: Queen's Printer, 1968), 104–105.

24. "Discussions with Provinces on Health Services Matters," Department of National health and Welfare Papers, Vol. 45.

25. Evidence of Canadian Medical Association, April 1962, Royal Commission on Health Services.

26. Evidence of British Columbia Medical Association, February 1962, Royal Commission on Health Services, Vol. 12, File 150.

27. Evidence of Canadian Medical Association, April 1962, Royal Commission on Health Services.

28. Ibid.

29. Evidence of Canadian Dental Association, March 1962, Royal Commission on Health, Vol. 14, Exhibit 192, 1962.

30. Evidence of Saskatchewan Registered Nurses Association, January 1962, Royal Commission on Health Services, Vol. 9, File 84.

31. See, for example, Evidence of New Brunswick Association of Registered Nurses, 9 November 1961, Vol. 8, File 44; Evidence of Manitoba Association of Registered Nurses, January 1962, Vol. 9, File 65; and Evidence of Association des Infirmières de la Province de Québec, April 1962, Vol. 15, File 219, Royal Commission on Health Services.

32. Evidence of Canadian Pharmaceutical Manufacturers Association, May 1962, Royal Commission on Health Services, Vol. 20, File 291.

33. Canada, Director of Investigation and Research, Combines Investigation Act, *Material Collected for Submission to the Restrictive Trade Practices Commission in the Course of an Inquiry Under Section 421 of the Combines Investigation Act Relating to the Manufacture, Distribution and Sale of Drugs* (Ottawa, ON: Department of Justice, 1961) 258.

34. Evidence of Canadian Medical Association, 16 October 1962, Royal Commission on Health Services, Vol. 6, File 67.

35. Canadian Press Report of Leslie Frost Interview, 29 March 1961, Royal Commission on Health Services, Vol. 8.

36. Evidence of Mrs. Marguerite Miles, Toronto, n.d., File 355; Evidence of Dr. C. Collins-William, Toronto, n.d., File 375, Vol. 22, Royal Commission on Health Services.

37. Evidence of Canadian Association of Social Workers, 28 May 1962, Royal Commission on Health Services, Vol. 6, File 61.

38. Evidence of Canadian Federation of Agriculture, 27 March, 1962, Royal Commission on Health Services, Vol. 14, File 190.

39. Evidence of United Church of Canada, April 1962, Royal Commission on Health Services, Vol. 22, File 352.

40. Evidence of Canadian Labour Congress, 17 October, 1962, Royal Commission on Health Services, Vol. 6, File 68.

41. Ibid.

42. Evidence of Newfoundland Federation of Labour, October 1961, Royal Commission on Health Services, Vol. 7, File 25.

43. Royal Commission on Health Services, *Report*, vol. 1 (Ottawa, ON: Queen's Printer, 1964), 29.

44. Ibid., 11.

45. Ibid., 19.

46. Ibid., 19, 24–25, 36, 41.

47. "Election 1963 Pamphlets," National Liberal Federation Papers, MG 28, IV–3, Vol. 1024, LAC; Bryden, *Planners and Politicians*, 136.

48. "Departmental Review of the Report of the Royal Commission on Health Services: Departmental Appraisal and Proposals and Recommendations," March 1965, 23, 25, 28, 59, 62, 77, 87–92. Quote is from 28. Department of National Health and Welfare Papers, Vol. 45.

49. Ibid., 142.

50. Bryden, *Planners and Politicians*, 159; "Discussions with Provinces on Health Services Matters," Meeting with Quebec Delegation, 12 and 13 April 1965, Department of National Health and Welfare Papers, Vol. 45; Finkel, *The Social Credit Phenomenon in Alberta*, 150–51.

51. Eugene Vayda and Raisa B. Deber, "The Canadian Health Care System: A Developmental Overview," in *Social Welfare Policy*, ed. Blake and Keshen, 316. In 1973–74, the federal grant to Newfoundland covered 81.5 per cent of the province's medical bills and 57.6 per cent of its hospital costs while the grant to Ontario paid 44.8 per cent of medical care and 49.4 per cent of hospital costs. "For medical insurance, each province received 50 per cent of the average national per capita medical care expenditure multiplied by its population."

52. The continued opposition of the premiers was clear in File 618.4, "Correspondence with Premiers," Lester B. Pearson Papers, MG 26, N-4, Vol. 199, LAC. Other than Saskatchewan and British Columbia, no provinces were clearly prepared to join the medicare program in February 1968. Nova Scotia and Newfoundland were believed by the federal government to be only prepared to join if Ontario did. But Ontario, New Brunswick, and Alberta were unprepared to join the program. Manitoba planned to defer participation for at least a year beyond July 1 in the hopes of convincing the federal government to concede support for a plan more in tune with Manitoba's free-enterprise views.

53. Ibid., 152–63.

54. Ibid., 164–67.

55. Department of National Health and Welfare, "Departmental Review," 2.

56. Evidence of United Electrical, Radio and Machine Workers of America, May 1962, Royal Commission on Health Services, Vol. 21.

57. Donald Swartz, "The Politics of Reform: Conflict and Accommodation in Canadian Health Policy," in *The Canadian State: Political Economy and Political Power*, ed. Leo Panitch (Toronto, ON: University of Toronto Press, 1977), 311–43; and Vivienne Walters, "State, Capital and Labour: The Introduction of Federal-Provincial Insurance for Physician Care in Canada," *Canadian Journal of Sociology and Anthropology* 19, 2 (1982): 157–72.

58. Paul Grescoe, "A Nation's Disgrace," in *Health and Canadian Society*, ed. Coburn, D'Arcy, Torrance, and New, 127–40.

59. James S. Frideres and René R. Gadacz, *Aboriginal Peoples in Canada: Contemporary Conflicts*, 6th ed. (Toronto, ON: Prentice Hall, 2001), 68–69.

60. Maureen K. Lux, *Medicine That Walks: Disease, Medicine, and Canadian Plains Native People, 1880–1940* (Toronto, ON: University of Toronto Press, 2001); T. Kue Young, *Health Care and Culture Change: The Indian Experience in the Central Subarctic* (Toronto, ON: University of Toronto Press, 1988).

61. Poen, *Harry S. Truman Versus the Medical Lobby*; Paul Starr, *The Social Transformation of American Medicine* (New York, NY: Basic Books, 1982).

RECONCILING THE TWO SOLITUDES?
The Debate Over Official Languages, 1963–1995

Matthew Hayday
University of Guelph

● RECONCILING THE TWO SOLITUDES? THE DEBATE OVER OFFICIAL LANGUAGES, 1963–1995

● **Introduction by Matthew Hayday**

▲ **Primary Sources**

■ **Secondary Sources**

INTRODUCTION

Matthew Hayday

The co-existence of two major language communities within one country has been the source of many of Canada's most heated political and cultural confrontations. Until the 1960s, the relationship between English- and French-speaking Canadians was at best one of ambivalent coexistence. However, it also frequently featured determined efforts on the part of the English-speaking majority to assimilate the francophone minority or otherwise eliminate their language rights. The New Brunswick and Manitoba Schools Questions of the late-19th century, the abolition of French-language rights in the Northwest Territories in the 1890s, and Ontario's passage of Regulation 17 on education in 1912 all attempted to limit the use of the French language outside Quebec. Although the *British North America Act* permitted the use of French in the federal legislature, simultaneous translation services were not provided until the 1950s. If francophones wanted to be understood by their English-speaking colleagues, they had to speak in English. Few French-speakers ever made their way into the senior ranks of the federal civil service. These circumstances clearly ran counter to the dominant francophone conception of Canada as a bicultural compact between two nations: English Canada and French Canada. Even in Quebec, which had a francophone majority, French was effectively the second-tier language. Most commercial signs in the major metropolis of Montreal were in English, and English was the language of management in most of the province's industries.

With the arrival of Quebec's Quiet Revolution, language issues were thrust onto the national stage in the 1960s. A university-educated French-speaking middle class led the charge for political and institutional reforms in the province, secularizing and modernizing a number of key sectors. Quebec's government nationalized the province's hydro-electric companies to create the massive new crown corporation Hydro-Quebec. The province re-created the long-moribund Department of Education (which had been dismantled in 1875) to lead wide-ranging educational reforms and a complete overhaul of the province's school boards. Huge sums of money were invested into improving health care in the province. The provincial government also created a new Quebec Pension Plan, and used the funds from the pension fund to invest in the province's economy. Many of these changes were intended to improve the status of Quebec's francophone majority, in a decade when the average French-speaker in the province earned far less not only than his or her anglophone counterparts but than most immigrant groups. While these governmental actions helped to foster the use of the French language in Quebec's workplaces, for many, the pace of change was not fast enough. Many intellectuals and journalists sounded the call for dramatic action to improve the lot of Quebec's French-speaking majority.

Prime Minister Lester Pearson responded to early calls for language reform by launching the Royal Commission on Bilingualism and Biculturalism in 1963. The B&B Commission had a mandate to "inquire into and report upon the existing state of bilingualism and biculturalism in Canada and to recommend what steps should be taken to develop the Canadian Confederation on the basis of an equal partnership between the two founding races." After its first round of hearings, the commission felt compelled to release a preliminary report, observing that Canada was passing through the greatest crisis in its history without being aware of it. The excerpts from B&B Commission co-chair André Laurendeau's diary describe his frustrations and fears about the state of the country. The commission would ultimately produce a six-volume report of recommendations for how to address questions of Canada's linguistic duality. The extract from Volume I of the commission's report lays out its general approach for creating a language policy for a country with very unevenly distributed language populations. The first editorial cartoon from the *Montreal Gazette* captures some of the mixed public reactions to the work of the B&B Commission.

The work of the B&B Commission led the federal government of Pierre Elliott Trudeau to pass Canada's *Official Languages Act* in 1969. The act declared English and French to be Canada's two official languages and guaranteed federal government services to the public in both languages. This move toward official institutional bilingualism provoked great controversy in English-speaking Canada, where many believed that the jobs of unilingual English-speakers would be at risk or that the federal government would force all Canadians to learn both languages. The article by Pierre Elliott Trudeau attempts to dispel some of these fears and clarify the intent of the act. Despite Trudeau's reassurances that the federal legislation was intended to promote linguistic equality, many Canadians feared that Trudeau and his senior cabinet ministers from Quebec had a hidden agenda. Individuals such as retired Lt-Cmdr J.V. Andrew and groups including the Single Canada League believed that the status of English in Canada was severely threatened by the federal government's policies. The excerpts from Andrew's book provide an example of some of the most extreme manifestations of these fears. The *Official Languages Act* was but the first stage in a broader federal agenda of constitutionally entrenching language rights. As part of the 1982 constitutional patriation package, the Trudeau government enshrined the two official languages and minority language education rights into the *Canadian Charter of Rights and Freedoms.*

Meanwhile, tired of being treated as second-class citizens in a province where they were the majority, Quebec's francophone majority was supporting concurrent actions by its provincial government to promote the French language. As the article by Kenneth McRoberts describes, the Quebec government passed a number of laws over the course of the 1970s and 1980s that made French the sole official language in the province, limited access to English-language education, and restricted the use of languages other than French on commercial signs. These policies, which included Bill 22, the *Official Language Act*, and Bill 101, the *Charter of the French Language,* aimed to promote the visibility and use of French in Quebec. As the editorial cartoons from the *Montreal Gazette* demonstrate, many Quebec anglophones felt that these policies went too far or were misguided, even after their implementation was somewhat softened in the 1980s. Groups such as the Alliance for the Preservation of English in Canada (APEC), which formed in response to Quebec's language laws believed that Quebec's language laws, were further evidence to support J.V. Andrew's pessimistic assessments about Canada's future. Many Canadian anglophones reacted with great hostility to what they perceived to be the erosion of the language rights of Quebec's English-speaking minority, which made it even more difficult to implement the federal government's language policies.

What were the impacts of these efforts to create new language regimes in Canada? Scholars working in the field of English–French relations and language policies have produced mixed assessments of the outcomes of these policies, depending on how they view the policies' main objectives. Kenneth McRoberts questions whether the Trudeau government's language policies met the needs of Quebeckers and fostered national unity. Conversely, Michael MacMillan stresses the success of these language policies in extending language rights for francophone minority communities and expanding the use of the French language in federal institutions. Both authors note the ongoing struggles related to resolving language questions in Canada. While supporters of Quebec and Ottawa's language policies point to how they have provided additional support for French language rights and/or fostered greater bilingualism, critics observe that questions of national unity and biculturalism remain far from resolved. With an increasingly diverse population, other critics question whether this focus on the English–French divide remains appropriate, or whether more attention needs to be paid to Aboriginal languages and other languages spoken by Canada's immigrant communities. In any case, questions of language promise to remain central to debates about the nature of Canada and its future.

QUESTIONS

1. The reports of the Royal Commission on Bilingualism and Biculturalism suggested that Canada was going through the greatest crisis in its history in the 1960s, an assessment that was also clearly the belief of commission co-chair André Laurendeau. What was the nature of this crisis? How did the B&B Commission and the federal government propose to fix it?
2. The language policies enacted by the federal and Quebec governments had differing objectives and approaches. In what ways did these policies conflict with each other? Did they have anything in common?
3. Why did Quebec and Ottawa's language policies provoke such hostility? What criticisms of these policies are suggested by the *Montreal Gazette*'s editorial cartoons?
4. Kenneth McRoberts and Michael MacMillan appear to disagree in their assessment of the success of the federal language policies of the 1970s and 1980s? What is the basis of their disagreement? Whose assessment do you find more convincing? Does your reading of the Trudeau document and the extract from the B&B Commission's report shed any light on the objectives of these policies and how they should be evaluated?

FURTHER READINGS

Michael Behiels, *Canada's Francophone Minority Communities: Constitutional Renewal and the Winning of School Governance* (Montreal & Kingston: McGill-Queen's University Press, 2004).

Daniel Bourgeois, *Canadian Bilingual Districts: From Cornerstone to Tombstone* (Montreal & Kingston: McGill-Queen's University Press, 2006).

Graham Fraser, *"Sorry, I Don't Speak French": Confronting the Canadian Crisis that Won't Go Away* (Toronto: McClelland & Stewart, 2006).

Matthew Hayday, *Bilingual Today, United Tomorrow: Official Languages in Education and Canadian Federalism* (Montreal & Kingston: McGill-Queen's University Press, 2005).

José Igartua, *The Other Quiet Revolution: National Identities in English Canada, 1945–1971* (Vancouver: UBC Press, 2006).

Richard Jones, "Politics and the Reinforcement of the French language in the province of Quebec, 1960–1986" in *Quebec since 1945*, Michael D. Behiels, ed. (Toronto: Copp Clark Pitman, 1987), 223–240.

Marcel Martel and Martin Pâquet, *Langue et politique au Canada et au Québec. Une synthèse historique*. Québec: Éditions Boréal, 2010.

▲ DOCUMENT 1: A PRELIMINARY REPORT OF THE ROYAL COMMISSION ON BILINGUALISM AND BICULTURALISM

Royal Commission on Bilingualism and Biculturalism

The members of the Royal Commission on Bilingualism and Biculturalism were astonished and greatly concerned by what they heard at their cross-Canada hearings in 1964. Seeking to instigate immediate action to address the linguistic tensions in the country, they hurriedly released a preliminary report in 1965, two years in advance of their first official report.

PREAMBLE

Ten Canadians travelled through the country for months, met thousands of their fellow citizens, heard and read what they had to say. The ten do not now claim that they are relying on this as a scientific investigation, nor do they have solutions to propose at this stage. All they say is this: here is what we saw and heard, and here is the preliminary—but unanimous—conclusion we have drawn.

The members of the Commission feel the need to share with their fellow citizens the experience they have been through, and the lessons they have so far taken from it. This experience may be summarized very simply. The Commissioners, like all Canadians who read newspapers, fully expected to find themselves confronted by tensions and conflicts. They knew that there have been strains throughout the history of Confederation; and that difficulties can be expected in a country where cultures exist side by side. What the Commissioners have discovered little by little, however, is very different: they have been driven to the conclusion that Canada, without being fully conscious of the fact, is passing through the greatest crisis in its history.

The source of the crisis lies in the Province of Quebec; that fact could be established without an extensive inquiry. There are other secondary sources in the French-speaking minorities of the other provinces and in the "ethnic minorities"—although this does not mean in any way that to us such problems are in themselves secondary. But, although a provincial crisis at the outset, it has become a Canadian crisis, because of the size and strategic importance of Quebec, and because it has inevitably set off a series of chain reactions elsewhere.

What does the crisis spring from? Our inquiry is not far enough advanced to enable us to establish exactly its underlying causes and its extent. All we can do is describe it as we see it now: it would appear from what is happening that the state of affairs established in 1867, and never since seriously challenged, is now for the first time being rejected by the French Canadians of Quebec.

Who is right and who is wrong? We do not even ask ourselves that question; we simply record the existence of a crisis which we believe to be very serious. If it should persist and gather momentum it could destroy Canada. On the other hand, if it is overcome, it will have contributed to the rebirth of a richer and more dynamic Canada. But this will be possible only if we face the reality of the crisis and grapple with it in time.

Source: *A Preliminary Report of the Royal Commission on Bilingualism & Biculturalism*, 1965, p. 13. Reproduced with the permission of the Minister of Public Works and Government Services, 2011, and Courtesy of the Privy Council Office.

That is why we believe it necessary to make this statement to Canadians.

We have to communicate an experience through which we have actually lived, and to show that simple realities of everyday life came to reveal the existence, the depth and the sharpness of the crisis.

Moreover, we are going to have to put our country's divisions on display, and we appreciate the dangers of doing so. But the feeling of the Commission is that at this point the danger of a clear and frank statement is less than the danger of silence; this type of disease cannot be cured by keeping it hidden indefinitely from the patient. Above all the Commissioners are convinced that they are demonstrating a supreme confidence in Canada; because to tell a people plainly, even bluntly, what you believe to be the truth, is to show your own conviction that it is strong enough to face the truth. It is in fact to say to the country that you have faith in it and in its future.

▲ DOCUMENT 2: THE DIARY OF ANDRÉ LAURENDEAU

André Laurendeau

André Laurendeau, former editor-in-chief of Le Devoir, *and one of Quebec's leading intellectual voices in the post-war era, kept a detailed diary while he was co-chairing the B&B Commission. The following entries express some of his frustrations and concerns that arose out of the commission's hearings and meetings.*

SATURDAY, FEBRUARY 22, 1964

[. . .]

Separatism

Faced with certain anglophones, I feel an inner urge towards separatism: "They're too deaf, they won't listen to anything but force." But when I get home, the separatists make me a Canadian again: they're too naïve, too unaware of political reality—or else strangely fickle and superficial . . . Among the nationalists who tend towards separatism in today's Quebec there is an extraordinary impatience—an all-or-nothing stance. I see it as an attitude of despair. Is it perhaps a reaction, specific to their generation, to the conditions imposed by modern society, and consequently an awareness of the need to mobilize the smaller community or nation? I would believe it more readily if they showed more signs of realism. But they don't seem to me to understand how society operates, or to take account of the passivity of the masses. (This expresses my thoughts very poorly. Quagmire again. Maybe the joy of separatism comes from the knowledge that at last it's possible to think clearly, if not accurately?)

[. . .]

MAY 5, 1964

Speak white!

Among the commissioners we have sometimes talked about this insult addressed to French Canadians speaking their own language in places where anglophones are in the majority. Frank Scott couldn't believe it existed: according to him, it's not even an English expression. It is obvious that it comes to us from the United States, and that it combines two insults.

Source: *The Diary of André Laurendeau*, André Laurendeau, 1912–1968. Toronto: James Lorimer & Co., 1991, pp. 51, 90–91, 146–147. Reprinted by permission of Patricia Smart.

Since that conversation with Scott, I've often asked Acadians or French Canadians from the West if they've had this expression thrown at them. If I'd thought of it sooner, I could have put together a veritable collection of foolish quotations. I note here the account of a French Canadian from Maillardville who attended our sessions last Tuesday. When he arrived in Vancouver in 1937 (I think he came from Saskatchewan), he met up with a very hostile milieu. He was constantly being told to "speak white" or "go back to Quebec." These days he encounters less aggressiveness. But at the factory where he works, and where there are two other French Canadians, it is not unusual that when they speak French they hear the comment: "Why don't you go back to Quebec?" All in all, it would seem that the fact of speaking French irritates anglophones more than the fact of being French Canadian. It would be interesting to go more deeply into the psychology that produces this insult: are they upset by hearing a foreign language? Or more specifically by hearing French? Do they feel left out? Do they have the impression that the French Canadians are making negative remarks about them? I have the feeling that the need for conformity plays a large role in all this.

This insult is used in all sorts of milieux, and there can be ideological dimensions to its use. A military man from Vancouver, a friend of Jean Marchand's, told Marchand of the violent reaction he provoked at a banquet some years ago. He was something like the vice-commander of a naval unit. One day, his superior officer suggested that he reply to a toast he would be proposing. At the start of the banquet the commander raised his glass, "to the King," to which our friend replied, "Messieurs, au Roi." Disbelief, anger, indignation on the part of all the officers present because of these three words spoken in French. This incident created difficulties for the military man, and wasn't in fact the only incident of this type in his career—with the result that at the age of 40 he retired and returned to civilian life. All these pressures and disagreeable events had made life impossible for him. Another detail about the same man. One day he decided to marry a French-Canadian woman from Vancouver, the daughter of a senator. The reaction of his colleagues: "You had a chance to enter our milieu; how can you be marrying a French Canadian?" I've heard fewer stories of this type in the Maritimes, perhaps because I didn't ask the question as often.

MONTREAL, JUNE 25, 1965. CONFIDENTIAL REPORT WRITTEN FOR THE COMMISSION . . .

II

I have been extremely struck by the practical opposition to French of the majority of anglophones we've met or whose texts we've read: a clear-cut refusal, or a refusal (except in Quebec) of the conditions that would make living in French possible in Canada. By the fact that in none of the anglophone provinces, not even in New Brunswick, is French clearly accepted as equal in law, and that nowhere does it seem even close to being accepted as such, that everywhere on the contrary, profound resistances exist: this is a significant fact. [. . .]

This would lead us to examine another problem: do English-speaking Canadians believe in the life and future of Canada? Which of these two facts is today considered or felt by them to be a more serious "threat": creating a space for both cultures, or evolving towards greater integration with the United States? "What does English Canada think, and what does it want?"

Neither an inquiry nor surveys can hope to reveal this: it's politics itself that will bring to light what for the time being seems obscure in the public conciousness. But we shall have to formulate our recommendations before this series of power struggles occurs beween the parties: therefore, we will make our own bets on the future. For my part, I am more aware now than at the beginning of the inquiry of being part of a minority, and also more aware of the hesitations and refusals of the majority. Consequently, I am less inclined to make daring hypotheses, because, as a French Canadian, I feel refused in nine out of ten provinces. Such is, I believe, the reaction of a large number of French Canadians, even outside Quebec. It's not a question of reacting in a sentimental way, but of weighing facts: we just can't foist on the majority of Canadians attitudes that they find repugnant.

It must not be forgetten that this is taking place after two hundred years of cohabitation, and almost a century of Confederation. Some French-Canadian demands (especially schools for minorities) are almost as old as the country itself. It would seem that the strongest (the majority, the colonial or economic powers) have found psychological mechanisms that allow them to forget on an ongoing basis the other side's expressed demands—until the next power struggle takes place.

▲ DOCUMENT 3: THE CANADIAN REALITY

Royal Commission on Bilingualism and Biculturalism

In 1967, the B&B Commission released the first volume of its report. The following extract outlines how the commissioners wrestled with the question of how best to guarantee the language rights of English- and French-speaking Canadians.

B. THE CANADIAN REALITY

250. A new status for Canada's official languages will thus be acceptable only if the proposed solution respects Canadian reality in all its breadth and diversity. The first aspect of this reality is the existence of an English-speaking and a French-speaking community, whatever the ethnic origin of their members, or their distribution throughout Canada.

251. Population studies show that 58 per cent of all Canadians have English as their mother tongue and 28 per cent have French. The mother tongue of the remaining 14 per cent is neither of the two official languages. These are the percentages we shall go by—always remembering, however, that they overestimate the strength of the "other" languages and reduce the size of the English-speaking group. Population studies also tell us there are areas of the country where one of the two official languages is spoken to the virtual exclusion of the other. They also remind us that there are vast regions inhabited by English-speaking or French-speaking minorities, some large, others small, some concentrated, others scattered. We shall therefore have to respect these two basic facts: in some areas one of the two official languages is completely dominant; in others the two language groups interpenetrate.

252. The adoption of uniform criteria for defining these unilingual areas is a factor in treating the two official languages equally. We believe each group would find the absence

Source: *Report of the Royal Commission on Bilingualism & Biculturalism, Volume I: The Official Languages,* 1967, pp. 84–87. Reproduced with the permission of the Minister of Public Works and Government Services, 2011, and Courtesy of the Privy Council Office.

of its language more acceptable in one area if the rule were applied to the other official language in other areas.

253. This idea could have far-reaching consequences. Narrowly and rigorously applied, it would lead in the direction of an official French unilingualism in Quebec and an English unilingualism in the other provinces, with bilingual federal institutions in the centre: it would be a triumph for the territorial principle based on provinces. Such a solution would doubtless have the advantage of simplicity and would follow the tradition established in several English-speaking provinces. However, it would lead to the recognition of only the majority's rights and to oppression of the official-language minorities. As an immediate consequence it would deprive minority groups *en bloc* (the English-speaking in Quebec and the French-speaking in the rest of the country) of essential language rights. It would place them in a situation of sharp inequality in areas where they have been long established; they would be affected in their daily lives, in activities and situations in which they are more directly involved than they can be in central institutions. We do not and should not approve equality in privation for members of the two groups when they form minorities at the provincial or local level. Injustices do not become acceptable because they are equally shared.

254. This approach could lead to the acceptance of a principle that institutions should be generally unilingual, and that bilingual institutions would be exceptions consented to only when there is no other choice. Such a principle would be particularly unjust and oppressive, for it would run counter to deep historical and social realities in our country. It would also be very difficult to apply, despite things we have been told, because minority bitterness provoked by French unilingualism in Quebec would be added to the present discontent aroused by English unilingualism of varying degrees in the English-speaking provinces. Perhaps each form of frustration would appear to some people as a just compensation for the other form, but the minorities thus deprived would find little consolation in that idea. Thus we reject any such means of trying to lessen the tensions affecting Canada.

255. Instead we shall take an approach determined by the realities of Canadian life. In the various fields and jurisdictions to be considered and in conformity with what we hope will be the future spirit of Canada, *we take as a guiding principle the recognition of both official languages, in law and in practice, wherever the minority is numerous enough to be viable as a group.* This is a positive conception of equality, under which language rights of official-language minorities are respected and come into force whenever circumstances permit; that is, when a language group is large enough to exercise them. Evaluation of the "circumstances" will be the only problem; each case will need its own assessment. It should not be a matter of applying the principle blindly without taking account of any difficulties in particular instances. In short, we have adopted an approach aimed at attaining the greatest equality with the least impracticality.

256. Questions will come up in all provinces of Canada, for every one of them, without exception, has a minority speaking one of the official languages. Every province demonstrates the linguistic complexity of Canada: from Newfoundland and British Columbia where the French-speaking minorities are less than 2 per cent of the population, to New Brunswick where the minority is 35 per cent, and Quebec where the minority of English mother tongue is 13 per cent. There are about 700,000 Canadians in Quebec whose mother tongue is English and some 850,000 scattered throughout the rest of the country whose mother tongue is French.

257. For the former it is a matter of obtaining clear and lasting confirmation of rights enjoyed and exercised for two centuries, but which a segment of Quebec opinion is now

challenging. According to the definition stated above, Quebec is officially bilingual through the provisions of section 133 of the B.N.A. Act. Moreover, a well-established tradition of respect for the rights of the English-speaking minority, and statues and regulations which go beyond section 133, have made Quebec bilingual officially and in practice—in relations between provincial administrative bodies and citizens as well as in local public activities where appropriate.

258. The situation is quite different for the French-speaking minorities. In some provinces, we find a degree of recognition of the French language; here we can speak of *de facto* bilingualism. For example, the Public Service Commission, since the 1961 Public Service Employment Act, has taken into account areas in some provinces where a significant minority speaks French, and several Canadian provinces, notably Ontario and New Brunswick, have granted a certain recognition to French consisting mainly of compromises, particularly in education. However, comparison of these situations with that in Quebec shows that this *de facto* bilingualism is very fragile. It is often at the mercy of intolerance on the part of local or regional majorities, and it puts constant strain on those minority groups inevitably forced to fight for its implementation. Actually, the language of the official minorities in these regions has survived only because of the intense determination of individuals and groups. Despite immense sacrifices and frustrations incurred by those concerned, the price has been inferior institutions which will condemn these groups to linguistic assimilation if the situation is not remedied quickly. Therefore we must find solutions assuring that both the French-speaking minorities outside Quebec and the English-speaking minority in Quebec are able not only to exist but to thrive.

NEL

▲ DOCUMENT 4: DOWN THE OTTAWA CHIMNEY

John Collins

This editorial cartoon, published in the *Montreal Gazette*, was published shortly after the publication of the first volume of the B&B Commission's report. What does it suggest about how some Canadians felt about a new policy on official languages?

▲ DOCUMENT 5: WHY ARE THEY FORCING FRENCH DOWN OUR THROATS?

Pierre Elliott Trudeau

ARTICLE BY THE PRIME MINISTER WRITTEN FOR THE CANADIAN PRESS

"Why are they forcing French down our throats?"

That question has been asked by English-speaking Canadians who are concerned about the government's bilingualism policy and about the *Official Languages Act* which was recently enacted by Parliament.

The question is based on a wide-shared misunderstanding of what our policy on bilingualism means. In fact, everyone in Canada will not be required to speak French, any more than everyone will be required to speak English.

You can grow up in parts of Quebec and never use English a day in your life. You can live in many parts of the country and never hear a single word of French. Most of the people who deal with the government of Canada speak only one language. It is because everyone in the country is not expected to speak both languages, and never will be, that the federal government must be able to speak to Canadians in either French or English wherever there are enough French speakers or English speakers to justify it.

Nothing is more important to a person than to understand and to be understood. The most common and the most effective tool we can use for this purpose is our language. Any policy which affects such an important aspect of our lives is bound to stir up some controversy.

But we should not mislead ourselves into magnifying the problem. One of our country's great strengths is the spirit of mutual understanding and tolerance that motivates Canadians. I feel certain that the great majority of our people accept and respect the differences that exist among Canadians—differences not only of language but of religion, colour and origin.

Nevertheless, some misconceptions have certainly arisen, and I am grateful to The Canadian Press and the daily newspapers of Canada for providing me with this opportunity to deal with a few of them.

For example, some people claim that the *Official Languages Act* will result in discrimination against those whose mother tongue is neither English nor French.

This is one of the most widespread and the most unjustified misconceptions. The Act itself states categorically that the rights and privileges of any language other than English or French, whether acquired by law or by custom, will in no way be diminished as a result of the Act. For instance, the right of people who do not understand English or French to be heard in court through an official interpreter will be maintained.

The recognition of two official languages in no way alters the position of people whose ethnic origin is neither British nor French. Indeed, the Act has nothing to do with ethnic origins or cultural origins. As Canadians we believe that the diversity of our cultural backgrounds is a great national asset. It is an enrichment for all of us that many of our citizens and their ancestors have come from Germany and Italy, Poland and the Ukraine, China and Japan, the Philippines and the West Indies, and so many other corners of the globe. We encourage Canadians of every background to preserve the values and traditions of the homelands in many ways, including grants for cultural events and organizations.

It would obviously be impractical for the government itself to operate in every language spoken by a group of Canadians. For practical purposes the government's working languages must be those spoken by Canada's two major language groups, which between them make up the majority of our population. That is why the Act declares that English and French will be the official languages of the government and Parliament. It imposes no restrictions on the languages or cultural activities of individual Canadians.

A second misconception is that the Act will prevent Canadians who speak only one language from working for the government, the Armed Forces or the Crown Corporations, or from being promoted to important government jobs.

There is no clause in the Act which states this or which will have this result. The object of the Act is to provide government services in both languages where required by the population.

This does not mean that everyone who works for the government must be bilingual. In many areas of the country, including almost all of Western Canada and much of Quebec, government services will be provided only in one language and people working for the government in those areas will need only that language.

Even in bilingual districts, many of those working for the federal government will speak only one language. Our goal in these districts is to have a sufficient number of government employees to serve an English-speaking or French-speaking Canadian in his own language.

In the past few years we have been building up our system for teaching a second language to public servants. Eventually it should be possible for anyone whose job requires a working knowledge of a second language to be taught it as a regular part of his career. In the meantime we are being careful not to handicap those who are already working for the government and who have not had an opportunity to learn a second language.

The federal government must and will continue to recruit its employees, at all levels, from all parts of Canada.

Some of those who oppose the Act have claimed that the Commissioner of Official Languages mentioned in the Act will be given unlimited powers which will make him a dangerous "super-snooper".

A glance at the Act would show that this is nonsense. In fact the Commissioner will be a kind of ombudsman similar to those which several Provinces have appointed to protect the human rights of their citizens. He is not a trial judge, much less an inquisitor.

His job is to listen to complaints about unfair language practices in federal government departments and agencies or in Crown corporations and, if he believes they are justified, to make recommendations to the departments to change their practices. If the departments ignore these recommendations, he can report the whole matter to Parliament. It is up to Parliament to decide what to do about it. Surely this does not give the Commissioner, or the government, excessive powers over individual Canadians.

The objective is, of course, exactly the reverse: to give individual Canadians greater power to check the abuses of government. The Act sets out standards of performance for federal government departments and agencies and provides remedies if these standards are not met. There are no provisions which impose duties on individual Canadians or, in any way, restrict the freedoms which we enjoy as private citizens.

Some opponents of the Act have argued that it violates or changes the Constitution (The *British North America Act*) and is therefore beyond the powers of Parliament.

In this article I am not going to set out a long and technical argument about constitutional law. The fact is that the Act deals only with the departments and agencies of the federal government. It does not deal with matters which, under the Constitution, are within the control of the Provinces. It does not alter any of the rights or privileges concerning the English or French languages which are already guaranteed by the Constitution. These constitutional rights and privileges will remain exactly the same after the Act comes into effect as they were before. The Act does not amend any article of the Constitution.

Even when misconceptions about the *Official Languages Act* are cleared up, there will be some Canadians who do not understand or accept the philosophy on which it is based.

For many Canadians, and particularly those who live in a region of the country where few people speak French, Canada has seemed to be an English-speaking country with a number of minority groups speaking other languages. There are places where such groups as Italian Canadians or Ukrainian Canadians or Chinese Canadians outnumber French speaking Canadians.

But if we look at Canada as a whole we find there are two major language groups in this country—English and French speaking. This has been the case throughout our history as a nation. No other group forms a majority in any Province. No other group has its own public educational systems or radio and television networks. No other group makes up more than a small percentage of our population. According to the most recent census figures, the three largest groups whose mother tongue is neither English nor French are German—3.1% of the population, Ukrainian—2.0% and Italian 1.9%.

To build and maintain a strong and united country, it is essential that both French and English speaking Canadians should be able to feel at home in all parts of this country, and that their rights as members of our major language groups should be respected by the federal government. That is the objective of the *Official Languages Act* and of our policy of bilingualism.

I believe that our two major languages are a great advantage for Canada. A country in which both French speaking and English speaking Canadians are fully participating in every aspect of our national life will be a richer and more interesting place to live. We will be more valuable and more effective members of the world community when we have learned to handle our two official languages and our many cultural traditions at home.

As I travel around the country. I find that the advantages of bilingualism are becoming more widely accepted by Canadians, particularly among the young. However urgent it may be to introduce such a policy, and I believe the very survival of our country depends on it, we should not expect to reap its full benefits overnight. That will require fundamental changes in attitudes and institutions which may take years, or even generations. In this historic process the *Official Languages Act* is an important forward step.

▲ DOCUMENT 6: BILINGUAL TODAY, FRENCH TOMORROW: TRUDEAU'S MASTER PLAN AND HOW IT CAN BE STOPPED

J.V. Andrew

A number of years after the passage of the Official Languages Act, *Quebec's Liberal government passed Bill 22, which made French the only official language of the province and restricted access to English-language schools to children who already spoke the language. The federal government had also begun implementing official bilingualism within its institutions, including the military. Many Canadians were vehemently opposed to this new policy. Writing in 1975 (although his book would not be published until 1977, after the Parti Québécois was elected in Quebec), retired Lieutenant-Commander Jock V. Andrew believed that the federal govern- ment's bilingualism policies threatened the very fabric of Canada. His book sold over 100,000 copies and Andrew would be regularly asked to speak on behalf of anti-bilingualism associations, such as the Alliance for the Preservation of English in Canada. The following extract outlines some of his concerns about Ottawa's official languages policies.*

THE CONSPIRACY

This is the story of a handful of men and a conspiracy. Perhaps you will want to decide for yourself what kind of men they are when you see what they have been doing to you and to our country.

Source: Andrew, J.V., *Bilingual Today, French Tomorrow: Trudeau's Master Plan and How It Can Be Stopped*. Richmond Hill, BMG Publishing, 1977, pp. 1–2, 91–95. Reprinted with permission of J.V. Andrew.

A political conspiracy has been taking place in Canada which, if it continues, will shortly lead to a Canadian civil war. This war will almost certainly involve the United States. Other countries, Russia and China included, will take whatever advantages they can from it. Many lives will be lost, and much of eastern Canada will be laid waste. When it is finally over, nothing will have been resolved that could not be resolved today, with no loss of life whatsoever.

What is it all about?

In 1968, Canada's newly-elected Prime Minister, Mr. Pierre Trudeau, set out with a half-dozen like-minded associates under cover of some very clever double-talk to convert Canada from an English-speaking country into a French-speaking country.

How could such a scheme even be contemplated? How could the second-largest country in the world, almost four million square miles of land and resources, be whipped out like a rug from under the 75% of the population that is English-speaking and be handed in its entirety to the Quebec-centred 25% of the population that is the French-Canadian race?

The fact is, the job is now more than half done. The planning for the remainder has been so well conceived that only the passing of a few years is now required to make the whole of Canada a French-speaking country.

In the ten years from 1968 to 1978, without firing a shot, Mr. Trudeau will have taken more of the earth's surface for his race than did Napoleon, Alexander the Great, and all the Roman Emperors combined. And with this achievement, Mr. Trudeau will have pulled the biggest swindle that has ever been pulled on a civilized country.

To give just a preliminary idea of the scope of Mr. Trudeau's success, he has, as of now (early 1975), legislated total and permanent French-Canadian control at all levels of each of the following:

The Canadian Government Public (Civil) Service.

All Canadian Government-owned Corporations, Commissions and Agencies.

The Canadian Armed Forces.

Canada's National Police Force, the RCMP.

Mr. Trudeau's goal at this minute is to secure French-Canadian control at all levels of Canada's ten provincial governments. Having gained that, he will automatically have control of the municipal governments of every city, town, and village in Canada. From that moment on, the French language can be imposed at leisure on every Canadian, and on every aspect of Canadian life under a formula that has already been tested in Ottawa, in Northern Ontario, and in New Brunswick.

In this book I have tried to show in detail what Mr. Trudeau is doing to Canada, as well as how he is doing it and why. I have also tried to show that what Mr. Trudeau is doing relates in no way whatsoever to his purported aim of resolving Canada's two-hundred-year-old, two-language problem. Indeed, through the use of Government-paid agitators, Mr. Trudeau has stirred up normally good-natured French-Canadians to such militancy that only a near-miracle can now prevent Canada's still dormant English-speaking majority from backlashing Canada into a full-scale civil war. What we have to do now, is to try to find that near-miracle.

There is a solution to Canada's increasingly serious two-language problem. It is a French-Canadian solution, and it is a good one. In fact, it is the only hope for a future of any kind for the people of Canada. We will examine that solution shortly, but first I want to explain why I am directing this book to American and British readers as well as to Canadians.

In the years that Mr. Trudeau has been in power, there have been effective efforts, both over and under the table, by the Canadian Government to suppress any public discussion in English-speaking Canada on the Canadian racial issue.

These efforts have included the control of television, of the newspapers, and of the publishing industry. This control, which I will cover in more detail later on, has been directed by Mr. Trudeau's chief strategist in the French takeover of Canada, Mr. Gerard Pelletier, formerly Secretary of State, subsequently Minister of Communications, and currently Canadian Ambassador to France. It is not an accident that Canadian publishers are being subsidized by as much as a million dollars each by the Department of the Secretary of State. Nor is it strange that the one tiny political group in Canada which has had the courage to oppose Mr. Trudeau's takeover of Canada, cannot at this moment find a printer in the whole of the city of Ottawa who is not afraid to print their reports of what is happening across Canada. By the time you have finished this first chapter, you will have no difficulty in seeing why Mr. Trudeau and Mr. Pelletier have been most anxious to keep English-speaking Canadians in the dark about what is being done to Canada.

My purpose then for writing for American and British readers, as well as Canadians, is quite simple. I hope to stir up enough interest in the United States and in Britain so that Canadians will not be able to avoid seeing what is going on in their own country.

In order to write for American and British readers I have made the perhaps unfair assumption that they would know nothing about what has been happening here in Canada. This assumption has permitted me to describe the whole story from start to finish. Canada has been so smothered with propaganda by the Trudeau takeover-team that such an approach might be useful for Canadians as well. If I have oversimplified, I hope I may be forgiven. [. . .]

Stage I—Resentment

It is a simple matter for Mr. Trudeau to tell Canadians that he has given them no cause for resentment. But let me outline for you some of the things that are being strongly resented by Canadians as the result of Mr. Trudeau's Bilingualism. I will use the first person singular, because by doing so I can best describe how I feel personally on these issues.

If I seem to dwell for some considerable time on resentment, it is because accumulated resentment will be the detonator of the explosion that will blast Canada into civil war. If some of the sentiment seems harsh, it is only because that is the way it is. It is better that these sentiments should be brought out into the light now while something can still be done to circumvent civil war here. Time is running out.

And so, with apologies in advance to my fellow human beings, I very much resent:
- That in eight years as Canada's Prime Minister, Mr. Trudeau has so succeeded in separating French- and English-speaking Canadians, that nothing will ever put them together again. He has in fact taken away the one common accepted means of communication, which was the English language, as imperfect as the arrangement may have been, and has in its place taught French-Canadians to resent the fact that English-speaking Canadians do not speak French.
- That as the result of the above-noted resentment introduced by Mr. Trudeau and Mr. Pelletier, the easy-going friendliness that existed between French- and English-speaking Canadians has vanished. Nowadays in Quebec and Ottawa as well as in parts of New Brunswick and Ontario, in stores, on buses, at gas stations, in public buildings, over the telephone and at the market, every new customer is first

343

categorized as French- or English-speaking by the all-French clerks or attendants, and then is served accordingly. English-speaking Canadians nowadays get curt, unsmiling service, while French-Canadians get almost the same geniality that heretofore used to apply to everyone in a clerk-customer relationship in Canada. But the business of categorizing their customers is causing such a strain, that even this geniality is not what it used to be.

- That French-Canada, having hidden in the weeds for two world wars is now being led by Mr. Trudeau to believe that it is fully entitled to come forward, declare Canada a two-language country, and then proceed to take over simply because French-Canadians are the only people qualified to speak the second, totally redundant language.

- That a French-Canadian Prime Minister who was only a technicality removed from being a draft-dodger in World War II, has the gall to stand at the Canadian Cenotaph on Armistice Day and talk about duty-to-country to a mother who had three sons killed helping save French-Canada from Hitler's forced labor camps.

- That English-language signs have been taken down across Canada and replaced with two-language signs, except in the Province of Quebec, where two-language signs have been removed and replaced with French-language-only signs.

- That the Canadian Government has been permanently legislated into the hands of the French-Canadian race by Mr. Trudeau. That my future and the future of my children and their children will be decided in policy formulated by people who now are, for all practical purposes, foreigners to me, and who are being directed toward the elimination of English-speaking Canadians throughout Canada.

- That the Canadian Armed Forces are being turned over in their entirety to the French-Canadian race, an occurrence that is particularly ironic in view of the limited participation of French-Canadians in the Canadian Armed Forces when they were needed during two world wars.

- That I and 75% of the rest of Canadians who speak English are being represented in Canada and abroad as living in a French-speaking, French-controlled country. The day is apparently rapidly coming when we all may be French-speaking, but it is not here yet. I have to concede the matter of total control being here today however.

- That the merit system has been replaced by the criterion of racial origin in the recruiting and promoting of people for, and within, the Canadian Forces and Canadian Government Service. Where merit goes as the standard, then principles go too. Without principles there is no honesty. Without honesty there is nothing, because communication becomes meaningless. If this sounds like verbiage, think of it in terms of the Nixon Administration.

- That at the identical time Quebec is resolving its two-hundred-year-old language problem by eliminating one of its two languages, Mr. Trudeau is inverting this self-same two-language problem onto the rest of the country. Knowing full well that it will not work, and that he doesn't intend it to work, he is trying to make Canadians believe that it will work.

- That English-speaking Canadians, having been done out of their jobs and their children's jobs in Canada's Federal Government, Crown corporations and Armed Forces as the result of a contrived need for a second language, are scheduled to lose their jobs and their children's jobs in their provincial and municipal governments, in stores, offices, and in factories, for exactly the same contrived reason.

- That deserving and qualified people are losing (or are not getting) all levels of jobs, to others whose only qualification is being French-Canadian.

- That the primary and sole objective of the Canadian Federal Government since Mr. Trudeau came to power has been to convert Canada to a French-speaking nation, and that the Government's sole objective will remain the same until every city, town and village in Canada has become French-speaking and French-controlled. The cost is obviously of no consequence.
- That thousands of millions of Canadian tax dollars have been piped into the Province of Quebec, both over and under the table.
- That no action has been taken by the Federal Government to deal with Canada's pressing economic problems. That Mr. Trudeau's policy of expanding the Federal Government is adding to these economic problems.
- That Mr. Trudeau is endeavoring to sever Canadian ties with Great Britain while simultaneously publicly advising the citizens of France that the future of their children lies in Canada.
- That Canadian taxes are being spent abroad to push the French language in other troubled countries, for the purpose of advancing the French international fraternity.
- That thousands upon thousands of permanent Canadian Government jobs have been established for the sole purpose of creating Bilingualism and advancing the takeover.
- That millions of man-hours are being wasted, and are scheduled to be wasted on linguistics. If those hours were used by Canadians in trying to learn some technology, Canada could be going somewhere other than into bankruptcy.
- That French songs and French lessons are being imposed on me through radio and television. That I am being told what I can listen to and what I should think. That our leaders in government would try to control my tongue and my pen. And with better reason than they can imagine.
- That in less than ten years, the City of Ottawa will be completely French-speaking, and every aspect of Canadian Government business will be French-speaking.
- That Ontario provincial tax-money is being spent to provide French schools which are, under the tutelage of Mr. Pelletier, becoming racist propaganda mills, concerned only with the advancement of the French-Canadian race.
- That on beautiful summer mornings in Canada's capital, I can no longer bid any stranger "Good morning", for fear of offending the newly indoctrinated language-sensitivity of some French-Canadian. Nor can I go down the street bidding people "Bonjour", for fear of offending the growing sensitivity of some English-speaking Canadian. Nor, might I add, do I particularly wish to go down the street bidding people "Bonjour" in what was, until Mr. Trudeau got hold of it, an English-speaking city in a predominantly English-speaking country.
- That in the City of Ottawa, in the once English-speaking Province of Ontario, even shopping is no longer a pleasure. The supermarkets are now manned and managed by French-Canadians, and as a result, the loudspeakers now blare out their commands to the staff in French. The two-faced labels of the boxes and bottles and cans on the shelves stare out at the customer with their French faces forward, and so if you want pears, you look for poivres, and if you want beans, you look for fevres. And the girls at the cash registers, just like Ottawa's bus drivers, and policemen, and shoe clerks, suddenly come all-over stone-faced as soon as they realize you are not French-Canadian. But were it not so, Mr. Pelletier's spontaneous citizens' groups would be raising hell with the owners.
- That life in Canada has been changed from a life of pleasantness and friendliness to a life of full-time resentment. In summary, I resent having to be resentful of what is being done to my country by a handful of slippery political conspirators.

▲ DOCUMENT 7: SOLITARY IN BILL 101

Aislin (alias Terry Mosher)

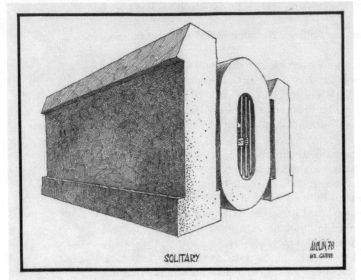

SOLITARY

In 1977, the Parti Québécois government of Quebec passed Bill 101: The Charter of the French Language. The legislation prohibited the use of languages other than French on commercial signs, required that all immigrants to the province attend French-language schools, and set strict requirements for the use of the French language in many public- and private-sector workplaces. What does this editorial cartoon suggest about how English-speaking Montrealers reacted to Bill 101? How does this contrast with the situation in the late-1960s?

Source: M983.227.16 | *Drawing, cartoon | Solitary in Bill 101.* | Aislin (alias Terry Mosher) © McCord Museum.

▲ DOCUMENT 8: BILINGUAL SIGNS

Aislin (alias Terry Mosher)

OUTSIDE, INSIDE...

SOYEZ RAISONNABLE, MONSIEUR ED! YOUR BILINGUAL SIGNS ARE A DISTINCT THREAT TO QUEBEC'S FRAGILE CULTURE!

UNLIKE MY NEW NEIGHBORS, I SUPPOSE?

BIENVENUE! / WELCOME!
CHEZ ED'S
PLAT DU JOUR / DAILY SPECIAL

Several years after the passage of Bill 101, the Supreme Court of Canada struck down a number of the law's provisions, somewhat relaxing the restrictions on access to English-language schools, and watering down some of the provisions on commercial signs. The Quebec government responded to these decisions with a new piece of legislation in 1988. Bill 178 still required that all outdoor signs be in French (apart from registered trademarks), but permitted bilingual signs inside stores. What do you make of cartoonist Aislin's take on this revised legislation?

Source: M989.363.96 | *Drawing, cartoon | Bilingual Signs* | Aislin (alias Terry Mosher) © McCord Museum

■ ARTICLE 1: OFFICIAL BILINGUALISM: LINGUISTIC EQUALITY FROM SEA TO SEA

Kenneth McRoberts

MAKING CANADA BILINGUAL

The Trudeau regime's ambitions for language reform went far beyond establishing bilingualism in Ottawa, however central that objective may have been. The ultimate goal extended to the whole of Canada. Wherever they live, Canadians, as Canadians, should be able to deal with the federal government in their own language, whether it be French or English. Moreover, in important areas, such as education, they should be able to receive services in either language from provincial governments too. As a result, the very presence of francophones throughout Canada would be strengthened.

In part, this conception of linguistic equality extending throughout the country stemmed logically from Trudeau's commitment to individual rights.[1] The notion of pan-Canadian linguistic equality, however, was rooted in Trudeau's primary political goal: to defeat Quebec nationalism. If all of Canada, rather than just Quebec, was to become home to the French language, he kept insisting, then the very basis of Quebec nationalism would be undermined. Indeed, Trudeau claimed that little else was necessary to do the job: the constitutional entrenchment of language rights alone offered 'a solution to a basic issue facing Canada today'.[2]

Once language rights were entrenched, Trudeau declared in 1968, then French Canada would stretch from Maillardville in British Columbia to the Acadian community on the Atlantic Coast and: 'Once you have done that, Quebec cannot say it alone speaks for French Canadians'.[3]

Demographic Trends: The Marginalization of French

To make all of Canada home for French, so that French Canada would stretch from coast to coast would have been a tall order. Historically, French Canada had

Source: McRoberts, Kenneth. *Misconceiving Canada: The Struggle for National Unity.* © Oxford University Press Canada 1997. Reprinted by permission of the publisher.

always been concentrated in Quebec, and the very presence of French in other parts of the country had been steadily receding ever since Confederation.

Only one of the four original provinces had a francophone majority. According to the 1871 census, 78 per cent of Quebec's population was of French descent;[4] French Canadians made up only 16 per cent of the population in New Brunswick,[5] 4.7 per cent in Ontario,[6] and 8.5 per cent in Nova Scotia.[7]

The addition of more provinces to Confederation did not break this pattern. When Prince Edward Island joined in 1873 it was overwhelmingly anglophone: according to the 1881 census, only 10 per cent of its population was of French descent.[8] Initially, the incorporation of western Canada had offered the promise of a new francophone base. When Manitoba became a province in 1870, English-speakers and French-speakers were about equal in numbers.[9] But by 1891, the francophones had shrunk to 7.3 per cent.[10] In 1949, the last addition, Newfoundland, only reinforced the established pattern: according to the 1951 census, barely 0.5 per cent of its population, 2,321 individuals, had French as their mother tongue.[11]

By the time Pierre Trudeau assumed office in 1968, the linguistic structure of Canada was more rooted than ever in territorial division. The marginalization of francophones in most provinces was dramatically revealed by the 1971 census, which for the first time supplemented its standard question on mother tongue with a question on the language Canadians normally used at home, a much more precise measure of the number of francophones. In New Brunswick, 31.4 per cent gave French as their home language, but the proportions were far smaller in the other provinces. The next highest, Ontario, was only 4.6 per cent, followed by 4.0 per cent for Manitoba, 3.9 per cent for Prince Edward Island, and 3.5 per cent for Nova Scotia. In the remaining provinces the proportions with French as their home language were truly infinitesimal: 1.7 per cent in Saskatchewan, 1.4 per cent in Alberta, 0.5 per cent in British Columbia, and 0.4 per cent in Newfoundland.[12] Even in 1971, then, the idea of a French-Canadian nation from sea to sea was totally unrealistic. French Canada never had stretched from coast to coast, and it certainly could not be *made* to do so.[13]

The steady decline in the French presence in most provinces had two causes. First, many provinces received large numbers of British immigrants; French immigrants were a rarity, even in Quebec. Immigrants of other origins tended to join the anglophone populations, even in Quebec, where the anglophones were economically much stronger than the francophones.

Second, the francophone minorities of most provinces lost ground through assimilation, especially as they left the relative isolation of rural communities to migrate to the major cities. In most cities, the overwhelming numerical superiority of anglophone speakers, reinforced by control of the principal economic activities, ensured that assimilationist pressures of urban life would favour English. Unlike the situation of the anglophone community of Montreal, the minority position of francophones was not offset by economic or political power. In fact, it was reinforced by economics and politics. Thus, as Table 1 shows, in every province but Quebec and New Brunswick, the majority of Canadians of French origin did not use French as their primary language at home.

And of course Canada's political institutions were themselves patterned on the assumption that French Canada was effectively concentrated in Quebec. For certain purposes federalism protected the position of francophones in Quebec, making them an electoral majority, but for the same purposes it doomed francophones elsewhere to political marginality. Nor did the terms of Confederation provide for offsetting measures.

We have also seen that historically all governments but Quebec acted as if territorial unilingualism and the provision of public services in a single language were operative principles of Confederation. In effect, they reinforced the social pressures working against French. When Manitoba was created in 1870, English and French were given equal status in the new legislature, reflecting their roughly equal numbers in the new province. However, after the very rapid decline in the francophone proportion of the province's population, the Manitoba government in 1890 formally ended the official use of French in provincial institutions and abolished denominational schools, thus in effect eliminating French-language education. Similarly, in 1912 the Ontario government passed Regulation 17, which required that English be the sole language of instruction after the third year of schooling. In the early 1930s, New Brunswick revoked Regulation 32, thus precluding French-language education in most of that province.[14] The pattern of provincial policy was clear.

● TABLE 1

Francophone Linguistic Retention Rate, 1971

	French Ethnic Origin	French Home Language	French Home Language as Proportion of French Ethnic Origin
Canada	6,180,120	5,546,025	89.7%
Newfoundland	15,410	2,295	14.9
Nova Scotia	80,215	27,220	33.9
New Brunswick	235,025	199,080	84.7
PEI	15,325	4,405	28.7
Quebec	4,759,360	4,870,105	102.3
Ontario	737,360	352,465	47.8
Manitoba	86,510	39,600	45.8
Saskatchewan	56,200	15,930	28.3
Alberta	94,665	22,700	24.0
British Columbia	96,550	11,505	11.9

Source: Statistics Canada, *Census of Canada, 1971*, Volume 1, Part 2, Tables 2 and 26.

For its part, the federal government had done little to counter this pattern. Typically, it did not call upon provincial governments to reverse their policies, nor was it very responsive to the entreaties of French-Canadian organizations such as the Conseil de la vie française en Amérique, which called upon Ottawa to use both official languages in its publications, to favour French-language radio in Western Canada, and to project a bilingual image of the country. Ottawa even refused the Conseil's request to issue bilingual cheques throughout Canada; until 1962, it did so only in Quebec.[15] The Conseil's requests were heeded only by the Quebec government, which in effect provided funds to the Conseil and to French-language organizations in other provinces. But with the rise of the new Quebec nationalism in the 1960s, Quebec government officials downgraded this support, focusing instead upon the state of French in Quebec.[16]

Under those circumstances, the Trudeau ideal of a pan-Canadian linguistic equality could not have been more ambitious. It sought to reverse the entrenched pattern of a century of Canadian history. Both demographic trends and political forces were stacked against it.

The B&B Commission

The goal of reversing the historical trend was shared by the Royal Commission on Bilingualism and Biculturalism. But the commissioners did not all subscribe to the premises underlying Trudeau's vision of a bilingual Canada, whether his emphasis on the individual or his determination that Quebec must have precisely the same status as the other provinces. In fact, leading members of the commission, especially André Laurendeau, approached the whole question of a bilingual Canada from a very different direction. In the process, they identified issues and forces that were to frustrate severely the Trudeau government's plans for a bilingual Canada.

The commission spelled out its approach at the beginning of its first volume, both in an interpretation of its terms of reference and in an introductory chapter, 'Bilingualism of Individuals and States'. It carefully distinguished between bilingualism as a trait of individuals and as a characteristic of countries. Very few individuals are truly bilingual: 'We know that complete bilingualism—the equal command of two languages—is rare and perhaps impossible'.[17]

If countries are bilingual it is because they contain groups of people for whom different languages constitute their primary means of expression. By the same token, the survival of this bilingualism depends upon the strength of these groups—'unilingual nuclei—that is, two or more groups of persons who habitually live and work in one language, resorting to the other language only to communicate with fellow citizens of that language'.[18]

It is not the responsibility of the bilingual state to propagate individual bilingualism, because 'if everyone in a bilingual state becomes completely bilingual, one of the languages is rendered superfluous',[19] and will disappear. Instead, a bilingual state must provide services to citizens in their own languages and ensure that members of the minority linguistic group are not disadvantaged. That may impose obligations upon the majority linguistic group 'to guarantee survival and equality for the minority group'.[20]

Thus, in interpreting its mandate to inquire into 'the existing state of bilingualism' in Canada, the commission declared that its first concern must be not with individual bilingualism but with the state of English and French, 'each being considered by itself' since 'the question of the life and vigour of each language must have priority. The problem of the first language must 'come first: it is vital; it is more essential for the human being than questions about a second language'.[21]

It was clear that in Canada the francophones were the minority group and that their relative disadvantage in Canada and isolation from francophones internationally would have to be addressed. It was also clear that this group was heavily concentrated in Quebec. Using a fateful phrase, the commission stated that it recognized, 'the main elements of a distinct French-speaking society in Quebec'.[22] In fact, the commission declared: 'Quebec constitutes an environment where the aspirations and needs of four out of five francophones in Canada can be satisfied. The mere fact of this concentration leads to a spontaneous French way of life and makes that way of life easier to organize.'[23]

With that interpretation of language and its roots in Canada, how was the commission to formulate a language regime that would strengthen Canadian bilingualism? What linguistic rights should Canadians enjoy in dealing with their governments? What obligations did the ideal of Canadian bilingualism impose on Canadian governments? Do these rights and obligations apply equally to all governments, federal and provincial? Should they be the same in all parts of the country?

The commission had to choose between two competing principles, each of which had found expression in other countries. According to the 'territorial' principle, language rights vary from one part of the country to another; the rights available to citizens depend upon the region in which they live. Under the 'personality' principle, language rights are the same throughout the country.

Each principle has its advantages and, over the years, has had its fierce advocates. The personality principle attaches uniform rights to citizenship and facilitates movement across a country. It favours geographically dispersed linguistic groups: however few in number the members of a language group may be in any locality they possess the full set of language rights. The territorial principle, on the other hand, offers language groups the security that comes from effective dominance over certain regions. In effect, a language group trades minority rights in one region for majority rights in another. Simply put, personality favours minorities; territoriality favours majorities.[24]

As it happened, the commission was well aware of the choice before it and of the ways in which the principles had been applied elsewhere. It had sponsored no fewer than 10 academic studies of language regimes in other countries.[25] Moreover, in its first book of recommendations, *The Official Languages,* the commission discussed four existing regimes in some detail: Belgium, which most clearly embodied territoriality; South Africa, the clearest embodiment of personality; Switzerland, which combined personality at the federal level with territoriality at the local (canton) level; and Finland, which featured a territorially limited accommodation of a second language.

The commission recognized that the experience of other countries seemed to commend the territorial principle to Canada. Canada's linguistic make-up was much closer to that of Belgium, which had adopted the territorial model, than South Africa, the clearest example of the personality model.[26] The territorial principle also had some advantages: 'The minority language is guaranteed priority in some areas and a large majority of the total population may be served in its own language.'[27]

However, the commission rejected territoriality in favour of the personality principle, arguing that the Canadian population was too mobile for such a scheme. More important, 'it would lead to the recognition of only the majority's rights and to oppression of the official language minorities'.[28] Beyond linguistic justice, the commission saw these official-language minorities as important forces for Canadian political integration. In its *Preliminary Report,* the commission had emphasized the symbolic importance of the francophone minorities. The bond that Quebec francophones had formed with these minorities was an important force for national cohesion.[29]

At the same time, the commission felt compelled to make some important concessions to territoriality, in recognition of the demographic structure of the country: 'We take as a guiding principle the recognition of both official languages, in law and practice, *wherever the minority is numerous enough to be viable as a group*' [emphasis added].[30]

So it called upon only two provinces, New Brunswick and Ontario, to adopt the Quebec model and to 'recognize English and French as official languages and . . . accept the language regimes that such recognition entails'[31] in effect, to become officially bilingual. Other provinces were to follow suit should their official-language minority reach 10 per cent. Otherwise, they should simply allow English and French in legislative debates and offer appropriate services in French for their francophone minorities.[32] Also, a constitutional amendment would require all provinces to establish schools in both official languages.[33]

By the same token, the commission recommended that the full provision of government services by federal and provincial governments in both official languages be limited to certain parts of the country. Apparently inspired by the Finnish example, it proposed a scheme of 'bilingual districts' in which the full range of government services—federal, provincial, and municipal—would be bilingual.[34] Federal and provincial governments would have to provide bilingual services directly through the offices they maintain in these districts, as opposed to relying upon communication with offices in their capitals. And all local governments in the district would need to provide bilingual services.

Finally, when they came to address language issues in Quebec, as opposed to the rest of the country, the majority of the commissioners tried to limit their application of the personality principle. They accepted the principle of formal equality between French and English in provincial governmental institutions. This was sanctioned both by the constitution, thanks to section 133 of the *BNA Act*, and the long-standing practices of the Quebec government. But the economy was a different matter. For commission co-chair André Laurendeau, in particular, the status of French in Quebec's economy and society was one of the most important questions facing the commission.[35] Indeed, the commission had sponsored several studies of such matters as the ethnic patterns of ownership in the Quebec economy and differences in income between anglophones and francophones in Quebec. These studies demonstrated overwhelmingly the inferior position of French and of francophones in Quebec; their publication was to have an explosive effect in Quebec, confirming as they did the arguments of many nationalists.

Laurendeau and some of his colleagues were convinced that these imbalances must be redressed and that governments must take direct responsibility for doing so. After detailing at length the inferiority of French and francophones in the Quebec economy, the commission proposed that 'in the private sector in Quebec, governments and industry adopt the objective that French become the principal language of work at all levels.'[36]

This departure from the personality principle when it came to the private sector was not lost on one of the commissioners: Frank (F.R.) Scott, McGill law professor and pillar of the Montreal English-Canadian community. In a spirited dissenting statement Scott declared: 'It seems to me that, consciously or unconsciously, the other commission members have departed from the principles laid down in Book I of our *Report*, where we defined "equal partnership" and rejected the territorial principle as being inappropriate for determining a language policy for Canada.'[37]

In short, the commission may have opted for the personality principle but not without important qualifications. Only two provincial governments were to join Quebec and become officially bilingual. Bilingualism in local offices of federal and provincial governments and in municipalities was to be restricted to selected bilingual districts. And when it came to the Quebec economy, the majority of the commissioners were not prepared to let the personality principle stand in the way of government measures designed to favour French over English, whatever might be the resulting logical contradiction, and dissension among the commissioners.

The Trudeau Government

The commission's concessions to territoriality were lost on Pierre Trudeau. Given his starting point of individual liberalism, the purpose of language policy could only be to protect the rights of individuals rather than to protect or promote linguistic collectivities. Only the personality principle was legitimate.

The centre-piece of Trudeau's language reforms was the *Official Languages Act*, passed in 1969. The Act called for notices, regulations, decisions, and similar materials to be published in both official languages; required departments, agencies, and Crown corporations to provide bilingual services in Ottawa-Hull, at its headquarters, in bilingual districts, and to the travelling public anywhere in Canada where demand warranted; stipulated the role of official languages in judicial proceedings; described the procedure for creating federal bilingual districts; and outlined the office, powers, and responsibilities of the commissioner of official languages.[38]

In its effort to implement official bilingualism throughout the country, Ottawa went well beyond the terms of the *Official Languages Act*. The 1960s and 1970s saw a major expansion of Radio-Canada's television and radio services beyond Quebec. Through the secretary of state, financial support was given to the organizations that represented, and provided services to, the official-language minorities. Finally, Ottawa began making extensive transfer payments to provincial governments to support both the education of official-language minorities in their own language and the instruction of children in the other official language.

At the same time, the Trudeau government dispensed with the B&B Commission's two main concessions to territoriality. First, even though the *Official Languages Act* contained provisions for the bilingual districts that the commission had envisaged, Ottawa failed to establish them. It did create two advisory committees to recommend which districts should be designated but rejected the advice of each of them.[39]

When the essence of the *Official Languages Act* was constitutionalized in the new *Charter of Rights and Freedoms*, no provision was made for bilingual districts. Instead the right to use either language to communicate with a federal office (other than a 'head or central' office) was made dependent upon 'demand' and upon 'the nature of the office'. Clearly, these two criteria will not produce uniform results in all departments of the federal government. In any one locality, demand may be sufficiently high for one type of federal service but not another. By their nature, some offices may be able to provide bilingual services quite easily whereas others may not. When the *Official Languages Act* was amended in 1988, all reference to official language districts was removed.

Second, the federal government made no formal effort to implement the commission's recommendation of a concerted action to strengthen the use of French in the Quebec economy. Even when, in 1974, the Bourassa government adopted a francization program for Quebec enterprises, as part of Bill 22, Ottawa did not follow suit.

The first commissioner of official languages, Keith Spicer, did say in his 1970 report that he would support 'within the Quebec sector of the federal administration, the often expressed will to make French Quebec's essential language of official, economic and social intercourse'.[40] Indeed, there was substantial progress in making French the essential language of work in federal offices located in Quebec. Less progress was made with federal Crown corporations. Nor did the federal government formally make working-language practices a criterion in awarding contracts to private enterprises, as the Quebec government did with its francization programs.

In part, Ottawa was constrained by its commitment to official bilingualism and the welfare of linguistic minorities. But Gilles Lalande, co-secretary of the B&B Commission and deputy commissioner of official languages from 1980 to 1985, wrote in 1987 that federal officials were also concerned that measures to strengthen French in Quebec might simply encourage Quebec nationalism (as the Trudeau orthodoxy would suggest). 'That is why federal authorities so consistently shied away from publicly acknowledging the need to consolidate the status of French in Quebec.' Lalonde called upon federal officials 'to pay more attention to Quebec's desire—unequivocally expressed in three high-profile pieces of legislation (Bills 22, 63 and 101)—to make French the normal and usual language of work, education, communication, trade and commerce within its borders'.[41]

To the extent the federal government did intervene in Quebec, it strengthened the position of the anglophone minority. Until quite recently, for instance, more than half of Ottawa's spending on the teaching of French and English as first and second languages went to Quebec's anglophone minority.[42] By the same token, in 1987/8, $2,220,000, 14 per cent of the Official Languages Communities program grants, went to Quebec anglophone groups.[43] In effect, Ottawa's language policy made no distinction between Quebec and the rest of Canada. In Quebec, as elsewhere, the focus was upon linguistic *minorities*.

Within this understanding of its responsibilities, however, the Trudeau government brought very substantial resources to bear. More recent governments have largely followed the same policies. As a result, very substantial progress has been made in ensuring that federal services are available in either language throughout the country, although there is still considerable room for improvement. The commissioner of official languages reported in 1994: 'On average, service can be obtained (sometimes not without insistence) in the official language of the minority three times out of four. In some regions, it is only one time out of two'.[44] Similarly, Radio-Canada could claim by 1981 that its networks of AM radio and television reached 94.5 per cent and 92.2 per cent, respectively, of the French-speaking population outside Quebec.[45]

Moreover, through the secretary of state financial support was given to the organizations representing official-language minorities, growing (in constant dollars) from $1.9 million in 1972 to $28 million in 1990, when it entailed more than 300 associations.[46] In 1987 the secretary of state identified five broad areas of activity: representation, institutionalization, services, community participation, and human resources development. On this basis, in 1989 financial support was provided to over 500 projects.[47]

On the other hand, there was only so much that the Trudeau government could accomplish within the federal government's own jurisdictions, since the bulk of government services, including the all-important matter of education, fall within provincial jurisdiction. Thus, the federal government launched a concerted campaign to induce the *provincial* governments to adopt its vision of a bilingual Canada.

The Predominantly Anglophone Provinces: Services but Not Official Bilingualism

Official Bilingualism

The Trudeau government attempted through a variety of tactics to have provincial governments adopt its framework of official bilingualism. The terms of the ill-fated Victoria Charter, the 1971 constitutional patriation package that died for want of Quebec's approval, showed the Trudeau government's determination that all provincial governments should follow the same formula of linguistic equality. The Charter set out a series of rights, but none of them had been agreed to by *all* provinces. Either language could be used in provincial legislatures, except in the three western provinces. Provincial statutes were to be published in both languages in Ontario, Quebec, New Brunswick, and Newfoundland. French and English were to have equal status in the courts of Quebec, New Brunswick, and Newfoundland. Finally, citizens could use either language to communicate with head offices in Ontario, Quebec, New Brunswick, Prince Edward Island, and Newfoundland. Of course, Newfoundland had the smallest proportion of minority language speakers of any province. In effect, the Trudeau government simply mustered as much commitment as it could to each element of official bilingualism. A provision enabled recalcitrant provinces to 'opt in' at a later point; clearly the hope was that they would be pressured to do so.[48]

In other cases, the federal government relied upon the various francophone minority organizations, which had become heavily dependent on federal funding, to lobby their provincial governments on behalf of official bilingualism. This practice was even formalized in a secretary of state *Grants and Contributions Manual, 1988*, which governed support for official-language communities. A list of the aims of activities that the secretary of state was prepared to support financially included 'the passing and implementation of legislation recognizing the equal status of the two official languages'.[49]

The B&B Commission, it will be recalled, had called upon only two provinces to become officially bilingual: New Brunswick and Ontario. The other provincial governments were simply to allow both languages to be used in legislative debates.

In the end, only one province, New Brunswick, adopted a formal scheme of official bilingualism in which French and English have equal status.[50] The B&B Commission's recommendations were incorporated in the *Official Languages Act* of New Brunswick in 1969 and later in section 16(2) of the *Constitution Act, 1982*: 'English and French are the official languages of New Brunswick and have equality of status and equal rights and privileges as to their use in all institutions of the legislature and government of New Brunswick.' Sections 17(2) and 18(2) provide for the use of both languages in the New Brunswick legislature; section 19(2) does the same for New Brunswick courts. In addition, section 20(2) establishes the right of the residents of New Brunswick to communicate with and be served by 'any office of an institution of the legislature or government of New Brunswick in English or French'.

Although no other province has gone that far, the Ontario government has come closer than the rest.[51] In a carefully staged incremental fashion it steadily raised the formal status of French in its institutions and expanded the range of government services to its francophone minorities. Starting with authorization of French in the Ontario legislature in 1970, the province adopted a policy on French services in 1972 and created the Office of the Coordinator of French-Language Services in 1977. In 1984 the government approved the creation of a French-language TVOntario network. Finally, the *French Language Services Act*, passed in 1986 under the Liberal government of David Peterson, declared that 'the French language is recognized as an official language in the courts and in education',[52] consolidating measures that had been adopted under the Conservatives. In addition, the law incorporates the B&B Commission's bilingual-districts scheme, designating 22 districts in which all ministries must provide French-language services (as they must at their head offices). Non-profit corporations may be designated under the Act to have similar obligations. Under the terms of the Act, both languages may be used in legislative proceedings and are used in records of debates, and, since 1991, legislation is adopted in both languages.

None the less, Ontario has steadfastly avoided any declaration that French and English are official languages. Even the NDP government of Bob Rae failed to do so. The present Harris government is certainly not favourably disposed; during its opposition days the Harris Conservatives championed a greater territorialization of language services in Ontario.[53]

During the 1980s, the three Prairie provinces were all forced to confront the issue of official bilingualism, in light of Supreme Court decisions upholding their obligations under nineteenth-century statutes. In each case, there was clear resistance among anglophones to official status for French.

In the case of Manitoba, the resulting conflict was especially acrimonious. In 1979 the Supreme Court ruled that the province was still bound by the *Manitoba Act, 1870* and that all laws passed since 1890 were unconstitutional since they had not been enacted in both official languages. The Manitoba government began translating all its statutes into French, but by 1982 it became concerned that the translation was not proceeding fast enough and began to fear that all its laws might soon be declared unconstitutional. Accordingly, Howard Pawley's government negotiated an agreement with Franco-Manitoban leaders to refrain from any court challenge on condition that English and French be declared official languages, that a specific number of statutes be translated into French, and that expanded French-language services be offered by the provincial government as well as municipalities and school boards. (All of this was to be constitutionally entrenched.)

The resulting bill provoked strong opposition among Manitoban anglophones. A final version of the legislation, released in January 1984, did not contain constitutional entrenchment and made it clear that, although English and French were to be designated as official languages of Manitoba, the province was not to be completely bilingual. None the less, the Conservative opposition stalled legislative proceedings and popular protests mushroomed. Finally, in February the government allowed the French-language rights bill to die on the order paper. In 1985 the Supreme Court confirmed that Manitoba's English-only legislation was invalid and ratified an agreement by which all pertinent statutes were to be translated by 1991.

The issue surfaced again in the late 1980s when the Conservative government of Gary Filmon introduced legislation to expand French-language services. In this case, Quebec's proclamation of Bill 178, which will be discussed later, was used as a pretext for withdrawing the bill. In 1990 a French-language-services bill was passed, but there has been no new attempt to declare French an official language.

As for Saskatchewan and Alberta, in 1988 the Supreme Court declared that they were still bound by provisions of the *Northwest Territories Act, 1891,* which among other things required that all statutes be enacted and printed in both languages. The court's judgement, however, gave the provincial governments the option of repealing the 1891 law and declaring all existing statutes valid even though they were enacted and printed in English only. Saskatchewan passed Bill 2, which affirmed the right to use English and French in the legislature and courts (in criminal cases), affirmed the validity (but not necessity) of enacting laws in both languages, and provided for the translation into French of statutes to be selected by cabinet.[54] For its part, Alberta passed Bill 60, which affirmed the right to use both languages in the legislature and in oral proceedings in certain courts but contained no undertaking to translate statutes nor allowed for the possibility of enacting laws in both languages.[55]

In the remaining predominantly English-speaking provinces, there apparently has been no movement towards making French an official language in government institutions.

French-Language Services

With respect to French as a language of public services as opposed to a language of government institutions, most provinces have in fact adopted reforms. That has been largely due to heavy prodding, and financial assistance, from Ottawa, in particular, extensive grants to provincial governments under the Official Languages in Education Program. In 1989/90 over $81 million was made available to the provinces for education for francophone minorities. (It should be noted that at the same time over $62 million was provided for the education of Quebec's anglophone minority.)[56]

In fact, in 1990 all the provinces had agreements with the federal government spelling out the terms of financial assistance for minority-language education; eight provinces also had agreements regarding other minority-language services.[57] In addition, under section 23 of the *Charter of Rights and Freedoms*, the provinces are required to provide minority-language schools. Some francophone groups have persuaded the courts to order provincial governments to comply.

As a result, all provinces now offer minority-language education; most of them provide some other French-language services as well. Although some provinces have been reluctant to allow francophone communities to manage and control French-language schools, in March 1990, the Supreme Court ruled that the provinces were in fact obliged to do so, under section 23 of the *Charter*. In principle, the provincial governments have been trying to comply with the decision, but their critics claim that many of them have been dragging their feet.[58]

Finally, the federal government has provided funds to provinces, largely on a cost-shared basis, to support public services to official-language minorities in areas other than education, including health care, social services, small business development, support for media, and legal services.[59]

In sum, over the last two decades the predominantly anglophone provinces have willingly or unwillingly expanded French-language services. But, with the exception of New Brunswick, they have been very reluctant to afford French an equal status with English. Even Ontario, which has moved furthest in the direction of official bilingualism, has stopped short of formally proclaiming such a regime. Nor should this resistance be surprising: it simply recognizes the demographic structure of the provinces. In Canada as a whole linguistic equality has a certain logic, given the 75/25 per cent ratio of anglophones to francophones. But among the provinces only New Brunswick approximates this. Elsewhere, the demography is simply too heavily weighted in favour of the majorities to afford any credibility to notions of linguistic equality.

Quebec Abandons Official Bilingualism

Meanwhile Quebec, whose *de facto* regime of official bilingualism had been the model for the B&B Commission and the federal government, has itself formally moved away from linguistic equality. Whereas the federal government set the protection of francophone and anglophone minorities as the goal of language policy and tried vigorously to persuade the provinces to act accordingly, the Quebec government has adopted the contradictory policy of protecting and advancing a linguistic majority. This policy has been propelled by two basic considerations.

First, the 1960s saw a new demographic vulnerability of francophones in Quebec. In the past, a high birth rate among Quebec francophones had always compensated for the tendency of immigrants to integrate with Quebec's anglophone population. But in the 1960s the francophone birth rate declined rapidly. By the late 1960s there was widespread concern among Quebec nationalists that the francophone proportion of the Quebec population would start falling from its historical level of 80 per cent. In Montreal, where most immigrants tended to settle, the historical proportion of francophones had been no more than two-thirds. If past levels of anglicization of immigrants continued, francophones might cease to be the majority. These fears were given a certain authority by the publication of demographic projections. Most notably, in 1969 the province's leading demographer, Jacques Henripin, predicted that if current trends were to continue, by the year 2001 francophones might constitute no more than 53 per cent of Montreal's population.[60] It was not difficult to argue that if francophones lost control of Montreal, the province's metropolis, their control of the province itself might be at stake.

Second, the 1960s saw the impact of changes in the social structure of French Quebec. During the 1950s there had emerged a new francophone middle class of salaried professionals whose work consisted of creating or disseminating and applying knowledge, which they could best do in their first language, French. Often their professional mobility was blocked by the preeminence of English as a language of work in the upper levels of the Quebec economy. This new middle class therefore had a particular interest in the quality of French and its general status in Quebec.[61] During the 1960s, the members of this class had obtained work in the rapidly expanding provincial state and public sector, but by the end of the 1960s such positions were no longer being created at the same rate. Increasingly, then, new middle-class francophones would have to look to the private sector for managerial opportunities. Confronted with the continued predominance of English in these positions, they increasingly called upon the Quebec government to intervene so as to alter the language practices of the workplace.

These twin pressures led successive Quebec governments to define a new language regime for Quebec. The first government to do so, led by the Union nationale under Jean-Jacques Bertrand, focused mainly on the access for immigrant children to English-language schools, the primary route to anglicization. Rejecting the nationalists' demands, in 1969 the government passed Bill 63, which established the right of all parents to choose the language of instruction of their children. To do so it had to override the organized objections of a large number of francophone nationalists, including a 50,000-person demonstration before the Quebec legislative buildings. In a vain attempt to appease the nationalists, the bill contained a provision calling for the creation of a commission of inquiry, under Jean-Denis Gendron, to investigate the state of the French language in Quebec.

The Liberal government of Robert Bourassa, first elected in 1970, found itself confronted with growing francophone concern over the twin issues of access to English-language schools and French as a working language. Meanwhile, the Gendron Commission, like the B&B Commission, pursued a broad-based investigation of language issues in Quebec, with public hearings and an extensive research program. In 1972 it delivered its report. Citing the central importance of 'collective action . . . to affirm or consecrate the French fact in Quebec', the commission recommended that French alone be proclaimed the official language, while French and English would be declared 'national' languages.[62] Although it did not make any recommendations about access to English-language schools, the commission proposed measures to make French the language of internal communication in the work world as well as measures designed explicitly to increase the proportion of francophones in managerial positions.[63]

The Bourassa government responded in 1974 with its Bill 22, which made French alone the official language of Quebec and its governmental institutions; access to English-language schools would be dependent upon children demonstrating a 'sufficient knowledge' of English; and a series of measures were to be adopted to induce private firms to 'francize' their operations. In effect, a government clearly committed to Quebec's remaining part of the Canadian federation imposed a regime under which only one language would have official status in a given territory and the state would openly seek to strengthen the position of the linguistic majority, restricting minority rights in the process.

The Parti Québécois government's Bill 101, passed in 1977, simply built upon the framework established by its federalist predecessors. Access to English-language schools was restricted on the basis of the parents' mother tongue (as measured by their language of education) rather than the child's knowledge of English. That is, a parent had to have been educated in English—and in Quebec. And private enterprises were to be obliged to pursue francization programs rather than simply urged to do so. To be sure, even Bill 101 assured Quebec anglophones of rights and services that exceeded those available to any of the francophone minorities, with the possible exception of those in New Brunswick.[64]

The differences in language policy could not have been clearer. Ottawa had vigorously tried to establish a language regime inspired by the personality principle and the ideal of linguistic equality and the protection of linguistic minorities. Quebec, on the other hand, was committed to a territorially defined language regime based on the promotion of its linguistic majority, even at the expense of minority rights. During the 1980s the Bourassa government even opposed in court the demands by francophone minorities to educational services under the *Charter,* for fear that a victory would hamper Quebec in its dealings with its anglophone minority.

The Bourassa government had been forced to recognize that abandonment of official bilingualism and the personality principle were the almost unavoidable response to linguistic conditions in Quebec. Only on the basis of French primacy could the Quebec state seek to reverse the historical inferiority of French in the province. It is difficult within a framework of formal equality between languages to legitimize state intervention on behalf of the *majority* language, even if it may be the one that is in an inferior situation or under assimilationist pressures. Frank Scott had demonstrated this point with devastating effect in his dissent from the B&B Commission's proposals to strengthen the position of French in the Quebec work world.

Moreover, the Quebec government could not ignore the fact that for Quebec francophones the most important linguistic issue was in fact the status of French in Quebec. Jean Marchand, member of the B&B Commission before entering federal politics with Trudeau and Gérard Pelletier, confirmed this in a revealing interview in the mid-1970s:

This is what I learned in the [B&B] commission when we went around meeting the people. We visited a small place in the Lake St John area [in Quebec]. I'd say: 'What's wrong?' And the people would say: 'The manager of the mill or whatever it was has been here for ten years—and he has never learned to say either "yes" or "no" in French. We all had to learn English.' The population in that area is 99.9 percent French.

So, for me, this was much more the cause of the trouble in Quebec than the fact that there was no bilingualism, say, at the Vancouver airport. Actually, at that time, nobody was travelling by airplane, or just a few people. I think that the main source of dispute or conflict or tension or friction—call it whatever you want—was Quebec itself and the federal institutions where there was surely no equality for all practical purposes.[65]

In fact, several months before the Bourassa government introduced Bill 22, Gérard Pelletier, who had been responsible as secretary of state for implementing the federal *Official Languages Act*, had given a major address in which he seemed to be calling for precisely such a measure. Before the Montreal Chambre de commerce, Pelletier had called upon the Quebec government to follow the approach that Ontario had taken when introducing French-language schools:

The provincial government [of Ontario] began by affirming that Ontario was first and foremost an English-speaking province and that all citizens, for their own good and the good of the province, should know English. After this cool and firm statement, it was also declared that this should not prevent the authorities from respecting the rights of Franco-Ontarians, nor should it prevent them, with the help of the government, from developing their own language or encouraging the study of French in the entire educational system.

I strongly wish that Quebec authorities would assert Quebec's character as firmly and as forthrightly, at the same time reaffirming their intention to respect the English-speaking minority as in the past. Who could object to this proposition which would have the advantage of being perfectly symmetrical with the stand of the neighbouring province? And who can deny the need to state as firmly and as frequently as possible the necessity of Quebec's remaining resolutely French?[66]

Yet, for Pierre Trudeau only official bilingualism would do; Bill 22's departure from that formula made it totally unacceptable. Indeed, in an address to the Quebec wing of the federal Liberal party in 1976, he branded the bill a 'political stupidity'.[67] By making French the only official language it greatly complicated the federal government's efforts to persuade the rest of the country that there are two official languages.

Trudeau did say that he would have accepted a designation of French as 'the main language', 'the language of work', or even 'the national language'. He even claimed to support 'the spirit' of Bill 22. None the less, as I have argued, it is difficult to see how, within the framework of official bilingualism, the Quebec government could have actively promoted one language, French, whether it be called 'the national language' or anything else. In particular, it would have had difficulty justifying any measures designed to make French prevail over English, as in the work world. Certainly, the Ontario model that Pelletier commended was not official bilingualism. In his own words, it was based on Ontario being 'first and foremost English-speaking'.

Not only did the Trudeau government denounce Bill 22, but the pursuit of its formula of official bilingualism at the federal level led to measures in support of Quebec's anglophone minority that have run directly counter to the Quebec government's promotion of French. For instance, under its program of financial support for minority-language community organizations, in 1987/8 Ottawa granted $1,200,000 to Alliance Québec, which has funded court challenges against Bill 101 and lobbied for changes in the bill.[68]

Indeed, when in 1988 the Mulroney government presented the draft of a revised *Official Languages Act*, the Quebec government strongly objected to a provision which authorized Ottawa to support organizations promoting bilingualism. Quebec City declared that support for such organizations would contradict the objectives of Bill 101. Finally, Ottawa agreed to negotiate an agreement with Quebec to ease these concerns.[69]

In sum, the Trudeau government had relatively little success in its concerted effort to secure provincial adoption of its model of official bilingualism. In fact, only one province is now officially bilingual. Others have openly resisted the notion or, in the case of Quebec, have abandoned it. Ottawa had much more success in inducing provincial governments to provide services in French to their francophone minorities. Still, provision of service beyond the minimum guaranteed under the education rights of the *Charter* much depended upon Ottawa's readiness to foot the bill through transfer payments. [. . .]

OFFICIAL BILINGUALISM AND SECURING NATIONAL UNITY

Taken as a whole, the results of the Trudeau campaign to implant its vision of a bilingual Canada have at best been mixed. Within its own institutions, the Trudeau government greatly enhanced the role played by francophones but failed to make the public service effectively bilingual. The predominantly English-Canadian provincial governments have expanded their services to francophone minorities but have generally balked at official bilingualism. Except for Quebec and New Brunswick, the assimilation of francophones has continued. Quebec has formally rejected official bilingualism while continuing to provide public services to its anglophone minority, which has itself declined. The federal government can point to success in its effort to expand personal bilingualism, especially among young anglophones. However, the continued decline in the number of francophones in most parts of Canada means that the enhanced bilingualism of anglophones will be of little use in their immediate communities.

Whatever success these various measures may have had in achieving their specific objectives, they must be judged against the underlying purpose of strengthening national unity. If French were to achieve equality throughout Canada, so the argument went, Quebec francophones would identify less with Quebec and more with Canada as a whole and its government in Ottawa. And as anglophone Canadians became more aware of the French fact, and perhaps even became bilingual, they would be united with francophones in a common attachment to a bilingual Canada. To what extent has this happened? And what have the consequences been for national unity?

Francophone Quebec: Bilingualism in Ottawa with Unilingualism in Quebec

It was obviously important for most Quebec francophones that the federal government become truly bilingual. As we saw, such lifelong Quebec nationalists as André Laurendeau were firmly committed to this ideal. To the extent the ideal was achieved, then, Quebec francophones were indeed likely to feel less estranged from the federal government. There were, however, real limits to these changes: in the public service francophones became much more numerous but they were not necessarily able to work in

French. These limitations were reported regularly in the Quebec media. But at least for the first time the federal government was moving in the right direction. Similarly for a good number of Quebec francophones, the fate of the francophone minorities was indeed important, and changes in the way governments treated them were all to the good.

Still, however much Quebec francophones may have cared about these questions and been gratified by the steps that were taken, the most important issue for them was the status of French in Quebec, as it always had been. Moreover, in the Quebec of the 1960s and 1970s, the issue was acquiring much greater urgency than ever before. Few Quebec francophones were prepared to subordinate the status of French in Quebec to improvements in the status of French elsewhere.

The accentuated concern with the status of French in Quebec did not necessarily lead to a rejection of the Canadian federal order. But it did render very problematic a conception of Canadian federalism in which language rights are the same everywhere and in which government policy is interested primarily in the fate of linguistic *minorities*, whether francophone or anglophone.

That was the underlying flaw in the Trudeau strategy. It presumed that dissatisfaction with the status of French in Quebec could be traded off against gains elsewhere. The error of this strategy was clearly revealed in the mid-1970s when, despite demonstrable improvement in the status of French both in Ottawa and some other provinces, the federalist government of Robert Bourassa responded to public pressures by abandoning Quebec's longstanding linguistic equality with Bill 22.

In effect, Quebec francophones could support official bilingualism in Ottawa and recognition of French rights in other provinces, yet also support the primacy of French in Quebec. There was a contradiction only if one believed, as the Trudeau government did, that linguistic equality should apply throughout Canada, provincially as well as federally.

The B&B Commission had recognized that the fate of French in Canada was, in the last analysis, dependent upon its vitality in Quebec, the home of 80 per cent of Canada's francophones. That is why it had proposed that concerted governmental action be taken to strengthen the place of French in the Quebec economy. In doing so, it had entered into a certain contradiction with its general endorsement of the personality principle, but at least it was struggling to address the full reality of the French language in Canada.

In denying a central element of this reality, the Trudeau government made its linguistic agenda irrelevant to the primary concerns of most Quebec francophones. It was left to the Quebec government, whether it be in federalist or sovereigntist hands, to address the status of French in Quebec. Indeed, when Ottawa did intervene in Quebec, it was on behalf of the anglophone community. In that respect the Trudeau government's language policy was in fact antagonistic to the primary concern of most Quebec francophones. Beyond that, Ottawa's insistence on linguistic equality and official bilingualism for federal and provincial governments alike brought into question the very legitimacy of measures such as Bill 22, which had the overwhelming support of Quebec francophones. Nor did Trudeau hesitate to make the point.

The result, then, was to make the federal order seem hostile to the primary linguistic concerns of Quebec francophones. To that extent, the Trudeau strategy of language reform became a source of conflict and division rather than the instrument of reconciliation it was intended to be.

Not surprisingly, Trudeau's strategy of linguistic reform failed to make Quebec francophones any less attached to Quebec as their primary national community, let alone to see themselves first and foremost as Canadians. Even if the federal government's efforts to strengthen the use of French outside Quebec should have made Quebec francophones see the rest of Canada as more hospitable to them, they well knew that nowhere else in Canada could there be as complete and dynamic a francophone society as in Quebec. Whatever the treatment of the francophone minorities in the other provinces, Quebec was bound to remain the centre of francophone life in Canada, as it always had been. Indeed, it was bound to remain, in the B&B Commission's own words, 'a distinct society'. No matter how vigorous Ottawa's efforts on behalf of the French fact elsewhere, Quebec francophones would continue to identify with Quebec and to want the Quebec state to have the powers necessary to protect and promote the French language in Quebec. The Trudeau strategy did nothing to change that.

Anglophone Canadians: Opposing Responses

In anglophone Canada, there were two very different reactions to the Trudeau government's language reforms. Some Canadians embraced the vision of a new bilingual Canada; others bitterly resented it. Both reactions generally precluded any recognition of Quebec's distinctiveness, a basic given for most Quebec francophones; either way, the result was strong indignation when Quebec then proceeded with its own transition to primacy for French. In these ways as well, the Trudeau linguistic strategy, with its emphasis on linguistic equality at provincial as well as federal levels, did as much to impede as to promote national unity.

For some English Canadians the Trudeau reforms offered an appealing vision of Canada. The decline of the British connection and the alarm at American domination had fostered the search for a distinctively Canadian identity. Bilingualism, especially as both personified and championed by Trudeau, seemed to be an answer. Canada would become a truly bilingual nation, and Canadians would be personally enriched by the experience of bilingualism. In that they would be different from and superior to their southern neighbour; indeed, Canada could provide leadership to the rest of the world by showing how linguistic antagonisms can be overcome.

Some English Canadians were more than prepared to support Ottawa's campaign to establish official bilingualism as widely as possible at the provincial as well as federal levels. To question this endeavour was to question Canada's national identity and to oppose a fundamentally progressive cause. By the same token, if English Canadians supported equality between French and English, so it was also their national duty to become bilingual themselves, or at least to ensure that their children did. This nationalist sentiment was at least partly responsible for the dramatic popularity of French immersion programs outside Quebec. Canadian Parents for French, an organization representing parents of immersion schoolchildren and funded primarily by the federal government, became a powerful lobby for official bilingualism and the Trudeau vision of Canada.[70]

When the Quebec government abandoned linguistic equality with Bill 22 and Bill 101, these English Canadians considered it a denial of the new vision of a bilingual Canada. Moreover, Quebec appeared to be acting in bad faith. Rather than taking measures needed to correct the historical disadvantage of French in Quebec, Quebec seemed to be violating a contract it had made with English Canada by which official bilingualism would be the rule throughout the country. Finally, it seemed to be a denial of the efforts made by some English Canadians to honour this presumed contract. Having supported official status for French and expansion of French-language services in their province, and often having enrolled their children in immersion programs as well, these English Canadians were outraged to discover that Quebec francophones seemed to be so indifferent to all their well-intentioned gestures.

Similarly, English-Canadian supporters of a bilingual Canada saw no reason to accept the continuing demands of Quebec nationalists for recognition of Quebec's distinctiveness. If the whole country was officially bilingual, Quebec was no longer unique. It was no longer the home of francophones. All of Canada was now their home. In effect, all of Canada had become like Quebec.

For other Canadians, however, the Trudeau vision of a bilingual Canada was not at all appealing. First, it constituted too radical a break with their own idea of Canada. In some cases, these responses clearly were uninformed and even bigoted. For instance, in his underground best-seller, *Bilingual Today, French Tomorrow* [see Document 6], Lieutenant Commander J.V. Andrew claimed that the designation of bilingual positions in the federal civil services was no less than a plot 'to hand Canada over to the French-Canadian race'.[71] But the reaction was not restricted to this rather paranoid fringe. After all, 17 MPs, including a former prime minister, John Diefenbaker, refused to support the *Official Languages Act* in 1969. At about the same time, the eminent historian Donald Creighton declared that there was no historical basis for recognizing French outside Quebec.[72] And in 1973, J.T. Thorson, former Liberal cabinet minister and president of the Exchequer Court of Canada, was moved to write a book entitled *Wanted: A Single Canada*[73] in which he drew upon the statements of prominent Québécois to demonstrate that Ottawa's language regime did not in any event respond to the discontent of Quebec francophones.

Second, the ideal of a bilingual Canada simply contradicted the reality of Canada as many English Canadians knew it, especially in the West. After all, in a 1985 survey, only 14 per cent of anglophones outside Quebec reported hearing French daily; most said they never heard it.[74] As the late Donald Smiley noted in 1980:

> A decreasing proportion of Canadians experience duality as an important circumstance of daily life. . . . On a day-to-day and a week-to-week basis most citizens have little direct contact with members of the other linguistic community. Because of this, the resistance of most non-francophones to a view that the essential nature of their country is dualistic is understandable, even when this resistance is expressed in such ungenerous sentiments as those of people not wanting French to be forced down their throats when demonstrably no one is trying to do any such thing.[75]

The fact of the matter is that in many parts of Canada the debate about official bilingualism has been a discourse with little connection to social reality. This was shown especially clearly when francophone groups, supported financially by the federal government, used the courts to impose long-defunct constitutional provisions. For instance, when in 1988 Saskatchewan francophone leaders denounced Bill 2 and insisted on a commitment to translate all statutes,[76] some central Canadian politicians and opinion leaders were quick to follow suit and denounce this abandonment of Saskatchewan's francophone community. Condemning the refusal to translate *all* the statutes, Ontario Premier David Peterson declared, 'This puts pressure on the kinds of things that many of us believe in, in terms of nation-building, which requires respect for the minorities.[77] Opposition Leader Bob Rae called it 'a sad day for the country when governments take away from individual rights as they have been expressed by the Supreme Court of Canada', and proclaimed that Ontario should declare itself to be officially bilingual.[78] (He failed to do so during his own term as premier.)

For its part, the B&B Commission had not called for such measures as translation of laws and bilingual records of debates in the case of such provinces as Alberta and Saskatchewan, It merely proposed the right to use either language in legislative debates. Both Saskatchewan's Bill 2, as well as Alberta's Bill 60, accorded this right.

More important, critics tended to overlook the reality of language use in present-day Saskatchewan. According to the 1991 census, in the province as a whole only 7,155 people, or 0.7 per cent of the province's population, spoke French at home.[79] Under those circumstances formal equality of French with English made little sense. And the condemnations of Saskatchewan for not agreeing to translate *all* its statutes or to begin publishing a French-language record of its legislative debates, let alone establish simultaneous translation, ignored the fact that at the time no one in the Saskatchewan legislature was fluent in French.[80] Nor was it at all clear how the perilous condition of Saskatchewan francophones would be helped by these measures.

It is not surprising that in many parts of Canada English Canadians have resisted the ideal of a bilingual Canada and the very extensive resources that were deployed to put it into effect. Nor should it be surprising that they have been angered by Quebec's insistence on making French the primary language in that province. It is as if Quebeckers, having imposed official bilingualism on the rest of Canada—at very considerable public expense—then decided not to accept it for themselves. At one point, francophones in Quebec and anglophones in other parts of Canada might in fact have been able to come to terms on territorially rooted language policy for provincial governments. However, the prominence the Trudeau government gave to official bilingualism in the early discussions of provincial language policy made that impossible.

NOTES

1. Richard Gwyn quotes one of Trudeau's senior francophone ministers: Bilingualism, for him, was far more than just something that was essential to the survival of French Canadians. For him, it was a *human right*, no different from freedom of speech, or freedom of religion. He would no more have compromised on it than he would have compromised on any basic human right [emphasis in original]. See Gwyn, *The Northern Magus*, (Markham, PaperJacks, 1981), 59.

2. Trudeau, *Federalism and the French Canadians*, Toronto: MacMillan, 1968), 56.

3. Speech to Quebec Liberal Convention, 28 Jan. 1968, reported in *Ottawa Citizen*, 29 Jan. 1968, as quoted in George Radwanski, *Trudeau* (Scarborough: Macmillan—NAL, 1978), 286.

4. Richard J. Joy, *Languages in Conflict* (Toronto: McClelland & Stewart, 1972), 91.

5. Richard J. Joy, *Canada's Official Languages: The Progress of Bilingualism* (Toronto: University of Toronto Press, 1992), 71.

6. Ibid., 93.

7. Joy, *Languages in Conflict*, 77.

8. Ibid., 78.

9. Joy, *Canada's Official Languages*, 106.

10. Ibid., 107.

11. Ibid., 69.

12. Calculated from *Census of Canada, 1971*, vol. I, part 3 (cat. no. 92–726).

13. In fact, this bleak prognosis had already been clearly established in 1967 by Richard J. Joy in his *Languages in Conflict*. Originally published by the author himself, the book was published in 1972 by McClelland & Stewart.

14. See Donald J. Savoie, *The Politics of Language* (Kingston: Institute of Intergovernmental Relations, Queen's University, 1991), 7.

15. Marcel Martel, 'Les Relations entre le Québec et les francophones de l'Ontario: De la survivance aux *Dead Ducks*, 1937–1969', Ph.D. dissertation, History Department, York University, 1994, 125–8.

16. Ibid., 105, and chap. 4.

17. B&B Commission, *General Introduction*, xxviii.

18. B&B Commission, Book I, *The Official Languages*, 12.

19. Ibid.

20. Ibid., 14.

21. B&B Commission, *General Introduction*, xxviii.

22. Ibid., xxxiii.

23. Ibid., xlvii.

24. Discussions of the two principles and their relative advantages appear in Kenneth D. McRae, 'The Principle of Territoriality and the Principle of Personality in Multilingual States', *International Journal of the Sociology of Language* 4 (1975): 35–45; André Donneur, 'La Solution territoriale au problème du multilinguisme,' in Jean-Guy Savard and Richard Vigneault, eds, *Les États multilingues: problèmes et solutions* (Quebec City: Presses de l'Université Laval, 1975); Jean A. Laponce, *Languages and Their Territories* (Toronto: University of Toronto Press, 1987); and J.A. Laponce, 'Reducing the Tensions Resulting from Language Contacts: Personal or Territorial Solutions?' in Daniel Bonin, ed., *Towards Reconciliation? The Language Issue in Canada in the 1990s* (Kingston: Institute of Intergovernmental Relations, Queen's University, 1992), 125–39.

25. The studies dealt with Belgium, Switzerland, South Africa, and Finland. See B&B Commission, Book I, *The Official Languages*, 210–11.

26. Of course, South Africa's claim to a 'liberal' language regime was based only on its treatment of *white* languages, a point that the commission merely acknowledged in a footnote (ibid., 80). Two traits distinguished South Africa from the territorially based Belgium and Switzerland: the proportion of the population that can speak the official languages and the territorial concentration of the languages. By its own evidence, Canada fell far short. Whereas 66 per cent of South African whites claimed to be bilingual, only 12 per cent of Canadians made this claim. The official-language minorities of the South African provinces represented proportions ranging from 23 per cent to 39 per cent. In 9 of the 10 Canadian provinces, they constituted less than 14 per cent. On this basis, the commission concluded that Canada would have difficulty pursuing 'a policy of the South African type, where a full range of governmental and educational services is provided in both official languages in all provinces of the country' (ibid., 84).

27. Ibid., 83.

28. Ibid., 86. By the commission's calculations, these 'official-language minorities' amounted to 'about 700,000 Canadians in Quebec whose mother tongue is English and some 850,000 scattered throughout the rest of the country whose mother tongue is French' (ibid., 87).

29. 'If, therefore, French-speaking Quebecers should decide to dissociate themselves from the fate of the French minorities, and particularly if they should adopt this attitude because they felt English-speaking Canada was not giving the minorities a chance to live, separatist tendencies might then be that much more encouraged.' See B&B Commission, *Preliminary Report*, 119.

30. B&B Commission, Book I, *The Official Languages*, 86.

31. Ibid., 97.

32. Ibid., 97–9.

33. Ibid., 147–9.

34. Ibid., 105–17.

35. According to B&B Commission co-secretary Neil M. Morrison, Laurendeau had very much wanted the first volume of the report to be devoted to the status of French in the work world rather than, as it turned out, the status of French outside Quebec, and lamented the fact that the volume 'does nothing for Quebec'. See N.M. Morrison, 'Bilingualism and Biculturalism', *Language and Society*, (Summer 1989), R–8.

36. B&B Commission, Book III, *The Work World*, 559.

37. Ibid., 565. Scott noted that for Ontario and New Brunswick the commission had proposed that task forces be created to determine what measures were necessary to put French on the same basis as English as a language of work. However, in the case of Quebec, the commission set out rigid guidelines for such a task force: 'So the principles differ depending on the provincial boundaries. This is a virtual acceptance of the territorial principle. My idea of "equal partnership" is that it operates in similar fashion across Canada, "wherever the minority is numerous enough to be viable as a group".' (ibid).

38. *Official Languages Act*, 1st session, 28th Parliament, C–120.

39. The fate of the bilingual-districts scheme is discussed in Kenneth D. McRae, 'Bilingual Language Districts in Finland and Canada: Adventures in the Transplanting of an Institution', *Canadian Public Policy* 4, no. 3 (Summer 1978): 331–51; Kenneth McRoberts, 'Making Canada Bilingual: Illusions and Delusions of Federal Language Policy', in David Shugarman and Reg Whitaker, eds, *Federalism and the Political Community* (Peterborough, Ont.: Broadview; 1989), 141–7; and Scott Reid, *Lament for a Notion*, (Vancouver: Arsenal Pulp Press, 1993), chap. 6.

40. Commissioner of Official Languages, *First Annual Report, 1970–71,* 4.

41. Gilles Lalonde, 'Back to the B and B', *Language and Society*, no. 19 (Apr. 1987): 24. Lalonde did not himself refer to the 'Trudeau orthodoxy'.

42. Léon Dion, 'The Impact of Demolinguistic Trends', 66. Between 1970 and 1978 the percentage was 58 per cent. See Fédération des francophones hors Québec, *À la recherche du milliard* (Ottawa: 1981), as cited in Wilfrid B. Denis, 'The Politics of Language', in Peter S. Li, ed., *Race and Ethnic Relations in Canada* (Toronto: Oxford University Press, 1990), 170. In the face of complaints from outside Quebec, the situation was altered somewhat. In 1989, of a total $225.7 million granted to the provinces and territories, 28 per cent went to the education of Quebec anglophones, 35.8 per cent for francophones outside Quebec, and 29.6 per cent to anglophones outside Canada. See Secretary of State: *Annual Report to Parliament, 1989–90,* Fig. 4, p. 45. See also the discussion in Denis, 'The Politics of Language', 171. Instances such as this would seem to refute Scott Reid's contention that the federal government's language policy is 'asymmetrical', that is, favouring French and francophones over

English and anglophones. See Reid, *Lament for a Notion*, 63. See also the critique in C. Michael MacMilan, 'Contemporary Challenges to National Language Policy: The Territorial Imperative', paper presented to the Canadian Political Science Association, 1996, 10–12.

43. Leslie Pal, *Interests of State: The Politics of Language, Multiculturalism and Feminism in Canada*. (Montreal: McGill-Queen's University Press, 1993), Table 7.5.

44. Commissioner of Official Languages, *Annual Report, 1994*, 7.

45. Société Radio-Canada, *Une décennie 1970–1980*, Services français de la planification du rayonnement, Oct. 1981, 14–15, as cited in Richard Chevrier, *Français au Canada: situation à l'extérieur du Québec* (Montreal: Counseil de la langue française, 1983), 19. To be sure, as Chevrier notes, francophone groups regularly complain about poor quality of reception and insufficient local production.

46. The 1971 figure comes from Denis, 'Politics of Language', 157. The 1987 figures come from Secretary of State, *Annual Report, 1989–90*, Appendix L.

47. Secretary of State, *Annual Report, 1989–90*, 73–81.

48. Richard Simeon, *Federal-Provincial Diplomacy*, 118, and Smiley, *Canada in Question*, (Toronto: University of Toronto Press, 1972), 76. The federal government was to publish statutes in both languages if a province should fail to do so.

49. Pal, *Interests of State*, 134.

50. See the review of linguistic reforms among the provinces in Donald J. Savoie, *The Politics of Language*, 7–15. Also for New Brunswick see Don Desserud, 'The Exercise of Community Rights in the Liberal-Federal State: Language Rights and New Brunswick's Bill 88', unpublished paper.

51. Don Stevenson, former co-ordinator of French-language services for the Ontario government, contends that with Bill 8 Ontario has for all intents and purposes become officially bilingual. See Don Stevenson, 'What Is an Official Language?', unpublished paper. To be sure, the formal declaration that English and French are official languages, as in New Brunswick, could be politically controversial, making this last step a very substantial one.

52. *French Language Services Act*, 2nd session, 33rd Parliament, Bill 8.

53. In his campaign for the Ontario PC leadership, Mike Harris had declared, "The people of Quebec and the people of Ontario say no [to official bilingualism]. We are English. We will provide French-language services, as was our commitment.' See Derek Ferguson, 'Tory Blames Bilingualism for Backlash,' *Toronto Star*, 26 Mar., 1990.

54. Bill 2 does not require that records of legislative debates be kept in both languages; it left this matter for the legislative assembly to resolve. Also, the right to use French in courts is restricted to criminal cases.

55. The 1988 court decision followed upon (but was unrelated to) a dispute over the right to use French in the Alberta legislature. A francophone legislator had demanded the right to do so, invoking the *Northwest Territories Act*, but his request was denied by the Speaker. Yet in the Saskatchewan legislature the occasional use of French (by non-francophones) had apparently not been challenged. The Alberta dispute is recounted in Timothy J. Christian, 'L' Affaire Piquette', in David Schneiderman, ed., *Language and the State* (Cowansville: Yvon Blais, 1991), 107–21.

56. Secretary of State, *Annual Report to Parliament, 1989–1990: Official Languages*, Appendix J.

57. Ibid., Appendix G.

58. See the review of provincial responses to the Mahé decision in Commissioner of Official Languages, *Annual Report, 1990*, 211–14. See also Daniel Bonin, ed.,. *Towards Reconciliation? The Language Issue in Canada in the 1990s* (Kingston: Institute of Intergovernmental Relations, Queen's University, 1992), 6.

59. See the account in Secretary of State, *Annual Report to Parliament, 1989–1990: Official Languages*, 73-82.

60. To be precise, Henripin and two colleagues predicted that francophones would be between 52.7 per cent and 60.0 per cent of Montreal's population and between 71.6 per cent and 79.2 per cent of Quebec's. See Hubert Charbonneau, Jacques Henripin, and Jacques Legaré, 'L'Avenir démographique des francophones au Quebec et à Montréal en l'absence de politiques adéquates,' *Revue de géographie de Montréal* 24 (1974): 199-202. Henripin has recently acknowledged that the estimate was erroneous owing to incomplete data. Indeed, the francophone proportion increased rather than decreased because an unexectedly large out-migration of anglophones. See Jacques Henripin, 'Population Trends and Policies in Quebec', in Alain Gagnon, ed., *Quebec: State and Society*, 2nd edn (Scarborough, Ont.: Nelson, 1993), 315.

61. These changes French Quebec are detailed in McRoberts, *Quebec: Social Change and Political Crisis*, chaps. 4 and 5.

62. Rapport de la commission d'enquête sur la situation de la langue française et sur les droits linguistiques au Québec, vol. 2, *Les Droits linguistiques* (Quebec City, Dec. 1972), 67–8 (my translation).

63. Rapport de la commission d'enquête, vol. 1, *La Langue de travail*.

64. Savoie, *The Politics of Language*, 16.

65. As quoted in Peter Stursberg, *Lester Pearson and the Dream of Unity* (Toronto: Doubleday, 1978), 146.

66. The Cultural Anguish of Quebec', notes for a speech by Gérard Pelletier to la Chamber de commerce de Montréal, 19 Feb., 1974, 7. This was the English version of speaking notes; in all likelihood the address was given primarily in French.

67. 'Je n' en ai pas contre l'esprit de la loi mais contre la lettre, en certain endroits. . . . Une de mes critiques les plus fortes n'est même pas source d'injustice, c'est ce que j'appelle de la stupidité politique. . . . Si on avait dit la principale langue ou la langue de travail, la langue nationale. . . . Cela aurait grandement facilité les choses aux libéraux de reste du pays, à qui nous disons qu'il y a deux langues officielles, le français et l'anglais.' 'I have nothing against the spirit of the law but against the letter, in certain places. . . . One of my strongest criticisms is not even in terms of injustice but what I call political stupidity. . . . If they had said principal language or language of work, national language. . . . that would have greatly helped things for Liberals in the rest of the country, to whom we are saying that there are two languages, French and English.' 'Le discours de M. Trudeau: Il faut qu'on se parle dans le blanc des yeux', La *Presse*, 8 Mar. 1976. Also see Pierre Elliott Trudeau, *Memoirs* (Toronto: McClelland & Stewart, 1993), 234, where he laments the fact that Bill 22 came at a time when 'we had managed at Victoria to get the provinces to accept a measure of official bilingualism even at the provincial level'.

68. Leon Dion, 'The Impact of Demolinguistic Trends on Canadian Institutions', in' *Demolinguistic Trends and the Evolution of Canadian Institutions,* special issue of *Canadian Issues* of the Association of Canadian Studies, 1989, 67.

69. Bernard Descôteaux, 'Ottawa négociera avec le Québec sur la loi des langues', *Le Devoir*, 8 June 1988, and Bernard Descôteaux, 'Ottawa et Québec s'entendent sur les langues officielles', *Le Devoir*, 18 Aug. 1988.

70. Pal, *Interests of State*, 166–71.

71. J.V. Andrew, *Bilingual Today, French Tomorrow: Trudeau's Master Plan and How It Can Be Stopped* (Richmond Hill: BMG, 1977), 11.

72. Donald Creighton, 'The Myth of Biculturalism,' in Donald Creighton, *Towards the Discovery of Canada* (Toronto: Macmillan, 1972), 256-70.

73. J.T. Thorson, *Wanted: A Single Canada* (Toronto: McClelland & Stewart, 1973), 149.

74. 1985 Canadian Facts survey cited in Michael O'Keefe, *An Analysis of Attitudes towards Official Languages Policy among Anglophones* (Ottawa: Office of the Commissioner of Official Languages, Policy Analysis Branch, Oct. 1990), 8.

75. Donald Smiley, 'Reflections on Cultural Nationhood and Political Community in Canada'; in R. Kenneth Carty and Peter Ward, eds, *Entering the Eighties: Canada in Crisis* (Toronto: Oxford University Press, 1980), 33.

76. 'Francophones Urge PM to Protect Their Rights': *Globe and Mail*, 5 Apr. 1988. When the Supreme Court reached a similar decision in Manitoba, francophone groups there instead tried to negotiate a package of French-language services in substitution for the translation of statutes.

77. 'Peterson Disappointed by Decision on New Act', *Globe and Mail*, 6 Apr. 1988.

78. Ibid.

79. Brian R. Harrison and Louise Marmen, *Languages in Canada,* (Scarborough: Prentice Hall & Statistics Canada, 1994), Table A.2.

80. Robert Andrew, the Saskatchewan justice minister, was reported to have said that none of the MLAs was functionally bilingual (*Globe and Mail*, 5 Apr. 1988). I have found no evidence to the contrary. In examining the record of Saskatchewan legislative debates between 28 Mar. 1988 and 28 June 1988 (which straddles the introduction and debate of Bill 2) I found no objection by the Opposition Party to Andrew's statement. The record did contain three instances of French-language paragraphs in what appeared to be prepared statements. Two of them were by members of Mr Andrew's party. The third was the first three sentences of a statement by Roy Romanow calling attention to the presence in the gallery of students from a French-language school in Saskatoon. For that matter, the whole debate over Bill 2 took place entirely in English.

■ARTICLE 2: LEGISLATING NATIONAL LANGUAGE RIGHTS IN CANADA

C. Michael MacMillan

With the advent of nationalist stirrings in Quebec, the federal government made a commitment to develop a comprehensive language policy. It struck a royal commission to examine the language question and to propose appropriate policies to redress perceived problems. The B and B Commission proposed 'a new concept of an officially bilingual country in which the two official languages will have new rights and better guarantees.' Official bilingualism was proposed as a policy that 'evolves from the sum of the rights expressly guaranteed to English and French by laws protecting their use.'[1]

The underlying principle was that of an 'equal partnership' between the English and French language communities. As a concept, 'equal partnership' had several dimensions. One of those was a commitment to language rights for both English and French speakers throughout Canada, so that each would be able to use their respective language in dealing with the state. Another dimension sought a more equitable balancing of the costs and benefits of Canadian political life for the two language groups, which required greater political autonomy for Quebec. This latter element was given a generally hostile reception outside Quebec and was never adequately developed, with the result that 'equal partnership' disappeared from the debate over official bilingualism.[2]

In justifying its proposals, the B and B Commission indicated that the basis for the privileged position of English and French rested not on their historical claims, but rather on their existence as complete societies (or nearly so) within Canada, meaning that most Canadians were able to live their lives within these language communities.[3] This general approach is consistent with the framework of language rights . . . , a framework which emphasized the grounding of such rights in an ongoing

linguistic community. However, the commission's explanation opened an avenue for criticism of the principle, because the proposition was progressively less true for francophone communities the further one travelled from the borders of Quebec. Recognizing this difficulty, the B and B Commission emphasized that the principle of equality itself was an essential grounding for these rights. Addressing the claims of francophone minorities outside the 'bilingual belt,' the commission averred, 'We believe that these French-speaking minorities have indisputable rights by virtue of the principle of equality, and that provinces consequently have certain immediate obligations to them.'[4] Thus, the feasibility of provision of the services associated with language rights was the sole question to be determined.

In developing its policy recommendations, the B and B Commission addressed this issue of feasibility in relation to the territoriality versus the personality principles. The principle of territoriality requires that language rights be recognized on the basis of territorial boundaries. Government services were to be available in the language of the majority of the people in the given territory. That would mean that in Quebec, government services would be French; in Manitoba, in English. The personality principle, on the other hand, recognizes an individual entitlement to government services in one's official language, independent of the territory in which one resides.[5]

Taking as its guiding principle the equal partnership of the two linguistic communities, the B and B Commission rejected the territorial approach, arguing, 'It would deprive minority groups *en bloc*. . . of essential language rights.' The general goal was to ensure that 'wherever similar conditions are found similar services will be offered'.[6] The 'bottom line' was feasibility. So long as there were sufficient numbers of people to warrant the service, then it was imperative that it be provided. On this basis, the commission urged those provinces that had substantial official language minorities (New Brunswick, Ontario, and Quebec) to become officially bilingual and the remainder to commit themselves to the provision of bilingual services as they deemed appropriate. It is noteworthy that the commission insisted that, in provinces with an English-speaking majority such as Ontario and New Brunswick government services must be available

Source: MacMillan, C. Michael, "Chapter 4: Official Bilingualism: Linguistic Equality from Sea to Sea" in *Misconceiving Canada: The Struggle for National Unity*. Toronto: University of Toronto Press, 1998, p. 70–99. Reprinted with permission of Michael MacMillan.

in English even in those parts of the province with a large French majority (and vice versa for Quebec). Thus, the commission maintained, the majority language must be available everywhere and the minority language where feasible.[7]

In its analysis of the conditions necessary for equality for the two language communities in Canada, the B and B Commission strongly emphasized the importance of education in one's own language. 'The school,' it insisted, 'is the basic agency for maintaining language and culture, and without this essential resource neither can remain strong.' Accordingly, the commission recommended that 'the right of Canadian parents to have their children educated in the official language of their choice be recognized in the educational systems.'[8]

Any comprehensive system of language rights must include the basic right to an education in one's own language. However, the question arises whether there is a right to a *choice* of language of instruction. This formulation poses the curious prospect that English-speaking British Columbians could assert a right to a French-language education. Since the basis for this right is the entitlement to preserve one's traditional language, the right should be more properly understood as an *option* right for the members of the official language communities, that is, the opportunity should be available to receive an education in one's mother tongue. It is not a right to receive an education in the official language that is not one's mother tongue. Typically minority language community members may at their discretion choose the other language school system. This is precisely what some anglophone Quebeckers have chosen for their children and, similarly, what many francophones outside Quebec have done. Although they may choose to participate in the other language school system, their right to do so does not flow from their language rights. All the same, governments may well choose to encourage second language education for reasons of national policy.

Official Languages Act (1969)

The major recommendations of the B and B Commission for federal language policy were embodied in the *Official Languages Act (OLA)* of 1969. Section 2 of the *OLA* (1969) declared that English and French are the official languages of Canada and 'possess and enjoy equality of status and equal rights and privileges as to their use in all the institutions of the Parliament and Government of Canada.'[9] With this section, the government recognized a duty to provide services in both official languages where numbers warrant and in head offices of the federal government. In conjunction with Section 2, the federal government made a commitment to increase opportunities for individuals to work in the French language in the federal government and to increase the percentage of francophones in the ranks of the federal public service to achieve equitable participation. It also attempted to develop, with provincial agreement, a plan for the provision of government services in both official languages in designated bilingual districts across the country.[10]

Strictly speaking, it would be more correct to say that the set of language entitlements, rather than language *rights*, expanded dramatically in the federal domain, as citizens did not explicitly have a *right* to these language services. This characteristic highlights, a certain continuity from the *BNA Act* to the *OLA* (1969), in that the associated language rights are not readily claimable by individuals or groups. In fairness, it should be emphasized that the federal language policy was self-consciously limited to areas of federal jurisdiction and that the government ultimately sought to entrench a more comprehensive set of language rights, binding on both levels of government, in the Constitution itself.[11]

In terms of justifying these policy innovations, the federal rationale was based not on any theory of language rights, but on grounds involving principles of equality, pragmatism, and considerations of national unity. Three years before the passage of the legislation, Prime Minister Lester B. Pearson justified the introduction of bilingualism in the public service as 'part of its fundamental objective of promoting and strengthening national unity on the basis of the equality of rights and opportunities for both English speaking and French speaking Canadians.'[12] This statement makes clear that the justification for language rights is 'goal based' rather than 'rights based.'[13] Specifically, language rights were treated as instrumental to the broader end of national unity. This goal was to be achieved by making the federal government more accessible to French-speaking Canadians, by enabling them to 'have a fair and equal opportunities to participate in the national administration and to identify themselves with, and feel at home in, their own national capital'.[14] Pearson's successor, Prime Minister Pierre Trudeau, implicitly invoked a similar rationale for federal language policy when he stated, 'We are dealing with straightforward political and social realities . . . If only because of sheer force of numbers, either group has the power to destroy the unity of this country. Those are the facts . . . These facts leave Canada with only one choice, only one realistic policy: to guarantee the language rights of both linguistic communities.'[15]

However, in explaining why failure to respect language rights was so disruptive, Trudeau graphically illustrated the importance of language rights for the *individual* (and sketched a compelling groundwork for a regime of language rights) when he remarked, 'but that is exactly why limiting a person's use of his language can cause in him such a trauma, because you are interfering with something almost as basic as breathing'.[16] This does not lead Trudeau, however, to formulate a cause for individual rights to language.[17] Trudeau's rationale for language rights was obviously restricted to the Canadian federal context. If we were to apply Trudeau's line of reasoning to the Quebec provincial scene, where the anglophone population constitutes but a small portion of the electorate, we would conclude that there is no basis for recognizing language rights for the English-speaking community there.

Four years later (1977), in the wake of considerable anglophone hostility to its language legislation, the federal government issued a statement of its rationale and principles for Canada's official language policy. It maintained that French and English were the official languages of the country and were to enjoy equality of status in the various activities of the federal government. In general, the government recognized a responsibility on the part of both federal and provincial governments to preserve the linguistic heritage of the country. It echoed Prime Minister Trudeau's basic rationale in asserting that 'Canada cannot continue to exist as a single country unless the English and French languages are accepted and recognized as the official languages of the country.'[18] It further echoed Trudeau in its use of oxygen as a metaphor for the significance of language to the individual, when it stated, 'It is a structure and an environment, like the air we breathe. When it is healthy we don't notice it. When it deteriorates, we are all affected by it.'[19] Despite this richly suggestive metaphor, the document did not expand upon a normative rationale for recognition of language rights.

The conclusion to be drawn from these various statements on federal language policy is that language rights were conceived and justified primarily in terms of *political necessity*.[20] They were *not* justified in terms of civil or political rights. Instead, they were inspired by a commitment to accord French language speakers, where feasible, the same opportunities to use their language in interaction with federal government institutions as were universally enjoyed across Canada by English speakers. The precise status of these opportunities received remarkably little attention. Meanwhile, the powerful metaphors invoked suggested the paramount importance of language to the individual, inviting comparison with conventional human rights. A distinct ambiguity has thus existed in the official discourse of language rights in Canada.

Task Force on Canadian Unity

If the federal language policy was supposed to resolve the national unity issue in Canada, its short-term effects were notably modest—if not counterproductive. Language issues were strikingly intense during the 1970s, both federally and within the province of Quebec. Nationally, negative public reaction to federal implementation of the language legislation gave the government pause for thought. Anglophones were angered by the rapid expansion of bilingual positions, while francophones were disappointed by the lack of progress in making French a language of work in the federal administration. This was exacerbated by 'Les Gens de L'Air' controversy, wherein the federal government, pressured by anglophone air pilots with significant support in English Canada, rescinded the decision of the transportation agency permitting the use of French in cockpit/control tower communications—much to the chagrin of Québécois.[21] In Quebec, the development of language legislation assigning priority to the French language was a standing contradiction to the federal policy and was greeted with consternation in much of English Canada.

In response, the federal government struck a task force to advise it on further policy initiatives required to reinforce national unity. Although its principal focus was on the place of Quebec in Canadian federalism, it nevertheless devoted significant attention to the language question. In 1979 the Task Force on Canadian Unity recommended entrenchment of the principle of equality of rights and status for the two official languages in the federal government. This would include rights to federal government services and to radio and television services in both official languages, and their equal status as languages of work within the federal administration. At the provincial level, the task force urged initiatives for extending the recognition or language rights to minority official language education, essential health and social services.

Rights to education in either official language were supported for citizens of both official language groups. The task force report stated, 'We firmly believe that children of all Canadian citizens who move to another province should continue to have access to educational services in the language, be it French or English, in which they would have obtained them in their former province of residence.'[22] In regard to Quebec, a distinction was made between English-speaking Canadian citizens and English-speaking immigrants. The former would have access to English language education in Quebec; the latter would not. The argument offered in support of the distinction focused on its utility for national unity, specifically a concern to avoid interfering with Quebec's efforts to assimilate immigrants to the French language, and it was, therefore, consistent with the official rationale for national language policy.[23]

The task force's proposals simultaneously broadened and diluted the concept of language rights. They offered a considerable expansion of the language rights recognized to that point, especially in regard to essential health and social services and access to radio and television services. At the same time, their careful distinctions among legislative jurisdictions and resultant entitlements raised challenges concerning the status of such rights.

The right to government services in either official language is a case in point. The task force report proposed to entrench such rights in the federal government wherever there was significant demand. However, the suggested linguistic rights within the provincial sphere were limited to education, criminal trials, and health and social services. These were described as 'basic rights,' strongly suggesting that rights to government services in one's language were of lesser importance.[24] Although the proposed list

represented critical components of a commitment to language rights, the omission of broad government services was a striking inconsistency. How could one maintain that a francophone in New Brunswick is entitled to French language services from the federal government, but not equally entitled to such services from the provincial government? Any rights-based case for the former would surely apply with equal force to the latter.

Obviously, a New Brunswick example is more intuitively compelling than an Alberta one, where the tiny francophone minority would presumably fail to meet a minimum size requirement. This underscores the point that a constitutionally entrenched language right to provincial government services would likely have very selective impact, since most provinces would be more like Alberta than like New Brunswick. Nevertheless, a statement indicating the circumstances under which provinces ought to acknowledge rights to provincial services in either official language would have been in keeping with the principle stated. On the other hand, the task force viewed these elements as sufficiently important to individuals to merit recognition. Beyond that, its proposals regarding provinces echoed the national practice of language rights accepted by Canadians, as identified in [original source].

This does not mean that the task force was indisposed to constitutionally entrenched language rights for provincial linguistic minorities. On the contrary, the task force emphasized its goal of stimulating the development of a social consensus on language rights *prior* to their entrenchment in a constitution. It judged that 'French-speaking minorities will make more headway as a result of social consensus and provincial legislation than they would from constitutional guarantees at this time.[25] Beyond that, the central issue for the task force was not language rights, but national unity. These proposals are best understood as an accommodation of linguistic sensitivities in Quebec and, to a lesser extent, the other province's. Within this context the task force report was politically judicious in balancing the recognition of language rights and the acceptance of such rights in the various political constituencies across Canada. Although it recognized a short list of language rights as 'basic rights', it ultimately opted for an approach that encouraged their evolution through the practices of Canadian politics.

Entrenching Language Rights in the *Charter of Rights and Freedoms*

In 1982 a major constitutional reform initiative culminated in the introduction of the Canadian *Charter of Rights and Freedoms*, a controversial document that has galvanized debates that still rage over the role of constitutionally entrenched rights in Canadian society. Although the language rights sections of the *Charter* were a secondary matter of attention at the time—at least in English Canada—there are some indications that they were a principal impetus in the entire initiative. In 1980 Prime Minister Trudeau explained the need for the *Charter* to a Quebec City audience as a political necessity to enable the government to entrench a set of language rights. The *Charter* thus functioned as a 'Trojan horse' to English Canadians to make them accept language provisions deemed necessary for Trudeau's design for national unity.[26]

The language provisions of the Canadian *Charter of Rights and Freedoms* considerably expanded the scope of language rights. In the *Charter*, English and French were recognized as the official languages of Canada and accorded equal rights and privileges in all the institutions of the federal government and the provincial government of New Brunswick, as well as in the courts of each entity. The *Charter* also recognized *individual* rights to the use of *either* official language, but on an expanded basis. It included the right to receive available government services from head offices of the federal government and other offices where there was 'significant demand'. This was an individual right of all Canadians, only indirectly linked to the existence of linguistic groups. However, it expressed the same limitation noted in the task force recommendations in that it applied to only one provincial government. Obviously, this reflected the lack of consensus among the provinces for such commitments and the constitutional fact that the provinces would control the administration of such rights.

Not all Charter language rights took the form of individual rights. An exception occurred in Section 23, in relation to minority language educational rights, where the specified right may be claimed only by those Canadian citizens whose mother tongue is that of the official linguistic minority of the province of residence, or where their children already have such access (subject to the precondition of sufficient demand). In this case, group membership is significant in at least three ways: the claimant must have membership, first, in an official linguistic group; second, in an official *minority;* and, finally, in a group sufficiently large to warrant the service in the first place, that is, a functioning community.

The group character was reinforced by a further distinction between minorities in Quebec versus those in the rest of the country. Outside Quebec, the only requirement concerned mother-tongue language; inside Quebec, there was a further requirement that one had received one's primary school instruction in Canada in English or French.[27] Thus, individuals in similar circumstances possessed different rights depending on their geographic location. Once again the special features of a group (in this case longstanding residents versus immigrants) determined the possession of such rights. Strictly speaking, these were the only groups who had constitutionally entrenched rights to an education in a particular language. However, these groups were simply categoric in that they did not involve organization or activity by the members. The group, as such, did not control or determine the availability or exercise of these rights. In practical terms, Section 23 of the *Charter* simply ensured that all Canadian citizens would have access to education in their (English or French) mother tongue throughout the country, where numbers warrant.

On balance the character of these language rights was best captured by Patrick Monahan's assessment when he asserted,

> Language freedom, as defined by ss. 16 to 23, is neither wholly individualist nor wholly communitarian. Instead, a complex and symbiotic relationship between individual autonomy and community values is posited. Community is both a prerequiste for individual freedom and a corollary of it. The complex and delicate linkage between individual and community is reflected most clearly in those provisions which make the exercise of individual rights expressly contingent on the presence of community.'[28]

When examined with regard to its language provisions, Canada's *Charter of Rights and Freedoms* clearly reflects the then-existing national agreement on the practice of language rights. As was evidenced in the previous chapter, a national acceptance has evolved of three components of language rights: federal government services in both official languages, minority language education, and health and social services. The *Charter* embraced the first two components, but not the third. In relation to government services, it recognized language rights where they were already legislatively acknowledged, federally and in New Brunswick. They were, however, extended by virtue of their new form as *constitutional rights*, and by their *individual* character. Second, the right to minority language education established a right that previously existed only as a series of federal-provincial agreements on funding minority language education. However, a consensus had already been achieved by the provinces in support of minority language education in the St Andrews meetings in 1978. In this respect, this constitutional provision also mirrored emerging practice in Canadian society. Nevertheless, the entrenchment of the minority's right to education in its own language enabled official language minority groups to make use of constitutional support to advance their claims. In terms of the survival of official language minority groups throughout Canada, this was probably the most important innovation of the *Charter*.

Thus, the language provisions in the *Charter* were an organic outgrowth both of prevailing public attitudes and political consensus that reflected the existing practice of language rights in Canada.

[. . .]

JUDICIAL INTERPRETATION OF LANGUAGE RIGHTS

The constitutional entrenchment of language rights has created an additional domain for the articulation of the status of language rights through judicial interpretation. The inclusion of language rights within the *Charter of Rights and Freedoms* created expectations that it would have a substantial impact upon tile status of language rights in Canadian society." One observer described the *Charter* language rights as 'Canada's first attempt to provide comprehensive constitutional guarantees to protect the English and French languages,' but noted that they were nevertheless 'marvellously ambiguous.'[29] Judicial interpretation would thus play a crucial role in defining the content of language rights in Canada.

Somewhat curiously the introduction of the *Charter* coincided with a retreat by the courts to a narrow interpretation of language rights. In the 1970s

the Supreme Court embarked on a more expansive reading of Section 133, a process that reached its zenith in the *Manitoba Language reference*, where the Supreme Court maintained,

> The importance of language rights is grounded in the essential role that language plays in human existence, development and dignity. It is through language that we are able to form concepts; to structure and order the world around us. Language bridges the gap between isolation and community, allowing humans to delineate the rights and duties they hold in respect of one another, and thus to live in society.[30]

Clearly, language rights were judged by the Supreme Court to be foundational elements of self-identity, citizenship, and community, and thus worthy of substantive interpretation. Somewhat ironically, this ringing endorsement of the importance of language rights was offered in defence of a rather modest set of constitutionally entrenched rights. However, such rhetoric could clearly provide a basis for an expansive approach to the interpretation of language rights.

The view expressed in the Manitoba reference, however, was not characteristic of the subsequent trend of the courts' decision making. In reviewing six decisions involving language rights, one legal scholar described a pattern of narrow interpretation whereby the courts 'uphold rights where their existence is unquestionable in the *Charter* or other parts of the constitution,' but otherwise 'interpret language rights narrowly.'[31]

The cases of the *Société des Acadiens* and *MacDonald* were more typical of the Supreme Court's approach in the *Charter* era. The question in the former case was whether the right to use either official language in judicial proceedings, as stated in Section 19(2) of the *Charter*, included the right to be understood in that language, meaning that court officers must be fluent in that language. In *MacDonald*, the point concerned the issuing of a speeding ticket in Quebec in French only, which the plaintiff challenged as a violation of Quebec's obligations under Section 133 of the *Constitution Act, 1867*. In *Société des Acadiens*, the majority on the Supreme Court restated its view of the distinctive character of language rights: 'Legal rights tend to be seminal in nature because they are rooted in principle . . . Language rights, on the other hand, although some of them have been enlarged and incorporated into the *Charter*, remain nonetheless founded on political compromise.'[32] Broadly speaking, the court's assessment was consistent with the established practice of language rights in Canada, though somewhat overstated. It is rather intriguing that language rights in the *Charter*, unlike the fundamental freedoms and legal rights that are the acknowledged 'seminal rights,' are *not* subject to the Section 33 override clause in the *Charter*.[33] Presumably, a case could be made that this suggests a rather different weighting of the relative importance of the two sets of rights noted above—one that assigns constitutional priority to language rights. In addition, the capacity of governments to override legal rights and civil liberties via Section 33 renders all these rights creatures of political compromise. However, these themes were not pursued in the various opinions offered.

As a lower order of right, the court generally has been disinclined to adopt a 'broad and generous approach' to the interpretation of the content of language rights as it had in relation to other legal rights. Here again, the perception that language rights were a product of political ·compromise led the majority of the court to assume that the wording of the language rights sections precisely reflected the framers' intent, and thus to adopt a narrow reading of their content. The majority reasoned that the absence of wording specifying the right to be understood in the official language of one's choice was grounds to conclude that it was not part of this right. The choice of the verb 'use' rather than the verb 'communicate' was taken to be indicative of a restrictive intent. Similarly, in *MacDonald*, the majority maintained that although Section 133 *permitted* the use of either official language in court proceedings, it did not *require* the use of both. Accordingly, governments were empowered to adopt whatever practices they deemed appropriate regarding the language of court proceedings.

A notable exception to these views was Judge Bertha Wilson, who argued, in minority opinions in both cases, that the language rights acknowledged in the *Charter* necessarily impose duties on governments for their implementation. The right to speak a language in the courts implies a right to be understood and therefore places a corresponding obligation on the government to ensure that the court can understand the languages uttered within its bounds.[34] Judge Wilson urged the Supreme Court to adopt a 'progressively expansive' interpretation of this language right that would embrace a right to be understood by the court directly in the official language of one's choice.[35] Judge Wilson's opinion was flatly contradicted by the federal government's submission to the court in the *Société des Acadiens* case, insisting that 'a broad and generous interpretation of language rights cannot be used.' One legal scholar concluded that the court majority took its lead from this federal government position, thus spelling the end of any expansion of language rights through the *Charter*.[36]

Minority language education rights is the major exception to this relatively cool reception by the courts to language rights. Initially, Section 23 of the *Charter* was used to overturn section 73 of Quebec's Bill 101, which limited access to its English education system to those whose parents or siblings were educated in English in Quebec (the Quebec clause). Section 23 of the *Charter* guaranteed Canadian citizens access to minority language education systems where they are in a minority in a particular province (the Canada clause). The court declared that the Quebec Clause completely negated the Canada clause without sufficient justification, and the offending section was overturned.[37] However, the judge emphasized the absence of compelling evidence and argument concerning the detrimental effects of the Canada clause on the position of the French language in Quebec, strongly implying that these elements could have been grounds for sustaining the position of the Quebec government. Subsequently, francophone minorities would find ample support in Section 23 for their efforts to obtain French language education outside Quebec.[38]

The courts have been relatively receptive to Section 23 minority language education rights. However, they have been inclined to view them as something other than fundamental rights. The prevailing judicial view is reflected in the following comment made by the Supreme Court:

> Sec. 23 of the *Charter* . . . is not a codification of essential, pre-existing and more or less universal rights that are being confirmed and perhaps clarified, extended or amended, and which, most importantly, are being given a new primacy and inviolability by their entrenchment in the supreme law of the land. The special provisions of s. 23 of the *Charter* make it a unique set of constitutional provisions, quite peculiar to Canada.[39]

This comment underscores the ambiguous constitutional status of our language rights. Lacking the weighty history and established legitimacy of traditional civil rights, they are nonetheless judged to be centrally important to Canadian political life.

The *Charter* language rights, as defined by judicial interpretation, are to be viewed as a demonstration of political compromise, rather than as inherent rights. Their content is thus to be determined by their expression in government legislation. Insofar as the *Charter* is concerned, this is largely in response to the accepted practice of language rights in Canada. As a result, both the constitutional status of language rights and the judicial interpretation thereof derive from the practice of language rights in Canada. The explicit language rights embedded in the *Constitution* continue to be treated as the stepchildren of political accommodation, and their content continues to be treated with considerable trepidation by the courts. Thus, unlike some other dimensions of the *Charter*, the courts have followed, rather than led, political opinion about language rights in Canada.

NOTES

1. Royal Commission on Bilingualism and Biculturalism, Report, vol. 1, *The Official Languages* (Ottawa: Queen's Printer, 1968), 74.

2. For an overview of this concept and its demise, and the impact of the B and B Commission, see Michael Oliver, 'The Impact of the Royal Commission on Bilingualism and Biculturalism on Constitutional Thought and Practice in Canada,' *International Journal of Canadian Studies* 7–8 (Spring–Fall) (1993): 315–32. The mandate of the commission instructed it to address the matter in terms of equality. Some passages hinted at a disposition to develop a human rights framework for policy, e.g., the observation that 'we are not asked by our terms of reference to deal with these fundamental rights,' in B and B, *Report*, vol. 1, xl.

3. Noted by Oliver, 'Impact of Royal Commission,' 320. Oliver reported that the commission defined 'society' as 'a complex of organizations and institutions sufficiently rich to permit people to lead a full life in their own language.'

4. B and B, *Report*, vol. 1, 98.

5. For an elaboration of these language policy options, see K.D. McRae, 'The Principle of Territoriality and the Principle of Personality in Multilingual States,' *International Journal of the Sociology of Language* 4 (1975): 33–54.

6. B and B, *Report*, vol. 1, 73, 74, xliii.

7. Ibid., 103.

8. Ibid., 122–3.

9. *Official Languages Act, 1968–69, Revised Statutes of Canada 1970*, c.O-2, s.2.

10. The ambitious plan to designate bilingual districts foundered on the twin shoals of provincial intransigence and the peculiarities of the minority language population distribution in the country. For an informative analysis of the failure of this scheme, see Kenneth D. McRae, 'Bilingual Language Districts in Finland and Canada: Adventures in the Transplanting of an Institution,' *Canadian Public Policy* 4 (3) (1978): 331–51.

11. 'The bill does not, of course, amend the constitution. I have often stated my belief that such amendment is necessary to guarantee the fundamental language rights of our citizens, and this is one of the subjects which is before the continuing conference on the constitution.' Statement by Prime Minister Trudeau, in House of Commons, *Debates*, 1st session, 28th Parliament, vol. 2 (17 Oct. 1968), 1483.

12. B and B, *Report*, Book 3, 353. The original statement was presented in the House of Commons (6 April 1966).

13. A goal-based theory is concerned with the welfare of any individual only insofar as that contributes to some generally desirable state of affairs. A rights-based theory places the individual at the centre of the evaluation. The distinction originates with Ronald Dworkin's, *Taking Rights Seriously*' (Cambridge: Harvard University Press, 1977), 172, and was applied by Marsha Hanen, 'Taking Language Rights Seriously,' in Stanley French, ed., *Confederation: Philosophers Look at Canadian Confederation* (Montreal: Canadian Philosophical Association, 1979), 307–9. I would take issue with Hanen's assertion that the federal policy is properly characterized as rights based, on the basis of the prime minister's statement noted above.

14. Rt. Hon. Lester Pearson, 'Statement of Policy Respecting Bilingualism,' House of Commons, *Debates* (1st session, 27th Parliament, (6 April 1966), 3915. This central concept of linguistic equality is examined in Chapter 6. Here I focus on the evolution of language rights per se within the federal domain.

15. Canada, House of Commons, *Debates* (31 May, 1973), 4303.

16. Ibid.

17. Prime Minister Trudeau nevertheless viewed language rights as 'fundamental,' sufficiently important to deserve constitutional entrenchment. See his statement in Canada, House of Commons, *Debates*, 1st session, 28th Parliament, vol. 8 (17 Oct. 1968), 1483. See also the speech from which the introductory quotation is drawn.

18. Government of Canada, *A National Understanding*, 41.

19. Ibid., 73.

20. This pattern of government justification also helps explain public perceptions about language rights reported in [original source]. The widespread view that language rights are primarily based on the preservation of national unity is completely consistent with the message presented by the federal government on their behalf.

21. This controversy is examined in considerable detail in Sanford F. Borins, *The Language of the Skies: The Bilingual Air Traffic Control Conflict in Canada* (Montreal: McGill-Queen's University Press, 1983).

22. Ibid.

23. Ibid. This distinction is critically examined in [original source].

24. Task Force on Canadian Unity, *A Future Together: Observations and Recommendations* (Hull: Supply and Services, 1979), 53.

25. Ibid.

26. This explanation is offered in Ken McRoberts, *English Canada and Quebec: Avoiding the Issue* (North York: Robarts Centre for Canadian Studies, York University, 1991), 15.

27. This is the 'Canada clause' of the task force proposal.

28. Patrick Monahan, *Politics and the Constitution: The Charter, Federalism and the Supreme (Court of Canada* (Toronto: Carswell, 1987), 112.

29. Joseph Eliot Magnet, 'The Charter's Official Languages Provisions: The Implications of Entrenched Bilingualism,' *Supreme Court Review* 4 (1982): 170.

30. Supreme Court, *Reference Re: Manitoba Language Rights* [1985] 2 *Supreme Court Reports*, 347.

31. Ian Greene, *The Charter of Rights* (Toronto: Lorimer, 1989), 207. Mandel observed a more self-consciously political role for the court. See Michael Mandel, *The Charter of Rights and the Legalization of Politics in Canada* (Toronto: Thompson, 1994), Chap. 3. This narrow conception would appear to be contradicted by the judgment in the *Ford* case concerning Quebec's Sign Law, Section 58 of Bill 101, in which the court assessed the validity of the Quebec requirement that all commercial signs be only in the French language. However, the *Ford* decision reflects an expansive reading of 'freedom of expression' rather than 'language rights' as such. That case is examined in some detail in [original source].

32. The quotation is from the case, *Société des Acadiens du Nouveau-Brunswick Inc. et al.* v *Association of Parents for Fairness in Education et al.* [1986] 1 *Supreme Court Reports*, 549. I have drawn it from Greene, *Charter*, 191. The second case concerning bilingual summonses is cited as *MacDonald* v *City of Montreal et al.* [1986] 1 *Supreme Court Reports*, 460. See his Chapter 7, 'Language Rights' for a useful summary of these and other Supreme Court decisions regarding language rights since the *Charter*.

33. McRoberts made the same point and further maintained that the language rights clauses are in fact the *raison d'etre* of the charter itself. *English Canada and Quebec*, 15.

34. Judge Wilson, *MacDonald* v *City of Montreal*, 521–4.

35. See Greene, *Charter*, 190–4.

36. Joseph Magnet, 'Comments,' in David Schneiderman, ed., *Language and the State: The Law and Politics of Identity* (Cowansville, Que: Les Éditions Yvon Blais, 1991), 146. The federal position is quoted on 144.

37. The case is cited as *A.-G. Que.* v *Association of Quebec Protestant School Boards et al.*, [1984] 2 Supreme Court Reports, 66.

38. See Wayne MacKay, 'Minority Language Educational Rights Vindicated,' in David Schneiderman, ed., *Language and the State*, 123–40. His discussion, however, emphasized that Section 23 is a useful, but not necessarily decisive, resource in the face of an intransigent provincial government.

39. *Quebec Association of Protestant School Boards et al.* (1984), 10 Dominion Law Reports (4th), 321 at 331; quoted in Pierre Foucher, *Constitutional Language Rights of Official Language Minorities in Canada* (Ottawa: Minister of Supply and Services, 1985), 347.

MEDIUM AND MESSAGE

Popular Culture, Mass Media, and National Identity, 1960s–2000s

Cynthia R. Comacchio
Wilfrid Laurier University

MEDIUM AND MESSAGE: POPULAR CULTURE, MASS MEDIA, AND NATIONAL IDENTITY, 1960S–2000S

● **Introduction by Cynthia R. Comacchio**

▲ **Primary Sources:**

■ **Secondary Sources:**

● INTRODUCTION

Cynthia R. Comacchio

Popular culture, as the very classification suggests, belongs to "the people." Despite its assumed inclusivity, factors such as those of class, gender, "race," age, region, religion, urban or rural location, and any combination of these, clearly affect both its content and the extent and nature of public participation. Historians are understandably interested in the subject, which concerns how culture is created, disseminated, and received on the level of everyday life in the past. As such, the kind of popular culture that Canadians create and consume is integral to self, group, and ultimately national identity. The recent flourishing of cultural and communications studies, especially in critical media research, has expanded the subject area enormously, ensuring that it is interdisciplinary, multi-disciplinary, and often transnational in approach. But Canadian scholars have long been active participants in the study of popular culture and media. More than half a century ago, University of Toronto theorists Harold Adams Innis (1894–1952), Marshall McLuhan (1911–1980), and George Grant (1918–1988) left a significantly "Canadian" imprint on the scholarly study of modern media, communications, and popular culture, entwined as they are with modern technology and mass media. In particular, Alberta-born and Cambridge University-educated philosopher Marshall McLuhan (1911–1980) was an inter-national pioneer in communications theory and critical media study. A controversial public intellectual, he is best remembered for his catchy slogans, "the medium is the message," and "the global village," both of which illustrated—well in advance of the Internet—suggested how national/regional identities are challenged by "borderless" com-munications technology.

By the early twentieth century, mass production was making new technologies more affordable to more Canadians, as well as more desirable, thanks to the expanding social influence of advertising and the related development of consumerism. Accelerated by the military demands of the two world wars, technology had effectively reconfigured popular culture into mass culture by the 1950s, making its experience more "democratic," and, as "mass" implies, more widespread than ever before. The historical study of popular culture and media allows us a sense of how social relations such as those hinging on economic and political issues, or those concerning gender, race, age, sexuality, and religion, operate in the everyday culture of everyday people. The question of technology, and who can access it, is also important in this context.

The history of popular culture is also the history of Canadian–American relations. Preserving and promoting what is believed to be "distinctly Canadian" has been a central issue in the larger, and largely unresolved, question of national identity, a matter explored by George Grant in his aptly named *Lament for a Nation* (1965). Sustaining cultural dis-tinctiveness remains daunting, given American proximity, cultural commonality, techno-logical entrepreneurship and media domination. Established in 1949 and reporting in 1952, the Royal Commission on the Arts, Letters and Sciences (The Massey Commission) opened the way to a new state involvement in cultural production and promotion and the regu-lation of media content. Yet, already by the end of the 1920s, Canada's fledgling feature film industry had been overtaken by Hollywood. American radio programming was being broadcast to, and enjoyed by, Canadian listeners across the land by the 1930s, sparking the instigation of the Canadian Radio Broadcasting Commission (1932–36) upon the recom-mendation of the Royal Commission on Radio Broadcasting (Aird Commission, 1928–29). The National Film Board of Canada was established in 1939, largely to produce documentary and educational films on Canadian subjects, by and for Canadians. Although its productions have amassed more than 5,000 international awards, the NFB did not begin to challenge the dominance of foreign films in Canadian theatres.

Similar developments can be traced in any number of areas of media and popular culture. During the Second World War, as comic books became increasingly popular among children and teenagers, trade exigencies cut off the supply of American comics, thereby opening the way to those "made in Canada." The homegrown comic book protagonists included the dashing and indestructible Nazi-fighter Johnny Canuck, and the first female super-hero—predating the American Wonder Woman by only a few months—"Nelvana of the Northern Lights." The transparently "Canadian" qualities of these two heroic wartime characters is summed up in their names alone. The reopening of the comic import gates saw the resurgence of the American DC and Marvel books; it was not until the 1970s that artist Richard Comely would unleash his Captain Canuck, but his season proved to be short lived.

The Canadian Broadcasting Corporation (CBC) expanded from radio into television broadcasting in 1952. The CBC's mandate was, and continues to be, to reflect back to us our own stories, nationally, regionally, locally, and in both official languages (via Quebec's Radio-Canada). By the 1990s, First Nations politicization, media attention to First Nations causes, and federal responses to these, brought about the first Indigenous community programming: Television Northern Canada was founded in 1992. It was superseded in 1999 by the Aboriginal Peoples Television Network (APTN). Despite the CBC's early state-funded monopoly, the Television Age that dawned in the 1950s was almost immediately identified with American TV networks, shows, and stars. The exception was Quebec, where Radio-Canada captured a unique francophone audience and "made in Quebec" television programming predominated.

In the realm of popular music, and in the context of the American rock n' roll that captured adolescent hearts in the 1950s, the first Canadian pop chart-topper and teen idol was Ottawa's Paul Anka, whose crush on his babysitter Diana inspired his hit single by that name, produced in 1957 when he was only 16. During the 1960s Canadian singer-songwriters such as Ian and Sylvia Tyson, Gordon Lightfoot, Joni Mitchell, and Leonard Cohen also acquired an international following, reassuring anxious Canadian fans that there was an identifiably Canadian popular music. Yet the rock music that revolutionized 1960s popular culture was also, by and large, the music of the so-called "British Invasion," epitomized by the Beatles, and also that of the American Billboard Top 100. By 1967, the Centennial year, an expanding, increasingly defensive, and not infrequently anti-American cultural nationalism brought about the establishment of the Canadian Radio-Television and Telecommunications Commission. In order to ensure support for Canadian popular music, the CRTC legislated that the playlists of radio stations had to be at least 30 percent Canadian: composed, performed, or produced in Canada by Canadians. The so-called Can-Con regulations were highly controversial, but they did succeed in encouraging Canadian record production and exposure for Canadian artists.

Although their own history predated Can-Con, it was not until 1970 that a Canadian song by a Canadian band—and one with a distinctly Canadian perspective—climbed the Billboard 100 to its coveted number 1 spot. Winnipeg band The Guess Who, fronted by Burton Cummings and Randy Bachman, made its mark with its "American Woman." Ironically, the song itself is a dramatic attempt to distinguish Canada from an American neighbour increasingly marred by its Vietnam involvement, and violent student protests and race riots at home. By the 1980s, bands such as the Kingston, Ontario–based Tragically Hip, and Newfoundland's Great Big Sea, featuring songs with historic and topical references to Canada, found ready national audiences without looking to make it big in the United States. With a sound that simply spoke to pop music tastes of the time and very little to their Canadian origins, singers Celine Dion, Alanis Morisette, and Shania Twain numbered among the top international performers of the mid-1990s.

Questions about national identity and cultural sovereignty, and consequently about our relations with our powerful southern neighbour, dominate our cultural history, especially in the arena of popular culture, where the borders are more permeable and the access and participation proportionately greater. The late-twentieth-century digital revolution, like the industrialization of the previous century, marked a watershed in communications and mass culture along the historic lines of the printing press, the telegraph and telephone, film, radio, television and the Internet itself. The purportedly border-free Internet carries a considerable proportion of American content, exposing the rest of the world to the kinds of "cultural domination" that have so long framed the Canadian identity conundrum. What Canadians have embraced as popular culture at various points in our history reveals a great deal about both changes and continuities in our perceptions of ourselves as citizens, as a society, and as a nation. The proliferation of digital technologies that transmit instantaneously and unremittingly around the world make McLuhan's theory that "the medium is the message" acutely relevant in our own time. Particularly since the 1960s, with the growing public appetite for television, as well as rapid advances in satellite communications, cable transmission, and internet and wireless technologies, Canadians have had to confront the complex matter of protecting a distinctive popular culture in view of not only American dominance, but also the elastic borders of the "global village" prophesied by McLuhan.

QUESTIONS

1. Why does George Grant connect the demise of Canadian cultural distinctiveness, and consequently Canadian sovereignty, with the rise of American technological entrepreneurship?
2. Historian Ryan Edwardson classifies the comic book superhero Captain Canuck as "a cultural artifact." What purposes have been ascribed to this artifact, in terms of how the images associated with him have been put to social and cultural uses?
3. What does Robert MacGregor's analysis of the Molson beer commercial phenomenon that came to be known as "Joe's Rant" suggest about the relationship of media, popular culture, and national identity?
4. Why does the government report on the CBC/Radio Canada see young Canadians as a particularly important audience in the early twenty-first century?
5. The "viewing share" chart quantifies Canadian preferences in television programming, but does it help to explain why viewers make these choices? What kind of evidence do historians need to make conclusions about this matter?

FURTHER READINGS

Ryan Edwardson. *Canadian Content: Culture and the Quest for Nationhood* (Toronto: University of Toronto Press, 2008).

Ryan Edwardson. *Canuck Rock: A History of Canadian Popular Music* (Toronto: University of Toronto Press, 2009).

Harold Adams Innis. *The Bias of Communication* (Toronto: University of Toronto Press, 1951).

L. B. Kuffert. *A Great Duty: Canadian Responses to Modern Life and Mass Culture in Canada, 1939–1967* (Montreal and Kingston: McGill-Queen's University Press, 2003).

Paul Litt. *The Muses, the Masses and the Massey Commission* (Toronto: University of Toronto Press, 1992).

Ted Magder. *Canada's Hollywood: The Canadian State and Feature Films* (Toronto: University of Toronto Press, 1993).

Marshall McLuhan. *Understanding Media: The Extensions of Man* (New York: McGraw Hill, 1964).

Peter Morris. *Embattled Shadows: A History of Canadian Cinema, 1895–1939* (Montreal and Kingston: McGill-Queen's University Press, 1978).

Paul Rutherford. *When Television Was Young: Prime Time Canada, 1952–1967* (Toronto: University of Toronto Press, 1990).

Mary Vipond. *Listening In: The First Decade of Canadian Broadcasting, 1922–1932* (Montreal and Kingston: McGill-Queen's University Press, 1992).

▲ DOCUMENT 1: LAMENT FOR A NATION, 1965

In the wake of the Conservative Party's resounding defeat at the polls in 1964, philosopher Grant argued that the Pearson Liberals' evident embrace of American science, technology and corporate capitalism would soon prove that Canadians could not sustain an indigenous culture. Ultimately, national sovereignty itself was doomed to collapse as Canada became an American satellite state …

… The confused strivings of politicians, businessmen, and civil servants cannot alone account for Canada's collapse. This stems from the very character of the modern era. … The aspirations of progress have made Canada redundant. The universal and homogeneous state is the pinnacle of political striving. "Universal" implies a world-wide state, which would eliminate the curse of war among nations; "homogeneous" means that all men would be equal, and war among classes would be eliminated. The masses and the philosophers have both agreed that this universal and egalitarian society is the goal of historical striving. It gives content to the rhetoric of both Communists and capitalists. This state will be achieved by means of modern science—a science that leads to the conquest of nature. Today scientists master not only non-human nature, but human nature itself. Particularly in America, scientists concern themselves with the control of heredity, the human mind, and society. Their victories in biochemistry and psychology will give the politicians a prodigious power to universalize and homogenize. Since 1945, the world-wide and uniform society is no longer a distant dream but a close possibility. Man will conquer man and perfect himself.

… Modern civilization makes all local cultures anachronistic. Where modern science has achieved its mastery, there is no place for local cultures. It has often been argued that geography and language caused Canada's defeat. But behind these there is a necessity that is incomparably more powerful. Our culture floundered on the aspirations of the age of progress. The argument that Canada, a local culture, must disappear can, therefore, be stated in three steps. First, men everywhere move ineluctably toward membership in the universal and homogeneous state. Second, Canadians live next to a society that is the heart of modernity. Third, nearly all Canadians think that modernity is good, so nothing essential distinguishes Canadians from Americans. When they oblate themselves before "the American way of life," they offer themselves on the altar of the reigning Western goddess. … As Canadians we attempted a ridiculous task in trying to build a conservative nation in the age of progress, on a continent we share with the most dynamic nation on earth. The current of modern history was against us …

… All the preceding arguments point to the conclusion that Canada cannot survive as a sovereign nation. … Perhaps we should rejoice in the disappearance of Canada. We leave the narrow provincialism and our backwoods culture; we enter the excitement of the United States where all the great things are being done. Who would compare the science, the art, the politics, the entertainment of our petty world to the overflowing achievements of New York, Washington, Chicago, and San Francisco? … In the mass era, most human beings are defined in terms of their capacity to consume. All other differences between them, like political traditions, begin to appear unreal and unprogressive. As consumption becomes primary, the border appears an anachronism, and a frustrating one at that.

Source: George Grant, *Lament for a Nation: 40th Anniversary edition* (Montreal: McGill-Queen's University Press, 2005), pp. 65–67, 84, 88. Reprinted by permission of the publisher.

● As Ryan Edwardson discusses in his article, the comic book series *Captain Canuck* was the creation of artist Richard Comely, with initial inspiration from Calgary teacher and cartoonist Ron Leishman.

Source: Richard Comely, *Captain Canuck* cover, no. 1, (first issue), (July 1975). Courtesy of Captain Canuck Incorporated.

▲ DOCUMENT 3: SIXTH REPORT, 2008

CBC/Radio Canada

In February 2008, the Standing Committee on Canadian Heritage, appointed by the Harper Conservative government, and chaired by Conservative Member of Parliament Gary Schellenberger, published its report on the CBC/Radio Canada. The multiparty committee was mandated to study "the role of a public broadcaster in the twenty-first century." The committee held 45 public meetings across the country, heard hundreds of witnesses, and received more than 50 written submissions.

CBC/Radio-Canada has played a major role in the development of the broadcasting system in Canada. It is at the centre of cultural, political, social and economic life in Canada. It brings Canadians closer together and allows them to share their unique experience in North America. This is a huge task for CBC/Radio-Canada, as it has to operate over a very large geographic area while reaching out to a linguistically and culturally diverse audience. The development of new communications technologies in the last 20 years has made the Corporation's work more complex. ... There is no question that the Canadian broadcasting system is facing tremendous changes that will continue to have unpredictable effects in the future. The multiplication of digital platforms, the increasing number of specialty channels and the transition to digital/HD television will all affect the future of CBC/Radio-Canada. The Committee gave special consideration to the impact of emerging technologies on the Corporation's mandate. ...

... We are asking CBC/Radio-Canada to be original, of high quality and innovative, and to represent the reality of all Canadians living in this immense land, and in many languages. There is absolutely no doubt that we must always bear in mind what a colossal task it is for our public broadcaster to satisfy these demands. ... The English-language network has seen its audience share decline for a decade now. The appearance of many specialised channels and the emergence of broadcasting by satellite in part explain the fragmentation of CBC/Radio Canada's television audiences. Nor should we forget that CBC/Radio-Canada television operates in a market in which American broadcasts exert a very strong attraction. ...

CBC/Radio-Canada's English-language television competes with all the other broadcasters for the viewers' attention. In 1993, English-language pay and specialty channels had 6.2 percentage points of the audience share; in 2004, that figure was 22.4. Conversely, CBC Television's audience share declined by 6.5 percentage points between 1993 and 2004. ...

For many northern communities, CBC/Radio-Canada plays a capital role because it is a point of contact with the rest of the world. During our hearings in Yellowknife, witnesses even indicated that the presence of a public broadcaster was an essential service. In many communities, CBC North's radio and television broadcasts are the only sources of entertainment and information the residents have. Some communities do not have a local cable network, and the cost of satellite broadcasting services is often prohibitive. ... The various Aboriginal organisations that appeared before our Committee requested a change to CBC/Radio-Canada's mandate to include explicit obligations to Canada's Aboriginal peoples. ... The Committee considers that matters should be rectified without delay. As a national broadcaster, CBC/Radio-Canada has the mandate to represent everyone in

Source: From the Report of the Standing Committee on Canadian Heritage, *February 2008, CBC/Radio-Canada: Defining distinctiveness in the changing media landscape.* Reprinted by permission of the Office of the Law Clerk and Parliamentary Counsel.

Canada, including the Aboriginal peoples. CBC/Radio-Canada is capable of doing more to serve the Aboriginal audience. It is a network's role to bring people together and to give the First Nations a voice. Partnerships with certain Aboriginal broadcasters could be strengthened.

... The ubiquity of digital media has forever changed the Canadian broadcast environment. Over the past decade, digital technology has significantly expanded the number of platforms from which audio and video programming can be accessed and received. The new services are characterised by their personalisation and on-demand accessibility from the Internet and mobile screens. Demand for these services is driven by the estimated 16.8 million adult Canadians who made personal non-business use of the Internet in 2005. That year, nearly 64% of Canadians 18 and older used the Internet at least once a day, a figure that jumps to nearly 73% in the 18–34 demographic. ...

Because of digital media's influence, traditional broadcasting is now about content delivery across as many platforms as can be made available, and the development of a global brand to attract audiences to that content. It is in the global milieu that Canada's public broadcaster must act, competing for audiences, advertising dollars, and the public's finite attention span for news, information and entertainment.

Audiences too have changed, now expecting the content they want, when, where and how they want it. Traditional broadcast television's former stranglehold on audiences has been weakened by competition from the Internet, specialty channels, iPods, video-on-demand, and audio and video streaming, to name just a few. As audiences fragment across multiple platforms, advertisers follow, seeking to take advantage of increasingly targeted niche programming and Web sites to deliver their messages. Advertisers spent in excess of $1 billion on the Internet last year in Canada. This has significantly impacted the traditional business model of conventional broadcasters for which advertising revenues are the foundation. ... Digital and broadband properties are now part of developing a global brand and remaining relevant to audiences, particularly younger audiences. The need for CBC/Radio-Canada to meet the new standard for content delivery was repeated by witnesses throughout the study. ... Witnesses pointed to new media, particularly the Internet, as a means for CBC/Radio-Canada to renew its commitment to Canadians and better reflect both the regions and individual voices. ... It is in this sense that digital media are seen to enable a redefinition of the "public" in public broadcasting.

... CBC/Radio-Canada established its web presence at CBC.ca and Radio-Canada.ca in 1995. ... The national public broadcaster is seen to be providing a reliable Canadian presence for news, information and Canadian content in a global media environment dominated by foreign content and market influence. Traffic has more than doubled to its two main Web sites, cbc.ca and radio-canada.ca, in the past five years, and they are among the most visited Canadian news and information Web sites. ... The Committee heard from some witnesses, however, that CBC/Radio-Canada needs to go further to develop a stronger national and global brand if it is to compete in the fragmented, global media environment. ...

Known as "digital natives" or "millennials", young people between the ages of about nine and 28 have a relationship with media that is different from previous generations. If Baby Boomers were the TV generation, Generation Y are the Internet generation, and they understand and use the new media tools in a different way. This group was born into the digital era, where previous concepts of bundling and scheduling have been replaced by downloading, streaming, peer-to-peer networks and on-demand programming. Their interactions with media are characterized by multi-tasking: they commonly use several media and platforms at the same time.

... More than 60% of young people have visited a social networking site, and nearly all of these have registered and created a profile. They have an expectation of interactivity and participation in media. When speaking of putting the public back into public broadcasting, younger Canadians will therefore be an important group of participants. ... CBC/Radio-Canada's online presence will be fundamental to its relevance to Canadian audiences in the future. According to the Canadian Internet Use Survey (CIUS), an estimated 16.8 million adult Canadians made personal non-business use of the Internet in 2005, and nearly 64% of Canadians 18 and older used the Internet at least once a day, a figure that jumped to nearly 73% in the 18–34 demographic ... More recently, a July 2007 Angus-Reid poll on Canadian technology habits reported that more than half of Canadians said that their lives are better because of the Internet (52%) and that they visit news Web sites at least once a day (55%) ... Among 18–34 year olds, 40% said that the Internet strengthens their sense of community with others, as did nearly one in three adult Canadians overall. ...

The Committee agrees that CBC/Radio-Canada requires a new media presence in order to remain relevant to Canadian audiences now and in the future. Innovative new media content and services are an essential part of renewing the Corporation's role as our national public broadcaster. ... The majority of witnesses, experts, academics and public and private organisations, supported an amendment to the CBC/Radio-Canada mandate commensurate with the view that the power of new media should be harnessed to fulfil Canada's public broadcasting objectives.

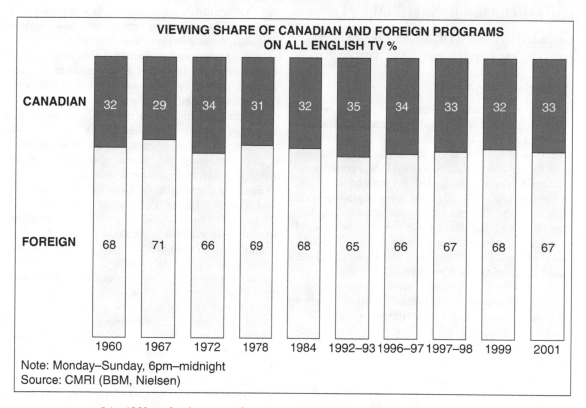

VIEWING SHARE OF CANADIAN AND FOREIGN PROGRAMS ON ALL ENGLISH TV %

	1960	1967	1972	1978	1984	1992–93	1996–97	1997–98	1999	2001
CANADIAN	32	29	34	31	32	35	34	33	32	33
FOREIGN	68	71	66	69	68	65	66	67	68	67

Note: Monday–Sunday, 6pm–midnight
Source: CMRI (BBM, Nielsen)

- In 1960, only six years after CBC-Radio Canada went on the air, two-thirds of Canadian prime-time viewing (6 pm to midnight) was dedicated to American programs. The same proportion has held from that time until the present, despite all technological advances and efforts by the federal government, especially the CRTC, to ensure both public funding and Canadian content.

Source: Canadian Media Research, Trends and Truth in Canadian Media, "60th Anniversary of Canadian TV: Why We Don't Have Hit TV Series," (18 April 2013). http://mediatrends-research .blogspot.ca/2013/04/60th-anniversary-of-canadian-tv-why-we.html. Used with permission from Barry Kiefl.

■ ARTICLE 1: THE MANY LIVES OF CAPTAIN CANUCK: NATIONALISM, CULTURE, AND THE CREATION OF A CANADIAN COMIC BOOK SUPERHERO

Ryan Edwardson

"Canada finally has her own honest-to-goodness comic magazine, with Canada's very own superhero—Captain Canuck!" (C.C. 1).[1] *Captain Canuck*'s 1975 release was the first Canadian comic book success since the collapse of the Second World War comic book industry. Captain Canuck, clad in a red and white suit and maple leaf emblems, used his strength—derived from a healthy diet and fitness—to fight for Canadian "peace, order, and good government." He avoided violence when possible, prayed before missions, and dedicated himself to protecting Canada and the world from evildoers. Canadian readers enjoyed the familiarity of national images, symbols, and locations infused with the action-adventure format established by American comic books. Yet, despite its popularity, the comic collapsed several times due to the economics of publishing in Canada and the problem of American cultural "dumping."

Captain Canuck is more than a comic book relic, however; it is a cultural artifact, a key item in the construction of modern Canadian cultural identity and consciousness. While in print, the comic presented popular cultural characteristics, myths, symbols, and stereotypes that legitimized the national identity and reinforced the conception of Canada as a "peaceable kingdom." Following the comic's publication run, Captain Canuck was revived by the Canadian government and incorporated as a national icon valuable for fostering national awareness and pride. It is an example of perpetual nation-building, an item of popular culture presenting national signifiers that, following its demise, was resurrected and recycled into a national signifier itself; it was fostered in a period of nationalism, empowered the national

Source: Ryan Edwardson, "The Many Lives of Captain Canuck: Nationalism, Culture, and the Creation of a Canadian Comic Book Superhero," *Journal of Popular Culture*, vol. 37, no. 2, (2003), pp. 184–201. Copyright © 2003 John Wiley and Sons. Reprinted by permission of the publisher.

identity, and later was integrated into the national myth-symbol roster.

"Nationalism," according to Ernest Gellner, "is not the awakening of nations to self-consciousness: it invents nations where they do not exist" (169). Benedict Anderson has furthered this idea, arguing that nations are imagined into existence because "the members of even the smallest nation will never know most of their fellow-members, meet them, or even hear of them, yet in the minds of each lives the image of their communion" (6). Comic books, as a visual medium, engage this act of imagination, in turn facilitating the mental construction of the nation and national identity. It is an act that may be an essential part of being Canadian. Canadian cultural historian Daniel Francis has argued (perhaps too generally but a valid observation nonetheless) that "because we lack a common religion, language or ethnicity, because we are spread out so sparsely across such a huge piece of real estate, Canadians depend on this habit of 'consensual hallucination' more than any other people" (10).

National identity, it can be argued, is also consumed into existence. Commodities can embody and popularize social identities and lifestyles—such as Nike and "Just do it" or the Body Shop and environmentalism—which are in turn confirmed through the consumption of those products (Klein). Through the consumption of commodities proposing certain myths, symbols, and values, national identities can be popularized and validated. In the area of Japanese national identity, Kosaku Yoshino has made some interesting insights into "a 'market' process whereby ideas of cultural differences are 'produced,' 'reproduced' and 'consumed'" (9). By drawing on Jean Baudrillard's argument that consumption "is a whole system of values, with all that expression implies in terms of group integration and social control functions" (81), one can see how cultural consumption provides a basis for identity construction. The material consumed carries a series of meanings that are either accepted or rejected by the consumer. [...]

[...] Consequently, in mass culture one can find mass national identity. Captain Canuck's red and white costume adorned with maple leaves signified his Canadianness, while his moralism, natural strength, and self-sacrificing persona reinforced conceptions of Canadians as polite, kind, moral, heroic peacekeepers. Distinctively national comic books, then, are vessels for transmitting national myths, symbols, ideologies, and values. They popularize and perpetuate key elements of the national identity and ingrain them into their readers—especially, given the primary readership, younger generations experiencing elements of that identity for the first time.

ALL IN THE FAMILY: CAPTAIN CANUCK'S COMIC BOOK LINEAGE

Late nineteenth-century Canadian newspapers often explored social, political, and cultural issues through comical caricatures, not only to highlight the editor's view, but to use as an aid for those lacking reading abilities. In the tradition of Miss Britannia, Canada often was cast as Miss Canada, the young daughter of the British Empire, or joined other masculine characters—including Britain's John Bull and America's Uncle Sam—as a youthful and sprightly Johnny or Jack Canuck.[2] Political parties, for example, attacked each other through newspaper cartoons that depicted Miss Canada in jeopardy, her virginal Victorian morality threatened by the older, seedy Uncle Sam. Jack or Johnny Canuck, on the other hand, embodied the "youthful" national spirit, ready to take on the world or, more often, confront Uncle Sam over an issue of trade or natural resources.

Comic books first appeared in the early 1930s, bringing together collections of reprinted comic strips. By 1938, stimulated by the popularity of Superman and similar superhero figures, they often included full-length original stories.[3] From the very beginning, the lack of a Canadian publishing industry and the cheap cost of American comic overruns ensured that the Canadian market was dominated by American comics. Stories of American heroes and villains supplied entertainment through exciting and spectacular figures, including Superman, the Flash, and Batman. They were a part of the American monomyth that "secularizes Judeo-Christian ideals by combining the selfless individual who sacrifices himself for others and the zealous crusader who destroys evil" (Land and Trimble 158). Yet Canadians share those "youthful, physically vigorous" and "morally upright" heroes, not only because their popular fiction is predominantly American in origin, but because their national, social, and economic developments have been similar. Thus, while the comics were of American origin, they engaged the imagination of Americans and Canadians by drawing on a shared North American monomyth of individualism, self-sacrifice, and personal humility. The fact that the superheroes existed in American cities like New York—or, at best, an undefined or imaginary "Anywhere, USA" metropolis—was a requisite part of reading comics in Canada.

In 1940, however, the American comics in Canada faced a challenge they were powerless to overcome: political policymaking. American comic book dominance was delivered a swift blow by Prime Minister William Lyon Mackenzie King's War Exchange Conservation Act, which limited the importation of "nonessentials"—including comic books—as a means of conserving American dollars for the war effort. Canadian companies, previously unable to compete against the "dumped" American comics, prospered in the protected market. Maple Leaf Publishing, Anglo-American, Hillborough Studios, and Bell Features and Publishing filled the Canadian demand for comic book entertainment. They produced superhero figures in mass quantities, relying on established American character types and war-inspired storylines. Out of the numerous heroes emerged Canada's first distinctly Canadian superhero, Nelvana of the North. The product of Hillborough Studios, Nelvana drew on the powers of the Aurora Borealis to fight superpowered Nazi agents. Nelvana's name came from an Inuit legend, but she was drawn as an Anglo-Saxon and clothed in a cape and miniskirt. In *Guardians of the North: The National Superhero in Canadian Comic-Book Art*, John Bell, Canada's foremost comic book historian, describes Nelvana as coming from the "same mold as the many white queens and goddesses that had appeared in popular fiction" (7). Nelvana was joined by Johnny Canuck in 1942, taking care of Nazis with his fast fists and solid jaw in adventure-packed (if slightly monotonous) comic book stories. Lacking superpowers but endowed with wit, charisma, and a strong right hook, Johnny Canuck traveled the world fighting Nazi tyranny. The war's end, however, brought the return of American comic books and the end of comic book Nazi antagonists. Canadian production quickly ended, once again unable to compete with the cheaper American material.

Until the 1970s, Canadians were limited to American comic books. There was little to ask for in the way of quality, as the comics supplied elaborate plot lines, skillful artistry, and exciting characters.

The comics were very American, however, in their symbols, figures, myths, and locations, right down to advertisements and the spelling of words. In Bell's assessment,

> what all Canadian comic-book readers of the 1950–1970 period had in common was a sense of alienation. For English Canadians, comics had become an American medium: the heroes were American, the settings were largely American, and even the alluring comic-book ads for toy soldiers and sea monkeys were American. Like U.S. television, comics seemed to contain an implicit message: Canada was a backwater bereft of heroes, bereft of guardians. For French Canadians, the medium was also dominated by the European francophone publishing houses. (*Guardians of the North* 19)

Indeed, in *Canuck Comics*, Bell notes that "Life in America, we just knew, was more exciting. Superman might visit his Fortress of Solitude in our Arctic from time to time, but never Toronto or Montreal, let alone Halifax where I lived" (13). It was a common experience for many Canadians. Reflecting on his own experience, Francis has described how

> in the universe I inhabited as a boy, there were no Canadian stars. There was no room; the skies were filled with the super novas of American history, politics, and pop culture. ... When I was looking for "role models" ... I found them on American television or in the myths of the American West or the comic books about U.S. marines in World War II. (112)

American cultural dominance increasingly came under criticism in the late 1960s, as a Canadian nationalist boom sparked an intense interest in cultural identity and concern over the lack of domestic cultural products. While American comics utilized ideas of heroism and self-sacrifice common to both Americans and Canadians, the dominance of American symbols and references drew scorn. Nationalists were especially keen to distinguish between conceptions of the American melting pot, tarnished by race riots and Vietnam violence, and the Canadian mosaic, a "peaceable kingdom" and multicultural haven of pluralism and understanding.[4] They called for cultural products reflecting distinct Canadian values, myths, and symbols.[5] Where were the

Canadian songs, movies, books, and even comic books? they asked.

"UP, UP, AND AWAY, EH?": THE BIRTH OF A CANADIAN SUPERHERO

Ron Leishman, a teacher and amateur cartoonist living in Winnipeg, Manitoba, first sketched a character he called Captain Canada in 1971. About a year later, Leishman met fellow comic book fan Richard Comely at a meeting of the Church of Jesus Christ of Latter Day Saints. They talked of creating a Canadian-themed comic book based on Leishman's Captain Canada, but the venture did not look promising. They were unable to get funding through government programs or loans, and in 1974 Leishman left to work in Alberta, followed by a two-year church mission in Belgium and France (Comely 2001).

Despite Leishman's absence, Comely did not give up on the plan. There were trademark problems with the name Captain Canada, so Comely changed it to Captain Canuck. The similarity to Johnny Canuck, however, was accidental; Comely was not aware of the national Nazi fighter until after the first issue of *Captain Canuck* was published (Comely 2001). "Canuck," the slang term for a Canadian, was distinctively national but not without its drawbacks. As one fan wrote in to the comic, "I thought it was some kind of a joke. Who would seriously think of naming a hero—even a comic book hero—'Captain Canuck'? Even if he is Canadian?" (12). The editor responded that "Canuck" was just "a casual term," and "like Yankee, it depends on how and when you say it." By placing the slang in a culturally positive context, Captain Canuck empowered the term, helping to popularize it as a valid nickname for a Canadian.

The first issue of *Captain Canuck* was published in 1975 with Comely as editor, artist, writer, publisher, production manager, and floor sweeper. Comely was, however, aided by Dave Abbott's "writing assistance," and he consulted Leishman on aspects of the comic. By the third issue, he was joined by George Freeman and Jean-Claude St. Aubin on penciling and coloring duties. Its release is regarded as the beginning of English Canada's "Silver Age" of comic book production (Bell, *Guardians of the North* 39). It was a milestone in Canadian comic book production. "Captain Canuck's very existence," Bell notes, "underscored the paucity of indigenous heroes that Canadian kids had experienced throughout the fifties and sixties" (*Canuck Comics* 39).

Captain Canuck was set in the future of the early 1990s, with Canada as the dominant world superpower—certainly a situation that could only occur in a comic book—facing evil forces seeking world domination. Tom Evans, a Mountie recruited into the Canadian International Security Organization, was of British descent, clean cut, strong and stocky, part "Indian blood,"[6] bilingual, and an ardent nationalist: a suitable candidate to protect Canada. As Captain Canuck, he literally embodied the Canadian flag, clad in a red and white costume adorned with maple leaves. Joined by the French Canadian agent "Kébec" and the super-Mountie "Redcoat," Captain Canuck was the first line of defense against supervillains seeking world domination. From futuristic Mounties to a maple-leaf-emblazoned snowmobile, Comely incorporated numerous Canadian references. Nelvana of the North may have fought superagents in the arctic while Johnny Canuck was overseas, but, in the first three issues alone, Captain Canuck's travels included dog sledding across the arctic, flying over "the magnificent Rockies," strolling "across the rooftops of scenic Montreal," and being abducted from "smog-ridden Sudbury" (Issues 1–3).[7]

Comely was "moved by the nationalism at the time" and proud of the comic's origin (Comely 2001). "We're 100% Canadian," the first issue announced, with the letters column in the third issue describing "national pride and patriotism [as] worthy attributes." *Captain Canuck* tapped into the nationalism of the period, and readers responded with great enthusiasm to having a distinctively Canadian comic: "as a Canadian I am proud to see our nation's greatness recognized," "here's to success in making *Captain Canuck* 100% Canadian," and "*Captain Canuck* has brought out the nationalistic spirit in all its readers, a pride this country now needs" (Issues 2, 3) are a few of the comments mailed in. He tried to make the comic as Canadian as possible, right down to the advertising. It was not easy, however. He contacted over 600 Canadian and 250 American companies, but had more success with the American advertisers. "Hopefully," Comely noted in the second issue, "it won't be too much longer before Canadian companies realize that it would be to their advantage to advertise in a 100% Canadian magazine like Captain Canuck." The lack of a Canadian publication industry posed problems, so distribution was handled by a U.S. company (*TIME* 1975, 10).

The myths and symbols were Canadian, but Comely's interest in conspiracy theories and his Mormon beliefs shaped the comic's content. "We're proud to say that there is nothing within that is degrading or offensive," the introduction to the first issue stated. Radical Communists bent on world domination were dealt with swiftly and with as little violence as necessary.[8] Captain Canuck prayed before missions and fought with God on his side. His abilities came from his moral character and natural health, a strong contrast to the supernatural powers of the American comic book characters. "Captain Canuck's tremendous strength and endurance come from a good wholesome diet and lots of exercise," Comely explained in the second issue. "His alertness and determination come from having a strong, clean mind." As the Canadian edition of *TIME* magazine noted in its 1975 review of the comic, "What distinguishes Captain Canuck from his American counterparts? Answer: The Canadian is polite and God-fearing and, although immensely strong, is not noted for his speed" (10). Concerned about the impact of excessive violence in society, in issue 2, Comely reprinted a four-page article on "How do movies and TV influence behaviour?" from a Mormon magazine. Comely was concerned with establishing a greater moral standard than existed in many mainstream comic books. He told *TIME* that "we need some moral fiber today and U.S. comics are tending more and more to violence and sexual innuendo … [Captain Canuck] will give thanks to God from time to time. [But] I don't want people to think I'm out to subvert them through a comic" (10).

At thirty-five cents, it was significantly more expensive than the popular twenty-five-cent American comics, yet Comely tried to provide plenty of value for the money. The early issues used a higher quality glossy paper and more complex coloring than their American counterparts. The issues contained a Captain Canuck story as well as a second feature story, often featuring two of Comely's other hero figures: "Jonn," a space commander stuck on a planet of iron-age warriors, or "Catman," a costume-clad vigilante. Occasionally there was "Beyond," a comical adventure series set in the Middle Ages. The early issues also included lessons on drawing and illustrating comic characters, a gallery for reader-submitted art, and small comic strip filler. With fewer ads, "at least 30% less than most super hero comics," issue 2 boasted, and a lower comic-to-ads ratio than the American comics, Comely offered a graphic-packed comic.

Captain Canuck was a source of inspiration for many Canadian comic book artists. Bell has noted that "the comic served to demystify the comic book business. Suddenly, the dream of creating Canadian superhero comics, which so many young artists and writers obviously harbored, became attainable" (Bell, *Canuck Comics* 39).[9] Yet *Captain Canuck* could not maintain production. Comely Comix, as the business was called, described itself as "a small struggling company with grand and lofty ideas" (C.C. 3)—an accurate claim for many Canadian publishing houses. Although "Canadian content" was fostered in television and radio through broadcasting regulations, and the arts community benefited from the Canada Council for the Arts, publishing had very little protection or domestic support.[10] The extensive coloring and higher quality paper added to the cost of production, but the biggest problem was the cost of producing a comic book in Canada. The market was small, funding sparse, distribution difficult, and printing expensive. As Comely explained to the readers in issue 2,

> I'm sure you're … aware that C.C. cost [sic] slightly more than U.S. comics. Sure, the higher quality increases the cost, but this is not the main reason. The small print runs and the fact that printing costs of comics are higher in Canada, cause our magazine to cost more than twice as much to produce than the U.S. comic magazines. I'm trying my best to bring cost down. One of the ways is to increase sales by distributing through out the U.S. as well as Canada.

Besides funding problems, the comic suffered from rigid characters, poor detailing, and unsophisticated plots with little tension or hook. In its review of the first issue, *TIME* magazine criticized its "amateurish quality" and "often clumsy artwork and story line" ("Canuck to the Rescue," 10). Issue number 3 was released in 1975, leaving the reader hanging on as Captain Canuck, badly wounded, was abducted in an ambulance by evildoers. Unfortunately, Comely Comix folded, unable to bear the costs of publishing *Captain Canuck*. It was a storyline cliffhanger that lasted for four years.

In 1979, Comely and partners, as CKR Productions in Calgary, Alberta, restarted the series at issue number 4. Comely wrote the stories, Ken Ryan was the business manager, George Freeman did the artwork, and Jean-Claude St. Aubain took care of the inking and coloring. Although this allowed Comely to focus on improving storylines, it isolated him from the aesthetic side of the comic. As of issue 5, Freeman was editing the comic with Comely as editor-in-chief.

This next generation of *Captain Canuck* maintained the focus on Canadian content. When confronted with the possibility of a Canadian civil war, for example, Captain Canuck announced that it would be stopped by "the War Measures Act! Then the Army would be everywhere!" (C.C. 6). Issue 11, set in Quebec City, had characters speaking French without translation for much of the issue, to the delight of some readers. One fan told the comic that he had "been interested in Captain Canuck over these years because of its potential to voice Canadian traditions and attitudes but never, in all that time, did I ever expect you to venture into such a sensitive area as Canadian bilingualism, especially when your magazine is so dependent on popularity for its existence" (13). Captain Canuck traveled to Halifax dockyards, Labrador ice fields, and visited his brother on a western Canadian ranch, interspersed with trips to more exotic places, including a lost South America city of gold and a multinational space station. "It is nice to see some Canadian landmarks for a change," a reader remarked, "such as Ottawa and Halifax. It is better than seeing New York and Washington all the time" (C.C. 9).

Under the new team, however, the revamped series integrated aspects of the established American comic book genre while shedding the elements that gave Comely's first three issues a grassroots feel. The religious undertone disappeared, and the conspiracy-driven plot lines were replaced by superhero supernaturalism and space-oriented themes. Captain Canuck no longer derived his strength from diet and moral cleanliness; history was rewritten, making him the product of an alien ray-beam that doubled his strength and speed (C.C. 5). Although this moved *Captain Canuck* in line with the established superhero genre, one fan complained that the change "lowers him to the level of the American super-heroes" (9). In addition, Captain Canuck became a freelance operative, serving both the Canadian government and a science-fiction-style international antiterrorist organization called Earth Patrol. Along with hoods and crooks, the Captain increasingly fought supernatural creatures and space aliens. Finally, perhaps in an attempt to spark circulation among American readers, Captain Canuck was removed from the future of the 1990s and, like most other superheroes, was relocated into the contemporary timeline—by that point, the early 1980s (13). Business manager Ken Ryan told readers that the time shift was for the best, as "a whole new lifestyle has been opened up for Captain Canuck—one that was not possible in the confines of the semi-futuristic period of the mid 1990s" (13).

The revitalized *Captain Canuck* was quite successful. In Bell's assessment, "*Captain Canuck* was transformed into one of the most accomplished alternative superhero comics ever published" (*Canuck Comics* 41). One fan confessed that "at first I only bought the comic out of Canadian pride, but now, who can resist?" (Special Summer issue 1980). In 1979, it was the bestselling comic book in Canada (C.C. 7), even though, at fifty cents an issue, it was still more expensive than many forty-cent American comics. A year later, *Captain Canuck* was the first Canadian comic to be distributed coast to coast in both Canada and the United States (10). There was even a *Captain Canuck* comic strip in the *Winnipeg Tribune*. Yet in 1981, with thirteen issues completed, Comely left *Captain Canuck*, returning to freelance design. In 1982, he released a new comic book titled *Star Rider and the Peace Machine*, but it only lasted two issues. With Comely's departure, Freeman was to take over the writing duties. Captain Canuck's time shift and the impact of Comely's departure did not have a chance to come to fruition, however, as CKR Productions only produced one more issue before financial difficulties caused it to shut down; *Captain Canuck* once again came to an end.

If Captain Canuck proved his heroism by never giving in to defeat, it reflected Comely's personal dedication to producing a Canadian comic book. In 1993, Comely and a new production staff released *Captain Canuck Reborn*, a new series with a different cast of characters and a new origin for Captain Canuck. The comic provided Comely with the opportunity to return to his original conception of *Captain Canuck*—a national superhero of natural strength and health in a comic with plenty of Canadian references and conspiracy theories.

In the new series, Darren Oak, along with his Native Canadian friend Daniel Blackbird, uncovered an international conspiracy to take over the world, led by none other than Darren's brother, Nathan, and his New World Order conglomerate. As a *Captain Canuck Reborn* commemorative trading card, released in 1993, explained,

> In a desperate attempt to rally a nation against an international conspiracy, Darren Oak becomes Captain Canuck. His big brother, Nathan, is involved in a devious plan to ignite civil war. Canada is to be HQ [Head Quarters] for a New World Order, but first they must gain complete control of Canada's government. Darren, armed only with truth and tremendous courage, must conceal his identity while he exposes the conspiracy. Inspired by a comic book, he becomes Captain Canuck.

Aided by Blackbird and other pro-Canada freedom fighters, Captain Canuck fought the New World Order on Parliament Hill, infiltrated a white-supremacist group in Lucyville, Alberta, and recovered from wounds at his home in Ourtown, Northern Ontario (C.C.R. 0–3).

Comely's skills as an artist, storywriter, and businessman had matured in the two decades since he first released *Captain Canuck*. Unfortunately, Captain Canuck once again fell victim to an enemy he could not defeat: the problems of publishing a comic book in Canada. The new series lasted for only four issues, ending in 1996 and taking with it a *Captain Canuck* newspaper strip that had started to run in various newspapers.

Captain Canuck was not only comic book entertainment, it was part of Canadian consumer culture. From the very first issue, readers were offered a barrage of items, including T-shirts, posters, iron-on crests, pens, pins, and doodle posters. Issue 7 introduced a series of merchandise with "New Captain Canuck paraphernalia to please even the pickiest patron!" There was even a Captain Canuck fan club, including a membership card and special merchandise for members only. The sale of Captain Canuck merchandise eventually made its way from the comic book and into Eaton's department stores in western Canada (Comely 2001). This was a key part of keeping the comic book going. According to Comely, "Captain Canuck merchandising made more than the sale of comic books. Printing costs were too high. The C.C. club, T-shirt licensing deal and other merchandise kept us afloat" (Comely 2001).[11] CKR Productions even went so far as to offer shares in the company to the readers. "This share bonus is not a gimmick!" the advertisement stated. "We've consulted the appropriate representatives of the Government of the Province of Alberta and we've received their cooperation and approval for our proposal to let you, the readers, actually own a part of the company" (14). It may have been a last ditch attempt to keep the company afloat, however, given that the offer was in the last issue of *Captain Canuck* to make it to press. This Canuck commodification was supported by publicity campaigns. Comely drove around Winnipeg in a yellow AMC Pacer with *Captain Canuck* emblazed on the side. As well, a 210-pound, 6'3" karate expert was hired to dress in a Captain Canuck costume and make public appearances at shopping centers and special events. Comely thought the events were quite successful (9, 11).

POST–COMIC BOOK LIFE AND THE TRANSITION FROM NATIONAL DEFENDER TO NATIONAL ICON

Nations need heroes, even fictional ones.[12] Not surprisingly, governments that lay claim to popular heroes, instituting them as representatives and manifestations of national might, validate the national identity and add cultural depth to an institutional hegemonic agent. Embracing popular culture, the Canadian government created a public showing of its comic book superheroes. From February 13 to June 7, 1992, the National Archives of Canada held "Guardians of the North: The National Superhero in Canadian Comic-Book Art," exhibiting Canadian comic books and paraphernalia, and detailing the development of Canadian comic art and superheroes. Canadian superheroes, the exhibition explained, were the "embodiment of our national spirit and identity" (Bell, *Guardians of the North* 50). Captain Canuck's natural strength and abilities, for example, were cited by the exhibition's catalogue as Canadian characteristics:

> … typifying Canadian reticence in so many things, some of these heroes possess no actual superpowers, relying rather on superior physical and intellectual skills to enable them to combat

their enemies. … In a sense, Canuck was the appropriate superhero for a middle power that was somewhat distrustful of heroism and very much aware of the limits of power. (v, 25–26)

The exhibition claimed that comics were much more than adventure stories: they probed Canadian society and reflected the issues within a national context.

> Why superheroes? Why comics? These are not just entertaining fantasy figures. They are important to our history because they are symbols of the Canadian identity. Their creators were probing issues of great concern to the Canadians of the day—World War II, national identity, our relationship with the United States. (v)

There is certainly some truth to this. As Alphons Silbermann has noted, "comics mediate, even as pure entertainment, certain mental values. Since the fact is that entertainment and information do not exclude each other, comics are latently or overtly open to any ideology" (21).

The National Archives exhibition was followed by Canada Post's recognition of five Canadian comic book heroes, institutionalizing them as important cultural icons. On October 2, 1995, Canada Post issued a booklet of ten stamps containing the "Canadian crusaders" Superman, Nelvana of the North, Fleur de Lys (who appeared in the late 1980s comic *Northguard*), Johnny Canuck, and Captain Canuck. Ironically, the government that would not provide funding for Captain Canuck two decades earlier now provided a different form of investment: a symbolic one. The Captain Canuck stamp commoditized his image in a new way, as an official national commodity—forty-five cents of federal currency added to the hats, pins, and pens Comely sold to keep the comic afloat.

Canada Post's inclusion of Superman as a Canadian superhero reflects an interesting part of the Canadian cultural psyche. Striving to establish strong cultural mythologies and heroes, it associates the nation with an internationally recognized, culturally important icon. This has been supported by some cultural nationalists, including Marsha Boulton, who gives him a section and a predominant place on the cover of *Just a Minute: Glimpses of Our Great Canadian Heritage*. Superman co-creator Joe Shuster was born in Toronto, Ontario, in 1914, and that alone was sufficient for Superman to be deemed

Canadian. Shuster left Canada for the United States when he was eight years old, and Superman was not created until a decade later with his friend Jerry Siegal. First a comic strip reflecting American New Deal politics and social consciousness, it was later reconfigured into a comic book action-adventure format. Let's not forget that Superman defended "Truth, Justice, and the American Way," not Canada's motto of "Peace, Order, and Good Government." Heritage Canada reaffirmed the government's claim to Superman through historical tampering, releasing a Superman "Heritage Moment" as part of its series of sixty-second television commercials that dramatize a moment in Canadian history. The spot showed a young Joe Shuster boarding a train, ranting about a new type of superhero he was creating, and passing a drawing of Superman to his friend "Lois" as she laughed about "you Canadian kids!" It was pure fabrication. And, as author Will Ferguson has slyly noted, Captain Canuck is from Canada, Superman is from Krypton (175).[13]

The image of Captain Canuck has become so associated with Canada that the nation itself has been placed in the costume. The April 28, 1997, Canadian edition of *TIME* magazine cast Captain Canuck on its cover, along with a banner declaring that "Canada is the new superhero of global trade (and even Superman is being produced in Winnipeg these days)."[14] Inside the issue, Canada—as Captain Canuck—lifted bar graphs and hurled pie charts detailing Canada's economic strength. In the context of *TIME*, Canada *became* Captain Canuck—Canada *was* strong and powerful. The magazine detached Captain Canuck's image from the comic book and resituated it in a new context and narrative, constructing a new denotative meaning that drew on the established connotation of heroism and strength.[15]

Soon after these developments, Captain Canuck was reconfigured yet again, his status as a national icon attracting the interest of the arts community. Featuring artwork from the *Captain Canuck Reborn* series, "Canada's Own Captain Canuck: Inked Drawings by Richard Comely" was exhibited at the Burlington Art Centre in Burlington, Ontario, during the summer of 1998. By exhibiting the artwork as individual pieces instead of as part of the comic book whole, the segmented, paneled aesthetics separated the artwork from the storylines. *Captain Canuck* was no longer just a comic book; it was now popular art

and material for aesthetic critique and display, the images providing content for the exhibition.

Captain Canuck—comic book superhero and national protector, embodiment of Canadian values, forty-five-cent postage stamp, Canada's alter ego, and, finally, popular art—survived not only fictional supervillains, but, perhaps even more heroically, the dangers of the Canadian publishing industry. *Captain Canuck's* history is a story of grassroots cultural production and a distinctly national superhero who became valuable to the government it fictionally protected. The comic's demise, however, may once again be temporary. In 1999, Mark Shainblum (writer and co-creator of popular 1980s Canadian comic book *Northguard*) and Sandy Carruthers, both contributors to the early 1990s *Captain Canuck* newspaper comic strip, attempted to bring back Tom Evans as Captain Canuck in *Captain Canuck: Utopia Moments*. Plans were made for a four-issue miniseries, but these have yet to come to fruition. An issue was compiled and released on a trial promotional run limited to one hundred copies, but has not progressed any further. Comely returned to the comic book scene in 2000 with a plan for yet another Captain Canuck. Establishing media contacts and setting up an Internet Web page, his project is still in the works. Things look hopeful, though. The Canadian publishing industry is not as weak now as it was twenty (even ten) years ago. Captain Canuck may again provide a generation of Canadian comic book fans with a sense of national identity in a cultural arena where New York overwhelms New Brunswick, and one rarely sees a maple leaf.

NOTES

1. Captain Canuck citations will be listed by issue number, not page number.
2. For examples, see J. W. Bengough, *A Caricature History of Canadian Politics*.
3. For a solid overview of the transition from comic strips to comic books, see Ian Gordon, *Comic Strips and Consumer Culture, 1890–1945*.
4. William Kilbourn popularized the term in Canada with the title of his edited collection of nationalist writing, *Canada: A Guide to the Peaceable Kingdom*.
5. Defining just what constituted "Canadian," however, was a more difficult task.

6. In issue 12, Captain Canuck slipped back in time and encountered a group of Micmac Native Canadians. In hopes of ingratiating himself with them, he pulled off his mask, showing them his "Indian blood," and was welcomed by them.

7. The location of issue 3 was identified in issue 4.

8. Interestingly, the Communist leader in issue 1 was drawn so similar to Lenin that a fourteen-year-old reader wrote into the comic about it in the second issue.

9. For an interesting look at comic books and fan mentality, see Matthew J. Pustz's *Comic Book Culture: Fanboys and True Believers*.

10. The 1972 Ontario Royal Commission on Book Publishing's *Canadian Publishers and Canadian Publishing* noted that there may have been "Canadian publishers," but that did not necessarily mean that there was "Canadian publishing" (60). "Commercial realism" and profitability prevented many Canadian publishers, foreign-owned or not, from publishing large quantities of distinctly Canadian content material (63).

11. Comely puts the number of C.C. club members at 1,200–1,500. The phenomenon of comic book commodification first took hold with Detective Comics's trademarking of *Superman* and the extensive merchandising of products during the 1940s, including a toy ray gun and wristwatch. Ian Gordon explains that "In the hands of a corporation, Superman was more important as a business asset than a fictional character" (134). Merchandising hit a high point in the 1990s—with the fusion of comic book characters and global media production—with characters such as Batman commoditized into billion-dollar industries. For more information, see Ian Gordon's *Comic Strips and Consumer Culture*, pp. 133–35 and 152–57.

12. Much can be said about the role of fiction in the stories of nonfictional heroes, of course. History is far from a precise science and, especially in the case of national history, is quite positive and supportive of its heroes. History, after all, is not only written by the victors but also by the heroes.

13. See Will Ferguson, *Why I Hate Canadians*, p. 175.

14. Part of the colorization process for *Superman* was handled in Canada.

15. Swiss linguist Ferdinand de Saussure's semiological work showed how a *signifier* (the communicative) is connected with a *signified* (mental concept, object, and so on) to construct a *sign* (the arbitrary signifying construct). Roland Barthes produced the most influential work on semiology and culture, first outlined in *Mythologies* (1957), *Elements of Semiology* (1964), and *The Fashion System* (1967). Extending Saussure's work on the denotative, Barthes explored the connotative, a subjective meaning produced by the meeting of the sign and the viewer. It is within the connotative that emotions, values, and so on are expressed.

WORKS CITED

Anderson, Benedict. *Imagined Communities*. London: Verso, 1991.

Baudrillard, Jean. *The Consumer Society: Myths and Structures*. London: Sage Publications, 1998.

Bell, John. *Canuck Comics*. Downsview, Ontario: Eden Press, 1986.

Bell, John. "Curator, National Archives of Canada." *Guardians of the North: The National Superhero in Canadian Comic-Book Art*. Ottawa: Minister of Supply and Services Canada, 1992.

Bengough, J. W. *A Caricature History of Canadian Politics*. Toronto: Peter Martin Associates, 1974.

Boulton, Marsha. *Just a Minute: Glimpses of Our Great Canadian Heritage*. Toronto: McArthur & Co., 1998.

Canada Post Corporation. Press release, 26 Sept. 1995.

Captain Canuck. Issues 1–3. Winnipeg, Manitoba: Comely Comix, 1975.

Captain Canuck. Issues 4–14. Calgary, Alberta: CKR Productions Ltd, 1979–1981.

Captain Canuck Reborn. Cambridge, Ontario: Comely Communications, 1993–1996.

Comely, Richard. Correspondence with author, summer 2001.

Ferguson, Will. *Why I Hate Canadians*. Vancouver: Douglas & McIntyre, 1997.

Francis, Daniel. *National Dreams: Myth, Memory, and Canadian History*. Vancouver: Arsenal Pulp Press, 1997.

Gellner, Ernest. *Thought and Change*. London: Weidenfeld and Nicolson, 1964.

Gordon, Ian. *Comic Strips and Consumer Culture, 1890–1945*. Washington, DC: Smithsonian Institution Press, 1998.

Klein, Naomi. *No Logo: Taking Aim at the Brand Bullies*. Toronto: Vintage Canada, 2000.

Land, Jeffrey, and Patrick Trimble. "Whatever Happened to the Man of Tomorrow? An Examination of the

American Monomyth and the Comic Book Super-hero." *Journal of Popular Culture* 2 (1988): 157–73.

Ontario Royal Commission on Book Publishing. *Canadian Publishers and Canadian Publishing*. Toronto: Queen's Printer and Publisher, 1992.

Pustz, Matthew J. *Comic Book Culture: Fanboys and True Believers*. Jackson: UP of Mississippi, 1999.

Silbermann, Alphons. "The Way Toward Visual Culture: Comics and Comic Films." *Comics and Visual Culture*. Ed. A. Silbermann and H. D. Dyroff. New York: K. G. Saur, 1986. 11–27.

TIME. "Canuck to the Rescue." Canadian edition, 9 June 1975: 10.

TIME. "Captain Exporter." Canadian edition, 28 Apr. 1997: Cover.

TIME. "Super Exporter." Canadian edition, 28 Apr. 1997: 34–40.

Yoshino, Kosaku. "Rethinking Theories of Nationalism: Japan's Nationalism in a Marketplace Perspective." *Consuming Ethnicity and Nationalism: Asian Experiences*. Ed. Yoshino Kosaku. Honolulu: U of Hawaii P, 1999.

ARTICLE 2: I AM CANADIAN: NATIONAL IDENTITY IN BEER COMMERCIALS

Robert M. MacGregor

Occasionally a television commercial causes social, political, and business ramifications far beyond anyone's initial expectations. In March 2000, a sixty-second television beer commercial became an overnight phenomenon. For approximately three months thereafter, the advertisement became a national and international focus of debates on Canadian nationalism and identity. Some issues concerning national identity will be discussed.

MOLSON CANADIAN "THE RANT"

Sometimes a single television commercial can have such an impact that it takes on a life of its own. A few examples of such advertisements include:

1. Coca-Cola's 1971 song "I'd Like to Buy the World a Coke" that became "I'd Like to Teach the World to Sing," a one-million-units-sales best seller.
2. LIFE brand cereal—Quaker Oats Company showing Mikey enjoying LIFE brand. "Hey Mikey" entered the lexicon.
3. The greatest commercial ever made—Apple Macintosh's "1984," showing Big Brother (IBM) in an Orwellian nightmare—caused the Macintosh revolution.
4. Clara Peller barked, "Where's the Beef?" for Wendy's and a popular culture phenomenon was born. American presidential candidate Walter Mondale used the phrase in his campaign (Ward Fawcett).

Molson's beer commercial, in a Canadian context, now stands as an example of a single advertisement that now joins the pantheon of selected "best" television presentations.

Montreal-based Molson Company, founded in 1786, is Canada's preeminent brewer and one

hundred percent Canadian owned, with sales in excess of $2 billion. One of its top-selling brands is called CANADIAN. Between 1994 and 1998, Molson had used the tag line, "I am CANADIAN." This line was replaced by "Here's where we get CANADIAN," widely criticized as flat-mouthed. Responsibility for reviving the CANADIAN brand went to Brett Marchand, an Alberta-born marketing executive who had been lured away from Campbell Soup in Philadelphia. Grassroots interviews clearly indicated a growing sense of national pride among the key niche, nineteen- to twenty-five-year-olds. The Toronto agency Bensimon Byrne D'Arcy recommended that Molson revive the "I am CANADIAN" slogan. The "Joe Rant" emerged as a passionate declaration of national pride, a definitive piece of popular culture. As they say, the rest is history.

I AM CANADIAN

Hey
I'm not a lumberjack, or a fur trader.
I don't live in an igloo, eat blubber, or own a dogsled.
I don't know Jimmy, Sally or Suzy from Canada.
Although I'm certain they're very nice.

I have a prime minister, not a president.
I speak English and French, NOT American,
and I pronounce it 'ABOUT', NOT 'A BOOT.'

I can proudly sew my country's flag on my backpack. I believe in peace keeping, NOT policing,
DIVERSITY, NOT assimilation
and that the beaver is a proud and noble animal.

A TOQUE IS A HAT,
A CHESTERFIELD IS A COUCH,
AND IT IS PRONOUNCED 'ZED,' NOT 'ZEE', 'ZED.'

CANADA IS THE SECOND LARGEST LANDMASS,
THE FIRST NATION OF HOCKEY
AND THE BEST PART OF NORTH AMERICA.
MY NAME IS JOE
AND I AM CANADIAN

Thank you.

The copy and visual elements of the advertisement addressed some of the commonly held stereotypes that others perhaps hold of Canadians. Whether it is language pronunciation differences, occupational, eating, and living factors, sports interests, or social and political policies, each of these is fleetingly presented. Two major symbolic icons are also invoked in the ad: the beaver and Canada's national flag, the maple leaf. The ad had been in movie theaters since March 17, 2000, and made its national television debut on March 26 during the Academy Awards broadcast.

A possible impetus to the immediate success of "The Rant" may have been Robin Williams's same-night, same-show rendition of the *South Park* film's song "Blame Canada." This song was nominated for an Oscar.

This song satirized Canada as a tool for satirizing Americans. In the song "Blame Canada," all four mums—Sheila, Sharon, Liane, and Ms. McCormick—sing the wows of parenthood. The last ten lines of the song are:

> Sheila: With all their hockey hubba baloo
> Liane: And that bitch Anne Murray too
> Everyone: Blame Canada
> Shame on Canada
> The smut we must stop
> The trash we must smash
> Laughter and fun
> Must be all undone
> We must blame them and cause a fuss
> Before someone thinks of blaming
> uuuuuus.

Trey Parker and Matt Stone did not create the flip-top headed characters in *South Park* to offend Canadians; they did so to take a jab at Americans' stereotyping of Canadians. They chose to "Blame Canada" before somebody thinks to blame us—Americans—for the sole reason American mentality is that way. Michael Moore wrote *Canadian Bacon* in 1995, a movie about invading Canada that focused on America's need to have an enemy. The song, the movie, and the Oscar presentation appeared to add to the poignancy of "The Rant" commercial and helped to reinforce some prevailing attitudes of Canadians about Americans.

Within days of the initial airing of "The Rant," dozens of Web sites sprung up, numerous parodies of groups and individuals appeared, and Jeff Douglas took on major celebrity status. The many parodies that appeared include: I am a columnist, I am an Albertan, I am a Newfie, I am Chinese, I am Pakistani,

I am Indian, I am Italian, I am Irish, I am Jamaican, I am Filipino, I am Torontonian, I am Manitoban, I am British Columbian, I am Not Canadian (parody on Québecers), and I am American. All of the parodies followed the same genre, and the American one read as follows:

I AM AMERICAN

I'm not particularly intelligent, open-minded, or generally well-liked.
I don't live in a clean place.
I don't eat nutritiously very often.
And I abandon my car on the side of the interstate until the tires are stolen.

I don't know Shakespeare, Da Vinci or Gutenberg. Although I'm certain they weren't American.

I drink watery beer.
I don't use utensils when eating.
I believe in guns for settling disputes, not discussions.

And I pronounce it AIN'T, not AREN'T.
I don't say, "you're welcome" in response to "thank you." I say "Uh Huh."
I can proudly sew my country's flag on my backpack ... until I go anywhere.

Burger King IS fine dining and Miss America is a virgin.
Ketchup IS a vegetable and WWF wrestling is real.

The UNITED STATES is the ONLY country in the world.

The FIRST nation of ignorance,
And the BEST part of South America!

My name is Johnny Bob Jimmy Joe Ray, I'm married to my sister,
AND I AM AMERICAN!

Joe, the actor, performed at National League Hockey games, appeared on most major television and radio talk shows, did business conferences, and eventually went off to Hollywood. The television commercial won a Bronze Lion at the 2000 Cannes International Advertising Awards, where thirty-two other commercials were on the short list in the alcoholic beverage category. In Canada, it was voted "Best of Show," winning the gold medal for television single over thirty seconds (*Marketing*).

In November 2001, "The Rant" won top honors at the advertising industry's CASSIE awards, picking up the coveted Grand Prix. The CASSIES are awarded based on how successfully the ad moves the client's business. In a release, the award's group said that the Molson Canadian campaign produced "amazing" results for the brand. From March 2000 to March 2001, the Canadian brand grew by 2.5 percent in market share, while archrival Labatt's Blue declined by 2.9 percent (Heinrich).

From a commercial and creative viewpoint, "The Rant" was an extremely successful advertisement. What was unseen initially were the eventual discussions that took place at the political and institutional levels. Ontario Minister of Consumer Affairs Bob Runciman quickly denounced the ad. He was quoted as saying:

> I felt it was saying things that didn't have to be said in terms of saying things of feeling good about our country. You can send out very strong messages about being Canadian—I'm certainly as pro-Canadian as anyone—but I don't think you have to kick anyone else in the shins to do that. I think that this is essentially an anti-American rant which taps into a national lack of self confidence when it comes to dealing with the United States. (Molson Canadian Commercial)

Several well-known Canadian historians, including Michael Bliss of Toronto and Desmond Morton of McGill, voiced their concerns about the negativity of "The Rant." Bliss believed that the advertisement was pathetic, depressing, and an embarrassment to Canada; it was nationalism without content. Morton said that "the mobilization of a sense of Canadianism to peddle beer is a frontal attack on the values Canadians share" (Walker).

Other well-known Canadians took an opposing view and voiced their support of the creative rendition. Bob Rae, former premier of Ontario, said:

> This speaks to every stupid question that Americans always ask Canadians. There is a very strong element of nationalism in Canada that never goes away. The closer we get economically, the more we like thumbing our noses and that's a lot of fun. (Kettle)

Rudyard Griffiths, director of the Dominion Institute in Toronto, saw "The Rant" as an example of tearing a page out of the book of American cultural imperialism—a change in the habits of cultural expression in Canada (a "ra ra-ism").

He believed:

> It's very retro and it's interesting that it's connected with a younger group. Canadian sovereignty has been more of an issue for those who came of age during the late 1960s and early 1970s. That was a time when Canada had a new flag, a hip and glamourous prime minister in Pierre Trudeau, and a world fair. As tensions over the Vietnam war tore at the social fabric of the United States, Canada emerged as a humane alternative society. There was a conscious rebranding of Canada as independent nation ready to take its place on the world stage. (Walker)

Throughout the public debates, two viewpoints were coalescing. The advertisement was seen as an expression of Canadian pride, and critics saw "The Rant" as a declaration of anti-American sentiment. Glen Hunt, who wrote the ad, saw the commercial as pro-Canadian and not anti-American. Brett Marchand, Molson vice president, believed what the ad said "… is what more Canadians wish people would do—scream that they are proud to be Canadian" ("Beer ad").

Marchand also stated that the ad elements—beer, hockey, and the environment, for example—represented "Canada's patriotic DNA." He believed that the young respondents interviewed for their views on Canada were likened to a "dormant volcano." "We definitely didn't expect it to have the impact it's had, beyond its value as a beer ad," Marchand continued. "You couldn't image [sic] the phenomenon it is in Canada. It's been on the front page of newspapers. There are radio talk shows across the country dedicated to the ad. I've been doing interviews almost from first thing in the morning until the end of the day every day. It really has struck a chord with a huge group of consumers." (Bach).

One federal politician who saw the social and political implications of the mass appeal of the ad to many Canadians was the Honourable Sheila Copps, Minister of Canadian Heritage. At the International Press Institute World Congress held in Boston on May 1, 2000, she used "The Rant" beer advertisement to present and discuss the importance of national cultural identity to Canadians. After the video of the ad was shown, she presented the following points to the audience:

> Yes, the ad pokes fun at the U.S., and yes, there is a bit of chest thumping—but it also pokes fun at Canadian efforts at self-validation by posing in contrast to Americans. The ad has spun off a huge raft of subsidiary jokes in which Canadians laugh at our teams, our cities and ourselves. The popularity of the ad raises a serious point, though. Some American business people firmly believe that culture is a good allocated solely by the private sector and free markets. When you are the world's cultural juggernaut, at best, this means serious challenges for other nations.
>
> For Canadians, culture is not just like any other good like pork rinds or brass tack. Culture is not just entertainment. It is the expression of the soul and the identity of the country. (*Speaking notes*)

Ms. Copps continued in the speech to discuss cultural pluralism, cultural diversity, and the disappearance of languages and dialects, encouraging free expression and cultural security. Near the conclusion of her speech, she stated,

> I'll undoubtedly catch flak from some commentors back in Canada for bringing "Joe Canadian" to Boston but I say what better place for a strong call for cultural identity by Joe Sixpack than here where Americans first stated their call for cultural recognition and fair representation. (*Speaking notes*)

The Minister of Canadian Heritage did not have long to wait. The next day, May 2, Mr. John Solomon (Regina-Lumsden-Lake Centre, NDP) rose in the House of Commons in Ottawa and proudly proclaimed "I am Canadian":

I AM CANADIAN

Mr. John Solomon (Regina-Lumsden-Lake Centre, NDP):

Mr. Speaker, I am not a Republican or a Democrat. I do not spend millions to run for office or hire American consultants or go negative. I do not know Stockwell or Tom or Joe but I am sure they are very nice. I have a health card, not an insurance card, I listen to Cross Country Checkup,

not Howard Stern or Rush Limbaugh, I speak for people, not multinational corporations. I believe in inexpensive generic drugs, environmental protection and fair trade deals. I believe that Canada can have an independent foreign policy. Canadian taxpayers are citizens too who value our social programs. And it is pronounced medicare, not Bill 11, okay? Canada is the home of public health care, curling, Codco and the NDP.

My name is John and I am Canadian.

Much of Mr. Solomon's "rant" compares various factors that clearly distinguish America from Canada, and clearly suggests his own political party's electoral platform (Solomon).

Three days later on May 5, Richard Marceau (Charlesbourg, BQ), member of the nationalist/separatist party, openly mocked Ms. Copp's Boston visit. His declaration clearly illustrated some of the tensions that prevail between the English and French populations in Canada. His statements were as follows:

Mr. Richard Marceau (Charlesbourg, BQ):

Mr. Speaker, on May 1, the Minister of Canadian Heritage went to the ridiculous lengths of promoting "Canadian" culture in Boston with a beer ad. How clever.

How can Quebecers define themselves within this selection of Canadiana when the beer in question is not even sold in Quebec? Molson long ago grasped the specific nature of Quebec and serves us in Laurentide.

We in Quebec have a real department of culture, not one for heritage. What we fear is not comparison with the Americans but assimilation with the Canadians.

In Quebec, when we say we are bilingual, that does not mean we just know a few pick-up lines. Our objective is to make Quebec known throughout the world, not to go other countries and put our foot in our mouth every chance we get.

Above all, when we in Quebec want some pro-Quebec advertising, we do not hire an American. (Marceau)

It is not the intent of this article to discuss the individual elements of the ad or to discuss the tensions between the English and French politicians. These will be analyzed in other articles as will the American dimensions—for example, stereotyping of Canadians and whether the ad was anti-American. Some considerations concerning national identity will conclude this article.

NATIONAL IDENTITY

"Who are we?" is a universal and perennial question. It is a particular question of concern to Canadians, most of whom believe that they are distinctive, and that to have a clear identity is to be different from Americans (Hedley). The advertisement highlights some of the perceived value differences: the protection of the state peace, order, good government, and inclusive social policies.

Douglas Kellner believed that today, in modernity, identity is more mobile, multiple, personal, self-reflexive, and subject to change and innovation. Yet in postmodern society, identity remained social- and other-related. Historically, in Canada the dominant ideology of "being a Canadian" was in the process of being defined as speaking English within a British-type institutional system. This British model, a latent unitarian model of identity, was reasonably successful in Canada but was never unchallenged. To varying degrees, tension has existed within the existing cultural diversity of the nation, and especially within the mainly French population of Québec. The symbolic order and cultural capital factors changed dramatically in the 1960s. One of the ways that changes were made to help assuage growing tensions and anxiety between the two founding nations was to change the symbolic character of the Canadian national identity. The Official Languages Act of 1969 made Canada a bilingual country, a Canadian Flag was adopted in 1965, Trans-Canada Airline became Air Canada, the Dominion Bureau of Statistics became Statistics Canada, "O Canada" was proclaimed as the national anthem in 1980, stamps were changed (elimination of the Queen's portrait), money was redesigned with more Canadian symbols, and the constitution was patriated. The point to emphasize here is to concur with Kellner's point that modern national identity more and more has a degree of flexibility to evolve. The state in Canada intervened substantially to reorient the symbolic national identity order. Some groups, not the Québec nationalists, perceived the changes to be an enrichment of society's symbolic system, and, as a result, their own symbolic identity. Some of these changes are reflected in "The Rant" beer advertisement (Breton).

Consumers, beer drinkers, and advertisement viewers are socially and culturally situated individuals seeking to make sense of their lives, identities, and relationships. Ads such as "The Rant" provided symbolic resources to be used for those purposes (O'Donohue). McCracken suggested that in looking at ads, consumers seek "concepts of what it is to be a man or a woman, concepts of what it is to be middle-aged … (or) a member of a community or a country" (122). Molson's sixty-second television commercial for its brand of beer, CANADIAN, appeared to motivate many people to be proud to stand up and shout, "I am CANADIAN!"

WORKS CITED

Bach, Deborah. "Better Ad Hyping Canada Strikes Chord Across Borders." *Baltimore Sun* 25 Apr. 2000. Available at http:// www.amarillonet.com.

"Beer Ad Gets 19,000 Fans Excited." 15 Apr. 2000. Available at http://www.canoe.ca/2000_NHL_Playoffs_OrrTor.

Breton, Raymond. "The Production and Allocation of Symbolic Resources: an Analysis of the Linguistic and Ethnocultural Fields in Canada." *Canadian Review of Sociology and Anthropology* 21.2 (1984): 123–44.

CASSIES, short for Canadian Advertising Success Stories, created in 1993. For more information see: http:// www.cassies.ca.

Copps, Sheila. *Speaking Notes for the Honourable Sheila Copps. Minister of Canadian Heritage.* International Press Institute World Congress, Boston, 1 May 2000.

Hedley, Alan. "Review Essay, Identity: Sense of Self and Nation." *Canadian Review of Sociology and Anthropology* 31.2(1994): 200–14.

Kellner, Douglas. "Popular Culture and the Construction of Postmodern Identity." *Modernity and Identity.* Ed. Scott Lash and Jonathan Friedman. Oxford, UK: Basil Blackwell Ltd., 41–77.

Kettle, Martin. "Mocked Canada Finds Hope and Glory in a Beer Ad." *Guardian.* 25 May 2000. Available at http://www.guardian.co.uk/Archive/Article.

Marceau, Richard (Charlesbourg, BQ). *House of Commons Debates.* Volume 136, Number 091, 2nd Session, 36th Parliament, Friday, May 5, 2000, 6443.

Marketing. Awards Issue 26 Mar. 2001, 7, 20.

McCracken, Grant. "Advertising: Meaning or Information?" Ed. Melanie Wallendorf and Paul Anderson. Provo UT. *Advances in Consumer Research* 14(1987): 1–2.

"Molson Canadian Commercial." 10 May 2000. Available at http://www.snopes.ca/in_boxer/petition/joerant .htm.

O'Donohue, Stephanie. "Nationality and Negotiation of Advertising Meanings." Ed. Eric J. Arnould and Linda M. Scott, Montreal. *Advances in Consumer Research* 26: 684–89.

Solomon, John (Regina-Lumsden-Lake Centre, NDP). "I AM CANADIAN" *House of Commons Debates*. Volume 136, Number 088, 2nd Session, 36th Parliament, Tuesday, May 2, 2000, 6282.

South Park. Prod. Scott Rudin, Trey Parker, and Matt Stone. Paramount Pictures and Warner Brothers, in association with Comedy Central, 1999.

Walker, Ruth. *Christian Science Monitor*. 4 May 2000 http://www.csmonitor.com.

Ward Fawcett, Adrienne. "The 50 Best." *Advertising Age*. Special Awards Issue spring 1995: 36–39.

Index